Resolute Rebel

CHET BENNETT

Resolute Rebel

General Roswell S. Ripley, Charleston's Gallant Defender

THE UNIVERSITY OF SOUTH CAROLINA PRESS

© 2017 University of South Carolina

Published by the University of South Carolina Press
Columbia, South Carolina 29208

www.sc.edu/uscpress

Manufactured in the United States of America

25 24 23 22 21 20 19 18 17
10 9 8 7 6 5 4 3 2 1

Library of Congress Cataloging-in-Publication Data
can be found at http://catalog.loc.gov/

ISBN 978-1-61117-754-1 (cloth)
ISBN 978-1-61117-755-8 (ebook)

This book was printed on recycled paper with
30 percent postconsumer waste content.

*To the memory of Anthony W. F. (Tony) Taylerson and
my maternal great-grandfather Private Gardner Lytle Davis,
Company A, First South Carolina Artillery*

CONTENTS

List of Illustrations, Maps, and Patents | ix
Preface | xi
Acknowledgments | xv

CHAPTER 1   *Family and Early Years* | 1
CHAPTER 2   *West Point* | 9
CHAPTER 3   *Prelude to War* | 16
CHAPTER 4   *Mexico, 1846* | 21
CHAPTER 5   *Mexico, 1847* | 27
CHAPTER 6   *Postwar, 1848–1849* | 37
CHAPTER 7   *Florida, 1849–1850* | 43
CHAPTER 8   *Twilight of a Career* | 47
CHAPTER 9   *A New Life in South Carolina* | 52
CHAPTER 10   *Secession* | 63
CHAPTER 11   *The Bombardment* | 73
CHAPTER 12   *Robert E. Lee in Command* | 84
CHAPTER 13   *General John C. Pemberton* | 96
CHAPTER 14   *Peninsula Campaign* | 108
CHAPTER 15   *Maryland Campaign* | 122
CHAPTER 16   *Return to Charleston* | 137
CHAPTER 17   *The Impending Storm* | 148
CHAPTER 18   *Attack of the Ironclads* | 158
CHAPTER 19   *The Defense of Morris Island* | 168
CHAPTER 20   *Attacks on Battery Wagner* | 179
CHAPTER 21   *Siege and Bombardment* | 190
CHAPTER 22   *The H. L. Hunley Arrives* | 202
CHAPTER 23   *Ripley Rebuked* | 212
CHAPTER 24   *The H. L. Hunley Lost at Sea* | 221
CHAPTER 25   *Ripley Returns and Reacts* | 228
CHAPTER 26   *Ripley in Crisis* | 238
CHAPTER 27   *Death of the Confederacy* | 251

CHAPTER 28 *Chaos and Flight to England* | 263
CHAPTER 29 *England, 1866–1869* | 271
CHAPTER 30 *Financial Struggles, 1869–1873* | 285
CHAPTER 31 *Literary Career, 1874–1875* | 293
CHAPTER 32 *An Eventful 1875* | 302
CHAPTER 33 *Ripley's "The Situation in America"* | 311
CHAPTER 34 *Inventor* | 323
CHAPTER 35 *Return to America* | 339
CHAPTER 36 *Death in New York and Honors in Charleston* | 349
            Epilogue | 357

Notes | 361
Bibliography | 387
Index | 399

ILLUSTRATIONS, MAPS, AND PATENTS

Illustrations

Ohio Historical Marker, R. S. Ripley | xii
Ripley's Birthplace | 2
St. Lawrence Academy | 6
General P. G. T. Beauregard | 69
Governor Francis W. Pickens | 85
General Robert E. Lee | 86
General John C. Pemberton | 97
Mumma Farm Outbuildings | 134
Colonel Alfred Moore Rhett | 143
Colonel David B. Harris | 169
Captain John C. Mitchel | 171
Francis Lawley | 273
Senator Louis T. Wigfall | 274
Secretary of State Judah P. Benjamin | 278
79/89 Gloucester Place | 280
Jackson Monument | 305
Stanhope Arms Pub | 312
Colonel William Hope, V.C. | 328
The New York Hotel | 341
Captain Thomas A. Huguenin | 352
Major John Johnson | 352
Grave Monument of General Roswell S. Ripley | 355

Maps

All maps by James L. Williams

Charleston Harbor | 74
Battle of Mechanicsville/Beaver Dam Creek | 116
Battle of Sharpsburg | 133
Attack of the Ironclads | 160

Patents

No. 2069 | 324
No. 5314 | 325–326
No. 5315 | 326
No. 4363 | 330
No. 1733 | 331
No. 2923 | 332
No. 1831 | 334
No. 3042 | 336
No. 817 | 336
No. 314,127 | 337

PREFACE

I first heard of Roswell Ripley in April 1961 while attending the College of Medicine at Ohio State University in Columbus, Ohio. It was the centennial of the Civil War, and I learned that Ripley, a Confederate officer born in the Columbus suburb of Worthington, was in command of the artillery at Fort Moultrie. Ripley's artillery fired on Sumter at the onset of the hostilities in that terrible conflict. I wondered how that came about, but over time Ripley's role slipped to the back of my mind.

Nearly thirty years later, in 1990, while researching my maternal South Carolina genealogy, I discovered that my great-grandfather, Private Gardner Lytle Davis, served with Company A, 1st South Carolina Artillery, and that his commanding officer was General Roswell S. Ripley. Believing Gardner must have at least known of Ripley, I wanted to learn more about this Ohioan and why he fought for the Confederacy. My paternal great-grandfather John Bennett, from Guernsey County, Ohio, was too young to serve. However, his brothers, David and Daniel, incredibly served on Folly Island with Company G, 62nd Ohio Volunteer Infantry, and the assaults on Battery Wagner.

Living in central Ohio, I thought it would be fairly easy to discover information about Ripley's early years. Worthington officials had erected a sign in front of Ripley's birthplace, a small brick house now painted white. A white wood sign at 623 High Street identified the Ripley House but with no explanation of who Ripley was or why his birthplace was recognized. On September 26, 2004, through the efforts of the Brigadier General Roswell S. Ripley Camp 1535, Sons of Confederate Veterans, and the United Daughters of the Confederacy, an Ohio historical marker recognizing Ripley was approved and erected on the site.[1]

No one at the Worthington Historical Society knew much about Ripley, and they referred me to a nine-page paper, *Worthington's Confederate General*, written by former mayor Richard T. Savage. Published in 1961, and although not an in-depth study, Savage presented a rather sympathetic view of Ripley, stating his belief that more should be known about "General Ripley, at least in the community where he was born."

I soon determined that no one had ever written a biography of Ripley, but I did learn that in 1963 Charles Martin Cummings received a doctorate in American history from Ohio State University for his dissertation, "Seven Ohio Confederate Generals: Case Histories of Defection." The amount of research Cummings

Ohio historical marker, Worthington, Ohio, for Brigadier General Roswell Sabin Ripley, C.S.A. Author's photograph.

conducted in completing his study is impressive. Although he hesitated to refer to the seven men as traitors, the subtitle of his dissertation indicates his bias against them. He minimized the fact that none of these men were in the U.S. Army at onset of the war. All had left Ohio years before the war, and their homes, families, and businesses were located in the South. Cummings contended that significant character flaws led to their "defection."

Cummings was viciously critical of Ripley. He minimized positive assessments, emphasized the most negative, and at times took quotations out of context to disparage Ripley. Cummings included photographs of the seven generals; all but Ripley are photographed in their Confederate uniforms and captioned with their name and rank. Cummings printed the most unflattering image of Ripley in existence. It is a postwar photograph of him in a business suit captioned, "Roswell Sabin Ripley, Business Failure." Later the *Ohio History* magazine printed Cummings's condensed and more balanced version of his dissertation entitled "Fruit of the Restless Spirit—Ohio's Confederate Generals."[2]

The brief biographical sketches found in volumes such as Stewart Sifakis's *Who Was Who in the Civil War* and Ezra Warner's *Generals in Gray* are incomplete, especially lacking information concerning Ripley's life after the war. Clifford Dowdey in *The Seven Days* malevolently wrote, "An opinionated man,

Ripley was even more contumacious than D. H. Hill: where Hill respected some superiors, Ripley was against them all."[3]

In contrast, many of Ripley's contemporaries described him much differently. According to Colonel E. M. Seabrook, a former staff officer, "He always endeavored to bestow upon his subordinates, officers and men, the full measure of praise due to them." Confederate general Samuel G. French, a former classmate at West Point, stated, "His cheerful presence dispelled all unnecessary solemnity. . . . his generous and unselfish disposition formed friendships among his classmates that lasted through life." George C. Eggleston, who served in an independent battery in Charleston, commented, "He was portly in person, commanding and almost pompous presence, and yet, when one came to know him, was as easy and unassuming in manner as if he had not been a brigadier general at all."[4]

There are probably two reasons a biography of Ripley has never been written. First, the twenty years he spent in England after the war were difficult to research. Second, Ripley had been so denigrated by historiographers, South Carolina's Governor Francis Pickens, and General P. G. T. Beauregard that many writers would not have thought it was worth their time or effort.

The negativity toward Ripley began with Governor Francis Pickens. Pickens fancied himself an authority on military tactics and bombarded Ripley with recommendations regarding troop dispositions around Charleston. Finally, Ripley, not very tactfully, suggested that Pickens's "interfering" was not at all helpful and caused "confusion and harm." Later Pickens retaliated in a letter to President Davis, claiming that Ripley said "extreme things" about Lee and feared Ripley's feelings toward Lee was calculated to do "great injury" to Lee's command. It has never been documented what Ripley is alleged to have said, or if he said anything along those lines at all.

However, Douglas Southall Freeman, Lee's biographer, became highly incensed and projected "extreme things" to a more serious level, claiming that "for some unknown reason, Ripley took a violent dislike to Lee." In addition, Beauregard's bitter diatribe against Ripley in the *Official Records,* repeated by Dowdey, Warner, and others, is the basis for the charge that Ripley could not get along with either his superior or subordinate officers. Significantly, the official National Park handbook *Fort Sumter: Anvil of War* includes images of Colonel Alfred Rhett, Major John Johnson, Captain John Mitchel, and Captain Thomas Huguenin. These men were Ripley's subordinate officers, and Ripley is not even mentioned in the Fort Sumter booklet.[5]

Ripley died of a stroke in New York City on March 29, 1887. The next day, the front page of the *Charleston News and Courier* read, "The Sad and Sudden End of Charleston's Gallant Defender." There is a great disconnect between the negative appraisals of Ripley and the consummate, sincere military honors bestowed upon him after his death. All of Ripley's subordinate officers who survived the war respected and honored Ripley at his death and memorial service. Despite the fact that Ripley had been absent from Charleston for over twenty years, he was still loved and honored by his officers and the people of Charleston. Ripley's burial with full military honors took place at Charleston's Magnolia Cemetery on April 3. The Survivors Association of Charleston District and friends of General Ripley began raising funds for a monument in his honor. They unveiled and dedicated the monument of polished Carolina granite on April 3, 1894, exactly seven years after his burial.[6]

ACKNOWLEDGMENTS

I began my research into the life of Roswell Sabin Ripley in 1989. That year, John Hennessy, then with the National Park Service at the Manassas National Battlefield, stressed the importance of presenting my personal opinions in a proposed Ripley article. That article was limited to Ripley's service in Charleston, South Carolina, and Stephen Hoffius was instrumental in its publication in the July 1994 issue of the *South Carolina Historical Magazine*.

As the Ripley family had moved from Worthington, Ohio, to Ogdensburg, New York, I expanded my research to the St. Lawrence County Historical Association in Canton, New York. They forwarded a copy of the April 1960 issue of the *Quarterly*, in which editor Atwood Manley discussed how the Owen D. Young Library of St. Lawrence University had acquired the Christopher Ripley/Charles Shepard Papers. Librarian Darlene Leonard provided copies of pertinent letters from the collection.

Archivist Suzanne Christoff, Manuscripts Curator Susan Lintelmann, and Archives Curator Alicia Mauldin-Ware offered assistance with Ripley's records at the United States Military Academy. Richard Baker, senior tech at the U.S. Army War College, Carlisle Barracks, furnished a copy of Ripley's photograph in their collection.

In 1995 I contacted the Beinecke Rare Book and Manuscript Library at Yale University concerning possible Ripley references. Bridget Burke, the library curator, was especially helpful and sent a bound copy of the R. S. Ripley Papers in their Western Americana Collection. The collection consisted of Roswell's letters to his mother and sisters during the Mexican War.

Ms. Tara C. Craig, reference services supervisor at the Butler Rare Book and Manuscript Library of Columbia University, copied the Ripley/Harper Brothers contract for *The War with Mexico*, and Keith Orejel, a Columbia graduate student, searched the Harpers' records for publication details. Robert Delap, rights and reproduction assistant with the New-York Historical Society Museum and Library, granted permission to publish their photo of the New York Hotel.

Thanks to Sarah W. Carrier of the David M. Rubenstein Rare Book and Manuscript Library at Duke University, and to Chuck Barber at the Hargrett Rare Book and Manuscript Library, University of Georgia. Sean Benjamin at Tulane University's Howard-Tilton Memorial Library contributed information from their G. T. Beauregard Papers.

Robert K. Krick furnished information regarding articles written by Captain Joseph B. Reese, Company F, 44th Georgia. Reese provided insight and supported Ripley's performance at Beaver Dam Creek during the Peninsula Campaign.

In Charleston, Matthew Lockhart, editor of the *South Carolina Historical Magazine,* Faye Jensen and the staff of the South Carolina Historical Society, as well as Jane Yates and Elaine Robbins at the Citadel Archives and Museum, were especially helpful. Ethel Nepveux gave much needed assistance in researching records at the Charleston County Court House.

In the early 1990s the Arizona Historical Foundation forwarded copies of the failed real estate deal between Ripley and Charles Poston. Linda Whitaker, director of the Arizona Historical Society, clarified the current location of the Charles Poston Collection.

Karen E. Kearns, curator of the American Historical Manuscripts and David Zeidberg, director of the Huntington Library, San Marino, California, furnished valuable material from the Thomas Haines Dudley Collection describing the protracted legal problems between Ripley and Greenwood & Batley, Machinists, of Leeds, England.

Years ago the University of Texas at Austin staff microfilmed the James H. Burton Papers, Ramsdell Collection, documenting the Burton/Ripley relationship. Recently, Margaret Schlankey, with the Briscoe Center for American History, University of Texas at Austin, referred me to Archivist Lisa Conathan, Manuscripts and Archives, Yale University Library, holders of the original Burton Papers.

C. Russell Horres Jr.'s account of Alfred Rhett's duel with Ransom Calhoun was quite informative regarding that incident. Antonio Rafael de la Cova shared Ripley information he gathered while researching his excellent book on the life of Colonel Ambrosio José Gonzales. Steve Hoffius and Robert Cuthbert furnished information pertaining to a real estate investment Ripley made in South Carolina near the end of the war.

J. Michael Comeau with the Massachusetts State Archives contributed significant information pertaining to Ripley's return of the 54th Massachusetts Infantry's colors and Ripley's correspondence with the governor. Karen Forgrave, with the North Family History Center, in Columbus, Ohio, located the New York ship arrivals lists for Ripley's three returns to the United States.

At the British Public Records Offices in Kew, now the National Archives (TNA), Mrs. E. F. Thomson discovered records from the Ordnance Select Committee pertaining to Ripley's Sharps carbine sales in 1855. Alison S. B. Mowat of Edinburgh, Scotland, supplied copies of letters, held in the National Library of Scotland, from Ripley and Francis Lawley to *Blackwood's Magazine.* My wife and I were fortunate to be invited to visit with Mrs. Mowat for afternoon tea on our trip to Scotland in 1993.

Charles Priestley, Tony Margrave, and Greg Bayne with the American Civil War Round Table, United Kingdom, freely and enthusiastically provided further help from London. Mr. Priestley contributed information and excellent photos regarding Ripley sites in London, Mr. Margrave copied Chancery records of the *Greenwood vs. Ripley* suit and discovered Ripley's role as sales agent for the Newport Oregon Coal Company in 1872–73. Mr. Bayne volunteered to read the chapters concerning Ripley's stay in England, providing helpful suggestions. Also, Ben Fellows, of the National Army Museum, United Kingdom. provided the difficult-to-locate image of William Hope, V.C.

Especially valuable was the research of W. H. J. Chamberlain and A. W. F. (Tony) Taylerson for their thoroughly detailed text, *Adams' Revolvers*. This fashioned a framework for the large gap in Ripley's life from 1853 to 1860. Tony continued to help me from London with research into Ripley's postwar life in England. He located Letters Patent granted to Ripley and William Hope between 1878 and 1883, and was instrumental in unearthing ordnance minutes concerning the "Hope cannon." Tony discovered a 1955 *Dagenheim Digest* interview with William Hope's granddaughter, which added never-before-known facts regarding Ripley's throat wound. My wife and I were able to meet with Tony and his wife, Felicia, for lunch in London and spent a pleasant afternoon with them. Unfortunately, not long afterward, Tony passed away.

A special thanks to Steve Hoffius for putting me in contact with Alexander Moore, the most helpful acquisitions editor of the University of South Carolina Press. When I began this study in 1989 I did not own a computer. I visited many state and university libraries, historical societies, the United States Military Academy Library, and the Manuscripts Division of the Library of Congress, poring over manuscripts and hand-cranking microfilm readers. I thank my son John for introducing me to the computer, without which I could not have completed this biography, and my grandson Andrew for his expert aid scanning the digital maps and images. Ashley Gerace provided constructive criticism of my early writing efforts.

I especially remember my mother, Ruby Donnan Davis Bennett, for instilling in me an appreciation of my southern Revolutionary War and Confederate ancestors. Last, but definitely not least, I owe much to my wife, Marcia, who remained positive and always offered encouragement through the long research period, writing efforts, and the prepublication process.

CHAPTER 1

Family and Early Years

In Worthington, Ohio, on Friday, March 14, 1823, Christopher and Julia Caulkins Ripley became parents of their first and only son, Roswell Sabin Ripley. Christopher and Julia also had two daughters, Lucia, born April 5, 1819, and Laura, born November 28, 1820. Roswell was most likely named after his maternal grandfather, Roswell Caulkins. Julia's sister, Chloe, had married Josiah Sabin, who was probably the source of Roswell's middle name. Later in Roswell Ripley's life, some references list his middle name as Sabine, but originally it was Sabin.[1]

Roswell Caulkins and his wife Eunice had moved to Ohio from Waterbury, New Haven County, Connecticut, in 1809. Their only son, Lovewell, and seven of their eight daughters, including the youngest two, Julia and Chloe, accompanied them. Three other families from New Haven County brought the migrating group to forty persons.

The arduous trip began on September 20 and ended forty days later in Ohio on October 30. The Caulkins family's destination was the five-hundred-acre tract in Berlin Township that Roswell had purchased for one thousand dollars in 1805. Lovewell visited the site, east of Delaware, Ohio, and north of Worthington, in 1807. He cleared three acres, planted fruit trees, and built a cabin for the family's arrival, before returning to Connecticut to assist the family's move. Julia, about fifteen years old at the time, wrote a narrative of the trip, parts of which are reprinted in the *History of Delaware County*. Julia stated that on September 22 they crossed the Hudson River near Fishkill, New York, in a leaking ferryboat. Julia described the steep ascents and descents over the Allegheny Mountains of Pennsylvania. An abundant supply of deer and wild turkeys, often shot by the women, provided ample meals. They crossed the Ohio River near Wheeling and proceeded through Zanesville and Granville to finally reach their destination near Berkshire in what would become Delaware County. Julia attended and later taught at the school in Berkshire.[2]

The Ripley family had been in New England since 1638. That year William Ripley, his wife, and their four children came from Hingham, Norfolk County, England, to settle in Hingham, Massachusetts. William's grandson, Joshua, married Hannah Bradford, the granddaughter of Governor William Bradford of Massachusetts, who came from England on the Mayflower in 1620. Thereafter, all Ripleys who descended from Joshua and Hannah would be "Mayflower descendants."

Roswell S. Ripley's birthplace, 923 High Street, Worthington, Ohio. Author's photograph.

Joshua's son, Ralph, was born on October 25, 1751, in Windham, Connecticut, and served as a quartermaster in the Backus Light Horse militia in 1776. Ralph was the father of Christopher, born December 12, 1781, at "The Mansion" in Windham. James Wolfe Ripley, Christopher's younger brother, was born on December 10, 1794. James attended West Point and received his commission after only one year, his term at school abbreviated because of the War of 1812. James served with the artillery until 1832 and then transferred to the ordnance department. He ultimately became the U.S. chief of ordnance during the first two years of the Civil War.[3]

In the early 1800s, the Hartford, Connecticut, brokerage firm of Kimberly and Brace hired James's older brother Christopher. On January 20, 1810, Christopher sailed from New York, bound for Denmark, on the 160-ton brig *Rachel* with a crew of ten. The owners placed the ship's captain, C. Howland, and Christopher in charge of the cargo, valued at $18,800. At that time the British, then at war with France, were seizing American ships in an attempt to prevent the United States from trading with Europe. The British feared those traded goods could ultimately aid the French. Unfortunately, on February 17 the English armed brigs *Violet* and *Rambler* seized the *Rachel* southwest of the Scilly Islands and escorted it to Plymouth Harbor. During the subsequent trial, the British alleged but were unable to prove that Howland and Ripley were in fact destined for Amsterdam and had burned the ship's records before its seizure. On March 20, 1810, the British Admiralty Court released Christopher, and by some means he secured a clerkship at the U.S. Consulate in London. He served in London from March 1810 until August 1812. In October 1812 Christopher returned to the United States, arriving at Baltimore, Maryland, with official papers addressed to President James Madison.[4]

In March 1813 as the War of 1812 continued, Christopher returned to Hartford and petitioned for an appointment in the U.S. Army. Alexander Wolcott endorsed his request, stating that Ripley "is a gentleman of fine character, ability and education." Three days later Christopher requested the rank of major, emphasizing his thirty months' experience as a clerk at the U.S. Consulate Office. His requested rank was denied, but on April 21 Ripley received an appointment as captain with the 37th U.S. Infantry Regiment. From April 30 to July 16, Ripley served as the recruiting officer in Hartford. On July 16 he received orders to march his twenty-two recruits, including some musicians and their instruments, to New London. From July 25, 1813, until April 15, 1815, Christopher was stationed at Fort Griswold in Groton. When the war ended, Christopher's request to remain in the military was denied.[5]

After his tour of duty, Christopher joined B. E. Deming at Stamford, Connecticut, in an unknown business venture. Letters "from the late firm of Ripley and Deming" indicate that the business failed. Following the firm's demise, in 1817 Christopher moved to Worthington, Ohio, and later met Julia Caulkins, who was teaching school in nearby Berkshire. On Monday, May 4, 1818, the Reverend Joseph Hughes officiated the wedding of Christopher and Julia in Berkshire. After their marriage, the couple made their home in Worthington.

According to local historians Robert and Jennie McCormick, Worthington in the early 1800s featured "a post office, a printing office, four taverns, four mercantile stores, a college, a Masonic hall and a number of manufactories for woolen cloths, hats, saddles, shoes, combs, etc." There is some evidence that during these years Christopher worked for James Kilbourne's Worthington Manufacturing Company. The firm produced caps, hats, woolen cloth, leather goods, and cabinetwork. The company also operated a retail outlet in Steubenville, Ohio. Christopher's friend Joel Buttles managed the company's store in Franklinton, now part of Columbus. In the early 1820s, the company experienced mounting financial problems and eventually collapsed.

These difficult times may have inspired Christopher to become more spiritually minded. In 1820 the rector of St. John's Episcopal Church and first bishop of Ohio, Reverend Philander Chase, baptized him. The following year, on June 10, the bishop baptized Christopher's daughters, Lucia and Laura. On June 4, 1823, with Bishop Chase in England seeking financial support for an Episcopal seminary in Ohio, the Reverend T. Morse baptized Roswell. In 1826 Christopher moved back to Leicester, Massachusetts, where he joined a nephew in an unknown business venture. Julia, Lucia, Laura, and four-year-old Roswell remained in Worthington until May 1827.[6]

In Worthington, Julia attempted to raise enough money to finance the family's return to New England. Evidently, she acted as an agent for Christopher's stake in the Worthington Manufacturing Company. On April 1, 1827, she wrote to Christopher, ardently hoping to meet him in six or eight weeks. She had been anxious about the route to be taken, as Christopher had recommended an overland trip by wagon. Julia claimed it was quite impossible, as her brother was totally unprepared with horses or wagon. Local friends advised the family to go by way of the Lake [Erie?] and Canal, and she planned to follow this advice. Julia asked her husband not to worry about the children, as she would be watching them closely. In her last letter from Worthington, written on May 3, 1827, Julia notified Christopher that the family would be leaving on May 8 for Portland (now Sandusky), Ohio. "Our driver, horses and carriage are excellent. . . . Lucia, Laura & Sabin are well," she wrote.

This letter is the earliest indication that the family addressed Roswell by his middle name, Sabin. When Julia and her children left Worthington in May 1827, Sabin would have been just slightly over four years old. It is unlikely he would have had any vivid remembrances of the city but must have heard reminiscences of Worthington from his parents and sisters.[7]

After moving to Massachusetts, Julia and the children did not have long to settle into the comforts of their home in Leicester. By May 1828 Christopher had uprooted his family and moved to Ogdensburg, New York. He claimed he came to Ogdensburg "with experience, intelligence and knowledge of the world, and with a stock of goods for retailing." In Ogdensburg, Christopher joined in partnership with his brother James, who was still an officer in the U.S. Army, and with Thomas Denney to establish the firm of C. Ripley & Company. Their company was located on North Water Street in Ogdensburg and engaged in "buying and selling goods, wares and merchandise." Christopher remained with the firm until March 21, 1831, when he severed his relationship.

Following this separation, Julia, Sabin, and his sisters remained in Ogdensburg, while Christopher moved to Montréal and gained employment with Molson Davies and Company, Commission Merchants. On July 3, 1831, Christopher wrote his wife that the company had offered him a "Western Agency," and in this capacity he obtained "consignments of Wheat, Flour, Beef, Pork and other Provisions . . . in the State of Ohio to be shipped to Montréal." He divided his time between the Montréal offices and buying trips to Rochester, Buffalo, Cleveland, and Columbus, Ohio. Joel Buttles and other acquaintances in central Ohio must have been helpful on these buying trips. Christopher's position with Molson Davies lasted three years. Although Christopher mentioned renting a house in Montréal and moving the family, this apparently never happened. However, a letter from Julia to her son, dated August 2, 1833, indicates that ten-year-old Sabin was attending a French school in Longueuil, a suburb of Montréal. Letters indicate that Sabin had written to his mother for permission to buy some pet birds and hoped to be rewarded for achieving good grades.

His mother denied his request, stating that their household was presently too unsettled for her to care for the "pretty birds" when he returned home. She closed with, "My dear son, I do not approve of offering rewards to children to induce them to study, for I think the love of learning and the idea of being qualified for future usefulness should constitute sufficient stimulus."

Sabin's mother encouraged him to write to his sisters in French and "give us specimens of your improvement." The opportunity to study in Québec and learn French obviously stemmed from his father's job with Molson Davies and is evidence of the family's dedication to their son's education. However, at Sabin's young age it must have been a traumatic separation from his mother. With his father on frequent buying trips, Sabin would have been separated from his parents much of the time.[8]

By early 1834, after three years with Molson and Davies, Christopher moved to New York City, where he became involved in various promotions to increase trade between Montréal and the western states. During this time, Julia and the children continued to live in Ogdensburg. Christopher, apparently still seeking his fortune, remained in New York City for only two years. His interest turned to speculation in land after receiving a letter from his brother James stating that "we cannot fail to do well in Illinois or Michigan by locating good lands, making some improvements and then selling out." This type of thinking ultimately led to Christopher's financial ruin.

His investment in Matildaville, a large tract of land near Ogdensburg, began in August 1836. Ripley and Palmer Cleveland prevailed upon Ripley's friend and former business associate in Ohio, Joel Buttles, to provide the $5,000 down payment required to purchase this 28,765-acre tract from George Parish and Company. They intended to resell the land quickly at a large profit to Cleveland's employer, the North American Mining Company. Unfortunately for the investors, the nation suffered a severe financial depression and panic in 1837, and the deal failed. For over a decade Ripley struggled to secure the balance of $20,170 he owed Parish for Matildaville.[9]

In 1836, although distraught and financially challenged by the Matildaville transaction, Christopher enrolled thirteen-year-old Sabin in the St. Lawrence Academy at Potsdam. In this village, about twenty miles from Ogdensburg, Judge Sewall Raymond founded the academy in 1816, and in 1825 he moved the school to a three-story stone building facing the public square in Potsdam. When Sabin

St. Lawrence Academy, Potsdam, New York, a preparatory school attended by young Roswell Ripley. From Franklin B. Hough, *History of St. Lawrence & Franklin Cos., N.Y.*, 1878, p 250.

enrolled in 1836, a second three-story school building had just been completed. Asa Brainard, a graduate of the University of Vermont, was the principal, having occupied the position since 1828.

Sabin wrote to his mother from the academy on October 3, 1836. He lamented having another bed crowded into his room and receiving more boarders. He was to start French in a day or two, was progressing slowly but thoroughly in arithmetic, and hoped to take up algebra next. He and his roommate, identified as "G.D.S.," had nearly used up all their provisions. As it was Sabin's turn, he asked his mother, "if it is convenient," to send a box very soon.[10]

On December 5, 1836, David Sheldon, who ran the boarding house where Roswell was staying, wrote to Christopher acknowledging the receipt of thirty-five dollars as payment for Roswell's board. Sheldon was gratified to learn that Christopher was "highly satisfied" with Roswell's improvement during the last term. Sheldon informed him, "Be assured that I shall not relax my exertions in his behalf for the present quarter."

Adding to the festivities of the approaching Christmas season, on December 8 the Ripleys' oldest daughter, seventeen-year-old Lucia, married Amaziah B. James. A young attorney in Ogdensburg, James originally became associated with the family because of Christopher's legal problems related to his speculation in Matildaville.

By February 9, 1837, things had deteriorated at Roswell's boarding house. His letter to his father began innocently, mentioning that his class had read the first three books of Livy and gone on to Virgil and Horace. He was enjoying all his studies, but "Mr. Sheldon has taken two Canadians into his family who both have the Itch [scabies]." The condition had spread to five other boarders, and Roswell claimed that neither Sheldon nor the boarders seemed to care about curing it. He asked his parents to send him some citrine ointment, adding, "I should like much to get out of this Itchy hole and so change my boarding place. If it does break out on me I shall be at home in less than no time."

It is not known to what extent the scabies infestation influenced Roswell's decision, but shortly after the outbreak, he left Sheldon's boarding house and St. Lawrence Academy. Not having heard from Roswell's father concerning his son's departure, Sheldon wrote Christopher a lengthy letter on March 1, 1837.

Sheldon claimed that during evening prayers, shortly before he left the academy, Roswell "left his seat, walked across the chapel, whispered to individuals as he passed; laughed our chapel teacher in the face who endeavored to check him, and when accused of it, promptly denied it." The principal, Asa Brainard, considered it grossly impudent to contradict a teacher, boxed Roswell's ears, and paddled him. A day or two later, when Sheldon returned home from school at noon, he found Roswell had taken his trunk and left the house. While Roswell waited for the arrival of the stagecoach to Ogdensburg, he browsed through various village stores in Potsdam. Sheldon went to the village, where he found Roswell's trunk outside a tavern. After Sheldon located Roswell, he persuaded him to return to the boarding house and instructed him to write his parents for permission to go home.

After dinner that night, Sheldon learned that while Roswell visited the village stores "he openly cursed and damned his teachers." Roswell admitted he did so because he was "enraged." Sheldon ordered his angry boarder to make a public confession in front of the school, but Roswell left again before the appointed time. Sheldon also claimed that Roswell had not been diligent or prompt in his studies and used profanity "to an awful degree."

In conclusion, Sheldon claimed that the incident would affect Roswell's character; he believed that if Roswell was allowed to question and defiantly curse authority publically and was not punished at home, "what may not be expected from him in [the] future? It is no enviable task to subdue a rebellious temper, to curb the headstrong will, but . . . I am confident thorough discipline will never prove injurious to anyone."[11]

There is no record of his parents' response to this incident. However, we have only Sheldon's description of the confrontation, and it would be interesting to know Roswell's version of the incident. Overcrowded living quarters, coupled with the scabies outbreak, produced a difficult environment. Not quite fourteen years old, Roswell responded inappropriately. This confrontation may be a prophetic sign of Roswell Ripley's rebellious temperament and his inclination to question authority later in life.

William Wordsworth's poem "My Heart Leaps Up When I Behold" is noted for the line "The child is father of the man," expressing the thought that how one acts or behaves when young determines what one will become when an adult. Although this may be the case, the noted biographer Sir Edward Cook warned writers not to draw too heavily on youthful experiences in explaining the adult. He admonished biographers who "magnify some childish incident as prophetic of what is to come thereafter."[12]

CHAPTER 2

West Point

Following the debacle at St. Lawrence Academy in the spring of 1837, nothing is known of Roswell's education for the remainder of the year. James H. Coffin served as principal of Ogdensburg Academy and in September 1837 indicated he would be happy to discuss Roswell's situation. However, there is no record that Roswell attended the local academy. Early in 1838 Christopher Ripley began a concerted effort to secure an appointment for his son to the U.S. Military Academy. In part, Christopher may have decided Roswell needed discipline and would benefit from the rigors of West Point.[1]

Christopher enlisted the aid of the U.S. commissioner for New York Indian Affairs, Ransom H. Gillet, who had represented the district in the 23rd and 24th Congresses. On February 26, 1838, Gillet wrote to Secretary of War Joel R. Poinsett seeking an appointment for Roswell to the academy. Gillet indicated that Roswell was active, intelligent, and worthy of an appointment, adding that his father, Christopher, had been a captain in the last war and was a very worthy citizen. This effort failed, as Roswell had not reached the minimum age of sixteen required for admission.

The next year, on February 9, Christopher resumed his fervent efforts to gain admission to West Point for his son. He informed Commissioner Gillet that he would be writing the secretary of war renewing the application for Roswell, who would be sixteen years old on March 14, 1839. Christopher asked Gillet to renew his recommendation and to speak with his friend Secretary of the Senate Asbury Dickins on the subject. Christopher wanted Gillet to call on the secretary soon and "have my son's name inserted on the register before the appointments for 1839 are made."

In 1838 Christopher had neglected to solicit his congressman's help with the appointment. So in February 1839, the same day he wrote to Gillet, he also sought the support of his congressman, James B. Spencer. The following day Christopher wrote to Secretary of War Poinsett personally, requesting his son's admission to the academy. He noted that Roswell was five feet eight inches tall, weighed 156 pounds, and had attended a French School near Montréal a few months in 1833, read French, had some taste for drawing maps and so forth, and had a good English education. "He is a robust, resolute, energetic, ambitious young man," the elder Ripley wrote. "He will regard an appointment as a valuable privilege, and is aware that it requires no small effort to sustain the character of a respectable

Cadet." Christopher wrote that his brother, Captain James W. Ripley of the Ordnance Corps, would probably write to Poinsett or speak with him about this application.

On February 16 twenty-two of Christopher Ripley's friends in Ogdensburg endorsed Roswell's application to the secretary of war. Senator Silas Wright supported these petitioners in a letter of February 26, stating that "the petitioners are my personal acquaintances and among the most respectable citizens of the county in which I reside." Poinsett also received a letter of endorsement, dated February 26, from James D. Doty, a former New Yorker who was then a congressman from Wisconsin. Commissioner R. H. Gillet's repeat endorsement arrived in early March.[2]

Christopher soon received a disappointing letter from his friend Asbury Dickins. The secretary had spoken with Poinsett and believed that Roswell would be given an appointment, but it would be for the following year. In the meantime, Dickins encouraged Roswell to study mathematics and French with "diligence," stating his belief that "nothing will have been lost by the postponement," as Dickins "had not known any instances in which boys of sixteen were able to keep up with their class." Much to Christopher's relief, his tidal wave of endorsements, petitions, and pleas succeeded. On April 6, 1839, Roswell Ripley received an appointment to the U.S. Military Academy, binding him to serve eight years. commencing from the time he entered the academy.[3]

As Christopher prepared to send his only son to West Point, he offered the boy some advice. If others excelled him, he was to be more diligent, persevering, and studious. If he excelled others, he was not to claim superiority by either conduct or language. If he was boastful, others would try to bring him down. He must be affable, obliging, and friendly.

In April the Ripleys received notification of a two-month preparatory school on the west bank of the Hudson River, one mile south of West Point. The school planned to accept a limited number of pupils in preparation for admission to the Military Academy. It is not known whether Roswell attended the school, but given the intensity with which his father had pursued the appointment, it is not likely Christopher would have permitted his son to miss this opportunity.[4]

R. S. Ripley reported to West Point on June 6, 1839, with "105 dollars in his possession." He passed his entrance examinations and formally entered the academy on July 1, 1839. Admitted the same day was Ripley's classmate, Ulysses S. Grant, who ultimately became the most noted graduate of this class. Roswell spent the months of July and August encamped with the newly admitted class. At the academy, first-year cadets, referred to as plebes, entered as Fourth Year Classmen and advanced to become the First Class their senior year. The plebes pitched their tents on grounds between their barracks and Fort Clinton overlooking the Hudson River. The administration intended the camp to duplicate, as much as possible, the actual conditions of a troop encampment. Life in camp could be very uncomfortable during the hot, humid summers at West Point. When it rained for a few hours, the cadets' soggy wool clothing became miserable to wear. Cadets of the Third Class, the class of 1842, mentored Roswell's class. The 1842 class included future Union generals John Newton, William Rosecrans, John Pope, Abner Doubleday, George Sykes, and Seth Williams. Future noted Confederate generals of that distinguished class were James Longstreet, D. H. Hill, Gustavus W. Smith, A. P. Stewart, Richard H. Anderson, and Lafayette McLaws.

Officers inspected the cadets in rank each morning and afternoon; their tents were inspected several times a day. The demerit system, referred to as delinquencies, had seven classes. A "first class" delinquency resulted in ten demerits, while a "seventh class" delinquency warranted one demerit. On July 6, just five days into the encampment, Roswell received three demerits for a "fifth class" delinquency. He had neglected to have his tent policed at morning drill. Young Roswell accumulated sixty-five demerits his first year; twenty of them resulted from four instances of "visiting after hours." Most serious were his two "second class" delinquencies, each worth eight demerits. These offenses occurred when he "neglected to salute an officer passing him" and later when he was caught "going beyond limits." He registered no "first class" demerits in his total of sixty-five. Considering Roswell's age and his previous difficulties at St. Lawrence Academy, his behavior had improved significantly. During the next three years he maintained better discipline and received ninety-five additional demerits, none of them "first class."[5]

When summer encampment ended, the cadets moved into their barracks and began the arduous West Point academic life. In his first year, Roswell did remarkably well academically. Each class was divided into four sections. The first section included the most competent cadets and used more difficult texts, while the fourth section covered only the minimum requirements. Ripley's fourth section was assigned alphabetically until the January examinations could permit reassignment by academic standing. Ripley did so well in mathematics and French that he advanced to the first section in September.

On May 10, 1840, Julia Ripley wrote to her son, noting that she had received "a few lines" from him delivered by Mr. Egert, who said "he found you in a very good condition, large, robust, and healthy; in short he describes you to your acquaintances here as a real military gentleman; your northern friends are a little proud of their representative at the Academy." She supposed that Asa Brainard, the principal of St. Lawrence Academy, was anxious to know whether his "predictions" about Roswell had merit. If Roswell proved to be respectable without Brainard's aid, she ventured, his predictions would be proven wrong. Julia was obviously referring to Brainard's negative appraisal of Roswell at the academy.

However, Julia was disappointed to learn that her son's demerits had increased during the previous month. "I fear you think too lightly of them," she wrote. "They have more influence in the estimation of character than you seem to be aware, especially among those who have no other criteria." She wanted him to be vigilant about his conduct in the future and asked, "will you be able to maintain a high standing at the next examination? You know that application and perseverance will ensure it."

Roswell's mother also informed him that his sister Laura had given birth to a daughter on May 8 and that "both mother and child doing well." The previous year Laura had married Charles Shepard, whose papers with the American Line Steamship Company are included in the Ripley/Shepard Papers at St. Lawrence University. This daughter, Roswell's niece Julia Adelaide Shepard, would witness the assassination of President Lincoln at Ford's Theater on Friday, April 14, 1865. To commemorate the centennial of Abraham Lincoln's birth, the April 1909 issue of the *Century Magazine* printed Julia's eyewitness account of the incident. Julia's younger brother, Roswell's nephew Charles William Shepard, enlisted in the 106th New York Infantry in 1862 and was killed at Cold Harbor, Virginia, on June 1, 1864.[6]

In June 1840, at the end of his first year, Ripley ranked seventh in a class of sixty cadets. The first-year curriculum consisted primarily of two courses, mathematics and French. As a member of the advanced first section, Roswell placed fourth in mathematics and ranked sixth in French. On June 19 Ripley was designated cadet corporal in the Battalion of Cadets and did not return to Ogdensburg for the summer of 1840. He and his classmates remained at the Point to mentor the incoming class of 1844. During the Civil War, Winfield Scott Hancock would become a most noted graduate of that class.

In July, as the second year began, Roswell received one demerit for "not having his tent cords properly secured," and as a file closer he received three demerits "for allowing a cadet to take his place in rank when not properly clad." Roswell finished his second year with thirty-one demerits, less than half the number he accumulated his first year. Unfortunately, on September 5 Roswell was absent from his quarters between 8:00 and 9:30 P.M. and was relieved of duty as corporal in the Battalion of Cadets.

In February 1841 Julia again offered more opinions and counsel: "There have been more parties this winter than usual, but I cannot see much use or amusement in them." She cautioned him against "chasing after enjoyment in a giddy whirl of fashionable life or attempts to simulate it.... It is probable that Cadet Ripley will be something of a Lion when he visits St. Lawrence. I think often of you studying away." Julia asked her son to bring home samples of his classroom drawings and wrote, "I found your 'Storm at Sea' among some of the old drawings the other day and put it up in my room. Have you found a Clergyman yet? ... how do you open your Sundays?"

During their second year the cadets faced a more diverse curriculum as ethics and drawing were added to French and mathematics. Roswell excelled in all subjects and moved from seventh place to fifth in his class. He finished eighth in math, ninth in French, and sixth in first-part drawing and ethics. The class now totaled fifty-three cadets, as seven members were found to be "deficient" or left school for other reasons.[7]

In May 1841, as the school year was coming to an end, an exasperated Julia criticized her son for not answering her questions in his letters. She chided, "I told you to let me know if you wanted your shirts before you went to Augusta, but you said nothing. Your father as usual is absent. ... I have often inquired of you respecting your present roommates. But you are not apt to answer all my questions."

Roswell apparently did answer his mother's concern about the lack of clergy, as she wrote, "I am happy to hear that you have a clergyman at W.P. of respectable talents. Suppose it is now no unpleasant task for the Cadets to attend Church."

During the summer break of 1841, Roswell planned to visit his uncle, Captain James W. Ripley, stationed at the U.S. Arsenal in Augusta, Maine. However, on June 14 the academy detailed Ripley to instruct a section of candidates for admission, so the trip could not begin until he completed this assignment. Julia wished to accompany her son "to see the Ripleys in Augusta, and then visit Leicester, our friends in Connecticut, and my birthplace." After their travels Roswell and his mother would return to Ogdensburg. "I presume you will find here a pleasant resting place from severe study and military routine, but you must not expect much gaiety, or many amusements of the noisy birthday sort."

In November 1841, during his third year at the academy, Roswell received a letter and more admonitions, this time from his father: "We were all pleased to hear of your good health, efforts, and progress. ... each individual Cadet ought to reflect that he is likely to be placed in situations unfavorable to health ... and ought to acquire the knowledge necessary for preserving it in such situations. ... Temperance, exercise, and good habits, will generally succeed. Abridge the habit of smoking Cigars until it is abandoned." Christopher Ripley wrote of the family's good health and then of his financial difficulties with George Parish as a result of his Matildaville investment. He cautioned his son "to steer as clear of debt as possible" and enclosed five dollars.

There is only one letter in the Ripley/Shepard Papers from Roswell, while at West Point, to his parents. On May 17, 1842, he wrote that his class had been engaged for a few days in putting some of its precepts into practice, such as finding height by means of a barometer and time of day by sextant. He added, "Our riding exercises have stopped for awhile, battalion drills for a week or two, and our class is now at the Battery. The weather has turned very pleasant and we shall soon resume our summer uniforms. The examination commences on June 6 and will probably last until the 20th." As requested, Roswell agreed to send his mother some of his drawings but cautioned her not to "look at them close, for they are not in the style for that." He was happy to report that he had not been "on the sick report since furlough, saving once when I had some creosote put in for the toothache."

Earlier, Roswell must have received some advice regarding his use of alcohol. He wrote, "So for the Temperance cause I am afraid that there is such a thing as running that as well as drinking into the ground. However it will be a year before I am called on to decide, and my opinion may very probably change before that." Unfortunately, alcohol would ultimately cause Ripley problems.

He closed this letter to his mother hoping that they could make a trip to Ohio to visit his maternal relatives. It is not known whether they made this trip, but a nostalgic journey with his mother to Worthington may have contributed to his memories of Ohio. Ripley had his birthplace, Worthington, Ohio, inscribed on his gravestone in Magnolia Cemetery, Charleston, South Carolina. Ripley evidently valued his Midwestern birthplace and did not want to be remembered in Charleston as a New England Yankee.[8]

During his third year Ripley maintained his fifth-place class standing. In drawing Roswell ranked fifth in his class and seventh in philosophy and chemistry. At the end of the school year in June 1842, only forty-one cadets remained from the fifty-three students who completed the previous year, and nearly one-third of his original classmates were no longer at the academy. Roswell's twenty-five demerits were the lowest of his years at the West Point.

The last preserved letter to Roswell at West Point was dated July 29, 1842. Both his father and mother contributed to the letter that summer before his final year. His father described his ongoing financial difficulties with George Parish and then offered more support and advice, while his mother inserted local news and regretted that she would not be able to visit him at West Point.

In February, Cadet Lieutenant Ripley received his appointment as captain of Company A, Battalion of Cadets. This rank gave him the honor of marching at the head of the company in the graduation parade of the class of 1843. In this final year Ripley dropped from fifth to seventh in a class that would graduate thirty-nine officers. He ranked eighth in engineering, ninth in mineralogy and geology, tenth in ethics, and unexpectedly, second in infantry tactics but only twelfth in artillery. Destined to become a much-acclaimed artilleryman, his class rankings for artillery and infantry are surprising. In addition to slipping in class rankings, Ripley's demerits rose to thirty-nine, although most were minor demerits for visiting after hours and tardiness.

Ulysses S. Grant graduated twenty-first in this class and finished a bewildering twenty-fifth in artillery and twenty-eighth in infantry tactics. Grant accumulated a total of 290 demerits compared with Ripley's 160 during the four years. Academic achievement, class standing, and conduct were obviously not predictive of Grant's development as a successful commander.[9]

In 1887 a West Point classmate, Samuel G. French, remembered Ripley as an excellent student who maintained his high class standing throughout the years. "He was generous, openhearted, and, though out-spoken, harbored no resentments. He usually saw the humorous side of every occurrence or question, and would illustrate it in a quaint manner, peculiarly his own. His cheerful presence dispelled all unnecessary solemnity in every assembly. Above all, he was honest, upright in all his dealings, and pure of heart."[10]

CHAPTER 3

Prelude to War

Most members of the graduating class, after being relieved of duty at the academy, returned home on leave to await orders. However, Brevet Second Lieutenants R. S. Ripley and J. J. Reynolds stayed at West Point and were assigned to the academy's Department of Artillery and Cavalry. On June 23, 1843, they received orders to report as assistants to Lieutenant Miner Knowlton, an instructor in the department. Their duty continued through the encampment months of July and August. As compensation for his extended duty at the academy, General Order No. 42 granted Ripley a leave of absence for September and October. On August 13 Ripley requested that his leave be extended through November 30. Major General Robert A. Delafield, superintendent of the academy, wrote to the Office of the Adjutant General supporting Ripley's extension request, "should the public service permit." The Adjutant General's Office granted the extension, Special Order No. 77, and Ripley spent the next three months in Ogdensburg.[1]

In November, Ripley received orders to join Company C, 3rd Artillery Regiment, under the command of Brevet Major Samuel A. Ringgold at Fort McHenry. Located on Whetstone Point southeast of the city, Fort McHenry defended the harbor at Baltimore, Maryland. The military and political pressure caused by the expanding Napoleonic Wars (1793–1815) led the United States to attempt to defend its extensive eastern coastline. On March 20, 1794, Congress passed "An act for the defense of certain ports and harbors of the United States." Fort McHenry survives today as one of the original sixteen forts proposed for the east coast.

Between 1829 and 1839 an extensive construction program upgraded Fort McHenry to its present configuration. The program for improving the fort began under the supervision of Roswell's uncle, Captain James W. Ripley, post commander from November 1828 to February 1829 and from June 1832 to October 1832. By 1833 Captain Ripley had supervised alterations in the inner fort's magazines and personnel casements; he had a "thick wash of water cement" applied to the exterior walls and raised the buildings to a full two stories. James Ripley could not have imagined his young nephew would be stationed at the fort in just ten years.[2]

When Roswell Ripley joined Company C, the nine other companies of the Third Artillery had been separated and sent to various forts primarily along the southeast coast. These assignments included Fort Moultrie, South Carolina; Forts Macon and Johnston, North Carolina; Fort Monroe, Virginia; and the Augusta

Arsenal in Georgia. Regimental returns for Fort McHenry in December list Ripley as being sick, but no details of his illness are given. In March 1844 Company C was sent to the Washington Arsenal but returned to Fort McHenry in April. During the month of July, Ripley served as acting adjutant at Fort McHenry.

In 1844 the United States Army had four artillery regiments, each composed of ten companies. One company, or battery, in each of these regiments was designated "light" artillery, suitable for accompanying an infantry regiment onto a battlefield. Sometimes referred to as "flying artillery," each "light" company usually manned four to six 6-pounder guns. Equipped with new, lightweight, horse-drawn guns, the mobile artillerists could maneuver and deploy quickly. These tactics would often bring the light artillery into the most dangerous positions on the battlefield. Ripley's commander, Major Samuel Ringgold, had been instrumental in the development of this concept and in the training of the artillerists who manned these guns.

On August 29 Major Ringgold notified the Adjutant General's Office of serious problems with the artillery at Fort McHenry. He cited insufficient men available to work even a reduced battery of four guns and therefore an inability to perform field exercises. The work was so severe that none of the discharged men reenlisted. Ringgold asked for twenty-two to twenty-four men to be attached to his troop. The July 1844 returns for the 3rd Artillery substantiated Ringgold's letter.[3]

These conditions may have prompted Ripley on September 26 to request a transfer from the artillery to the 1st Regiment of Dragoons, but the Adjutant General's Office denied his request. Being unsuccessful in transferring to the dragoons did not end Ripley's efforts to leave Fort McHenry. In October he secured a transfer to Company A stationed at Fort Johnston near present-day Southport, North Carolina. Ripley's short tour of duty in North Carolina ended in December. In January 1845 he again changed companies, this time moving to Company B garrisoned at the Augusta Arsenal in Georgia. Ripley remained in Augusta for nine months, serving under Captain John R. Vinton and First Lieutenant F. O. Wyse.[4]

At this time tension was rising between the United States and Mexico over the annexation of Texas. The Mexican State of Tejas had declared its independence from Mexico on March 2, 1836. That year, on April 21, the Texans' overwhelming defeat of Santa Anna at the Battle of San Jacinto validated the revolution and their independence. For nine years Mexico refused to recognize the Republic of Texas, although the republic gained recognition from the United States, Great Britain, France, and other European governments. On March 1, 1845, during Ripley's posting at the Augusta Arsenal, the United States extended an offer of annexation to the Texas Republic. On the Fourth of July 1845, the republic voted to accept the offer and gave up its independence. The Mexican government considered the annexation a declaration of war, and the government instructed Brigadier General Zachary Taylor to move troops into Texas for its defense. On July 31 Taylor's forces reached and encamped on the banks of the Nueces River near Corpus Christi. Despite this tension, the Polk administration made no significant effort to prepare for war. Military appropriations were not increased, and there was only a nominal increase in the size of the army. The standoff continued for the remainder of 1845 with Texas being admitted to the Union in December.[5]

On September 4, 1845, after nine months in Augusta, Ripley received Special Order No. 84 appointing him assistant instructor in mathematics at the United States Military Academy. Five days later he departed Augusta, bound for West Point. It is not recorded whether Ripley sought this position or whether the academy requested his appointment based on his academic achievement at West Point. There is only one known reference to Ripley's performance as an instructor at the academy. The source, Orlando Wilcox, described Ripley as "one of our old unpopular West Point instructors." Unfortunately, Wilcox did not say why Ripley was "unpopular." As a new instructor, Ripley may have been ineffective in the classroom. Conversely, he may have been unpopular because he was too strict and demanding for the cadets. Ripley's assignment at the academy, whether intended to be temporary or not, lasted only through the end of the year. It is only conjecture whether his "unpopularity" led to his brief stay.[6]

Following his departure from the academy, difficulty arose when the Office of the Adjutant General realized that the company to which Ripley had been assigned already had three officers. On January 24, 1846, by Special Order No. 6, the adjutant general ruled, "as Lieut. Ripley [is] a brevet let him be ordered to report to the Chief of the Coast Survey." Assigned to the survey, Ripley spent February through May in Baltimore and Washington. During this time he would have been involved with the first U.S. Coast Survey to chart Chesapeake Bay and the Harbor of Annapolis. Ripley's duty with the Coast Survey was interrupted when his former commanding officer at the Augusta Arsenal, Captain John Vinton, asked for a court of inquiry to be held on that post. On February 20 Vinton requested Ripley's presence as a "witness before the Court of Inquiry."[7]

Roswell wrote to his mother from the Augusta Arsenal on March 9, 1846, stating that he left Baltimore about February 27. He wrote that Baltimore had been an exceedingly pleasant and happy place during his previous duty at Fort McHenry. Ripley's friends were most happy to see him, and he was pleased with the kind reception he received. He related that his trip to Augusta was "for the purpose of attending a Court of Inquiry instituted to investigate certain charges made against my late commanding officer, by his obstreperous Lieut. Wyse." Ripley stated that he "found Captain Vinton very well and very glad to see me." Ripley had not given his testimony as yet but was expected to do so in a few days.

He would be required to remain in Augusta until the court finished its deliberations. He was "sick of this continued squabbling, and I think it high time that something more than mere reprimanding should be done." Ripley contrasted Augusta's "delightful weather" to the conditions he left at Baltimore, "cold in the extreme and snowing something like St. Lawrence."

Roswell told his mother of meeting by chance a family friend, Mrs. Lewis, in Washington while he was still with the Coast Survey. She claimed to be very glad to see him but scolded him for not trying to get in touch with her. She "talked of writing home about me, and ended by abusing me for wearing a moustache, all of which I conceived to be my business, not hers. It is a pity indeed, but I believe that our faults grow with our age."

Roswell stated that he was applying for an appointment with either of two regiments being organized for the Oregon service. He believed service during the Oregon boundary dispute with Great Britain would afford him a chance to increase his rank. He realized the risk and hazard would be great, but "I <u>must</u> rise in some way or another."

In early April, after finishing his court of inquiry duty in Augusta, Ripley returned to the Coast Survey. A letter to his mother on April 7 from Barnum's Hotel in Baltimore, began, "I have just returned from Washington, although [I am] supportive of Jas. K. Polk, I think he's rather a fool, not for going to war, but for not making preparations for the emergency." (During the war, Ripley's opinion of Polk would improve significantly.) In closing, Ripley stated, "We shall get on the bay in the course of a few days."

The crisis over the Oregon Territory faded as negotiations between Great Britain and the United States resulted in a peaceful agreement. All attention turned to Mexico. By the middle of May, Ripley was relieved of duty with the Coast Survey and ordered to Fort Columbus in New York Harbor. There he joined Company G, 2nd Artillery Regiment, after being promoted from brevet to full second lieutenant. He regretted leaving his companions in the 3rd Regiment and hoped he would be transferred back to that unit. Ripley believed he would soon be bound for Mexico, where he wished he had been a month ago: "Our fellows have given a glorious account of themselves at Palo Alto and Resaca de la Palma." Ripley mentioned that he had a daguerreotype taken in Baltimore and would ship it home soon: "It is in moustache and beard. . . . I may say it does not do me quite justice, but is a likeness of me in my bad humor." He hoped duty in the field in Mexico would help repay his education at the Military Academy.[8]

On Monday, June 8, 1846, Roswell wrote to his father that on Thursday, with fair winds, it was presumed "we shall be off." He would be shipping out on the six-hundred-ton *Henry Pratt,* built for the Canton trade. The officers' accommodations were not very good but "very commodious" for the men. He would try to follow his father's suggestions "relative to health, though I do not think there is much danger. My experience in the South will have done me some good." He believed that one problem would be the quantity of water one must drink "and it is not the best." However, "very few of us have been seriously unwell and none of us have been snatched off. I hope and trust that it will be granted to us to meet again before very, very long."

Ripley obviously did not know just how seriously his health would be endangered in Mexico. The Mexican War had an even higher mortality rate than the Civil War, with many more men dying of disease than in combat. While only 1,548 officers and men died of wounds sustained in action, reportedly 10,970 died of illness.[9]

When a new regiment of riflemen arrived at Fort Columbus, Ripley noticed that ten or twelve of the men were dismissed or resigned cadets. Second Lieutenant Ripley was especially angered when one of his former classmates, who resigned from the academy after about two years, was appointed first lieutenant. Ripley believed that the greatest injustice has been done to the regular army and thought the present government did not respect graduates of the U.S. Military Academy.

There is an undated note Ripley probably included with this last letter before shipping out. Obviously written just prior to his departure, the paper lists Ripley's outstanding debts, "which are heavy in consequence of the roving life which I have lately led and which has been most expensive. The fitting out obliges me to leave them unpaid," and he wanted to leave a trace of them "in case I should be carried off."

Roswell owed eight establishments at West Point, Boston, New York, and Washington, as well as Barnum's Hotel in Baltimore, a total of $464. He regretted that he had not been able to pay at least some of the bills, noting, "shall I live, do my best for it." He did not want his mother to see the list and cautioned against "troubling her about it. I had thought of getting my life insured in her favor, but these bloodsuckers would have charged more for the war clause than the whole thing amounted to."

On June 11, 1846, the *Henry Pratt* sailed from New York Harbor bound for the Gulf of Mexico. Just before the ship weighed anchor, Roswell wrote a quick note to his mother informing her that he and three hundred men and nine officers were leaving New York in stormy winds. Roswell acknowledged receiving all of his mother's recent letters and one from Laura.[10]

CHAPTER 4

Mexico, 1846

July 21, 1846: "We are here at last after a tedious passage of about 40 days, having been set back by the Gulf Stream, headwinds and calms, save during the last week." In this letter to his mother, Ripley reported that the troops had been "exceedingly healthy during the trip." The *Henry Pratt* lay at anchor for several days off Brazos Santiago, "pitching about in fine style." Ripley attributed the delay at anchor to limited means of transportation. After struggling against a heavy sea during their disembarkation, all were "overjoyed to get our feet once more on shore." The "immense crowd" of volunteer forces already at Los Brazos appalled Ripley. He noted that the volunteers showed little discipline, and six regiments of the best of them had become disgusted and were rumored to be leaving.

On July 25 Company G, 2nd Artillery, moved inland from Los Brazos to the base at Point Isabel, where Ripley found a company of the 4th Artillery, including "some old friends and acquaintances." Ripley wanted to join the army in the field and did not want to be guarding "a depot of pork and hard bread." While he waited, a company of the 1st Artillery arrived, bringing more old friends. Ripley was irritated that "many of our West Point friends are here in the Volunteers as well as the regular army. They are trying to make something of them, but I think the case is nearly hopeless."

Ripley wrote that his former company at Fort McHenry, under the command of Major Samuel Ringgold, had arrived some time ago and proceeded inland. At Point Isabel, Ripley took a stroll through the hospitals that were caring for the wounded from the Battles of Palo Alto and Resaca de la Palma. Although not a pleasant sight, Ripley found a couple of Ringgold's old soldiers who were recovering and were glad to see him. Ripley spent time with them and congratulated them on their recovery. He heard from all his former companions in the fight, even about the way his old horses behaved, which he found to be interesting.

Ripley did not mention Major Ringgold in his letter, and possibly Roswell's recovering friends did not know Ringgold's fate. Ripley later learned that his former commander was mortally wounded in action at the Battle of Palo Alto. While directing his artillery, a Mexican cannon ball tore through both of Ringgold's thighs, as well as the body of the horse on which he was mounted. Ringgold was moved to Point Isabel, where he lingered for three days before dying.[1]

After a week at Point Isabel, Ripley's company of the 2nd Artillery and two companies of the 4th Artillery marched eight miles to the mouth of the Rio

Grande. During this time Ripley served on the battalion quartermaster staff and with a company of the 4th Artillery. In a day or two, the companies split up, boarded steamers for Camargo, and proceeded slowly upstream against a rapidly moving current. The steamers stopped briefly at Matamoros, where Ripley again encountered many old friends and enjoyed a pleasant afternoon.

After this short layover, the steamers continued on and in five days arrived at Camargo, which the officers found to be a miserable, dirty little town: "The Mexicans on the banks were very kind and treated us with much consideration, that is to say, sold us what we wanted at very high prices," Ripley wrote. Most of the regular force was there as Ripley joined the 1st Brigade of the Army Artillery Battalion.

After about three weeks of routine camp duty, General Taylor arrived, reviewed the troops, and ordered General William J. Worth's brigade to advance. On August 18 they passed the San Juan River and the encampment of Duncan's Battery of Artillery. The following night the battalion, now accompanied by Duncan's Battery, traveled eight miles over rough roads and an occasional bog before stopping at the village of Mier. There they awaited the arrival of the 8th Infantry and a train of pack mules. After he obtained permission, Ripley saddled his horse and rode out to survey the terrain with Captains Duncan and Meade of the topographical engineers. George Gordon Meade, with whom Roswell rode that day, achieved fame in July 1863 as commander of the Union army at Gettysburg.

Captain John R. Vinton and Roswell's old company at the Augusta Arsenal had captured and were now occupying the village of Mier. After the addition of Vinton's company and the 8th Infantry, the brigade headed for Cerralvo. While en route they found a considerable quantity of ammunition and lances, which they destroyed. The brigade arrived at Cerralvo with no other incidents except for the loss of a few knapsacks stolen by rancheros from the back of a strayed mule.

On August 27 Roswell described Cerralvo as a most picturesque village of about two thousand inhabitants and with houses of white, sunburnt brick. It resembled a village in old Spain except for "the Indian-like appearance of the inhabitants." Ripley had enjoyed painting and regretted that he had nothing with which to sketch the scenic village. Although the residents appeared to be alarmed and a little distrustful, "they are coming in with articles for sale. They intend to beat us by breaking our bank, for they charge exorbitantly."

Roswell did not believe Mexico was necessarily an unhealthy country and thought "tarantulas, scorpions, centipedes and rattlesnakes, which are abundant," posed the greatest danger. He obviously was unaware of how unhealthy it actually was, or would become, as diseases in the camps at Camargo killed an estimated fifteen hundred volunteer troops. Roswell believed that they would be at Cerralvo for a few more weeks, waiting for the rest of the army to arrive, before beginning the advance toward Monterrey.[2]

The remainder of the army reached Cerralvo on September 9, and the push toward Monterrey would begin on September 13 with General David E. Twiggs's First Division. As Ripley's position as battalion quartermaster had been "legislated out," he returned to his company. On September 11, while still encamped near Cerralvo, Roswell claimed, "the army is in excellent health and fine spirits and pretty confidant of having a hard fought action at or near Monterrey. Our encampment is as pleasant as could be and perhaps the largest American encampment ever seen, stretching over the whole of the tableland above the village of Cerralvo. Many old friends are present and it seems as if the Military Academy has been transferred to Mexican soil." Roswell lamented the lack of mail from home since he left Point Isabel and thought the family may have gone to Ohio. For the family to make the long arduous journey to Ohio indicates that ties remained strong between the Ripleys in Ogdensburg and the Caulkins family in Ohio. This tie to his mother's family helps explain Roswell's nostalgia for Worthington and Ohio.[3]

The U.S. assault of Monterrey began on September 20 against the Mexican forces under the command of General Pedro de Ampudia. This would be Ripley's first combat experience, which he described in a letter to his mother. When the attack of September 21 began, Ripley, who was then on the commissary staff of Worth's Brigade, had to "remain behind for a short time to park the train, etc." When they heard the opening fire of musketry, "we started off to join the General. As we turned the hill at a gallop we came upon the field at once." He noted that "a dead Mexican officer, Mexican soldiers and horses" littered the way.

Ripley had probably observed the aftermath of the battle between the Mexican cavalry of Lieutenant Colonel Juan de Najera and McCulloch's Texans. This victory allowed the Americans to control the important Saltillo Road, and paved the way for the assaults on Federation Hill and Independence Hill next to it. After defeating the Mexicans on Federation Hill, they would attack the fortification known as the Bishop's Palace on Independence Hill. Control of the Bishop's Palace, overlooking the city of Monterrey, would give the artillery command of the town.

Ripley heard the thunder of the enemy's guns, and his company moved into a nearby gorge. As they took their positions, a gun on their right sent several 9-pound shot into their line. The position became untenable and caused the company to fall back about half a mile. Soon a detachment from the Artillery Battalion, the 5th and 7th Infantry, and McCulloch's Texans received orders to assault the enemy battery. They succeeded in capturing the battery and turned the Mexicans' guns on the palace and a battery inside. According to Eisenhower, on September 22, "At three o'clock in the morning, the Artillery Battalion and some 200 Texans advanced, stormed, and carried the Palace battery." Ripley went up the hill "in the gray of the morning under a shower of balls," but claimed they had very few casualties. Reaching the main body of troops, he found Captain Vinton at the head of the advance and during a lull in the action went down to the base camp for provisions. After preparing the train, he started for the hill and passed through a field on the rear of the hill, where shells began to fall around him. He spurred his horse and galloped as far up the hill as possible. He dismounted and reached the top in time to see "the charge of our fellows, the fall of the Mexican flag, and the Stars and Stripes floating in its place."

On the morning of September 23, the Americans turned the palace guns on the city of Monterrey. In the afternoon they advanced into the city streets under a hot and heavy fire. The infantry, able to get into the houses and behind walls, were somewhat protected, but the horse artillery and staff were much more exposed as every street appeared to be swept with fire. A mortar the Americans brought into town began dropping shells on the defenders that night, and the next morning "a flag of truce bore proposals for a surrender." Representatives of the two forces, early in the morning of September 25, signed surrender documents that also called for a truce of eight weeks.[4]

On October 6 Ripley wrote to his cousin Adeline (known as Adie), the daughter of his uncle James. To his mother he had described the march from Cerralvo to Monterrey as being pleasant, but to Adie he admitted that his time was unpleasant enough, as he was quartermaster to the 1st Brigade. Therefore, he had to remain in the rear for a good portion of the time, "talking broken Spanish to a crowd of Mexican arrieros," the men who packed and unpacked the mules when the army moved from place to place.

Mexican forces had evacuated the town, and it now served as quarters for the Americans. Ripley believed that the beauty of the area was unrivaled and a description impossible: "The splendid combination of rugged mountains and fertile valley, with the river San Juan and the magnificent foliage of the southern climate, all make a scene, which is unsurpassed in my experience."

On the twenty-sixth, Ripley reminded his mother that his safety had not been an issue during the eight-week truce. We are "safely housed in Monterey, lying on our oars, waiting for more troops to come up and for the expiration of the truce." Ripley had recently had a "slight touch of fever and ague" and had recovered, but he could hardly find enough energy to perform his duties. Many others quartered in the city experienced chills and fevers, which, although minor, took a greater toll on their energy than anything the enemy had done.

Lately, Roswell's duties had been changing so much he found them difficult to describe. When the First Brigade left Cerralvo he was appointed brigade commissary, but during the action at Monterrey, "I acted as Commissary, Quartermaster, Aide de Camp and soldier." After the battle, he served for a short time as division commissary but then was appointed acting assistant adjutant general of the First Brigade. "What the next turn of the wheel will bring me remains to be seen," he wrote.

Lieutenant Colonel Thomas Staniford, commander of the First Brigade, had spent time in Ogdensburg and often spoke with Ripley about his days there. Staniford, along with Clark, adjutant of the 8th Infantry, and Dr. Deleon of the medical staff, composed Ripley's "very pleasant" mess. The Mexican cooking contained a little too much garlic and red pepper for Ripley's taste, but he enjoyed the "most delicious Spanish chocolate and other little delicacies." He spent most of his time doing paperwork but made up for it with "a good deal of pleasure riding." His division was the only one quartered in Monterrey, while the remainder of the troops encamped about three miles away; riding to and from their camp made a pleasant trip.

Ripley had no idea where they would be ordered next but did not doubt they would beat the Mexican army wherever they met "unless there was a huge disparity of force." He only wondered whether the government could stand the expense or whether the public would accept the loss of volunteer lives. In contrast, he thought the lives of the regular troops meant nothing to the politicians. He agreed with General Taylor's determination not to advance "with less than 25,000 men, 10,000 to be regular troops, [but] where they are to come from is to be seen."[5]

Early in November, General Taylor decided to push farther into the interior of Mexico toward Saltillo. Ripley, accompanying the lead elements, stated that the advance consisted of Duncan's Battery, the 8th Infantry Regiment, and Blanchard's company of volunteers, altogether about a thousand men. He also described the march of nearly seventy miles as being unpleasant because of a shortage of water and thought the "men must have suffered extremely."

After passing through a narrow valley bordered on both sides by the rugged Sierra Madre Mountains they arrived at Saltillo, a city of about twelve thousand inhabitants. As they entered the city, Ripley believed the men who gathered to witness their arrival far outnumbered the American troops. The women did not impress him: "as for Mexican beauty, the less said about that the better."

Understandably, the Mexicans did not want their homes taken by the military and used as officer's quarters, but they were ordered to "turn out, or be turned out, as we are getting into quarters and making ourselves as comfortable as possible." Colonel Staniford and Ripley were quartered in General Ampudia's house, which Ripley thought was nice "for a Mexican house, but with gaudy paintings, all in more profusion than taste."

Roswell complained that the nearby cathedral was the biggest problem, as its bells rang from morning till night. He intended to stay home rather than travel, for November in the mountains "is monstrous cold, and the wind of the coldest kind." He lamented having received only one letter and hoped more were on the way somewhere between Point Isabel and Saltillo: "In this far-off land a letter from our friends is a Godsend."

Roswell thanked Lucia for her "kind letter" and appreciated their "anxious interest" in his welfare. He asked them to remember, just as they had told him, "there is a Providence who watches over all, and if it be his will that I should fall in the service, bow before his judgment and say, thy will Oh Lord be done."

Roswell described Saltillo as being larger than Monterrey but not as pleasant. He enjoyed being in General Ampudia's old quarters, "sitting in chairs and being under a roof." There were many senoritas, but "as they don't understand my Spanish well enough to appreciate any attention, I have not spent much time cultivating their acquaintance."

Ripley and other officers were surprised when every piece of mail from home was loaded with various accounts of the bloody battles of Monterrey, "so different are they that [we] can hardly recognize them." The officers were amused by these accounts and thought Americans would believe anything if it would "flatter either their personal or national vanity." Rumors circulated that Santa Anna had assembled thirty to thirty-five thousand men near Potosi, but Ripley believed that "it is impossible, or almost so, for him to move and if he does it would be only to get a good sound thrashing. And please don't trouble yourselves so much about my safety."[6]

CHAPTER 5

Mexico, 1847

On New Year's Day 1847, Ripley wrote to his mother from his office, a room he described as also being his "bedroom and parlor." Wishing all at home a happy New Year, he supposed they were enjoying a good fire in "our frozen land of the North and perhaps talking a little bit about me." The only excitement in Saltillo since his last letter was a rumored attack in early December by Santa Anna's forces in San Luis Potosi. Within days, approximately four thousand troops under the command of Generals John E. Wool and William O. Butler began to reinforce the garrison at Saltillo. After the reinforcements arrived, it soon became obvious that Santa Anna had no intention of attacking; however, the new troops remained near Saltillo.

On Christmas morning General Wool had notified the garrison at Saltillo that "the enemy was in his front and he expected to be attacked either that day or the next. We were all agog and Christmas dinners stood a fair chance of being lost." The First Brigade had dinner earlier, and as they finished their last mouthful of pie, an orderly rushed in informing the staff that General Wool wanted them at his headquarters in twenty minutes. Ripley and others at his table quickly mounted and rode to Wool's headquarters. The moment they arrived they were ordered forward to examine the field chosen for the battle. As Ripley and the staff reconnoitered the proposed battlefield, Wool's messenger arrived to inform them that the threat was over. For the remainder of December 1846, Ripley was engaged in ordinary garrison duties.

When General Winfield Scott arrived in Mexico, Ripley believed that the strategy would probably change. He thought that all field artillery would be ordered to the coast, regimented, and transported to Veracruz. If all the artillery moved, Ripley planned to give up his staff appointment and go along. As Ripley anticipated, on January 10 his division was ordered from Saltillo to the mouth of the Rio Grande.

On February 12 he wrote to Lucia from Camp Palo Alto on the Rio Grande. Ten days after leaving Saltillo the division finally reached Camargo, passed through the city as quickly as possible, and encamped near the Rio Grande. A week later they embarked for Palo Alto, where Ripley learned that his brigade had been reorganized. Ripley refused a position as commissary to the battalion and joined his company. To his sister Lucia, he confided, "I have been busily engaged since our arrival doing nothing." He wished that "this confounded war was over, running about after them takes away the romance of the thing."[1]

General Scott's objective was indeed Veracruz, which he planned to take by amphibious assault. The city would then serve as his base of operations for the offensive against Mexico City. Beginning in mid-February, Scott began moving his forces by sea hundreds of miles down the east coast of Mexico. They would ultimately rendezvous at Punta de Anton Lizardo, just twelve miles from Veracruz. On March 9 the men transferred from the transports to steamers and canal boats, and then headed for Isla Sacrificios, the actual launching site for the amphibious landing. Ripley's division would be the first wave ashore in the largest amphibious invasion yet attempted in U.S. history. Ripley and the men embarked in surfboats, dropped astern of the *Princeton*, slipped the hawsers, and pulled steadily to shore.

Although Ripley expected a severe struggle, they were unopposed, landing and forming on the hills without receiving a shot. The men bivouacked overnight on the beach, their sleep interrupted by a sharp skirmish between the pickets of both sides. Although balls whistled over their heads, no one in the regiment was wounded. During the night the remaining troops landed, and in the morning the investment of Veracruz began.

Ripley described the morning attack and his artillery position on the crest of a sand hill facing the enemy about two miles from the city. The enemy opened fire with their long guns, "finally got our range and burst a shell or two in our faces, after which we retired behind the crest of the hill." Scott's forces completed the investment of Veracruz the next day, but strong winds prevented bringing their heavy guns ashore. Ripley expected to get their "bull dogs" ashore soon, and then the enemy "must be careful walking about the city for shells will fall there thick and fast."

On March 27 Ripley wrote that he had no doubts Veracruz would be taken. About six days earlier, under fire from the enemy, the batteries were finished. Mexican officials were summoned, and after they refused a truce, "we immediately opened fire with 10 mortars. The enemy returned about as hot a fire of shot, shell, and rockets as one could be under, but thanks to the excellence of our field works only a few were injured." Unfortunately, a shell killed Captain Vinton not long after the action began. Ripley was told that the concussion from a ball, passing inches from Vinton's head killed him without leaving a mark on his body.

In a letter on April 3, Ripley described the Mexicans' formal surrender. He was on duty with the inspector general to assist in receiving paroles of the prisoners and saw the entire ceremony. The Mexican troops marched through the city gates and onto a plain, where they halted by a flag of truce. After the Mexicans piled their arms and accoutrements, Ripley and his fellow officers tallied the rolls of the various regiments. They noticed the changes in the countenances and bearing of the men: "Some appeared indifferent; others tried to look dignified and unconcerned, but were unable to hide their mortification, and others giving way to grief. One Commandante de Batallon could not restrain his tears. Their paroles being given they marched off without music, a sad procession, while we marched into town with bands playing and colors flying."

Ripley described the Mexican military quarters as being well riddled but with comparatively little loss of life. "The citizens had suffered dreadfully in life and property," which Ripley blamed on Mexican General Juan Morales for refusing to call a truce and evacuate the town. They then had no choice but to bombard or storm the city. The day following the surrender, Ripley's company moved closer to town and into Fort Concepcion. He did not know whether some of the artillery companies would remain in the city, but if so, "I hope you will not be affected by the exaggerated reports of the deadly vomito [yellow fever]." Ripley reassured his family that in all probability his company would move inland with the siege train toward Jalapa and Puente del Rey, which, he had been told, were "splendid and delightful places."[2]

The American forces leaving Veracruz on April 8 followed the National Highway to Mexico City by way of Jalapa, Perote, and Puebla. Ripley accompanied the rear division leaving Veracruz and claimed that their first day's march, under a burning sun and on a sandy road, was quite difficult. The men were forced to carry their knapsacks and "being without water, suffered exceedingly."

Early in March, after their defeat at the Battle of Buena Vista, Santa Anna and his army struggled back to Mexico City, where the Mexican general learned that Veracruz had fallen. Anticipating General Scott's decision to move against the capital, Santa Anna planned to block Scott's progress along the National Highway. At Cerro Gordo the highway passed by this heavily fortified hill nearly one thousand feet high, its steep cliffs overlooking Rio Del Plan. On his right, about a mile in front of Cerro Gordo, Santa Anna placed artillery batteries on three cliffs between the highway and Rio Del Plan. General Gideon Pillow's Pennsylvania and Tennessee volunteers were to launch an attack on these artillery batteries.

Pillow, a Tennessee Democrat, was a close friend and confidant of President Polk, and helped secure his nomination at the Democratic convention in 1844. A practicing attorney and politically appointed brigadier general in his state's militia, Pillow had no formal military training. Scott's deployment of Pillow's volunteers to attack these formidable batteries is questionable. After Pillow's attack degenerated into chaos, it had no effect on the outcome of the battle and resulted in the needless loss of life; relations between Scott and Pillow then began to suffer.[3]

On April 23 Ripley informed his mother that he recently had been promoted to First Lieutenant and briefly described his participation in the Battle of Cerro Gordo. He was in command of an 8-inch howitzer that enfiladed the right of the enemy's entrenchments. His role has been described as the "laborious and bold movement performed by Lieutenants Ripley of the artillery, Tower of the engineers and Laidly of the ordnance department." These officers successfully carried an 8-inch howitzer across the river to the south side, planting it on the heights to support the assault of General Pillow's brigade.

On May 2 Ripley described his actions in greater detail to his sister Laura. General Worth had ordered him to report to the engineer officers for service with an 8-inch siege howitzer. To cooperate with General Pillow and his volunteers' attack, Ripley planned to place the howitzer on the enemy's right and enfilade their entrenched line. Ripley had three companies of New York volunteers, twenty picked artillerists, a party to carry ammunition, and several ordnance men at his command. Ripley and his men spent the afternoon examining the route and removing as many obstructions as possible. Ripley made no mention of needing to carry the howitzer across a river.

General Pillow asked Ripley to do his best to get the howitzer in place, as his attack depended on Ripley's success. At about 6:00 P.M. the men began hauling the heavy howitzer inch by inch over steep heights and through rugged, narrow gullies. By 2:00 A.M. the men were completely exhausted and were compelled to halt about one third of a mile from the foot of the heights, where they were to place the howitzer.

At daybreak the men renewed their backbreaking task and arrived at the foot of the hill at about 7:00 A.M. Ripley wrote that the heights were most discouraging, nearly one hundred feet high and in some places at an angle of 60 or 70 degrees. However, "the men went cheerily to work" and by 8:30 the howitzer was in position. They spent some time clearing the ground and bringing up ammunition, and at about 9:15 began shelling the Mexicans. Ripley continued his shelling until both sides in his front quit firing, which he thought indicated that Pillow's troops had carried the position. Only later did Ripley discover that Pillow's assault had failed.

Ripley claimed that his struggle to get the artillery in place turned out to be of little importance in the victory at Cerro Gordo because Pillow, "volunteer-like, did not know what he was doing and changed the plan of attack." The army acknowledged Ripley's actions at Cerro Gordo, promoting him on April 18 to brevet captain for "Gallant and Meritorious Conduct."[4]

Ripley informed Laura that the next morning he and his men descended from their position, rejoined the regiment, and marched on to Jalapa. The advance continued, and on April 22 they took possession of the castle of Perote, which the Mexicans had abandoned. After the rest of the army caught up with the advanced regiments, Ripley believed that they would push on to Puebla and establish quarters there before the final drive on Mexico City.

In this letter Ripley was surprisingly negative regarding his military career: "Were it not for the war and for the empty honor of the thing, or rather the dishonor of leaving the country before it is finished, I should be almost tempted to throw away my commission and try something else for pay and rations, so much deep injustice has been done to the army in the late appointments." He then closed by apologizing for his "grumbling."

On May 15 General Worth's forces reached Puebla, and a few days later Ripley wrote home. There had not been much action along the way "except for a skirmish at Amozoque with Santa Anna's Cavalry." The next day they marched into Puebla, "a very fine town, but like all Mexican towns is filled with many loafers and leperos [uncouth, low-class people]." Puebla, then the second-largest city in Mexico, did not resist American occupation, and for a time hostilities were suspended. A convent in Puebla served as Roswell's quarters, "a most exquisite monkery of a place with pictures of crucifixions and enough saints to satisfy all catholic flummery."

General Scott arrived on May 28 and began organizing his forces and bringing up reinforcements. During the summer, while both sides prepared for future hostilities, private and public attempts were made for a negotiated peace. On July 27 the arrival of reinforcements in Mexico City emboldened its defenders and ended the peace efforts.[5]

In late August, Ripley wrote to his mother from the outskirts of Mexico City. He mentioned the Battles of Contreras and Churubusco, "the hard-fought actions of the 19th and 20th." He claimed that against overwhelming odds, by good management and bold maneuvering, as well the valor of the veterans, new regiments, and volunteers, they brought "the city to our mercy." Ripley's opinion of volunteers obviously was improving, and he noted that the American forces did not make a "triumphant entry" into the capital to allow the Mexicans to negotiate for peace. He wondered whether this "magnanimity" was advisable, as many believed the enemy was trifling with the Americans. If so, with American artillery and the captured artillery and ammunition of the enemy, they could force an entry with small loss. Although the negotiators were meeting at four o'clock that afternoon, Ripley had little confidence that an agreement would be reached. According to Mexican War historians Robert Self Henry and John D. S. Eisenhower, the armistice lasted from August 24 until September 6.

Roswell marveled at the scenery of Mexico: "The country through which we have passed since entering the valley of Mexico, and that in which we are located at present is beautiful. Tacubaya, about a mile and a half from here, is General Scott's headquarters. The view from the palace is magnificent. Mexico [City], in the midst of the lakes and surrounding marshes, is in the forefront and in the distance on every side are the snow-capped mountains of Mexico. Directly in front of the palace are cultivated fields and orchards, and throughout the valley and countryside are many villages."

Roswell informed his mother that he had been serving as an aide-de-camp on the staff of General Pillow since leaving Puebla. He suggested that she could follow his participation in the recent action by reading Pillow's battle report, most of which he claimed to have written. Although Roswell had little personal contact with the general before accepting the invitation to join his staff, he found Pillow a very agreeable man to serve.

General Pillow had indeed done well at Contreras and Churubusco. General Scott complimented his work and seemed well satisfied with his performance. General Worth commented on the "gallant bearing of General Pillow," with whom he had coordinated well at Churubusco. After these two costly battles, General Scott believed a truce would give his battle-weary troops time to regroup and, surprisingly, secure peace "without totally humiliating" the Mexicans. Worth and Pillow both openly opposed Scott's armistice with the Mexicans. When Pillow could not dissuade Scott from implementing the armistice, he brazenly wrote to President Polk describing the armistice as "measures so disreputable to the Government."

The political differences between Scott, an active Whig, and Democrats Pillow and Polk damaged their relationship. In fact, in May 1846 President Polk referred to the three general officers still in Washington—Scott, Wool, and Adjutant General Roger Jones—as violent partisan Whigs who did not have the success of his administration at heart. After the armistice failed, Pillow disagreed with Scott over the necessity of capturing Molino del Rey, as he believed the machinery thought to be there for a cannon foundry had been removed. Scott dismissed Pillow's objections and ordered the September 8 assault to be led by Worth and one of Pillow's brigades. Ironically, as Pillow predicted, after the fierce two-hour battle Worth found no cannon foundry at Molino del Rey.[6]

After Contreras, Churubusco, and the capture of Molino del Rey, Scott still was on the outskirts of Mexico City. Needing to fight his way into the capital, Scott sent his engineers to reconnoiter the better of two possible attack routes. On September 11 Scott gathered the engineers and general officers to consider alternatives for the attack. Scott began the conference by advocating a direct assault on the formidable fortress of Chapultepec. Only then did he ask for the opinions of his staff officers. Pillow gave an eloquent argument for the alternate route, and four of Scott's engineers, including Robert E. Lee and Zealous B. Tower, agreed with Pillow. However, P. G. T. Beauregard sided with Scott and that settled the issue; the attack would be a direct assault on Chapultepec.

The next day Scott's siege guns opened fire on the Mexican Military Academy atop Chapultepec. Its brick buildings towered from the crest of this two-hundred-foot hill, and although the barrage did considerable damage, it became apparent that infantry would need to storm the fortress. Pillow was not pleased, as his volunteers would be leading the assault from Molino del Rey. Pillow first turned his attention to his artillery. He had Ripley and Beauregard work through the night repairing the batteries at Molino del Rey, enabling them to open fire at dawn.

On September 13 at 8:00 A.M., Pillow, on horseback, led the advance. Near the base of the hill, ricocheting grapeshot struck Pillow in his left ankle, breaking it and severing tendons on his foot. After the successful attack, Pillow had his men triumphantly carry him in a blanket up the hill and into the academy. Astoundingly, in a letter to his wife, General Pillow, described himself as the "Hero of Chapultepec." The fall of Chapultepec led to the occupation of Mexico City and an end to all major hostilities.

As the animosity between Generals Scott and Pillow intensified, Scott asked Pillow to alter his self-serving Contreras and Churubusco battle reports. However, the reports were anonymously leaked to the *New Orleans Daily Picayune* under the byline "Leonidas." Pillow was suspected of writing the reports himself because of the "sycophantic manner in which everything is told."

After the battle of Chapultepec, two small Mexican howitzers were mysteriously removed from their carriages and loaded into Pillow's personal baggage wagon. Although Pillow denied any knowledge of the affair, he may have intended to take them back to his home in Tennessee. Pillow ordered staff officers Ripley and G. W. Rains to remove the howitzers; however, being unable to find the gun carriages in the dark, they left the guns in Pillow's wagon, but told him they had done so. When the guns were found, Scott refused to believe Pillow's explanation of the affair. An indignant and embarrassed Pillow demanded a court of inquiry, and Scott convened a court on October 23 to investigate the charges. The court ruled that Rains and Ripley made an "error in judgment" and cleared Pillow, except for the fact that the officers told him that the howitzers were still in his wagon. Therefore, he was guilty of attempting to shift blame to them, which was deemed "ungentlemanly conduct."

In late October, Ripley sat down to "scratch a few lines of remembrance to all my loved friends at home," and claimed to have sent letters "after all our battles." Unfortunately, if Ripley wrote home in September describing the action at Chapultepec, his letter is not included in the collection at Yale. A letter may have described his actions on September 13 that resulted in his promotion to brevet major for "Gallant and Meritorious Conduct."

Ripley lamented not having received a letter from home since he left Puebla. In Mexico City, he claimed to be "comfortably settled in the Calle de San Francisco in General Pillow's house and have had little to do." Ripley believed the City of Mexico was filled with many beautiful buildings and many things of interest. In his spare time, he had been able to do some sightseeing and horseback riding.

He also had been attending the theater and other such "gentleman of leisure" activities: "Really, having your general's leg broken is very comfortable, far more so than your own, and we all ran our chances in this Valley of Mexico."

Ripley supposed that the American forces would remain in Mexico for years to come. It would be in a city "far preferable to many of our out of the way posts in the United States, but then it is very far from home." He told of their heavy losses, noting that many of his "nearest and dearest friends have fallen." He was sending a daguerreotype "taken at Puebla, when I was in full beard and looking, as you will see, extremely savage. I thought you would like it, although I must say it does not flatter me, and has the usual sour look of such pictures. However, it will serve as a remembrance in place of anything else." He did not mention of the howitzer incident.

Soon after the army gained control of Mexico City, a group of officers met on October 13 to form a social club for their entertainment and relaxation. "The *Aztec Club,* where good cheer may be had by members at moderate rates, and good company for nothing," originally had 160 members. The initiation fee was "$20.00 payable in advance." The home of the club was in the residence of Señor Boca Negra the former Mexican ambassador to the United States. The members believed there was as much comfort in their club "as in the princely mansions of the wealthiest Mexicans." The list of members included future Confederates P. G. T. Beauregard, Barnard E. Bee, Maxcy Gregg, Joseph E. Johnston, Robert E. Lee, Samuel McGowan, John B. Magruder, John C. Pemberton, and Gustavus W. Smith. The gregarious Roswell S. Ripley was member number 122. Future Union generals who were members included Ulysses S. Grant, Joseph Hooker, and George B. McClellan, as well as a future president, Franklin Pierce. Interestingly, General Pillow is not listed as a member of the Aztec Club.[7]

Secretary of State James Buchanan suggested Nicholas P. Trist, a Democrat and chief clerk in the State Department, for a mission to Scott's headquarters with full powers to negotiate a peace treaty with Mexican authorities. Pillow quickly established contact with Trist when he arrived at Puebla. Pillow, who pretentiously believed he was Polk's "other self," tried to insinuate himself into the treaty-making process. Soon, the disgusted Trist avoided Pillow and worked closely with General Scott in the negotiations.

In October, Pillow retaliated against this perceived indignity by informing President Polk of an attempt to bribe Santa Anna into signing a peace agreement in July. He also wrote an insulting letter to Scott's adjutant asking for the commanding general's redress of the howitzer findings. When Scott refused, Pillow appealed directly to Secretary of War William L. Marcy. On November 22, infuriated by Pillow's insubordination and arrogant disregard of regulations, Scott placed Pillow "in a state of arrest confined to the limits of the city." General Worth was soon implicated by allegations that he allowed his private reports and letters, detrimental to Scott, to be published. Worth appealed to President Polk, essentially accusing Scott, his old friend and fellow Whig, "of conduct unbecoming an officer and gentleman." Scott then relieved Worth and placed him under arrest. Worth's chief of artillery, Lieutenant Colonel James Duncan, suffered the same fate.

On November 27 Ripley wrote that there was little news of interest except for quarrels among the general officers, noting that Pillow and Worth had been arrested for what General Scott termed disrespect: "The fact is the old gentleman is getting too large for his coat." He added, "The President must act and act speedily, or we shall be in as bad a state as the Mexicans," who had been fighting among themselves throughout the war.

Regarding his social life, Ripley "attended a benefit held for Cañete, the 1st actress of the Spanish Company." The officers presented Señora Cañete with a purse of $2,000 for her dramatic performance in *Don Juan Tenorio*, held at the National Theatre. The house was crowded with many women present, but because the officers had not "acquired the habit of speaking Spanish politely, we make but little headway in society."

Two weeks later in December, after horseback riding in the fields of Contreras and Churubusco, Ripley returned to camp and was pleased to find three letters from home. In his return letter, he said he believed that he "would be back in the United States by the end of January for the trial of Generals Scott, Worth, Pillow and Colonel Duncan." He would try to get back to New York but thought he might not be allowed to proceed farther than Washington. He did not know what the government would do, but he did not think that they "will be sufficiently insane to proceed on General Scott's frivolous charges. The government may be content with bringing Scott, the cause of all this trouble, to Washington." There he could "cogitate the probability of his running for the Presidency."

Ripley's last letter of 1847, dated December 27, wished all at home a merry Christmas and a happy New Year. "The city is getting a little gayer now than formerly and on Christmas Eve we had a fashionable ball at the house of one of the Mexican *Bon Ton*," he wrote. "I was the only officer present and had a delightful evening. The Mexican ladies were not at all fearful of the northern Barbarian. On Christmas a large party dined at Mr. Benfield's, an Englishman who fed us very well indeed, very much like a home dinner party."[8]

Ripley's letters to his mother and other family members provide insight into his personality, interests, and character. The fact that so many of his letters were saved and that he voiced his disappointment when slow mail service delayed the delivery of letters from home indicate that his family ties remained strong.

Ripley obviously appreciated Mexican scenery and architecture, and he regretted that he could not use his artistic talent to depict these subjects on canvas. At times he revealed his unique sense of humor. When he encountered old friends and acquaintances, their mutual pleasure at meeting once again is evidence of his social skills and gregarious nature. Ripley had the ability to reevaluate people and situations and, when appropriate, change his opinion. He gradually, though possibly reluctantly, acknowledged the efforts of the volunteer troops in Mexico. After the Battle of Cerro Gordo, Roswell had been critical of General Gideon Pillow. He markedly raised his opinion of the general after becoming Pillow's aide-de-camp. Undoubtedly, the potential for his personal advancement owing to Pillow's political connections and friendship with President Polk, influenced Ripley's opinion of the general.

Ripley's letters also reveal some of his biases and prejudices. He professed a belief in the superiority of Anglo-Saxons, wrote disparagingly about the Mexicans, though he later moderated this belief, and viewed the Roman Catholic Church somewhat disdainfully.

CHAPTER 6

Postwar, 1848–1849

By the end of December 1847, President Polk had received news of General Scott's attempt to bribe Santa Anna, as well as the arrests of Pillow, Worth, and Duncan. Polk believed that these incidents demonstrated "the vanity and tyrannical temper of General Scott and therefore his unfitness to command." On January 13, 1848, Secretary of War William L. Marcy issued the order removing General Winfield Scott from command of the army; however, Marcy's letter did not arrive in Mexico until February 18. His letter also stipulated that Worth, Pillow, and Duncan were to be released from arrest and Scott's charges against them were to be investigated by a court of inquiry. The political makeup of the court and the members' lack of rank angered Scott.

The court of inquiry convened on March 13, 1848, at Puebla, then adjourned to the City of Mexico. General Worth withdrew the charges against Scott, a fellow Whig, and Scott dropped his charges against Worth and Duncan. The politically charged battle would now be between Pillow and Scott, with attorney Pillow conducting his own defense. Pillow faced two charges. The first accused him of writing, or arranging to have written, the self-serving "Leonidas" article published in the *New Orleans Daily Picayune*. The second charge listed eight specific instances of "conduct unbecoming an officer and a gentleman." Pillow's request to move the proceedings to the United States was granted, and on April 21 the court adjourned to reconvene in Frederick, Maryland.

Upon leaving Mexico, the courtroom rancor abated as Pillow joined members of the court aboard ship for a pleasant trip to New Orleans. The general stopped for a few days at "Clifton," his home four miles west of Columbia, Tennessee, then continued on to Maryland accompanied by his wife. By June 5, 1848, Pillow was in Frederick confident and anxious to attack the opposition. As the court began calling a series of witnesses, including Secretary of War Marcy, Pillow's expertise in the courtroom soon overwhelmed his professional military opponents. Nicholas Trist watched in disbelief at the conduct of the court, claiming to have seen General Cushing "furtively communicating with and giving advice to Pillow." Trist believed Pillow to be an "intriguer of incomprehensible baseness of character" and watched in amazement as Pillow skillfully reduced Scott's charges to pulp. Major Archibald W. Burns, Pillow's division paymaster, admitted responsibility for the "Leonidas" article, thereby weakening the main charge against Pillow. Scott's case began to unravel, and Pillow summed up his defense on June 20. Although Pillow's critics admitted his courtroom presentation was clearly superior, they dismissed the findings as a "whitewash." Even so, Scott's reputation as the foremost military figure of the era had been questioned, and he had been damaged as a potential Whig presidential candidate. Although Pillow won the court battle, he too lost credibility with the public, and his image suffered within his own party.

From January through June 1848, Roswell Ripley continued to serve as an aide-de-camp to General Pillow. In that capacity he must have been present for the court of inquiry; however, no letters from Ripley to his family describing the proceedings have been found. Pillow's friendship with President Polk must have impressed and influenced young Ripley, and Pillow always made a practice of recommending his accommodating friends for higher positions and favors. After the completion of the court of inquiry, Pillow went to Washington for a conference with the president. While there he secured a second brevet for his chief of staff, Joseph Hooker, and an extension of leave for Ripley.

Pillow deemed it imperative to have a "correct version of the Mexican War—a work of high authority" written and published as soon as possible. He entrusted this project to Ripley and sequestered him at his home near Columbia. To give Ripley time to complete the book, Pillow secured a series of questionable and highly unusual leaves of absence for his aide-de-camp. In May 1848 Pillow arranged Special Order No. 69, granting Ripley a six-month leave beginning on July 15. On December 26 Ripley wrote to Adjutant General Roger Jones requesting a sixty-day extension of this leave. Secretary of War Marcy annotated Special Order No. 2: "The Adjutant General will extend the leave of absence as asked for," beginning on January 15, 1849.

In early February, Ripley again wrote to General Jones and requested another extension of his leave, this time "for the term of four months, as I have pressing business, of a private nature which requires my attention for that time." He added that from the time he entered the service until July 15, 1846, he was constantly on duty and for two years absent on Foreign Service. He believed that the length of his uninterrupted service would allow the department to view his application for the extension as a reasonable request.

Pillow was becoming worried that time was running out for Ripley to finish his history and would be ordered back to his regiment. He had managed to keep Ripley's whereabouts unknown from Marcy and instructed Polk's private secretary, Knox Walker, to "tell anyone in Washington who got nosy that Ripley was in Maury County, engaged in an interesting *negotiation* with a *young lady*."

On February 22 Marcy added compelling support to Ripley's request: "The President insists that the leave asked for be granted." If this did not sufficiently intimidate Jones, it was accompanied on the same day by a note from the president's staff: "The President desires that the extension of Captain Ripley's leave be sent to him today." By this time the adjutant general, totally disgusted with Ripley's extended leave requests, wrote, "Lt. Ripley violates the regulations, and utterly disregards the propriety of the service in making his applications thru channels of communication not authorized by the regulations." Jones reluctantly added, "The leave is to be extended as directed by the President." This became Special Order No. 14, dated February 22, 1849, and brought Ripley's combined leaves of absence to one full year, ending on July 15, 1849.[1]

Only one letter, written while Ripley was working on his history, is known to exist. Ripley wrote to Pillow on March 8, 1849, while visiting in Nashville and staying with Judge Maney, probably Tennessee State Superior Court Judge Thomas Maney. The letter primarily referred to Tennessee politics and Pillow's possible candidacy for the 1850 governor's race. Pillow ultimately decided not to run for office.

The relationship between Ripley and Pillow was such that Roswell brashly admitted, "Until today [I] have done no work at all. I shall commence today to do something, but have at the same time many inducements to do nothing in this vicinity, and shall take your advice and return to Columbia in a day or two."

The letter indicated that he had been distracted by an active Nashville social life: "The young ladies are pretty as usual and agreeable of course. I've seen Miss Laura Martin, a Miss Phillips, and to tell you the truth I don't care if I never see the former again. Miss Laura Brown is in excellent health and good spirits, and as lovely as usual. Miss Betty Brown has got religious and talks about it very pratingly. But it's a sin to criticize the young ladies on paper." As he closed his letter, the subject of his book, so important to Pillow, finally came up. Ripley asked the general, "If you can recollect the day on which you arrived at Perote let me know. If you cannot write immediately, and happen to be in town either Friday or Saturday, telegraph the date to me at Judge Maney's."

President Polk completed his one-term presidency and left office on March 4, 1849, touring several Southern cities on his way home to Tennessee. On April 5 a huge crowd greeted Polk at the public square in Columbia, where he received a long and warm welcoming speech from his old friend Gideon Pillow. A week later Pillow invited President Polk and his family to dine at Clifton, his estate west of Columbia. In his diary the president described the large dinner party, composed chiefly of his and Pillow's relatives, as being very pleasant, adding, "Major Ripley of the U.S. Army was one of the guests." The president offered no appraisal of Ripley, and did not comment on the progress of Ripley's history of the war. Ripley would have been delighted at the opportunity to dine with President Polk and most certainly would have written his family about the dinner, but no correspondence has been found describing the event.[2]

Gideon Pillow was not the only one interested in having the Mexican War documented. Numerous literary publications such as the *Southern Quarterly*

Review, Democratic Review, Literary World, and the Whig Party's *American Review* all realized the significance of the war and discussed the appropriate time for it to be written. Many recognized that time must be allotted for the proper research and analysis of official records and documents. However, according to the *American Review,* if one waited too long, "the spirit of the time may not be so easily recaptured."

Most believed that only soldiers who had fought in the war with Mexico could write an authentic history of the conflict, but the distinction between a soldier's personal experiences, his dashing narratives, and accurate history often became blurred. Personal accounts written by soldiers, no matter how expanded by references, were proving to be unsatisfactory histories of the war. According to historian Robert Johannsen, "It is ironic that the one history written by a soldier that stood out as an exception aroused so much controversy, and was seen as so flawed with bias that its contribution to the historiography of the war was clouded from the beginning." Johannsen was referring to Ripley's two-volume history, *The War with Mexico,* published by Harper & Brothers in 1849. "Still," Johannsen continued, "it occupied a position apart from all the other efforts and indeed won praise as the only complete history yet written of the entire war and as the only one worthy of the library."

Although *The War with Mexico* emphasized military operations, Ripley also discussed the political and diplomatic events that led to the war. In writing his history, Ripley utilized congressional documents, official battle reports, and correspondence of American and Mexican officers. His familiarity with military tactics gave his battle accounts authenticity. Unfortunately, Ripley's history of the war was clouded from the beginning by his close association with Gideon Pillow. It was rumored that Pillow collaborated with Ripley and possibly wrote some sections of the book. These charges resulted from Ripley's alleged criticism of General Scott and claims that he exaggerated General Pillow's importance in winning the war.

Ripley claimed that he intended to give a general and impartial account of the events and that the observations and conclusions were exclusively his own. They "may, and probably will, be at variance with the opinions of many officers of the American army; but as they appeared to me to be correct, I have thought proper to insert them, and to trust to the accompanying arguments for their support," he wrote.[3]

Historian John D. S. Eisenhower deemed Ripley's *The War with Mexico* to be one of several "works of special value for background, eyewitness information or perspective." In his history Ripley was more complimentary of the Mexicans. In describing the Battle of Cerro Gordo, Ripley wrote that "although the eight-inch howitzer from the right bank of the river opened upon their flank, the greater number of Mexican troops stood manfully to their post, and plied their guns and muskets vigorously." He praised the Mexican forces for their valor but did not cite his prominent role and the obstacles encountered in the placement of that cannon. Nor did he acknowledge that he had been brevetted to captain for accomplishing this difficult maneuver.

Most significantly, his book reveals Ripley to be a staunch Democrat and profoundly anti-Whig. Nevertheless, he did not allow politics to dampen his praise of General Zachary Taylor's military ability and popularity, even though Taylor was a Whig. Ripley firmly supported President Polk and the Democratic Party's policies regarding the annexation of Texas, its statehood, and the Mexican War. In contrast, Northern abolitionists, such as William Lloyd Garrison, James Russell Lowell, and John Greenleaf Whittier, opposed annexation and the war.

According to Johannsen, "The most outspoken opposition to the Mexican War came from the abolition movement (under the mistaken notion that the war was being fought to extend the area of slavery)." In *The War with Mexico*, Ripley wrote that a party in the Northern states advocated the abolition of black slavery, and because of the existence of that institution in Texas they opposed annexation. In addition, Mexican General Juan N. Almonte concocted with some abolitionists of black slavery schemes by which the abolitionists would assist Mexicans against the U.S. government if war broke out. To document this allegation, Ripley reprinted two letters, addressed to General Almonte, that were found in the Mexico City post office. These letters allegedly were from abolitionists to General Almonte and were among numerous letters from various abolitionists to other Mexican officials.[4]

By May 1849, after about ten months of extensive research and writing, Ripley completed his history and traveled to New York to negotiate its publication by Harper & Brothers. Disclosing that he wrote the book "during a respite from ordinary professional duties," Ripley feared that "the time has been too short for the undertaking, but the time at my disposal has nearly expired and it must be presented as it is."

On June 4, 1849, Ripley signed a contract with Harper & Brothers and agreed "to read the proofs and prepare between ten and fifteen drawings for lithographing" within ninety days. Ripley divided the book into two volumes based on the two phases of the war. Volume 1 totaled thirteen chapters; the twenty chapters of volume 2 began with the siege of Veracruz. Included in the volumes were fourteen detailed topographical maps. The publisher required Ripley to pay for the stereotype plates and for putting the drawings on stones, which it supposed would cost "about seven hundred dollars." The publisher was to furnish the paper, printing, and binding, and pay the author "seventy cents per copy sold, plus 12 copies for his own use." The publisher would pay Ripley "semiannually by notes at four months." The publisher's records failed to disclose the number of volumes printed and sold, or the financial results of the publication.

In his history Ripley surprisingly concluded that "the effect of the war on Mexico has been and will continue to be greatly beneficial, and it may be that in the future Mexico will truly follow the example of the northern republic. By this war the United States acquired an immense extent of territory, the value and consequence of which are yet to be determined." Ripley thought that the military success of General Zachary Taylor and his "single-hearted devotion to the service of the country" led to his election and gained the presidency for the Whig Party.

After Ripley signed the contract in New York City, nearly six weeks remained on his leave of absence, which was due to expire on July 15, 1849. He would have been in a position and had ample time to spend some of his remaining leave with his family in Ogdensburg, but there is no record supporting this likely scenario.[5]

CHAPTER 7

Florida, 1849–1850

While Roswell Ripley served as an aide-de-camp to General Pillow, including the year he spent writing the history of the Mexican War, he was on detached service from Company K of the 2nd Artillery. The majority of Company K departed Chapultepec, Mexico, on June 10, 1848, and arrived at Governors Island, New York, on August 16. The company received orders on October 8 to proceed to Fort Marion in St. Augustine, Florida; the men arrived about a week later. Ripley completed his leaves of absence on July 15, 1849, and received orders to rejoin Company K at Fort Marion. By that time his company had been in Florida for nearly nine months.[1]

By the summer of 1849, Florida had endured two wars against the Seminole Indians. In 1818, in reprisal for Indian depredations, the government sent General Andrew Jackson into northern Florida to burn the Seminoles' villages, drive them farther south, and gain control of their farmland. That action became known as the First Seminole War. In 1823 the Treaty of Moultrie Creek forced the Seminoles to the edges of the Everglades and onto a reservation with land poorly suited for farming. By 1835 living conditions on the reservation had markedly deteriorated, and the government decided to solve the problem by removing the Seminoles from Florida. They were to be forcibly relocated in the West, but many of the tribe refused to leave.

Chief Osceola personified the Seminoles' resistance and determination to keep their land. In December 1835 he precipitated the Second Seminole War when he killed the local Indian Agent, organized raids on white settlements, and ambushed and slaughtered military patrols. President Andrew Jackson responded by sending General Winfield Scott and fourteen companies of infantry to Florida. The war dragged on for over six indecisive years, finally ending in a stalemate in August 1842.[2]

After seven relatively peaceful years, in July 1849, just before Ripley's arrival, five defiant young warriors broke out of the reservation and went on a pillaging and killing spree. Labeled "The Indian Scare of 1849," military patrols scoured the region and attempted to restore order. When Ripley arrived in Florida, he received orders to proceed with a detachment of one corporal and ten privates down the coast to old Fort Pierce on the Indian River. Ripley and his men traveled along the shoreline in one of the surfboats used in the landings at Veracruz, arriving in late July. After participating in several patrols, on August 17 Ripley and his detachment returned to his company at Fort Marion.[3]

In early September, Ripley and Company K left Marion for Fort Pierce and additional patrol duty. The company remained at the fort during September and October, and then marched to Russell's Landing on the Indian River. On November 27 the company headed for Kissimmee and Big Cypress Swamp.

In the 1840s the Everglades blanketed nearly all of south Florida from present-day Orlando to the Florida Keys. In addition to extensive marshlands, the Everglades included true swamps, most notably the Big Cypress, which covered an area the size of Delaware. During the Second Seminole War, a U.S. Army surgeon from South Carolina, Jacob Rhett Motte, wrote descriptive accounts of the swamp and presented a clear picture of the difficulties Ripley and his men would face.

As described by Motte, conditions were intolerable, as the men were forced to wade waist deep through swamps and were subject to drenching rains or the scorching sun. "It is in fact a most hideous region, swarming with rattlesnakes, moccasins, and other deadly reptiles . . . a perfect paradise for Indians and alligators," Motte wrote. Swarms of mosquitoes made life miserable, and although Motte and physicians of that era were unaware of the fact, the mosquitoes spread malaria, dengue, and yellow fever. The troops had to drag their canoes, rifles, ammunition, and provisions through deep and clinging mud or over razor-edged saw grass that ripped their clothes and their skin. Jagged pinnacle rocks, which Motte compared to "a thick crop of sharply pointed knives," shredded their boots. The troops spent so much time slogging through the swamps and wetlands that their ankles swelled and gruesome inflamed sores covered their legs.

After spending about two weeks on patrol in Big Cypress, Ripley and Company K returned to Fort Pierce on December 13. Six days later Ripley marched his company to Russell's Landing, where they remained until year's end.[4]

On January 7, 1850, Ripley and his company left Russell's Landing, following orders to march to Post No. 4 on the "Attah Hatchee." During February, March, and April, regimental returns for the 2nd Artillery listed Ripley as commanding Company K at Fort Drum in Brevard County, near Big Cypress. However, during this time Ripley's only surviving letter to his family was from Russell's Landing, dated February 12. Ripley informed one of his sisters that he had been there for a few weeks because of illness but in a day or two would be well enough to return to the "Attah Hatchee." According to Ripley, some in his company were stationed at Russell's Landing, but most of his command were on the line completing a road to Tampa.

Ripley believed that his family would be surprised to learn there were three ladies in camp; two were married and "one young, pretty demoiselle" had come to Florida to spend the winter with her brother and sister, Captain and Mrs. Jordan.

It was strange to see a "pretty miss in this region of discomfort, and yet she bears it well, as do the other ladies."

Ripley asked his sister to tell their mother that he had the contract with Harper & Brothers and would hold on to it. He had been in correspondence with Henry Hilton about the publishing arrangement and cautioned their mother not to "build too many castles in the air about the profit of the work, for it will take a good many books to make a fortune out of it." He mentioned that $818 would come from the profits for "the stereotype plates," as well as "some $250 on lithographing." This amounted to a $368 increase over Ripley's costs as estimated in his contract. Aware of his book's potential for controversy, he added, "I am in hopes that it will go down pretty well, although some Whigs and neutral presses are making furious assaults on it." He wanted his family to look for any reviews of the book, especially those by Whigs.

Ripley was optimistic that he and many of the troops would be leaving Florida in the near future, as "the Indians have agreed to emigrate and are now coming in at the different military posts west of the Kissimmee." Ripley left Florida later in the year; however, not all of the Indians agreed to emigrate, and more violence erupted in 1855.[5]

In January 1850 one of the first reviews, in the *Southern Literary Messenger,* reported favorably on Ripley's *War with Mexico*. The reviewer admitted that he was unable to compare official documents with Ripley's narrative but noted that "the high character of Major Ripley as an officer and a gentleman furnishes a sufficient guaranty of the accuracy of the work." The reviewer believed that the "author's style was cautious and the general tone was pleasing." Prior to Ripley's effort, many partial and loosely written histories of the war had been published, and the reviewer was glad to see "one at last which is worthy of the library." The reviewer also believed that the volumes contained excellent maps of the engagements, all of which would have been done by Ripley.

M. C. M. Hammond, a Mexican War veteran and an early historian of the conflict, authored one of the anticipated "furious assaults" on Ripley's book about a year later in the *Southern Literary Messenger*. Hammond credited Ripley with a bold, ambitious, and quite well-written effort, "the only complete history yet written of the entire war." Hammond was surprised that Ripley discussed the political issues pertinent to the war and permitted his "political creed to bias his judgment regarding military operations and achievements." Hammond believed a writer of military history should deal with politics in general, not in detail, and should not criticize political parties or leaders. A military work advocating one set of political principles "cannot be considered an impartial history," Hammond maintained.

Although Hammond claimed that he did not believe them, he repeated allegations that Ripley did not write the book. Hammond boldly asserted that the army in general believed this claim, and some believed that Ripley never saw the book until it was published. Hammond had no doubt that the military portion of the book was written by Ripley: "The military terms, the tactical phraseology and the air of assumed authority are certainly Ripley's."

Hammond believed that Ripley had thoroughly researched the material and complimented his inclusion of information from Mexican sources. He thought the narrative was vivid and forcible and the battles depicted correctly. He admitted that the book would be "highly valuable for future reference" and doubted the same data could be collected again.

Hammond was convinced that the second volume of Ripley's history was "replete with disparagement of Scott" and full of Ripley's prejudices. He closed his review by sincerely recommending that Ripley "revise his work, suppress the many illiberal passages, and assume a more elevated and impartial tone." If Ripley would revise the book as suggested, it would be "interesting and instructive reading, and become a standard authority in our collections." Hammond concluded that if Ripley's history did not have at least some merit, he would not have spent as much time "considering its errors." Needless to add, Ripley did not revise his history.

According to Johannsen, "Ripley's comments on Scott and Pillow in today's light hardly seem out of the ordinary, but in the heavily charged atmosphere of 1849 they were viewed as an attempt to inflate Pillow and destroy Scott."

On May 8, 1850, Ripley and Company K were transferred to Fort Capron, located opposite the Indian River inlet, where he remained in command through the end of September. On October 1, 1850, Ripley transferred from Company K to Company A of the 2nd Artillery, ending his tour of duty in Florida. Ripley's service in Florida, where he functioned primarily as a company commander of infantry, lasted approximately fourteen months. He departed Florida and its anticipated pleasant winter, moving north to Baltimore and returning to his original duty station, Fort McHenry. Ripley spent the last months of 1850 at Fort McHenry and would now be closer to his family and home in Ogdensburg, New York.[6]

CHAPTER 8

Twilight of a Career

Ripley's stay at Fort McHenry, his third tour of duty in the Baltimore area, lasted only six months, from October 1850 through March 1851. In April 1851 Company A, 2nd Artillery, transferred to Fort Monroe, Virginia. Located at the tip of the peninsula between the James and York Rivers, the site had long been recognized for its strategic location, but nothing had been done to erect a permanent fort. Construction of Fort Monroe had begun in 1819, motivated by the burning of Washington by the British in 1814.

In 1824 ten artillery companies were garrisoned at the fort, creating the Fort Monroe Artillery School of Practice. Two of Ripley's commanding officers, John R. Vinton and Samuel A. Ringgold, attended the artillery school, as did Roswell's uncle, James W. Ripley, in 1824. Frequent garrison moves ultimately led to the dissolution of the artillery program, and on April 19, 1834, the War Department put Fort Monroe on the same status as other military posts.

Between 1829 and 1835, President Andrew Jackson visited Fort Monroe and its environs several times for official functions, as well as for rest and relaxation. Jackson was the first but not the only president to visit Fort Monroe. In 1851 Brevet Major Roswell Ripley had been at Fort Monroe only three months when, early in the morning of June 21, President Millard Fillmore arrived by steamer. At 5:00 A.M. the officers of the garrison assembled at Brevet Brigadier General James Bankhead's quarters and accompanied the commander to the wharf to greet the President. When Fillmore disembarked, the fort's artillery welcomed him with a twenty-one-gun salute. Future events indicate that Ripley may very well have met personally with President Fillmore, a fellow New Yorker.[1]

After serving three months at Fort Monroe, Ripley left on July 30, 1851, for a seven-day leave of absence. He may have returned to Ogdensburg, where his sixty-nine-year-old father was ailing. For fifteen years, Christopher Ripley struggled to sell or develop the 28,765-acre Matildaville tract near Ogdensburg that he had signed to purchase from George Parish in 1836. Joel Buttles, a family friend, entrepreneur, and prominent citizen of Columbus, Ohio, provided the down payment of $5,000. After the quick sale of the tract to the North American Mining Company collapsed, Christopher tried to sell the tract to speculators in New York City. This failed, but he did succeed in selling some smaller parcels to settlers moving into upstate New York.

Christopher next dreamed of converting the remainder of the tract into "New Germany." He advertised widely and even distributed broadsides in Germany. When this also failed, he unsuccessfully tried to develop a "French Colony" for prospective French-Canadian buyers. In his study of the Ripley papers, Atwood Manley concluded, "There was scarcely a proposition to advance the sale of this land that escaped Ripley's mind."

If Joel Buttles was aware of Ripley's untiring efforts to sell the property, he was unimpressed. On July 20, 1842, after a weeklong trip from Columbus, Buttles arrived in Ogdensburg by steamboat and attempted to recover the $5,000 he had advanced Ripley. Buttles met with Ripley and his sons-in-law, Charles Shepard and attorney A. B. James, and offered to settle for $5,000 but was refused. Surprisingly, Buttles then appointed A. B. James as his attorney to avoid the "labor and expense" of making the long trip from Columbus to Ogdensburg.

However, in September 1843 and again in May 1845, Buttles did return to Ogdensburg. He believed that Ripley had at least $2,000 worth of land and money that belonged to him, and offered to let Christopher keep the money if he would deed him the land. Ripley stubbornly refused. Buttles then asked attorney James to get a deed for the property from Christopher.

Unfortunately for both Ripley and Buttles, Parish refused to relinquish a deed to any portion of Matildaville. As Christopher had not made the total payment stipulated in the contract, Parish declared the contract forfeited, repossessed the remainder of the land, and kept Ripley's down payment and all his additional payments. Seeking to recover at least something from Parish, Christopher began litigation but was unsuccessful.[2]

In 1850, bitter and impoverished, Christopher was advised by counsel to resign his rights to the property. He did not have the means to fight the wealth, power, and influence combined against him. Christopher declared that he was a victim of injustice, but he either did not understand the contract or refused to admit he had failed to fulfill it.

The 1850 census listed sixty-eight-year-old Christopher and fifty-five-year-old Julia in New York, with real estate valued at $2,510. No occupation was given for Christopher, and apparently their income came from three borders in the household.

On September 14, 1851, about five weeks after he returned from his leave in early August, Roswell Ripley learned that his father's health was deteriorating rapidly and hurriedly left for Ogdensburg. Christopher died on September 17 and was buried two days later in Ogdensburg Cemetery. Roswell may not have arrived home before his father's death but probably was there for the interment. Christopher's pride in his War of 1812 military service was emphasized when on September 23 the *St. Lawrence Republican* announced the death of "Capt. Christopher Ripley." That same day, Roswell extended his twenty-day leave for sixty additional days. As the family mourned Christopher's passing, Roswell Ripley and his brother-in-law, A. B. James, attempted to salvage what they could of Christopher's estate. On December 6 Ripley returned to Fort Monroe, where he remained until the end of the year.[3]

The year 1852 would be even more eventful for Ripley. Shortly after he returned to duty from his bereavement leave, he requested more time off. On January 12 he arrived in Washington, D.C., and registered at the Willard Hotel, moving a few days later to the National Hotel. Located at the corner of Pennsylvania Avenue and 6th Street, the National would serve as quarters for John Wilkes Booth in 1865. On April 14 Booth left the hotel for Ford's Theater. That night, Roswell's niece, Julia Shepard, witnessed the assassination of President Lincoln.

On January 23, with his leave expiring, Ripley was still in Washington. He petitioned the Adjutant General's Office (AGO), for a ten-day extension of his leave "in consequence of the obstruction of both routes from Baltimore to Fort Monroe." Ripley delivered the request in person to the AGO and "was verbally authorized by the adjutant general to defer returning to his station for a few days." Adjutant General Roger Jones, who had been angered and frustrated by President Polk's influence in granting Ripley's extended leaves of absence in 1849, must have been irritated to be dealing with him again. Nevertheless, he had little recourse but to grant the extension, as ice obstructed the waterways to Fort Monroe.

Two days later Jones received an astonishing request from Ripley: "I have the honor to apply for a leave of absence for six months from the 1st of February 1852." General Bankhead at Fort Monroe approved the request when he informed the AGO, "Company A, to which Major Ripley belongs, now has two officers. We respectfully submit to a higher authority, [but] I have no special objection to it." However, on February 6 the AGO denied Ripley's application and stated they could "discover no good reason for an indulgence which exceeds that usually granted to officers." Major General John Wool, another Whig now with the AGO, wrote the disapproval, adding, "If the leave now applied for (six months) be granted, Major Ripley will have received about 23 months of leave in the space of about four years." As Whigs and supporters of General Scott, Wool and Jones would not have appreciated Ripley's *War with Mexico* and probably would not have wanted to approve Ripley's request for political reasons, even if it had not been excessive.

On February 12 Bankhead discovered that Ripley's six-month leave had been denied. As the major had not returned to Fort Monroe, Bankhead asked the AGO whether he should press charges against Ripley for being absent without leave. In doing so, Bankhead reversed his previous position. He now claimed that Ripley was needed because there were only two officers with his company. Previously, Bankhead thought that staffing the company with only two officers was not a problem.

On February 18, now aware of Ripley's continued absence from Fort Monroe, Jones wrote to Bankhead that he did not think Ripley would be detained for over ten days and that he was not authorized by the AGO to be gone so long. Understanding that Ripley was still in the city and not knowing by what authority, Jones directed Ripley to report to him in person. Ripley reported to the AGO the next day and claimed that President Fillmore's secretary of war, Charles Conrad, sanctioned him to remain in Washington for a "fortnight longer." Conrad then notified the AGO on March 2 that a senator "required Major Ripley's assistance in certain measures he was preparing." Therefore, Conrad authorized the two-week extension for Ripley to remain in Washington.

Ripley's fortnight extension, granted by the secretary of war, lasted longer than two weeks. As of March 22, Ripley still had not reported to Fort Monroe. General Bankhead again wrote to the adjutant general informing him that he had not heard from Ripley and wanted to know how long Ripley was to be on leave. He did not want to question the authority of the secretary of war but surmised that Conrad did not know Ripley still had not reported for duty. Bankhead also suspected the secretary did not know that since the army's return from Mexico in 1848, Ripley had been on leave of absence nearly one-half of that time.[4]

The member of the senate, who according to the secretary of war required Ripley's assistance, turned out to be Democrat James Shields of Illinois. On March 31 Senator Shields wrote to the adjutant general, asking Jones to do him the favor of writing to Colonel Bankhead to let him know that Major Ripley had been detained in Washington with Jones's permission. Ripley "leaves today, and this will prevent any unpleasant occurrences."

In 1846 the war with Mexico provided an opportunity for personal advancement, and the Senate, on July 1, 1846, commissioned Shields a brigadier general. Polk would have been pleased with Shields's appointment, as he wanted Democrats commissioned as volunteer generals to balance what he believed to be a Whig monopoly of the West Point officer corps. Shields returned to Illinois, recruited a twelve-month volunteer force, and arrived in Mexico in August. The new general and his volunteers participated in the Siege of Veracruz and the Battle of Cerro Gordo. At Cerro Gordo, a one-and-a-half-inch piece of grapeshot tore through Shields's right chest and exited his back near the spine; miraculously, he survived this horrendous wound. While serving in Mexico, Shields received many favorable comments from his troops, one noting that he had "won the hearts of the men by shaking hands with several of the privates." Another commented, "He preserves his dignity and commands respect although he is entirely sociable and communicative."[5]

Following the war, Shields incurred President Polk's wrath after a speech in South Carolina in which he praised General Winfield Scott's military abilities. In 1848, when Shields ran against the incumbent Democrat for the Senate seat from Illinois, Polk attempted to derail his bid by appointing him governor of the Oregon Territory. Shields declined the governorship and ran successfully for the Senate. Senator Shields served as chairman of the Committee on the District of Columbia and on the Committee on Military Affairs in the 32nd Congress.

It is unlikely that Secretary of War Conrad and Senator Shields would have become involved in Ripley's leaves of absence for frivolous reasons. Shields would have known Ripley as an artilleryman, Pillow's aide-de-camp, and the author of a history of the war. Shields evidently valued Ripley's opinion, consulted with him, and may have even originally requested Ripley's leave for his trip to Washington.

Ripley probably assisted Senator Shields with two items noted in the *United States Senate Journal* of March 1852. On March 17 Shields "presented a memorial of officers of the army stationed at Fort Monroe, that the quarters of officers at the permanent military posts might be furnished." This memorial was referred to the Committee on Military Affairs. On March 23 Shields's Committee on Military Affairs submitted to the Senate a report, "No. 140, accompanied by a bill, S. 304, to improve the efficiency of the artillery."

Senator Shields and Ripley must have worked together on these matters, but Ripley's contributions did not seem to require his presence for more than three months. Learning from his father and from General Pillow, Ripley used influence and connections to secure another lengthy leave of absence but apparently was oblivious to the animosity he generated. Although not the six months he originally asked for, Ripley spent considerable time away from Fort Monroe. On April 5, 1852, Ripley finally returned to his duty station but did not remain there long. He left on April 24 for Fort Moultrie, South Carolina, returning to command the unit he had left in Florida, Company K of the 2nd Artillery Regiment. With so much controversy and contention regarding Ripley's leaves of absence, General Bankhead probably was not sorry to see him leave.[6]

CHAPTER 9

A New Life in South Carolina

Roswell Ripley arrived at Fort Moultrie late in April 1852. Located on Sullivan's Island facing the entrance to Charleston Harbor, Fort Moultrie was the third fortification built on the island to protect Charleston from a naval assault and bombardment. The third fort of brick and masonry was completed in 1809; however, unrelenting beach erosion began to undermine a portion of the fort's foundation. In 1831 the Corps of Engineers began work to strengthen and preserve the fort. The following year the "Nullification Crisis" over high protective tariffs favoring Northern industries resulted in South Carolina's threatened secession and an increase in the garrison at Moultrie.

During this emergency Captain James W. Ripley preceded Roswell to South Carolina by nearly twenty years. According to Cullum, in November 1832 "Captain Ripley was ordered to Fort Moultrie to keep peace in Charleston harbor during South Carolina's threatened nullification." Although James Ripley served only about five months in the Charleston area, he made a very favorable impression on Charleston native and Unionist Joel R. Poinsett. Poinsett became secretary of war in the Van Buren administration, and his relationship with James Ripley may have been a factor when he appointed James's nephew to West Point in 1839. On April 5, 1833, Poinsett wrote to President Andrew Jackson, "We part with Captain Ripley with great regret. His indefatigable exertions to resist the lawless attacks have won the esteem and respect of the friends of the Government in this city." Poinsett hoped that Ripley would be rewarded for "the zeal he has displayed in the defense of the Union." How greatly different would be the role his nephew would play in April 1861.[1]

Ripley remained in command of Company K at Fort Moultrie from April until November 1852. At that time Colonel Samuel Cooper, then the adjutant general, issued Special Order No. 194, directing Ripley to report to Company I of the 2nd Artillery stationed in Florida. When relieved of duty on November 20, Ripley asked for and received twenty days' leave to "attend to important private business." On December 6, apparently on his way to Florida and with only four of his twenty days off remaining, Ripley wrote to Adjutant General Cooper from Savannah, Georgia. Up to his old tactics, he "reluctantly" requested a three-month leave of absence "to attend to private business of much importance." By this time, another officer had reported to Company I in Florida, so Ripley offered to withdraw his request for three months' leave if his orders to report to Florida could be canceled. General Bankhead, from the headquarters of the 2nd Artillery Regiment at Fort Monroe, agreed to the cancellation but asked the AGO to order Ripley "to immediately join his proper Company E at Fort Moultrie." Ripley successfully avoided the assignment to the swamps of Florida, returned to Moultrie, and resumed his "private business of much importance."[2]

This "important private business" involved courting the twenty-eight-year-old widow Alicia Middleton Sparks. Alicia descended from Edward Middleton, a forefather of the prominent Middleton family of South Carolina. John Middleton, Alicia's grandfather, was born in England sometime after 1754. During the American Revolution, John left England for South Carolina and served against the British as a junior officer. In 1783 John Middleton married Frances Motte, daughter of Jacob Motte, one of the wealthiest and most influential men in the colony. Jacob owned Mount Pleasant Plantation, from which the town, directly across the Cooper River from Charleston, ultimately derived its name.

In 1784 Frances Motte Middleton gave birth to the couple's only son, Alicia's father, also named John. Young John was sent to England, was educated there, and spent much of his youth with his Middleton uncles. In England, John married Mary Burroughs in 1806 and later that year returned to South Carolina, where he had inherited the family's Crowfield Estate and other plantations.

Alicia Middleton, the youngest of John's five daughters, was born on January 16, 1824. One of her older brothers, J. Motte Middleton, developed a large rice plantation, Ogeechee Estates, near Savannah. During the war Motte served in the Charleston area, and after the conflict played a role in Roswell and Alicia Ripley's financial problems in England.

Alicia Middleton married Dr. William Alexander Sparks on May 31, 1842. Dr. Sparks was the son of Alexander Sparks, an exceedingly wealthy plantation owner with thousands of acres near Society Hill, South Carolina. On March 25, 1848, Alicia gave birth to a daughter, Marie Alice Sparks. Appointed consul at Venice by President Polk, Sparks died of cholera in that city on August 19, 1849. In April 1852, when Ripley arrived in Charleston, Alicia Sparks was a socially prominent and eligible young widow, as well as the mother of a four-year-old daughter.[3]

There is no record of how or where Ripley met Alicia, but during his leisure time at Fort Moultrie the affable young officer, intent on impressing Alicia, would have taken advantage of Charleston's fine dining, theater, and other entertainments. In addition, in the early 1800s Moultrieville on Sullivan Island's southern shore began to flourish as a resort destination. Steamboats crossed the Cooper River "throughout the day at convenient hours" carrying passengers between Sullivan's Island, Mount Pleasant, and Charleston.

The Moultrie House, a two-story resort hotel with accommodations for two hundred, began its first year as a summer resort on July 8, 1850. Located on the oceanfront just east of Fort Moultrie, this elegant hotel provided magnificent views of Charleston Harbor and the Atlantic Ocean. The massive hotel fronted the beach, and at each end wings extended from the main building. The spacious dining room, with multipaned floor-to-ceiling windows, was noted for the finest of foods. Folding doors could be opened to turn the first-floor rooms into a ballroom where weekly dances were held in season. The hotel touted their "Billiard Saloon" with four tables and a "well arranged bar with the choicest of liquors." Carriages were available for drives on "the unrivaled beach," where "sea-bathing cannot be surpassed."

The hotel soon gained a national reputation as one of the most luxurious, exclusive resorts on the East Coast. Wealthy planters, businessmen, and professionals thronged to Sullivan's Island in the summer for the cooling oceanfront breezes and the entertainment of Moultrie House. Both popular and notorious for its "flirtations," it was the place at which to be seen and to spend the South Carolina lowcountry summers. The nightlife and entertainment of the Moultrie House, being so accessible to the fort, would have been irresistible to Roswell, and it is likely that he met Alicia at the resort.[4]

In July 1852, nearly three years after the publication of *The War with Mexico*, the *Charleston Mercury* printed a column reviewing Ripley's two-volume history. The paper did not mention that Major Ripley was then stationed at Fort Moultrie, nor did it disclose who recommended the book for their "most favorable consideration." The review saw the book's "chief charm [as] its soldierly spirit of candor and faithfulness," adding, "We have long awaited such a book." As Ripley endeavored to impress Alicia during the summer and fall, the positive assessment of his book in the *Mercury* would bring his acclaim as an author to her attention.

It soon became apparent why Roswell desperately wanted to avoid reporting to Company I in the Florida swamps. The whirlwind romance had gone so well that Ripley's "important business" now included his wedding to Alicia Middleton Sparks. Returning to Fort Moultrie during the second week of December, Ripley and Alicia finalized their wedding plans, and the marriage took place on December 22, 1852.

On the last day of December 1852, Ripley finally began the process he had been contemplating for many years. In the first of two letters to Adjutant General Cooper, he offered to resign his commission on April 30, 1853. In that era, terminal leave could be granted to an officer planning a career after his military service ended. In his second letter Ripley applied for a leave of absence from January 1 until April 30, at which time his resignation would take effect.

By this time Ripley had definitely become disillusioned with the military. Just four years after graduating from the academy, he had expressed concerns about his military career. In a letter to his sister, written in May 1847, he claimed that he was "almost tempted to throw away my commission and try something else for pay and rations." After his service in Mexico, his incremental leaves of absence totaling one year, facilitated by General Pillow and President Polk, heightened his appreciation of civilian life. After that year of freedom from the regimentation of the military, it would have been a shock to serve in the hazardous and unhealthy swamps of Florida.[5]

Ripley's frequent leaves of absence brought him temporary relief from tedious and unexciting garrison duty and sharpened his desire for civilian life. In peacetime, the dismal prospect for advancement in rank and a static pay grade may also have influenced Ripley's decision. His fellow officers, those who were devoted to General Winfield Scott, would not have appreciated Ripley's history of the war and the alleged disparagement of the commanding general. Even if some officers may have treated him disdainfully, Ripley's strong personality would probably have kept him unthreatened.

Finally, the death of Ripley's father in September 1851 removed the last barrier to his resignation. Considering Christopher Ripley's dreams of pursing his own military career and all the effort he expended getting his son an appointment to West Point, Roswell's resignation would have been a major disappointment to his father.

General Bankhead, commanding the 2nd Artillery at Fort Monroe, did not view Ripley's letters of December 31, 1852, favorably. In forwarding Ripley's request to General Cooper, Bankhead stated that he could not approve the leave of absence because Ripley "has taken advantage of that indulgence more than any officer of my command." When Ripley learned that his resignation had been accepted but that his request for leave would not be granted, he attempted to withdraw his resignation. If his leave were to be denied, he would resign as soon as he was prepared for his postmilitary career. General Cooper ignored Ripley's request to withdraw his resignation, audited Ripley's military finance and property accounts, so that "the proper report may be made to the Secretary of War." All accounts were in order, no charges remained unpaid, and as a result the adjutant general proceeded to process Ripley's resignation.

Undeterred, Ripley wrote to his influential friend Senator James Shields for help. On January 16 Shields brought Secretary of War Conrad into the controversy, asking him to allow Ripley to "recall his resignation." Now registered at the Charleston Hotel, Ripley wrote a third letter to the AGO. On January 21 Ripley reiterated his request for four months' leave, dating from December 31 and giving him a separation date of May 1. Senator Shields's appeal to Conrad succeeded, and Ripley's resignation was recalled. On January 24 Conrad wrote to the AGO stating that Ripley's resignation would take effect on May 1. Evidently, Ripley was to be on leave until that date.

Even though the situation appeared to be settled, in late February Ripley traveled to Baltimore, Maryland, and registered at the Eutaw House. Astonishingly, on March 2 Ripley asked the adjutant general to change his date of resignation from May 1 to that very same day, March 2. Ripley had already received the four months' leave he originally requested, only to now be asking for immediate termination.

What behind-the-scenes maneuvering took place is unknown, but on March 19 the AGO informed Ripley, "the date of acceptance of your resignation has been changed by the President from the first day of May to the second day of the present month." This indicates that while in Baltimore, Roswell visited Washington and prevailed upon Shields and Conrad to involve President Millard Fillmore, a Whig who was to leave office on March 4, in his resignation process.[6]

Ripley remained in Baltimore for several more months and in September gained a position on the staff of Charles G. Baylor's *Daily American Times,* which had begun publishing in August. The highlight of the family's stay in Baltimore occurred on November 1, 1853, with the birth of his daughter, Alicia Middleton Ripley. He remained on the newspaper's staff until March 1854, after which the family returned to South Carolina.

Finally finished with the monotony and exasperations of a peacetime military career, Ripley could relax and enjoy civilian life in his adopted home of Charleston. However, the need to now support his wife and two daughters significantly altered Ripley's perspective on life. For this reason he turned to a business with which he was most familiar, the arms industry, and he likely had been developing contacts during the year. Ripley's intelligence, sociability, and knowledge of the industry would be an advantage in selling firearms on commission.[7]

In 1848 Christian Sharps developed and patented a breech-loading percussion rifle, which was manufactured for him in small numbers by several companies, including Robbins and Lawrence of Windsor, Vermont. Robbins and Lawrence gained recognition for producing small arms with fully interchangeable parts. In 1851 Sharps assigned his patent to the newly formed Sharps Rifle Manufacturing Company of Hartford, Connecticut, and Ripley would launch his sales career with this new company.

In the spring of 1853, Ripley would have followed developments in the Crimea intently. With the Turkish Empire in decline, Russia saw a chance to improve its access to the Mediterranean. In October 1853, after Russia occupied the Danube principalities, Turkey declared war on Russia. In 1854 an Anglo-French fleet sailed into the Black Sea to support the Turks, and in October the British landed troops on the Crimean Peninsula. The war continued throughout 1855 and finally ended in 1856, when the besieged Russian position became untenable. During the Crimean War the British military desperately needed arms and proved to be fertile ground for Ripley's sales efforts.[8]

In 1854 British officers arrived in the United States to inspect arms-manufacturing machinery and evaluate U.S.-made firearms. This may have been Ripley's first contact with the British and an opportunity to interest them in Sharps rifles. In preparation for sales trips to England, on December 20, 1854, Ripley applied for a passport. Now thirty-one years old, he was described as being five feet, ten-and-a-quarter inches tall, with "light" eyes and a fair complexion.

The British Ordnance Select Committee evaluated small arms, and their reports hold numerous references to letters received from "R. S. Ripley, Major, U.S." None of Ripley's letters have survived, but brief abstracts of his letters, recorded by British ordnance officers, are available. On January 20, 1855, Ripley wrote to the ordnance department asking them to conduct trials of the Sharps breech-loading rifle. In late February, Ripley arrived in England and submitted twelve self-priming Sharps carbines to the ordnance department. The carbines passed firing tests at Hythe, the British army's school of musketry, and on March 24, 1855, the British War Department received Ripley's proposal to provide the cavalry with Sharps carbines.

In April and May, Ripley continued correspondence with the ordnance committee, answering a request for "Bullets and Rifle Powder for cartridges for Hythe" and for four thousand rounds of ammunition. On May 9 and 11 the War Department approved "an offer made to Major Ripley, by Captain William M. Dixon, R.A., Director of the Small Arms Manufactories at Enfield, of £4 each for 550 Sharps breech-loading carbines." A week later Dixon requested that Ripley provide "suggestions regarding the Sharps carbines," and on June 7 the parties signed a contract for the carbines. On July 26 Dixon asked Ripley for an additional "1000 cartridges for the Sharps Breech Loading Carbine."[9]

Captain Dixon noted on May 28 that the British government had recently placed a large order for Victoria carbines to arm the Turkish Irregular Cavalry. Dixon believed the weapon to be almost useless, and as very few of them would be left for "our own cavalry," Dixon recommended purchasing one thousand to fifteen hundred more Sharps carbines. Dixon believed that the Sharps breech-loader was much superior to anything yet invented, had been well tested, and could be obtained in large numbers on short notice. Captain Dixon, whose military rank did not reflect the importance of his position, became a vital ally in Roswell Ripley's sales efforts.

On June 5 an aide to the general commanding in chief, Viscount Hardinge, notified Dixon that the viscount considered the Prince carbine to be superior to the Sharps and was against purchasing more of the American carbines. Hardinge favored a continuation of trials between the two weapons, but it does not appear that Dixon complied with the viscount's request.

On November 6 the viscount, much to his chagrin, learned only incidentally that orders had been given for the purchase of an additional six thousand Sharps carbines to arm both British and Turkish cavalry. Hardinge's aide notified Dixon that "his Lordship has been no party to this and views it with regret, and recommended the further manufacture of them should be stopped."

Dixon defended his Sharps order based on the large number of carbines needed by the British, Turkish, and their mercenary allies. With no carbines in stock, Dixon believed that only Sharps could be obtained quickly, in large numbers, and would actually be arriving from America soon.[10]

Early in the Crimean War the British decided to modify their older handcraft methods of arms manufacturing and adopted an American system, which relied more on machinery and the principle of interchangeable parts. In 1854 and 1855 the British began buying U.S.-made rifle milling and stock-making machinery for the modernization of the Royal Small Arms Factory at Enfield, northeast of central London. On April 2, 1855, Captain Warlow, who was in the United States with the British Arms Commission, conferred with James H. Burton, the acting master armorer at the Harpers Ferry Arsenal in Virginia. They discussed a possible appointment for Burton at Enfield, and on April 19 Burton, although still working at Harpers Ferry, began making drawings of arms-making machinery for the British government. On May 31 the British selected Burton to be the chief engineer at Enfield, and on August 15 the armorer sailed from Boston for Liverpool. Burton reached Enfield two weeks later to meet with Dixon. As chief engineer, Burton would have worked closely with Dixon and may have encouraged and supported the British officer's preference for Ripley's Sharps carbines.[11]

The year 1855 had been a successful one for Ripley. He had been in the right country at the right time, had a product in demand, and sold the British a substantial number of Sharps carbines. During the year Ripley also began an association with British gunsmith Robert Adams, whose revolver had been adopted by Queen Victoria's War Department and was being used extensively in the Crimea. The Adams revolver, with patented improvements by F. B. E. Beaumont and James Kerr, competed directly with Samuel Colt's revolvers for sales to both the U.S. and British governments. It is not known how long Ripley remained in England, but he probably returned home to spend the 1855 Christmas season with his wife and young daughters.

Early in 1856 Ripley began sales efforts in the United States for the London Armoury Company, Ltd., the manufacturer of the Adams revolver. In early June, Ripley offered the five-chambered, self-cocking revolver to the U.S. Ordnance Department. On June 17 the government accepted his offer to supply about one hundred of the pistols, as well as his proposal to arrange for free trials of William Beasley's British barrel-rolling machinery at the Springfield Armory. Adams, Beaumont, and Kerr planned to obtain U.S. patents for their "improved" revolver, and Ripley also developed business relationships with Kerr and Beaumont. In

August, Ripley and Kerr were in the New York City to obtain legal documents for his patent application.

Later that month Ripley and Kerr approached the Massachusetts Arms Company in Chicopee Falls regarding the production of Adams revolvers. Production was to begin after their patents were granted, finances arranged, and Colt's master patent expired in 1857. George Peabody, the respected American merchant and financier, who had been residing in London for many years, returned to Chicopee Falls in August while Ripley and Kerr were negotiating with the Massachusetts Arms Company. Most likely the discussions also involved Peabody, for later in 1856 he entered his interests with the British Patent Office along with Ripley and Adams. On August 28 Kerr granted Ripley a general power of attorney to manage his patent after it was issued. Adams granted Ripley a like power from London in September, and Beaumont completed the triad on January 1857.[12]

On September 1, 1856, on behalf of the London Armoury Company, Ripley and Kerr placed an order with the Robbins and Lawrence Company for stock machinery, barrel-boring machinery, turning lathes for barrels, milling machines and drill presses; machines capable of manufacturing 200–250 Minié rifles per day. The order also included finishing and edging machines for bayonets and machinery for ramrods. Robbins and Lawrence addressed all correspondence to Ripley, who had registered at the New York Hotel. On September 18 Robbins and Lawrence informed Ripley that the machinery had been delayed and could not be shipped until Wednesday, September 23. That would be too late for the *Arabia*, the steamer on which Ripley planned to have the machinery shipped. Then, in early October the company notified Ripley of additional delays.

Forced to remain in New York while dealing with Robbins and Lawrence, Ripley used the delay to search for more business. Early in September he called on Captain Duncan N. Ingraham, chief of the U.S. Navy's Bureau of Ordnance and Hydrography, and left an Adams revolver for the captain to inspect. With artillery still a prominent interest, Ripley asked Ingraham if the Navy Department would send him the dimensions and weight of the 9-, 10-, and 11-inch guns then in use by the navy. There is no evidence Ripley received an answer to his request, but it is unlikely Ingraham would have provided Ripley with the specifications.

Undoubtedly frustrated with the Robbins and Lawrence delays, Ripley finally returned to England in early November. James Burton, at Enfield, listed in his diary the visits of "Major Ripley" on November 20 and December 10. Burton recorded these visits but did not disclose what they discussed. Ripley most likely stayed in England over the 1856 Christmas and New Year's holidays, as on January 19, 1857, he again visited Burton in Enfield. On this occasion, Archibald Hamilton, president of the London Armoury Company, accompanied Adams, Kerr, and Ripley as they examined the lock and barrel finishing machinery. Barrel rolling and finishing machinery interested the men because U.S. arms manufacturers, despite their sophistication in arms machinery in general, trailed England in barrel technology.[13]

Soon after this visit to Enfield, Ripley returned to New York and once again registered at the New York Hotel. In early February he claimed a box of pistols being held at Customs and on February 9 delivered the box containing 113 Adams revolvers and spare parts to the quartermaster's store at the New York Arsenal. Ripley asked the quartermaster to forward the revolvers to his commanding officer, Captain R. H. K. Whitely. Priced at eighteen dollars each, with three dollars' estimated duty, Ripley stated that the revolvers were those the ordnance department ordered on June 17, 1856. Colonel H. K. Craig, the chief of ordnance, told Whitely to inspect, test, and certify all the pistols he approved.

On March 1, 1857, Ripley acknowledged Captain Ingraham and the bureau's order for fifty Adams revolvers to be manufactured by the London Armoury Company. Apparently, Ripley had just received Ingraham's order, nearly six months after he left the sample revolver in the bureau's office in September 1856.

By March 9 Captain Whitely had finally tested all of Ripley's 113 revolvers, firing each one ten times with the maximum practicable powder charge. He reported that three weapons suffered multiple discharges, blowing off their rammers, and a number were temporarily jammed. Some revolvers had other defects, and a few of the spare parts were not interchangeable. All in all, Colonel Craig viewed the report favorably.

Ripley wrote to Craig on March 14 proposing to sell five hundred additional revolvers to the U.S. Ordnance Department. Now described as Beaumont-Adams revolvers, these pistols were to be made by the Massachusetts Arms Company in Chicopee Falls. Craig strongly endorsed Ripley's proposal and forwarded it to the secretary of war. He was impressed with the revolver, noting that "the price is considerably less than the Colt pistol, to which it is quite equal, and in some respects superior." As evidence of Ripley's sales ability, the War Department approved the purchase of the five hundred additional revolvers.[14]

It is not clear whether Ripley returned to South Carolina later in March, but by May 1 he, along with Alexander McConochie and his son James, filed papers in New York incorporating "The Adams' Revolving Arms Company." The McConochies, commercial merchants and insurance brokers, represented the local financing and distributing organization Ripley needed. These three were to be the sole trustees of the company and would manufacture the revolvers in Chicopee Falls, with all other business conducted in New York City. The three trustees divided the capital stock, valued at $15,000, equally among themselves. Somewhat surprisingly and possibly for legal reasons, the certificate of incorporation listed Ripley as being a citizen of the city and state of New York.

Unfortunately for Ripley, the London Armoury Company was having problems filling the Bureau of Ordnance and Hydrography's order for fifty Adams revolvers. In late May, Captain Ingraham wrote to Ripley twice complaining of the delayed delivery. Ripley informed Ingraham that he had been expecting them for some time and was told they would be finished soon. Ripley offered to substitute revolvers made by the Massachusetts Arms Company, but Ingraham refused. As a result, on May 27 Ripley notified Ingraham that he would await the arrival of the revolvers, thereby delaying his next trip to England. By the end of July, Ripley still had not received the pistols. He advised Ingraham that he was sailing the next day for England and acknowledged Ingraham's right to cancel the order. As correspondence between the two men ceased, the captain may indeed have done just that. Ripley obviously had expanded his sales efforts beyond Sharps rifles but was continually plagued by production problems.[15]

The *Atlantic* steamed out of New York harbor on August 1, 1857, for Liverpool, and after arriving, Ripley continued on to London, where he listed the prestigious George Peabody & Company as his forwarding address. On August 18 Ripley called on James Burton at the Royal Small Arms Factory in Enfield, bringing general news from Burton's friends. More important, Ripley was interested in learning more about experiments with explosive bullets that Burton had witnessed on February 19. Burton had written to Ripley describing the hollow-pointed bullets filled with chlorate of potash and antimony and sealed with yellow wax.

Ripley also would have been interested in news that A. Bower of Liverpool met with Burton on June 30 for professional advice regarding machinery for a "Small Arms Factory proposed for the Viceroy of Egypt." Burton's diary reveals that Ripley returned to Enfield on September 7 asking about this proposed machinery. Ripley and Bower had become acquainted on the return train from Enfield to London on August 18 and had discussed the arms factory project. Although Ripley sensed potential business with Bower and the machinery for Egypt, there is no record this meeting resulted in future sales. On October 20 Burton wrote that Ripley came to his office to discuss barrel roll machinery and four days later noted that Ripley was leaving Liverpool for the United States.[16]

A financial crisis in 1857 tightened credit and affected Ripley's business, but not to the extent the Panic of 1837 devastated his father's Matildaville investment. On February 13, 1858, the *Chicopee Journal Weekly* reported that the Massachusetts Arms Company had begun hiring more men and was beginning to fill their Adams revolver contracts. By June 1858, according to the same paper, Ripley's Adams Revolving Arms Company of New York had contracted with the Chicopee Falls company for five thousand revolvers. W. H. J. Chamberlain and A. W. F. Taylerson, the authors of *Adams' Revolvers*, believe that Ripley left the country in the summer of 1858, but no record of his activities has been found.

In an 1861 interview published in the *Charleston Mercury,* Ripley stated that he had been in Europe during much of the Crimean War engaged in the manufacture and supply of arms for the British government. The interviewer concluded that Ripley had enjoyed an excellent opportunity to learn about the latest technology in arms manufacture and artillery. Since that time, Ripley claimed, he had had been engaged in engineering and mining; however, no additional information about Ripley's mining activities in the late 1850s has been found.[17]

After the birth of his daughter, Alicia, Roswell Ripley spent a significant part of the 1850s on business travel to New York, New England, and Great Britain. In being away from his family for protracted periods, Ripley followed in his father's footsteps, replicating Christopher's long absences away from home on business. Ripley most likely would not have sensed anything unusual about his behavior, but one wonders what his wife and daughters thought of his prolonged absences.

CHAPTER 10

Secession

No record of Ripley's activities in 1859 has been found, other than the mention of some mining and engineering efforts in the *Mercury* interview. However, The Lincoln-Douglas debates of 1858 would have been of interest to Ripley as the two candidates for the Illinois Senate argued aspects of slavery. Then in October 1859, John Brown launched his violent, abolitionist-financed raid on the U.S. Armory at Harpers Ferry, Virginia. Brown and his followers planned to seize weapons from the armory, invade the South, and forcibly free, at any cost, as many slaves as possible. While this sent panic and fear across the South, many in the Northeast hailed Brown as a hero and martyr after he was tried and hanged. The murderous Harpers Ferry raid would have intensified Ripley's loathing of abolitionists; he clearly foresaw the inevitability of secession and ultimately the Civil War.[1]

On March 3, 1860, Ripley met with Governor William Henry Gist at his Rose Hill Plantation near Unionville, South Carolina. Ripley presented a written proposal to the governor and his cousin, States Rights Gist. Ripley also planned to submit his ideas to the governors of Georgia and Alabama for their consideration. Ripley advocated the construction of a Southern armory, capable of producing between eight and twelve thousand "stands of arms" per year, in one of these three states. Ripley believed that a substantial armory would require a five-year contract with each of the three states and cost $50,000 per year. Ripley believed that the South faced two serious problems, the first being the time needed to build the armory and begin manufacturing arms. The greater problem was the lack of persons in the South having experience or knowledge of the arms industry. If the governors agreed it was advisable to build an armory in one of their states, Ripley asked them to present his proposal to their respective legislatures. After meeting with Governor Gist, Ripley planned to travel to Savannah, Georgia, where he could be contacted at the Pulaski House.[2]

Ripley received the first reply to his proposal from Governor A. B. Moore of Alabama. The governor responded on March 23 that he viewed the proposal favorably and planned to submit it to the General Assembly of Alabama at its next session. Moore cautioned that he could not guarantee that the legislature would consider the matter positively, even if he recommended it. He was convinced there should be an armory in the "cotton growing States" and thought Ripley's plan was better than any of which he was aware.

On April 3, while he was in Savannah, Georgia's governor, Joseph E. Brown, replied with specific concerns about Ripley's proposal. The previous Georgia legislature had voted to appoint one or more commissioners to study the establishment of an armory in Georgia. Therefore, Brown was not at liberty to make an arrangement that could bind Georgia to an out-of-state armory. If the Georgia commissioners did not present a suitable plan, Governor Brown agreed to present Ripley's proposal to the legislature.[3]

While Ripley pursued his quest for a Southern armory, the Democrats and Republicans held their nominating conventions for the presidential election in November. In April the Democratic Party met in Charleston, and Senator Stephen A. Douglas led in the lengthy balloting. When the party refused to include a plank in its platform calling for federal protection of slavery in the territories, delegates from the Deep South walked out of the convention. The Northern Democrats reconvened in Baltimore and nominated Douglas, while the Southern Democrats, now referred to as "National Democrats," also convened in Baltimore and nominated John C. Breckinridge. To complicate the situation and further divide the Democratic Party, a third splinter group, the Constitutional Union Party, nominated John Bell of Tennessee. Although he trailed William H. Seward on the first two ballots, the Republicans nominated Abraham Lincoln.[4]

To keep Governor Gist informed about his armory proposal, Ripley forwarded copies of the replies he had received from Alabama and Georgia. Ripley, who was still in Savannah, planned to keep Gist informed as the summer progressed, but no other correspondence has been found.

On November 7, from the Continental Hotel in Philadelphia, Ripley wrote his last known prewar letter. Writing to General States Rights Gist, the acting adjutant and inspector general of the South Carolina Militia, Ripley acknowledged that he was in Philadelphia on business relating to the armory he had spoken with Gist about in March. Ripley thought he would be in Columbia before the end of November, which would suffice for a bill covering an armory, but added "what you want first is arms." Ripley delayed his return to South Carolina while he investigated the availability of arms in the United States and abroad. Authors W. H. J. Chamberlain and A. W. F. Taylerson have noted that the Continental Hotel was not far from the Sharps company's Philadelphia rifle works and that Georgia had received a shipment of Sharps rifles in February 1861. They postulated that Ripley may have acted as an agent for Georgia but could not prove the connection.

Ripley advised General Gist that except for national arsenals, good arms were scarce in the United States and that if arms were needed soon, they might need to be obtained abroad. He believed that French arms were available but not as good as English arms or others. Ripley reminded Gist that there were about fifteen thousand serviceable weapons in Charleston and that he should make certain they were not removed from the state. Ripley believed there was no doubt Lincoln would be elected but cautioned against overt acts, such as disputes about customs or the post office until Lincoln assumed office; then, he wrote, "Mr. Lincoln will walk into a house gutted of its best furniture."[5]

W. B. Cisco related that on November 5, 1860, the South Carolina General Assembly met and following verification of Abraham Lincoln's election, unanimously voted for a "sovereignty convention" whose delegates were to be elected on December 6. This convention was scheduled to meet on December 17 and to vote on whether South Carolina would secede. As recounted by E. B. Long, in Charleston on December 20, all the 169 convention delegates voted in favor of secession. "In the evening the formal signing took place in Institute Hall, while Charleston went wild with joy . . . church bells rang, cannon roared . . . military companies paraded, and as night came on bonfires were lighted in the principal streets." South Carolina was proclaimed "to be a free and independent country."[6] Ripley's armory plans obviously had not kept up with the escalating political events.

On the day before Christmas, three representatives of South Carolina boarded a train for Washington. These commissioners, Robert Barnwell, James Adams, and James Orr, were appointed to negotiate the transfer, from the United States to South Carolina, the lighthouses, forts, magazines, and all real estate within the boundaries of the state. The commissioners arrived in Washington on December 26 and met with Assistant Secretary of State William H. Trescott, a native of Charleston. Trescott arranged for the three Carolinians to meet the next day with President Buchanan.[7]

Early on the night of December 26, realizing the vulnerability of his exposed position at Fort Moultrie, Major Robert Anderson, acting without orders, stealthily transferred his command to the unfinished Fort Sumter. As the Union forces abandoned Fort Moultrie, Anderson ordered his men to spike the guns, burn the gun carriages, disable the hot shot furnaces, and destroy all ammunition they could not transport to Fort Sumter. When the news reached Washington, President Buchanan, Secretary of War John B. Floyd, and the commissioners were stunned, certain that Anderson had created a major dilemma for all.

On December 28 South Carolina's governor, Francis W. Pickens, who had recently assumed office, considered the evacuation of Fort Moultrie a violation of the understanding between Washington and the representatives of South Carolina and, more important, an act of war. On January 1 the commissioners wrote a lengthy letter to Buchanan stating that South Carolina had sent them to negotiate a settlement but that Anderson's actions constituted a threatening, ominous act. The president refused the letter, and when he and his Cabinet members learned that South Carolina had retaliated by seizing Fort Moultrie, Castle Pinckney, the United States arsenal, customs house, and post office, a peaceful settlement became nearly impossible. Perceiving their mission to be a failure, the Carolinians planned to leave Washington the next day.[8]

Learning of the evacuation of Fort Moultrie, Ripley immediately volunteered his services to his adopted state, and on December 27 Governor Pickens appointed him major of ordnance, South Carolina Militia. On January 2, 1861, he was assigned to the command of Brigadier General R. G. M. Dunovant on Sullivan's Island. General Dunovant placed Ripley in charge of the artillery at Fort Moultrie, assigning him to repair the damages done by the departing Union forces and restore the fort to fighting condition. Pickens recalled that when questions arose over rank, Ripley waived all formality and agreed, if necessary, to "serve as a private at the heavy ordnance."

Without notifying Major Anderson, the first attempt by the U.S. government to reinforce Fort Sumter came on January 5, 1861, when the *Star of the West* steamed from New York Harbor bound for Charleston. Governor Pickens received several telegrams from informants in Washington alerting him that reinforcements were headed for South Carolina. Anderson's forces occupying Fort Sumter heard rumors to that effect but discounted them. The unarmed steamship, carrying two hundred reinforcements, arrived off Charleston Harbor on January 9 and was shelled by batteries on Morris Island. After receiving two insignificant hits, the ship steamed past the island but then came within range of Fort Moultrie. Even though the rearmament of Fort Moultrie had only just begun, Ripley fired at the approaching steamer but without effect. He fully expected to receive a withering return fire from Fort Sumter, but Anderson, unsure as to the mission of the steamship, declined to return a covering fire. Forced to abort its mission, the *Star of the West* headed for New York.[9]

As work progressed on Fort Moultrie, Governor Pickens recommended Ripley for promotion, and on January 28 the South Carolina Senate confirmed his appointment as Lieutenant Colonel of the First Battalion of Artillery. Ripley's efforts to restore Fort Moultrie did not begin smoothly because of problems with Major Walter Gwynne of the Engineer Corps. On January 31 Ripley, who now outranked the engineer, informed General Dunovant that because of problems with the construction of barracks for Captain Calhoun's company, their orientation and instruction would be unnecessarily delayed. The next day Ripley requested that Major Gwynne be ordered to report to him, so that he could approve or emend the engineer's plans and prevent future "ill-advised and annoying measures." If the engineer refused this request, Ripley believed that "he should be relieved of duty." However, Gwynne insisted he would take orders only from the South Carolina War Department. Ripley claimed that the damage done during the last twenty-four hours must now be repaired and that he expected "Major Gwynne will refuse to do it, while exercising his quasi-independence."[10]

That same day, Ripley gave Gwynne specific instructions on what needed to be done regarding the barracks for Calhoun's company. He also ordered work on the northeast bastion and the hospital, while directing that palmetto logs should be used in place of planking on Moultrie's wall facing Fort Sumter. Gwynne was also to consult with Ripley regarding the dimensions of the fort's embrasures. As these works were of the most urgent necessity, Ripley ordered the engineer to lose no time in completing them, indicating that he would give other instructions when that work was finished.

Astonishingly, Gwynne responded by asking for a leave of absence. Ripley again wrote to General Dunovant informing the general that under the present urgent circumstances he could not grant Gwynne's request: "I shall order him to proceed at once, and in case he does not, I shall order him to report to you under arrest." Ripley believed that the engineers, "if not completely removed, should be prevented from causing frequent difficulties." These allegations and recriminations ended, suggesting that the situation must have been resolved to Ripley's satisfaction.[11]

By February 1, 1861, Mississippi, Florida, Alabama, Georgia, Louisiana, and finally Texas had seceded from the Union and joined South Carolina. Three days later delegates from these seceded states convened in Montgomery, Alabama. The delegates adopted the Provisional Constitution of the Confederate States on February 8 and elected Jefferson Davis of Mississippi provisional president of the Confederacy.

As these states seceded, they confiscated Federal forts and other government property within their boundaries. Most of these forts were not garrisoned or were manned only by an ordnance sergeant or caretaker. In San Antonio, Texas, General David Twiggs surrendered all U.S. military posts in the Department of Texas to the state. The lack of a strong government response to these seizures emboldened the Confederacy.[12]

On the "beautiful afternoon" of February 6, while Ripley supervised the repairs of Fort Moultrie, a group of men and women, accompanied by the rector of St. Phillip's Church, visited the fort to present the new South Carolina flag to the garrison. The flag was raised to an artillery salute; and, in the words of the *Charleston Mercury*, its "silver crescent gleamed out in the setting sun, and seemed to give promise of a glorious future." When the flag reached the top of the staff, "it was warmly cheered by the men, and Major [sic] Ripley came forward and complimented the ladies on their gift. The ladies were provided refreshments and the flag was handsomely toasted."[13]

This was not the only pre-Confederate flag at Fort Moultrie, as the ladies of Charleston had also sewn a "handsome silk" parade flag for the 1st South Carolina Artillery. Ripley designed the flag himself, and his wife presented it to the artillerists of Fort Moultrie. After the surrender of Fort Sumter, the parade flag became one of the three flags to fly over the fort during the war.[14]

In early February, Ripley had been asked to estimate the requirements for forty-eight hours of continual firing against Fort Sumter. At the time he had an unspecified number of columbiads and only six 32-pounders. He reported that the "32-pounders can be effectually fired once in two minutes and calculated that at best the six cannon could fire 7,200 shots in 48 hours." However, despite his frequent pleas, he had only about one-third of the required ammunition. Ripley added that he did not believe forty-eight hours of firing would cause the surrender of Fort Sumter. At the end of the cannonade his forces would be "out of ammunition and no nearer Fort Sumter than at the beginning." Interestingly, he added, "unless the Commanding Officer chooses to surrender to avoid civil war."

Ripley doubted that brave or desperate men could be deterred by forty-eight hours of turmoil and confusion and believed that every artillery officer "who knows the effect of projectiles at long range against masonry" would support him. At this time Ripley regarded a forty-eight-hour bombardment of Fort Sumter as a desperate effort, resulting in the loss of what ammunition they had and having little effect on either side. Ripley's warnings must have been instrumental in increasing the firepower of Fort Moultrie and Sullivan's Island for the eventual bombardment.[15]

On March 1 the Confederate government assumed control of the military operations in Charleston. The Confederate secretary of war, Leroy P. Walker, ordered General P. G. T. Beauregard to report to Governor Pickens in Charleston and take command of the Provisional Forces of the Confederate States. Beauregard was directed to report back to the War Department on the status of the defenses of Charleston Harbor.

In a letter to Secretary Walker, Ripley applied for a commission as "Colonel or Lieutenant Colonel of Artillery in the Army of the Confederate States of America." Striving to be reasonable in his request, Ripley mentioned the second rank, as he did not want his application to take precedence over an officer who had more active service in the artillery than he did. General Beauregard strongly supported Ripley's request, as did Major J. H. Trapier and Congressman W. Porcher Miles.

During the first week of March, Beauregard and Ripley corresponded in detail regarding locations for artillery batteries and the caliber of guns to be installed, especially those covering the approaches to Fort Sumter. In a letter to Beauregard's aide-de-camp, Ripley described the momentous difficulties he faced preparing Fort Moultrie with the forces under his command. Asked to send two 32-pounders from Moultrie to a five-gun battery, Ripley replied that he had no way to send the guns, no gin to dismount or mount them, and no artificer to build the traverses or pivot pins. He claimed he had "290 indifferent artillerymen, 53 volunteers at a five-gun battery, and 318 helpless infantry recruits." Most had no arms, little clothing, and "were totally and entirely unfit to meet the enemy." He complained that he lacked laborers and had to use his men building defenses instead of drilling. Beauregard claimed that he was fully aware of the difficulties

General P. G. T. Beauregard. In command of the Department of South Carolina, Georgia and Florida, Beauregard worked well with Ripley until Ripley criticized and denounced engineer D. B. Harris, a friend of Beauregard's, for incompetence regarding Charleston's defense works. From the National Archives.

Ripley faced, "but from your zeal and known ability to surmount obstacles I have no doubt you will give a good account of yourself and command."[16]

On March 4 Abraham Lincoln was inaugurated president of the United States. In his inaugural address he stated that "no state, upon its own mere motion, can lawfully get out of the Union. . . . The power confided in me will be used to hold, occupy, and possess the property and places belonging to the government." Louis T. Wigfall, who had resigned his Texas senatorial seat but remained in Washington, immediately telegraphed Governor Pickens to be vigilant. He believed that Lincoln's inauguration meant war and that reinforcements would soon be sent to Fort Sumter.

Even though South Carolina's original commissioners had been unsuccessful in mediating the situation, in early March the Confederate government sent three envoys to Washington in an attempt to negotiate a peaceful settlement of the crisis. William H. Seward, now Lincoln's secretary of state, would not recognize the three emissaries officially but met with them clandestinely through intermediaries. Seward claimed that he wanted to settle the standoff peacefully and gave the Southern commissioners reason to believe that he could convince Lincoln to evacuate Sumter. The secretary of state, even though he knew the administration had not decided to abandon the fort, convinced an intermediary, Associate Justice of the Supreme Court John A. Campbell, that Sumter was to be evacuated within five days. Campbell immediately notified the commissioners, and they dispatched the good news to the government in Montgomery.[17]

On March 20 the three Confederate commissioners in Washington telegraphed Beauregard asking whether Sumter had been evacuated as Seward had supposedly indicated. That same day they telegraphed the government in Montgomery that there had been no change in the situation: "If there is faith in man we may rely on the assurances we have as to the status." How seriously the Confederacy wanted to believe Seward's semiofficial promises regarding Sumter was apparent when Secretary Walker, the next day, asked Beauregard "to afford Major Anderson and his men safe conduct out of the harbor." Toward the latter part of March, the Confederates interpreted Seward's promises and the vacillation in Washington to be devious maneuvering. If the government was unwilling to withdraw Anderson peaceably, Beauregard predicted, the uncertainty would end as soon as preparations were completed to compel him to surrender.[18]

Delegates to a state convention, meeting in Charleston on Saturday, March 30, were given a tour of the fortifications around Charleston Harbor. Several hundred guests of General Beauregard boarded two steamships, the *Carolina* and the *General Clinch,* for the harbor excursion. The ships cast off from Southern Wharf at 10:00 A.M., and as the ships moved into the harbor, the Palmetto Band, on the forward deck of the *Clinch,* gave an inspiring rendition of "Dixie." General Beauregard, aboard the *Carolina,* chatted with the guests and pointed out sites of interest. Confident and seemingly unaware of the impending crisis, all enjoyed the beautiful spring weather and fresh sea breezes.

The ships first visited Fort Johnson, then stopped at Moultrieville wharf on Sullivan's Island. After passing through Moultrieville, the contingent arrived at Fort Moultrie. Within the fort, the big guns on the parapet welcomed the convention delegates with a thunderous salute. According to the *Charleston Mercury,* the group dispersed over the fort to examine the massive defenses that had been added to the walls under the guidance "of the energetic and indefatigable Lieut. Col. Ripley." The artillerymen, at their batteries, went through the "manual of heavy artillery with remarkable precision." The group inspected the quarters, magazine, and bombproofs, and was given a demonstration at the hot shot furnace where several 8-inch shot were heated bright red, "suggestive of unpleasant results." The visitors were impressed "with the high state of discipline and efficiency to which the gallant Ripley has brought the garrison."

Leaving Sullivan's Island, the ships steamed down Maffitt's Channel to the band's rendition of "La Marseillais" in honor of General Beauregard. As the ships passed the Moultrie House, the 1st Regiment Rifles with colors flying saluted the passing steamers. Soon after, a champagne lunch was served to the enthusiastic guests in the steamers' lower cabins. The steamers returned at dusk, and as the groups disembarked, "the band played 'Dixie' quite as vigorously as if they had never stopped."

At Fort Sumter, the State Convention's harbor cruise and the extensive firing of cannon from Fort Moultrie, Morris Island, and Cumming's Point had definitely been noticed. From this cannonade, Captain J. G. Foster of the engineers updated the number of guns and mortars in the Confederate batteries around the harbor. In his report to General Joseph G. Totten, he noted that three of the mortars fired the day before had been practicing to obtain the range and length of their fuses to reach Fort Sumter.[19]

As late as March 28, much to Secretary Seward's satisfaction, General Winfield Scott advised the evacuation of both Sumter and Fort Pickens in Florida. Both men were convinced this would prevent other slaveholding states from seceding. Undeterred by Scott and Seward, Lincoln decided to resupply Fort Sumter. On March 29 Lincoln ordered Secretary of War Simon Cameron, in concert with the secretary of the navy, to prepare a naval expedition ready to sail as early as April 6. At various northern ports the steamers *Pocahontas, Pawnee,* and *Harriet Lane* were provisioned and readied for departure. On April 1 Lincoln ordered the commandant of the naval yard in Brooklyn to outfit the *Powhatan* for sea "at the earliest possible moment under sealed orders."

The next day the commissioners in Washington informed their government in Montgomery that the "war wing" was asserting influence on the president, sarcastically adding, "Their form of notice to us may be that of the coward, who gives it when he strikes." The preparations incensed the commissioners, who were now convinced Seward had knowingly deceived them. In the words of W. A. Swanberg, "Seward . . . in all of his dealings, carried on without Lincoln's knowledge, had been so reckless and unscrupulous that they put the whole administration in a deceitful light."[20]

On April 2 Secretary Walker ordered Beauregard to absolutely "prevent the re-enforcement of Fort Sumter," saying that he should treat the situation "precisely as if you are in the presence of an enemy contemplating to surprise you." Walker stressed that the government did not have any confidence in assurances from Washington regarding the evacuation of Sumter. Nevertheless, Beauregard was to take no action until the Confederate commissioners were withdrawn from Washington. At that time, the War Department would provide the commanding general with specific instructions.

In his inaugural address Lincoln had warned the South, "You can have no conflict, without yourselves being the aggressors." If there was to be war, Lincoln intended to force the Confederacy into firing the first shot. Governor Pickens and the South Carolina commissioners believed that the destruction and abandonment of Fort Moultrie was actually the first blow in the war, followed by the *Star of the West*'s unsuccessful attempt to reach Fort Sumter. The U.S. government's refusal to negotiate and the planned resupplying of Fort Sumter would be the final affront. The desire to negotiate in order to avoid a war, originally espoused by South Carolina, was fully embraced by the Confederacy. The Confederates failed to realize, in part because of the possibly unintended duplicity of Secretary of State Seward, that the issues were not open to negotiation; nor did the Lincoln administration even recognize the Confederate government's existence. In effect, Lincoln had drawn a line in the sand, and the Confederates would be goaded into firing on Fort Sumter.[21]

CHAPTER 11

The Bombardment

President Lincoln was determined to notify Governor Pickens that he intended to reprovision Fort Sumter, thereby placing the responsibility for any resultant hostilities directly on the governor. He communicated only with the governor of South Carolina, refusing to recognize or acknowledge the Confederacy, or deal with its commissioners.

On the evening of April 6, Robert Chew, a State Department clerk accompanied by a U.S. army captain, boarded a train in Washington. Bound for Charleston, they were to present Lincoln's ultimatum to the governor. Lincoln chose to belittle the governor by sending his note, lacking a formal salutation, unsigned, and delivered by a low-level clerk and low-ranking army officer. Chew was instructed to refuse any response from Pickens, thereby indicating that Lincoln was uninterested in anything the governor might have to say. Chew delivered the note to Governor Pickens and General Beauregard on the night of April 8. The governor was astonished by this lack of protocol and disregard for his office. He and Beauregard were stunned and angered by the ultimatum, feeling with some justification that the U.S. government had been devious in dealing with the Confederacy. At about the time Chew delivered his note to the governor, Major Anderson finally received his first communication from Secretary of War Simon Cameron, informing him that he would be reprovisioned by April 11 or 12.[1]

When the relief force sailed for Charleston on April 10, the Confederate commissioners notified Beauregard, "Diplomacy has failed. The sword must now preserve our independence." The commissioners also forwarded newspaper articles claiming that the Fort Sumter relief expedition intended to land a force that would overcome any opposition. Secretary Walker instructed Beauregard to demand the evacuation of Fort Sumter and, if refused, to use whatever force was necessary to force its surrender.

During the next few days, Ripley worked diligently to complete preparations at Fort Moultrie and strengthen the other batteries on Sullivan's Island. To the chagrin of Major W. H. C. Whiting of the engineers, Beauregard had ordered the Dahlgren gun on Sullivan's Island to be dismounted. Whiting informed Beauregard that the gun, then on Sullivan's Wharf, must be remounted or sent to Morris Island, which would take much longer. On April 10 Beauregard acquiesced and ordered Ripley to remount the gun, position it at the west end of the island, and

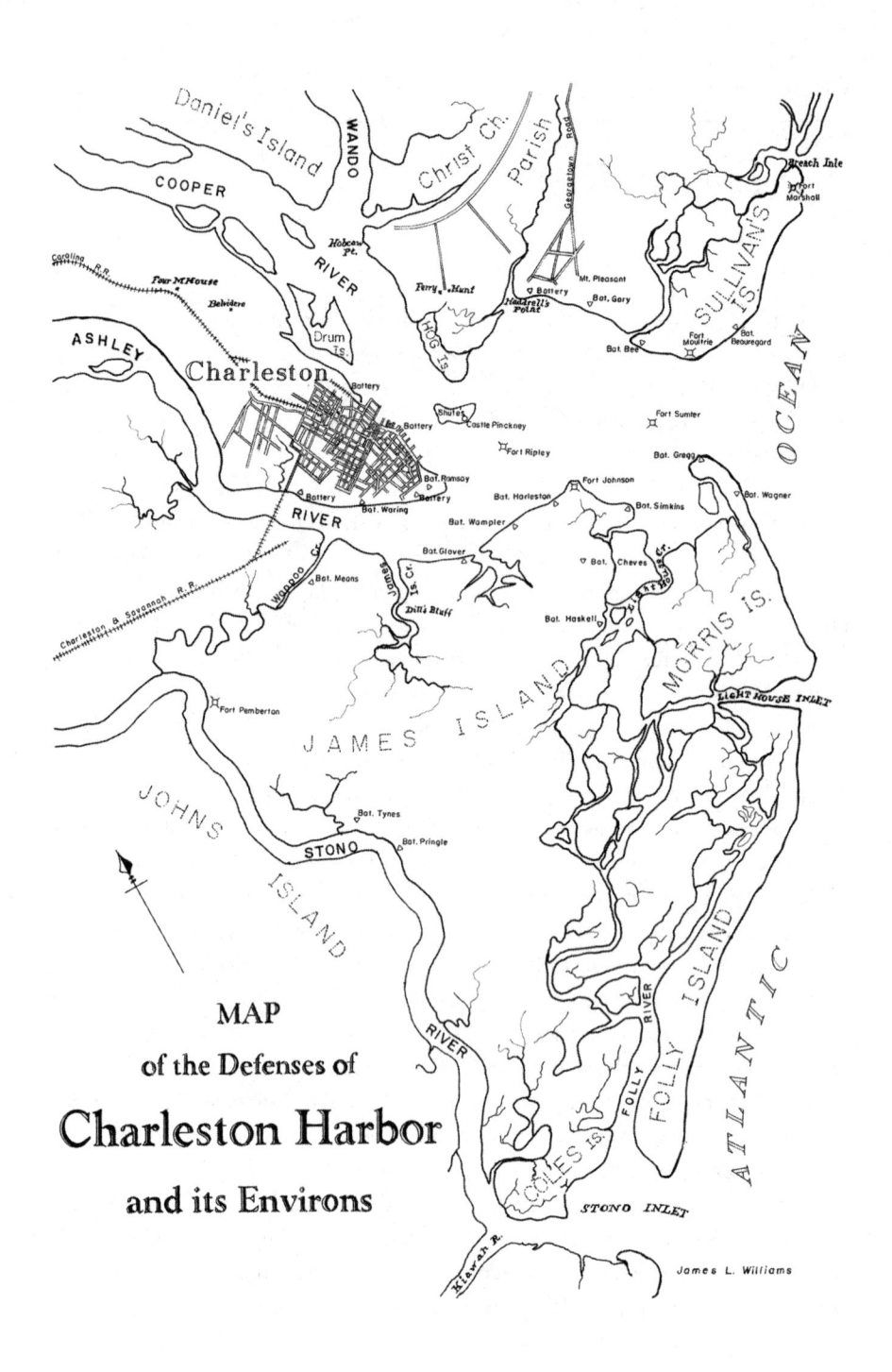

MAP
of the Defenses of
Charleston Harbor
and its Environs

James L. Williams

build a parapet for it. The Dahlgren was to enfilade the western end of Fort Sumter, which could be a disembarkation site for the relief fleet.[2]

On April 11 at 3:30 P.M., three of General Beauregard's aides rowed a small boat out to Fort Sumter. They delivered an ultimatum from the Confederate government demanding the evacuation of the fortification commanding the entrance to Charleston Harbor. Anderson, after consulting his fellow officers, refused to evacuate but admitted to the Confederates that they faced being starved out in a few days.

That same day, Ripley encountered a small boy with a box clutched tightly in his hand, running breathlessly toward Fort Moultrie and asking where he could find Colonel Ripley. Years later, Ripley recounted that he had ordered "cocked hats" for the officers in anticipation of the possible bombardment of Fort Sumter. The boy had heard that Fort Sumter would be fired upon that night, and he needed to get the hat to the colonel so that he would be in "full regalia" for the attack.[3]

At 9:30 P.M., April 11, Ripley manned the batteries of his command, heated the hot shot furnaces, and readied all for action, either against Fort Sumter or the approaching relief fleet. Ripley now had a tremendous array of heavy artillery under his control, and a significant portion was trained directly upon Fort Sumter. In all, Ripley's command included three 8-inch columbiads, two 32-pounders, and six 24-pounders at Fort Moultrie; two 24-pounders and two 32-pounders of the enfilade battery; and one 9-inch Dahlgren, two 32-pounders, six 10-inch mortars, and two 42-pounders at the Point. A floating battery of four guns commanded by Confederate naval captain John R. Hamilton completed Ripley's artillery.[4]

Captain Hamilton achieved considerable notoriety following his resignation as a lieutenant in the U.S. Navy in December 1860. A native of South Carolina, Hamilton sent in his resignation while serving aboard the USS *Wyoming* at Panama. In addition, Hamilton urged all Southern officers to resign their commissions and join the navies of their native states, even suggesting that officers in command of ships surrender the vessels at Southern ports. A special committee of the House of Representatives concluded, "Such conduct is nothing less than treason and has no parallel since Benedict Arnold." After the war Ripley and Hamilton would be in close contact in England.[5]

Between midnight and 1:00 A.M. on April 12, General Beauregard's aides, under a white flag, again rowed out to Fort Sumter. In an attempt to avoid firing on the fort, the aides asked Major Anderson how long he and his men could remain at Sumter before the lack of provisions would force them to evacuate. Anderson consulted nearly three hours with his staff officers and then informed the aides that he would not be forced to leave until April 15. The Confederates realized that this would allow time for a relief force to arrive, if one was actually on its way, and concluded that a bombardment of the fort would be necessary. The aides left but notified Anderson that artillery would open fire on Sumter in one hour.

During the night Fort Moultrie kept a strict watch on the approaches to Fort Sumter but saw no signs of the relief fleet. While Beauregard's aides were waiting on Anderson's decision, a false alarm awakened Ripley an hour or two before the bombardment was to begin. Ripley grabbed his cocked hat and rushed to his battle station. He later humorously related, "That was my uniform—a cocked hat and my nightgown." However, the false alarm gave him time to return to his quarters and dress properly for the attack.

After the signal rocket flashed at 4:30 A.M., three lanterns were raised on a staff at Fort Moultrie to alert all batteries that the bombardment was to begin. Moultrie's batteries had been readied and aimed prior to the signal rocket, and the first shot, which struck the masonry of Fort Sumter, was fired from an 8-inch cannon near Ripley's battle station. Ripley later commented that he definitely felt the gravity of the situation and said to himself, "That begins the war. What will be the end of it?"[6]

The firing commenced from every battery, at first very slowly as it was still dark. At daylight the firing quickened and continued throughout the day. Describing the bombardment, a *Mercury* correspondent reported that Ripley was in his shirtsleeves working the guns himself. Fort Sumter first responded against Cummings Point and then began firing against the floating battery with great precision. At 8:00 A.M. Ripley visited the batteries west of Fort Moultrie and commented on the admirable conduct of the officers and men. At 8:30 A.M. Sumter finally opened fire on Moultrie with casement 32- and 42-pounders. Ripley countered with nine guns of his "Sumter" battery and then added two more guns from the oblique battery. During the morning the channel guns were readied for action against the anticipated arrival of the relief fleet, but the fleet did not appear. On three occasions that afternoon, hot shot fired from Fort Moultrie set Sumter's quarters on fire, but each time the fires were temporarily extinguished.

Ripley admitted that the principal fire of the enemy was directed against Moultrie all afternoon. The barracks were almost entirely destroyed, and beds and bedding in many instances torn to shreds. One shell actually struck Ripley's quarters, demolishing nearly everything in his apartment.[7]

Sandbags, piled many feet deep, made it difficult for Sumter's gunners to damage Fort Moultrie's walls. In addition, after the bombardment ended, Sumter's artillerymen learned that cotton bales had protected Fort Moultrie's embrasures. Immediately after the Confederates fired a cannon, a cotton bale was lowered to cover the opening. What appeared to Union gunners to be direct hits actually bounced harmlessly away from the embrasures, and the gun would fire again after the cotton bale was raised.

During the barrage a crowd, apparently of noncombatants, gathered on the beach in front the Moultrie House. Allegedly, unknown to any of the officers, two veteran sergeants, frustrated by apparently causing so little damage to Moultrie, directed two 42-pounders at the spectators and fired two shots. Each shot fell about fifty yards short but bounded over the crowd and crashed into and through the once-elegant hotel The gathering of spectators understandably ran for cover.[8]

Captain Abner Doubleday, a New Yorker and an 1842 graduate of West Point, served with Major Anderson at Fort Sumter. Doubleday remembered the incident quite differently. Claiming that the Confederates were using the hotel as a depot and barracks, Doubleday saw what he thought were troops in front of the hotel and deliberately aimed two 42-pounder balls at the hotel. The balls crashed through the whole length of the building and sent the occupants fleeing. Later, Doubleday treated it as a joke, claiming that he fired at the hotel because the landlord had given him a "wretched room there one night" and he could not resist the opportunity to "get even with him."[9]

Except for the mortars, firing ceased as night fell and it began to rain. At dawn on April 13, the mortar fire continued, and to it Ripley added fire from the enfilade battery, as well as two or three guns from Fort Moultrie's "Sumter" battery. Ammunition for the floating battery and the Point battery was saved to repel any attempt to reinforce Sumter. Ripley began to increase his fire during the morning, and at about 9:00 A.M. smoke was seen from the quarters at Sumter. At once, Ripley had the entire "Sumter" battery open fire. Ripley believed that his artillery fire had never been equaled in distance and precision. "The shot, both hot and cold, crashed into the quarters at Sumter," making it difficult for the enemy to extinguish the fires, and lit new fires to windward. Although Ripley believed that "the enemy was worsted," he ordered all batteries to increase their fire.[10]

Doubleday had known Ripley at West Point and was aware that his fellow New Yorker was in command at Fort Moultrie. Doubleday claimed that Ripley "took pains to denounce me as an Abolitionist, and to recommend that I be hanged by the populace as soon as caught." He spoke despairingly of Ripley for joining the Confederacy but added, "being a man of talent and a skillful artillerist, he did us a great deal of harm." Doubleday noted that the hot shot from Moultrie came so rapidly that "it was impossible for us to contend with them any longer. . . . the wind drove the smoke in dense masses. It seemed impossible to escape suffocation." Doubleday crawled out of one of the embrasures and sat on the outer edge, "but Ripley made it lively for me with his case shot spattered all around." A slight change in the wind prevented many smoke-inhalation fatalities from the fire.

Ripley admitted that during the second day of the bombardment his hot shot furnace had sustained three direct hits, rendering it less efficient but still functional. He also ordered his command, especially Captain Hamilton's floating battery, to be economical with their ammunition as he expected a channel fight against the Union relief fleet, which never materialized.[11]

Former Texas senator Louis T. Wigfall, after resigning his Senate seat, remained in Washington and concluded that Fort Sumter would have to be taken by force. To be near the action, he returned to South Carolina, his native state, and arrived in Charleston on April 1. About a week later, General Beauregard appointed Wigfall to his volunteer staff.

During the second night Wigfall noticed that Sumter's flag was down and mistakenly believed that Major Anderson had seen the futility of continuing to fight. Wigfall decided to make an unauthorized trip to the fort to personally officiate Anderson's surrender. The former senator left from Cummings Point in a small, leaky boat paddled by three African American oarsmen. Wigfall and Private William G. Young made their way across the rough waves of the harbor with two of the oarsmen paddling and the third now baling the rapidly filling boat. Lookouts at Fort Moultrie spotted the boat, and Ripley, not knowing who was in the boat but aware that it was unauthorized, fired a warning shot across the boat's bow. When it did not obey his warning shot, Ripley ordered the boat sunk and continued firing. Some "damn politician" was meddling in military affairs, and Ripley "intended to sink him." Fortunately for Wigfall, Young, and the three-man crew, the cannon missed the small boat.[12]

Unaware of Wigfall's misguided but well-intentioned mission, at about 2:00 P.M. Beauregard sent Captain Stephen D. Lee and two aides, William Porcher Miles and Roger Pryor, from Moultrie to Fort Sumter. They were to officially negotiate surrender terms with Anderson. Despite the confusion caused by Wigfall's trip, Anderson agreed to surrender and the final conditions for the evacuation were approved that night.

On Sunday morning, April 14, Charleston gaily celebrated the surrender. Finally, they believed, Anderson and the Union forces would be gone, and Sumter's rightful owners would occupy the fort. Thankfully and somewhat surprisingly, there were no deaths on either side, and the Confederates treated the defeated enemy with courtesy. Brandy was brought to the fort and thankfully accepted; medical aid was offered but refused. Beauregard graciously permitted Anderson to fire a salute to his flag. In the harbor, nearly anything that could float and carry people was readied to witness the firing of the salute and the lowering of the Stars and Stripes. The Confederates furnished the departing Union forces with a steamer to ferry them out to the waiting Union ships.[13]

In his official report detailing the bombardment of Fort Sumter, Ripley praised nearly everyone of his command, including the acting military storekeepers. He singled out several men who were in command of individual batteries for special acclaim: Lieutenants Wagner, Rhett, and Yates, and Captain J. R.

Hamilton. Despite their previous differences, Ripley credited Major Gwynne for Moultrie's strong defenses.

After the evacuation, the honor of occupying Fort Sumter was given to the South Carolina Palmetto Guard, under the command of Colonel Roswell S. Ripley. Shortly after the Confederates arrived, the smoldering barracks once again broke into flames. As thirty thousand pounds of gunpowder remained sealed in the fort's magazine, the risk of a catastrophic explosion was great. For nearly twenty-four hours the Palmetto Guard, assisted by two fire-engine companies from Charleston, fought to control the blaze.[14]

After the fires were contained, Ripley was in charge of rebuilding and repairing the extensive damages. Although he had the embrasures in the upper casemates filled in with brick, he had embrasures in three of the casemates at the main salient armed and mounted two casemate howitzers to protect the quay and pier. He strengthened the eastern and western magazines with stone and buttressed each to a height of fifteen feet. He restored the hot shot furnaces and rebuilt the barracks with brick, but at a lower height. Sumter was supplied with a gasworks, bakery, forge, fire engine, shoe factory, cisterns for rainwater, and even a "machine for converting salt water into fresh water." Ripley established telegraph contact with headquarters in Charleston by way of James Island. Miss Emma Holmes and several friends sailed out to Sumter and witnessed the ongoing construction. She described Colonel Ripley as "rather above the medium size, but very stout & quite a jolly looking soldier in his loose white linen suit."[15]

On May 3 Governor Pickens addressed a letter of thanks to Ripley, extolling his work during the bombardment of Sumter and his proficiency with heavy ordnance. Pickens believed that Ripley's efforts enabled Moultrie to withstand the fire from Fort Sumter. "You have acted nobly and heroically, and South Carolina will never forget the services you have rendered at this most trying period of her history," Pickens wrote.

Ripley replied to the governor from his post at Fort Sumter, sending him the "Flag of South Carolina" that had been presented to the garrison in February. It flew over Fort Moultrie during the bombardment and had been pierced four times by shots from Sumter. Ripley indicated that a "prominent citizen of Virginia" cut out one of the four perforations to show people evidence of the battle.

Governor Pickens's reply, upon receipt of the flag, appeared in the *Mercury*. The governor would keep the flag as a memorial to Ripley and the "noble garrison" under his command. The governor recalled that Ripley always said he could stand the fire as long as Major Anderson could, adding that "your eye always kindled with enthusiasm for the day of trial and . . . you proved yourself his *superior* in every military point of view."

Pickens, who valued Ripley's artillery expertise, was later distressed to hear rumors that he contemplated resigning. In a letter to President Davis in mid-May,

Pickens stated that if Ripley resigned, the people of Charleston would feel very uneasy: "Ripley is by far the most efficient and thorough officer here, and has been working night and day to put Sumter in fighting order. I owe him more than any other single man, and the people of Charleston know it."[16]

The *Times* of London sent their veteran war correspondent, William Russell, to the United States to cover developments following secession. After a month in Washington, Russell headed south and arrived in Charleston following the fall of Fort Sumter. He met with General Beauregard and his chief engineer, Major Whiting, who conducted Russell around the harbor, showed the correspondent the batteries, and explained the bombardment in detail. Soon after meeting Russell, Beauregard notified President Davis that his plans for the defense of Charleston were complete.

Davis envisioned a new role for Beauregard and instructed him to meet in Richmond for reassignment. Beauregard entrained for Richmond, arriving on May 30, and at their conference Davis placed Beauregard in command of the Confederate forces in northern Virginia. This was in response to the Federal invasion of Virginia, the occupation of Alexandria, and the anticipated attack on the rail center at Manassas.

When the text of Russell's *Times* report describing the bombardment of Fort Sumer reached Charleston, many in the city were incensed. They criticized Russell for crediting only Beauregard and Whiting for the Confederate success. On June 6 a critical review of Russell's article appeared in the *Mercury*. The review praised Whiting as "a scientific engineer" and admitted that the batteries he had anything to do with were well designed. They gave Beauregard credit for the confidence he inspired, his prudence, and the success of the bombardment.

However, the *Mercury* wanted praise for the officers and soldiers of South Carolina as well as the newly arrived Confederates. The review argued that Majors Trapier and Gwynne, as well as Colonel Ripley, had for the most part completed the Moultrie and Sullivan's Island batteries before Whiting and Beauregard arrived. The *Mercury* noted that Beauregard approved the plan then in place with only "minor and immaterial suggestions." Beauregard turned his attention to the channel and added batteries to those already in place, none of which saw action, as the relief fleet never entered the channel. In summary, the *Mercury* argued that the main works employed were due principally to Major Trapier and Colonel Ripley. These officers, the *Mercury* contended, should receive full credit for their "timely, efficient and valuable services." This difference of opinion as to who deserved the credit for the defense of Charleston would grow with time, and the praise Ripley received from the people of Charleston would not please Beauregard.

Ripley's popularity surged in the months after the bombardment, and on July 20 the *Mercury* featured a front-page review of his military career. The article concluded, "When many others were absent, or unexpectedly lukewarm, Col. Ripley came forward for the emergency. All were impressed by his energy, zeal and efficiency. His devotion never flagged under discouraging circumstances, his watchfulness never tired and his humor never failed. He inspired his troops with confidence. Under his inspiration, Sumter . . . has again arisen, a Southern fortress."[17]

In July word reached Charleston of the Confederate victory at Manassas, but the news was tempered by the death of Charleston native General Barnard Elliot Bee. Five days later a special railroad car conveyed his remains to Charleston, where they lay in state at city hall. Roswell Ripley, along with four other Confederate officers, and a Cuban volunteer, Ambrosio J. Gonzales, served as pallbearers. In 1856 Gonzales had married Harriett "Hattie" Elliott, of the Bee-Elliott family and with the onset of war actively supported the Confederacy. Beauregard appointed Gonzales, his friend and boyhood schoolmate, an aide-de-camp following the evacuation of Fort Sumter. After Beauregard's transfer to Virginia, Pickens named the Cuban his special aide-de-camp.[18]

After the First Battle of Manassas, Castle Pinckney in Charleston Harbor was chosen as one of the repositories for a small number of Federal prisoners. Ripley ordered Captain Charles E. Chichester's company, the Charleston Zouave Cadets, to garrison the fort and guard the prisoners. With the Union blockading fleet in plain view of the Castle, some were concerned that the prisoners might exchange signals with the fleet. This concern increased when a powerful pair of opera glasses was discovered in a box sent to one of the Union officers. Ripley seized the glasses and refused to have them delivered.

In an 1895 pamphlet, Chichester's wife recalled with pleasure General Ripley's unexpected visit to the Castle one summer evening. The couple had just seated themselves for dinner when the officer of the day announced, "General Ripley and Aide." At the time Mrs. Chichester had "a red and green table cloth, with plain white dishes and glass tumblers, all of which looked bright and cheerful by lamplight." Ripley "remarked in his quick manner, 'Why! Why! I had no idea you had such an attractive place.'" That day Chichester had "raked up a good supply of fresh oysters, which they had raw and stewed, with hot coffee, hot biscuits, and good butter." Ripley and his aide "enjoyed the oysters and ate a hearty supper, lingered around the table in pleasant conversation, seeming loath to tear themselves away."[19]

Governor Pickens and the *Mercury*'s praise of Ripley was no doubt spurred by the recurring rumors of his possible resignation. Although at first Ripley modestly agreed to serve his adopted South Carolina at any rank, he became frustrated when his celebrated performances at Forts Moultrie and Sumter were not formally recognized in Richmond. He had not been promoted and his frustration increased during the summer, reaching a critical point near the end of July.

In late July worried "patriotic and representative citizens of Charleston" appealed to Colonel Ripley. In their letter eight prominent South Carolinians, expressed concern "for the safety of their native city, the State and the South." The petitioners urged Ripley to "pause, and if possible, to refrain." The writers realized that the lack of promotion was an issue but believed his accomplishments would ultimately be recognized. They concluded their plea, "hoping they would not be called on to mourn your departure from us. With highest respect and gratitude for services already rendered."

The citizens of Charleston were relieved when on August 15, 1861, Ripley received his promotion to brigadier general. The next day the *Mercury* announced the confirmation of his appointment by Congress, and on August 21 Ripley assumed command of the Department of South Carolina and its coastal defenses.[20]

On September 7 the F. M. Jones shipyard on South Bay expressed its regard for Ripley when it launched the 162-ton schooner *General Ripley*. The announcement described the ship as having a "good carrying capacity," and its sleek design promised speed. The Charleston group that owned the ship intended to use it as a blockade-runner. "Most of our citizens, no doubt, know she is named in compliment to the popular commander of our forces on the coast," the *Mercury* noted. In October the ship made one documented trip with a cargo of rice.

The owners changed the ship's name to the *Island Belle* and on November 4 obtained a certificate of British registry in Nassau. The *Island Belle*'s life as a blockade-runner was quite short: on New Year's Eve 1861, it was captured by the USS *Augusta* just southeast of Bull's Island. The schooner, flying British colors, was supposedly bound for Baltimore from Trinidad de Cuba carrying a cargo of sugar and molasses. The *Augusta* claimed the ship as a lawful prize running the blockade at Bull's Bay. The schooner's captain was permitted to remain on board, and with a prize crew from the *Augusta* the schooner sailed for New York.[21]

After he assumed command, it did not take Ripley long to formulate a plan for the defense of the South Carolina coast. On September 1 he submitted a four-point program asking for the authority to raise a force of fifteen hundred men for service on the coast. He asked to increase the currently enlisted South Carolina infantry to ten full companies and raise the battalion of artillery to a full regiment. He sought to establish improved inland transport and communications between various points along the coast and requested a steam-powered guard boat to assist blockade-runners. Finally, he asked for lines of credit totaling $175,000 for Major Trapier, his chief engineer; Captain Lee, his quartermaster; and ordnance officer Captain F. L. Childs. The funds were to be used solely for coastal defense preparations, and Secretary of War Walker granted Ripley the authority he sought.[22]

Ripley also began working with Jno. Fraser & Company, which, partly in anticipation of war, had set up offices in Liverpool, England. A South Carolinian, Charles K. Prioleau, manager of the Liverpool office, became a naturalized British citizen. On September 23, 1861, the company wrote to Secretary of War Judah P. Benjamin, who had recently replaced Walker, that at the insistence of General Ripley they were ordering, from England, 100,000 pounds of cannon powder for the government and an additional 100,000 pounds for South Carolina. The company also ordered an additional 250,000 pounds "at their own risk." Secretary Benjamin replied that he heartily approved of the arrangements made between the company and General Ripley.[23]

During this time Captain Childs served as the chief ordnance officer of the Charleston Arsenal. His relationship with Ripley deteriorated when Childs began refusing to follow Ripley's orders even under threat of arrest. Although he previously acquiesced to Ripley's orders, Childs wrote to his wife that he had just received word from the chief of ordnance in Richmond, Colonel Josiah Gorgas, and from Benjamin that the Charleston Arsenal was under their control and not under the control of the Department of South Carolina. This did not end the issue, as Ripley viewed it to be an officious, bureaucratic waste of time.[24]

On October 24 Major Barnwell informed Ripley that Childs had, in effect, refused to store 290 Enfield rifles at the arsenal. Ripley wrote to Childs complaining of this lack of cooperation and expressed his irritation that Childs had referred the matter to Richmond. Ripley asked Childs to inform him whether he had received instructions on the subject. As the rifles could not be stored here [likely Ft. Sumter] "they should be stored at the arsenal, with no hindrance and without further delay."

Childs replied that Major Barnwell's report was incorrect and forwarded Ripley's letter to Gorgas. Childs complained that Ripley did not like the decision that he was accountable only to Richmond. He grumbled that Ripley had no right to send such a letter to him and viewed the words "with no hindrance and without further delay" as an insult. Gorgas referred the matter to Secretary Benjamin and added that Captain Childs was entitled to protection from General Ripley's rude letter, "for which there is no excuse, and if not restrained will ultimately produce difficulties in his command." Whether Ripley's letter was in fact rude is debatable, but Gorgas's comment was prophetic.[25]

CHAPTER 12

Robert E. Lee in Command

In early August 1861, Assistant Secretary of War Thomas A. Scott, at the behest of President Lincoln, ordered General Thomas W. Sherman to proceed to New York City. He and Captain Samuel F. Du Pont of the U.S. Navy, along with various Northern governors, were to coordinate an expedition of twelve thousand men to attack a point along the Southern coast. Many in Charleston thought that there would be an attack before winter. Harriott Middleton, a third cousin of Alicia Ripley, corresponded regularly with her cousin Susan Middleton and on August 24 wrote that General Ripley believed they would attack Charleston. Although the assault would be at Port Royal Sound, the ultimate goal was indeed Charleston.[1]

In October, while Childs and Gorgas were complicating Ripley's command with what he considered bureaucratic red tape, Governor Pickens was meddling in military affairs. Although the Confederate government ostensibly was in charge of coastal defenses, Pickens assumed the role of supplying troops, labor, and arms for the resistance. The governor had a complex temperament; although he could be hospitable and generous, it was said that "he was often overbearing, proud, envious, stubborn, and often appeared to be insincere."

Throughout the month of October, while Union naval forces were on the move, Pickens and Ripley exchanged numerous dispatches over the raising and equipping of troops. The governor barraged Ripley about the disposition of forces along the coast, and in late October an exasperated Ripley replied to the governor's latest harangue.

Ripley respectfully suggested that "from such interference as this, nothing but confusion and hindrance can arise. . . . I receive suggestions, or directions from your Excellency to move companies of cavalry and light artillery to Beaufort, Edisto, or other places as if they were completely equipped . . . when in fact the whole command is but simply recruits, partially armed and in bad condition." Ripley's frank appraisal of Pickens's efforts as interference would not have been favorably received, and the governor would retaliate.

Pickens was besieged with problems, and his popularity with the state's executive committee and aristocracy deteriorated. D. F. Jamison, president of the South Carolina Convention, became the chief critic of the governor. Secretary of State Andrew Magrath disassociated himself from Pickens, the gubernatorial secretary resigned, and William H. Trescott called attention to Pickens's "blunders." According to one observer, "Pickens is such an ass that he will drive away

Governor Francis W. Pickens was originally a strong supporter of Ripley. He began advising Ripley on the deployment of artillery, cavalry, and infantry but turned against him when Ripley characterized his instructions as interference. Courtesy of the South Caroliniana Library, University of South Carolina, Columbia.

... every decent counselor. He has caused the most infinite degree of blundering and has offended many."[2]

On October 19 the U.S. invasion fleet began assembling at Hampton Roads, Virginia. For ten days troops and supplies continued to arrive, and by October 29 a total of fifty-one vessels, fifteen men-of-war, and thirty-six transports carrying nearly thirteen thousand troops had formed for the voyage south. Despite gale-force winds, which temporarily dispersed the fleet on November 1, the ships gradually straggled toward Port Royal. Over the next few days Captain Du Pont's fleet arrived off the Carolina coast, and he planned to attack on November 5. Unfortunately for Du Pont, his flagship ran aground and bad weather the following day forced postponement of the attack until November 7.

On November 1 Secretary of War Benjamin notified Pickens that he had received "reliable information" that the attack would be made at Port Royal Sound. Ripley reported to Adjutant General Samuel Cooper, now holding that office in the Confederacy, that an enemy fleet of forty-one vessels had been sighted between Tybee Island and Port Royal. Ripley advised Cooper that he was sending reinforcements to General Thomas Drayton, in command at Fort Walker on Hilton Head and Fort Beauregard across the sound. On November 5 Ripley reported that the enemy was concentrating off Beaufort and an attack was imminent. He

General Robert E. Lee was in command of the Department of South Carolina, Georgia and Florida from November 1861 until March 1862. He worked with Ripley during both the Peninsular and Maryland Campaigns. In 1865 he welcomed Ripley's assessment of the situation in South Carolina after Sherman invaded the state. From the National Archives.

requested General Alexander R. Lawton to reinforce Hilton Head and asked General J. R. Anderson to send him two regiments and a field battery. Ripley would start for Port Royal as soon as the reserves were organized and planned to attack the invaders as soon as possible.[3]

That same day General Robert E. Lee was appointed commander of the military department encompassing the coasts of South Carolina, Georgia, and East Florida. The *Mercury* announced, "Gen. Robert E. Lee, of Virginia, late in command of the Dept. of West Virginia, arrived in Charleston yesterday [November 7], and proceeded at 3 o'clock by special train to the scene of the action at Port Royal." Word of the invasion reached Charleston by telegraph, and the bombardment could be heard in the city.

In early November, Ripley rode out from Charleston to meet General Drayton at Fort Walker. On a road about a mile and a quarter from the fort, Ripley and his staff unexpectedly met the general. As they talked, they came under fire from enemy ships before moving to shelter. Drayton asked Ripley whether he had come to assume command; he had not but would return to Coosawhatchie, a small settlement on the Charleston-Savannah rail line, to find reinforcements immediately. Drayton then described the day's action and how all was going against them. As one of Ripley's aides reported, Drayton solemnly assured Ripley he would never leave the fort "unless a corpse and every man killed." When Ripley arrived in Hardeeville, "courier after courier galloped in with the same astounding news, our men had retreated." Ripley asked whether the retreat was orderly and was horrified to learn it was in great disorder. In his official report, Drayton described the withdrawal as being orderly but with a large loss of equipment. In his endorsement of Drayton's report, Ripley respectfully maintained that no good would result from discussing the "inaccuracies" in Drayton's version of the battle and withdrawal.

On his way to the entrance of Port Royal Harbor, Lee fortuitously met Ripley returning from Fort Walker. Ripley informed Lee that the troops were withdrawn to prevent their capture but unfortunately had lost most of their clothing, tents, and provisions. Lee had no choice but to inform Richmond that the enemy had landed at Hilton Head and were in complete control of Port Royal Harbor. Lee would attempt to consolidate his troops and protect the railway linking Charleston and Savannah.[4]

After Beauregard's transfer to Virginia, A. J. Gonzales, now with the rank of lieutenant colonel, began serving as special aide-de-camp to Governor Pickens, and was charged with inspecting South Carolina's coastal defenses. The Cuban conceptualized the idea of "sea-coast flying artillery," which could be quickly moved by train to any point along the coast. Unfortunately, Gonzales incessantly sought a commission as brigadier general from President Davis, and his self-aggrandizing appeals finally alienated the president.

Gonzales advertised in the Charleston newspapers his availability for a more active role in his adopted state's defense. Ripley appointed Gonzales one of his volunteer aides-de-camp and placed him in command of an artillery siege train of "four eight inch howitzers and a full complement of horses, ammunition wagons, travelling forge and equipment." Gonzales impressed Ripley with his efforts, and the general wrote the war department supporting the Cuban's request for a general officer's commission. Gonzales never attained his coveted rank, but Ripley supported the Cuban's appointment as chief of artillery with the rank of colonel.[5]

A detailed description of the Battle of Port Royal appeared in the *Mercury* a few days after the battle. Owner-editor Robert Barnwell Rhett, one of Ripley's supporters, asserted that the action at Port Royal was "one of the best fought and conducted battles." Rhett claimed that if General Ripley had been in command two months sooner, all would have been better prepared. With the time he had, "General Ripley did all that untiring energy and skill could accomplish." In reality, because of a shortage of men and matériel, it is doubtful that anyone could have stopped the juggernaut that hit Port Royal Sound.

On November 17 Lee assigned Ripley to "prosecute vigorously the completion of the water and land defenses of Charleston." Ripley gave Lee a detailed description of the disposition of the troops in the Charleston area, stating that they were placed to cover the railroad bridges in the direction of Savannah and would be able to move either towards Charleston or Savannah, depending on the site of attack. Ripley warned that the troops were very raw and would require "severe discipline and constant watching; it will take some time to make them efficient."[6]

General Lee on November 21 informed the adjutant general and the secretary of war that he had inspected the batteries and posts along the coast from South Carolina to Florida. He proposed defending only the entrance to Cumberland Sound and Brunswick, Georgia, as well as "the water approaches to Savannah and Charleston."

A few days later Ripley informed Lee that the enemy had landed on Otter Island and Fenwick's Island, which allowed Federal access to the Ashepoo and Edisto Rivers. Ripley advised Lee that it would take time to obstruct these rivers, and if Union forces moved inland, they could threaten the Charleston-Savannah railroad. Lee's immediate response was dismissive: "The enemy can land on all the islands he can approach with his armed vessels, but he will hardly find it to his advantage to hold them after they have been pillaged." This surprisingly suggests that Lee believed Union forces would land on the coastal islands primarily to pillage them, and it seems to minimize the islands' role in preventing river access to the interior, the rail line, and Charleston itself. Lee did advise Ripley to find laborers to obstruct the two rivers.

After meeting General Lee, Pickens wrote to President Davis with his opinion of the new commander. The governor was impressed with Lee's "high bred cultivated bearing" and had "a very high estimation of his science, patriotism and enlightened judgment." Pickens wrote, "If he has a fault it is over caution." At the same time, Pickens could not refrain from offering the president some military advice. He believed that Lee should have "some man like General Evans to make guerilla dashes."

Still smarting from Ripley's rebuke of his "meddling" the previous month, Pickens took his first swing at Ripley when he said, "Ripley is unfit for anything but to fight in batteries, such a fort as Sumter; with eighty-nine guns and mortars of the largest caliber, there is no man his superior." Further, Pickens claimed that "between General Drayton and Ripley there are the most unpleasant feelings, and they can never act in harmony." This seems to be in conflict with Ripley's reticence to criticize Drayton's "inaccuracies" in his battle report following Port Royal. On November 29 President Davis informed Pickens that Generals Nathan G. Evans and John C. Pemberton would be sent to assist General Lee.[7]

In early December, Lee notified Ripley he could not direct certain companies from Colonel R. G. M. Dunovant's regiment for the protection of the Combahee. Nevertheless, he was pleased with Ripley's installation of four rifled and banded

32-pounders at White Point Battery and his placement of four 12-pounders for the defense of the Ashepoo and Combahee. Lee instructed Ripley to send two 24-pounders now in his possession to General Drayton and to send four navy 32-pounders to Coosawhatchie for Lee's disposition. Lee also did not want any powder or ammunition taken from Fort Moultrie, Fort Sumter, or the Stono, apparently continuing to value the importance of the Stono River's access to Charleston. Lee was also "highly gratified" with Ripley's successful experiments with musket and blasting powders.

Ripley responded to Lee on the fifth that he thought it best for Charleston's defense to go forward as far as safely possible from the city. Ripley repeated this thought later in his letter but realized that two to four more regiments would be required to establish a longer defensive front. Ripley also expressed concern that at any time the enemy could attack up the rivers, strike the railroad, and cut the communications between Charleston and Savannah. Lee must have asked for the date of Ripley's commission as brigadier general, for at the close of the letter Ripley listed the date as August 15.

Lee basically agreed with Ripley's desire to defend the Ashepoo, Paw Paw and Combahee Rivers, and to prevent the enemy's occupation of Edisto Island; but he doubted it would be possible to obtain sufficient regiments for that purpose. Lee approved Ripley's site for a battery at Wilton's Bluff on the Edisto River but was concerned about the placement of the river's obstruction. Lee claimed that he "understood" the planned obstruction would be above the battery, while a preferable site was located about three hundred yards below the battery: "The benefit of placing the barrier below the battery is apparent in the obstruction you adopted for the Coosawhatchie, now under construction by General Gonzalez [sic].... I suggest that you adhere to the same plan."

At about the same time, Lee was more critical in notifying General Pemberton that his site for the obstruction to the Ashepoo "now in the process of execution is not the most advantageous point." Lee also advised Pemberton where he should locate his defensive entrenchments.

On December 10 from his headquarters at Coosawhatchie, Lee divided the coast of South Carolina into five military districts. Lee appointed Pemberton to command the Fourth District, extending from the Ashepoo to Port Royal, then on to Ferebeeville. Pemberton's headquarters were located at Coosawhatchie with Lee, while Ripley, in command of the Second District, was headquartered in Charleston. His district began at the South Santee River, included Charleston, and extended south to the Stono River. His command temporarily included the Third District from the Stono to the Ashepoo River.[8]

While Lee was organizing the defense of coastal South Carolina, what came to be known as the "Great Fire of Charleston" broke out at about 9:00 P.M. on the night of December 11. A sudden and unfortunate change in the weather, from two weeks of calmness to heavy gusts of wind, occurred almost simultaneously with the start of the fire. Dust, smoke, sparks, and flaming bits of wood were borne in blinding showers, brightly lighting the city.

By 10:00 P.M. the fire raged in several different points in the lower part of the city, where the exceedingly flammable wooden buildings were close together. The fast-spreading flames induced a horrible panic, and hundreds of families were suddenly driven from their homes. Furniture and bedding were carried into the streets and vacant lots. Small children and the sick were placed on the bedding; however, falling sparks and burning shingles soon caught the bedding on fire and the refugees had to be rescued.

At Castle Pinckney the entire garrison watched anxiously as some of the men were from that part of the city. Captain Chichester sent a detail of men by boat to the city to help fight the fire. As the fire spread, a second and finally a third detachment followed the first. By midnight the fire had become so enormous that the efforts of the entire city fire brigade were of little consequence. As a result, Ripley's regiments stationed at the Charleston racecourse hurried to aid the beleaguered firemen. The gale continued to spread the fire from Market, East Bay, and State Streets to Meeting and Queen Streets. Meeting Street, from Market to Queen, was one mass of flame. The Mills House and the Charleston Hotel were evacuated but ultimately survived the fire.

Around 3:00 A.M. the steeple of the Circular Church fell thunderously into the street. Ripley reportedly rode into "the very teeth of the fire, his coolness and vigilance were conspicuous, as we know they would be on the field of battle." The *Mercury* believed that Ripley's decision to blow up intervening buildings saved the Catholic Orphan Asylum, Roper Hospital with its hundreds of patients, and many houses beyond the hospital.

The following day the *Mercury* reported the extent of the fire in detail, listing the five churches destroyed, the loss of St. Andrew's Hall, where the Ordnance of Secession had been signed, and Institute Hall, where the ordnance was ratified. Most significantly for the war effort, the Cameron and Company's Phoenix Iron Works were a total loss. Large quantities of shot, shell, and other ordnance stores, including valuable machinery for rifling cannon and making percussion caps, were lost.

A fire relief committee was organized, and by Christmas Day $130,162.74 had been received. Contributions came from nearly every state in the Confederacy. Donations from local residents were not published, but out-of-state contributors were listed. The largest contribution, $1,443.50, was from the citizens of Raleigh, North Carolina. General Lee donated $300, and General Beauregard sent $40 from Virginia.[9]

The conflagration did not distract Lee as he continued preparing the defenses around Charleston. As mentioned, Lee had proposed defending the water approaches to Charleston, and some considered the Stono to be the "backdoor" to the city. Lee notified Secretary Benjamin that batteries were now in place at Wappoo Creek on the Stono in addition to those at Cole's Island at the mouth of the river. Cole's Island was some distance from Charleston, whereas Wappoo Creek, or Cut, was much closer to the city.

On December 20, the first anniversary of secession, Ripley reported that the U.S. Navy had begun sinking between thirteen and seventeen stone-laden ships across the bar in the main channel into Charleston Harbor. Intended to render the navigation of a difficult channel more hazardous, Ripley noted positively that Maffitt's Channel and the North Channel were still open to the blockade-runners. In forwarding this information to the secretary of war, Lee described this action by the Federals "as unworthy of any nation, the abortive expression of revenge and malice." Lee believed that this act indicated the U.S. government's "despair of ever capturing a city they design to ruin." He concluded that it now was certain an attack on Charleston was not contemplated and the Confederates must prepare for assaults "elsewhere on the Southern coast."

On Christmas Day, Ripley informed Lee that he was cooperating to the fullest extent with the recently arrived General Evans. He enclosed a memorandum of the troops in Evans's district and a list of the troops in his Second District. Ripley described the difficulty of raising troops, securing laborers, and problems due to "the crippled mechanical resources of the city."

Lee complimented Ripley on his efforts to reinforce and support General Evans, and Evans confirmed that Ripley readily granted his requests. In the same letter, Lee emphasized that if Ripley thought the enemy intended to attack Charleston through the Stono approaches, he was to resist with all available forces. This is the third time Lee expressed his resolve to defend the Stono River approach to Charleston. Lee also praised Ripley for his "judicious" steps in securing the rice crop, and hoped Ripley would do the same with "other provisions, corn, provender, etc."

As December drew to a close, Ripley advised against removing men from the Stono, as the enemy was "sounding and making other demonstrations" in that area. He did not believe they would be attacked unless the point was undefended.[10]

On the eve of the New Year, Governor Pickens wrote to Lee, listing the troops he believed were in the military districts. He claimed his figures differed significantly from those Lee had received from district commanders including Ripley. Pickens suggested that the officers in each district were not sending Lee "a full report of the troops mustered in." He also admitted he had promoted two officers, General Beauregard's son R. T. Beauregard and J. B. Ferguson, much to the displeasure of the officers in Ripley's command, particularly the junior officer of artillery. Pickens did not mention whether Ripley was angered, but the general would have fully supported his junior officers and resented Pickens's continued interference in military matters. Revealing his ignorance of military protocol, the governor claimed that he did not understand why his appointments should create such a problem with "the junior officers at Fort Sumter."

It appears that the relationship between Pickens and Ripley, tenuous since Ripley admonished the governor for interference causing "confusion and harm," had deteriorated markedly. No record of a direct confrontation between the two has been found, but Ripley must have informed the governor that granting promotions to young Beauregard and Ferguson was inappropriate.

A week later, on January 7, Pickens wrote to President Davis excoriating Ripley, "I take the liberty to inform you that I fear the feeling of General Ripley towards General Lee may do injury to the public service. His habit is to say extreme things even before junior officers, and this is well calculated to do great injury to General Lee's command." None of the "extreme things" Pickens claimed Ripley said have been found. That this was "well calculated to do great injury to General Lee's command" is at best conjecture and illogical. Pickens attempted to soften this criticism by adding, "I do not think General Ripley means half what he says in his energetic way, but others construe it differently."

Pickens then claimed that there were many important omissions in Ripley's reports to Lee regarding troop strengths. Pickens did not think Ripley was "at all exact in relation to infantry." He added, "I have sent forward lately from this camp [in Columbia] five new regiments, not yet reported to Lee by Ripley. Pickens pompously informed Davis that he had "sent General Lee a correct return."

To further denigrate Ripley, Pickens described Lee as a perfect leader, quiet and retiring and "all that a gentleman should be, . . . a thorough and scientific officer. The two are in contrast." All would agree that of the two, Lee was the refined gentleman, but it would be difficult to criticize Ripley's ability as an artilleryman. Continuing to meddle in military affairs, Pickens advised President Davis that for the safety of Charleston, the forces under General Pemberton should be positioned closer to Adams Run.

Regarding the troop-strength discrepancies, Ripley had received reports from the newly mustered soldiers in the 16th and 17th South Carolina Regiments indicating that they lacked sufficient muskets, cartridge boxes, knapsacks, and bayonet scabbards; some companies had no ammunition. Ripley would not have considered these regiments fit for duty and would not have included them in his reports to Lee. The 18th and 19th South Carolina Regiments were still disabled by a measles epidemic, and the 20th had not been armed as late as February.[11]

For the first two months they worked together, indications are that the relationship between Lee and Ripley was fine and confirms that Ripley cooperated fully with both Lee and Evans. In view of their documented cooperation and no written evidence of what Ripley was alleged to have said against Lee, it is difficult to give Pickens's damning letter unquestioned credibility. This is especially true considering Ripley's letter critical of Pickens's interference in October. Pickens's vituperative letter to Davis followed soon after he apparently had been criticized for promoting the younger Beauregard. Later, Ripley disagreed with Lee over the defense of Cole's Island, but this difference of opinion had not yet arisen. In late 1861 Lee and Ripley both considered Cole's Island and its access to the Stono River important for the defense of Charleston.

Early in the New Year, Lee expressed his concern to Adjutant General Cooper that he had inadvertently overstated the strength of the coastal defenses. He intended to "express hope rather than confident assurances" that when completed and manned, the defenses of Charleston and Savannah could successfully resist the enemy. He admitted that there was much work to be done and he had not received as many troops from South Carolina and Georgia as he expected. Lee concluded that the enemy would attempt to seize the Charleston-Savannah rail lines, prevent reinforcement between the cities, and then alternately attack each city.

On January 17 General Lee responded to Ripley's letter concerning operations against the enemy at North Edisto. Lee claimed that when he gave his approval, he did not sufficiently understand the plan to know whether it would succeed. Ripley was to judge the plan and "the means to effect it." Lee also informed Ripley that Evans believed the enemy was preparing to land on Bohicket Creek near Seabrook Island, then push across Johns Island "to silence your batteries on Cole's and Battery Island, and thus ascend the Stono." Evans apparently had insufficient troops to defend this attack route, and Lee asked Ripley to support Evans once more.

A few days later rumors surfaced that Union forces were planning to sever the Wilmington and Charleston Railroad line above Charleston and the Charleston-Savannah line below the city. Lee asked Ripley to take measures to insure the safety of the railroad within his district. By mid-February the projected Union movement across Johns Island had not materialized, but the enemy did land on Edisto Island. Again, Lee asked Ripley to reinforce and support Evans.[12]

Although the defense of Charleston occupied most of Ripley's time, the affable general managed to find time for a limited social life. In early February there was a party given at Fort Sumter. Several men and women went to the fort by steamboat and planned to return to Charleston at 9:30 that night. After a night of music, dancing, and pleasant conversation, the party began to disband on a lovely moonlit night. The Ripleys and the Captain Duncan Ingraham party left "in style in a row boat." When the others made it to the steamboat, the harbor was at low tide and the boat aground in the mud. The party tried to occupy their time with talk and laughter; some slept but most spent a miserable time until the high tide at 3:00 A.M. enabled the steamboat to depart.[13]

In the middle of February, concerned with a possible attack on Savannah, Lee established headquarters in that city. Lee again turned to Ripley for assistance, asking in the event of an attack on Savannah for "two or more good companies, skilled in the management of heavy guns" for temporary service in batteries on the Savannah River. Ripley hoped Lee would agree that companies could not be spared but thought a number of men, "who are not perfect" but had some practice, could be sent with little risk.

Ripley informed Lee that Colonel Hagood had asked for more artillerymen at the Stono, but he had been unable to provide General Evans with the guns and men requested. In closing, Ripley mentioned that the citizens of Charleston feared the city would be attacked, and "I am not going to allay it, hoping they may volunteer at once." Two days later a notice in the *Mercury* indicated that Ripley was raising a company for the defense of Charleston and the vicinity. Enrollment would be at the Pavilion Hotel.[14]

Ripley began building a fixed battery in Charleston Harbor on the middle ground between Castle Pinckney and Fort Johnson. With a sandbar at the site, the water was only eight feet deep. Ripley proposed using rubbish from the great fire to ballast the timber caissons. Lee supported Ripley's effort and suggested that the Middle Ground Battery, which would be named Fort Ripley, be casemated with heavy timber and railroad iron.[15]

On February 18, in a lengthy letter to Lee, Ripley commented on the "disaster in Tennessee." He believed the defeat at Fort Donelson would lead to a longer war, but it is unclear whether he realized how the disaster would later affect the defense of South Carolina. One wonders if he was aware of the role that his former benefactor, General Gideon Pillow, played in the debacle.

Ripley presented his ideas regarding the defense of Charleston, Savannah, and the coast. He claimed the weakest point on the all-important Savannah-Charleston rail line was near Charleston, "perhaps our most important city." He was concerned that Charleston did not have enough men to defend it if attacked, and although "my opinion of these matters has not been asked," he was charged with the defense of this military district and believed it was his "duty to submit his considerations to the commanding general."

Lee acknowledged Ripley's dispatch and stated that if the enemy decided to attack Charleston, they would advance in great force. Lee was in favor of abandoning all exposed points, as far as possible, within reach of the enemy's gunboats and taking interior positions, where they could meet the enemy on more equal terms. Lee pointed out that the batteries at Cole's Island would not be a factor in preventing the enemy from advancing up the Edisto River, and unless arrangements were made to withdraw the guns, they would be lost. Lee also believed that if the enemy's gunboats reached Cole's Island in force, the batteries "might be suppressed, and the Stono River seized as an avenue of approach to Charleston." It follows that the abandonment of Cole's Island would also result in the seizure of the Stono as an approach. Lee added, "If it is necessary to maintain these batteries, they should be made as strong as possible."

Lee's object in writing to Ripley was "to ascertain your opinion, whether, without weakening the plan of defense, our lines could be contracted, and exposed or distant points abandoned. . . . I wish you therefore to review the whole subject, and see what changes or improvements can be made, both as to the importance and strength of the positions retained." Lee obviously valued Ripley's judgment and solicited his opinion regarding the defense of Charleston. This dispatch also indicated that Lee was not committed to abandoning Cole's Island and, if necessary, would strengthen the island's batteries. There seems to have been little contentiousness between Lee and Ripley, remarkably at odds with the Pickens diatribe of early January.[16]

It has long been known that the acclaimed Civil War historian, Douglas Southall Freeman, revered Robert E. Lee. After three decades of research, he produced the four-volume biography *R. E. Lee* and a three-volume work entitled *Lee's Lieutenants: A Study in Command*. In his biography of Lee, Freeman concluded that "for some unknown reason Ripley took a violent dislike to Lee." In *Lee's Lieutenant's,* Freeman contended, "For Lee, during the winter of 1861–62, he [Ripley] had acquired a contemptuous dislike. So bitterly had he denounced Lee, even before junior officers, that Governor Pickens had written in protest to President Davis."

Freeman apparently based his conclusion on Governor Pickens's letter to President Davis cited earlier. Exactly what "extreme things" Ripley is alleged to have said about Lee have never been found or published. Whatever Ripley may have said about Lee, it is a rush to judgment and difficult to conclude that Ripley had a "violent" or "contemptuous" dislike of Lee.

Another interpretation of this situation is that Ripley had severely admonished Pickens for his continued meddling in military affairs, and this was the governor's attempt to even the score. The word of a meddling governor, described by his peers as an insincere, blundering ass, was readily accepted by Freeman, apparently without verification, and repeated by historiographers ever since.

While Lee, Ripley, and Evans were evaluating the defense of Charleston, Lee received a notice from President Davis, dated March 2, requesting his return to Virginia "with the least delay" if circumstances in South Carolina permitted him to leave.[17]

CHAPTER 13

General John C. Pemberton

On March 3, 1862, at the request of President Davis, General Robert E. Lee departed Savannah for Richmond. The next day, newly promoted Major General John C. Pemberton assumed command of the Department of South Carolina and Georgia.

Pemberton, a native of Pennsylvania and a graduate of West Point's class of 1837, had a less than illustrious record at the academy. He finished twenty-seventh out of fifty in his class and accumulated 167 demerits. Despite his mediocre class standing, his father's influence gained Pemberton a more desirable placement with the artillery. In 1848 he married Martha "Pattie" Thompson of Norfolk, Virginia, and the Old Dominion became his adopted home.

When Virginia seceded from the Union, Pemberton was torn between his commitment to his country, his family in Pennsylvania, and his wife and children in Virginia. He hesitated to resign his commission, as his family in Pennsylvania "begged and pleaded" for him to maintain his allegiance to them and the Union. Finally, Pemberton's wife wrote him to ask why he was still in Washington and not with his family in Virginia. He then resigned and made his way to Richmond.

No evidence has been found to confirm that before the war Pemberton was a strong pro-Southern, states' rights advocate, as asserted in the postwar writings of Confederate generals Jubal Early and Richard Taylor. Pemberton's son supported Early's and Taylor's claims by writing that his father "was from earliest manhood a firm believer in the doctrine of State sovereignty." Possibly they wanted to enhance Pemberton's poor postwar image and rebut those who questioned his devotion to the South during the war.

After arriving in Virginia, Pemberton received a series of spectacular promotions. His ascent has been attributed to being a favorite of Jefferson Davis, the advocacy of General Joseph E. Johnston, influence exerted by his wife's Virginia family, or a combination of these factors. On May 8, 1861, Pemberton became a lieutenant colonel of artillery in the Provisional Army of Virginia. On June 15 he was designated a major of artillery in the Confederate States Army, and two days later he was promoted to brigadier general, completely bypassing the intermediate ranks of lieutenant colonel and colonel. After Pemberton arrived in South Carolina his astonishing ascent in rank continued, despite having accomplished nothing of major importance during his short time in the state. Nevertheless, he

General John C. Pemberton, a superior officer for whom Ripley had little respect. Ripley strongly disagreed with Pemberton's plans for the defense of Charleston and requested a transfer. Ultimately, most who were involved in the defense of the state demanded that Pemberton be relieved of command. From the Library of Congress.

outranked the other brigadiers in the department, and Robert E. Lee probably endorsed his promotion to major general.

By comparison, on June 17, 1861, when Pemberton was promoted to brigadier general, Ripley's crucial efforts in restoring Fort Moultrie and reducing Fort Sumter had been ignored. Even after supervising the rebuilding of Fort Sumter, Ripley remained a colonel and was not promoted to brigadier general until August.[1]

The February 1862 capture of Forts Henry and Donelson in Tennessee was a catastrophic defeat for the Confederacy. Their loss opened Tennessee to the Federal army and necessitated the transfer of some regiments from the southeastern coast to reinforce western defenses. Later, conditions in Virginia led to the transfer of troops to the Old Dominion. These troop movements compromised the defense of the coast and caused a readjustment of the defensive lines in South Carolina.[2]

In July 1861 James L. Orr organized an infantry regiment at Sandy Springs, Anderson District, in northwest South Carolina. Known as Orr's Rifles, the regiment was sent to Charleston in August. Originally in reserve at Summerville, the regiment was sent to Sullivan's Island under the command of General Ripley. After Orr was elected to the Senate in December, Colonel Jehu Foster Marshall assumed command of the regiment.[3]

In mid-February, Marshall submitted his appraisal of the island's defenses to Ripley "with the earnest hope that we may be ready to give the enemy a different reception from that of Fort Henry." He proposed building a new fort at the eastern end of Sullivan's Island to protect it from Long Island to the east. Marshall suggested that the fort could be constructed with bricks from the burnt district in Charleston, or palmetto logs and sandbags. Marshall favored strengthening Battery Beauregard, just east of Fort Moultrie, where he found 8-inch shells in short supply and many to be defective. At Fort Moultrie, Marshall found a shortage of powder and shell, requested ten thousand pounds of powder and five hundred shells, and advised Ripley to keep a six-month supply on hand. Ripley followed Marshall's suggestion and began construction of a fort, located just west of Breach Inlet, which was later named after the colonel.[4]

On March 10, 1862, William H. Trescott, a Charleston native who had been an assistant secretary of state in the Buchanan administration, wrote to W. Porcher Miles, the chairman of the Committee on Military Affairs. "Whatever Gen. Pemberton's reputation and whatever he has done (unknown here certainly) to be made Major General," Trescott complained, "it is a great and crying injustice to allow him to outrank Ripley in this military district."

Shortly after assuming command, Pemberton examined defenses on James Island in Ripley's district. He recommended that Ripley strengthen some positions and "construct certain other works on the island." Ripley "appreciated" the importance of Pemberton's requests but found them impossible to accomplish with his available labor force. The administratively inclined Pemberton then inexplicably began reorganizing all the military districts as defined by Lee. He divided one district into two, with the Fifth District becoming a new Sixth District; plus he made geographical changes in some of the districts.

On March 21 Pemberton inquired how Ripley's fortifications were progressing on James Island and hoped to see his brigadier in a few days. He asked Ripley to assist in transporting rice to locations where it would be readily available, an undertaking Ripley had judiciously begun months before, duly notifying General Lee of the fact.[5]

For several weeks in March, Ripley ran an "Important Notice" in the *Charleston Mercury*. He requested that anyone having "models or plans of ball-proof covered vessels, propelled by steam" to submit them as early as possible to Ripley's headquarters. It is not known whether Ripley's notice influenced the ultimate development of the *Palmetto State* and *Chicora* torpedo rams later in the year, but it indicates Ripley's resourcefulness.[6]

In addition to his more serious duties, Ripley had other, mundane day-to-day activities. An interesting Northern impression of Ripley is found in the diary of a captured Union officer, Lieutenant Colonel Frank T. Bennett of the 55th Pennsylvania Infantry. The colonel and another officer were captured on March 16 and sent by General Evans to Charleston. After the prisoners reached Ripley's headquarters, he refused to see them and had them taken to the guardhouse. They were put in a "very pleasant, well-furnished, carpeted room," and soon Ripley and one of his aides visited them. Ripley asked Bennett whether he "had been supplied with the necessary comforts, bid us good day and left. The visit was so sudden, so short and the general's manner so very different from what I expected." The Pennsylvanian described Ripley as "a large, burly man, very abrupt in his manner, and I should say very harsh." Bennett knew that Ripley was from Ohio—an old army officer who fought for the rebels, "in their insane attempt to overthrow the Government," an arguably flawed belief held by some Northerners.

Bennett grumbled, "Alas for us! We should have fared better in the hands of a native of the South." Soon afterward, the officers were taken through the burnt district to what Bennett described as a vermin-filled, dank jail cell. The colonel blamed Ripley for the transfer and their poor provisions, but by early May conditions had gradually improved. The prisoners were placed in a two-room cell, with separate sleeping and living rooms, for which Bennett credited the jailer, as if he had acted independently of Ripley.

About this time, J. T. Morrill, former master of the steamer *Osceola* wrote to Secretary of War Edward. M. Stanton describing the conditions of his imprisonment in Charleston. Morrill complained of cramped quarters, poor rations, and severe treatment. He claimed the prisoners considered Ripley to be their worst enemy and exceedingly bitter, "though a Northern man." Morrill alleged that Ripley delayed distributing clothing sent by the U.S. government for its "destitute soldiers in enemy's hands."[7]

In early March, Foster Marshall received news of the naval battle between the Confederate ironclad *Virginia* and the Union *Monitor*. This convinced him that Federal ironclads could steam unimpeded past Forts Moultrie and Sumter to attack Charleston. He believed as soon as they were built, enemy ironclads would be in Charleston Harbor. Marshall submitted, for Ripley's "careful consideration," plans for obstructing the shipping channels into the harbor. By 1865 Charleston Harbor and its shipping channels featured barrel, boiler, and frame torpedoes (mines) as well as rope obstructions running from Fort Sumter to Battery Bee just west of Fort Moultrie. There was a row of pile-driven obstructions in the Middle Ground fronting Fort Ripley and Castle Pinckney. Marshall was prescient in regard to the assault by Federal ironclads, but underestimated the power of Ripley's artillery and his resolve to thwart the attack.[8]

When Pemberton concluded that he had to shorten his defensive lines, he precipitously withdrew his forces and abandoned the position at Georgetown. He then ordered the removal of all guns from the batteries on Cole's Island, thus exposing the Stono River. Unfortunately, the new lines of defense, farther up the Stono and much closer to Charleston, had not been completed.

Colonel Johnson Hagood was in command of the substantial defenses on Cole's Island. These works consisted of a system of nine detached batteries extending the full length of the shoreline. The batteries were interconnected by a covered trench for the passage of troops, and each battery had a "bomb-proof" to shield the artillerymen and their infantry support. A total of twenty-one guns were placed in the nine batteries, with most batteries having from two to four guns. Complying with Pemberton's orders, in two days Hagood had all of the artillery, except for five cannon, loaded on flats and ready to be towed up the Stono River to other positions on James Island and the Charleston area.[9]

At Georgetown, district commander Colonel A. M. Manigault was to dismount the artillery rapidly and at night if possible. Heavy logs simulating cannon were to be placed in each battery after the guns were removed. All guns were to be transported by rail to Charleston, where Manigault and his infantry would report directly to Ripley.

Governor Pickens was furious when he learned of these withdrawals. He wired Lee complaining that the premature abandonment of Cole's Island, before the inner lines were prepared, allowed the enemy an easy approach to Charleston. He argued that the guns should remain on Cole's Island until the works on James Island were finished. Pickens criticized the abandonment of Georgetown because the inhabitants had not been warned of the evacuation and were dangerously exposed to a Union attack.

On April 4 Lee advised Pemberton to comply with the governor's requests, at least until the planters and others could remove their property and anyone who wished to leave could safely move out of the area. To preserve harmony, Lee politely asked Pemberton to consider informing the governor of any future plans to abandon a position along his lines of defense.

Pemberton did halt, at least temporarily, the removal of the batteries from Cole's Island, but Manigault had accomplished his withdrawal from Georgetown before the commanding general could delay the evacuation. Twenty cannon were being transported by rail to Charleston, and Manigault had already reported to Ripley; but he did inform Pemberton that he believed the remaining companies of cavalry and infantry were sufficient for the protection of the Georgetown area.[10]

Governor Pickens was not the only Carolinian incensed by Pemberton's actions. W. H. Trescott expressed his concern to Miles: "Pemberton has . . . interfered most injudiciously not only to Gen. Ripley's great dissatisfaction, but to the universal discontent of the whole country. Every spot of land, every marsh, every island, every creek, has been examined, measured, sounded by Gen. Ripley and those under his command . . . and now General Pemberton is to ride over this country at a hard gallop, look over a map which he can't understand, and all must be abandoned." Claiming to have observed Ripley closely, Trescott testified to "his energy and ability. I care not what his faults may be, his work stands there to prove his capacity and fidelity." This command, he said, "should be his fully and entirely. . . . I did hope that Gen. Lee would take this view, but I have been disappointed."

Finally, Pemberton agreed that if Ripley was confident that Cole's Island could be held, he would not insist on the removal of the guns until a number of them could be placed farther up the Stono at Elliott's Cut. In early April the 24th South Carolina Infantry, commanded by Colonel Clement Stevens, replaced Hagood's regiment on Cole's. A month later Pemberton followed through on his original order, and the removal of the guns began in earnest. Within a week, Stevens's men dismantled most of the batteries and prepared the guns for shipment to Elliott's Cut and other positions.

After removing the artillery, Pemberton considered Cole's Island to be an advanced post defended by only a regiment or companies of infantry. The infantry was not to defend the island against gunboats, only against "parties of the enemy in small boats." If gunboats approached, the infantry would be withdrawn. Ripley must have thought Pemberton's strategy to be absurd. In effect, Federal gunboats were given an open invitation to the Stono; they would not be attacking in "small boats."[11]

On Sullivan's Island, Colonel Marshall and his regiment were kept busy in April rescuing cargo from beached blockade-runners. When the owner of the *Laura* did not attempt to salvage the cargo of his ship, Marshall's men salvaged over six hundred bushels of salt and received Ripley's approval to reward the men with ten sacks of salt per company. Later, Marshall salvaged Jamaican rum, candles, soap, sweet oil, wrapping paper, bags, and coffee from the wreck of the abandoned schooner *Rosalie*.

However, Marshall was unhappy with his relatively easy duty on Sullivan's Island and wished to be assigned to a post where he could confront the enemy. He wrote to President Davis, the secretary of war, and his former commanding officer, Senator James Orr, asking to be sent to Mississippi or Tennessee. Marshall also pleaded with Ripley to be assigned to Corinth, Mississippi, but was denied when Ripley claimed he could not spare or replace him. Evidently, Ripley and Marshall had been working quite well together, which helps refute claims that Ripley could not get along with anyone.

Despite Ripley's attempts to retain the regiment, Orr's Rifles was sent in late April to Virginia, serving with the 1st, 12th, 13th, and 14th South Carolina Infantry Regiments in the illustrious Gregg's/McGowan's Brigade, Army of Northern Virginia. Unfortunately, Marshall was killed in action on August 29, 1862, at the Battle of Second Manassas.[12]

Late in April, during this contentious relationship with Pemberton, Ripley pleaded to be transferred away from the major general. On April 22 William Trescott directed his efforts on Ripley's behalf, wiring Miles that Ripley had asked to be relieved and sent to Virginia. Trescott believed he could not be replaced but wanted to either give him power equal to his responsibilities in Charleston or let him take the field.[13]

Ripley had been using a swift, shallow-draft, wood-burning steamboat, the *Planter*, as a dispatch boat. The boat also transported men and matériel around the harbor and along the Carolina coast. In early May the *Planter* began making trips up the Stono River to transfer guns and ammunition from Cole's Island to James Island. On May 12, after two weeks of hauling ordnance, the *Planter* returned to Charleston Harbor. The steamboat docked at Southern Wharf, loaded twenty cords of firewood, two hundred pounds of ammunition, and four cannon. Ripley claimed the cannon had been damaged in the bombardment of Fort Sumter and "had been condemned and laid aside." As heavy guns were scarce, Ripley ordered them banded and transported to Fort Ripley on the Middle Ground. Against Ripley's orders, the *Planter*'s master, C. J. Relyea, along with the Charleston Harbor pilot and their engineer, went ashore to spend the night.[14]

Those remaining on board—the wheelsman, Robert Smalls, and his crew of five—were slaves. Over the past several months, Smalls had developed a plan to steal the boat, and at 3:00 A.M. on May 13, the crew fired the boilers and eased away from the wharf. Smalls had hidden his wife and child, along with four women and another child, on a ship at the nearby North Atlantic Wharf. After the women and children were aboard the *Planter*, the steamboat gave the proper signals and steamed past Forts Ripley and Sumter. The crew hauled down the Confederate ensign, hoisted a white flag, and headed out to sea.

After the *Planter* reached the safety of the USS *Onward* and the Union blockading fleet, Smalls was joyfully received and taken to Captain Du Pont at Port Royal. Although the loss of the *Planter* was embarrassing, it was insignificant compared to the intelligence Smalls relayed to Du Pont. Neither Du Pont nor Major General David Hunter knew that the Confederates had transferred so many troops from the state and had weakened the coastal defenses. More important, Smalls informed Du Pont that the batteries on Cole's Island had been abandoned, leaving the Stono access to Charleston basically unguarded.[15]

As the appalling loss of the *Planter* registered with the Confederates, George Cary Eggleston provided some insight into Ripley's reaction to the event. Eggleston, a native of Indiana, was living in Virginia at the onset of hostilities and enlisted in the Confederate army. After the war Eggleston had a notable career in journalism, wrote nine novels, and compiled a collection of his experiences in the Confederate army, published as *A Rebel's Recollections*.

During the winter of 1861–62 and through the next spring, Eggleston served in Charleston as sergeant major and the "acting adjutant" of an independent battery. In this capacity he reported directly to Ripley and called upon him numerous times, giving him an excellent opportunity to study Ripley's character and behavior. Eggleston described Ripley as "portly in person, of commanding and almost pompous presence," but when Eggleston got to know Ripley, he found him to be as easy and unassuming as if he were not a brigadier general at all.

On the morning after Robert Smalls and his crew stole the *Planter*, Eggleston spent an hour or two at Ripley's headquarters, passing the time looking at the harbor through Ripley's telescope. While viewing the harbor activity, Eggleston noticed a ship's launch, bearing a white flag, approaching Fort Sumter. Ripley heard the sergeant major comment about the launch and rushed to the telescope. Eggleston recalled that Ripley, probably still seething over his missing dispatch boat, told his signal officer, "Tell Fort Sumter if that's a Yankee boat to burst her wide open, flag or no flag." However, as soon as the message was sent, Ripley had it recalled and sent instructions more "in accordance with the rules of civilized warfare."

According to Eggleston, General Ripley had less regard for red tape than any brigadier he had ever met. One day the sergeant major reported to Ripley that much of their harness was worn out. Ripley suggested the battery call a board of survey and have the harness condemned. Eggleston thought that would be impossible, as the independent battery had only two commissioned officers. A board required three officers, and the officer calling for the board could not legally participate.

"Oh the deuce!" Ripley replied. "What's the difference? If yours is not fit, there's plenty of new in the arsenal." Ripley told Eggleston to have his captain call the board and have it consist of the battery's lieutenant, Eggleston, and another sergeant. Ripley admitted that it was not legal to put anyone but a commissioned officer on the board but told Eggleston to do it anyway: "Write 'sergeant' so nobody can read it, and I'll make my clerks mistake it for lieutenant." Ripley told Eggleston that the board should conclude that "the harness is not worth a damn, or words to that effect. Send in your report and I'll approve it, and you'll have a new set of harness in three days." Ripley did not worry about technicalities when the efficiency of a battery was at stake: "We're not lawyers, but soldiers." Eggleston firmly believed Ripley always promoted "the good of the service at the expense of routine. He was not a good martinet, but he was a brave, earnest man and a fine officer, of a sort of which no army can have too many."[16]

In early May, W. P. Miles, W. D. Porter, and Judge A. G. Magrath were convinced that losing Ripley at this critical period would be disastrous. The three wired Lee and recommended placing Ripley in direct control of Charleston District, independent of Pemberton. Lee, as expected, informed them that their request could not be granted as long as Pemberton was in command of the Department of South Carolina and Georgia. Lee determined that one of the generals must be removed and regretted relieving the "dissatisfied" general "as his ability and knowledge of affairs in Charleston Harbor would be essential in time of an attack." However, Lee believed it would be "best to comply with Ripley's repeated requests and relieve him from his present command." After all this, Lee surprisingly asked Miles, Porter, and Magrath which course they would recommend.[17]

It did not take long for Union forces to take advantage of their unexpected gift from Robert Smalls. Within a week, barges arrived at the mouth of the Stono and began sounding the channel. On the twentieth, three gunboats successfully passed into the confluence of the Stono and Kiawah Rivers, and then steamed up the Stono, firing in all directions at the fleeing Confederate pickets. Exasperated, Ripley sent dispatches to Pemberton from the Stono, describing the Union gunboat attacks and reminding Pemberton that the evacuation of Cole's Island was "not in accordance with my views." Ripley stated that he was unaware of the commanding general's plans for the defense of the Stono after the batteries on Cole's Island were abandoned and suggested, "I should be happy to receive instructions."[18]

Ripley certainly would have agreed with shortening the defensive lines as more and more troops were transferred from the coast to Virginia and Tennessee. However, Ripley believed that Cole's Island should have been a point in the contracted lines. Lee had mentioned on several occasions that he intended to defend the water approaches to Charleston and advised Ripley to strengthen the batteries on Cole's Island if he thought it imperative that the island be held.

About this time, Lee informed Pemberton that he believed Confederate troop strength around Charleston was double that of the enemy but asked whether Pemberton had any reliable information regarding the strength of the Federal forces. Lee presumed the enemy would not attack "unless provided with iron boats" and feared he was losing the service of troops needed for the defense of Virginia who were unnecessarily retained in South Carolina. If Pemberton agreed with Lee's assessment, he was asked to forward without delay a good brigade to Richmond under General Ripley "if he can be spared." How could Pemberton not agree? He had previously ordered Ripley to "hold yourself in readiness to move with two regiments of infantry to Virginia should the requisition be made."[19]

Ripley, who questioned Pemberton's decisions and judgment, had his doubts confirmed by subsequent events. Pemberton evidently was obsessed with saving his artillery at any cost, even if it meant the destruction and loss of Charleston. To be out of the range of Union gunboats, he evacuated Cole's Island, fearing it could be overrun and the artillery destroyed or lost. Pemberton instructed Ripley not to have any heavy guns in front of the lines unless they were equipped with horses and able to be moved at any time: "The field artillery will not be kept on the lines, but will be kept in park."

Pemberton then advocated defending Charleston from in and around the city itself. He believed all harbor installations, including Forts Sumter and Moultrie, should be abandoned and destroyed after the guns were removed as secretly as possible. He thought that sooner or later ironclad gunboats would destroy the brick, stone, and mortar forts, and bizarrely claimed that "however great might be the injury to the city itself from bombardment," he could keep the Union army's feet "from polluting its streets." Pemberton completely ignored Charleston's importance as one of the last remaining ports in the Confederacy and that it must be kept open for the blockade-runners. Ripley was justifiably appalled by Pemberton's plan.

Equally appalled was Robert E. Lee, who responded quickly to Pemberton's ill-conceived proposal. He notified Pemberton that he should pay close attention to the fortifications of Charleston Harbor and stressed the importance of defending Charleston to the last extremity. The loss of Charleston would close off the Confederacy from the rest of the world. Lee wanted the harbor and the city defended, but if the harbor was taken, the city was to be "fought street-by-street, house-by-house as long as we have a foot of ground to stand upon."[20]

Another divisive issue in May 1862 had a much earlier origin. Difficulties between Major Alfred Rhett and Colonel Ransom Calhoun began at Fort Moultrie with the perceived affronts Rhett received from Calhoun following the bombardment of Fort Sumter. Calhoun, who later was on temporary duty in Virginia, angered Ripley by bypassing him and appealing directly to General Beauregard to adjudicate an issue. The Civil War diarist Mary Chesnut believed that Calhoun wrote an insulting letter either about Ripley or to him. Rhett's hatred for Calhoun escalated in April when Calhoun returned from Virginia and criticized Rhett for his actions at Fort Sumter. Their dispute would rage on through the summer, result in a duel, and later in the year embroil Ripley and much of Charleston.

Governor Pickens, in a rambling letter to Lee on May 23, referred to the problems between Calhoun and Rhett, which he claimed were creating dissension and widespread disloyalty at Fort Sumter. He offered no solution to the problem but commented on the disposition of troops and ordnance inspections, while advocating that only "native-born artillery" and "native infantry" be stationed at Sumter. Pemberton investigated the situation and concluded, as did Calhoun, that there was no disloyalty.[21]

On May 24 Pemberton informed Lee that Ripley had been ordered to Virginia, along with Moore's South Carolina and Gibson's Georgia regiments. The general's replacement, General H. W. Mercer, was to contact Ripley immediately to learn the disposition of troops and the location of defensive works around the harbor and city. Although they disagreed, Pemberton asked Ripley to share with Mercer his ideas for completing the city's defenses and his knowledge of the city's resources.[22]

During this time Ripley developed a close relationship with the British consul in Charleston, Robert Bunch, who was sympathetic to the Southern cause. In late May a Charleston Unionist sent an anonymous letter to the editor of the *New York Herald* claiming that he saw Consul Bunch leave for trips to the British cruisers off Charleston. Each time Bunch returned with "six or eight Charleston pilots," he would be escorted to Ripley's office, where he remained for nearly an hour. The Unionist believed that Bunch brought intelligence of the blockading fleet to Ripley, as vessels often ran the blockade immediately after the consul's visits. The writer claimed that the United States should question why Bunch was allowed to hold a consulship.[23]

On Thursday morning, May 29, Ripley, along with his chief of staff, Captain Leo D. Walker, and his aides Captains Frank Ravenel, Rollins Lowndes, William Kirkland, and Julian Mitchell, left Charleston for Richmond. The *Mercury* attributed Ripley's difference of opinion with Pemberton as the cause of his departure. The disagreement centered on the abandonment of Cole's Island and access to the Stono River. The paper claimed that Ripley did not want to be responsible for the defense of Charleston when he had so little input into its strategic planning. The *Mercury* stated these facts but offered no opinion, only commenting that "the future will tell the tale."

The lengthy, two-column article described in great detail Ripley's services to Charleston since secession. The positive summary noted that Ripley had "labored devotedly and intelligently for our security," adding, "Night and day his office has been open, and his zeal and energy has never flagged. . . . His military knowledge is high and his judgment is excellent. Although brusque in manners and unpopular with some he has inspired the utmost confidence and respect with all those associated with him in military matters. . . . in our opinion Gen. Ripley is an officer of great skill and energy. Whatever the loss to Charleston, will be a gain to the army of Virginia."[24]

Soon after Ripley left Charleston, the Union army, under the command of Generals David Hunter and Henry Benham, began its assault on James Island from the Stono. On June 16 at the Battle of Secessionville, they would test the defenses Ripley and Pemberton had struggled to complete. Despite being greatly outnumbered, the Confederate defenders and their well-placed artillery prevailed.

In his excellent, definitive history of the Battle of Secessionville, Patrick Brennan has written that the Confederate victory proved that Pemberton was correct in the abandonment of Cole's Island "despite the rumblings of Roswell Ripley and assorted South Carolina politicians." Brennan described in detail the failings of those in command of the Federal offensive. It could be argued that if generals more capable than Hunter and Benham had been in command and the attacks better coordinated, the outcome of the battle might have been different. The Federal army would then have been on the doorstep of Charleston, and Pemberton's abandonment of Cole's Island may not have been the correct decision at that time.

In the end, Pemberton was the beneficiary of Hunter and Benham's ineptitude. It should be mentioned that Ripley was not the only Confederate officer in favor of defending Cole's Island. General Beauregard, General States Right Gist, Colonel Johnson Hagood, Major of Engineers John Johnson, and others criticized the move.[25]

CHAPTER 14

Peninsula Campaign

On July 26, 1861, General George B. McClellan arrived in Washington, just five days after the ignominious defeat of General Irwin McDowell's army at the First Battle of Manassas. McClellan had recently triumphed in western Virginia, a region inhabited by a large number of Unionists unsympathetic to the government in Richmond. The region would later secede from the Old Dominion to become West Virginia. The Union forces defeated a greatly disadvantaged Robert E. Lee, who had nearly everything against him: the weather, sickness, and several quarreling, politically appointed generals. After Lee returned to Richmond, he was soon dispatched to the command in South Carolina.

Hailed as the "Young Napoleon" for his triumph in the West, McClellan began the reorganization and strengthening of McDowell's defeated army, which would later be referred to as the Army of the Potomac. On November 1 McClellan was appointed general-in-chief of the Union army, replacing the aging Winfield Scott.[1]

All winter Radical Republicans called for McClellan to attack the forces of General Joseph E. Johnston in Virginia, just across the Potomac from Washington. However, McClellan preferred not to attack what he believed to be a superior number of well-entrenched Confederates. Instead, in the spring he planned to transport his army down the Potomac, outflank Johnston, and attack Richmond from the southeast.

President Davis believed that McClellan was planning a spring offensive, and urged Johnston to begin moving his army to a better defensive position closer to Richmond. As a result, McClellan was forced to move his base farther south to Fort Monroe. This fort had remained in Union possession after Virginia seceded and was located only seventy-five miles from Richmond.

In early March, now even more dismayed by McClellan's inactivity, President Lincoln demoted his general-in-chief of the army. McClellan would now command only the army under his direct control, the Army of the Potomac. At about that time, President Davis recalled Lee from South Carolina to command the military operations in Virginia.[2]

In mid-March 1862 McClellan's reorganized and well-equipped army of nearly 122,000 men began embarking for Fort Monroe. On April 2 McClellan established his headquarters at Fort Monroe and thirty-six hours later issued orders for the first 55,000 of his newly arrived men to advance against Yorktown.

In time, McClellan concluded that the Yorktown defensive works were more formidable than he had previously supposed and came to believe he would have to take Yorktown by siege.

Now with a clearer idea of McClellan's intentions, Lee wired Johnston to begin moving his men south toward the Peninsula. Johnston's troops began arriving at Yorktown on April 7, but a week later, after surveying the situation, Johnston concluded that the works were indefensible against McClellan's superior numbers. In contrast, Lee and Davis believed that Richmond should be defended as far from the capital as practical and ordered Yorktown to be held as long as possible. During nearly a month of siege, McClellan managed to bring up an impressive array of heavy artillery and planned to open a devastating bombardment on the morning of May 5. Fortunately for the Confederates, during the night of May 3–4 Johnston withdrew his army.[3]

Now able to proceed, McClellan moved toward Richmond, and as he advanced, his army became split into two wings divided by the Chickahominy River. To take advantage of the geographical division of the Federal forces, on May 30 Johnston decided to counterattack. The next morning he struck McClellan's left wing south of the Chickahominy. He aimed the assault at Fair Oaks Station and Seven Pines just seven miles east of Richmond. The battle was scheduled to begin at first light but started late and quickly became disorganized. Later in the day General Johnston chose to observe the action around Fair Oaks and positioned himself on top of a knoll, out in the open. A bullet struck him in the right shoulder, and just moments later a large fragment from an exploding shell struck him in the chest, knocking him from his horse. Johnston would survive, but his second in command, General Gustavus W. Smith, assumed command for the remainder of the battle. That night General Smith notified Lee that he intended to renew the action the next day, utilizing his right wing under the command of Major General James Longstreet. Smith also asked Lee for any assistance he could make available.[4]

On May 30, the day before Johnston planned to attack McClellan, General Lee ordered Ripley, who was still on his way to Virginia from Charleston, to report for duty with General Johnston when he arrived. Unless Johnston ordered otherwise, Ripley's regiments were to take transportation to their encampment at the Fairfield Race Course near Richmond.

On June 1 at 5:00 A.M., Lee responded to General Smith's advisement that he planned to renew the attack. He believed Smith was correct in planning to attack, but he should first determine how best to hit the he enemy. Lee commended Smith for calling upon him for reinforcements and only wished he could do more, but he indicated that he would send Ripley and any available forces from North Carolina. Lee hoped that some of Major General Theophilus Holmes's North Carolina troops could be a factor at Seven Pines. Lee closed, "It will be a glorious thing if you can gain a complete victory. Our success on the whole yesterday was good, but not complete."[5]

G. W. Smith's second-day offensive began on time but soon bogged down. Longstreet planned to use four of his brigades and two brigades of General Benjamin Huger's division, which had not been engaged the previous day. Ripley's brigade was to form a reserve on Nine-mile Road for Smith's division, now under the command of General W. H. C. Whiting. As the battle progressed, Smith redirected Ripley's brigade, which was expected in Richmond at about that time, to move to the front on Williamsburg Road. However, the battle ended before noon, and was over by the time Ripley and his men reached the field. By 2:00 P.M. on June 1, Davis relieved General Smith as commander of the Army of Northern Virginia and replaced him with Robert E. Lee.[6]

Only two regiments accompanied Ripley from Charleston, and when these two regiments were absorbed into Lee's Army of Northern Virginia, only Colonel William Gibson's 48th Georgia would remain with Ripley. Added to the 48th Georgia would be the 44th Georgia, as well as the 1st and 3rd North Carolina Regiments. These four regiments formed Ripley's brigade and would serve as the 5th Brigade of Daniel Harvey Hill's division. Generals Robert E. Rodes, George B. Anderson, Samuel Garland, and Colonel Alfred Colquitt were in command of Hill's other four brigades.[7]

There was not another general in the Confederate army under whom Ripley could have served who would have been more contemptuous of him than the misanthropic Harvey Hill. It has been suggested that Lee reluctantly formed a negative opinion of Hill because of his disagreeable temperament and his snarling "so regularly and acerbically at the world around him," as historian Gary Gallagher put it. Of Lee's generals, Hill was one of his most outspoken critics. Hill would be especially critical of Lee's performance at Malvern Hill and of his Maryland Campaign. Lee must have been pleased when he eventually found an opportunity to transfer Hill out of the Army of Northern Virginia.[8]

Ripley was at a marked disadvantage with Harvey Hill because the Carolinian detested Northerners and nearly everything about the North. Hill, an 1842 graduate of West Point and a veteran of Mexican War, resigned his commission following the war. Hill then taught mathematics at Washington College in Virginia from 1848 to 1854, and algebra through calculus at Davidson College from 1854 until 1859. During this time, Lippincott & Company published Hill's *Elements of Algebra,* which was filled with demeaning anti-Northern assessments, all of which he sarcastically wrote into his algebraic word problems. Hill was suspicious of Northerners who fought for the Confederacy and had been particularly critical of the Confederate chief of ordnance, Josiah Gorgas, a native of Pennsylvania. Hill suspected foul play in the ordnance department as it was "very rotten . . . a Yankee concern throughout." And now Hill was saddled with a Yankee brigade commander.[9]

To make matters worse, during the Mexican War Ripley had been an aide to General Gideon Pillow, and Harvey Hill hated Pillow, a political general with no military training who had strong ties to his fellow Tennessean President Polk. Hill said of Pillow, "Mr. Polk seems studiously to have selected the most worthless and inefficient men that he could find." Hill's hatred of Pillow peaked over an incident following his return from a regimental reconnaissance. Hill received conflicting orders from his colonel, Bennet Riley, and from General Pillow. Not knowing that Pillow was temporarily in command of the brigade, Hill obeyed his colonel and not Pillow. Allegedly, Pillow used what Hill described as harsh and insulting language for disobeying orders, and "I shook my sword at him and forbade him to use such language again." Pillow then arrested Hill, but when Colonel Riley interceded, Pillow released Hill and "retracted his offensive language." Hill was not mollified.

When General Winfield Scott was recalled from Mexico, Hill reacted vehemently. He believed the recall was "owing to the intrigues of that arch-scoundrel Pillow." Hill clearly was sympathetic to General Scott, and as Pillow's aide, Ripley would have been guilty by association.

Following the war, Polk and Pillow ensconced Ripley in Tennessee for about a year, giving him time to write *The War with Mexico*. A controversial book at the time, some viewed it as an attempt to damage Scott's reputation. As Hill strongly supported Scott, *The War with Mexico* gave him another reason to detest Ripley. Harvey Hill definitely would not have been happy to see his Yankee brigade commander, but there probably were few men he would have welcomed cheerily.[10]

Three days after Ripley arrived, General Longstreet notified Harvey Hill that he had ordered Ripley "to put all the force on the road that he can." Ripley commented on the inexperience of his regiments, noting that they arrived in Richmond shortly after the Battle of Seven Pines, and had not been given time to perfect "their organization and discipline as a brigade." He pointed out that his regiments were immediately ordered to the front to perform picket and outpost duty with little relief.

Colonel Gibson's 48th Georgia had never been in action when they arrived with Ripley. The 44th Georgia, new troops under the command of Colonel Robert A. Smith, arrived in Richmond from Goldsboro, North Carolina at about the same time. The 1st and 3rd North Carolina, under the command of Colonels M. S. Stokes and Gaston Meares respectively, had been in the service in Virginia for a short time, but they too had never been in action.[11]

Private Joseph B. Reese was an educated and quite literate member of the 44th Georgia. On April 14, 1862, while the unit was in Goldsboro, his company, the Putnam Volunteers, appointed him correspondent for the *Countryman* of Turnwold, Georgia. In this capacity, Reese was "to keep the friends of absent soldiers posted as to their whereabouts and condition." Reese was promoted to lieutenant after the Peninsula Campaign and captain in May 1863. He later was wounded at Gettysburg, the Wilderness, and Winchester, but survived the war.

Reese described the conditions Ripley's brigade endured during their first three days and nights in the field: "The place where we camped was very low and marshy, over shoe deep in mud and water and the rain still falling." On their first deployment "the picket line in some places is a half-leg deep in water—none less than shoe deep."[12]

On June 12 Longstreet asked Hill to send one of his brigades to the pinewoods occupied by Ripley's brigade and relieve him for a day. Soon after, Ripley received orders to attack the enemy's outposts and deployed a skirmish line extending from White Oak Swamp across the Williamsburg Road to the York River Railroad. The two North Carolina regiments and the 44th Georgia each sent out three to six companies of skirmishers, with the 48th Georgia being held in reserve. Throughout the day Ripley's skirmishers advanced in a rainstorm against the 73rd and 69th New York regiments of General Daniel Sickles's Second Brigade. Although the heavy rainstorm prevented an accurate reconnaissance, the Confederates pushed the enemy pickets back to their works. Ripley reported that the Federal defenses appeared to be strengthened and the enemy in force behind their lines but without artillery. At 9:00 P.M. the skirmishers were recalled, with the exception of the 1st North Carolina and the 48th Georgia, which held the advanced line of pickets. Following this skirmish, Longstreet asked Hill to relieve Ripley with another brigade whenever he thought it proper.[13]

On June 20 General McClellan informed Lincoln, "There is reason to believe that General R. S. Ripley has recently joined Lee's army with a brigade or a division from Charleston." He either did not know or chose to ignore that Ripley brought just two regiments from Charleston. McClellan would have wanted Lincoln to believe that Ripley brought a brigade or division to substantiate his own supposed inferiority in numbers. McClellan, believing he was facing forces vastly larger than his, would decide he must take Richmond by siege. He emphasized that Lee was daily increasing his defenses and had no intention of evacuating Richmond. "I find him everywhere in force," McClellan claimed.

At about this time Lee was formulating an audacious plan to attack McClellan instead of settling into the defense of a besieged Richmond. In a bold move he would send for General Thomas J. "Stonewall" Jackson and his army from the Shenandoah Valley. When General J. E. B. Stuart completed his reconnaissance cavalry ride around McClellan's entire army, Lee learned the Union's right flank was near the north bank of the Chickahominy not far from Mechanicsville. More important, McClellan's right flank did not extend far enough north to block the roads that Jackson and his Army of the Valley would use to turn the Federal flank. On June 23 Lee held a war council with Generals Ambrose Powell Hill, D. H. Hill, James Longstreet, and Jackson, who made the grueling trip from the valley. Following this meeting, Jackson, who had begun moving his troops on June 18, would now have only three days to get his army to Richmond and launch the initial attack scheduled to begin at 3:00 A.M. on June 26.[14]

East of Richmond, McClellan's army remained astride the Chickahominy River. The left wing, nearly two-thirds of his army, was south of the river, while the nearly thirty thousand men of the right wing were situated north of the river. It was this right wing, under the command of General Fitz John Porter, that Lee planned to attack.

On the morning of June 25, even after learning of Jackson's approaching army from a Confederate "deserter," McClellan advanced units of his left wing against Lee's forces south of the Chickahominy. This engagement, the Battle of Oak Grove, was the beginning of the Seven Days or Peninsula Campaign. The Confederate lines held, and Lee decided to proceed with his plan to attack Porter north of the river the next day, as described in General Orders No. 75.[15]

In the early morning darkness of the twenty-sixth, D. H. Hill moved his five brigades toward the Mechanicsville Bridge. Seven artillery batteries, three of which were temporarily attached to the division, accompanied the brigades, bringing his total force to nearly ten thousand men. At about 2:00 A.M. Ripley's brigade began its march from Williamsburg Road, about five miles east of Richmond. By 8:00 A.M. the brigade reached the bridge and took up positions hidden behind a crest of hills overlooking the Chickahominy. While they awaited Jackson's opening attack, Hill's and Longstreet's divisions, positioned near the Mechanicsville Bridge, remained in the boiling sun well into the late afternoon.[16]

Jackson, arriving from the north, was to initiate the attack on Porter's northern, right flank, after which General A. P. Hill's Light Division was to cross at Meadow Bridge and join the assault. Longstreet and D. H. Hill would cross at the Mechanicsville Bridge, with Hill to support Jackson and Longstreet in support of Powell Hill. All four divisions would then sweep the Federals down the north bank of the Chickahominy. By mid-afternoon Jackson still had not arrived to begin the assault on Porter, and Ripley's brigade remained concealed behind the crest of hills waiting for the attack.

After waiting most of the day for Jackson, General A. P. Hill, without informing anyone, impetuously took matters into his own hands. Wearing his red calico battle shirt, he drove his brigades over Meadow Bridge and launched an attack on the Federals at Mechanicsville. Hill's brigades swept through Mechanicsville and drove the Yankees to fixed positions on high ground above and east of Beaver Dam Creek. Ellerson's gristmill was located farther down the creek, which flowed southward into the Chickahominy. The Federals, east of the creek, were well entrenched in fortifications extending for over a mile and supported by six batteries of artillery. On the west side of the creek, the defenders had felled timber and created abatis to impede the Confederate advance. Still waiting for Jackson's attack on the Federal flank, Powell Hill's advanced brigades were being pounded by enemy artillery. When Lee crossed over the bridge to confer with Hill, he must have been stunned to learn that Hill had acted on his own, as Jackson had not initiated the assault. Lee was now obliged to continue Hill's premature attack.[17]

Powell Hill first attempted to turn the Federal right flank, where Jackson should have begun his assault. After repeated attacks were repulsed, Hill rode to the front and decided that continued assaults on the Federal right would be hopeless. Hill then ordered a fourth brigade, under the command of General William Dorsey Pender, to form on the right and attack farther down Beaver Dam Creek toward Ellerson's Mill. Pender's approach led the brigade directly into a hail of artillery and musket fire. The 38th North Carolina of Pender's brigade became entangled in the abatis on the creek bank and was suffering huge losses. Around 4:00 P.M. Ripley's brigade was ordered to cross the Chickahominy in advance of the division and effect a junction with the troops of A. P. Hill. By 6:00 P.M. the enemy had been driven from the bridgehead far enough to allow the head of the column to cross.[18]

Learning that A. P. Hill was "hotly engaged," Harvey Hill pushed Ripley's leading brigade to his support. Immediately after crossing the bridge, Ripley communicated with Powell Hill, who ordered him to "turn the enemy's left, lower down the creek." In the meantime, D. H. Hill received orders from Lee and from President Davis to send a brigade forward. While advancing with Ripley's brigade, Hill met General Pender, "whose forces had just been roughly handled." Pender told Hill that "with the assistance of two regiments of Ripley's brigade, he could turn the position at Ellison's [sic] Mill by the right, while two regiments should advance in front." D. H. Hill reported that it was about dark when he ordered Ripley to Pender's aid.

Ripley reported that while his troops were in motion following A. P. Hill's orders, he received orders to assault the enemy from Lee and D. H. Hill. Ripley indicated that Hill directed him to "send two regiments to support General Pender, on my right, and attack the battery in front with the remainder of my force." With night coming on, it was deemed "important to attack the position at once, and the advance was ordered along the whole line."

Following Harvey Hill's orders to attack the battery in his front, Ripley utilized Colonel Gibson's 48th Georgia and Colonel Meares's 3rd North Carolina regiments. Ripley described driving the enemy back from his advanced positions and closing in on the batteries and their heavy infantry support. The battery poured a heavy and incessant fire of shell, canister, and musketry on Ripley's troops. The ground was rugged and intersected by ditches and hedges and covered with abatis in front of the enemy's position. "A millrace, with scarped banks and in some places waist-deep water, ran along the front of the enemy." Ripley reported that his troops reached the millrace despite being under heavy fire and sustaining severe losses.

Lieutenant Colonel William L. de Rosset of the 3rd North Carolina led four companies of skirmishers who, despite becoming fragmented in the darkness, reached the millrace in a ravine only eighty yards from the battery. The 3rd North Carolina lost only eight killed and thirty-nine wounded, which de Rosset attributed to the enemy's firing too high. Most of the regiment's casualties were at the extreme range of grapeshot; few occurred after they closed on the battery.

After being slowed by the damaged Chickahominy bridges, Captain A. Burnet Rhett's South Carolina Artillery finally arrived, but it was now nearly dark. Nevertheless, Rhett began an effective fire against the enemy, which soon relieved Ripley's infantry from the "storm of shell and canister which had been poured upon them," as Ripley later described the scene. Some time after nightfall, "under cover of the cannonade, our troops were withdrawn to a point of woods a few hundred yards" distant. The 3rd North Carolina and the 48th Georgia, along with a portion of Pender's brigade, held this position, but the fragments of the two regiments sent to Pender's aid were rallied farther in the rear. At about midnight Colquitt's brigade arrived within supporting distance, and around 2:30 A.M. the two brigades were relieved and marched to a position on the turnpike beyond Mechanicsville. They remained there all night, at first under artillery fire, then through morning until about 11:00 A.M., June 27.[19]

The two regiments Ripley sent to support Pender on his right, Colonel Stokes's 1st North Carolina and Colonel Smith's 44th Georgia, suffered extremely heavy casualties in attacking Ellerson's Mill. According to Private Marcus D. Herring of the 1st North Carolina, "on reaching the open field, Colonel Stokes, attempted to throw the regiment into line, under fire for the first time." The regiment moved forward but was soon ordered to lie down and to fix bayonets. Then, "in a storm of flying missiles the regiment went forward on a run, in the open and in the direct range of drilled soldiers. The carnage was terrible. Before we got to the works we came to a deep cut or canal, halted and commenced firing," but were soon ordered to fall back. Colonels Stokes and Smith were mortally wounded. The North Carolinians had 36 killed and 105 wounded. Their major was killed, the lieutenant colonel wounded, and 6 company captains and lieutenants killed or wounded; the Georgians lost 71 killed and 264 wounded.[20]

Private Reese participated in this frontal assault at Ellerson's Mill and wrote an account for the *Countryman* on June 28. When Ripley was ordered in, the battle was raging furiously, with both artillery and infantry heavily engaged. One of Hill's aides dashed up to Ripley, directly in front of the 44th Georgia, and said something to the general who quickly turned his horse and ordered Colonel Smith

Map of the battle of

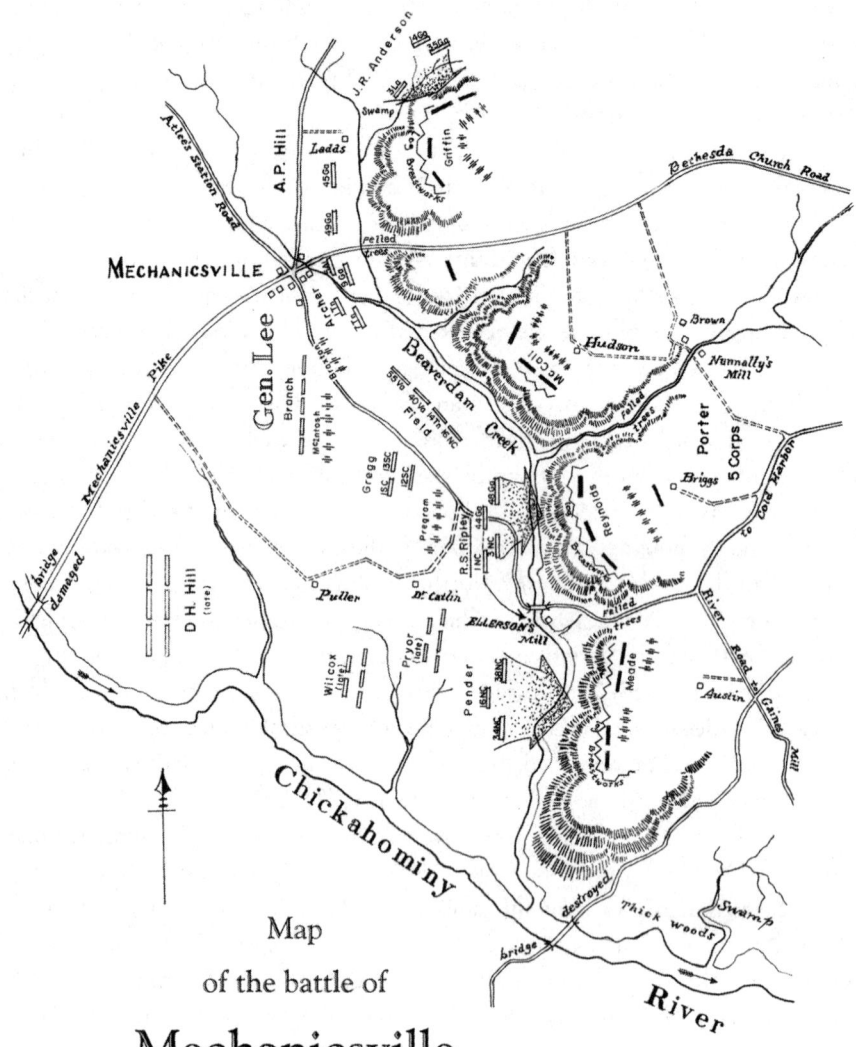

Mechanicsville

June 26, 1862

Confederate
Federal

James L. Williams

to "charge that battery immediately in front." When within 200 yards they "went double-quick with a yell to within 50 yards of the battery." Several pieces of artillery had been firing on the regiment with shell and grape for 150 yards before the Georgians stopped to fire a shot.

Fortunately, the regiment ran into a millrace, which protected them somewhat from the heavy and continuous fire of the enemy, although many were killed and wounded. The survivors stood in water up to their cartridge boxes and fought for two hours before concluding that the regiment was too badly shot up to attempt another charge. Reese crawled out of the millrace and up to the top of a little hill, where he "heard that our gallant Colonel is dead, having received three wounds in the fight."[21]

The acclaimed Civil War author Clifford Dowdey wrote a well-received book describing the Peninsula Campaign. Apparently taking a cue from Freeman, Dowdey attacked Ripley at every turn. He began by claiming, "An opinionated man, Ripley was even more contumacious than D. H. Hill: where Hill respected some superiors, Ripley was against them all." Ripley was indeed opinionated, but Dowdey exaggerated the issue by claiming that Ripley did not respect any of his superior officers.

Dowdey continued, "Judging by Ripley's reports and his actions, his only purpose was to charge straight ahead, taking the batteries by assault." Ripley was actually on his way to the left flank as ordered by Powell Hill, when Harvey Hill countered those orders, directing him to assist Pender, and then, with his remaining forces, assault "the batteries in front." Dowdey surmised that "leading troops in combat constricted the play of [Ripley's] faculties" and self-indulgently contended that Ripley "evidently had not considered the changes made since the Mexican War, advancing in splendid array, as if against smoothbore cannons and muskets accurate at little more than sixty yards." This was a preposterous claim as Ripley had been selling Sharps rifles to the British before the war and was well aware of the improvements in ordnance. Dowdey asserted that nearly half the Confederates lost were the result of "Ripley's Napoleonic heroics." However, it was Harvey Hill who ordered Ripley's frontal assault. Burnside at Fredericksburg, Grant at Cold Harbor, and Lee on the third day at Gettysburg would order similar, costly frontal assaults.

In his final report, A. P. Hill rightly claimed, "It was never contemplated that my division alone should have sustained the shock of this battle, but such was the case, and the only assistance received was from Ripley." Powell Hill possibly did not know that D. H. Hill had countered his orders for Ripley to turn the Federal left.[22]

On August 3, 1862, Reese wrote to the *Countryman* from Camp Ripley, Richmond. He had chanced upon a July 24 copy of the *Macon Telegraph*, which featured S. Boykin's article "Battle Pictures." Boykin claimed, "The gallant Col. R. A. Smith remonstrated in vain with General Ripley when the 44th Georgia was ordered to charge a battery. Obedience, however, is a soldier's duty."

Reese adamantly denied Boykin's account: "This is not so. I happened to be within four steps of Col. Smith and Gen. D. H. Hill, and the latter ordered the charge." Colonel Smith *"did not remonstrate"* but repeatedly asked General Hill to point out the battery he wished to have taken. When Hill impatiently turned for another regiment to make the charge, Colonel Smith angrily replied, "No never, this regiment will charge the battery."

Reese concluded that Boykin's account did General Ripley a grave injustice. Reese believed Ripley to be a brave soldier and a man of discretion. Although he was "blustery and rough in his manner," he loved his men too much to attempt to win "everlasting laurels" at the expense of the lives of his troops. "Besides," Reese continued, "he put himself with his men, and on the charge he went, showing a willingness to take his chance with the men." Reese admitted that he could not assess General Hill's abilities as an officer, but he hoped that in the future, every man would be accorded his proper place in the history of the war. Reese placed the blame on D. H. Hill for ordering the frontal assault that resulted in the death of so many Georgians and praised Ripley for personally accompanying the ill-fated regiments. However, Captain Fleming Jourdan of the 44th Georgia's commissary staff did not share Reese's positive opinion of Ripley. In a sarcastic letter to his wife, Jourdan described Ripley as their "fat, whiskey-loving general."[23]

Early in the morning of June 27, Ripley's severely damaged brigade moved beyond Mechanicsville, then accompanied the division along the road to Cold Harbor. After arriving there, the brigade was held in reserve for a short time. A battalion of the 1st North Carolina Regiment, under Captain H. A. Brown, and only a fragment of the 44th Georgia remained to accompany the 3rd North Carolina and the 48th Georgia. Hill's division was ordered to the front on the extreme left of the Confederate line, with Ripley's brigade occupying the extreme right of the division.

After crossing densely wooded, swampy ground, the brigade reached its designated position, only to find the line already occupied by Confederate troops. As Ripley evaluated his position, he received a request for aid from General R. H. Anderson and dispatched the 48th Georgia to his right, leaving primarily the North Carolinians of Colonel Meares and Captain Brown on the left. At Gaines' Mill for nearly two hours, the brigade, or what was left of it, was under a heavy barrage; however, casualties were light as the thick woods provided protection and sheltered them from view.

Just before dark the enemy attempted to turn Ripley's left but was checked by artillery and a succession of charges by different brigades. Ripley praised the 3rd North Carolina, under Colonel Meares, and Captain Brown's 1st North

Carolina for their good service. The 48th Georgia "was masked by troops in its front" and did not see action.

Hill and Rodes also reported that the heavily wooded and swampy area, with tangled undergrowth, made troop movements difficult and caused confusion, overlapping of brigades, and the separation of regiments. Apparently disregarding the conditions and the fact that Ripley's brigade was held for a time in reserve, Hill took the opportunity to denigrate his Yankee brigadier. He contended that Ripley's brigade "was not engaged, owing to that officer not keeping it in hand and not pressing vigorously to the front."[24]

Following the Battle of Gaines' Mill, Captain Campbell Brown, an adjutant to Major General Richard S. Ewell, described a chance meeting he and General Ewell had with Ripley around midnight. Ewell and Brown sat down at that late hour to finally eat a portion of their lunch, but before they finished Ripley arrived and "was of course asked to join us." Brown was interrupted before he could finish his share, so Ripley ate the remainder of Brown's lunch and the captain "went without until the next day." Even then, "rank had its privileges."[25]

Ripley and his troops remained on the field during the night and early the next morning moved toward the Grapevine Bridge. The brigade "bivouacked within 1½ miles of that point Saturday and Sunday." As a result, it was not engaged at the Battle of Savage Station on June 29.

At this point in his report, Ripley confused his dates and days of the week. He claimed that early on Monday, July 1 (in fact, June 30), the brigade moved with the division across the repaired Grapevine Bridge. The division followed the enemy's line of retreat until reaching White Oak Swamp Creek, where they found the enemy in position on the far side of the creek. Ripley brought his brigade to a supporting position of the division's artillery, "which engaged the enemy until nightfall, driving him from his position and enabling the pioneers to repair the bridge."

On the morning of July 1, the division crossed the bridge and followed the retreating Federals until they reached the enemy's position on the elevated plateau, Malvern Hill. By this seventh day of the Peninsula Campaign, Lee had driven McClellan completely down the peninsula to that low hill, advantageously positioned about one mile from the James River and eight miles from the Union base, now at Harrison's Landing.

That afternoon Harvey Hill ordered Ripley's brigade to advance "through a heavy fire of artillery to a dense wood in close proximity of the enemy's position, where it lay for a time in reserve." Possibly Ripley intended the next sentence in his battle report to be humorous as he quipped, "At about 5 o'clock I was ordered to take position in a jungle near the hill on which the enemy was established and to the left of General Anderson's brigade." Ripley's regiments, aligned from right to left, were the 48th Georgia, 3rd North Carolina, and the 44th Georgia, of which officers had rallied about 170 men from the disaster at Ellerson's Mill and brought them back to the brigade. On the far left were the remnants of Captain Brown's 1st North Carolina.

Hill ordered Ripley to reconnoiter the enemy's position, and he found them in strong force immediately in their front, with a well-advanced battery supported by strong lines of infantry. At about 6:30 or 7:00 P.M. Hill ordered the brigades on Ripley's right to begin the attack. Ripley's brigade advanced with those of G. B. Anderson and Rodes, with Colonel John B. Gordon leading that brigade for the wounded Rodes. Ripley claimed that the three brigades mounted the hill "in gallant manner." However, at the brow of the hill they "met a furious fire of shot shell and musketry" that killed Colonel Meares at the head of his Carolinians. There was much confusion because of the loss of officers, and with night approaching the brigades fell back. Fresh troops were ordered in, and they too were repulsed. In his final report Ripley praised his three colonels who were killed in action, Smith and Stokes at Ellerson's Mill and Meares at Malvern Hill. He also credited officers de Rosset, Brown, and others who "made good, to as full extent as possible," the loss of their colonels.[26]

The Battle of Malvern Hill was in fact more fragmented and disorganized than described by Ripley. Sears opined, "D. H. Hill suffered 1,756 casualties in this series of fruitless charges, even more than he had lost at Gaines' Mill, and this time he had nothing to show for it." Although he did not mention Lee by name, Hill criticized the "blundering management of the battle . . . the want of concert with the infantry decisions. . . . none of our troops drew trigger except McLaws' division, mine and a portion of Huger's." Hill's artillery ran out of ammunition and had to be sent back for a fresh supply. Hill believed that if his artillery had been present with a good supply of ammunition, they could have beaten the force immediately in their front.

D. H. Hill's total casualties for the Peninsula Campaign were horrendous: Colquitt, 554; Rodes, 570; Garland, 844; G. B. Anderson, 863; and Ripley, 908. The grand total was 3,379 killed, wounded, and missing. Hill eulogized his "hero-martyrs," Colonels Stokes, Smith, and Meares of Ripley's brigade. Of Ripley's four regiments, three lost their commanding colonels in reckless frontal assaults on heavily supported Union artillery positions ordered by General D. H. Hill.[27]

General Evander McIvor Law discussed the Peninsula Campaign in an article published after the war. His appraisal of Pender's and Ripley's attacks on Ellerson's Mills is enlightening. Upon examining the position afterward, he believed that "to attack it from the front seemed the extremity of rashness, yet Pender's brigade was pushed recklessly forward. . . . Ripley's brigade was sent to Pender's support and shared the same fate. . . . I could not repress a feeling of astonishment that any commander who had a knowledge of the ground would have attempted a direct assault upon it." A casual reader could fault Ripley for such an egregious attack; that is, if one did not know or ignored the fact that D. H. Hill ordered Ripley's direct frontal assault.[28]

Hill's only regret may have been that Ripley—the hated Yankee, aide to the despised Gideon Pillow, and author of what Hill presumed to be a "slanderous" attack on Scott—was not among the fallen.

CHAPTER 15

Maryland Campaign

Lee had hoped to split the Union army and destroy it in detail before McClellan could return to his last base of operations at Harrison's Landing. In this he failed, but the Peninsula Campaign was a strategic success, and for the time being Lee had saved Richmond. The capital rejoiced and bestowed acclaim upon Lee never to be equaled by any other Confederate. During the week following Malvern Hill, Ripley's brigade and the other brigades of Harvey Hill's division gathered dropped arms and accoutrements, and buried Confederate and Union dead. In addition they gathered Union prisoners and transferred the wounded of both armies to area hospitals. In mid-July the division returned to its old camp near Richmond.[1]

Robert E. Lee was not pleased with the performance of three of his six major commanders during the Peninsula Campaign and transferred Generals Benjamin Huger, John Magruder, and Theophilus Holmes out of the Army of Northern Virginia. On July 17 Harvey Hill replaced Holmes as commander of the North Carolina district, where his fellow North Carolinian had served before bringing three new brigades to Lee's army. Hill was not immediately replaced as commander of his division, and on paper it continued to be referred to as D. H. Hill's Division.

Private Calvin Leach, of the 1st North Carolina Infantry, noted in his diary that at 10:00 A.M. on Sunday, July 20, Ripley held a general review of the brigade. With Hill transferred to the North Carolina district, Ripley worked with Lee planning lines of defense on the peninsula between the Darbytown Road and Charles City on the James River. Late in July, Ripley informed Lee that he had gathered a "force of laborers" and was ready to begin building the defensive works between those two points. Ripley asked Lee to have a "proper engineer officer" contact him regarding the works. Lee assigned Captain W. P. Smith of the Engineer Corps to give Ripley the help he needed.[2]

With McClellan's army having been driven back down the peninsula to their base at Harrison's Landing, President Lincoln and his newly appointed general-in-chief, Henry W. Halleck, decided that McClellan should evacuate the peninsula and join forces with General John Pope's newly formed Army of Virginia. Pope had recently been recalled from the western theater of operations and was reportedly moving his army south toward the Virginia Central rail lines at Gordonsville. On August 3 Halleck officially ordered McClellan to bring his army north immediately, unite it with Pope, and open a new campaign. McClellan bitterly protested this decision, but Halleck was adamant.[3]

Despite these orders, on August 5 McClellan attempted to restart the Peninsula Campaign by reoccupying Malvern Hill with approximately seventeen thousand cavalry and infantrymen. Colonel L. S. Baker of the 1st North Carolina Cavalry detected the Union advance on the night of August 4 and dispatched an officer who notified Ripley of the incursion at 3:45 A.M. Ripley immediately authorized Baker to call up two infantry regiments and a section of artillery that were on picket duty four or five miles to the rear of the cavalryman. If Baker needed more assistance, he was authorized to call up the remainder of the nearby brigade. At about 11:00 A.M. Ripley arrived on the scene.

Lee ordered the divisions of Generals Longstreet and McLaws, and Hill's brigades under General Ripley, to advance to Long Bridge Road. Lee intended "General McLaws and Ripley's divisions, reinforced by that of General D. R. Jones . . . to form the left wing, while General Longstreet formed our right." Evidently, in the absence of General Hill, Lee placed Ripley temporarily in command of the division. Lee understood that the intensely hot day slowed the troops' progress, and even though they were marched slowly, men still fell by the wayside, some with heat stroke. A portion of Ripley's troops had not been issued rations, which caused further delay.

As a result, the sun had nearly set before the enemy's pickets were cleared and the left wing was ordered to extend to the far left. Ripley's brigades were ordered forward to the junction of Long Bridge and Charles City roads and formed a line of battle at that point. Ripley and the left wing then threatened the Union's line of communications, while Longstreet's brigades pushed directly toward Malvern Hill. As the advance continued, the enemy abandoned Malvern Hill and Confederate cavalry moved to occupy it.[4]

Following the repulse of McClellan's attempt to restart the Peninsula Campaign, Ripley asked Lee for instructions regarding the placement of his brigade. As Ripley's position at the crossing of the White Oak Swamp on the Charles City Road seemed to be appropriate, Lee suggested keeping two regiments and a battery there for the present time. Lee also agreed with Ripley's proposal of placing strong pickets "at the shops." Lee concluded that this would give Ripley time to see if a "change for the better can be made, or if a stronger position farther down cannot be found."

Later that day, in reference to McClellan's return to Malvern Hill, Lee emphasized the importance of having "the Charles City road better cared for." Lee "wished" Ripley would station a regiment on the road to support the cavalry and, if Ripley saw fit, to include a section of artillery. Lee suggested a position at or near Riddle's Shops and expected the health and comfort of the troops to be considered when selecting the camp; however, the camp should be advanced as far as the waters of White Oak Swamp. Breastworks were to be erected for the regiments' defense, pickets were to be changed every twenty-four hours, and Lee gave Ripley the option, if he so desired, to lighten the duty by changing regiments weekly. By all indications, Lee and Ripley had a positive and supportive relationship in planning these defenses.[5]

On August 10 Major General G. W. Smith reported for duty, and as he outranked Ripley, Lee assigned him to command the brigades of D. H. Hill's division. After Lee became dissatisfied with Hill's performance in North Carolina, Smith did not remain in command long. About a week later Lee notified President Davis that he feared "General Hill is not entirely equal to his present position." Four days later Davis issued orders for Hill to resume command of his old division. However, before Hill's reappointment, Lee ordered Ripley "to mass Smith's division behind the North Anna."[6]

On Lee's orders, Ripley and Colquitt's brigades continued to move northward. There had been a significant change in Ripley's brigade as the 4th Georgia Infantry replaced the 48th Georgia. On August 19 Ripley's regiments were loaded onto boxcars and transported to Orange Court House. The brigade remained in camp until August 27, when they marched to Rapidan Station and Culpepper Court House. At Amissville two days later, Jedediah Hotchkiss, Stonewall Jackson's chief topographical engineer, met with Ripley, "who had just come up with his Georgia brigade." The brigade went on to Warrenton and Gainesville and then to Manassas, where the second battle at that site had just ended. On September 1 the brigade marched on to Centreville, where the 44th Georgia did picket duty during the night.

The next day the brigade moved to Stewart's farm, where General Lee tripped and fell, suffering a painful injury to both his hands. The nearest surgeon was summoned, and Dr. N. S. Walker of Ripley's 44th Georgia splinted Lee's injured hands. The doctor also gave Lee a bottle of liniment, which greatly relieved the discomfort. Lee returned the bottle at Sharpsburg and told Dr. Walker "to keep it for the next patient with a sprained or broken finger or hand."[7]

Coming from Petersburg to resume command of his division, Harvey Hill lagged far behind Ripley and Colquitt. After reaching Hanover Junction, Hill took command of McLaws's division and the three remaining brigades of Rodes, G. B. Anderson, and Garland. On August 26 Hill headed north, and although he drove his men mercilessly, they did not arrive in time to participate in the Battles of Second Manassas or Chantilly, the battles that drove Pope and his forces back toward Washington.

During Hill's forced march, the Georgia brigade of portly Howell Cobb covered sixty miles in three and a half days. Cobb viewed the march as poorly directed and "inhuman." In Cobb's opinion, Hill was a "weak, self-conceited heartless and cruel ass . . . as despicable a wretch, as ever disgraced any army." Hill's reunited division finally joined Lee at Chantilly on September 2.

Pope's recent poor performance resulted in his removal, and George B. McClellan, replaced him, once again in command of the Union army. With Pope defeated, Lee wanted to relieve the military pressure on Virginia by invading Maryland. He planned to carry the war into the North even though his army was in rags, many without shoes, and food was in short supply. He intended to advance through Frederick, Maryland, to South Mountain and then move northward toward Hagerstown near the Pennsylvania border.

In early September two unspecified brigades of Hill's division drove Union forces away from the mouth of the Monocacy and crossed the Potomac River into Maryland. The next night, Hill followed Jackson's command and encamped within a few miles of Frederick. In the morning, Hill's troops marched into Frederick, seized the rail station, cut telegraph lines, and encamped near town, where they remained until September 11.[8]

Lee soon learned that the Federals had not evacuated nearby Harpers Ferry and Martinsburg, Virginia, as he had expected they would in response to his invasion. As a result, on September 9 Lee countered with an audacious but complicated battle plan. Despite receiving reports that McClellan was advancing northward from Washington against him, Lee issued Special Orders, No. 191, and divided his army into four groups. Counting on the ever-cautious McClellan to advance slowly, Lee's ultimate goal was to capture the arsenal and garrison remaining at Harpers Ferry before reuniting his divided army.

Lee sent Jackson, along with A. P. Hill, to seize the Baltimore and Ohio Railroad and capture any Union forces at Martinsburg, as well as any troops escaping from Harpers Ferry. They would then advance on Harpers Ferry from the west. Generals McLaws and R. H. Anderson were to approach Harpers Ferry from the north and seize Maryland Heights. General John Walker's small division was to advance on the arsenal and garrison from the south and occupy Loudoun Heights. This daring offensive was to be completed by September 12, when these divided forces were to quickly reunite before McClellan could attack and destroy them piecemeal.[9]

On September 10, at the onset of this complex campaign, Harvey Hill's division became the Confederate rearguard. Lee placed them in charge of his immense wagon train moving north on the National Road toward Boonsboro and Hagerstown. Lee received a report claiming Union forces were moving southward from Chambersburg, Pennsylvania, toward Hagerstown. In response he ordered Longstreet, immediately in Hill's front, to continue advancing toward Hagerstown. This seriously troubled Longstreet, as Lee's army would then be split into five groups and dispersed even more widely.[10]

Three days later, with the supply train halted at Boonsboro, Lee ordered Hill to guard the roads leading north from Harpers Ferry. His brigades were also to assist the cavalry in guarding Turner's Gap, the main pass from the east over South Mountain. Also on the morning of September 13, General J. E. B. Stuart's cavalry fought a delaying action at a gap in Catoctin Mountain; it then retired from the crest and moved toward Middletown, just east of Turner's Gap. With the Union army moving toward the South Mountain passes, Lee's divided army faced a major crisis. Amazingly, near mid-day on the September 13, a Union infantryman found a copy of Lee's Special Orders, No. 191, and passed the papers up the chain of command. McClellan now knew Lee's plans and that he had divided the Army of Northern Virginia into at least four separate wings. McClellan planned to attack and destroy them in detail.[11]

Stuart informed Harvey Hill that in the delaying action at Catoctin Mountain he had observed only two brigades of Federal infantry, but the enemy kept its troops "well concealed," indicating that more units could be involved. However, Hill claimed that Stuart reported only that two brigades of Yankees "were pursuing us, and one brigade would be sufficient to hold the pass." Stuart did not list this advisory in his report, but he did not write the report until February 1864. Hill apparently doubted the accuracy of Stuart's report and sent two brigades, Garland's and Colquitt's, to Turner's Gap. He ordered the brigades of Ripley, Anderson, and Rodes to the vicinity of Boonsboro.

Around midnight on September 13, Hill dispatched Ripley to meet with Stuart and obtain information concerning roads and gaps in and around South Mountain. As General Hill had been lying with his command in the area for two days, Stuart intimated that Hill, on his own, should have had a better idea of the topography with which he was dealing. Stuart claimed that he gave Ripley all his information "cheerfully" and explained the gaps "by map." Ripley reported that earlier in the evening Hill had ordered him to march his brigade to an eminence northeast of Boonsboro and take a position there along with a battery of his artillery. Interestingly, Ripley did not mention his midnight meeting with Stuart in his report.[12]

Sometime that night at Hagerstown, Lee and Longstreet received a dispatch from Stuart claiming that McClellan had obtained information regarding his widely dispersed army. With the capture of Harpers Ferry two days behind schedule, it became paramount for Hill to hold the South Mountain passes, and to that end Longstreet was to start for Boonsboro at dawn the next day to support Hill. Longstreet did so under protest, believing he would be too late and his men too exhausted to be effective.

Early on the morning of the fourteenth, Hill personally examined Turner's Gap and concluded that he would need a larger force to hold the pass than he had previously believed. Turner's Gap, where the National Road from Frederick to Hagerstown crossed the mountain, was quite narrow and could easily be defended by a small force, but it was vulnerable to attacks on both flanks. In fact, the area to be defended covered three miles of mountaintop and included Fox's Gap about one mile south of Turner's Gap. Stuart barely acknowledged Fox's Gap, which he referred to as Braddock's Gap, but he did leave a small cavalry detachment under Colonel Thomas L. Rosser, along with Stuart's Horse Artillery, to occupy the gap. Stuart then proceeded farther south to join the main portion of his command at Crampton's Gap.

Turner's and Fox's Gaps were interconnected by at least four old looping mountain roads, as well as by several farm lanes the enemy could utilize to attack Hill's outnumbered forces. Deep ravines, steep slopes, and rounded peaks marked the heavily wooded terrain, with its dense undergrowth of mountain laurel. It presented a difficult, rough terrain over which to maneuver troops.

After assessing the situation, Hill ordered Anderson's brigade to join Garland and Colquitt at Turner's Gap. He ordered Ripley to send a regiment from his brigade to Hamburg Pass three miles north on their left, for which Ripley sent his new regiment, Colonel George Dole's 4th Georgia. At that early hour Hill was reluctant to order Ripley and Rodes up from their position at Boonsboro.[13]

Hill climbed a lookout point near Turner's Gap and viewed firsthand the huge Union force spread over the valley below him. He now had no doubt he was in for a desperate battle. Hill positioned Colquitt's brigade on each side of the turnpike at Turner's Gap. At approximately 7:00 A.M. on September 14, Federal forces began their assault but angled off toward Hill's right and Fox's Gap. Hill rushed Garland's brigade to repulse the large enemy force attempting to gain control of a road leading to the Confederate rear. General Garland was killed, and his men suffered heavy losses in securing the road. Colonel Duncan K. McRae of the 5th North Carolina replaced Garland, and Anderson's brigade arrived in time to relieve Garland's embattled troops. Harvey Hill mourned the loss of General Garland but was "pleased to report" that the Yankees lost "General Reno, a renegade Virginian . . . killed by a happy shot from the 23rd North Carolina."

Under this heavy Federal onslaught, Hill ordered Ripley and Rodes up to Turner's Gap, noting that they arrived soon after Anderson. Hill sent Rodes north to seize and occupy a peak with a commanding view of the turnpike and gap. He then sent Ripley to the right to support G. B. Anderson's North Carolinians. Ripley traveled the Braddock Road and met with General Anderson who was to extend farther south on the road to make room for Ripley's men. Ripley claimed that when in position he and Anderson were to attack "the enemy, then occupying the heights to the south."[14]

Hill stated that at about three o'clock the brigades of General Thomas F. Drayton and Colonel George T. Anderson arrived from Longstreet's Corps. Hill claimed that he called Drayton, Anderson, and Ripley together and directed them "to follow a path until they came in contact with Rosser," supposedly near Fox's Gap, "then change their flank . . . and sweep the woods before them." Hill previously indicated that Ripley's three remaining regiments had gone to the support of G. B. Anderson, so the brigades of Colonel Anderson and Drayton, a total of eight regiments, would have to travel some distance to reach Rosser's and Ripley's regiments already supporting G. B. Anderson.

Ripley's report, which is improbable in places, claimed that while he was taking position, "General Hill arrived, and with him Brigadier General Drayton's command." Ripley knew Drayton from South Carolina and met with him at the Port Royal disaster. Strangely, Ripley made no mention of Colonel G. T. Anderson's brigade of five Georgia regiments, possibly not realizing that the colonel commanded a brigade, though Anderson would state that his brigade was positioned between Ripley's and Drayton's.

According to Ripley, General Hill directed General Anderson and his command "to extend still farther on the road making room for Drayton's troops, and the attack should be made as soon as all were in position." Ripley reported that "General Drayton's command was rapidly forming" when the enemy attacked him in force. This attack, before Drayton was completely deployed, drove him from the field and seems to have preempted the planned attack by Ripley and Anderson.

Hill reported, "Anderson soon became partially and Drayton hotly engaged, but Ripley did not draw trigger; why I do not know." Hill mentioned the 4th North Carolina's failed attempt to "carry a Yankee battery," so the "partially engaged" brigade Hill referred to might have been that of G. B. Anderson. Hill recorded that three Yankee brigades attacked Drayton, "and his men were soon beaten and went streaming to the rear. Rosser, Anderson, and Ripley still held their ground and the Yankees could not gain our rear." Adding to these confusing and contradictory reports, Hill included Ripley's brigade as one of those holding its ground.[15]

The battle reports referring to South Mountain filed by Ripley and Hill contain contradictions and improbabilities, while neither Drayton nor G. B. Anderson filed a battle report to be found in the *Official Records*. Their reports might have provided some insight into the reports of Hill and Ripley. However, Colonel G. T. Anderson did file a report of the action but one critical of Ripley.

Anderson contended that Ripley ordered "the whole line to move by the right flank" before Drayton had formed his line. He believed that Ripley's order to move by the right flank precipitated the separation and disorganization of the brigades. Ripley was probably following Hill's order to extend farther on the road "to make room for General Drayton's troops." Anderson then stated that at about this time the enemy opened a heavy fire on Drayton and drove him from the field.

The rout of Drayton's troops was reversed only by the arrival of Hood's brigade from Longstreet's Corps.[16]

Hill recorded that Ripley "did not draw trigger," but his criticism of Ripley was rather subdued. That would change. Twenty-four years later, Harvey Hill authored an article entitled "The Battle of South Mountain, or Boonsboro" published in the *Century Magazine*. Hill wrote, "At about 3:30 P.M. the advance of Longstreet's command arrived and reported to me, one brigade under Colonel G. T. Anderson and one under General Drayton. They were attached to Ripley's left, and a forward movement was ordered. In half an hour or more I received a note from Ripley saying he was progressing finely; so he was, to the rear of he mountain on the west side. Before he returned the fighting was over, and his brigade did not fire a shot that day."[17]

In preparation for this article, in June 1885 Hill wrote to his fellow North Carolinian William L. de Rosset. He asked the former colonel for his opinion of Ripley and what he could recall of the battle. De Rosset claimed he regretted that his "desperate wounds" at Sharpsburg prevented him from filing a report. He believed that he could have answered Hill's questions better then than he could now, twenty-three years later.

Probably aware of Hill's loathing of Ripley and to ingratiate himself with Hill, de Rosset claimed, "After the 'Seven days fight' it was a common subject of conversation, among officers and men, that Ripley was not under infantry fire during the week." As cited earlier, Joseph B. Reese of the 44th Georgia witnessed Ripley at Ellerson's Mill and unequivocally refuted de Rosset. Ripley "put himself with his men, and on the charge he went, showing a willingness to take his chances with the men."

As for Boonsboro, de Rosset recalled that when "the brigade reached the summit it filed off to the right. Marching by obscure roads, about a mile from the Pike we changed directions to the right & soon found ourselves at the foot of the mountain, probably 3 or 4 miles south of the Pike. Here we were informed that G. B. Anderson was on our right, near by, not connecting, & Ripley remarked to me, Colonel, we are cut off from the main body of the army."

At this point, de Rosset claimed, Ripley took command of the two brigades, his and G. B. Anderson's, and assigned de Rosset to command his four regiments. Ripley then ordered the brigades to "move up the mountain with a heavy skirmish line in front." De Rosset claimed that he placed Major Stephen Decatur Thruston of his regiment in charge of the skirmish line and the brigade moved forward "keeping in sight of the skirmish line as near as possible."

When near the top of the mountain, Thruston notified de Rosset that "there was a heavy body of troops in his front, which he took for the enemy." When de Rosset notified Ripley of this, he alleged that Ripley ordered the brigade "to fall back down the mountain which was done," thus accusing Ripley of retreating to avoid a fight. "The brigade lay on its arms 'til near dark, then near midnight, we were quietly withdrawn and put in route for Sharpsburg." De Rosset claimed that only later did he learn that the troops seen by Thruston were G. B Anderson's, who upon reaching the top of the mountain, changed front to the left and were crossing Thruston's front.[18]

After de Rosset was wounded at Antietam, he probably did not know that Major Thruston (later promoted to colonel) of the 3rd North Carolina wrote a letter to their governor, Zebulon Vance. In his letter, written not quite two weeks after the battle, he described the action at Boonsboro. Thruston gave a significantly different version of the brigade's movements. He reported "marching by the right flank along the Western Turnpike; we reached the summit where this pike crosses, here changing direction to the right. We moved along the ridge to ___ Gap." Thruston must have been referring to Fox's Gap but didn't recall its name as he wrote his report.

Thruston wrote that the brigade was "formed in line of battle preparatory to an attack on the enemy, who was here massed in heavy force." He reported that the brigade rested for an hour or more at this position and then again moved by the right flank to give place to General Drayton's brigade. Thus, Thruston corroborated Ripley's explanation of the move by the right flank. As Ripley made room for Drayton, he became separated from the newly arriving brigade. Thruston also did not mention Colonel G. T. Anderson's brigade in his letter. At about the same time, the three brigades of Yankees attacked Drayton, which also is not included in Thruston's letter.

Thruston wrote that Ripley, not de Rosset, ordered him to form a battalion of skirmishers from four companies of his regiment, which he deployed about two hundred yards in advance of the brigade, covering its entire front. The major advanced his skirmishers "in line of battle up the side of a steep and rugged mountain covered by an almost impenetrable growth of ivy." After about a half-mile, Thruston's skirmishers contacted a similar line from General G. B. Anderson's brigade on their right. The major made a reconnaissance in person and discovered that his regiment and Anderson's brigade were nearly at right angles to each other, rendering them ineffectual. This is an absolute refutation of de Rosset's claim that Ripley withdrew the brigade to the base of the mountain when his skirmishers confronted the enemy.

Thruston notified Ripley, who, because they had collided with Anderson, ordered the brigade to regroup and "to fall back to the base of the mountain, which was done in good order." The lines of skirmishers were properly positioned, and the regiments again moved up the mountain by a steep and narrow road. They halted when they reached the top of the mountain at about 9:00 P.M. The brigade rested "in this position within 200 hundred yards of the enemy until 11 P.M., when we took the road to Sharpsburg."[19]

Hill's magazine account also implied that Drayton and Anderson's "attachment" to Ripley was completed and the "forward movement" ordered and begun, after which Ripley mismanaged the attack and "was progressing finely ... to the rear of the mountain on the west side." In reality, before Drayton and Colonel Anderson's "attachment to Ripley" was completed and the "forward movement" begun, three Union brigades attacked Drayton while he was in the process of forming up.

Bridges sharpened and embellished Hill's charge that Ripley was "progressing finely to the rear of the mountain on the west side." According to Bridges, Ripley marched his brigade "on a weird, wandering trip through the mountain laurel—away from the scene of the action." Bridges also claimed that Ripley moved the brigade from place to place to avoid fighting and then "marched it to the western base of the mountain, held it there for a time, and did not take it back up again until after dark. His brigade did no fighting that day."[20]

It is true that Ripley's brigade did not fire a shot that day, but surprisingly Private Calvin Leach made no mention in his diary that Ripley took the brigade completely back down the west side of the mountain. Leach wrote on Sunday, September 14, "Today the battle of Boonsboro was fought in the top of the [mountain] where we crossed it on Friday." The brigade moved up the mountain road "toward the roaring of the cannon." According to Leach, the brigade stopped about halfway up the mountain, took off their knapsacks, rested for a moment, and loaded their guns. Then they marched to the top of the mountain, where Leach could see the Yankees in a line of battle. Union artillery was firing on his regiment, and Confederate artillery returned the fire. Leach claimed that the enemy tried to flank them on the right, but his regiment moved by the right flank and "marched on the top of the mountain keeping even with the enemy. Going over rocks and clifts [sic] and some of the worst places I almost ever saw." Leach claimed that they marched backward and forward across the mountain and "to the top of it by the left flank in a line of battle." Leach never mentioned marching down to the base of the mountain and back up again. Surprisingly, all his entries refer to the "top of the mountain." Leach stated that the firing stopped at about ten o'clock and they "marched silently off and left the field behind."[21]

Ripley, the senior brigadier in command of what amounted to a division of four brigades, was not totally in control of the situation and the units became separated. The brigades were not on a parade ground, and Ripley lacked the experience to lead four brigades strung out over the difficult terrain so graphically described by Leach. As a result, G. B. Anderson and Ripley's brigade were not significantly engaged that day. Ripley submitted a report that does not accurately describe what he did after the attack on Drayton and as a result is subject to criticism. South Mountain was definitely not Ripley's finest hour; however, over the years historiographers have mercilessly attacked Ripley's performance, even to the extent of claiming that he deliberately took his men back to the base of the mountain to avoid fighting. This is not true.

In 1914 Judge George D. Grattan, who had been a captain and assistant adjutant general. on the staff of General Colquitt, offered an interesting evaluation of Ripley's actions: "General Ripley's brigade was sent to Anderson's assistance, but by some mishap lost its way in the thick brush, and never rendered any service." Grattan suggested that possibly the Federals observed Ripley "marching around from place to place" and thought there was a large force in their front. Alarmed by Anderson's attack "and the appearance of Ripley moving on the mountain side, they fell back to the original line of Fox's Gap, and the whole of General Reno's corps remained idle."[22]

As the action on South Mountain was ending, Lee summoned Hill and Longstreet for a meeting. He asked them whether they could hold their current position for another day, and both emphatically answered no. During the night all the remaining brigades stealthily moved down the mountain to Boonsboro and toward Antietam Creek and Sharpsburg.

In the haste of the withdrawal, Harvey Hill and Ripley forgot the regiment they had ordered to Hamburg Pass, where Colonel George P. Doles's 4th Georgia spent "all day there without molestation." When Colonel de Rosset discovered that the regiment was missing, he dispatched a courier to notify them of the move. The 4th left hurriedly, and none too soon, for as they passed through Boonsboro, the enemy was entering it.[23]

As the brigade neared Sharpsburg on September 15, it crossed the Middle Bridge over Antietam Creek, marched a short distance to the right, and formed a line of battle facing the creek. Ripley reported that General Longstreet, during the temporary absence of the division commander, ordered him to post his, Anderson's, and McRae's brigades "on the heights overlooking the river [Antietam Creek], with the right resting on the road from Boonsboro to Sharpsburg, facing the river." The three brigades bivouacked in this position for the remainder of September 15 and 16. On the morning of the sixteenth, the enemy appeared in force and began an "annoying artillery fire" from 9:00 A.M. until nightfall.

On the evening of the sixteenth, Ripley received orders to move his brigade to the left of the division, cover a road leading from his left to the Sharpsburg-Hagerstown turnpike, and support artillery in that vicinity. Very early on the seventeenth, enemy batteries on the eastern banks of the Antietam opened a severe enfilading fire on Ripley's troops. Unfortunately, the brigade occupied a position

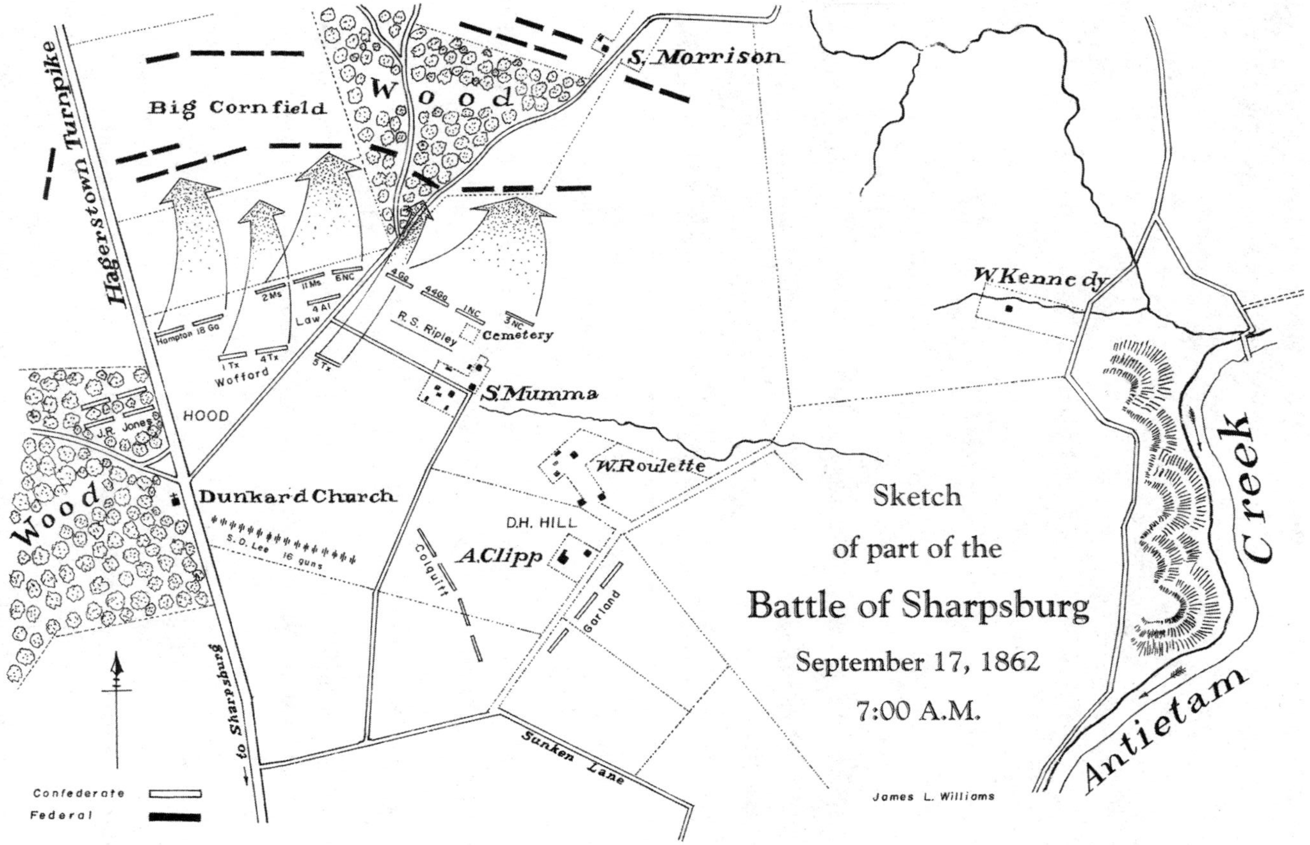

Sketch
of part of the
Battle of Sharpsburg
September 17, 1862
7:00 A.M.
James L. Williams
Hagerstown Turnpike
Big Cornfield
Wood
S. Morrison
W. Kennedy
Antietam Creek
Hampton 18 Ga
1 Tx
4 Tx
Wofford
2 Ms
11 Ms
6 NC
4 Al
Law
5 Tx
4 Ga
44 Ga
1 NC
3 NC
R. S. Ripley
Cemetery
S. Mumma
HOOD
J.R. Jones
Wood
Dunkard Church
S. D. Lee 16 guns
W. Roulette
D.H. HILL
A. Clipp
Colquitt
Garland
Sunken Lane
to Sharpsburg
Confederate
Federal

Mumma Farm outbuildings, Sharpsburg, Maryland. At the Battle of Sharpsburg, near these buildings, Ripley was shot in throat. Author's photograph.

in clear view of nearly all the Union artillery. Lying under the barrage without flinching for over an hour, the brigade suffered serious losses before called into action.

While under this artillery fire, Ripley sent a squad from de Rosset's 3rd North Carolina to set fire to the Mumma farmhouse and outbuildings. He ordered the buildings, one hundred yards in the brigade's front, burned to prevent their use as cover. Ordered to advance, at about 8:00 A.M. the brigade moved toward the flaming buildings.[24]

The 4th Georgia was positioned just to the right of the Mumma graveyard, and to the right of the graveyard were a large barn and numerous other burning buildings. Passing through this conflagration, the brigade became somewhat disoriented and the regiments became intermixed. Beyond the burning buildings, the brigade "reformed and opened a rapid fire upon the enemy." While Ripley was reforming the brigade, he was disabled by shot to the neck, but the troops continued forward under the command of Colonel Doles. Ripley left the field to be examined and have his wound dressed.[25]

Hill, probably begrudgingly, reported, "Brigadier General Ripley received a severe wound in the throat from a Minié-ball, which would have proven fatal but for passing through his cravat. After his wound was dressed he heroically returned to the field, and remained to the close of the day with his brigade." Ripley probably survived because the missile was well spent when it struck him, and passing through his cravat most likely had little to do with the outcome. Ripley was extremely fortunate that the bullet somehow missed his carotid artery, jugular veins, trachea, and larynx.

Ripley reported, "After an absence of an hour and a half, I returned to the field with such force I could collect from detachments, and found my brigade relieved and in position west of Sharpsburg. I remained with it until afternoon when, finding myself faint and exhausted, I relinquished the command to Colonel Doles."[26]

Not satisfied with his biased attack on Ripley's performance at South Mountain, de Rosset continued his rant against Ripley at Sharpsburg. In his 1885 letter to Hill, de Rosset claimed that he confronted Ripley as the battle was beginning. "When we advanced that morning Ripley was with me. After 4 messages sent him, he came down and asked me what I wanted. . . . In all the engagements I had been in, I felt the need of advice from him and had never seen him." De Rosset told Ripley that the rank and file were complaining that they had not seen him under infantry fire since he took command and believed that he kept to the rear to avoid the fire. Ripley "blusteringly replied that he would show them he was no coward & would go along with me into action."

This says much about de Rosset's insecurity as he berated his commanding officer for not being with him "in all the engagements." This is in sharp contrast to the concern expressed by Lieutenant Colonel Thomas Ruffin Jr. of the 13th North Carolina for the safety of General Garland at Fox's Gap. Ruffin urged Garland to leave the scene of heavy firing and argued with Garland about the difference in their respective duties. Shortly afterward, Garland was killed. De Rosset went on to criticize Ripley for leaving the battlefield after receiving a "slight wound in the throat."

Ripley was not the only target of de Rosset's wrath. He was "disgusted beyond measure" with Colonel Doles and claimed that the "other Georgia regiment was utterly useless. This was the regiment that ran like dogs at Mechanicsville." De Rosset did not specify the regiment but was possibly referring to the 44th Georgia. According to Reese, Ripley accompanied this regiment, and they had suffered horrendous casualties at Ellerson's Mill.

Surprisingly, Douglas Southall Freeman, a serious Ripley critic, wrote, "At Sharpsburg, Ripley's personal conduct, as always, was courageous and bold. In the thick of the action he was struck in the neck by a Minié ball. . . . his wound was dressed, but within an hour and a half he was back with his men and was able to keep the field until action was concluded."[27]

Union casualties were estimated to be 12,469 out of nearly 75,000 engaged. Of approximately 40,000 Confederates, about 13,724 were casualties for a grand total of over 26,000 for both armies. Outnumbered nearly two to one, Lee ended his Maryland Campaign and withdrew his damaged but unbroken army back across the Potomac. They would continue the war for over two and a half more years.[28]

CHAPTER 16

Return to Charleston

Ripley began his recuperation at the brigade's camp on Opequon Creek, not far from Winchester, Virginia. Here on September 21, 1862, with the bullet embedded in his throat, he wrote his account of the Battles of Boonsborough and Sharpsburg. Notice that Ripley had been wounded reached the Charleston newspapers by the twenty-third, and the next day the *Mercury* announced they had received a private dispatch from the general claiming that his wound "was a slight one in the neck and that he still keeps in the saddle, and at the head of his column." One would think Ripley must have known his wound was "slight" only because the embedded Minié ball miraculously missed every significant anatomical structure in his neck.[1]

From June through September, while Ripley struggled through the Peninsula and Maryland Campaigns, Governor Pickens turned his wrath on General Pemberton, asking for his removal. The feeling was mutual; Pickens had so intimidated Pemberton that the latter wanted to leave Charleston as badly as Pickens wanted him replaced. In early June, President Davis and Pickens exchanged telegrams. Pickens notified Davis that he feared Charleston would be sacrificed because of Pemberton's total incompetence and his lack of knowledge of the region. Davis asked Pickens to suggest a replacement, and the governor replied that he would be pleased with Beauregard, who at first claimed his health was not the best and could not leave his army. Numerous other candidates were considered, and the process of appointing a successor dragged on. In July, General G. W. Smith was selected, but reported himself unfit for duty.[2]

Growing impatient, Pickens wrote to Davis on July 29 and again urged the selection of an "efficient" officer to replace Pemberton. Pickens could not resist adding his military advice, specifying the number and caliber of rifled cannon, columbiads, and mortars he thought were needed. He also advocated the reoccupation of Cole's and Battery Islands.

Another month passed without the appointment of a replacement. Pickens wrote again, responding to a letter from the president notifying him that he (Davis) had interviewed Pemberton and believed he was determined to hold the city of Charleston. The governor frankly told the president he was mistaken. When Pickens and the Executive Council had met with Pemberton the previous April, the general did not believe he would be able to keep the enemy out of Charleston but was willing to give General Ripley full authority to complete the works, saying, "if any man could do it he could, as he is full of energy and talent." Pickens claimed Pemberton had no plans to defend the city until General Lee ordered him to do so. No one was more astonished than Pemberton, and only then did he seriously prepare for Charleston's defense."[3]

On August 29 Special Orders, No. 202, assigned Beauregard to command the Department of South Carolina and Georgia. Pemberton, not wanting to be subservient to Beauregard, pleaded for reassignment, preferably to Virginia. On September 17, the day Ripley was wounded at Sharpsburg, Pemberton was instructed to proceed to Richmond for further orders. However, Beauregard was delayed and did not arrive in Charleston until September 24, requiring Pemberton to stay until then. On October 1 Pemberton received orders to assume command of the separate military department of the state of Mississippi and that part of Louisiana east of the Mississippi River.[4]

Following Ripley's departure for Virginia in May, the difficulties between Alfred Moore Rhett and Ransom Calhoun escalated. On August 7 Rhett was with a group of officers at the esteemed Charleston Club when the conversation turned to the abilities of the West Pointers in the command at Charleston. Captain Arnoldus Vanderhorst believed they owed much to this group, but Rhett was at times critical of West Pointers, probably in part because Calhoun was a graduate of the academy.

Vanderhorst must have known that for over a year Calhoun and Rhett had been at odds and seems to have baited Rhett. Vanderhorst claimed that Davis and Beauregard regarded Colonel Calhoun highly and had the temerity to ask Rhett what he thought of Calhoun's qualifications. Rhett frankly told him that Calhoun was a "damned puppy." A heated confrontation between Rhett and the captain ensued, escalated out of control, and ended with Vanderhorst challenging Rhett to a duel.

Horres related that on August 9, at a farm "near the present site of the Citadel," the duelists, armed with smoothbore pistols, fired two rounds; neither was hit. The "issue was declared settled without satisfaction." Calhoun learned that Rhett had insulted him and that Vanderhorst had fought a duel on his behalf. As it was customary and expected for the slandered to challenge his defamer, Calhoun, through an intermediary, accused Rhett in early September of insulting him many times and demanded redress. Rhett obliged him with a duel.

The duel, again with smoothbore pistols, was scheduled for September 5 at the Charleston Oaks Club north of Magnolia Cemetery. According to Rosen, spectators included "three state senators, the speaker of the [state] House of Representatives, and surgeons." At 5:00 P.M. "both parties fired almost simultaneously." Calhoun missed, Rhett did not, and "Calhoun died within the hour."[5]

The incident became quite a scandal, and although both men had supporters, most sided with Calhoun. Emma Holmes wrote on September 6, "The Rhetts have been hitherto hated enough, now the name is almost execrated. It is universally hoped he will be arrested, court-martialed and broken of his commission." On September 18 the Charleston coroner's inquest ruled unanimously that Major Rhett had feloniously killed Colonel Calhoun. Coroner E. M. Whiting issued arrest warrants for all parties involved, and a board of inquiry convened to hear testimony that would last nearly two months.[6]

A surgeon's certificate for fifteen days' leave had been issued to Ripley following his wounding at Sharpsburg, and on September 29, while recuperating in Richmond, Ripley learned that Beauregard had relieved Pemberton in South Carolina. Ripley soon informed Beauregard that he would like to be involved in the defenses of Charleston, and as they had had good results before, he hoped that if "associated again we should be as fortunate."

Ripley mentioned that his brigade was now under the command of Colonel George P. Doles of the 4th Georgia, whom he characterized as one of the oldest and best colonels in the service and deserving of promotion, "so no objection could arise on that score." Ripley informed Beauregard that the South Carolina and Georgia delegation in Richmond wanted him assigned to the department, and if requested, he believed the order "would be issued speedily." Ripley added that he would be fit for duty in a few days.[7]

The following day South Carolina representatives James L. Orr, W. Porcher Miles, Milledge L. Bonham, and others cosigned a letter to President Davis indicating that they were concerned the enemy would soon attack Charleston. They cited a need for experienced artillery officers, declaring, "We desire most respectfully, but earnestly request that General Ripley may, if not incompatible with public interest, be assigned to duty in the Department of South Carolina and Georgia." The representatives thought that Ripley's presence would increase the confidence of the people and the troops, and would be of great importance in Charleston's defense. They added that Beauregard and Ripley would be the most desirable combination for the city's defense.[8]

Shortly afterward, Beauregard notified Adjutant General Cooper that he would be pleased to have General Ripley assigned to his command for the defense of Charleston. As of October 8, Ripley still had not been ordered to South Carolina, and Brigadier General W. D. Smith, who was in command of the First Military District, died of yellow fever. Beauregard then began pressing authorities in Richmond for the reassignment of Ripley, and Secretary of War George W. Randolph asked Lee to telegraph him if he objected to Ripley's transfer. On October 10 Ripley received orders to proceed to South Carolina.[9]

The *Mercury* announced on October 15 that General Ripley had arrived and "was back again at the scene of his former triumph and labors, and we greet him with a hearty welcome." The article claimed that for his knowledge, good judgment, and energy, Ripley had the endorsement of Generals Beauregard, Lee, Joseph E. Johnston, and Pemberton.

Ripley reported on the sixteenth, and Special Orders, No. 195, assigned him to command the First Military District. General States Rights Gist had temporarily replaced W. D. Smith after his death, and with Ripley's arrival Gist returned to command the forces on James Island. Ripley was to focus his attention on the defenses of Charleston Harbor and have them completed as soon as possible. He was to call on Beauregard for any men and matériel needed for a prolonged resistance to any attack.[10]

Ripley asked Gist to determine what additional forces were needed for the defense of Charleston against a land attack across James Island. Gist estimated that they would need 21,850 infantry, artillery, and cavalry, but was especially concerned about the lack of heavy artillerists. Gist mentioned that he had several battalions on the mainland but that they were without guns and even if 12- and 24-pounders were supplied, he would have no artillerists to man them.

Three days later, while Beauregard inspected fortifications in the Savannah area, Federal troops were detected in the vicinity of Pocotaligo and Coosawhatchie between Savannah and Charleston. Ripley ordered Gist to move three regiments and a light battery, about two thousand men, by train to Pocotaligo to assist the local commander, Colonel W. S. Walker. By 9:00 P.M., while the troops were en route, Walker reported that he had driven off the Federals in possession of the rail lines at Coosawhatchie. By the next day the affair was over, and the enemy had reembarked.[11]

As requested, on October 25 Ripley informed Beauregard of what he would need to withstand a prolonged attack. He reiterated his belief that the attack at Secessionville would not have occurred if Cole's Island had not been abandoned. He expanded his reasons for strengthening Cole's Island, arguing that it would have forced "the base of the enemy's operations to the Edisto, keeping much difficult ground and several rivers between him and the city." With the enemy in possession of the Stono, their base of operations was within a few miles of the city, requiring extensive works and a strong force on James Island.

As to the men and matériel required for a successful, prolonged defense, Ripley gave Beauregard the numbers compiled by General Gist. With the current effective force of 4,189, they lacked nearly 17,000 troops. These numbers were accurate if a combined attack by land and sea was attempted, but Ripley doubted a combined attack would be made. He strongly believed a naval attack by the enemy's ironclad fleet was their greatest danger and discussed the pros and cons of obstructing the channels into the inner harbor. The obstructions would delay the ironclads and keep them longer under fire from the outer forts. He touched on the development of explosive obstructions but was concerned that they had not been sufficiently developed to materially help in defending the harbor. He concluded that the main defense would be the forts and batteries around the harbor. Ripley's report included a detailed analysis of the various works around the harbor and any additional measures needed to improve them. His thorough report, finished less than two weeks after assuming command, exemplifies his efforts in the defense of Charleston Harbor.

The report began with Morris Island, where Battery Wagner extended across the island at a distance of about twenty-four hundred yards from Fort Sumter. It had five mounted guns and two guns awaiting carriages. The garrison included two companies of artillery and a regiment of infantry. Ripley believed it needed "two or more long-range guns to enable the garrison to reach transports lying inside the bar." He also called for a light battery of four pieces and another company of artillery.

Breach Inlet Battery on Sullivan's Island had eight guns for the protection of the narrow inlet east of the island. One company of South Carolina infantry and two companies of the 20th South Carolina Volunteers garrisoned the installation. Although he believed the battery was quite strong and would be difficult for the enemy to drive out the garrison or dismount the guns, he recommended the addition of a long-range rifled gun.

Beauregard Battery, on Sullivan's Island, protected Fort Moultrie from a land approach from the east. It had six guns, and Ripley recommended the addition of a long-range gun but believed the present garrison was sufficient. These three outworks were designed to prevent approaches by the enemy over Morris or Sullivan's Island.

Ripley evaluated Fort Moultrie and indicated that it has mounted thirty-seven guns commanding the various channels in crossfire with Fort Sumter. Unfortunately, the fort was old and of significant value only against wooden ships. Moultrie's effect against ironclads would only come from the shock of its full battery. Ripley suggested that the six smoothbore 32-pounders, now on the fort's water faces, be rifled and banded.

Ripley considered the enfilade batteries on Sullivan's Island to be very powerful as they were armed with one 8-inch and five 10-inch columbiads. Four additional heavy guns were being added; when completed, they would require the assignment of another company to the garrison. The 20th South Carolina Volunteers and a battery of light artillery were stationed on Sullivan's Island for the support of these various positions. Ripley doubted that the enemy would attempt an amphibious landing and was against increasing the island's permanent garrison. In the case of a naval bombardment, troops outside the forts were to be positioned within Beauregard Battery. However, some of these troops, along with the light battery, were to be placed behind the sand hills to the east to prevent a landing at Breach Inlet. Ripley advised stationing troops in reserve at Mount Pleasant for the support of troops on Sullivan's Island. For this he advocated two full infantry regiments with a battalion of cavalry and two batteries of light artillery.

Fort Sumter, the main defense of the channel, required and was receiving special attention. Ripley advised strengthening the barbette batteries with as many 10-inch guns as could be procured. He advised Beauregard to rifle and band as soon as possible all 32-pounders in good condition and supply them with bolt shot for ironclad vessels. In addition, the second-tier casemates should be armed with rifled guns "as soon as they are embrasured." Ripley preferred 10-inch guns but feared they would be too heavy for the arches. Three 10-inch mortars required new beds, and all others were useless unless provided with elevating screws. He also reported that the Ordnance Department was constructing a cupola for filling shells with molten iron.

In an ominous precursor of future difficulties, Ripley lamented, "Much of the engineer work lags, and under the present arrangement" all the commanding officer can do is report. He suggested that officers of the different departments should push the work on this fort and be speedily supplied with the required matériel.

Ripley lauded the Confederate navy's ironclad gunboats, stating that, if properly manned, they would "assist in increasing the chances for a successful defense." In a final note of concern, Ripley worried that for a prolonged resistance they did not have enough powder or ammunition, not more than 100 rounds per gun. If possible, he believed that at least 150,000 pounds of powder should be available.[12]

Toward the end of October, Ripley received a letter from Colonel George Doles, now in command of his former brigade. Doles stated that the commanders and men of his regiments wished to serve in South Carolina or Georgia. Ripley remarked that, "knowing the character of the officers and men of the brigade," this unit should be included if a call was made to Virginia for troops. This did not happen, and Doles's brigade remained with the Army of Northern Virginia.[13]

While Ripley worked on the posts around Charleston Harbor, Alfred Rhett's board of inquiry continued in session. On October 30 Ripley testified on behalf of Rhett, whom Governor Pickens believed was a favorite of the general. Ripley testified that he knew there were problems between the two officers since August 1861. At that time Calhoun considered but did not bring charges against Rhett. Under cross-examination Ripley testified that he would definitely bring charges against any junior officer who was insubordinate to him. Ripley also knew that during the past spring Rhett wanted to leave the regiment rather than serve under Calhoun. Ripley testified that in the past the Articles of War against dueling were not enforced when other officers had fought them.

Rhett testified on his own behalf, claiming that Calhoun had offended him repeatedly and that it was Calhoun who challenged him to the duel, leaving him

Colonel Alfred Moore Rhett was favored by Ripley but much criticized for the dueling death of Ransom Calhoun. He commanded at Fort Sumter during the 1863 ironclad attack. After the war he married Ripley's stepdaughter, Marie Sparks, and participated in Ripley's impressive memorial service and burial. From John Johnson, Defense of Charleston Harbor, 1863–1865 (1889), facing p. 49.

Colonel ALFRED RHETT, First Regiment S. C. Artillery, Commanding Fort Sumter 1862-63. From a Photograph

no choice. However, the board ruled that it could not exonerate Rhett because he fought the duel as an officer, a violation of the Twenty-fifth Article of War, and ruled that the investigation should continue.[14]

Although Alfred Rhett may have been a favorite of Roswell Ripley, some of the Middletons did not like him at all. Harriott Middleton, Alicia Ripley's third cousin, criticized Rhett for attending a grand review at Fort Sumter during the furor over the duel: "I had no idea he would go about and amuse himself." Harriott wrote that a court-martial might follow the present inquiry but "few people seem to think he will be punished in any way for what seems to us so gross an offense."

Harriott's words were indeed prophetic. In January 1863 Beauregard closed the proceedings, ruling that it would be unjust to convict Rhett for dueling when other duels had been fought and no one was tried. However, he ruled that in the future any duels would be subject to the Articles of War.[15]

On October 31, the day after Ripley testified before the board, he reviewed the 1st Regiment, South Carolina Artillery, garrisoned at Fort Sumter. The *Mercury* reported that on this "bright and balmy day" with a large number of ladies present, Ripley "looked as fine as a fiddle and performed his part with style. The splendid corps at the post appeared to be at a great advantage before their original and honored commander." A band added much spirit to the occasion, and after the exercises on the parade ground, "guns were fired for the benefit of the ladies." A luncheon topped off the occasion.[16]

Rather surprisingly, about a month after Ripley returned to Charleston, Governor Pickens wrote him a welcoming letter. He believed that Ripley would add a new chapter to the laurels he had achieved at Fort Moultrie. Ripley was now where his "talents were eminently suited." If he succeeded in defending the harbor against the enemy's heavy ironclads, he would be "at the head of the Artillery Captains of America."[17]

Early in November, less than a month after Ripley returned to Charleston and while he was evaluating the defenses of Charleston Harbor, Colonel Ambrosio Gonzales filed a scathing report against him. Gonzales, a childhood friend of Beauregard's, now served as Beauregard's chief of artillery. Gonzales criticized the condition of a company on the South Carolina siege train and censured Ripley's conduct. Beauregard directed Ripley to correct the condition of the company but reprimanded Gonzales for the report as the "tone and temper shown are not those of an official paper intended for the files of this office." De la Cova, in his excellent biography, surmised that Gonzales's report, which has not been found, "probably mentioned Ripley's alcoholism problems."

Ripley was definitely quite social, had a fondness for alcohol, and apparently favored whiskey; but the contention that he was an alcoholic is questionable. He was quite functional and his accomplishments and productivity weaken the accusation. However, his drinking gave his detractors an opportunity to criticize him. Ripley, who befriended and aided Gonzales in early 1862, must have been infuriated that his supposed friend, a colonel, had attacked him so vehemently. The report effectively ended their friendship.[18]

During the last two weeks of November, Major F. L. Childs, in charge of the Charleston Arsenal, again began thwarting Ripley's efforts. Now he not only defied Ripley but also questioned and refused to obey Beauregard's orders. The commanding general explained the situation in a letter to Adjutant General Cooper.

On November 20 Beauregard decided that not enough heavy-caliber guns could be obtained for the defense of the harbor. Following Ripley's advice, he planned to have many of the 32- and 42-pounders already in place dismounted, banded, and rifled. The arsenal's first attempt to band and rifle a 32-pounder took over four weeks. With a total of at least twenty more guns to be modified, it was evident that it would take much too long for the armory to complete the job with the "pressing emergencies of our situation." Ripley notified Beauregard that he could have the cannon modified in less than half the time taken by the ordnance department if Beauregard would place the matter under his control. Believing the work needed to be done as soon as possible, Beauregard issued Special Orders, No. 229, Part III of which granted Ripley that control and allowed him to make requisitions directly upon the arsenal or other sources for any matériel needed.

Ripley quickly had several 42-pounders dismounted and transferred to Messrs. Eason & Company's foundry. When Ripley called on Major Childs to provide two sets of 42-pounder bands, Childs refused and questioned Beauregard's intent to "devolve any portion of my duties upon Ripley." Childs argued that Ripley violated "the reiterated orders and regulations of the Ordnance Bureau." Beauregard tersely informed Childs that S.O., No. 229, issued from his headquarters, "shall be carried into effect."

To resolve the impasse, Beauregard asked both Ripley and Childs how quickly the work could be done under each officer's supervision. Ripley claimed that he could have the two guns currently at the foundry done in nine days, then turn one or two guns out every five or seven days. Beauregard deemed Ripley's response to be better than Childs's proposal and chose Ripley to "direct these important alterations."

In protest, Childs visited Beauregard on or about November 23 and stated that the ordnance department would not pay for alterations unless he ordered them. Beauregard informed Childs that he would get the money either from the state or the city of Charleston, as the altered guns were intended only for the defense of Charleston Harbor. On November 26 Childs again rejected Ripley's requisition for bands until he could talk with Beauregard.

Ripley went to the arsenal with an armed force to compel Childs to comply. When Childs again refused to issue the bands, Ripley arrested him. The next officer in rank pointed out the bands, which were taken to the foundry and the awaiting guns. Although under arrest, Major Childs continued to work at the arsenal but was confined to the city. Ripley preferred charges against Childs, but Beauregard deferred ordering a court-martial until he received instructions from the War Department.

Then, on November 30 Beauregard included an addendum to his letter to General Cooper. He did not think that Childs appreciated the gravity of his offense and "seems to think that the ordnance department was created solely for the special benefit of its officers." Beauregard claimed that he would press charges himself and requested that the War Department order "the assembling of a court for his immediate trial."[19]

On December 11 Childs informed his wife that "Col. Gorgas is highly indignant at the conduct of Ripley and Beauregard." Gorgas had a poor opinion of Ripley, with which Childs agreed. "Beauregard is probably arrogant, but not malicious," he added. Childs continued working at the arsenal through February, and on April 17, 1863, to the relief of Beauregard and Ripley, Childs received orders to relieve Colonel Langnel, commander of the Fayetteville, North Carolina, Arsenal and Armory.[20]

With the approach of the 1862 Christmas season, Ripley held a "grand dinner at the Hotel," most likely either the Charleston Hotel or the Mills House, as both had survived the great fire the previous year. Ripley arranged to have six carriages available to take the guests home. The French ship *Milan* was in harbor and its captain, who had previously been impressed with an earlier party at Fort Sumter, asked for a copy of the elaborate bill of fare. He claimed that he wanted to show it to "those damned Yankees at Washington who tend to believe you are all starving down here."

In December, Susan Middleton mentioned to her cousin that "when the Federal fleet left Port Royal some time ago, Ripley spent the whole night on the parapet at Fort Sumter." The general thought, or so Mrs. Ripley told a friend, that with a high tide and bright moon, "they [the Yankees] might be mad enough to make an entrance under such favorable circumstances. So he kept a look-out for them himself." Susan asked Harriott whether she liked "Timrod's verses to Ripley? If they are poetry, he must be a poet indeed, to be inspired by that bull-headed fighter."[21]

Henry Timrod, a native of Charleston, had abandoned the study of law to become a private tutor, while successfully writing poetry. He worked for a time as a war correspondent for the *Mercury* with the army in the West. Timrod departed Charleston just after the Battle of Shiloh, carrying letters of introduction from Ripley and others to present to General Beauregard. Susan referred to the poem "Ripley" by Timrod, who was then considered the "poet laureate" of the Confederacy. The poem had been printed in an early December edition of the *Mercury*, in honor of Ripley's return to Charleston.[22]

On Christmas Eve Colonel Keitt presented Ripley with a beautiful bay horse from the Honorable John P. Kinard, who had been quartermaster of Colonel Keitt's 20th South Carolina Infantry. Kinard expressed his gratitude for Ripley's "zeal, ability, and skill he devoted to our State and our common cause." Ripley acknowledged Kinard's "splendid present" and asked Colonel Keitt to give Kinard his warmest regards. Ripley owned a horse before Kinard's gift; his stable would eventually hold four horses, with the addition of a horse in April and one in July.[23]

In October 1862 Ripley returned to Charleston, requested and welcomed by Governor Pickens and General Beauregard, as well as by many appreciative subordinate officers and local citizens. He had survived Colonel Gonzales's report, the confrontation with Major Childs, and the turmoil of the Rhett inquiry. The year 1863 would be even more tumultuous.

> RIPLEY
> By Henry Timrod
> Rich in red honors, that upon him lie
> As lightly as the summer dews
> Fall where he won his fame beneath the sky
> Of tropic Vera Cruz;
>
> Bold scorner of the cant that has its birth
> In feeble or failing powers;

A lover of all frank and genial mirth
That wreathes the sword with flowers;

He moves amid the warriors of the day,
Just such a soldier as the art
That builds its trophies upon human clay
Moulds of a cheerful heart.

I see him in the battle that shall shake,
Ere long, old Sumter's haughty crown,
And from their dreams of peaceful traffic wake
The wharves of yonder town;

As calm as one would greet a pleasant guest,
And quaff a cup to love and life,
He hurls his deadliest thunders with a jest,
And laughs amid the strife.

Yet not the gravest soldier of them all
Surveys a field with broader scope;
And who behind that sea-encircled wall
Fights with a loftier hope?

Gay Chieftain! on the crimson rolls of Fame
Thy deeds are written with a sword;
But there are gentler thoughts which, with thy name,
Thy country's page shall hoard.

A nature of that rare and happy cast
Which looks, unsteeled, on murder's face;
Through what dark scenes of bloodshed hast thou passed,
Yet lost no social grace?

So, when the bard depicts thee, thou shalt wield
The weapon of a tyrant's doom,
Round which, inscribed with many a well-fought field,
The rose of joy shall bloom.[24]

CHAPTER 17

The Impending Storm

The day after Christmas 1862, Ripley wrote a circular with instructions for the commanding officers of the forts and batteries around the harbor. These instructions were to be carefully followed if the officers had little warning of an attack. Commanders were to immediately begin strengthening their gun carriages and preparing their ordnance. Ripley called for the inspection of all elevating screws, eccentric wheels, and traversing gears, which were to be kept in order. Ammunition was to be inspected and apportioned to the guns of the battery, with a greater portion going to the heavier guns. When an alarm sounded, the officers and men were to go immediately to their guns, which should be ready for action when they arrived. Ripley believed that most of these things were already in practice but also that "constant vigilance is our only security."

With the threat of an attack, the first battery or fort nearest the enemy was to give the alarm, by day a fired gun and a dipping of the flag and by night a fired gun and a rocket. The enemy was to be engaged accurately and as soon as possible, with each commander determining the number of guns brought to bear. Ripley went into detail on the use of the distance buoys in the harbor to determine range and elevation. Wooden vessels were to be hit "near the water-line just abaft of the smoke-stack." Ironclads should be hit on the turrets at the intersection with the deck, which would impair turret revolution, or on the ports of the turrets to throw the machinery for closing the ports "out of gear." Fire was to be concentrated on the leading vessels, but if any of the vessels succeeded in passing, firing should be controlled by the commanding officers of the battery. Obviously, the fire should be directed at the vessel nearest the battery involved.

Ripley designated "circles of fire" through which enemy vessels would be forced to pass on the main ship channel. The guns of the first circle of fire would be those of Beauregard Battery, Fort Moultrie, and Battery Bee opposite the northeastern, eastern, and northwestern faces of Fort Sumter. Sumter would complete the first circle. All mortars of Sumter and Moultrie would be trained on the center of this circle. The mortar batteries were to be fired when the targeted vessel was about two ships' lengths from the point of impact.

If the attacking fleet was large, Ripley ordered the mortars of Fort Sumter to remain trained on the same point in the first circle. If the fleet was small, the mortars of Fort Sumter were to be trained on vessels that passed through the first circle and on the center of the second circle of fire. The second circle was to be formed by the heavy guns of Forts Johnson and Ripley, Castle Pinckney, Battery Bee, and the northwestern and western faces of Fort Sumter. The guns of Fort Johnson, Fort Ripley, and Castle Pinckney were to open fire on the leading vessels when they were within range. The guns of Sumter and Bee should continue firing on the leading vessels if they remained in range.

If any vessels passed through the second circle, they would enter the rapidly forming third circle of White Point Battery and Battery Glover, along with any guns of Forts Johnson and Ripley and Castle Pinckney as could bear. Obviously, the fire was to be concentrated on the leading vessels. Ripley stressed the importance of accuracy when the enemy was between batteries and that care be taken not to fire on their own works. If the Confederate navy was engaged, Ripley wanted battery fire discontinued when a ship was in close quarters with an enemy ironclad.

Ripley expected the plunging fire from the barbettes of Sumter to be especially effective. He advocated hitting the roofs of the turrets with "square-headed bolts, followed by shells filled with molten iron." He stressed the importance of maintaining furnaces for melting iron and heating shot. If any disabled vessels attempted to escape the fire, or if any vessel came to their aid, "let every gun and mortar that will bear be turned upon them by battery."

Ripley believed the main objective of the enemy would be to run by the batteries and that every effort be made to crush them in each successive circle of fire they entered. The commanders would be told the location of the torpedoes (mines), and every effort should be made to drive the vessels into them. The obstructions would also be designated and, Ripley commanded, "under no circumstance will the enemy be permitted to reconnoiter them."

Ripley announced that his headquarters would be at Fort Sumter, and should anyone require special directions, he would send them by telegraph and signal. Ripley ordered all officers involved in this "honorable" defense to study the circular: "With careful attention, coolness, and skilled gunnery, success is far more than probable." The circular indicated that Ripley did not intend to just open fire on the enemy but had developed a concise plan involving all his batteries and integrating his ordnance: mortars, smooth-bore guns, and rifled cannon.[1]

January 1863 was a busy month for Ripley, who was involved in many aspects of managing the First Military District. Colonel Charles H. Simonton notified Ripley of serious problems with the commissary on James Island. The men were on half rations of coffee, flour, candles, and soap. More important, their only food was "inferior quality" beef, rice, and grits. Simonton learned that fresh pork, bacon, and excellent beef were available if Ripley allowed Captain Ryan, the post commissary officer, to make direct contracts for the items. With his disgust for red tape, Ripley of course acquiesced; and Major Guerin, chief of subsistence in the department, responded positively when Ryan contacted him.

However, the process was stopped when orders from Richmond relieved Ryan from duty. Ripley thought that the commissary situation on James Island was bad but that "I have never heard the fault lay with Captain Ryan." Ripley believed that restrictions adopted by the department in Richmond were the cause of the problem and asked Beauregard to intercede on Ryan's behalf: "It is very certain that under the arrangements made at Richmond, the troops . . . are in fact only living from hand to mouth."[2]

Early in the month Ripley ordered Colonel L. M. Keitt to examine the countryside between Mount Pleasant and South Santee River, inspect the troops, and record their positions. Keitt studied the area and reported that there was little likelihood Charleston would be attacked from that direction. However, he believed there were opportunities "for plundering expeditions from Bull Island." Keitt recommended establishing a fixed battery on the Santee River and to cover it and close the river to all but ironclad boats. He also wanted measures taken to prevent African Americans from being induced to desert to the enemy. Ripley endorsed Keitt's report, forwarded it to department headquarters, and also suggested he would increase the cavalry force in that area. Beauregard decided that the cavalry could not be spared and disapproved the proposed artillery for the Santee River.[3]

Ripley reviewed the garrison at Fort Sumter on January 19. Spectators included the Marquis of Hartington; Colonel Charles Leslie, commander of the British steamer *Petrel,* and Frank Vizetelly, artist and correspondent for the *Illustrated London Times.* Vizetelly had recently arrived in Charleston and established his residence at the Charleston Hotel. After presenting his credentials to Beauregard and Ripley, he went to work sketching the harbor forts, with the French sloop *Milan* and the HMS *Petrel* at anchor in the harbor.[4]

Private Augustine T. Smythe, an intelligent and literate member of the Signal Corps described the foreign vessels and the *Petrel*'s armament. Colonel Leslie was disappointed that he was unable to hold gunnery practice for Generals Beauregard and Ripley, but noted that the other night "there was quite a pleasant entertainment on the English frigate" attended by Ripley and his staff, several of Beauregard's staff, and a great many ladies.

Also in January, Ripley responded to General Gist's concerns that there were not enough artillerists to man the guns. A few days after the Sumter review, he ordered Company E, First Charleston Battalion, to move from its camp in a lumberyard to White Point Garden. They were to man the guns in the battery and drill as heavy artillery. Ripley's order was promptly carried out the next day.[5]

During the month of January, vessels of the South Atlantic Blockading Squadron, headquartered at Port Royal Harbor, made numerous incursions up the Stono and other rivers along the coast. One of the most prominent vessels involved was the gunboat *Isaac Smith*, which ranged freely up and down the Stono, shelling the Confederate forces on James Island.

In response to these incursions, Beauregard ordered Ripley to prepare boats or barges with muffled oars for a surprise night attack on the *Smith*. Indications are that Ripley developed a better plan. He preferred placing eight or ten guns in masked positions on the west side of the Stono, having the guns placed quickly overnight, and then concealed. Beauregard approved Ripley's plan if the ground provided cover for such an attack. Beauregard left the details of the attack to Ripley, who selected Lieutenant Colonel Joseph Yates of the 1st South Carolina Artillery to coordinate the plan.

The "secret expedition" was composed of artillery companies from the Palmetto Light Artillery Battalion and the 1st South Carolina Artillery, as well as companies from the 20th South Carolina Infantry acting as sharpshooters. The Federal gunboat, mounting a single 30-pound Parrott in the bow and eight 8-inch columbiads, came up the Stono, passed the masked batteries, and anchored slightly above them. Batteries on the James Island side of the river immediately fired on the gunboat, and as the ship attempted to flee down the river, three shots from a masked battery disabled it. The *Smith* dropped anchor and unconditionally surrendered its entire crew "consisting of 11 officers, 105 sailors, and 3 [African Americans]." Yates reported the enemy's loss to be 25 killed and wounded while his command had 1 man mortally wounded.[6]

The capture of the *Isaac Smith* was not without problems. Ripley received a dispatch from Yates informing him that he was out of ammunition and that there were two more Union boats on the Stono. Yates first thought to destroy the gunboat and retire, but Ripley telegraphed him that he was sending a boat with ammunition at once. The light-draft *Sumter*, bringing forty 8-inch shells, was to be alongside the *Isaac Smith* in about three hours. Ripley planned to have the *Sumter* tow the prize gunboat to Fort Pemberton at flood tide.

This unique capture of a heavily armed gunboat by land batteries not only exemplifies Ripley's resourcefulness but also his willingness to praise and credit his subordinates. Ripley believed that "the successful capture of the steamer reflects the highest credit on the officers and men engaged" and heartily concurred with the commendations forwarded by their respective commanders. Ripley sent the captured commander's sword, along with flags from the steamer, to Beauregard. The *Isaac Smith* was repaired and rechristened the *Stono,* but while attempting to run the blockade, it was forced aground near Fort Moultrie. The *Stono* was refloated later and used as a gunboat in Charleston Harbor.[7]

Buoyed by Ripley's performance in general and his part in the successful capture of the *Isaac Smith*, Beauregard petitioned General Cooper to promote "Brigadier General Ripley as Major General." Beauregard praised Ripley's performance in the reduction of Fort Sumter at the onset of the war and recognized that he held important commands in the battles around Richmond and in the Maryland Campaign.

Beauregard reasoned, "In his present command, as important if not more so than is entrusted to any Major General in the service, he is daily giving the Country and myself, the benefit of his administrative talent and resources, and the untiring energy and zeal in the discharge of his duties as Commander of the First Military District. . . . In numbers his command is that of a Major General." Cooper, likely remembering Ripley's past U.S. Army leave manipulations and his involvement of Secretary of War Conrad and President Fillmore in his resignation process, failed to approve the request.[8]

At about 5:00 A.M., the day after capturing the *Isaac Smith*, Confederate naval forces attacked the Blockading Squadron off Charleston harbor. The *Chicora* and the *Palmetto State* damaged, but did not sink, the *Mercedita* and set fire to another vessel. Beauregard notified General Cooper that the enemy's whole fleet was dispersed north and south and that he planned to proclaim the blockade of Charleston had been lifted.

Beauregard claimed that the rule of public law required foreign nations to be notified that a new blockade was in place before they were obliged to obey it. He then informed the consuls of France and Spain that the blockade had been lifted. Both sailed out of the harbor with Ripley and verified that the blockade appeared to be over. The British consul independently verified that the blockading squadron had been dispersed. However, the respite was short-lived, and the blockade was reapplied that afternoon.[9]

Despite the disappointment in the reinstitution of the blockade, a degree of normalcy returned to Charleston in February. The French frigate *Milan* remained in the harbor, and a "magnificent" dinner was held for Captain Dubuquois and the French consul, Monsieur St. Andre. Ripley would have been among the thirty attendees, and nearly all present thought that "an alliance offensive and defensive has been made, or will very shortly be made, by our Minister, Mr. Slidell, with the French government." Officers of the *Petrel* believed the British government would recognize the Confederacy during the month. To their chagrin, France and England would never recognize the Confederacy.[10]

In 1862 Harriott Middleton, who usually spent summers with her family at Flat Rock, North Carolina, escaped the war in Charleston and moved to that popular retreat. Susan Middleton moved to Columbia at about the same time and continued to relay news and gossip from Charleston. Although popular, Ripley was not free of criticism. In February, Susan alleged that Ripley was engaged in speculation and had shipped a load of cotton through the blockade, clearing "$30,000 in the transaction." In a thrust at the socially active Ripley, when someone at a staff ball asked Beauregard whether he danced, he replied that he did but "this does not seem to me to be a time for dancing."[11]

An incident later in the month confirmed Ripley's strong anti-Union fervor. The steamer *Flambeau* approached Fort Sumter flying a white flag. When notified, Ripley ordered Sumter to keep the ship "at a proper distance." Unknown to Ripley, batteries on Sullivan's Island had fired at the steamer, and the fourth shot caused it to drop anchor. The indignant captain claimed to be bringing mail for the commander of the HMS *Petrel* and for Union prisoners captured on the Stono. The captain was informed that in the future, Sumter would hoist a white flag in response to any such attempt. Only then could they send a boat to meet a Confederate vessel at the mouth of Maffitt's Channel.

Ripley investigated the shots fired from Sullivan's Island and found the commanding officer had indeed seen *Flambeau*'s white flag. However, after the *Flambeau* launched a boat for the purpose of taking soundings in the channel, he opened fire. Ripley concluded that the enemy had used the situation to reconnoiter and that the shots fired were justified. Ripley denounced "the practice of allowing the enemy to communicate with this port by flag of truce and it should be stopped."[12]

Beauregard sent Lieutenant Colonel Alfred Roman to inspect Fort Sumter, then under the command of Colonel Alfred Rhett. Ripley had appointed Rhett to the command after the dueling charges were dismissed in January. Roman reported that Sumter was "a model of order and good management, the best school of discipline and military bearing, and held by the first and most efficient military garrison of the South. The seven companies of the First South Carolina Artillery now at Fort Sumter have no rivals."

Ripley instructed General Gist to make a thorough, personal inspection of all the works on James Island and the adjacent St. Andrew's Parish. Gist responded on March 3 with a detailed report on the condition of defenses at Fort Johnson and Batteries Glover and Means. He studied the three miles of James Island defensive lines, Secessionville, and Fort Lamar, as well as Fort Pemberton on the western edge of James Island at a bend in the Stono River. Gist hoped the advanced line of defense could be reestablished upon Cole's Island and the Stono once again freed from Yankee gunboats. Gist believed this would reduce to one-third the garrison required for the defense of James Island. This could be categorized as wishful thinking; because of Pemberton's ill-fated move, Cole's Island was lost forever.[13]

In early March, Gist offered his opinion that Savannah was probably not going to be attacked even though the enemy had concentrated their fleet at Port Royal. Gist was concerned that Confederate forces were too widely dispersed covering Savannah and Charleston, and believed the enemy probably knew or could easily determine that Charleston was almost without troops. According to Gist, it would take at least six days to concentrate their forces at some point on the railroad or in Charleston, the most important point. Ripley concurred and recommended that Beauregard should keep a permanent force of infantry in position on James Island, not to be moved unless the enemy attacked elsewhere. Beauregard responded dismissively, "The general commanding will be happy to have the opinions of his subordinate officers at the proper time." This brusque reply may very well be indicative of the schism developing between Ripley and Beauregard.[14]

Around this time Susan forwarded to Harriott in Flat Rock a bit of gossip possibly confirming Ripley's $30,000 profit from running cotton through the blockade. She wrote, "Ripley has offered Mr. Wm. Ravenel 25,000 dollars for the Roper House and has been refused." The Roper House was built in 1838 and named after its original owner. It still stands, an elegant, three-story structure on East Battery facing Charleston Harbor and Fort Sumter.

A week later Susan informed Harriott that she had heard of an "infernal machine" developed by Ripley: "He has filled an old boiler with 10,000 pounds of gunpowder and is to sink it in the channel." A wire, which Ripley had ordered from New York over a year earlier, had finally arrived and would lead from Fort Sumter to the sunken boiler. When a Yankee vessel was over the "contrivance," an electric spark from the fort would blow "whatever is passing above to atoms."[15]

On March 12, 1863, in a seemingly spiteful response to Gist and Ripley's report, Beauregard appointed a board of general officers to meet in Charleston as soon as possible. Beauregard may have decided that if Ripley and Gist had time to send him suggestions, he would give them something to occupy their time. The committee included Generals Ripley, Gist, and J. H. Trapier, with Ripley serving as president.

They were to discuss six points raised by the commanding general for the defense of Charleston. The first four points involved a detailed summary of the works and heavy ordnance needed for an "efficient defense" of the harbor. Point five asked whether additional artillery and infantry were needed. Point six concerned the number of African Americans called for in the past four months, the number received, and the average number employed monthly.

Undaunted, the committee met promptly and reported to Beauregard on March 16. The board answered points one and two together. They acknowledged that General Pemberton had requested heavy ordnance for the defense of the outer harbor but had placed most emphasis on a chain and boom obstruction then being constructed at the mouth of the harbor. Pemberton intended the obstruction to detain an attacking fleet and keep it under fire from the forts. In early October 1862, after much time had been spent on the obstruction, it proved to be a failure. When Beauregard assumed command, he ordered fifty-one 10-inch columbiads added to ten ordered by Pemberton, plus a number of 10-inch seacoast mortars.

The board reported that since June 1862 the ordnance department in Charleston had received from Richmond seventeen 10-inch columbiads, two 42-pounder banded and rifled guns, two 7-inch banded Brooke guns, two 12-pounder banded and rifled guns, and eight 10-inch seacoast mortars. Three other guns were imported during this time period. The board criticized the Charleston Arsenal Works for failing to cast the 15-inch guns authorized three months earlier. The board blamed the delay on a disagreement between ordnance officers and the arsenal mechanics. In summarizing points one and two, the board concluded that there was a deficiency of thirty-eight 10-inch columbiads.

As for point three, the board decided that the works constructed and planned for the water approaches to Charleston could be adequately armed with the guns on order. The generals agreed that no heavy artillery should be ordered until the current orders were filled. The board recommended adding four more 10-inch columbiads to Battery Bee and two more columbiads to both Fort Moultrie and Castle Pinckney. They believed that the advanced post at Battery Marshall required the addition of two movable long-range guns. Works at Light House Inlet and the seafront at Battery Wagner should be strengthened. For the lines of defense in Christ Church and St. Andrews Parish, the board decided that the siege train should be added to the guns already in place. The siege train currently had eight 8-inch siege howitzers and four rifled 12-pounders; the board believed its armament should be increased as much as possible with guns of a similar caliber.

Regarding point four, the board advocated the erection of new works in the vicinity of Fort Johnson. They envisioned building five detached works, about 100 to 150 yards apart along the James Island shore, each armed with one 10-inch columbiad. The generals concurred that if possible, the enemy should be expelled from Cole's Island. If retaking Cole's Island was "impracticable," labor should be procured, with troops, African Americans, or both engaged to build strong a work at Grimball's plantation on James Island. In addition, a short line of defense should be erected from Secessionville (Fort Lamar) to Grimball's. The board unanimously deemed the location of Fort Pemberton to be a mistake, as it could not prevent enemy incursions onto James Island farther down the Stono. The board also advised the strengthening of White Point Battery.

With respect to point five and the need for additional forces, the generals reminded Beauregard of the detailed study Ripley and Gist had compiled and submitted to him in October 1862. The effective force had increased from 4,189 to 10,513, partly because of regimental conscripts and recruits but principally because of the reinforcement of Brigadier General Thomas L. Clingman's command. Seven hundred infantrymen, it was noted, were acting as heavy artillery. The board estimated that the present forces probably still lacked 16,563 men and concluded that two strong brigades should be added without delay. They estimated the strength of the enemy to be between 35,000 and 40,000 men, while Admiral Du Pont's fleet had at least six monitors and one ironclad battery.

Responding to point six, the board estimated that 11,000 black laborers had been requisitioned during the past four months, for an average of 2,750 per month. The numbers actually received during the entire four-month period was 2,833; however, 843 were sick and had to be returned. The average monthly labor force for the previous four months had been 755, a shortage of nearly 2,000 laborers per month.

A short time later Beauregard accepted the report and especially regretted the delay in producing the 15-inch columbiads. Beauregard approved the suggested increase in the strength of the siege-train battery, claiming that he had long contemplated the need for the shore batteries at Fort Johnson but that they were delayed by the lack of labor. The "scarcity of Negro labor has materially crippled the artificial defenses of Charleston," he wrote.

Beauregard admitted that it would be of great importance to repossess the Stono. He lamented the abandonment of Cole's Island before works at a narrower part of the river above Cole's Island had been strengthened. The poor location of Fort Pemberton now gave the enemy access to both sides of the Lower Stono. To also defend Savannah, Beauregard could only supply, on short notice, ten thousand of the projected sixteen thousand men needed at Charleston.[16]

In addition to this laborious committee work, Beauregard ordered Ripley to "organize and train at least six boarding boat parties" for the purpose of carrying out night attacks against any monitor successful in penetrating the harbor. The oars of the boats should be muffled, and not surprisingly the crews were to be volunteers only. The parties would be armed with revolvers, provided with blankets to cover all the monitor's apertures, and given sledges to drive iron wedges under the turrets to prevent them from revolving. The boarding parties were to carry bottles of "burning fluid" to throw into the tower and leather bags of powder to throw down the smokestack. Within two months, Ripley had enough volunteers from Keitt and Colquitt's regiments to man any number of boats provided. Ripley planned to have the men instructed by naval officers, but if asked, he would take charge of the project himself. There seems to be no record as to whether this rather strange idea ever came to fruition.

Beauregard responded to a letter from Congressman W. Porcher Miles, claiming that he was now charged with defending Charleston and Savannah with fewer men and against more of the enemy than confronted Robert E. Lee: "I have now done all that I could to procure more troops from the Confederate Government and from this State. If I meet with a disaster under the present circumstances the responsibility will not rest on my shoulders." The commanding general once again added that Ripley should have been promoted to major general.

On March 27 Ripley warned the commanders of the subdivisions within his First Military District that "the approach of the enemy northward from Port Royal might indicate a speedy attack on the city of Charleston." He urged all guards and pickets, as well as the commanding officers, to exercise the utmost vigilance.[17]

On April 5 the British war correspondent Frank Vizetelly hurried north from Savannah to Charleston and sent a dispatch to the *Illustrated London News:*

> At length the long expected moment has arrived.... I have every faith in the result of the coming encounter, for never at any time have the Confederates been more determined to do or die than they express themselves now. Every preparation has been made, every appliance pressed into service by General Ripley to give the foe a warm reception.... his zeal and success seem perfectly wonderful. As he expresses it, he will "fight it low down" until not a brick nor stone is left for another to rest upon before he gives in. If the mail-clad monsters now in the offing are repulsed, it will be to General Ripley and the brave men under him that victory will be due.[18]

CHAPTER 18

Attack of the Ironclads

During these months, while Ripley was engaged in strengthening the defenses of the First Military District, the Federal South Atlantic Blockading Squadron, under the command of Rear Admiral Samuel F. Du Pont, increased their presence at Port Royal Harbor. At times as many as fifteen ships maintained the blockade of Charleston, and the squadron placed ships at nearly every important sound and inlet along the Carolina and nearby Georgia coast.

In early January, Secretary of the Navy Gideon Welles ordered the *New Ironsides* and the "Passaic class" monitors *Passaic, Montauk, Patapsco, Weehawken,* and *Nahant,* each with a two-gun revolving turret, to Port Royal. Welles believed this would enable Du Pont "to enter the harbor of Charleston and demand the surrender of all its defenses or suffer the consequences of a refusal." Welles believed Savannah should be attacked next, "under the panic produced by the fall of Charleston."

Not being especially seaworthy, the monitors were towed from Hampton Roads, Virginia, to Port Royal. After their arrival the *Montauk* and *Passaic* were put into action southeast of Savannah on Ossabaw and Wassaw Sounds. In late January the *Montauk* bombarded Fort McAllister on the Ogeechee River, not far from Savannah. In that action the *Montauk* received thirteen hits from the rebel artillery in what Du Pont termed "preliminary experiments in view of the attacks to be made upon Charleston."[1]

Du Pont, "after very mature deliberation," decided to also test the monitors *Patapsco, Passaic,* and *Nahant* against Fort McAllister. In early March, Welles notified Du Pont that his squadron would include, in addition to the *New Ironsides* and monitors, the fixed, double-turreted, ironclad floating battery the *Keokuk.* Given Port Royal's proximity to Savannah and the heavy Federal attacks in that area, it was not clear to Beauregard where the enemy would strike next. As a result, he struggled to defend both Savannah and Charleston.[2]

By the middle of March, the seven monitors were undergoing repairs and taking on provisions. According to one of the navy engineers, the three monitors that recently attacked Fort McAllister were "struck by scores of balls, but none of them were damaged, and all proved to be impregnable." Du Pont "crawled on all fours" to see for himself and saw it differently, especially with regard to the *Montauk,* which had been in three attacks and was actually heavily damaged. When the *Keokuk* arrived eleven days later, Commander A. C. Rhind reported that the vessel was good and safe at sea and had steamed to Port Royal without a convoy. In late March, Beauregard learned that Du Pont's squadron was rendezvousing at the North Edisto, and on April 1 the *Passaic, Patapsco, Montauk,* and *Keokuk* also received orders to proceed to the rendezvous.[3]

On March 31 the *Mercury* reported that the French war steamer *Milan* had been ordered "to leave the harbor without delay. Rough weather prevented the departure yesterday, but the steamer would be leaving today, carrying off the French Consul, Vice-Consul, their families and effects." The reason for the hasty departure would soon be obvious.[4]

Early on Sunday, April 5, the attacking fleet of monitors, ironclad vessels, transports, and Admiral Du Pont's flagship, the *New Ironsides,* arrived off the Charleston bar. To acknowledge the fleet's presence, the men of the 1st South Carolina Artillery at Fort Sumter fired a salute, hoisted the Confederate flag, the South Carolina flag, and their regimental colors. Ripley had supervised the training of these 550 men and eighty guns, now under the direct command of Colonel Alfred Rhett.

The first attempt to attack was postponed because of the presence of a heavy haze, but on a clear and mild April 7, the attack began. Du Pont planned to steam past the Morris Island batteries directly toward Fort Sumter. He intended to steam past Sumter, reach its northwest side, and take up a position within Charleston Harbor. The nine attacking vessels formed a single line in the following order: *Weehawken, Passaic, Montauk, Patapsco,* and the flagship *New Ironsides,* followed by the *Catskill, Nantucket, Nahant,* and finally the *Keokuk.*[5]

Neither side fired a shot until the lead monitor neared Fort Sumter. Evidently, Fort Moultrie fired the first shot at the out-of-range *Weehawken,* and the *Passaic,* second in line, answered Moultrie. The *Weehawken* then began firing at Sumter before it reached a Confederate marker buoy placed at a distance of 1,120 yards from the fort. At this point the *Weehawken* entered Ripley's first "circle of fire," and Sumter began firing on the leading monitor. Batteries Bee and Beauregard, as well as Fort Moultrie, also shelled the *Weehawken.*[6]

At about this time Du Pont's flagship began having trouble, floundered, nearly "bottomed out," and drifted backwards in the main channel. The Confederates believed the flagship now floated near a huge boiler-torpedo, eighteen feet long, three feet in diameter, and filled with three thousand pounds of powder. In March, Ripley ordered the torpedo's construction and, a few days before the attack, positioned it at a specific point in the main ship channel. Anchored there, it would be exploded by an electric current passed by underwater electric cable from Battery Wagner.

All attempts to generate an electric current were unsuccessful, and Ripley's torpedo failed to explode. Assistant Engineer De Lisle originally thought the failure might have been due to a leak in the boiler, a break in the underwater cable,

Defense of Charleston Harbor
April 7, 1863

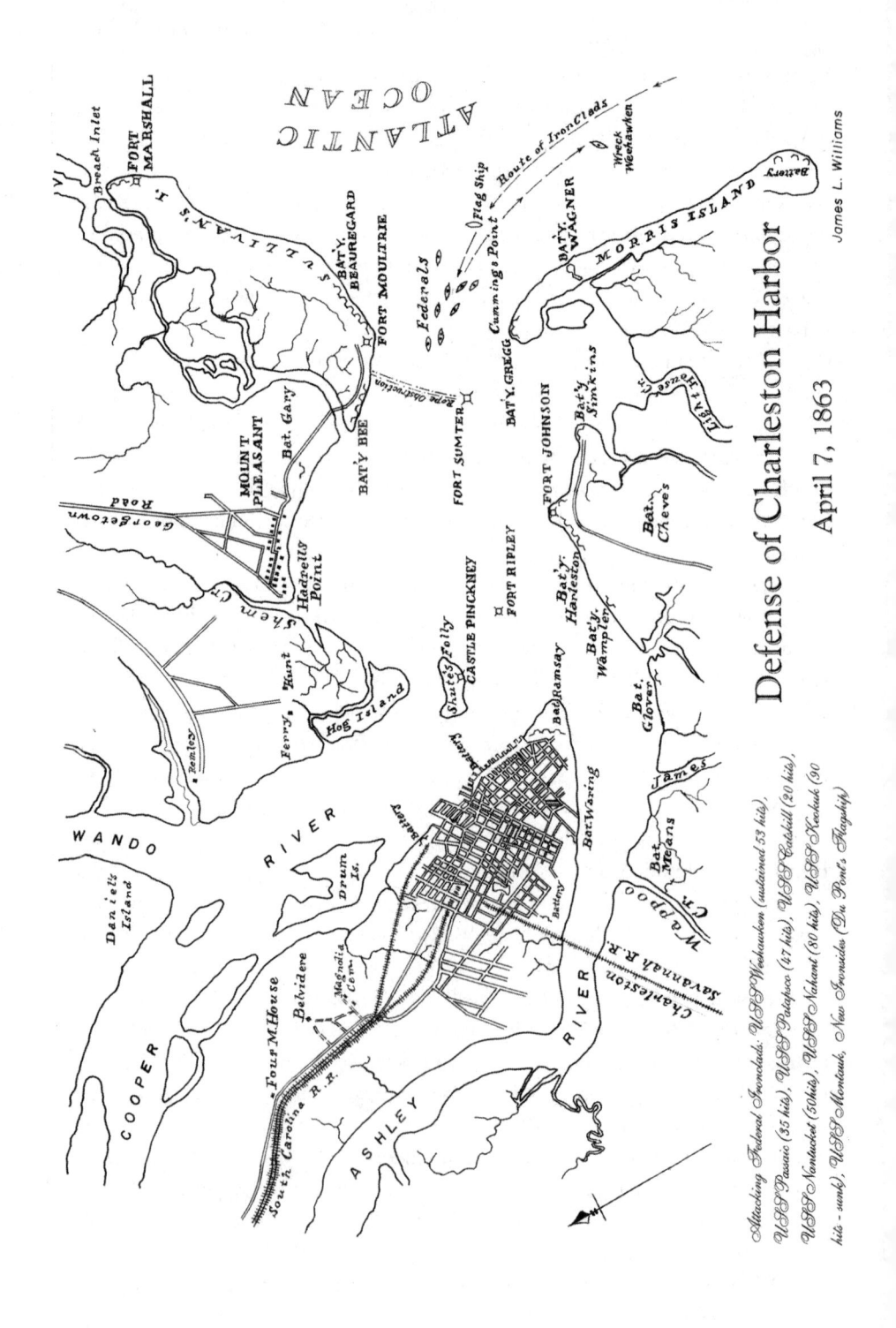

James L. Williams

Attacking Federal Ironclads: USS Weehawken (sustained 53 hits), USS Passaic (35 hits), USS Patapsco (47 hits), USS Catskill (20 hits), USS Nantucket (50 hits), USS Nahant (80 hits), USS Keokuk (90 hits – sunk), USS Montauk, New Ironsides (Du Pont's Flagship) or a defect in the fuse. He later determined that the cable was intact and blamed the failure on fuse design. This apparently was Ripley's "infernal machine" that Susan mentioned in her note to Harriott on March 13 cited above.[7]

Around the time the flagship faltered, the *Weehawken* encountered formidable rows of rope obstructions extending from Fort Sumter to Fort Moultrie. When a torpedo exploded under or near the *Weehawken* and lifted it slightly out of the water, its captain feared the obstructions included more torpedoes and backed the vessel off. This caused the *Passaic, Montauk,* and *Patapsco* to stop about six or seven hundred yards from Fort Sumter. At this point the vessels began firing on the fort, and one shell pierced Ripley's 1st Artillery Regimental flag near the crossed canons at the flag's center.[8]

At first, in the belief that the monitors would run past the forts and enter the harbor, Fort Sumter returned the fire rapidly and by battery. As the battle progressed, the fire became more deliberate, accurate, and effective. Captain Rodgers of the leading *Weehawken* described the Confederates' shooting accuracy as being "very great, having been attained, no doubt, by practice at range targets." Probably as a result of Ripley's rigorous instruction, Rodgers's vessel was struck at least fifty-three times.

Captain Drayton of the *Passaic* reported that his ship "was struck by heavy shot twice in quick succession at the base of the turret rendering it totally useless for the remainder of the action." This was exactly as Ripley had advised in his January circular issued to all facilities in the harbor. Another shot struck the upper portion of the turret and broke all eleven steel plates and "considerably mashed" the pilot's house. Hit thirty-five times, the *Passaic* was "shattered."[9]

The captain of the *Montauk*, the third vessel in line, reported much less damage and reported that his monitor was struck only fourteen times. When the *Patapsco* tried to keep from colliding with the *Montauk*, it backed off and was enveloped in a concentrated fire from Sumter. The *Patapsco* fired its rifled gun only five times before receiving several heavy blows to its turret, rendering it immovable. Forty-seven projectiles struck the *Patapsco,* while its crew could fire only ten shots.[10]

Soon, Du Pont signaled for the squadron to ignore the flagship's struggles, and as ordered, the second wave of three monitors and the *Keokuk* steamed slowly by the floundering flagship. The *Catskill* was the first to pass the *New Ironsides*. After entering Ripley's predetermined "circle of fire," it was soon hit by shots from Fort Sumter. *Catskill* returned the fire and claimed to have dismounted one of Sumter's barbette guns. Its captain admitted, "The crossfire from the forts and batteries was most severe," and his ironclad was struck about twenty times. He was surprised to see the monitors so badly damaged in such a short time.

The *Nantucket* followed immediately behind the *Catskill* and at first drew fire only from Battery Beauregard. About thirty minutes later, when positioned to fire on Fort Sumter, the commander reported that he received fire from three forts, "and most terrific it was for forty-five to fifty minutes." The *Catskill*'s 16-inch gun fired only three shots before being disabled by shots striking "very near the port and driving in the plating." Its crew fired the 11-inch gun only twelve times during the entire seventy-five-minute attack. The commander admitted the Confederate fire was excellent throughout the engagement: "Any one vessel could not have withstood the concentrated fire of the enemy's batteries." Shells struck the *Nantucket* fifty-one times, and the vessel received many more hits by shell fragments.[11]

The *Nahant* was the last of the monitors to enter the action. Placed just ahead of the *Keokuk*, the *Nahant* soon received a "terrible and almost unprecedented fire from Forts Sumter and Moultrie." About thirty minutes into the battle, the turret became jammed after three heavy shots hit its base. The *Nahant* reported that in forty minutes of "close action" it was struck heavily—thirty-six times.[12]

The shape of the ironclad floating battery, the USS *Keokuk,* differed remarkably from the monitors. It had five feet of slanting hull above the water line, its two turrets were thinner clad than those of the monitors, and the plating on the slanting hull was not as thick as it could have been.

When Du Pont signaled Commander Alexander Rhind to advance the *Keokuk,* he ran past his lead monitor under a concentrated fire from Forts Sumter and Moultrie. For the thirty minutes he held his position, about 550 yards from Moultrie, the ironclad received ninety shots to the hull and turrets. Rhind reported that nineteen shots completely pierced Keokuk's hull at or just below the waterline. The turrets were pierced in many places, and a forward port shutter was shot away. In short, the vessel was completely riddled.

During this "extraordinary fire," hot shot and rifled projectiles of every caliber were poured into the *Keokuk*. The shelling disabled the forward gun turret and wounded many of the gun crew in the aft turret. Finding it impossible to keep the Keokuk afloat much longer, the commander reluctantly withdrew and anchored in smooth water, out of range of Ripley's artillery. During the night Rhind kept the *Keokuk* afloat, but rough seas in the morning were destined to sink the ship. A tug arrived and managed to save the crew, but was unable to save the ship. Rhind noted, "at about 7:30 A.M. she went down rapidly, and now lies completely submerged to the top of her smokestack."[13]

The Confederates had overwhelmed and convincingly repulsed the ironclads' attack. Colonel Rhett, in command at Fort Sumter, lacked formal artillery training but was an able and dedicated student of his superior officer. Reports indicate that Ripley's artillery repeatedly struck the ironclads at the points he stressed in his circular to the batteries. The accuracy of the harbor's artillerists most likely resulted from Ripley's rigorous instruction and supervision.

On April 7, as soon as possible after the repulse, Ripley visited Fort Sumter. He reported that one 10-inch gun and chassis had been disabled, one 8-inch gun had burst, and two rifled guns were dismounted but now replaced. The walls were badly shaken in two or three places and four men badly wounded. He believed that Rhett and his officers were doing all they could to repair the damage and asked the engineers to provide material and laborers as soon as possible. He appealed to the populace to furnish petticoats and pillows to make sandbags. Ripley quipped that "the *Keokuk* is probably for sale" and that if the attack were renewed, "the men will shoot better tomorrow than today.[14]

On April 9 the *Mercury* printed an enthusiastic account of the defeat of the ironclads. The article gloried in the sinking of the *Keokuk* and claimed that where it rested the smokestack and pilothouse were visible above the water. "All the batteries in the harbor were commanded by Gen. Ripley, probably the best artillery officer in the Confederate service, whose arrangement of works and guns have been put on trial," the article added.

Although Ripley planned to make his headquarters at Fort Sumter, the heavy fire on Sumter prevented his reaching that fort, and as a result he stationed himself at Battery Bee, "buoyant with hope and sternly lit with the joy of battle, while giving his directions, and watching the grand and novel struggle." The article continued, "General Beauregard, accompanied by General [Thomas] Jordan and Staff Officers, was a radiant and confident spectator of the fight from the East Bay Battery promenade. This successful repulse . . . must add to the fadeless wreath he already wears, and unites his triumph with the distinguished and successful services of Gen. Ripley to the people of South Carolina and Charleston." The egoistic Creole general was not pleased and must have bristled when referred to as a "confident spectator."[15]

As a result of this perceived slight, General Jordan called on the offices of the *Mercury* the next day. On April 10 the paper printed the following amends: "The new works constructed for the defense of Charleston since the return of General Beauregard were, of course, ordered by him. Chief Engineers Major Harris and Colonel Echols planned and directed them." The *Mercury* added, "The special arrangement of the guns in each work (especially in Sumter and Moultrie) was left to the experience of General Ripley as an artillerist, after consulting however, with the General Commanding."[16]

Ripley's official report recounted the attack by the "ironclad fleet of the Abolitionists." Before the attack he was proceeding by boat to Battery Bee and "watched the cannonade from that point." He described the order of the monitors as they progressed to ranges varying from nine hundred to fifteen hundred yards from his batteries. After about an hour the *Keokuk* left the monitors and, with "more boldness" than shown by any of the enemy's fleet, proceeded to the front. The vessel approached to within nine hundred yards of Fort Sumter and received the "full attention" of the powerful batteries. The effect was soon apparent. Ripley described the damages he observed on the *Keokuk,* and in less than forty minutes it withdrew as fast as its "disabled condition would permit." The monitors dropped out one by one, moved down the channel, and anchored out of range.

Following the attack, Ripley reported on the injuries sustained and the conditions at each fort and battery. He brought into the attack seventy-six assorted cannon, thirty-seven of which were above the caliber of 32-pounders. Ripley's artillerists expended 2,229 projectiles, of which more than 1,600 were over the caliber of 32-pounders. Ripley devoted over a page of his four-page report to profusely praising the officers and men of his command. He concluded, "In this, the first trial of the Abolitionist iron fleet against brick fortifications . . . they were beaten before their adversaries thought the action had well commenced."[17]

Despite the successful repulse, Beauregard was not pleased with the expenditure of more than twenty-two hundred rounds during the two-and-one-half-hours battle and believed there had been great waste, "which if repeated will end in our disaster." He believed more stringent orders must be given and rigidly enforced. Firing had to be slow, deliberate, carefully aimed, and within short range. He hoped that "officers will not again throw away so much precious ammunition." Apparently the topic had been discussed in Charleston. Susan Middleton wrote, "discontented people of Charleston are finding fault with Ripley for his waste of ammunition in the late fight. The economists say the victory cost us 100,000 dollars, and might have been won for much less."[18]

After the ironclads had been driven off, both sides directed their attention to the wreck of the *Keokuk.* Commander Du Pont wanted to destroy the ironclad to prevent the Confederates from raising it or salvaging its guns but could not devise a credible plan of action. At ebb tide, the tops of the *Keokuk*'s turrets were visible, and on April 12, after the ironclad fleet steamed southward, Colonel Rhett visited the wreckage. He noted that the hull of the vessel had been penetrated multiple times, and 10-inch round shot and rifled bolts had made clean holes through the turrets. Rhett removed several U.S. flags, three officers' swords, and pistols from the turrets to present to Beauregard. The quantity of bloody clothes and blankets indicated that some of the turret crew sustained serious injuries. At about the same time, Lieutenant W. T. Glassell of the CSS *Chicora* visited the *Keokuk* to observe the effect of Ripley's batteries on the turrets. He recovered two U.S. flags, two pennants, and three signal flags, which he forwarded to Ripley and then on to General Beauregard.[19]

Confederate naval officers who visited the wreck determined that the recovery of *Keokuk*'s guns would be impossible. However, after visits to the site by Lieutenant S. C. Boylston and later by Beauregard's chief engineer, Major D. B. Harris, it was decided that although difficult and hazardous, the guns could be removed. Beauregard assigned Ripley the task of organizing and supervising the mechanics for the salvage operation.

Ripley selected Adolphus W. La Coste, a local civilian and rigger by trade and an employee of the ordnance department. Ripley had been involved with La Coste in mounting guns in batteries around the harbor. After a long conference among the officers, Beauregard placed La Coste in charge of the work crew. A covering force of men from Fort Sumter, in boats some distance down the channel, protected the crew of ten or twelve skilled workers.[20]

John Johnson, in his book *The Defense of Charleston Harbor,* described the mechanics' efforts and the recovery of the guns in great detail. The turrets were conical in shape, twenty feet in diameter at the base and fourteen feet at the top. Each turret was armed with an 11-inch Dahlgren gun measuring nearly thirteen and one-half feet long, three feet in diameter at the breech, and weighing sixteen thousand pounds. At ebb tide, only the top four and one-half feet of the turrets were above water.

The first step in the recovery took nearly two weeks. Operating only at night for secrecy, the crew used chisels, sledges, and crowbars to remove a large section of roofing from the badly damaged turrets. Each gun could be seen resting below on its carriage, mostly but not totally underwater. Thick iron plating, confining each gun to its carriage, had to be cut through and removed before the guns could be hoisted from the turrets. By early May the gun of the first turret was ready to be hoisted from the wreckage.

The crew added projecting outriggers to an old but solid lightship hulk, then affixed a block and tackle to it. The ship was moored to the first turret, inside of which several of the crew, waist deep in water, had lashed a sling around the Dahlgren. The gun was hoisted breech first, and after much difficult maneuvering by the crew, the muzzle of the gun finally cleared the open roof of the turret.

As dawn approached, the transport ship *Etiwan* arrived to carry the gun to a wharf in Charleston. Having gained considerable experience removing the first gun, the crew was ready to hoist the second gun just three nights later. On May 7 the *Mercury* announced the recovery of both guns, noting, "General Ripley himself went down to superintend the removal of the second gun." The whole recovery process took a little over three weeks.

One of the two Dahlgrens was transported to Fort Sumter and mounted at the eastern angle of the barbette battery. On September 2 it was transported to Battery Ramsey at White Point Garden, where it remained until the evacuation of Charleston. The other Dahlgren was mounted in Battery Bee on Sullivan's Island. These two guns, according to Johnson, were the heaviest in the harbor, with the exception of two rifled English Blakely guns. In summarizing the action on April 7 and the recovery of the *Keokuk*'s guns, Beauregard wrote, "two 11-inch Dahlgren pieces, now in battery, were recovered under the supervision of General Ripley and by the mechanical resources and energy of Mr. Adolphus La Coste, employee of the district ordnance department."[21]

From Georgetown, on the coast northeast of Charleston, Lieutenant Colonel Joseph A. Yates notified Ripley of a new threat to that region. On April 27, the Federals discovered that a coastal town identified as "Murray's Inlet" [probably Murrells Inlet] was a port of entry and export. At the time there were five schooners in port that had recently run the blockade, plus a large amount of baled cotton stored on the wharves. Before being driven off, the Yankees shelled the port and burned one of the vessels. Yates expected the enemy to return and destroy the other vessels along with the cotton.

The pending recall of four companies of infantry from Yates's Fourth Military District complicated the situation. If Yates lost those companies without receiving replacements, he would "be obliged to abandon the whole coast from Georgetown to Little River" on the North Carolina border. Withdrawing pickets from nearby Waccamaw Neck would invite the enemy to seize "an immense quantity of grain now there [and] perhaps all the Negroes . . . numbering on the Neck 4,431."

Yates asked Beauregard to delay the order until he could relieve the four recalled companies. Ripley endorsed and sent the request to Beauregard, adding that he had forwarded 32-pounder rifled guns to Yates and intended to reinforce the colonel temporarily with artillery and infantry when the guns arrived in Georgetown.

Beauregard approved holding the companies temporarily but condescendingly added that he "desires it be impressed on your mind that the preservation of Murrays [sic] Inlet as a port of entry for blockade runners is not regarded as of very great military importance." He added that no points now occupied should be left uncovered to maintain the inlet as a port of entry. Although Murrells Inlet may not have been of "very great military importance," the planters in the region would have suffered economically if the inlet could not be used to export their cotton and grain.[22]

Compounding the manpower problems in South Carolina was a directive from Secretary of War James A. Seddon on May 2. Seddon notified Beauregard that he believed the enemy was abandoning attacks on the eastern coast and was now concentrating strong forces on the Mississippi. Beauregard was to send as soon as possible eight thousand or ten thousand men to General Pemberton at Tullahoma, Tennessee.

Beauregard immediately notified Seddon of the "remarkable increase" in the enemy's fleet in South Carolina, but the secretary of war was unimpressed. Reluctantly, Beauregard relieved General S. R. Gist from duty in his department and placed him in command of a four-regiment brigade with a field battery of four guns, all to be selected by Ripley. They were to proceed with the least possible delay and report to General Pemberton, now at Jackson, Mississippi.

Ripley assigned Colquitt's 46th Georgia, Stevens's 24th South Carolina, Watters's 8th Georgia Battalion, along with Ferguson's Light Battery to form Gist's brigade. General Hagood, commanding the Second Military District, was to supply Gist with the fourth infantry regiment. In addition, Beauregard ordered General W. H. T. Walker's brigade to report to Pemberton by way of Selma and Mobile, Alabama.[23]

Senator W. Porcher Miles pleaded with Seddon not to "strip us of troops," as there was evidence of an impending attack, saying, "don't invite it." Beauregard also pleaded with Seddon but to no avail. Seddon requested more troops, and Beauregard, with Special Orders, No. 105, sent General Evans's brigade and a newly formed brigade under the command of General Johnson Hagood to Jackson, Mississippi. Ripley was to select the light battery to be brigaded with Hagood.[24]

Ripley forwarded a plea recommending that "the order for the movement of troops from his command be suspended." He believed that "the enemy is in force on Folly Island and entrenching [and that] from his command of Stono Inlet, owing to the abandonment of Cole's Island last year by General Pemberton, the enemy can, with his superior transportation, attack either Morris or James Island before we could possibly concentrate a reduced force." Even in his absence, Pemberton was causing problems for South Carolina.

Seddon refused all pleas from Senator Miles, Governor Bonham, Mayor Charles Macbeth, Beauregard, and Ripley. "The Mississippi is vital," he wrote. "I send from every point that can spare any troops." He steadfastly believed, or claimed to believe, that even at these reduced troop levels the Confederates outnumbered the enemy on the coast. The secretary of war astonishingly urged "the organization and arming, for local defense, of all citizens capable of bearing arms. . . . Well officered and with tried soldiers interspersed, they would be scarcely less effective for defense than regular soldiers."[25]

CHAPTER 19

The Defense of Morris Island

In early March 1863, before the ironclad attack on Fort Sumter and the enemy occupation of Folly Island, General Beauregard decided "to have the southern end of Morris Island fortified and armed." These defensive works were to be constructed across from Lighthouse Inlet and north of Folly and Little Folly Islands. Beauregard decided that even though James Island had been considered the best route to attack Charleston, it was now probably too heavily defended for the enemy to assault along that front. He concluded that the enemy would probably move from Stono Inlet along Folly Island and then to Morris Island to take Fort Sumter, "but they may find that to be a piece of folly."[1]

During March and April, because of the shortage of black labor, Colonel R. F. Graham, in command of the 21st South Carolina Infantry on Morris Island, furnished parties of infantry for construction of the proposed works. Armament was sent over and some progress was made, but it was extremely slow. Ripley believed one of the reasons for the inaction was the carelessness and inattention of the engineer officers. Graham reported that at times working parties were present, but no engineer officer was available to direct their operations; several times the engineer officer left the work for days.[2]

There had been a chronic shortage of African American labor, and it was exacerbated by recent enemy incursions, renewing the planters' fears that their valuable property could be seized. Ripley decided that the engineers tolerated the situation and made no significant effort to expedite the construction of the works. When soldiers were put on work details, a problem arose between the engineer and the infantry officers. The infantry officers, who were in direct command of the work details, outranked the engineer officers. Technically, they could not be ordered by the engineer officers to do anything and at times ignored or altered input from the engineers. This lack of urgency, inefficiency, and pettiness infuriated Ripley.[3]

In early May, when the enemy began entrenching on Folly Island, Ripley became concerned. Later in the month, in a letter to General Thomas Jordan, Beauregard's chief of staff, Ripley criticized the lack of progress on the works at the island's southern end and blamed the engineers under the command of Lieutenant Colonel David B. Harris. Exasperated by the lack of progress and aware of the enemy's expanding presence on Folly Island, Ripley notified Jordan that he planned to "send a strong and efficient company under a competent officer" to the

Colonel David B. Harris, Beauregard's chief engineer. Criticized by Ripley as incompetent and inept in constructing Charleston's defenses, he was a major cause of Ripley and Beauregard's deteriorating relationship. From the Library of Congress.

southern end of Morris Island. Ripley's soldiers were to complete the batteries and magazines ordered by Beauregard for that location.[4]

Colonel Harris, a Virginian and 1833 graduate of West Point, served in the artillery for only nine months. From March 1834 until August 1835, he was an assistant professor of engineering at the USMA during Beauregard's plebe year. He then resigned his commission and worked for two years as an assistant engineer on the James River and Kanawha Canal. After a short stint as a tobacco merchant, from 1845 until 1861 Harris listed his occupation as a planter in Woodville, Virginia.

After Virginia seceded, Harris volunteered his services to the Confederacy, although it appears he had not been actively engaged in engineering for some time. Harris renewed his acquaintance with Beauregard and became a close friend and an integral part of his staff, serving with the Creole at the Battle of First Manassas. Quiet and reserved, Harris's temperament was the opposite of that of the jovial but occasionally irascible Ripley. Beauregard described Harris as the chief engineer of the department, "on whom I placed the utmost reliance," and who "always thoroughly understood and entered into my views." One wonders whether Ripley was aware of the close personal relationship between Beauregard and Harris. Regardless, his response to the situation and criticism of Harris and the engineers would have been no different. Ripley was no sycophant.[5]

Ripley's accusations provoked excuses and denials from officers of the engineer department. Harris and his staff—Major William H. Echols, Captain John Howard of the volunteer engineers, Captain Langdon Cheves, and J. Fraser Mathewes—all admitted that the work had been delayed. Harris claimed it was not the fault of the engineers but resulted from the lack of labor and insufficient transportation to get workers from James Island to Morris Island. Harris claimed he did not wish to respond to Ripley's accusations in the same spirit in which they were made.[6]

All of Harris's staff agreed with the labor and transportation issues, but Mathewes claimed that the poor health of the workers was a problem and that the tides restricted the work to only seven hours a day. Major Echols admitted that Ripley and his officers could probably induce the soldiers to work harder and possibly could arrange for more transportation. Only Echols thought Ripley could possibly get the works finished sooner.

Langdon Cheves, satisfied that the works were progressing in accordance with Harris's instructions, claimed they were proceeding as rapidly as the available work force and the insufficient supply of material would permit. Nevertheless, on May 28 Colonel Graham notified Cheves that his work detail would now report for duty to Captain John C. Mitchel, commanding a company of the 1st Regiment, South Carolina Artillery. Under the "direct instructions of Brigadier General Ripley," they were to continue the works on the south end of the island, which would be nearly identical with those ordered by the engineers. Cheves's ten remaining hired laborers went to work on a portion of Battery Wagner.[7]

Captain Mitchel was a native of Ireland who came to America as a young man. His father, a prominent Irish nationalist, was tried by the Crown for treason and banished to Australia. After his arrival in the United States, young Mitchel received an engineering education at Columbia College in New York and was employed in railroad construction in Tennessee at the onset of the war. Mitchel came to Charleston and received an appointment as a lieutenant in the battalion of artillery stationed at Fort Sumter. Ripley, obviously aware of Mitchel's engineering background, had no qualms about entrusting the construction of the works to him.

By June 14, under the supervision of Ripley and Captain Mitchel, significant progress had been made on the works at the southern end of the island. That day, Ripley notified Jordan that Lieutenant Colonel Joseph A. Yates detected enemy activity on Little Folly Island, shelled the enemy for about forty-five minutes, and believed he had stopped their operations.[8]

On the eighteenth Lieutenant Colonel Alfred Roman, Beauregard's assistant inspector general, reviewed Ripley's complaints against the engineers and determined that Ripley's removal of Cheves and the appointment Captain Mitchel to replace him violated General Orders, No. 95. In essence, all field and military works in the department "will be ordered, planned, located, and constructed . . . only under the orders of the engineer and his assistants." All plans, instructions, and explanations had to be relayed from the engineers to the officers in command of the work details. Those officers had to then supervise the execution of the orders by the laborers. Roman suggested that Captain Cheves be reinstated, with proper steps taken to insure the transportation of all material required by the engineers and the number of laborers doubled. Roman concluded that no blame could be attached to the engineer department and astoundingly claimed Ripley's

Captain John C. Mitchel. A native of Ireland and a trained engineer, he was Ripley's choice to finish the lagging works on Morris Island— a choice overruled by Beauregard. From John Johnson, The Defense of Charleston Harbor, 1863–1865 *(1889), facing p. 223.*

Captain JOHN C. MITCHEL, First Regiment S. C. Artillery, Commanding Fort Sumter.—Killed July 20th, 1864. From a Photograph.

actions were "calculated to delay, instead of advancing, the completion of the works he was so anxious to have in operation." Two days later Beauregard's chief of staff documented the commanding general's views exonerating the engineer department and placing Cheves once again in charge of the works on Morris Island.[9]

It seems that Beauregard applied a double standard in this situation. Previously, he encouraged and supported Ripley's efforts against the inefficiencies of the local ordnance officer, Major F. L. Childs. Beauregard allowed Ripley to issue orders directly to Childs and ultimately placed the ordnance officer under arrest, all in an attempt to subvert the bureaucracy of Colonel Josiah Gorgas's ordnance department. It was an entirely different matter, and not tolerated in the least, when the issues involved Beauregard's friend Lieutenant Colonel D. B. Harris and his engineer department.

On June 20, apparently before Ripley received word of Cheves's reinstatement, he found that it would be another month before labor from the upper districts of the state could be obtained. Not sitting idly by, Ripley informed Jordan of his successful conversations with planters and other citizens in the area to send enslaved blacks to work on the fortifications. Despite the approach of the rice season, Ripley believed that sending the "proper agents" among the planters on the Cooper River could secure from two to three hundred able-bodied African Americans for one month to six weeks.

Ripley also advised the commanding general that if Cole's Island could not be retaken, the most important work on James Island would be the erection of a battery to shorten that defensive line. If Beauregard approved his suggestion, he would attempt to secure laborers and provide them with the proper guardianship, provisions, and employment. Ripley even suggested that Captain Ramsey of the engineers be assigned to the work and ordered to report on the project to Ripley's headquarters. Ripley failed to remember that Beauregard did not appreciate unsolicited advice. Previously, he had informed Ripley that he would "be happy to have the opinions of his subordinate officers at the proper time."[10]

While Ripley was embroiled with the engineers on Morris Island, Lieutenant Colonel Arthur J. L. Fremantle, an officer in the British Coldstream Guards, arrived in Charleston during his tour of the Southern states. The Englishman kept a diary of his three months' visit, which he published in 1864. Although the institution of slavery at first repulsed Fremantle, he soon developed a "great admiration for the gallantry and determination of the Southerners," as contrasted with "the foolish bullying conduct of the Northerners." Fremantle arrived in Charleston at 5:00 A.M., June 8, and registered at the Charleston Hotel.

On the same morning at 9:00 A.M., Fremantle called on Beauregard's offices and was disappointed to learn that the commanding general was on an inspection tour of Florida. He then called on Ripley, whom the colonel described as "a jovial character, very fond of the good things of life; but it is said that he never allows this propensity to interfere with his military duties," which he performed with "both zeal and talent." Despite "his Northern birth," Freemantle wrote, "he is generally popular."[11]

Fremantle, who admittedly had "roughed it" for ten weeks, thought that Charleston looked comparatively comfortable and luxurious, although he was certain the inhabitants must be suffering "great inconvenience." The lighting and paving of the city had deteriorated, most shops were closed, and those that were open had very few goods. The burned-out section of Charleston, destroyed by fire in December 1861, appeared to be a vast wilderness in the center of the city. However, he noted, "The people . . . all seem happy, contented, and determined." Both the Mills House and the Charleston Hotel were crowded, but rooms were available for eight dollars per day.[12]

Captain Henry Wemyss Feilden, a British officer on Beauregard's staff, called on Fremantle the following day and accompanied his fellow countryman to Ripley's office. Feilden attended Sandhurst and served with British regiments in India and China. In December 1860 Feilden sold his commission and with the outbreak of war began planning to join the Confederate cause. His motivation, in addition to his sympathy for the South, was the opportunity to improve his financial status. With the proceeds from the sale of his commission, Feilden purchased household goods worth £1,000 for resale at a profit in South Carolina. In late January 1863 Feilden successfully ran the blockade into Charleston, traveled by rail to Richmond, and in February received an appointment as captain and assistant adjutant general in the department of his choice. In early March, Feilden returned to Charleston and joined General Beauregard's staff.[13]

During their visit Ripley took Feilden and Fremantle by boat to inspect Fort Sumter. Fremantle described in great detail the structure, condition, and armament of the fort. Ripley proudly pointed to the prize ordnance at the fort, "a fine new 11-inch gun, fished up from the wreck of the *Keokuk*." Fremantle added that Ripley "has the reputation of being an excellent artillery officer, and although by birth a Northerner, he is a red-hot and indefatigable rebel. Nearly all the credit of the efficiency of the Charleston fortifications is due to him."

At noon Colonel Rhett treated his visitors to a luncheon in one of the casemates before they returned to Charleston. At five o'clock that evening Fremantle dined with General Ripley and his wife. While his host termed the event a "blockade" dinner, Fremantle thought the meal was "sumptuous." Also in the dinner party were General Jordan, Colonel Rhett, and others.[14]

On June 11 Ripley took the colonel to Morris Island and Battery Wagner, which Fremantle described as being a powerful, well-constructed fieldwork, mounting nine heavy guns and extending across the island at the point nearest Fort Sumter. Fremantle noted that Ripley pointed to the fort with pride but was unimpressed with Morris Island, "a miserable, low, sandy desert" with a range of low sand hills at its extreme southern end. About ten guns and mortars were placed behind the low hills, manned by two companies of regular artillery "under the command of Captain Mitchell [sic] (the 'patriot's' son), to whom I was introduced. He seemed a quiet, unassuming man, and was spoken of by General Ripley as an excellent officer." Mitchel informed Fremantle that he expected to fire on the enemy on Little Folly Island within the next few days, hoping to drive them off.[15]

As they were returning from the Morris Island inspection Ripley opined, "the proper manner to attack Charleston was to land on Morris Island, take Forts Wagner and Cummins [sic] Point, and then turn their guns on Fort Sumter." By Friday, June 12, Beauregard had returned from Florida, and Fremantle called at his office. During the conversation Beauregard agreed that General Grant was having considerable success in the West, especially for "a man of no great military capacity."[16]

At 7:00 P.M. Sunday night, Walter Blake, an Englishman with a plantation on the Combahee River, and Fremantle called on Ripley at his office. Ripley related that the shelling between Morris and Folly Islands continued vigorously, aided by the enemy's gunboats. He could well understand Blake's problems on the Combahee, where raiders burned property and carried off hundreds of his slaves. Ripley called these light-draft gunboats "river-gropers" that were forever "pushing up the numerous creeks, burning and devastating everything." He told his guests how his men captured one of these "critters," the *Isaac Smith,* on the Stono. After his informative and entertaining week in Charleston, Colonel Arthur Fremantle paid his respects to Beauregard and Ripley, and departed for Richmond.[17]

On June 25 Ripley responded to Beauregard's reinstatement of Langdon Cheves, directing his lengthy reply to General Jordan. Ripley believed that Beauregard based his conclusions on Lieutenant Colonel Alfred Roman's report on the subject and complained that evidently all Roman did was "peruse the reports" of the engineer officers and their employees. Apparently, Roman and Harris made only a cursory visit to the causeway under construction. Roman then filed his report without making a thorough study of why the works were progressing so slowly.

Ripley contended that it was the engineers' duty to set out the work, mark what was to be done, and see that it was understood. About a month after Beauregard originally ordered the work, Ripley and General G. W. Smith observed a party of over fifty men, accompanied by their officer, present and ready to work but with no engineer officers available to direct them. Moreover, these men had never been informed as to what work was to be done. With so little work having been completed and the enemy on their doorstep, Ripley decided to direct the work himself.

Ripley contacted Colonel Graham, who advised him that no engineer officer ever informed him of the proposed work, even though it was to be done by his troops. Everything the colonel knew about the fortifications he learned from Ripley. When Ripley questioned Cheves at Battery Wagner, the engineer claimed that he knew nothing of the work, as it was not "under his charge." Ripley then contacted the engineer office in Charleston and was told that, in fact, "all the works on Morris Island had been placed under Mr. Cheves."[18]

As nothing had been done on the batteries for days and very little done for weeks, Ripley denied removing Cheves from any "works on which he was engaged." Ripley asked Cheves to report to him because the work was to be done by Ripley's officers and men and needed to be completed at once. Cheves did not answer Ripley's note and then verbally refused to proceed with the work or "furnish any assistance." Cheves claimed that he had been displaced and as a result turned his efforts to other works on the island and to the causeway. Ripley countered that this might be fortunate because, "as these [works] had been for so long unfinished," they provided incontestable proof that the Engineer Corps could not do the work "with which they were charged."

Ripley then railed against Cheves for precipitously discharging his employees, allegedly because they had no shelter. Ripley doubted this weak excuse and accused Cheves of sending the men away to prevent him from finishing the works after the engineers' months of "dilatory action."[19]

Cheves claimed that transportation problems had prevented the engineers from receiving construction material needed for the magazines and batteries.

Amazingly, Cheves also asserted that timber available for the magazines could not be brought to the site because his mules had not been fed. Ripley countered that there had always been a supply of corn on the island and no other animals had suffered.

Ripley criticized Roman for adopting the engineer's transportation excuses without determining how much the engineers actually had at their disposal. Ripley claimed that, in fact, the engineers had more transportation available than Roman's report recommended should be allocated. When Ripley received no reply to his written concerns of May 24, he ordered Mitchel to begin construction on or about June 1. By the eleventh, Mitchel had the magazines completed, supplied the batteries, and on the twelfth opened fire on the enemy. Ripley argued that if the matter had been left to the engineers, the works would still not be completed.[20]

Regarding the "reinstatement" of Cheves to manage the works on Morris Island, Ripley stated that Cheves would actually be returning to the duty he had abandoned. Ripley did not object to Cheves's return but insisted that the work be done in reasonable time and that any delays be for legitimate reasons.

Ripley next wanted to "respectfully" bring a matter concerning the engineers to Beauregard's attention. Colonel Roman, in his report, referred to the "district engineers." Ripley argued that under the present arrangement, the district engineers appeared "to consider themselves absolutely independent of instructions from . . . the district commander and the commanding officer of the forts and works."[21]

Beauregard had fully agreed with this point of view when he and Ripley were struggling with Childs, Gorgas, and an inefficient ordnance department. At that time Beauregard commented, "Childs seems to think the ordnance department was created solely for the special benefit of its officers." As of June 25, Ripley still had not received from the chief engineer, or any engineer, a plan, drawing, or description of works going on in his command. Ripley closed his reply to Jordan with two questions:

> First, is the district commander forbidden from constructing any defensive works, which he feels to be necessary, unless they are planned and erected by engineer officers?
>
> Second, is the district commander expected to yield his conviction of the necessities within his command to any officer of the engineer department even though that officer is of inferior rank?[22]

Beauregard answered that Ripley was not prohibited from constructing works but that his plans must first be submitted to the commanding general for approval to prevent any "unnecessary" construction. If the commanding general approved, orders would be issued to the engineers.

As for the second question, district commanders had no control over works under construction other than as provided in General Orders, No. 95, and Special Orders, No. 56. The Special Orders permitted commanders to finish uncompleted works if they followed the original plans whenever possible. However, Ripley had never received any plans or drawings from Harris and the engineers.

Beauregard instructed the chief engineer of the department, Colonel Harris, to communicate verbally or in writing with district commanders concerning the plans and instructions of any works to be constructed within their district. Nevertheless, Beauregard absolved the engineers of any blame or neglect in the delays.[23]

It appears that Ripley's rebuke of the engineers may have had repercussions in a portion of the community sympathetic to Beauregard, Harris, and Cheves. During this contentious time, an unnamed person or persons supposedly expressed their concern to Beauregard about Ripley's conduct on the recent occasion "of a drinking frolic, either in the city or on a vessel in the harbor." The vague accusation did not, or could not, pinpoint where the "frolic" had occurred. Evidently it was well known, as Fremantle had written, that Ripley occasionally engaged in "rollicking habits." On June 24 Beauregard's chief of staff directed Colonel Roman to inquire into the facts of the case and report the findings to the commanding general. The timing of this accusation, in the midst of the criticism of the engineers, seems unlikely to have been by chance.

Roman's investigation included an interview with Ripley conducted by *Mercury* editor R. B. Rhett and Mayor Magrath, who reported to Beauregard on the thirtieth that Ripley "would not be intoxicated, nor allow himself to be excited or influenced by liquor so as at any time to interfere with the proper discharge of his duties." They hoped these assurances would restore Beauregard's confidence and regard "if they have been disturbed." Beauregard accepted the assurances as proper and satisfactory and on July 1 directed Roman to cease any further investigation into the allegations.[24]

Believing the engineering issue finally closed, Ripley reported the findings of a reconnaissance conducted by Colonel C. H. Simonton's command on James Island to General Jordan. On June 28 Ripley concluded that there were about three thousand enemy troops on Folly Island, another six hundred men on Cole's Island, and a small force on Little Folly. Through Ripley's personal observations and his knowledge of Colonel Simonton's abilities and means for reconnaissance, he believed those figures were correct.[25]

Although the divisive turmoil with the engineers should have been over, during the first week of July, Harris, Echols, and Cheves attacked and denied Ripley's charges. Harris agreed that he had never given Ripley any plans or drawings but disingenuously claimed that Ripley never asked for the information; therefore, Harris assumed that Ripley "attached no consequence to what he now considers a grievance." Echols disputed the number of steamboats Ripley claimed were available for transportation and implicated the quartermaster department in that problem.

Cheves argued that Ripley had indeed removed him from duty, as all the available labor was taken from him and placed under the command of Captain Mitchel. Ripley claimed that as Cheves was not actually working on the battery, he did not remove him but only appointed Mitchel to do the work. Cheves admitted he "probably" had told Ripley he knew nothing of the work, as it was "not under his charge," when in fact it actually was. Cheves challenged Ripley's accusation that at one time fifty men were ready to work but without an engineer officer to instruct them. Cheves asserted that the men knew what to do but that their excuse was "a pretense to cover up their laziness."[26]

Enemy activity on July 8 and 9 brought this divisive issue to a halt, at least temporarily. An armed reconnaissance, ordered by Ripley on July 6 and conducted by Colonel Yates, confirmed that the enemy remained in force on the nearby coastal islands. This information gave Beauregard a valid reason for not sending another brigade from South Carolina to other theaters as requested by General Cooper in Richmond.

On the morning of July 9, nineteen vessels and four monitors were spotted off the bar outside Charleston Harbor. The same day, Simonton reported that eighteen vessels and one monitor had appeared on the Stono, with four gunboats advancing up the river as far as the obstructions. He later claimed the enemy was landing troops on Battery Island and the pickets were exchanging fire. Simonton notified Ripley that he might be facing an attack and had a critical need for infantry on his western lines. Later, Ripley determined that this was a diversion from the main attack on Morris Island.[27]

Later on the ninth, Beauregard notified Governor Bonham and Mayor Magrath that an attack on Charleston was imminent, and he believed that Fort Sumter would be attacked from Folly and Morris Islands. Beauregard asked the governor to order all available troops to the defense of the city and admitted to the mayor that "an indispensible battery" on Morris Island was not finished. Blaming the state for not providing an adequate supply of laborers, he asked the mayor whether he could furnish a supply of free black laborers in this emergency, as "material results may be achieved, even at this late hour, by a sufficient labor force handled in an energetic way." Beauregard also notified Major General W. H. C. Whiting in Wilmington, North Carolina, of the impending attack, asking him to send one or more regiments if possible.

Ripley also was convinced that the main attack would come against Morris Island, in part because of a captured diary forwarded to him earlier by Lieutenant Colonel J. G. Pressley of the 25th South Carolina Infantry. The diary described the enemy's building of masked batteries on Folly Island in preparation for the attack. Ripley asked his adjutant, Captain W. F. Nance, to send the first battalion that arrived in Charleston to Morris Island unless instructed otherwise.[28]

At this time the works at the southern tip of Morris Island were nearly finished, with eleven detached and unconnected artillery batteries supported by infantry in rifle pits at nearby Oyster Point. The artillery, built into small hillocks, consisted of eight guns of assorted calibers and types, and three 10-inch mortars. The works were manned by 220 artillerymen of the 1st South Carolina Artillery under the commands of Captains Mitchel, J. Ravenel Macbeth, and Lieutenant Edward Frost. Four hundred men of the 21st South Carolina Infantry and fifty men from the 1st South Carolina Regiment provided infantry support. Their objective was to prevent the enemy from gaining a foothold on the island, but if unable to do so, the Confederates would fall back to Battery Wagner and hold out as long as possible.

Facing south, about three miles north of the works was Battery Wagner, an irregular-shaped fortification built of earth and revetted with palmetto logs. Wagner extended completely across the island from Vincent's Creek on the west to the ocean shore on the east. The fortification had a large salient projecting southward between the oceanfront and the land wall. Wagner's land wall faced south toward Folly Island and extended westward across the island to Vincent's creek. Two 32-pounders, one smooth bore and the other rifled, along with a 10-inch columbiad, were mounted on the salient's seafront, providing fire on the ship channel. Two cannon, on the salient's land face, added crossfire to three carronades, two shell guns, and one 10-inch seacoast mortar facing the land approaches to Wagner. This massive firepower in relatively compact quarters would provide a devastating barrage against infantrymen advancing up the beach. In front of Wagner's south face was a deep moat designed to fill with seawater at high tide. A three-thousand-square-foot bombproof, built into the fort, reportedly could protect up to 900 men. Ripley's forces at Battery Wagner included 107 artillerymen from Captain Chichester's Artillery and Captain J. R. Mathewes' Artillery Company. Two hundred twelve men of Colonel Graham's 21st South Carolina Regiment provided infantry support. In all, Graham's command on the island totaled nearly 1,000 infantry, artillery, and cavalrymen.[29]

CHAPTER 20

Attacks on Battery Wagner

In June 1863 the Federal command along the southeast coast underwent changes as Rear Admiral John A. Dahlgren succeeded Du Pont in command of the South Atlantic Blockading Squadron. Then, on June 12 Major General Quincy A. Gillmore replaced David Hunter as commander of the Department of the South, and selected General George C. Strong, a young and energetic brigadier, to lead the assault on Morris Island. In preparation for the invasion, on the night of July 9 Strong marched his regiments to the north side of Folly Island, where assault boats were waiting. The brigade, led by the 7th and 6th Connecticut regiments, proceeded overnight up the Folly River toward Light House Inlet and the partially completed Confederate batteries. Shortly before dawn Admiral Dahlgren prepared his monitors to support the attack.[1]

On July 10 at 6:00 A.M., Beauregard telegraphed General Cooper in Richmond that at 5:08 A.M. enemy batteries on Folly Island opened fire on Morris Island. Soon after, he notified Cooper that enemy forces had successfully landed and were gaining a foothold on the southern end of the embattled island. An hour later he telegraphed General H. W. Mercer in Savannah and General Whiting in Wilmington that the enemy was attacking in force and requested both generals to send reinforcements to Charleston as soon as possible. General Thomas L. Clingman's brigade was put in motion from North Carolina, and soon two of General Alfred H. Colquitt's regiments and much of General William B. Taliaferro's brigade entrained from Georgia.[2]

For more than an hour the Confederate batteries effectively exchanged fire with the Federal opposition, but after Dahlgren's monitors, *Catskill, Nahant, Montauk,* and *Weehawken,* moved into position, they flanked the batteries and unleashed a devastating barrage. As a result, fire from the Confederate batteries gradually became sporadic and less accurate. As the cannonade progressed, a concerned Beauregard asked Ripley whether the Morris Island batteries were firing against the monitors or at the enemy forces approaching by land. He cautioned Ripley against "throwing away" ammunition against ironclads at long ranges and implored Ripley to place a large number of Rains torpedoes in front of Wagner at the appropriate time.[3]

As the Union infantry came ashore, Confederate artillerymen were unable to depress their guns low enough to fire on the advancing enemy. The 6th and 7th

Connecticut Regiments led the attack, followed by the 3rd New Hampshire, 76th Pennsylvania, and 9th Maine, plus a few companies of the 48th New York. The Confederates in the rifle pits fired fusillades at their attackers, but the leading regiment, the 7th Connecticut, reached the works of the beleaguered defenders. The attack soon degenerated into fierce hand-to-hand combat and began to overwhelm the Confederate infantrymen. Meanwhile, Colonel John L. Chatfield's 6th Connecticut outflanked the batteries and overpowered the outgunned artillerymen. After seizing the batteries, they pushed on to link up with the 7th Connecticut engaged at the rifle pits.

Lieutenant Colonel Yates, in command of the Morris Island artillery, telegraphed Ripley that the batteries were lost, and now only Colonel Graham's infantry engaged the enemy. Ripley asked his adjutant, Captain W. F. Nance, to send three companies of the Charleston Battalion to the island if possible and soon requested sending all infantry available with a full supply of ammunition and camp rations. Nearly surrounded and with many taken prisoner, the surviving defenders of the works fled toward Battery Wagner. When two companies from the 7th South Carolina Battalion arrived as reinforcements, they were swept back toward Wagner in the rout.

Ripley notified General Jordan that Cummings Point Battery was firing over Wagner at the pursuing Federals and that Fort Sumter had just opened on the enemy. He also advised Jordan that monitors were shelling Wagner and decided that the battery was now so crowded it would not be wise to send more troops to the island at that time.[4]

Ripley reported that in the severe struggle all eleven artillery pieces at the works, along with their ammunition, were captured. Most important, the defenders lost 294 men killed, wounded, and missing. Captains Langdon Cheves and Charles T. Haskell, as well as Lieutenant J. S. Bee were killed. Colonel Graham lost nearly one-third of his available force, and 60 percent of the artillerymen were captured.

Finally, the day's oppressive heat, as well as fire from Brooke rifles mounted in Fort Sumter's barbette wall, slowed the Federal advance. As Strong's pursuing regiments neared Wagner, the battery opened fire with grape and canister, halting the column. As the action ended, the Federal troops fell back and organized a picket line across the island.

Later that day Ripley visited Battery Wagner and at 1:30 A.M. on the eleventh he wired Beauregard and his staff at the Mills House. He reported that Colonel C. H. Olmstead's Georgia command, the 1st Georgia Volunteers and the 12th and 18th Battalions, were now in position. He added that the guns were all in order and recommended placing obstructions in the nearby creeks and additional torpedoes in front of Battery Wagner.[5]

At dawn on July 11 more than twelve hundred men from the 7th Connecticut, 9th Maine, and 76th Pennsylvania launched a second furious assault against Wagner. The attackers, led by the fatigued Connecticut regiment, received volleys of rifle fire from Wagner's pickets before the Confederates retreated back toward the battery. The Connecticut troops made it into and through the water-filled moat, then were pinned down on Wagner's exterior slope. Canister and grape, fired over the men trapped on the fort's sloping wall, stopped the supporting regiments in their tracks. The pinned-down 7th Connecticut could not advance and received an even deadlier fire during their desperate retreat from the wall. The Federal attack became a complete disaster.

Ripley reported that the defenders "gallantly and decidedly repulsed" the attack. Confederate burying parties interred over 100 attackers killed within their lines and took 130 prisoners, while Confederate casualties totaled only 6 killed and 6 wounded. For the remainder of the day, the enemy strengthened its position and buried their dead. However, all was not quiet as three gunboats and three monitors continued to bombard Battery Wagner. General Johnson Hagood and his men arrived the next day, bolstering the defenses and taking command on James Island.[6]

The July 11 edition of the *Mercury* praised the repulse of the enemy but claimed that saving the city required "prompt, daring, and desperate valor." The editor advocated "at any cost of life and labor," and as soon as possible, that the enemy be quickly driven from the island before they could establish a permanent foothold. The paper, evidently unaware of Ripley's frustrated attempts, illogically proposed to retake the island and then quickly builds proper works at its southern end. The editor preferred this to staking the city's defense solely on Battery Wagner.[7]

Whether influenced by the *Mercury*'s editorial or not, the next day Beauregard convened a meeting to discuss this issue. In attendance were Generals Ripley, Clingman, and Taliaferro, to whom Ripley assigned the command of Morris Island. Governor Bonham and William Porcher Miles, Charleston's representative to Congress, also were present. They first discussed how many troops would be required to retake the island. The officers at Wagner estimated that five thousand men would be needed. Generals Ripley and Taliaferro, who had just examined the ground, placed the number at four thousand. After further discussion, Ripley and Taliaferro informed the group that, unfortunately, the officers at Wagner believed that even if the island were retaken, it could not be held for long.

Despite this negative note, the board discussed the number and condition of the vessels needed to transfer the additional troops for a counterattack. After acknowledging the significant transportation problems, Ripley declared that any attempt to recapture the ground held by the enemy would be desperate and impractical. Taliaferro and Clingman agreed, and the commanding general came to the same conclusion. Beauregard decided that a failed counterattack could result in a "grave disaster, loss of life, and an irreparable loss of strength" and should not be attempted. The only recourse was to defend Batteries Wagner and Gregg and the northern end of the island as long as possible.[8]

Georgia's Colonel Olmstead recalled Ripley's visit to Morris Island on July 12 following the attack. Ripley was elated with the repulse of the enemy and wanted to examine the ground in front of the fort. As additional torpedoes had been planted the day before, Olmstead stationed a sentinel, Private Donnolly of the 1st Georgia, to prevent anyone from the garrison straying onto the dangerous ground.

As Ripley started around the battery, he spurred his horse and unknowingly rode toward the newly mined area. The Irish-born Donnolly emphatically ordered Ripley to stop, raised his musket, and took "dead aim at the general." For a moment Olmstead believed that "there was a strong possibility of a vacancy among the brigadiers of the Confederate army," but an officer rushed forward, knocked Donnolly's gun away, and explained to Ripley why he was being halted. Questioned later, the unsophisticated Georgian admitted that he was going to shoot the general "to keep him from being blown up with the saltpeter, to be sure."[9]

In response to these attacks and the heavy troop movements into the Charleston area, Mayor Macbeth conferred with Beauregard, and they decided that all women and children should leave the city. Mrs. Ripley had been forewarned of this probability and had reached Columbia by July 9.[10]

Certain that additional Federal attacks would be attempted, Ripley stressed the importance of improving the defenses at Wagner. General Taliaferro ably supervised these improvements, carried out under a constant bombardment from enemy gunboats and monitors. When Clingman's four regiments arrived, three were sent to James Island, while the 51st North Carolina was posted to Battery Wagner. On July 14 Colquitt's two regiments arrived, reinforcing Hagood on James Island. At this time, detachments from Captain William De Pass's Palmetto Artillery Battalion and from Company A, 1st South Carolina Artillery, reinforced the light artillery at Battery Wagner.

The Federals were also active and for several days strengthened their positions on the island. Nevertheless, Ripley reported on July 16 that Generals Hagood and Colquitt would lead an attack against Union forces on James Island. For this offensive, Lieutenant Colonel John G. Pressley formed the 25th South Carolina Infantry and marched toward Secessionville and Battery Lamar. Upon his arrival, Pressley reported to General Colquitt, who at the time was meeting with Generals Ripley and Hagood at Lamar. Ripley and the other generals impressed Pressley as being "as cool and in as good spirits as if there was no serious work in hand."

Pressley personally observed Ripley's composed, hands-on participation with his subordinate officers in the field.

In this limited offensive, the Confederates drove an estimated two thousand Federals from James Island, inflicted serious losses in killed and wounded, and captured fourteen soldiers of the 54th Massachusetts Regiment. This black regiment, recently organized and funded by wealthy Boston abolitionists, had been recruited throughout the North and arrived at Port Royal on June 3.[11]

General Gillmore and Admiral Dahlgren met on the sixteenth to plan the next attack on Wagner. During their discussions the naval commander became concerned when he realized Gillmore seemed overconfident and seriously underestimated Battery Wagner's strength. The general was certain an infantry assault could easily overrun the battery after a daylong bombardment and evidently did not realize the protection afforded the garrison in the bombproof. More important, he failed to appreciate the difference between pulverizing the masonry of Fort Pulaski in April 1862 and the ability of the sand and palmetto log construction at Battery Wagner to absorb the terrific pounding.

Ripley became concerned when, on July 17, while the bombardment of Wagner continued throughout the day, the enemy withdrew all vessels from the Stono and concentrated their troops on Little Folly and Morris Islands. On the morning of July 18, five wooden gunboats, later joined by five monitors and the *New Ironsides,* opened fire on Battery Wagner. By noon all Federal artillery, land based and naval, began a massive bombardment of the battery. Taliaferro estimated that Wagner received a deadly crossfire of more than nine thousand shells from the artillery on the southern end of the island and the naval forces to the east. The fort actually absorbed the heavy bombardment well and protected most of the garrison, which suffered only eight killed and twenty wounded.[12]

Ripley was convinced that the enemy planned to assault Battery Wagner at dusk. Therefore, he had the guns at Sumter and Battery Gregg prepared to fire over Wagner into the columns of the advancing enemy. Beauregard decided to relieve General Hagood on James Island and have him replace or support General Taliaferro at Wagner. However, while Hagood was en route, the enemy launched a ferocious onslaught up the island directly at Wagner.

Taliaferro positioned his men with great care, with infantry support from companies of the Charleston Battalion, along with the 51st and 31st North Carolina Regiments. Artillerymen from Company A of the 1st South Carolina Artillery and companies from the 63rd Georgia and the 22nd Georgia Battalion manned Wagner's artillery. On the beach outside the fort, a detachment from Company A, 1st South Carolina Artillery, manned two 12-pounder howitzers.[13]

For the Federal assault, three brigades under the command of General Truman Seymour were readied at the southern end of Morris Island. General George

C. Strong's brigade, now with the added strength of 650 men in the 54th Massachusetts, was to lead. This regiment replaced the four companies of the 7th Connecticut that had participated in the original attack. General H. S. Putnam's brigade of the 100th New York, 7th New Hampshire, and 62nd and 67th Ohio, along with General Thomas G. Stevenson's brigade, completed Seymour's command.

On the evening of July 18, Colonel Robert G. Shaw's 54th Massachusetts transferred from Folly Island to Morris Island. Generals Seymour and Strong had previously determined that Shaw's regiment would be given the honor of leading the assault. Despite his regiment being without food or rest, the idealistic Shaw accepted the honor enthusiastically. Assuming the bombardment had devastated and demoralized Wagner's defenders, Gillmore expected an easy victory, regardless of which regiment led the assault. General Putnam, commander of the second brigade, disagreed, protesting that the Union troops were "going into Wagner like a flock of sheep."

The decision to have the 54th Massachusetts lead the attack was not taken lightly. If they were not used on an equal footing with white troops, abolitionists and many Radical Republican politicians would claim discrimination. On the other hand, if the abolitionists thought the black troops were used to shield white troops, were used too aggressively, or were expended as cannon fodder, their criticism would be unrelenting.[14]

Shaw moved his regiment from the rear of the division, where they were positioned with Stevenson's brigade, to the front of the column. The 54th Massachusetts at that time was actually the strongest regiment in terms of manpower of any among the three Union brigades. The 6th Connecticut and the 48th New York would immediately follow the 54th Massachusetts. Shaw's men moved under the cover of darkness toward Wagner with the colonel leading the first battalion of five companies. Sergeant John Wall of the leading battalion carried the national flag, while the following five companies of the second battalion flew the state's regimental colors.

The assault, scheduled to begin at 7:45 P.M., was to be a simple bayonet charge; rifles were loaded but not capped. The men moved at quick time until they were within one hundred yards of the fort and then began their all-out rush. At this time, Taliaferro ordered the battery to open fire with muskets and canister. The two howitzers outside the battery, manned by Company A, 1st South Carolina Artillery, cut devastating swaths through the ranks of the attackers. When Sergeant Wall, the color bearer of the first battalion was wounded, Sergeant William C. Carney gathered up the national flag and carried it forward.

After stalling briefly, Colonel Shaw rallied his remaining men and charged through the water in the moat and up the sloping walls at the center of Battery Wagner. Some of Shaw's men gained the top of the breastworks, and the colonel was killed near the summit of the parapet. The attackers were soon driven down the slopes of the works and pinned there by canister from the beach howitzers. Carney was finally forced to retreat, and although wounded four times, he saved the national flag. However, the 54th Massachusetts regimental colors, carried by the second battalion, were lost in the vicious struggle. The reinforcements from the 6th Connecticut and the 48th New York soon met the same fate as the 54th and were also forced to retreat.[15]

General Strong's remaining regiments attempted an attack through a defile choked with wounded and retreating men from the first three regiments. These last three regiments soon received a storm of musket fire, canister, grape, and shell, which broke them into small groups. Strong, realizing the futility of the attack, was mortally wounded while ordering the brigade's retreat.[16]

As the first attack was being repulsed, General Putnam belatedly ordered the second brigade into action. Led by the 7th New Hampshire, the brigade charged the salient on Wagner's seaward side. Elements of the 67th Ohio, aided by survivors from the first brigade, seized temporary control of the salient but lost all momentum to advance. While rallying the men who had gained the lodgment within Wagner, General Putnam was killed. General Hagood, with Colonel Harrison's regiment, arrived in time to assist in containing the enemy still holding the southeastern salient of Wagner. Doomed by the piecemeal commitment of their troops, this last Federal attack also failed.[17]

Finally, at 1:00 A.M. on July 19, the carnage came to an end. Ripley praised the efforts of General Taliaferro who "had been in command and on trench duty for five days." He had directed all the operations of his "heroic garrison," who bravely met and repulsed the enemy with a "terrific slaughter." On the morning of the nineteenth, General Hagood relieved General Taliaferro.

Overnight the Confederates remained in position within Wagner and early the next morning saw the results of their devastating barrage. In Ripley's opinion, "The carnage of the enemy in the confined space in front of battery Wagner was extreme. The ditch and glacis were encumbered with the slain of all ranks and colors, for the enemy had put the poor Negroes, whom they had forced into an unnatural service, in front to be . . . slaughtered indiscriminately. The white colonel who commanded them fell, with many officers of the regiment, and the colors under which they were sent to butchery by hypocrisy and inhumanity fell, draggled in blood and sand in the ditch, a mournful memorial of waste."

Colonel Harris thought the scene in front of Wagner was "pitiless" and was greatly moved by the wounded and dying black soldiers. Harris believed that the 54th Massachusetts had been put in front to shield the white troops. He reached this conclusion because the blacks were not issued any equipment to help them scale the battery's sloping sand walls, and they carried nothing with which to spike the Confederate cannon.[18]

After Hagood relieved Taliaferro, the defenders repaired breaches, replaced guns, and in general strengthened the works at Wagner. Sections of Wagner's fatigued garrison were replaced almost nightly as Ripley rotated fresh troops to the battery. Those transferred included the return of Captain C. E. Chichester's company, then on Sullivan's Island, plus units from Castle Pinckney and Forts Pemberton and Ripley.

On July 22 General Taliaferro resumed command of Battery Wagner. For several weeks, about every three days, Ripley rotated Generals Hagood, Taliaferro, and Colquitt, along with Colonel L. M. Keitt as commander of the battery. Also on the twenty-second, after a failed attempt the previous day, the two sides agreed to exchange wounded prisoners, which would take place between ships off Morris Island. In the interim the Union suspended their fire on Wagner, and the Confederates continued their repairs.[19]

In the latter months of 1862, the Adjutant and Inspector General's Office issued General Orders, No. 93. Accordingly, the Confederate Congress authorized President Davis to recognize and award a medal for special acts of gallantry and courage on the battlefield by enlisted men and officers. Commissioned officers were to be chosen by the same method used by the British in awarding the Victoria Cross. Lack of funds and difficulty in procuring the medals delayed their presentation, and ultimately they were never issued. To avoid not recognizing their valor, those worthy of this distinction were to be inscribed on a "Roll of Honor." The roll was published only three times: October 1863, August 1864, and December 1864.[20]

Ripley's report of the events from July 8 to 19 cited the signalmen under the command of Lieutenant F. Markoe Jr., who had praised his men "for their zeal and gallantry in performing their duties under the heavy and continuous fire of the enemy." Probably no noncombatants faced greater risks than the Signal Corps. They were perched on the highest, most conspicuous spot on Battery Gregg and exposed to artillery fire and the deadly aim of sharpshooters. Ripley endorsed Markoe's assessment, and with his recommendation the men were listed on the Roll of Honor. According to John Johnson, in addition to the signalmen five other officers and enlisted men were placed on the Roll of Honor for their actions at Battery Wagner. The roll was to be read to every regiment in the service at the first dress parade after its receipt.[21]

The steamer *Alice,* under a flag of truce, proceeded as scheduled on July 24 to meet Federal vessels off Morris Island and exchange wounded prisoners. Ripley's brother-in-law and aide-de-camp, J. Motte Middleton, accompanied the steamer under the command of Colonel E. C. Anderson. Ripley appears to have worked well with Motte and praised the services of his brother-in-law during this period. After the war Motte Middleton, possibly unavoidably, would complicate Ripley's financial problems.[22]

Ripley showed his resourcefulness by proposing an unconventional tactic to drive the enemy vessels from the ship channel. He first spoke privately with Beauregard, who initially dismissed the plan. Ripley continued to seek support for his idea and discussed it with Confederate naval officers, Captain J. R. Tucker, commander of the naval forces in the harbor, and Lieutenant Commanders John Rutledge and Alexander F. Warley. As these officers thought his idea should be considered, Ripley sent a written proposal to Beauregard, who referred the plan to Commodore D. N. Ingraham and Captain Tucker. If they approved the plan, Beauregard asked them to meet him in conference.

Ripley's plan was a variation of an old naval tactic, setting a sailing ship on fire and sailing it into a compacted enemy fleet. He observed the enemy fleet lying in a group extending from Battery Wagner out to the bar. The *New Ironsides* and monitors were in front with about twenty or more transports, store ships, and gunboats in the rear. Ripley complained that the enemy disembarked troops, sent stores ashore, and prepared to reduce the Confederates' fortifications, all "under our sight," and little had been done to stop them.

Ripley proposed seizing a private steamer, packing its magazine with ten thousand pounds of gunpowder, combustibles, and loaded shells, and sending it against the Federal ships. He would equip the steamer with outriggers connected to the magazine and set to explode on contact; the crew would ignite time fuses in the event no contact was made. Ripley countered Beauregard's criticism of the plan's uncertainty by claiming its uncertainty was not as great as the certainty that nothing else would be tried with effect.

Regarding objections to the expense of his proposal, he suggested that "the blockade running steamers in port are almost useless to our defense and in case of a catastrophe everyone of them will be sacrificed." Recognizing the mission was extremely dangerous, Ripley included a plan to enable the "fire-ship's" crew of four or five to escape. After the helm had been lashed and time fuses lit, each crewmember, who was tethered to a trailing boat or boats, would jump overboard and haul himself to his boat. They would also escape this way if the contact outriggers were nearing an enemy ship. Although Ripley expressed concern for the men's safety, their escape was certainly problematic.[23]

Beauregard called for a conference in the evening of July 24 with Generals Ripley and Jordan, and with Commodore Ingraham and Captain Tucker representing the navy. Ripley, Ingraham, and Tucker initially believed that there was a 20–30 percent chance of success. Beauregard believed the possibility was much less, and as Ingraham and he reevaluated the plan, they concluded the chance for success was only 5–10 percent. Nevertheless, Beauregard authorized Ripley to make all necessary inquiries to carry out the plan if it ultimately was approved.[24]

On July 25 Beauregard telegraphed General Cooper at the War Department about Ripley's proposal and asked whether it should be tried. Never enthusiastic about the plan, Beauregard probably discouraged Cooper from endorsing the plan when he added that the "probable cost will be nearly a million dollars." As of July 28 Beauregard still had not received an answer from the adjutant general.

In early August, Captain Tucker asked Beauregard whether it would be better to send the private steamers abroad than keep them for the defense of the harbor or use one as the "fire-ship," Obviously annoyed, Beauregard replied that it was now time for them to attack the *New Ironsides* or other ironclads that were destroying the works on Morris Island. If the navy planned to hold the steamers in the inner harbor as a last line of defense, it would be better to release them at once and send them abroad for military supplies. This effectively ended Ripley's innovative but rather implausible plan to attack and drive off the Federal fleet with an exploding "fire-ship."[25]

In the summer of 1863, Ripley expressed his concern for his wife and the future of his nine-year-old daughter by selecting John Middleton and Theodore D. Wagner to be Alicia's trustees. On August 6 Ripley purchased a three-story brick tenement building in Charleston from Alexander Robertson for $25,000 and placed it in trust for his daughter. The building, known as the "South Tenement of Vanderhorst North Row," was located on a lot bounded on the west by East Bay Street, on the north by the "Middle Tenement of Vanderhorst North Row," on the south by a street connecting East Bay Street to Vanderhorst Wharf, and an unnamed property to the east. The income from the property would go to Mrs. Ripley, but at age twenty-one, or if married with her parents' consent, Alicia would receive income from the property.[26]

That Ripley had $25,000 to invest strongly suggests that he had other sources of income. On April 23 Augustine Smythe had written that the "*Thistle* tried to run the blockade night before last, got into it and had to come back. She and the *B* tried it again last night, but failed again. The *Thistle* is owned chiefly by General Ripley and Colonel Keitt. These are the only vessels now in port."

On May 1, 1863, from Liverpool, Charles K. Prioleau wrote to Ripley's attorney, Theodore D. Wagner, "It was hard luck for Wigg. He is somewhat excited about the sale of the *Thistle* and I am afraid you will have trouble about it. Some man named Butcher has written Wigg that he is the victim of a conspiracy, and General Ripley now owns a fourth of the *Thistle,* which if true does not look well." Prioleau went on to write that Wigg did not accuse Wagner of anything "worse than acting hastily, and being deceived by false information." If there was a conspiracy involving Ripley, it certainly would not "look well" for him, but it is not known whether Butcher's accusation was valid.

In fact, there are two *Thistles* mentioned in Stephen R. Wise's excellent account of the blockade-runners, *Lifeline of the Confederacy.* Wise wrote that *Thistle (I)* was built in 1859 at Port Glasgow, Scotland, and owned by George Wigg for the Navigation Company until March 1862. At that time, after running aground, it was sold to John Ferguson and renamed the *Cherokee*. While trying to leave Charleston on May 8, it was captured and taken into the U.S. Navy. Wise's sources evidently do not mention either Butcher or Ripley, and the timeline does not fit with Smythe's April 1863 letter or with Prioleau's letter to Theodore Wagner in May regarding Wigg, Butcher, Ripley, and the "conspiracy."

Thistle (II) was built at Port Glasgow, Scotland, in early 1864. The owner was listed as Fraser, Trenholm & Company. This second ship was captured in June 1864 bound for Wilmington from Charleston. While difficult to determine, as neither ship fits the appropriate timeline, it would seem that if Ripley was an investor in one of the *Thistles,* it may have been the *Thistle (I)*.[27]

CHAPTER 21

Siege and Bombardment

Following the failed infantry assaults, General Gillmore began the siege of Battery Wagner. To facilitate the siege, a zigzag line of trenches, protected by wire entanglements and artillery, was dug relentlessly closer to Wagner. The Union navy continued to batter Wagner, while new artillery emplacements and breaching batteries were constructed on the southern end of Morris Island. Wagner would be under increasingly heavy fire, and Gillmore's breaching batteries intended to bombard Fort Sumter into submission.[1]

On July 24 General Taliaferro notified Ripley that the enemy's batteries were now so close they could soon dismount his land-face guns. His 10-inch gun had been disabled, and if Ripley could arrange the transportation, he wanted to withdraw the garrison that night. One of Taliaferro's officers, Captain C. E. Chichester, disagreed. As he had personal knowledge of Wagner's construction, he believed that although its form had changed, the depth of sand outside the bombproofs and magazines was still practically intact. Chichester hurriedly rowed into the city and went to Ripley's headquarters, where allegedly he convinced Ripley that the situation was salvageable. Ripley sent the information to Beauregard for his approval, assigned Chichester to duty as Taliaferro's chief of artillery, and sent him back to the battery with orders for it to be held.[2]

It was essential to hold Wagner as long as possible, for it was only a matter of time before Fort Sumter would be silenced by the new Morris Island batteries. Time was needed to transfer artillery from Fort Sumter to strengthen the defenses of the inner harbor and James Island. Beauregard instructed Ripley to inform Taliaferro that Battery Wagner was to be held and "fought to the last extremity." Beauregard charged Ripley with making all arrangements for the evacuation of Wagner when further resistance became fruitless. In the effort to strengthen the new defenses, Beauregard instructed Ripley to remove five of the 8-inch naval guns from the casemates at Fort Sumter. They were to be sent by way of Fort Johnson to Battery Cheves, a newly erected battery west of Wagner on the eastern end of James Island.[3]

Beauregard asked Ripley to report the number of guns removed from Sumter and where they had been transferred, and in the future to provide a daily list of the removal and disposition of Sumter's guns. On July 27, possibly still annoyed by the earlier criticism of the engineers, Beauregard assailed Ripley with numerous issues and recommendations regarding ordnance placement. Ripley was to inform Commodore Ingraham of the circumstances involved in the bursting of a 6.40 Brooke gun. He was to list the number of times the gun was fired, the charge used, the elevation, the exact nature of the fracture, and so on. In addition, one of Beauregard's "inspectors," questioned the adequacy of the infantry guard posted for two field pieces at Battery Simkins on James Island.[4]

The following day Colonel A. J. Gonzales, Beauregard's chief of artillery and ordnance, submitted urgent proposals to Beauregard and Ripley for the disposition of heavy artillery from Fort Sumter. Beauregard dismissed the Cuban's suggestions, and Ripley "respectfully" returned them to the colonel. Ripley also corrected Gonzales: "rifled guns, with the proper projectiles, are better for shelling at long range than smoothbores, and can be fired as fast with proper aim." Ripley advised against indiscriminately removing ordnance and reducing Sumter's offensive capability too severely. He worried about his men and thought the unlimited removal of artillery would have a negative effect on their morale.

In another move, Beauregard directed Ripley to remove six 8-inch columbiads from Sumter, send one each to Battery Simkins and Battery Haskell, and two to Battery Cheves on James Island. Ripley sent the other two to a new battery east of Fort Moultrie. Battery Cheves was also to receive five 8-inch naval shell guns from Moultrie.[5]

In early August, Ripley informed Beauregard that an enemy gunboat threatened the relief of Wagner's garrison by attacking the steamer bringing a replacement battalion and stores to Cummings Point. As Sumter and Moultrie were too far distant to protect Cummings Point, Ripley suggested that a "movable" force was needed to prevent future interruptions. Ripley criticized the navy's inability to prevent enemy access to nearby creeks, which allowed them to send signals regarding his operations. Beauregard agreed with Ripley and proposed stationing an ironclad near Cummings Point nightly. Ingraham and Tucker claimed that a coal shortage prevented this. They intended to cooperate with Ripley but believed it would be best to keep the ironclads within the harbor.[6]

At about the same time, Beauregard asked Ripley to send a rifled 32-pounder from Sumter to Battery Wagner, replacing one that had burst, and to send one of Sumter's mortars to Battery Gregg. He also directed Ripley to furnish, at once, Fort Sumter and Sullivan's Island with enough provisions and ammunition for a prolonged defense. Nevertheless, he directed the expeditious transfer of all guns and ammunition that could be spared from Sumter to Sullivan's Island. In response to a possible enemy landing in Georgia, Ripley was to have General Taliaferro and two regiments, with three days' cooked rations, ready to move to Savannah on a moment's notice.[7]

While the enemy continued to strengthen the batteries on Morris Island, Beauregard's deluge of directives continued. Ripley received two separate lists of instructions and complaints from two of Beauregard's staff officers. The first notice concerned five changes in the disposition of ordnance within his command. Ripley was to transfer an 8-inch shell gun on a columbiad platform from Battery Glover to the southeast angle of Redoubt No. 1 on James Island. This gun would replace a 32-pounder smoothbore that was to be moved to the southeast face of the same installation. Second, one of the five 8-inch shell guns taken from Fort Sumter, originally destined for Battery Cheves, was to be installed at Battery Haskell instead. Third, the naval carriages for the five shell guns previously mentioned were to be taken from the arsenal to their proper positions, four to Cheves and one to Haskell. Next, Ripley was to send a staff officer to Cummings Point and transport a 10-inch carriage, currently on the water's edge, to the city. Along with the carriage, he was to send the large quantity of spent Yankee shot and shells that had been recovered. Finally, Ripley was to send the four bronze rifled cannon returned by the siege train, plus any ammunition with them, to the weakest point on the eastern lines on James Island.

The second more critical directive that day stemmed from Beauregard's visit to Morris Island and Fort Sumter, where he noticed matters needing attention and asked Ripley to "carry out his views." First, Battery Gregg was in need of many small things, such as fuse gauges, and "more importantly 9-inch shells," which had been requested but never filled. Second, at Battery Wagner, despite the tremendous bombardments they had endured, Beauregard found fault with the lack of paperwork between relieved officers and their successors, and ordered that all relieved officers should remain at their posts until the paperwork was completed. He also complained that the general officers had not been keeping a book of orders to transmit to their successors. Beauregard directed Ripley to have a book of orders prepared, including all backorders, and sent to Morris Island. The book was to be kept up to date and turned over to the relieving commanding officer; the inspector was to examine the book weekly. Beauregard complained that the battery often lacked sufficient provisions and ammunition and counseled the obvious: "an ample supply of both should always be on hand."

As Beauregard's relationship with Ripley had become more contentious, to further chastise Ripley, Beauregard advised him to visit Morris Island personally at least once or twice a week, although there is no record that he had not been making visits. He also directed Ripley to send a staff officer at least every other night to report any irregularities. Ripley, who had a great disdain for bureaucratic red tape, must have bristled at this increased paperwork, especially considering the artillery barrage the battery was receiving. As his biographer has written, Beauregard's "greatest weakness as a soldier [was] to think of war as something that was in books and was fought in conformity to a fixed pattern. Too many times he would go by the rules of the book."[8]

Beauregard became more involved in the direct management of the First Military District and inundated Ripley with orders for the removal of Fort

Sumter's ordnance. He proposed removing two 8-inch columbiads from the east face to make room for traverses and the placement of the 7-inch Brooke gun taken from the northwest salient angle. One of these 8-inch columbiads was to be sent to either Battery Bee or Fort Moultrie. He did not specify the destination of the other.

The 7-inch Brooke gun at the northwest salient was to be replaced by a 10-inch columbiad now situated next to it. A 42-pounder on the northeast face near another 10-inch columbiad should be removed to Battery Bee. This would allow for the addition of traverses in the rear of the two 10-inch columbiads to protect them against fire from Morris Island. He ordered a traverse constructed at the northwest salient to protect the 10-inch columbiad from fire coming from that direction.

Fort Sumter's two rifled 32-pounders in casemate were to be mounted at once on the south face in place of the two 24-pounders. Those two guns should be sent to the city for banding and rifling. The mortars in the gorge should be lowered to the parade level, but Beauregard, apparently not certain how many mortars were in the gorge, ordered only three to be kept at Sumter, while "the others, not already disposed of (if any), should be sent to Battery Simkins or Sullivan's Island."[9]

As previously noted, Ripley had informed Beauregard that the inactivity of the Confederate navy allowed "the enemy to infest our creeks and give signals of our operations." Two days later Beauregard himself "discovered" this to be the case and found it necessary to enlighten Ripley. It appeared that "the enemy has a picket at night in the Marsh Creek battery, at or near the battery, to observe and report when our steamers are at Cumming's Point." He called for Ripley to prevent this and thought it "may be best done by the navy."[10]

The next night Ripley ordered a combined force from the 25th South Carolina and a naval party from the steamer *Chicora* to attack the Union pickets at the mouth of Vincent's Creek. In a brief skirmish the pickets were driven off, and the Confederates captured a boat, along with a wounded Federal captain and ten noncommissioned officers and privates.[11]

While the Union army dug their siege lines relentlessly toward Battery Wagner, General Gillmore established a massive artillery stronghold on the southern end of Morris Island. Twelve batteries, totaling over thirty guns, were trained on Fort Sumter. About twenty guns concentrated their fire on Battery Wagner, with a few guns directed against Battery Gregg. In addition, two monitors bombarded Sumter, while the remaining ironclads and wooden gunboats directed their fire against Wagner.[12]

Ripley chronicled the Confederates' day-by-day resistance in August, noting that the heavy fire received on the nights of August 8, 9, and 10 had impaired the transfer of troops to and from the island. On the eleventh the bombardment began at 7:00 A.M. and continued all day, but caused little damage to Battery Wagner. Ripley observed a marked increase in Union firepower beginning on the morning of August 12 and claimed that the Federals had opened on Fort Sumter at seven o'clock that morning with a 200-pounder Parrott from a distance he estimated to be nearly five thousand yards. Ripley noted that Sumter was struck seventeen times and was badly damaged when any of the projectiles hit light masonry, but little damage was done to either the heavy concrete or sand revetments. At nightfall, Wagner opened with eight guns on the enemy directly in its front, and Sumter joined the steady fire through the night.[13]

When the enemy attempted to repair and advance their siege trenches, fire from Battery Wagner repulsed the work details. The enemy fell back to its rear batteries and with support from the ironclads shelled both Wagner and Gregg. In the afternoon the heavy Parrott guns opened on Sumter with several shells damaging the gorge wall. Ripley recorded a lull in the action on August 14, but firing resumed that night. Sumter received five hits from the enemy's land batteries and one from a gunboat, but little damage was done. Some firing continued on the fifteenth, but the enemy's batteries were unusually quiet on the following day.[14]

In mid-August, Beauregard directed Ripley to transfer a mortar from Fort Sumter to Battery Gregg and send the other two to Battery Haskell when they were no longer of use at Sumter. More important, as soon as possible, Ripley should transfer every gun not needed for the defense of Sumter to Sullivan's and James Island.

The quiet of the sixteenth was truly the lull before the storm. August 17 is recorded as the first official day of the heavy bombardment of Fort Sumter from Morris Island. The action began early, and by mid-morning the *New Ironsides* and six monitors joined the shelling of Sumter. Ripley believed that Sumter received three 200-pounder Parrotts and one 100-pounder from a distance of two to three miles. John Johnson, the engineer in charge, who was slightly wounded that day, later wrote that there were eleven variously sized rifled guns involved in the attack, significantly outgunning the defenders. When the firing slacked off in the early afternoon, Ripley's staff rowed him to the fort to inspect the damage. Over a twenty-four-hour period, the Federals fired 948 shells at Sumter; nearly 700 struck the walls or inside the fort, but more than 200 passed harmlessly overhead.

Sumter sustained major damages, but surprisingly the casualties were few. Half of the parapet for the gorge was demolished. A major section of the second and third floors of the western barracks were in ruins, and seven guns had been disabled. The relatively quiet night allowed some repairs to be made, and a large amount of stores and ammunition was transferred to works on Sullivan's Island. The garrison lowered two 42-pounders from the ramparts to the parade grounds for shipment to the inner harbor defenses. With the destruction of Sumter now assured, the role of the garrison was to save anything of value and delay the end as long as possible.[15]

The barrage continued relentlessly for the next two days, further damaging the northwest face, collapsing an additional section of the gorge wall, and disabling the remaining guns on the northeast face. The two guns remaining on the west face, the 7-inch Brooke gun in the southwest angle, and all of the gorge guns were disabled. During these two days the Federals fired 1,656 shot and shell at Sumter with slightly over 80 percent hitting the target. Despite this tremendous battering, only one man was killed and seven wounded. During the night the garrison transferred more ammunition from Sumter to Sullivan's Island.

Battery Wagner received a similar bombardment from the enemy's smaller guns, which disabled two guns, but the sand-and-log battery absorbed the shelling with little damage. Union forces attempted to extend their approaches closer to Wagner, but Confederate artillery and sharpshooters armed with British Whitworth rifles and telescopic sights slowed the advance.[16]

Around 5:00 P.M. on the third day of the bombardment, Ripley's men again rowed him out to Fort Sumter under a heavy fire, and he "remained there for some time examining its condition." The *Mercury* reported that the garrison still maintained "the admirable discipline for which it has always been credited. Guards were turned out, and the usual etiquette observed as strictly as if nothing was going on."[17]

On the fourth day of this huge bombardment, the Federals completed their breaching batteries on Morris Island and now had eighteen rifled 100-, 200-, and 300-pounders firing on Sumter. The fort received 748 shots that day, with 408 striking outside and 241 inside; however, there were only three minor casualties. That night 25,000 pounds of powder and other ammunition were transferred out of the fort.[18]

During this barrage a young artillery lieutenant, W. Gordon McCabe, arrived in Charleston for temporary duty. Shortly after McCabe's arrival and before new guns arrived from Richmond, Ripley appointed McCabe to his staff as an acting adjutant. In this capacity on the day after he arrived, McCabe "ran the gauntlet" to Fort Sumter. The lieutenant wrote a letter to a young friend, James Barron Hope, describing the "situation" in Charleston. His boat to Fort Sumter was one of three making the trip and the only one not sunk by enemy fire. He described the destruction at Sumter in vivid detail: "Within the fortress . . . great timbers are crashing, great arches of masonry are falling, but the officers are seen coolly walking the parapet, and the men laughing, chatting, and singing, except when some poor fellow is brought by on a stretcher." McCabe thought that the whole north wall would soon fall and that "there is scarcely a gun in the fortress that can harm the enemy . . . but the red-cross banner is floating now as proudly as ever from its shattered battlements."

McCabe wrote, "So far I find my position here very agreeable, and the officers here are very kind to me in every way. General Ripley commands all the defenses of Charleston . . . He looks very much like 'Count Fosco,' except his face, which is as honest and hearty as an old Tom Brown's." McCabe was referring to Count Fosco, the corpulent "villain" in Willkie Collins's 1860 novel *A Woman in White* and to *Tom Brown's School Days,* Thomas Hughes's 1857 novel. "I like to hear his bluff, jovial voice," McCabe added, "as he gives orders with the rapidity and accuracy of an old soldier." However, McCabe described Beauregard as appearing "very much worn, and the light in his eyes rather dim."[19]

During the bombardment on August 21, Colonel Rhett, Lieutenant Johnson, and the other officers at Sumter held a conference at noon to discuss their situation. Beauregard and Harris inspected the fort at sundown and Ripley visited for an inspection at 10:00 P.M. The fort had received 750 shots that struck either inside the fort or on its outer walls; despite being heavily protected, five more guns were disabled. The garrison shipped 9,700 pounds of powder, artillery implements, subsistence, and other stores from Sumter; and a fresh crew of workers arrived at the fort.[20]

Johnson divided the first Union bombardment of Sumter into two phases, the first of which ended on August 23 after one week of shelling. At the end of the week, the only gun in serviceable condition was the 11-inch Dahlgren salvaged from the *Keokuk*. More powder and ordnance were shipped out, and although Sumter was not totally silenced, for all practical purposes it was a demolished, shapeless ruin.

The second phase of the first bombardment began on August 24 but slackened for nearly a week, enabling more powder and a large number of shells to be shipped from the fort. In addition, the garrison began digging out and removing guns buried in the fort's massive debris. During this time more than twenty-five guns and mortars were recovered and sent to the inner harbor and islands.[21]

Near the end of the month, Beauregard's chief of staff notified Ripley that despite being required to reduce the size of Fort Sumter's garrison, he must instruct the commanding officer to hold the fort to the "last extremity." For the garrison of two to three hundred men, Ripley was to choose from the best companies in his command, selecting one company of artillery supported by two full companies of infantry. Three guns were to be mounted and kept serviceable at all times. Two hundred pounds of powder were to be kept for each gun, but all other powder and any "valuable projectiles" were to be removed from the fort. As the removal of as many guns as possible to the inner harbor would continue and the garrison reduced in size, Jordan suggested that Colonel Rhett might opt to transfer his command to Fort Johnson. If so, Major Stephen Elliott should replace him.

In closing, Jordan expressed Beauregard's genuine "pride and gratification" with the defense of Fort Sumter made by Colonel Rhett, his officers, and the men of the 1st South Carolina Artillery. He praised their discipline and the organization of the regiment: "In the annals of war no stouter defense was ever made, and no work ever . . . encountered as formidable bombardment as that under which Fort Sumter has been successfully held." Although unmentioned by Beauregard, Ripley was most instrumental in training and supervising these men, resulting in their compelling performance.[22]

On the last day of August, Beauregard communicated a long list of "wishes" to Ripley. The requests varied from the sublime to the most basic and some that would definitely increase Ripley's paperwork. He was to compile a complete list of the guns removed from Fort Sumter since April 7. Another list was to be made of all guns that had burst or been otherwise permanently disabled. Beauregard reminded Ripley to supply Castle Pinckney and Fort Ripley with sufficient provisions and ammunition. Previous orders relative to supplying Morris, James, and Sullivan's Islands, if not yet carried out, were to be executed at once. Ripley was to direct Colonel Rhett to use his sharpshooters, at night if necessary, to protect the rope obstructions in the ship channel. When the new batteries on James Island west of Fort Johnson were fortified with guns, they were to be manned and supplied with ammunition. Every night all harbor batteries should be prepared to open fire on a moment's notice. All heavy gun carriages and chassis were to be removed as soon and as rapidly as possible. Finally, after the remaining guns at Sumter became disabled or were unserviceable, the artillery company was to be replaced by a company of infantry. The commanding general also instructed Ripley to file a weekly report of any operations in his district.[23]

On August 21 General Gillmore issued Beauregard an ultimatum, demanding the evacuation of Fort Sumter and Morris Island, or else he would open fire on Charleston. Beauregard was absent when his headquarters received the note at 10:45 P.M.; as it was unsigned, his staff returned the message. At 1:30 A.M. on the twenty-second, an 8-inch Parrott, nicknamed the "Swamp Angel," located in the marshes between James and Morris Islands, opened fire on the city. Beauregard considered it "an act of desperation and barbarity" and protested the attack, as did the British and Spanish consuls. Gillmore relented and suspended the barrage for twenty-four hours to allow civilians time to leave the city. The following day the firing resumed, but with the thirty-sixth shot fired at Charleston, the "Swamp Angel" burst, ending its bombardment.

The *Richmond Examiner* reported the bombardment of Charleston, and on August 30 the *Mercury* reprinted the Richmond paper's response to the "barbarous shelling." To prevent future bombardments, the *Examiner* proposed transporting a few thousand Yankee prisoners from Libby Prison in Richmond to

Charleston and confining them in warehouses in the city: "As there is no prospect for a speedy renewal of exchange, these prisoners might as well be defending Charleston.... This kind of retaliation will teach Gillmore how to conduct a siege according to the rules of civilized warfare."[24]

Throughout August, while the Federal artillery and navy pulverized Sumter, the bombardment of Wagner continued, with Union sappers digging their trenches ever closer to the Confederate rifle pits fronting Wagner. Confederate sharpshooters occupied the rifle pits two hundred yards in front of Wagner and for some time succeeded in slowing the Federal advance toward the battery. However, on the night of August 26, two Union regiments, totaling nearly four hundred men, overwhelmed the eighty-six defenders of the 61st North Carolina and seized the rifle pits. With the loss of this forward position, it was only a matter of time before another concerted Federal attack would gain the battery. Wagner's determined resistance bought time for the Confederates to strengthen the defenses on James Island and to build new batteries along the inner harbor. Even with the impending loss of Battery Wagner, the Confederate defense of the harbor was stronger than it had been in early July.[25]

In mid-July, Beauregard responded to questions from Secretary of War James Seddon and attempted to explain how Union forces gained a foothold on Morris Island. He claimed the catastrophe was not preventable because "stronger works could not be erected for lack of labor, though every effort was exhausted to secure Negroes from the day I took command of the department up to July 1, 1863." He also claimed that he was unable to get ordnance essential for the works and that "I did not have a garrison sufficiently strong for Morris, James and Sullivan's Islands at the same time." Beauregard must have regretted this last claim, for it engendered an angry response from Secretary Seddon.

Seddon asserted that he had no "disposition to criticize military operations, or point out errors and omissions which can no longer be avoided or remedied," but he believed the enemy's success in gaining a foothold on Morris Island was not due to the lack of infantry but resulted from not having an adequate work of defense at the lower end of the island. He also criticized Beauregard for being unaware that the enemy had erected powerful, concealed batteries on Folly Island. Seddon maintained that these were the true causes of the enemy's success and definitely "not the want of men." He concluded that the failure of the enemy to swiftly capture Forts Wagner and Gregg proved that a shortage of men was not the problem.

Beauregard claimed to be totally surprised by Seddon's criticism and decided he would not suffer censure alone. He sent Ripley a copy of Seddon's letter, along with an exhaustive list of thirty-two interrogatories covering minute details of Ripley's district. Beauregard also asked Ripley about the size of the infantry force in Georgia, how many were transferred to Charleston, and when they arrived.

Beauregard, who was in charge of the entire department, probably should have known this without quizzing Ripley.

The commanding general demanded a full and detailed report on the subjects at Ripley's "earliest convenience." Of these questions, the most contentious may have been Nos. 9 and 31. In No. 9, Beauregard asked Ripley whether there could have been a better disposition of their troops and, in No. 31, whether the works had been completed and armed with the troops on hand and, if so, would Charleston have been safe until reinforcements arrived for a prolonged defense.

Ripley dutifully answered the thirty-two questions the following day but admitted that a full and detailed report covering the several months preceding the attack would take more time. Ripley answered No. 9 by admitting that he did not know whether there could have been a better distribution of the troops at hand but stated, "[If] we had concentrated on Morris Island, the enemy would have at once turned on James Island."

Most likely Ripley's answer to question No. 31 did not please Beauregard and further damaged their relationship. Ripley claimed that if the works for the defense of Morris Island had been completed and armed, the troops of his command, with a few reinforcements, could have held the southern end of the island until larger forces arrived. If no other attacks were attempted, the whole assault would have been repulsed.[26]

More problems arose for Charleston's defenders when, on September 1, General Cooper notified Beauregard that Union advances in Tennessee and incursions into Virginia had compromised the supply of niter and metal. Cooper chastised Beauregard for the recent bursting of two rifled guns in the Charleston batteries and the daily expenditure of large amounts of ammunition. Cooper suggested that the heavy guns were fired at too great an elevation and with excessive charges, and then urged Beauregard to economize ammunition without compromising Charleston's defenses.

The next day Beauregard informed Ripley of the potential shortages of niter and metal, and instructed him to notify his battery commanders of the situation. Beauregard criticized Ripley's batteries at Fort Moultrie, alleging that they wasted almost every pound of powder and iron they fired because the ironclads attacking Fort Sumter were beyond Moultrie's effective range. Beauregard ordered Ripley to prevent Sullivan's batteries from firing at ironclads farther than that at which the *Keokuk* was sunk but delightedly asserted that the enemy's fire on Fort Sumter was "an evident waste of ammunition and a useless expenditure of ordnance."

Ripley countered that the action of the monitors was intended to batter down the east face of Sumter and that they succeeded in demolishing "nearly the whole of the scarp wall," leaving only the sand embankment for protection through several of the arches. Although there were no serious injuries at Sumter,

Ripley claimed that there were two or three because of the carelessness of certain commanders who left their troops in the Moultrie House, which the enemy shelled. Disputing Beauregard's assessment of his batteries, Ripley claimed that they were actually quite accurate and that "the monitors were struck probably one hundred times . . . at distances varying from 800 to 1,300 yards," seriously damaging two or three of them. The amazing difference of opinion regarding the effectiveness of Moultrie's fire is inexplicable and contributed to the contentiousness between the two generals.[27]

Beauregard and Ripley exchanged messages on September 3, when the commanding general asked Ripley to place calcium lights on Sullivan's Island to illuminate the recently placed rope obstructions opposite Fort Sumter. He also instructed Ripley where to mount the three rifled and banded 42-pounders recently removed from Sumter. Ripley did not believe the enemy would attempt to occupy Sumter, so if Beauregard approved, he proposed reducing Sumter's garrison to two companies of infantry. In granting his approval, Beauregard selected Major Stephen Elliott to replace Colonel Rhett, who was given command of the inner batteries, Castle Pinckney and Fort Ripley.

During these first three nights of September, Ripley continued to ship ordnance and stores from Sumter and credited J. Fraser Mathewes and Lieutenant Julius M. Rhett for having nine more guns readied for transfer to the inner harbor. Colonel Rhett documented Ripley's visit to Fort Sumter around 1:00 A.M. on the fourth.[28]

In early September, Augustine Smythe wrote about Ripley's "serious loss last night" when his "fine sailboat, used to visit the forts," was captured. Ripley had sent the boat to Morris Island on business, but on the return trip, while bringing back Major Warley, who had been slightly wounded at Wagner, a Yankee barge captured the boat, the crew, and Major Warley. Smythe believed that this was especially unfortunate, as the crew was very well acquainted with all the harbor fortifications.[29]

Ripley summarized the final days of the stubborn Confederate defense in his report of September 22. Early in the month Union land batteries, along with the *New Ironsides* and monitors, poured a devastating fire on Batteries Wagner and Gregg. Fifteen to twenty Union barges, approaching from the junction of Schooner and Vincent's Creek, attempted an amphibious infantry landing at Cumming's Point but were repulsed. The Confederate batteries had held for fifty-seven days under a furious cannonade, but now the Union lines reached to within yards of Wagner's salient. Most of Wagner's guns were disabled; transportation and supply were most difficult; and the possibility of reinforcing the garrison was out of the question. Therefore, on the morning of the sixth, orders were given to prepare for evacuation. Ripley "determined not to subject those brave men—the flower of our force—to the desperate chances of assault."

Instructions were sent for the demolition of the armament and magazines of both batteries as they were being abandoned. Transport steamers and small boats assembled at Cumming's Point to embark the men. The evacuation on the night of the sixth began at nine o'clock and was completed by midnight. At eleven o'clock, while the evacuation was in progress, Colonel Keitt turned the command of Wagner over to his current chief of artillery, Captain Thomas A. Huguenin. Keitt and a small rear guard nervously waited at Battery Gregg for Huguenin and four others to spike the guns and explode the magazines. Some time after 1:00 A.M. the party from Wagner, without Huguenin, arrived and explained why the explosions and demolition had failed. Keitt, in the belief that Huguenin, who had an injured knee, had been captured or possibly killed, ordered the boats to pull away. As the captain limped onto the beach, he witnessed the last of the boats rowing away and feared he had been abandoned. However, in the darkness a launch appeared offshore; Huguenin waded out and was taken aboard.[30]

In the morning, an erroneous report claiming Huguenin had been killed reached Ripley. Around 8:00 A.M., when he finally reported to Ripley's headquarters, Huguenin is said to have received a very characteristic greeting from the general: "In his bluff, military manner Ripley said, 'Huguenin is that you? Why I thought you were dead. I am glad to see you.' It appears in South Carolina, short greetings serve in times of war."[31]

Huguenin had met Ripley at Fort Moultrie early in the war and considered him to be "the best artillerist I ever saw, who knew his profession from the smallest detail up to the most important." While in Ripley's office giving the general and Colonel Keitt an account of the evacuation, Ripley received an order from Beauregard to arrest Huguenin for not blowing up the armament and magazines. Ripley and Keitt were "much annoyed" by this as they had heard Huguenin's story, and Colonel Keitt knew exactly why the captain was unable to execute the order. Ripley and Keitt told Huguenin to wait in the general's office and write his report, while they would go to Beauregard's headquarters and explain the whole matter. Beauregard immediately countermanded the arrest order and sent Huguenin "a kind message."[32]

CHAPTER 22

The H. L. Hunley *Arrives*

After the loss of Batteries Wagner and Gregg, Fort Sumter became the advanced fortification against Union forces attacking Charleston. It was the symbol of Southern secession and the people of South Carolina, and the Confederacy strongly supported Beauregard's decision to hold it at all costs. Serving in the crumbling remnants of the fort was considered an honor. Despite the withdrawal of his artillerists, Major Stephen Elliott was committed to defend the ruins of Sumter with his infantrymen "or die in the attempt." When Admiral Dahlgren demanded Sumter's surrender, Beauregard replied, "such demands are puerile and unbecoming, take it if you can."[1]

The following day Dahlgren launched an amphibious assault against the fort, and although Gillmore had a similar plan, because of the lack of cooperation between the two services, the general opted out of a combined attack. Late at night on September 8, Federal tugs towed five groups of boats, carrying about 450 men, to within eight hundred yards of Sumter. Dahlgren planned a diversionary attack at the northwestern front of the fort while the main assault would be directed against Sumter's southeastern wall. In the darkness, in haste and somewhat in disorder, the boats were cast off, and evidently only two of the five groups actually disembarked. Having anticipated the night attack, Major Elliott had prepared his men well and repulsed the disorganized landing without a loss. Federal losses totaled fifty killed, wounded, and missing, while over one hundred officers and men were captured and sent to the city. The fairly easy Confederate victory reinforced the Rebels' resolve to hold the fort to the last.[2]

On September 9 Beauregard sent two rather basic directives to Ripley. He was reminded to inform his artillery officers that in any engagement with ironclads, they were to concentrate their fire as much as possible on the vessel nearest to the battery. If the nearest vessel was forced to retire, they were to fire on the next vessel in order. If the *New Ironsides* became a target, all fire should be directed on it.[3]

Three days later Ripley sparred with Beauregard. He acknowledged receiving a copy of the directive from Adjutant General Cooper to economize ammunition and asserted that every battery commander had already been instructed to do so. He vowed that they would continue to conserve ammunition; nevertheless, he wrote, "I know of no way to repel the attacks of the enemy except by the use of heavy artillery, which must on certain occasions be at long range." He asserted that while his men "lie quiet to save powder and projectiles, guns are dismounted by the un-resisted fire of his ironclads and land batteries."

Surprisingly, Beauregard seconded Ripley's remarks and forwarded them to both Cooper and the ordnance department. Beauregard criticized Gorgas and his department, adding that more ammunition could be saved if the fuses sent to Charleston were of better quality. Despite repeated complaints, he claimed, currently only about one-fifth of the fuses "burst properly or with accuracy," causing a waste of ammunition.[4]

During the last weeks of September, Beauregard deluged Ripley with orders nearly every other day. Some communications contained up to eight separate points, varying from the important transfers of ordnance from one battery to another, to mundane minutiae. Ripley was ordered on September 19 to keep Fort Sumter always supplied with one month's provisions and to report exactly what supplies were currently at the fort. Beauregard emphasized that the Moultrie House was not to be destroyed as it served as an object to draw the enemy's fire. Ripley also received orders to keep all sandbags in the embrasures wet during any artillery action. On a positive note, Ripley was to ask Generals Hagood, Colquitt, and Taliaferro for the names of any officers and men who had distinguished themselves for "zeal and gallantry in the discharge of their duties on Morris Island," and to ask Colonel Rhett and Major Elliott for any distinguished performances by the garrison at Fort Sumter.[5]

Near the end of September, Ripley informed Beauregard that local regiments of the six-month State Troops were in such poor condition that, for all practical purposes, they were useless for the defense of Charleston. Of two regiments present, only about 50 percent of the men were listed as effectives, as "surgeons' certificates of disability come in by scores." These men had recently been enrolled and were quartered in healthy and comfortable locales. They were basically unarmed, had not seen duty, and had received only the most basic drills. With the prospect of continued losses from disease, the difficulty in obtaining arms, the amount of subsistence they consumed, and "the almost utter hopelessness of making them into good troops," those men who were subject to conscription should be assigned to current South Carolina regiments on duty in the department. All others should be discharged and sent home, as any help they could give their families or the black population would be more important than anything they could do as soldiers. Swelling the aggregate forces, they added "nothing whatever to our real strength," Ripley argued. Beauregard agreed with this assessment and planned to forward it to the War Department "to show the condition of the State troops I have to depend upon for the defense of this place."[6]

In responding to General Cooper's charge of September 1—that misuse of several rifled heavy guns led to their bursting—Beauregard asserted that the cause was the inferior quality of the metal and the long ranges that had to be reached, not their misuse. In early October, Gorgas, angered by this and Beauregard's criticism of his department's fuses, lashed out against Ripley and Beauregard. He claimed that an imported 600-pounder Blakely gun had burst "due to a want of forethought, unpardonable in an officer as experienced as General Ripley." His criticism of Beauregard involved the commanding general's firing twenty-one-gun salutes to celebrate a victory by General Braxton Bragg in the West, despite knowing that powder and ammunition were to be conserved.[7]

Evidently, Beauregard and Ripley's relationship had not totally deteriorated, for on October 2 Beauregard petitioned General Cooper for Brigadiers Ripley, Mercer, and Taliaferro to be promoted to major general. Of Ripley, Beauregard wrote, "As is known to the War Department, Brigadier General Ripley is the 6th or 7th brigadier general in date of commission now in the service; he is an officer of unquestionable professional ability and attainments—an artillery officer of the largest experience, he has exercised a Divisional Command for nearly a year, and I believe his sphere of influence would be enhanced by his promotion." Cooper did not grant promotions to any of the three.[8]

By October 7 Beauregard had completed the "rearrangement" of his cannon, at least for the time being. In the last of these directives, Beauregard expressed his dissatisfaction that a defective 32-pounder rifled gun at Fort Moultrie, previously ordered transported to the city for rerifling, remained in place. He also complained that the 11-inch gun at Battery Ramsay required the refitting of its trunnion. Beauregard ordered Ripley to execute both of these orders at once. A dismounted smoothbore 32-pounder in Redoubt No. 1 and three guns of the same caliber on the water face of Fort Pemberton were to be transferred to the new lines on James Island, as "determined by the chiefs of artillery and engineers," Gonzales and Harris. Beauregard evidently was not interested in any input from Ripley.[9]

That same day Beauregard responded to comments attributed to U.S. Secretary of State William H. Seward. On August 12 the secretary presented his foreign diplomats with his version of why the ironclad attack on Fort Sumter had failed. Seward claimed that the monitors, after successfully passing through the fire of Confederate batteries, were forced to retire after rope obstructions fouled their propellers. Despite previous documentation, Beauregard surprisingly asked Ripley and the commanders at Fort Sumter and Sullivan's Island whether Seward's version was correct. Beauregard also asked whether the enemy had suffered any losses during the attack, as Seward claimed the ironclads passed through the cannonade with "singular impunity."[10]

Ripley believed that Seward's statement was simply false. He admitted that the rope obstructions would probably have fouled the screws of the ironclads, "but no Abolition ironclad came within 300 yards of them." Of the entire fleet of ironclads, only the *Keokuk* came within nine hundred yards of Fort Sumter and one thousand yards of the batteries on Sullivan's Island. Badly damaged by Ripley's batteries, the *Keokuk* sank the next morning. The fleet made no attempt to renew the attack and left the harbor on April 12. In his reply to Beauregard, Ripley included substantiating reports from Colonels Alfred M. Rhett and William Butler. These officers claimed that several of the ironclad crew members were either killed or injured and had not passed through the "cannonade with singular impunity."

To ask Ripley for clarification of the April 7 attack, Beauregard either believed Seward's version to some extent or questioned the accuracy of Ripley's original report. According to the *Mercury*, the Creole and his staff were "radiant and confident spectators of the fight from East Bay Battery," a considerable distance from the action.[11]

The October 10 issue of the *Mercury* described General Ripley's "Grand Review" of his forces on James Island, and "the sight was one not soon forgotten." Noting the columns of troops that passed in review, the account declared that since the war began, "Charleston has not seen so splendid an array." "Seemingly interminable" lines of infantry followed long trains of artillery. Brigades of gray-clad veterans "accustomed to victory" marched with their "bayonets glittering in the sunlight, and their stained and tattered flags fluttering in the breeze." General Ripley, at the close of the review, expressed his satisfaction with the "discipline and appearance of the forces in that portion of his command." Obviously, after the loss of Morris Island and Batteries Wagner and Gregg, the *Mercury* was attempting to boost its readers' morale by lavishly praising the strength and resolve of the Confederate forces.[12]

On October 10 Ripley informed Beauregard of problems in rifling, banding, and preparing heavy ordnance in his district. Soon after the ironclads had been repulsed, Ripley tried to work with the commanding officer of the ordnance department, Major J. T. Trezevant, who had replaced the difficult Major F. L. Childs. As nothing had transpired for several weeks, Ripley arranged to have the work done outside the arsenal, but it was understood that the arsenal should pay the account when the work was completed. Reminiscent of Ripley's difficulty with Childs, after the project was underway Trezevant received orders from Colonel Gorgas that no accounts ordered by either Beauregard or Ripley should be paid.

As Ripley knew "the importance of the matter, and the necessity of improving our ordnance," he directed a foundry to proceed and provided the funds himself. Since then, four 8-inch columbiads, one 42-pounder, and several other guns of smaller caliber had been rifled and double banded. A quantity of bands for 8-inch and 42-pounder guns and a quantity of iron were on hand to continue the work. Ripley claimed that the rifling and double banding had been a success and that 140-pound projectiles had been thrown, with ordinary charges, to the full range of a 64-pound shot at similar elevations. Four of these guns were in position for the defense of the harbor and the double-banded 42-pounder was on board the ironclad *Charleston*. As the superiority of the guns was so great, Ripley hoped to have the remaining columbiads "remodeled in the same way." Ripley did not believe that ordnance work for the defense of the harbor should be paid for by private sources. Therefore, he asked the secretary of war to instruct the chief of ordnance to settle his account.

Beauregard endorsed Ripley's request on October 26 and sent it to General Cooper, who three days later forwarded the information to the chief of ordnance. Considering the importance of the guns, Beauregard added, he would have used public money had it been available, and he was not "deposed to have it in the power of Capt. [Major] Trezevant to stop the work at any time by the threat of refusal to pay." Trezevant argued that he was acting under instructions from Gorgas and claimed he could have banded the guns but did not have the iron on hand.[13]

The issue was not settled until March 14, 1864, when the second auditor's Office of the Treasury Department awarded Ripley $3,225 for furnishing 12,900 pounds of iron on July 1, 1863, as well as reimbursements of $2,500 on August 20 and $9,350 on October 15, for payments Ripley made to local firms for rifling, welding bands, and banding 8- and 10-inch columbiads. If, as alleged, Ripley invested in blockade running, he spent some of his profits for the defense of Charleston.[14]

In early August, during the siege of Battery Wagner, Baxter Watson and B. A. "Gus" Whitney met in Charleston with Beauregard and Captain John R. Tucker of the navy. They presented their credentials and the plans for their "submarine boat" recently tested in Mobile, Alabama. The inventors impressed Beauregard with their plans, and as the blockade was slowly strangling Charleston, Beauregard asked them to transport the boat to the city as soon as possible.

The submarine, now christened the *H. L. Hunley* after its principal investor Horace L. Hunley, arrived by train on August 12 and soon was launched into Charleston Harbor. Beauregard decided that the crew from Mobile was too passive and that the boat should be used more aggressively against the blockade. By August 26 the Confederate navy had seized the *Hunley,* and Lieutenant John Payne, CSN, volunteered to command the submarine. On August 29 he and his volunteer crew made several practice dives around the harbor, but while docking at Fort Johnson, disaster struck. Awash with its hatches open, the boat plunged to the bottom, drowning five crewmembers. Only Payne and one other crewmember survived.[15]

Within seventy-two hours of the *Hunley*'s sinking, Beauregard telegraphed Ripley: "Fish Torpedo still at the bottom of bay, no one working on it." Realizing that Ripley was more familiar with the resources in Charleston required for raising the boat, Beauregard asked him to take measures to raise the boat immediately, put a knowledgeable person in charge of the work, and inform Lieutenant Payne of the orders. Ripley hired two civilian hard-helmet divers, David Broadfoot and Angus Smith, who had previously anchored underwater contact mines in the harbor at night.

On September 9, unimpressed with Lieutenant Payne's supervision of the salvage operations, Beauregard directed Ripley to relieve the lieutenant. If the boat still had not been raised, Ripley was to place the salvage under the direction of "Ferguson, Mathewes, or other competent persons, as you may determine."

The work of Broadfoot and Smith was actually progressing well, and Ripley resisted relieving Payne, possibly because the lieutenant was the only officer who had any knowledge of the workings of the submarine. After two weeks of working in the dark in about forty feet of water, Broadfoot and Smith had raised and transported the *Hunley* to the city. Ripley notified Beauregard on September 14 that "the torpedo submarine boat" was on a Charleston wharf "in charge of Lieut. Payne, C.S.N." Unfortunately, the *Hunley* would experience another disastrous, accidental sinking before it successfully attacked and sank a Federal ship.[16]

About a week after the salvage of the submarine, Hunley asked Beauregard to return the boat to him. Hunley stated that he would furnish a crew from Mobile who were familiar with managing the boat and would attempt to destroy an enemy vessel as soon as possible. Beauregard agreed and ordered Ripley to have the boat cleaned, readied for service, and turned over to Hunley within two weeks.

In early October a second crew, under the command of Lieutenant George E. Dixon, arrived in Charleston from Mobile. The new crew completed many practice dives under the CSS *Indian Chief* anchored in the Cooper River. However, on October 15, in the absence of Lieutenant Dixon, Hunley for some unknown reason decided to take command of the vessel himself. Hunley, who rarely served aboard the boat, attempted a dive under the *Indian Chief*. It was later determined, as the boat submerged, that operational errors committed by Hunley doomed the vessel and prevented it from resurfacing.

Beauregard, now even more anxious to break the stranglehold of the blockade, again called upon the divers, Broadfoot and Smith, to salvage the boat. The commanding general issued orders to Colonel D. B. Harris to supply Smith with certain tools, ropes, and chains to facilitate the recovery. Angus Smith now joined Ripley in experiencing difficulties with Harris, after the chief engineer delayed Smith's request for material from his department. Evidently, the divers lost a government-owned chain and anchor during the first salvage of the *Hunley*, and Harris decided to qualify Beauregard's order to supply the salvagers with material. Harris required Smith to have a representative from the engineer department present at all times to assure the material was "properly cared for." Smith refused the material under this arrangement and notified Beauregard's staff that Harris was obstructing his efforts. Smith's embellished complaint generated an immediate response from Beauregard, who ordered Harris to comply immediately with the previously issued orders.

The following day Ripley issued orders for Lieutenant Dixon to travel to Mobile on business connected with the "submarine torpedo boat." After returning with fellow engineer William Alexander, the lieutenant would take command of the *Hunley*. On October 18 dragging operations found the boat, this time in about nine fathoms of water. Delayed by bad weather, the boat was finally raised on November 7, and the following day Horace Hunley and his crew were laid to rest in Magnolia Cemetery north of Charleston.[17]

In the third quarter of 1863, during the attacks on Morris Island, Ripley received $135 as "Commutation of Quarters and Fuel" as the lone occupant of a five-room house on Rutledge Street. In October, in an effort to be closer to the important works on Sullivan's Island, Ripley moved his headquarters across the Cooper River to Mount Pleasant. There he began receiving his commutation for quarters and fuel, as well as a forage allowance for his four horses. Future references indicate that Ripley maintained his residence on Rutledge, but the exact address is unknown.[18]

On October 22 Harriott Middleton wrote to Susan after reading Colonel Arthur Fremantle's diary, published in the *Richmond Weekly* from *Blackwood's Edinburgh Magazine*. She believed it to be "so extremely interesting. It is hardly more than a recital of facts, but no eulogy could more exactly describe the men about whom he writes."[19]

While Broadfoot and Smith struggled with their salvage effort, on October 26 Union artillery began the second heavy bombardment of Fort Sumter. It lasted day and night, with varying intensity, until December 6. Because of this continued bombardment, the Confederates anticipated another amphibious assault on Sumter. On October 30 Beauregard directed Ripley to have all batteries bearing on the fort ready at night to sweep its exterior walls on a signal from Major Elliott or whenever hostile boats approached. Possibly irritated by what he interpreted to be the Creole's micromanagement of the First Military District, Ripley acknowledged receiving Beauregard's orders and informed the commanding general that he and Elliott had discussed the issue and agreed on a signal, and that his batteries had received pertinent orders "some hours" ago.[20]

On November 1 Beauregard, possibly in spite, ordered Ripley to "rearrange" ordnance around the harbor without delay. An 8-inch columbiad in Castle Pinckney was to be exchanged for a 10-inch columbiad at Fort Ripley and positioned near the main ship channel. The rearrangement of ordnance on Sullivan's Island included transferring two 24-pounder smoothbores and one 8-inch seacoast howitzer from Fort Moultrie to Battery Marshall, two 24-pounder smoothbores to lines in Christ Church, one 8-inch seacoast howitzer to Battery Beauregard, and one rifled 32-pounder from the west face of Moultrie to the battery between Batteries Beauregard and Marshall.

Beauregard further ordered the transfer of Battery Marshall's dismounted smoothbore 32-pounder to the two-gun battery located between Batteries Beauregard and Marshall. The 12-pounder siege carriage at Battery Marshall was to be sent to the arsenal for modification so as to accept a banded 12-pounder at Battery Marshall that had no carriage. From the Charleston Arsenal four 12-pounder bronze howitzers were to be sent to Battery Ryan on James Island. One 12-pounder bronze howitzer was to go to Battery Tatom, and one 24-pounder rifled and banded gun to Secessionville. Two 24-pounders already at Secessionville were to be alternately removed for banding at the arsenal.[21]

During this hectic time, Charleston proudly received a formal visit from President Davis. Following the Battle of Chickamauga, September 19–20, General Braxton Bragg and his subordinate generals bitterly disputed why their victory was not more decisive. A majority of the generals petitioned the president to remove Bragg from command. Davis decided to mediate the situation personally and traveled to Bragg's headquarters. Without solving the problem, Davis began his return to Richmond by train, stopping along the way to deliver speeches and, it was hoped, to boost morale.[22]

A welcoming committee from South Carolina, headed by Governor Bonham, met the president in Savannah and escorted him to Charleston, where they arrived on November 2. Beauregard, his staff officers, and civic leaders met Davis at the railway station and escorted him by carriage to City Hall, passing through throngs of cheering citizens anxious to see their president. The next day Davis, accompanied by "Generals Beauregard and Gilmer, Colonel Harris and a number of other officers, visited Sullivan's Island and inspected the fortifications," with which "his Excellency" was highly pleased. After seeing all the works on the island, the president and his party had lunch with Ripley and then returned to the city. It is doubtful whether Beauregard's recently ordered ordnance "rearrangements" had been completed. On November 4 Davis visited the works on James Island, and early the next morning the Charleston Light Dragoons and a company of infantry escorted Davis, Beauregard, and several staff officers to the northeastern depot. A crowd cheered Davis as he bid farewell to Charleston, "pleased with his reception and the condition of our defenses."[23]

During Davis's visit, Beauregard received a telegram from Major William Norris, chief of the Signal Corps in Richmond, indicating that the enemy intended to make an amphibious landing at night on Sullivan's or James Island either that week or the next. Beauregard forwarded the telegram to Ripley and "wished" Ripley would "make all necessary arrangements for this contingency." Beauregard suggested that Keitt's 20th South Carolina, alternating with "some other good regiment," be posted on Sullivan's at night, returning to their encampments before daylight to avoid detection. The next day Ripley replied that he would make the proper dispositions but feared he was deficient in "quick acting and quick moving artillery." He therefore requested that two light batteries be sent to him at once.

Beauregard then turned his attention to Fort Sumter and directed Ripley to have two hundred men ready each night to send to Sumter by rowboats in the event of an attempted Federal landing. He issued the same orders to General Taliaferro for the transfer of men from Fort Johnson. Later, Beauregard "recalled" his strange order to use rowboats; instead he would have a steamer ready to send to Mount Pleasant for the men.[24]

In early November, Ripley issued a circular addressing in detail Beauregard's concern regarding an enemy attempt to land on Sullivan's Island or the shore of Mount Pleasant. Totaling four pages in the *Official Records*, Ripley's detailed instructions were to be "carefully studied by the commanders of regiments, batteries and companies."

The entire shore of Sullivan's Island, from Breach inlet to west of Fort Moultrie was to be picketed at night at intervals not exceeding one hundred yards. Ripley determined that the picket duty was to be performed by the regiments under the command of General Clingman and Colonel Hamilton, and specified the ground to be covered by their troops. Each regiment and battalion, positioned in line of battle after dark, was to sleep on its arms. These troops were to be in the advance of, but between the fixed batteries and the light artillery, with care taken not to mask the fire of those batteries. Ripley specified where Keitt's regiment should be positioned each night, and as soon as possible he would distribute light artillery batteries where needed. Artillery batteries were to be on strict alert and their commanders were to be in communication with the picket commanders in their front. The whole remaining strength of the Sullivan's Island forces was to be in readiness for instant service.

Ripley went into great detail about how signal rockets, chemical "blue lights," Roman candles, and tarred "light balls" should be handled during a night attack. As soon as the pickets had cleared the illuminated area of attack, the light batteries bearing on the point of the enemy's landing were to open on the beach, principally with grapeshot, intending "to strike the beach within about 50 yards from the shore." No troops were to fall back beyond the first line of sand hills, and "the batteries are to be defended and protected at all hazards." Ripley ordered any battery in danger of being taken by assault to fire a rocket, and all available troops would be ordered to support the threatened battery.

Ripley described the procedures required to repulse any attacks on the western end of the island, west of Battery Rutledge, which could require reinforcements from Mount Pleasant. The batteries were to pour a heavy fire of canister if a landing was tried, but the batteries were also to be ready to fire on the enemy's ironclad fleet if a passage was attempted. Ripley devoted attention to the defense of Mount Pleasant with watch fires kindled on the shore from Battery Gary to Shem Creek. He proposed leaving three hundred infantry in the village and would have cavalry patrol the beach. In conclusion, Ripley requested that all officers study and understand these general instructions.[25]

Ripley's timely and detailed response to Beauregard's request for a plan of action is impressive. His attention to detail in these lengthy and comprehensive instructions to his subordinates confirms his thorough understanding of the measures required and validates his competence in the defense of Charleston. However, if a major amphibious assault on Sullivan's Island was ever planned, it was not attempted.

CHAPTER 23

Ripley Rebuked

Throughout November the Federal land-based batteries and ironclads continued their bombardment of Fort Sumter. The attacks came principally at night, but the enemy began using a high-powered calcium light to better illuminate their target and increase the effectiveness and accuracy of their fire.

On November 13 Ripley received orders from Beauregard to determine the exact location of the enemy's calcium light by triangulation between certain batteries on James Island and on Sullivan's Island. A converging fire was to be maintained on the light until it was extinguished.[1]

In another directive to Ripley that day, Beauregard referred to an earlier order in which he had instructed Ripley to protect Battery Marshall from flank and reverse fire as soon as possible. Beauregard claimed the engineers had developed a plan for the work and hoped there would be no deviation from the plan by any orders issued by Colonel D. H. Hamilton, whose troops were engaged in constructing the work. The commanding general added that if Ripley believed there was any undue delay owing to the engineers not laying out the works, or if they lacked tools, he should be informed.

This reopened the disruptive issue caused by Ripley's complaints earlier in the year regarding the lack of progress on the works at the southern end of Morris Island. Beauregard believed the engineer officers were to provide tools and instruction to the officers of the line but were not responsible for any delays in the progress of the work. Beauregard maintained that any delay was the responsibility of the officers in charge of the troops doing the work, not the engineers.[2]

Ten days later Ripley responded energetically, pointing out that it had been "some weeks" since he brought to Beauregard's attention the necessity of protecting an exposed flank of Battery Marshall. That flank, Ripley argued, could be enfiladed by reverse fire from monitors or ironclads positioned in Maffitt's Channel. Ripley had directed Colonel Hamilton to examine the flank and report what works were needed to protect it. Hamilton determined the tools needed and the number of troops required for the work, but the engineers could not provide either the tools or enough labor.

Ripley was forced to order tools from the quartermasters, but misunderstandings among the officers in that department caused delays, both in obtaining the tools and in determining whether they could even be found. In time, enough tools were obtained for Hamilton to begin work on the project. Ripley reported the colonel's findings to headquarters and received instructions to employ troops to do the work.

Some weeks after the works had been proposed, the chief engineer, Lieutenant Colonel Harris, visited the battery. Discovering the work was about to begin, Harris laid out a piece of the fortification without consulting Ripley and in direct opposition to Hamilton's plans. Ripley reported that Harris planned to build "a miniature citadel," which would be used as a fortification of last resort but would not protect the exposed flank as originally intended.

Under orders to protect the western flank of Battery Marshall from enfilade and reverse fire, Colonel Hamilton refused to employ his troops in building "Harris' citadel." Ripley fully agreed with Hamilton's decision, but when the commanding general heard of this impasse, he immediately telegraphed Ripley; no work was to be done on Battery Marshall unless approved and directed by the engineers. Ripley replied that to the best of his knowledge Beauregard's order had been obeyed but that the work, whether "faulty or meritorious," had progressed slowly.[3]

About this time, Ripley received a warning that an amphibious attack on Sullivan's Island was imminent. To meet this threat Ripley consulted with General Clingman and Colonel Hamilton about constructing some temporary works, which he had described in his circular of November 8. The circular had been transmitted to the commanding general and to Ripley's knowledge had not been disapproved. Ripley claimed that Harris began interfering with these lines, "unmistakably at variance" with those he had planned with Clingman and Hamilton. As these works were to be temporary, he informed Beauregard that this interference might not be important, but it was one in a series of actions by the engineers under General Orders, No. 95, in which commanding officers of areas for which they are responsible had to submit to inferior and oftentimes incompetent engineer officers or dispense with any defensive works at all. Ripley protested against a system that placed "the success of our cause" in the hands of officers in a department "characterized by inactivity[,] oftentimes-faulty dispositions," and wasted labor.

Ripley brought up the thirty-two interrogatories Beauregard had saddled him with in August while investigating the defense and loss of Morris Island. He audaciously criticized the nature of Beauregard's questions and reminded his superior that the issue had been completely taken away from him and placed entirely in the hands of the engineers. Ripley believed strongly in his evaluation of the engineers and their deficiencies, and would continue his resolute complaints, although he must have known that his opinion would not be well received.

Ripley claimed the engineers had been dilatory following the evacuation of Batteries Wagner and Gregg. They deliberated for four or five weeks, delaying work on the batteries at Sumter, and did not supply enough material to construct even simple bombproofs at the fort. Ripley cited the slow progress of works on James and Sullivan's Islands, and the now faulty disposition of and slow progress on the works at Battery Marshall. As for the lack of available labor, Ripley pointed out that recently there were days when gangs of idle blacks, who could have been employed on Sullivan's Island, roamed the streets of Charleston. He maintained that only in times of imminent danger was anything of importance accomplished. It seemed to Ripley that whenever anything was done to remedy the deficiencies of this department, it excited the interference of the chief engineer, "who pursues a course of action looking much like obstruction. As he is unable or unwilling to complete a project, he endeavors to prevent others from doing so, and in this he has always been supported."[4]

Ripley pointed out that several times since April, headquarters had directed engineer officers to communicate with district and other commanders and furnish them with information concerning the progress of works in their commands. In the previous five months, Ripley claimed, he had not received a single report on works in his district. Any information he sought was given "with extreme unwillingness and delay." At times guns were shifted and cut off from their fields of fire without discussion of the situation with the commanders. In some instances the engineers seemed not to care if the guns were appropriate for their intended service.

Ripley asserted that if the defensive works were progressing well, if the labor was used properly, and if the works would actually accomplish what was intended and the defense not given to those whose fitness was questionable, he would "submit to the system without further remark." However, as that was not the case, he deemed it his duty to bring the matter again to the attention of headquarters and believed "some change in the system should be adopted."[5]

Ripley reiterated the engineers' lack of work in protecting the southern end of Morris Island but admitted, "It is true that the ultimate cause of our weakness can be traced to a different source," but those who neglected a necessary work and prevented its execution by others must share the responsibility for the loss and the injuries now being inflicted on Charleston.

Over the next several days, Ripley obtained endorsements of agreement from General Clingman and Colonels Hamilton and Keitt. Clingman stated specifically that the engineers should be under the command of the district or post commanders and cited for special criticism regarding the "misapplication of labor" and the extraordinary failure to put it to use. Hamilton agreed that the engineers' work at Marshall had been "conducted in a most dilatory manner and still remains unfinished, impairing the effectiveness of several guns for immediate service." Also, Hamilton did not believe the new work would protect the battery from flank and reverse fire, as originally intended. Based on his observations, Keitt briefly and simply supported Ripley's evaluation. By the end of November, Ripley submitted his evaluation of the situation and recommendations, along with these three supporting endorsements, to Beauregard.[6]

Instead of responding to Ripley's concerns regarding the lack of progress on the works at Battery Marshall and the independence and ineffectiveness of the engineers, Beauregard angrily instructed his assistant inspector general, Lieutenant Colonel Alfred Roman, to conduct an "exhaustive inquiry into the movements of the enemy on Folly and Morris Islands, ending in the events of July 10, 1863." Roman sent Ripley thirteen interrogatories to which he was to return written answers:

1. State what were the enemy's movements at the entrance to Charleston Harbor, and more particularly at the south end of Morris Island, between the 1st and the 10th of July last.
2. What were the movements of the enemy on and about Folly Island?
3. What were his forces on the island?
4. How was the attack made by the enemy?
5. What forces had we on Morris Island, and under whose command were they? Who commanded the artillery forces? Who commanded the infantry forces?
6. Was the attack of the enemy a surprise, or was it anticipated? If a surprise, to what extent?
7. At what point did the enemy land on Morris Island, on the morning of July 10, and at what o'clock?
8. State the disposition of our troops, and by whose order so disposed?
9. How was the artillery supported?
10. In what formations and in what numbers did the enemy advance on our positions?
11. At what o'clock did our troops fall back, and by whose order?
12. When our troops fell back, what was the enemy's position, and what their estimated forces?
13. State the different directions from which the enemy's guns opened on us, both by sea and land.

Ripley immediately notified General Jordan that he had informed Roman he would answer the interrogatories when the necessary papers, which had been sent for, were on hand. Ripley sarcastically suggested that, "as valuable as the facts may be, any conclusions derived and expressed" by Lieutenant Colonel Roman "can have no more importance than the opinion of any individual of his estimable character." Ripley denigrated Roman's military knowledge and experience and deemed the inquisitional nature of the inspector general's interrogatories to be inappropriate under "any general custom of service or the provisions of any military law." Ripley asked this paper to be filed with any report on the subject;

however, General Jordan refused and unofficially returned the letter to Ripley two weeks later.[7]

On November 28 the situation deteriorated further when Beauregard relieved Clingman's brigade and ordered it "without delay" to Weldon, North Carolina. Within hours an exasperated Ripley replied, "The troops must be replaced or I will not be responsible for the position from day to day." Later, Ripley advised Jordan that Clingman would not be able to move until the following day and asked what troops would replace the transferred brigade. He added that the enemy's 300-pounders were firing on Moultrie and repeated that Clingman should not be withdrawn until his command was reinforced.

Dispatches between Ripley and Jordan continued throughout the day, with Jordan finally informing Ripley that Beauregard had no troops to replace Clingman. Jordan stressed that Clingman must move after dark to prevent the withdrawal from being detected.

The following day Ripley received word that the 17th and 26th Regiments of Evans's brigade would be ordered to his military district. The hostility was palpable when Jordan added, "You will be held responsible, as are all other military commanders, to handle the resources at your disposition to the best advantage in an emergency." The double standard in Beauregard's earlier response to the transfer of troops from his department to other fronts is enlightening. The Creole complained to W. Porcher Miles, "If I meet with disaster under the present circumstances the responsibility will not be on my shoulders."[8]

Ripley submitted his detailed answers to Lieutenant Colonel Roman's thirteen interrogatories on December 4. Ripley's answer to the sixth question, about whether the attack was anticipated or a surprise, and Ripley's unsolicited concluding statement following the thirteenth question must have angered Beauregard.

Ripley answered the sixth question by stating that as the attack had been anticipated, it therefore was not a surprise. In March, Beauregard had ordered the southern end of the island fortified, and in April he predicted an attack on Morris Island from Folly Island. Ripley stated that by May 24 enemy activity on Folly Island confirmed their intentions, "unless we were fully prepared to receive his attack." Efforts were made to prepare works that could be held by a small force, but the engineers were put in control of the issue and little was accomplished. Ripley asserted that in another sense the attack was a surprise, as the enemy had attacked before the defenders were in "proper condition" to receive the attack. Ripley admitted that the commanding general had ordered reinforcements from other points to the island but that they did not arrive in time to do anything more than cover the retreat from the end of the island.

Ripley concluded that the batteries on the south end of Morris Island were simple, detached works, without communications, and separated from each other in some cases by intervals of two hundred or three hundred yards. "From the time construction began and until their capture," he wrote, "no very vigorous measures were carried out by those who were in charge of making them secure against such an attack."[9]

Beauregard instructed Roman to inform Ripley that he found part of his answer to the sixth interrogatory to be irrelevant. Due to this irrelevancy, Beauregard posed eight additional questions comparing Morris Island with Sullivan's Island:

1. Which of the two islands, Morris or Sullivan's, offers greater natural advantages for a combined attack by land and sea?
2. What forces of each arm do you consider would have been required on the 10th July, 1863, to have secured the safety of each island?
3. What forces of each arm had you on each of those islands at that period?
4. What forces of each arm have you now on Sullivan's Island, and in your district, within one hour's march of that island?
5. How many soldiers were available to work on the defenses of Morris Island prior to the 10th of July, 1863?
6. How long would it have taken you at that period (admitting you had the sole control of the available working forces on Morris Island of soldiers and hired men, the latter being 10 in number) to have made the defenses ordered on the south end of the island as strong as Battery Marshall is at present?
7. When were the works ordered, and when commenced?
8. To what extent would the construction of those works, prior to the 10th of July last, have permitted a reduction of the forces you state would have been required to insure the safety of that island?

Other than creating a great amount of paperwork for Ripley and rehashing previous disputes, it is difficult to see the purpose of many of these queries.[10]

Undaunted, four days later Ripley dutifully submitted detailed answers to Roman's latest questions. However, in the introduction to his answers, Ripley "regretted" that the commanding general "does not clearly see the relevancy of part of my answer to the sixth interrogatory." As he was "in the dark" as to the purpose of Roman's inquiry, Ripley believed his answers should be as complete and detailed as possible. Ripley planned to submit thorough answers to this latest series of questions and, with some sarcasm, added, "should more be expressed than is deemed relevant by the commanding general, those portions of the answers . . . can be made use of by whoever draws conclusions." Ripley answered that for all practical purposes it would have taken six or eight weeks to construct works similar to those now present at Battery Marshall. However, he suggested that if he had been in charge, he would have employed the men differently than they were at the time. He critically added that Battery Marshall was still not a model of defensive works and that over the past three or four months the engineers had not taken very energetic measures to strengthen it.

Ripley continued his criticism, seemingly unaware or uncaring that his appraisal of Harris and the engineers would infuriate Beauregard. Obviously annoyed by these interminable questions and possibly viewing them as harassment, Ripley added, "almost every fact called for by your questions has been communicated to the headquarters of the department in official reports or correspondence. . . . prospective opinions concerning the fortifications and preparation of the south end of Morris Island were not often asked from the district commander." When opinions "were given and action taken, . . . the action was checked and the opinions neglected."

Ripley argued that "retrospective opinions," such as those Roman called for, should "only be compared with those expressed at or before the time." He called Roman's attention to his correspondence beginning on May 24, 1863, and concluded that the attack came before the works were finished, although they had been ordered four months earlier, and that "the probabilities of the point being attacked grew stronger day by day." None of Ripley's answers or his criticism of the engineers would have pleased Beauregard. The commanding general did not hesitate to circumvent Colonel Gorgas and Majors Childs and Trezevant of the ordnance department; Harris and the engineers were beyond reproach.[11]

Despite the controversy, Ripley rigorously continued his duties. On December 18 he reported detailed results to General Jordan of five test firings of a double-banded and rifled 10-inch gun at Battery Bee. Ripley was satisfied that the firing did not impair the condition of the gun, that the projectiles took the grooves in every instance, and that the line of fire was accurate. The range was limited to 1,100–1,800 yards as the projectiles were flat-headed bolts, not pointed shells, but the velocity appeared to be equal to a round ball. Ripley believed the results demonstrated the efficiency of the gun in its present location.

Later in the month Ripley reported that at nightfall of the previous day four large parties of the enemy, thought to be regiments, were proceeding from Battery Wagner toward Cumming's Point, their intention unknown. Ripley directed the batteries on Sullivan's Island and at Fort Johnson to open fire on them at 9:10 P.M. He determined that the results were fair, limited somewhat by the "often-reported" defective fuses.[12]

During this clash between Beauregard and Ripley, in November Lieutenant Dixon and William Alexander returned to Charleston from Mobile. Dixon began his efforts to convince a reluctant Beauregard to put him in command of the submarine and allow him to enlist another crew. Awarded the command, Dixon requisitioned a barrel of lime and a two-pound box of soap, five brushes, and was granted the use of ten black laborers to begin the work of cleaning and repairing the salvaged vessel. To serve on the *Hunley*, Dixon and Alexander selected five members from the crew of the *Indian Chief* to join three volunteers from Mobile. As soon as the submarine was serviceable, Dixon instituted an intense orientation program for the crew and began practice dives.

On December 14 Beauregard officially ordered Lieutenant Dixon to take command of "the submarine torpedo-boat, *H. L. Hunley*, and proceed tonight to the mouth of the harbor, and sink and destroy any vessel of the enemy with which he can come in contact." Beauregard ordered all officers to give Dixon any assistance he requested.[13]

In Columbia on December 23, Susan Middleton could not resist forwarding gossip to her cousin Harriott regarding a "shameful incident" (by the standards of that era) taking place in the capital: "Columbia is greatly scandalized just now at Dr. Gibbes having a guest in his house, General Jordan's friend and 'relation,' the beautiful 'Mrs. Mason,' of whom you no doubt heard of last winter in Charleston. Colonel Mason, the brother of the Captain Mason, whose wife she claims to be, declared that she has no more right to their name than to a great many others!" Jordan's friend, the "beautiful Mrs. Mason," returned to Charleston in 1864 and would add to Roswell Ripley's problems.[14]

The controversy between Ripley and the engineers remained unresolved through December. Apparently frustrated and tired of struggling with Beauregard's engineering policies, on December 29 Ripley applied to Jordan for a leave of absence of forty days, noting, "I have had no leave since January 1st 1861 except fifteen days on Surgeon's certificate immediately after the battle of Sharpsburg."[15]

In early January, Ripley waited for Beauregard to approve his request for leave and for a response to his suggestions for improving the current policy for constructing defensive works around Charleston. On the third Ripley notified Jordan that the enemy was deploying barges north of Battery Marshall but that their intent had not been determined. Ripley continued his criticism of the engineer's ineffectual efforts, stating that the works at Battery Marshall remained far from complete and in generally bad condition. Two days later Ripley reported that Battery Beauregard had fired on an approaching enemy vessel, and he strongly urged erecting telegraph lines to increase security on exposed outposts on Sullivan's Island.[16]

On January 6, 1864, Beauregard claimed that constant pressure involved in the defense of Charleston prevented him from responding to Ripley's suggestions and allegations, submitted in November. Beauregard stated that Ripley could not legitimately communicate the subject matter in his paper to headquarters. Ripley's allegations against staff officers within the department headquarters essentially "impeached the orders, measures, plans and the general conduct of operations for the defense of Charleston by the commanding general." Beauregard suggested that Ripley could only bring to the commanding general's attention any instances of lack of energy or intelligence on the part of officers within his command. Otherwise he could prefer specific charges against Colonel Harris, which would then be "brought to a court martial."[17]

Even though Beauregard had officially rebuked Ripley on January 6, three days later he forwarded his personal evaluation of Ripley's answers to Colonel Harris, seeking the engineer's "remarks." Beauregard disapproved of Ripley's "innuendoes against the engineers of this department" and deemed Ripley's detailed answers to be "vague and unsatisfactory, studied and labored." He especially criticized Ripley's answer to interrogatory six, which involved the time required to construct works, comparable to those of Battery Marshall, on the south end of Morris Island. Beauregard estimated that the proposed works would require nine to eleven months to complete.

Beauregard claimed that Ripley's answer of six to eight weeks to complete the construction "shows a total want of practical knowledge in the construction of field works, and still more justifies my action in intrusting the planning and superintending of such works in this department, not to district commanders, as had been done before I assumed command." This does not ring true as Ripley had chafed under the injudicious defense plans for the First Military District formulated by General Pemberton. Ripley was now subservient to Harris, Beauregard's planter/engineer, with little input as to the construction of the works he was to defend.

Beauregard maintained, "The successful defense of Charleston against such great odds is the best answer in favor of the system of defense followed in this department." The commanding general wrote that this refutes the "ungenerous and uncalled for vague accusations of General Ripley against that gallant, meritorious and unassuming officer and gentleman, Col. D. B. Harris." Beauregard's letter clearly indicated his high regard for Harris and confirmed that his relationship with Ripley was irreparably damaged.[18]

Apparently Beauregard and Harris were less troubled than Ripley by the loss of Morris Island, Batteries Wagner and Gregg, the reduction of Fort Sumter to a pile of rubble, and the bombardment of the city of Charleston. The lower part of the city was shelled on and off until Charleston was evacuated in February 1865. The citizens either left Charleston or moved north of Calhoun Street to be out of range of the bombardment. The area south of Calhoun became an uninhabited ghost town.[19]

Correspondence and reports in the *Official Records* for January 1864 indicate that Beauregard denied Ripley's request for leave at the end of the year. It is surprising that Beauregard did not take this opportunity to temporarily rid himself of his difficult general.

CHAPTER 24

The H. L. Hunley *Lost at Sea*

Censured and denied his request for a leave of absence, Ripley continued his duties from Mount Pleasant and Sullivan's Island. During the first months of 1864, Ripley kept his thoughts and any criticisms of the engineers' efforts or lack thereof to himself. On January 9, the same day Beauregard disparaged Ripley in his letter to Harris, the Creole belatedly responded to correspondence from Colonel Gorgas the previous November. The chief of ordnance had objected to banding and rifling 8- and 10-inch columbiads by a private firm in Charleston.

Although Beauregard was emphatically against Ripley's involvement in the construction of the works he was assigned to defend, he may have wanted Ripley close at hand to refute Gorgas's contentions. The commanding general referred to and relied on Ripley's evaluation of a rifled and banded 8-inch columbiad at Fort Moultrie cited above. Beauregard argued that Ripley believed this particular columbiad was "the best gun in the battery," as it had been in four or five engagements, fired more than one hundred times using shells and bolts of over one hundred pounds, and was expected to last for a long time.

Beauregard also cited Ripley's report on the firing of a Brooke gun at Fort Sumter; in the report Ripley noted that even though the fifteen-pound charge of powder was less than the maximum recommended, the gun cracked through the vent and Ripley was forced to condemn it. Beauregard commended Ripley's astute adjustments in the composition of the powder used and decreasing the amount to ten pounds, but using a different mixture of coarse-grained and common cannon powder.

Beauregard reminded Gorgas that he had not objected to banding 8- or 10-inch columbiads, provided there would be only a few of each caliber required for special service. Beauregard concluded that the guns selected by Ripley for banding had been captured at Forts Moultrie and Sumter at the start of the war and were made of the very best iron. Gorgas must have seethed when Beauregard described the cannon as being "superior to those now being manufactured by the Ordnance Department of the Confederate States." Beauregard's two-page rebuttal of Gorgas relied almost entirely on Ripley's expertise.[1]

On January 1 Harris finally responded to Beauregard's request for his evaluation of Ripley's answers to the eight interrogatories posed on December 12. Harris's responses were similar to Ripley's but differed significantly on question six. The chief engineer claimed that with the work force then available it would have taken twelve months to construct a fortification, comparable to Battery Marshall, on the south end of Morris Island. Knowing Ripley's opinion of Harris, he would have derisively agreed with the engineer's estimate of the time involved. Beauregard probably judged correctly that Ripley's proposed time was underestimated and that the true figure would fall somewhere between the two conflicting claims. Probably accounting for the huge difference between the two estimates is the fact that the engineers did not actively seek additional labor nor manage the work as aggressively as Ripley would have.[2]

During this time Ripley was forced to deal with a "mutinous disaffection among the troops" of the 22nd South Carolina Infantry and the 1st Regiment (Regulars) South Carolina Infantry on Sullivan's Island. They believed their enlistment terms had expired, but they had not received confirmation from the authorities. Ripley appointed Colonel H. L. Benbow of the 23rd South Carolina to investigate the situation, and the colonel recommended a thorough reorganization of the officers of the 22nd South Carolina. He also advised permanently removing to a secure site several men of the 1st Regiment who were confined for mutinous conduct. Ripley agreed, ordered the confined men of the 1st South Carolina sent under guard to the provost marshal in Charleston, and forwarded Benbow's report to Beauregard.[3]

In early January, Lieutenant Dixon moved his operations from Charleston across the Cooper River to Mount Pleasant, where repairs were being completed on the *Hunley*. Dixon, Alexander, and two Alabama volunteers joined the crew from the CSS *Indian Chief* quartered in "an old abandoned house" near the Mount Pleasant city docks. With operations now in Mount Pleasant, Dixon was more closely associated with Ripley, whose headquarters was also in Mount Pleasant.

Being somewhat isolated from the mainstream of the Confederate military in the area, Dixon's crew cooked their own meals and ate at a separate mess. Ripley approved and signed Lieutenant Dixon's special requisition for a "camp kettle" and "mess pan" as well as Dixon's requisition for "one and two/sixths cords of wood" for cooking and heating the crew's frigid winter quarters.

To be closer to the blockading vessels in the harbor, Dixon moved the *Hunley* from the docks of Mount Pleasant to Breach Inlet, adjacent to Battery Marshall. However, the move required the crew to walk nearly seven tiring miles from their quarters in Mount Pleasant to reach the inlet. During the afternoons, Dixon and the crew boarded the *Hunley* for practice dives in Back Bay, located behind the battery. In late January or early February, probably facilitated by Ripley, Dixon secured quarters for the crew at Battery Marshall, ending the long walks the crew endured each day before they could practice.[4]

While Dixon was moving his base of operations to Breach Inlet and the crew was practicing their dives, Ripley continued his daily mundane duties. On

January 19 Beauregard's assistant adjutant, Captain Feilden, counseled the obvious: Ripley was to not place any obstacles in the way of the blockade-runners entering Charleston Harbor. The blockade-runners were notified that they would not be fired on if only one steamer attempted to enter the harbor each night. As one would expect, Ripley was to advise his command of this policy.[5]

Early in the war, during the Peninsula Campaign, both sides used observation balloons for reconnaissance against the enemy. On January 25 Ripley notified General Jordan that enemy "balloons have gone up for the last three nights from Capers Island" northeast of Charleston and Dewees Inlet. As the balloons had not been sent up during the day, Ripley reasoned that they were looking for Confederate campfires. With a touch of humor, Ripley gave "directions to insure they see a number of them after tonight, and shall commence rocket practice. Shall also send a reconnoitering party in that direction." Two days later Ripley notified Jordan that he had nothing further to report about the balloons but that Vanning's and Peterkin's companies "are building campfires and rocketing at night." Ripley would report if and when he observed any additional balloon activity.[6]

Early in February, Beauregard notified Ripley that the "enemy was making a heavy movement" in Florida and ordered Colquitt's brigade to proceed to Savannah. About the same time, Jordan informed Ripley that he was to have two regiments, with three days' provisions and a supply of ammunition, ready to move against an enemy demonstration on John's Island, but Jordan added that he thought the movement was "probably" a feint.

To counter an attack against General Henry A. Wise's forces on Johns Island, Generals Ripley, Taliaferro, and Hagood received orders to create a diversion. At 2:00 A.M. they were to open all guns in their commands against Morris Island and "keep up the fire for one hour and a half." Preceding the cannonade, three rockets were to be fired from every available rocket site on the island. The following day Beauregard congratulated General Wise for his successful repulse and pursuit of the enemy, forcing them to evacuate Johns Island.

On February 14 Beauregard ordered Ripley to send a "good regiment of infantry" from Sullivan's Island to Green Pond, South Carolina, approximately halfway between Charleston and Savannah. They were to proceed with as little delay as possible and "carry tents, cooking utensils, and baggage."[7]

In the meantime, when the weather permitted, Dixon and his crew carried out frigid night practice dives from Breach Inlet. After dark they took the submarine out to sea and steered for the nearest blockading vessel until conditions forced them to return to their dock. They also conducted an underwater endurance test and survived staying submerged for two hours and thirty-five minutes without opening the hatches to allow fresh air into the *Hunley*'s cramped quarters.

While training his crew, Dixon took time to write to a close friend in Mobile who had been urging him to return to Alabama. Dixon wrote of his activities in

Charleston and described Sullivan's Island as follows: "a more uncomfortable place could not be found in the Confederacy. I am fastened to Charleston and its approaches until I am able to blow up some of their yankee [sic] ships. For the last six weeks I have not been out of range of the shells and am often forced to go within very close proximity of the yankee [sic] battery.... I believe [that if] there is any post of honor or fame where there is danger, I think it must be Charleston, for if you wish to see war every day and night, this is the place."[8]

About this time Susan wrote to Harriott confirming Dixon's assessment: "The enemy are pounding away again against Fort Sumter and the city, they say not a pane of glass is to be found in Broad Street. Shells have burst lately in Mr. Charles Lowndes and Daniel Hayward's houses and in front of the Alston's."

William Flynn, a carpenter and citizen of Charleston who had been employed by Harris's engineer department, deserted to the enemy and provided some interesting observations of Charleston under siege. Flynn informed the enemy of Confederate troop dispositions and enumerated the size and position of guns in the city. He believed that Union artillery had been throwing shells too far toward the Ashley River and that many were falling on the burnt district. He offered that General Ripley was in command at Mount Pleasant and advised where the artillery should be trained "to make Beauregard's quarters very uncomfortable." Flynn noted that everybody had left the city "except the very poor that cannot get away." He believed that few people had been killed by the bombardment but that many houses had been ruined. All of the necessities of life were extravagantly high priced, and "Rebel money has depreciated until it is worth only $22 for $1 in gold and $18 for $1 in silver"—interesting figures compared with current prices for gold and silver. On a positive note, Flynn claimed that the blacks captured at Battery Wagner were not treated cruelly.[9]

Around the middle of February, a Federal sloop-of-war, the USS *Housatonic*, anchored about three miles offshore but within sight of Breach Inlet. Dixon decided to attack this "target of opportunity" on the first calm night. From his headquarters at Mount Pleasant, Ripley issued daily watchwords and the correct replies for the week of February 15. On the seventeenth the watchword would be "Green" and the correct response "Briar." That afternoon, Dixon and his crew made adjustments on the *Hunley* in preparation for that night's attack on the *Housatonic*.

Dixon spoke with Lieutenant Colonel O. M. Dantzler of the 20th South Carolina, who then was in command of Battery Marshall. As they parted, Dixon informed the colonel that if he succeeded in his attack, he would "show two blue lights." In response, a beacon was to be lit on shore to guide the *Hunley* safely home to Breach Inlet.[10]

On February 19 Colonel Dantzler reported to Ripley's aide, Captain William Nance, and to General Beauregard that the "torpedo-boat" stationed at Breach

Inlet went out on the night of the seventeenth and had not yet returned. The night of the attack, a signal from the boat signifying a successful attack had been observed, and in reply Dantzler's men lit a beacon on shore to guide her return. The officer of the day on the eighteenth mistakenly believed the boat had returned and informed Dantzler that it had. In his message on February 19, Dantzler apologized for not notifying his superiors sooner, but as soon as he realized that he had been misinformed, and the *Hunley* was missing, he telegraphed Nance.[11]

Ripley immediately notified Jordan that the *Hunley* had not returned and added, "Unless she has gone to Charleston, the boat has probably been lost or captured. I have no reason to believe the crew would have deserted to the enemy. They were not however under my directions, and I fear it is more likely she has gone down judging from past experience of the machine."

On February 20 Ripley forwarded to Jordan a message he had received from Dantzler. In it the colonel reported "a gun-boat sunk off Battery Marshall; smoke stack and rigging visible. A tugboat and barge are around her. . . . it may be she was blown up by the missing torpedo boat." This report, by Dantzler and Ripley, was the first to recognize that the *Hunley* may actually have sunk an enemy gunboat.[12]

While the fate of the *Hunley* remained uncertain, Ripley continued to receive orders and carried out his routine activities. That same day Beauregard instructed him to relieve the detachment of the 18th South Carolina who were then stationed at Fort Sumter and replace them with a like number of men from his district. Two days later Ripley received news that the enemy had been defeated with heavy losses in a battle at Olustee, Florida. With the increased Federal activity south of Charleston, Ripley was ordered to send the Holcombe Legion to Savannah with three days' rations and one hundred rounds of ammunition.

It is likely, as military action was moving south toward Florida and away from Charleston, that Ripley chose this time to once again request a leave of absence but now for only thirty days. In this request, dated February 22, he reiterated that he had not had any leave time since the beginning of the war except for the surgeon's certificate following his wounding at Sharpsburg. Evidently, Ripley was granted his request, as there are no reports or correspondence in the *Official Records* referring to him during March 1864.[13]

Where Ripley went for rest and relaxation during his leave is not known, but it is unlikely that he stayed in Charleston. In the 1850s he spent time in Savannah, at times staying at the Pulaski House, so he and his wife may have gone to Georgia. Perhaps he and his family went upstate to Flat Rock, in the mountains near Asheville, North Carolina. During the early 1800s, that area became a popular destination for many affluent lowcountry families escaping yellow fever, malaria, and the sweltering heat of summer. More likely, Roswell joined his wife at her Sparks in-laws' plantation in the quieter area of South Carolina near Society Hill.

As February drew to a close, Beauregard notified General Cooper that a gunboat had been sunk off Battery Marshall. He supposed that the "Mobile torpedo-boat, under Lieut. George E. Dixon, Company E, Twenty-first Alabama Volunteers, which went out for that purpose," sank the boat. Beauregard regretted to inform Cooper that the torpedo boat had not been heard from since. By the end of the month, Union prisoners revealed that the gunboat sunk was the USS *Housatonic,* and Beauregard notified Cooper that the "submarine torpedo boat" had indeed sunk the *Housatonic.* As the *Hunley* had not returned or been captured, Beauregard believed that there was little hope for the "safety of that brave man and his associates."[14]

While the tragedy of the *H. L. Hunley* was unfolding, Ripley joined a group of prominent South Carolinians in their efforts to incorporate a land-development company. The investors included John Fraser & Company, Chamberlain & Company, entrepreneur William Gregg, W. C. Bee, W. Ravenel (presumably William, a partner with Bee in a blockade-running firm), Charles J. and Thomas H. Colcock, John A. and E. M. Seabrook, R. B. Rhett Jr., and others.

The trustees of the group, Henry Seabrook and Thomas H. Colcock, planned to purchase a 575-acre tract of land, known as the "Foot Point Plantation," from John A. Seabrook for $100,000. A second source claims the tract was 525 acres. The same day, for $65,000, the trustees purchased an adjacent tract of 344 acres, now known as "Victoria Bluff," from Charles J. Colcock. All this acreage was undeveloped and included the attached marshes situated on the east side of the Colleton River in St. Luke's Parish, Beaufort District. This acreage, purchased for a total of $165,000, was divided into thirty-three shares selling for $5,000 per share. The most heavily invested was John A. Seabrook, who purchased six shares. Roswell Ripley and his aide, Captain E. M. Seabrook, each bought one share, as did most investors.

The first petition to the legislature in February, "for an act of incorporation, failed for a lack of certainty and technical objections." On March 18 the associates presented their second submission for a charter to the state senate and house of representatives. The company planned to establish a town at Foot Point with a capitalization of $500,000 but did not receive its charter until December 5, 1864.[15]

The fact that the site, in the words of one recent account, "is on deep water up to the very wharves" motivated the investors to establish a town at Foot Point. In the 1800s "it was regarded as a ideal site for a great commercial city," and as late as 1969, because of its deep-water harbor, the German company BASF considered building a chemical plant in the area. This attempt failed primarily because of the efforts of environmentalists.[16]

In late March 1866 Seabrook and Colcock deeded the company to the investors, but by then Ripley was attempting to leave for England. It is not known whether he recouped any of his investment. With the Confederacy near collapse and its economy in shambles, this speculative deal was reminiscent of Christopher Ripley's failed Matildaville investment during Roswell's youth.

CHAPTER 25

Ripley Returns and Reacts

Ripley returned from leave on April 5, 1864, and asked Beauregard whether he had any additional instructions for the "proper management" of his military district. The commanding general replied that he did not but hoped he would soon be able to return one of Brigadier General Evans's regiments to Ripley's district. Beauregard also advised his returning brigadier that the enemy was preparing an expedition against either Charleston or Wilmington and urged Ripley to maintain "due vigilance."[1]

On April 9 Ripley submitted memoranda to Beauregard's chief of staff on the fortifications of Sullivan's Island, as well as "certain remarks" related to the defense of some points in his command. Ripley reminded Jordan that in November he had submitted, in what he thought were plain terms, some of the reasons the works on Sullivan's Island were progressing so slowly. About a month and a half later, Ripley's communication was returned and he was told he had no right to make such criticisms. Ripley was advised to "report any want of energy" in the engineers' operations or "prefer charges against the chief engineer, or other officers of the department." Ripley claimed he had complained frequently of the engineers' "want of energy" but to no avail. He could not prefer charges against the engineers because he "had no knowledge of directions or orders issued to the officers in question." Ripley "remained quiescent under the system adopted," and the works progressed slowly during December, January, and February. At about that time orders were issued to increase the work on Battery Marshall.

When Ripley returned from his leave of absence of nearly forty days, he found the command reduced to about twenty-nine hundred effectives. Work on Battery Marshall had apparently been going on for only about two weeks, and Ripley wanted a work of appropriate strength completed soon. As there had been little change in his absence and with a possible enemy expedition against Charleston, Ripley believed that it was his duty to examine his command and submit appropriate memoranda. Ripley sarcastically hoped his "communication is not of such a character as I have no right to make; if so it can be treated as was that of the 23rd of November, 1863." He hoped the memoranda might be of some use and prevent the future interrogations or calls for "retrospective opinions." Ripley's memoranda covered seven pages, describing in great detail the state of the fortifications on Sullivan's Island. For each position he described the condition of the works, guns, and carriages, including the direction and extent of their fields of fire. These thorough memoranda are another example of Ripley's attention to detail.²

At Battery Marshall thirteen gun sites were distributed among six separate batteries: the northeastern outwork, northeast flank, eastern battery, southeast curtain, color battery, and the southwest battery, with the ordnance and any vacant sites listed for each battery. These batteries covered from the northwest to the southeast shores of Long Island and Breach Inlet (incorrectly identified as "Beach Inlet" in the *Official Records*), along the beaches of Sullivan's Island, and seaward over the channel. Ripley listed most guns as being in fair to good condition but noted that one rifled 12-pounder "required attention."

Despite being previously rebuked, Ripley again criticized the engineers on their current work at Battery Marshall. Ripley approved the two magazines, one in the nearly completed western bombproof, but was incensed that it had taken seven months to complete and had been altered three separate times. Ripley was disappointed that work had only just begun on the eastern bombproof. He "regretted" its irregular shape, with too many "nooks and corners," which would make it difficult to "manage men in the hurry and confusion of an action." He wanted these and all bombproofs on the island whitewashed for better light and to improve sanitary conditions.

Ripley argued that although the work at Battery Marshall had been proposed the previous November, five months had passed and the work "has not been prosecuted with energy." As no heavy fire could come from certain directions, Ripley believed that some of the battery's walls were being made much thicker and higher than necessary, requiring more laborers and taking much too long to complete. Ripley praised the garrison for being "good soldiers, attentive to their duties." Whatever the merits of these detailed memoranda, Beauregard would not have been pleased.³

Ripley next examined the four "Detached Two-Gun Batteries" between Batteries Marshall and Beauregard, each having either two 24-pounders or two 32-pounders, all smoothbore and in barbette. He considered two 32-pounders to be in good condition but all other guns to be in only fair condition. Their field of fire was seaward and south along the beach of Sullivan's Island, right and left, covering about 120 degrees. Ripley noted specific deficiencies in each battery and the need for renovation of the parapets and slopes of each of the four batteries as soon as possible. He added that each battery should be provided with double or triple chevaux-de-frise to prevent them from being carried by a surprise attack.⁴

Battery Beauregard had a diverse array of eleven guns divided between three positions, all in barbette. The work was in good order, garrisoned by two companies of Captain Thomas A. Huguenin's 1st South Carolina [Regular] Infantry. The two guns of the east face were in fair condition and covered the beach channel and about 120 degrees of the beach. The parapets and traverses at the northern end of the east face were badly in need of repair.

The three guns in the east face redoubt were in only fair condition. They covered northward along the east face and to the east for about 90 degrees to the right and left. Ripley claimed the redoubt's bombproof needed sod roofing and general repairs.

Battery Beauregard's southern batteries contained six guns, no two of which were alike. Most of the guns were in good condition and covered from the east to southeast, east along the beach, and seaward to the southwest. In view of the needed repairs, Ripley recommended certain modifications in the battery.[5]

Moving west along the beach, Ripley evaluated the work between Batteries Beauregard and Rutledge. He reported that the whole distance from Beauregard west to the bombproof had been almost blown away and badly needed "renewing." Ripley "regretted" that the battery, intended for a rifled 32-pounder ordered two months earlier, had not been completed. The work did have four iron 6-pounders in good condition and trained on the beach, but the parapet in front of two of these guns badly needed repair. Continuing westward toward Battery Rutledge, his inspection found the bombproof at the angle next to Battery Rutledge unfinished. From the angle to Battery Rutledge the work looked to be in good condition but needed sod. At night, detachments from Rutledge manned the guns.

Battery Rutledge was armed with three columbiads, three seacoast mortars, and one rifled cannon. The easternmost columbiad swept the eastern beach and fired seaward toward Morris Island. The rifled cannon and the other two columbiads were cut off from firing on Morris Island but could fire seaward and toward the harbor.

The three seacoast mortars could fire seaward and toward Morris Island; however, the mortar batteries were in very bad condition as repeated concussions had nearly destroyed their parapets. Rutledge's bombproof was strong, well ventilated, and spacious, its magazine in good condition. Rutledge also had a bombproof hospital with room for twenty or thirty cots. Ripley advised constructing a covered passageway between these points for protection when under fire. Ripley commended Captain C. H. Rivers and units of the 1st South Carolina [Regular] Infantry and 27th South Carolina Volunteers for having Rutledge in "fine order" with the exception of the mortar batteries.[6]

Old Fort Moultrie, so familiar to Ripley, had been remodeled to protect it from the enemy's heavy artillery. Fourteen cannon were divided among the eastern and western outworks and two faces, southeast and southwest, as well as a northwest half bastion.

The mortar battery on the east was in what remained of an old outwork and badly needed attention. It currently held a seacoast mortar in good condition, directed seaward and toward Morris Island. Six guns were positioned at the southeast face; all were judged to be in good condition, directed toward Morris Island and seaward. The three seacoast mortars of the western outwork batteries also were directed seaward and toward Morris Island but badly needed repairs. The two guns in good condition on the southwest face covered west and seaward. The half bastion had two smooth bores in only fair condition.

Ripley described Moultrie's construction projects, which included a nearly completed officer's bombproof in the old east curtain, still needing a layer of sod, and a bombproof gallery on the west needing more sand to be finished. The covering of the sea face was progressing well and would soon be "impervious to any artillery." Ripley approved the service magazine and bombproof along the south rampart even though they, probably unavoidably, had cramped gun chambers. The western gallery and bombproof were completed and the magazine fully protected. Ripley was pleased to see that the traverses between the guns on the seaward faces were very strong and complimented Captain B. S. Burnet and his four companies of the 1st South Carolina [Regular] Infantry for their proper care of materials and ammunition.[7]

Moving to the west, Ripley evaluated Battery Marion and its seven guns. The five guns in Marion's eastern batteries were unable to fire on Morris Island and were directed seaward and toward the harbor. Most were in good condition, but an 8-inch columbiad was in only fair working order. Most traverses were in proper condition, but certain parapets needed repair and the bombproof needed additional work. As the bombproof was quite spacious, Ripley thought it could be used for quarters or a siege hospital.

The two remaining seacoast mortars at the west end of Marion could fire on Morris Island and seaward. The mortars and their bombproof seemed to be in good condition, but Ripley thought the traverses, parapets, and revetments all needed repairs badly. Ripley praised Major William S. Basinger and the 18th Georgia Battalion for taking proper care of the ordnance.[8]

The inspection of the fortifications on Sullivan's Island ended at Battery Bee. Of the ten gun emplacements, only seven were filled. Positioned at the eastern end of the battery was one of the prized 11-inch Dahlgrens. All guns were listed in good condition, but their location prevented firing on Morris Island; as a result, their direction of fire was toward the sea and harbor. In addition to the Dahlgren, there were five columbiads and a 10-inch rifle. At Battery Bee, Ripley pinpointed specific problems with some of the merlons, parapets, and certain traverses, all of which were at the eastern end of the battery. The magazines and bombproof were in good condition. Major Warren Adams's two companies of 1st South Carolina [Regular] Infantry were well-supplied and their "material well cared for." Ripley closed with a strong health warning regarding the low places west of Fort Moultrie. These needed to be "filled up or drained . . . as the summer season will bring sickness if the matter is not attended to."[9]

Shortly after submitting his memoranda, Ripley received negative news regarding his command. In response to Federal threats in northern North Carolina, General Cooper began to transfer troops from South Carolina northward. Beauregard ordered Ripley to send General Nathan Evans's brigade, except for the 18th South Carolina, to Wilmington, North Carolina. The portion of the brigade in Ripley's district was to move at once with baggage, five days' rations, and forty rounds of ammunition. Also ordered to North Carolina were the Holcomb Legion, the 23rd and 29th South Carolina Regiments from Sullivan's Island, and the 26th from Charleston.[10]

Ripley notified Jordan that he had executed the order and that the movement of the troops would take place as soon as possible. However, he informed the chief of staff that "there is not one infantry soldier left in this command," and as the works on Sullivan's Island were not prepared, the enemy could attack and carry the position at any time. Beauregard responded that he was fully aware of Ripley's defenseless condition and regretted the depletion of his command. He advised Ripley that he had ordered the 18th South Carolina Volunteers, of Evans's brigade, from Florida and two companies of the 20th South Carolina, then in the Fourth District, to report to Ripley.

Ripley was not happy. He was fully aware of the problems with Evans's brigade, particularly the 18th South Carolina. He "respectfully" did not want the 18th and had no confidence in any troops of that brigade. He suggested that the 25th or the 27th South Carolina, then stationed on James Island, be substituted for Evans's troubled regiment. Ripley reiterated that he had no infantrymen on Sullivan's Island; there were only forty at Mount Pleasant and many were invalids. Beauregard denied Ripley's request, as the regiments could not be spared from James Island. He attempted to mollify Ripley by replacing the 18th Regiment with the 11th South Carolina when it returned from Florida and then sending the 18th to Colonel Rhett in the city.[11]

Beauregard, who earlier had been ordered to Weldon, North Carolina, along with the troops, finally left on April 20 when his replacement, Major General Samuel Jones, arrived in Charleston. One of the few members of Beauregard's staff not accompanying him to North Carolina was the twenty-five-year-old Englishman Captain Henry Wemyss Feilden. During his short tour, the young adjutant became an enthusiastic supporter of Beauregard, writing, "There is not another General in the service as thoughtful as our dear General. There is no doubt he has the best military head of any man in this Confederacy." Beauregard, before leaving for North Carolina, personally introduced his young aide to General Jones. Major John F. Lay, Beauregard's inspector of cavalry, also remained to join Jones's staff.[12]

In response to Ripley's request for a cavalry company, Jones agreed to send him one as soon as it reported. Jones wanted to meet at Ripley's headquarters on the April 27 to inspect the most important points in Ripley's district. At this point there is no evidence of any discord between Ripley and Jones, although Ripley would not have been pleased to learn that on May 6 Jones asked General Cooper whether Harris could return to Charleston. Jones valued Harris's long service in the department, his knowledge of the local topography, and the present defensive works. If Harris could not return, Jones wanted a "competent engineer officer" appointed as soon as possible.[13]

In May the manpower situation worsened, and the tone of the messages became desperate. The Confederates were running out of troops to shuffle to the north from South Carolina, Georgia, and Florida. Jones ordered officers, clerks, and employees organized into companies of forty or fifty men. They would be drawn from various offices in and around the city and would include men from the adjutant and inspector general, quartermaster, engineer, medical, commissary, pay, and ordnance offices. The chief of each department was to forward a list of all persons able to perform military duty.

On May 8 Feilden notified Ripley that the Macbeth Artillery would be sent from his district to western North Carolina. A few days later General Taliaferro, in command on James Island, notified Feilden that during the night the enemy opened a heavy fire on Secessionville, which continued into the morning. Taliaferro now added his voice to Ripley's criticisms of the engineer's lagging defensive works. He complained of the unfinished bridge connecting Secessionville with new lines and the incomplete connections between Battery Haskell and Fort Johnson. Taliaferro claimed that the bridge and connections had been commenced in November, it was now early May, "and I have reported their condition so often I despair of seeing them completed." Jones ordered Major Echols of the engineers to "complete the bridges with the least possible delay." Jones's reproach of the engineers was stronger than any ever voiced by Beauregard regarding Harris.[14]

Through Captain Feilden, Ripley pleaded with Jones to return two companies of the 20th South Carolina, recently at Branchville, to his district. Ripley planned to use these men in relief of a portion of the 20th, who were now sick at Fort Sumter. Jones did approve Ripley's request for Captain Ellison S. Keitt's company of cavalry at Georgetown to report to him. They had been attached to the 20th Regiment and were familiar with the Charleston area.[15]

In the middle of May, faced with the bold and bloody advances of General Grant in Virginia, General Cooper deluged Jones with requests for more and more infantry. Cooper requested that the 12th Georgia Battalion, then on James Island, and the 18th Georgia Battalion, also from Ripley's First Military District, be sent north. He also asked for two additional South Carolina regiments and two Georgia regiments on their way to Charleston from Dalton, Georgia, to proceed immediately to Virginia. To Ripley's disappointment, Cooper ordered Keitt's 20th

South Carolina to also start for Virginia, and two days later he ordered Jones to send a "good brigade of infantry from Florida" to Richmond.[16]

Growing desperate, Jones informed the mayor of Charleston that he was in great need of a few additional troops until others he had ordered arrived. He asked the mayor to allow him to send to James Island as many members of the Fire Battalion as could be spared. Jones vowed that he would not keep them "an hour longer than necessary." Jones also appealed to the navy for assistance, informing Flag Officer Tucker that having been ordered to send so many troops to Virginia, he could not man all the guns then in position. He even sent a battalion of "detailed men" and all the clerks in his headquarters to James Island, which by then was without an infantry garrison.

On May 18 Ripley notified Feilden that he was temporarily retaining the 18th Georgia Battalion despite orders to send them to Charleston to entrain for Virginia. When the order came for the battalion, some were on picket duty and the balance at the guns and mortars of Battery Marion. To comply with the order, they would have to abandon their guns, and Ripley had no forces available to relieve them. Colonel Keitt telegraphed Ripley for instructions and was told to send the steamer back to the city and retain the troops. Ripley believed that there must be some misunderstanding at headquarters about the 18th Georgia Battalion, which had been on duty as artillery since nearly the beginning of the war. They had been at Battery Marion since the previous August and had been frequently engaged, and during the last few days had seen action against monitors and batteries on Morris Island. Ripley felt it was his duty to retain the battalion until it was relieved by other competent troops.

It was not to be. The 12th Georgia left Charleston for Virginia on May 18, and Ripley's prized Georgia artillerists left the city the next day. Jones notified Ripley that the calls from Richmond for more troops were most urgent, but on May 20 the 32nd Georgia from the Florida District would be sent to Sullivan's Island. The next day Jones urged Ripley to get the 20th Regiment to Charleston that night, as the train would depart for Richmond early the next morning. He also asked Ripley, if he was "not too busy," to come over to his headquarters in Charleston.[17]

Later, Ripley filed a report describing concerted attacks by the monitors on Fort Sumter during this period. The assaults began on May 13 when two monitors approached within eighteen hundred yards of Fort Sumter and were aided by a cannonade from batteries on Morris Island. Ripley was in fact on Sullivan's Island at the time and personally directed all batteries that could be brought to bear on the monitors. That fire drove the monitors about five hundred yards farther off Sumter. The monitors retired at dusk, but firing from Morris Island lasted through the night.

The monitors returned the next day and renewed their attack, again aided by a "vigorous" bombardment from Morris Island. With the monitors now somewhat closer to Sullivan's Island, Ripley directed a heavier fire on them, driving one out of the action, with the other moving "to the extreme range of her guns." Notified that the fire from Morris Island was interfering with working parties at Sumter and causing damage, Ripley ordered all guns that could bear to open a heavy fire on Morris Island. As a result, the island ceased firing on Sumter and redirected their guns at Ripley's position on Sullivan's Island but "without any effect upon the position under my command."

Ripley realized that the enemy had been using the position of the merlons on the Sullivan's Island batteries to screen its monitors from some of his fire. As a result, he directed the engineers to open as many embrasures as possible in the direction of the sea approach, thus giving him better command of the monitors' former positions. After a day's lull in action, the monitors returned to their previous positions "with apparent confidence"—that is, until Ripley's "batteries opened, which they did with full effect." At 1,800 yards distant, the monitors immediately "hauled off, pursued by our shot until they were about 3,500 to 3,800 yards off." Ripley's artillerists fired ninety-two shots at different ranges, thirty-five of which were direct hits. One monitor's pilothouse was "knocked to pieces, and both monitors were evidently seriously damaged." They had been "severely hit by heavy shot in their turrets, on their decks, and between wind and water."

Ripley branded this latest attempt against Sumter a failure, which "demonstrated the power of our heavy batteries and the skill of our artillerists, officers and men." After this action, Ripley believed that three monitors had left the area in a southerly direction, ostensibly for repairs. Ripley closed his report with a subtle criticism of the engineers. He claimed the position of the merlons limited his forces' offensive power to a great extent, and the elevating apparatus for their heaviest gun (a 10-inch rifle) prevented its use "with full effect when the enemy was in its field of fire." He vowed to correct the problem. Ripley praised the efforts and preparation of the units under the command of Major William S. Basinger, 18th Georgia Battalion, and Captain Thomas A. Huguenin, whose reports described the action in greater detail.[18]

On June 13, 1864, Major General Sam Jones notified Major General John G. Foster, commanding general of U.S. forces on the coast of South Carolina, that five generals and forty-five field officers, all prisoners of war, had been sent to Charleston for "safe-keeping." They were turned over to General Ripley, who was to provide them "with commodious quarters in a part of the city occupied by non-combatants, the majority of whom are women and children." Jones informed Foster that this was "a portion of the city which has been for many months exposed day and night to the fire of your guns." Ripley enclosed a copy of this letter when he sent a similar notice to General Alexander Schimmelfennig, commander of U.S. forces on Morris and Folly Islands.

Generals Beauregard and Gillmore exchanged similar correspondence in August 1863 when Gillmore suggested that noncombatants be removed quickly from the city. Foster justified the continued shelling because Charleston was a depot for military supplies and contained an arsenal as well as foundries and factories for the manufacture of munitions. Foster notified Jones that he had forwarded his letter to President Lincoln, asking him to place in Foster's custody an equal number of prisoners of similar grades to be exposed to Confederate fire.[19]

Foster forwarded copies of Ripley's and Jones's letters to Major General Henry W. Halleck, Federal chief of staff, and sent one of his personal staff to Fortress Monroe to await Halleck's reply. The staff member was to bring the requisite number of prisoners to South Carolina pending Lincoln's approval of Foster's proposal. On June 21 Halleck informed Foster that the secretary of war had directed him to send an equal number of Southern generals and field officers to be placed "where they will be most exposed to rebel fire" and "treated with the same severity that they treat ours." Two days later the list of fifty-one Confederate prisoners from Fort Delaware was published. Number fifty on the list was Major F. F. Warley, who was captured in Charleston Harbor on September 4, 1863. He was the slightly wounded officer, captured when the Yankee barge seized Ripley's sailboat, as previously related by Augustine "Gus" Smythe.[20]

A few days later Ripley visited the quarters of the Federal prisoners in Charleston and found them being attended by a couple of black servants. Thinking this was not proper, Ripley stopped the practice and asked for a decision from General Jones as to how far "we are bound to supply them with cooks" and other attendants.

On July 1 the five Federal general officers held prisoner in Charleston—H. W. Wessells, T. Seymour, E. P. Scammon, C. A. Heckman, and Alexander Shaler—proposed an exchange of prisoners of war. These generals had just learned that five Confederate general officers had arrived at Hilton Head and were to be treated in the same manner. The generals asked for the Confederates to receive "every kindness and courtesy you can extend to them," as they were "pleasantly and comfortably situated as is possible for prisoners of war . . . receiving every privilege we could desire . . . nor are we unnecessarily exposed to fire." By the end of the month, General Foster informed Jones that the secretary of war had authorized the exchange of prisoners held by the respective camps, rank for rank, or their equivalents. This special arrangement was to involve only the officers in question.

On August 10, following the exchange, General Seymour told a different story. In a letter to Colonel William Hoffman, commissary-general of prisoners, Seymour now claimed they were treated "as outlaws and felons . . . referred to with vindictive and retaliatory spirit." Prison conditions improved only after the generals protested vigorously. Outrageously, he claimed that Federal prisons were elegant accommodations with every convenience, admitting all kinds of luxuries.

Seymour also informed Hoffman that Southern authorities were "exceedingly desirous for an immediate exchange of all prisoners" and that he and General Wessells had interviewed Ripley in Charleston on this point. They determined that the urgency and anxiety of the Confederates was proof of the "failing strength of their cause." They had informed Ripley that it would be "the poorest possible policy for our Government to deliver to them 40,000 prisoners, better fed and clothed than ever before in their lives and perfectly equipped for the field by Northern generosity, while the United States received in return an equal number of unfortunate men worn out with privation and neglect, barely able to walk, often drawing the last breath and utterly unfit to take the field as soldiers." Seymour concluded that it was wiser not to reinforce the enemy, "although hard upon our poor fellows, to let them stay yet longer where they are now." There obviously was no general exchange of prisoners.[21]

CHAPTER 26

Ripley in Crisis

The third major bombardment of Fort Sumter began in May and continued through June and July. In early May, Captain John C. Mitchel replaced Lieutenant Colonel Stephen Elliott in command of Sumter and nearly every day reported the number of shells fired at the fort, the hits and misses, casualties, and the health of the garrison. On the morning of June 2, Mitchel informed Ripley that a 300-pounder Parrott shell had dismounted an "important" 24-pounder, flank-casemate howitzer, damaging it beyond repair. Mitchel believed there were two similar guns with carriages at Moultrie and sought to have one transferred to Sumter.[1]

Later in the month Ripley gained an ally in his struggle to have Charleston's defenses completed without delay. General Jones emphasized that because of their weakened numbers, the works at the most important points must be finished soon. Jones asked Ripley to obtain as many hands from the rice planters in the area as possible but stressed that proper care and attention must be given to the African Americans, who under no circumstances should be retained if they were needed for harvesting crops.

The situation became more serious when on the night of July 1 the enemy landed in force on James and John's Islands. The following day Jones informed General J. E. Johnston in Georgia that Charleston was most seriously threatened and asked him to send troops if at all possible. Early the next day Ripley received orders from Jones to hold three companies of the 32nd Georgia Regiment and two light batteries from Mount Pleasant for transfer to James Island "at a moment's notice." The enemy assaulted Fort Johnson on July 3 but was repulsed with heavy losses, including 140 men and their commanding colonel taken prisoner.[2]

In early July, Captain Thomas A. Huguenin was on a leave of absence when he received a telegram from Ripley ordering him to return to Charleston immediately. When Huguenin reached the city, he reported to Ripley's office and was informed of the recent attack on Fort Johnson. In addition, a fleet of vessels and transports appeared off Dewees Inlet threatening to attack Battery Marshall. Ripley ordered Huguenin to take his boat to the battery, where he would find a company of cavalry awaiting orders. The captain was to take the cavalry across Breach Inlet to Long Island, form a picket line to detect any movement toward Sullivan's Island, and then return to his command at Battery Marshall. Huguenin recalled Ripley's words as he left the general's office: "I don't want any surprise on Sullivan's Island like there was on Morris Island. I put my trust in you and I feel satisfied I will not be mistaken." To Huguenin's surprise, he added, "How would you like to have command of Sumter?" Huguenin assured Ripley it was the "dearest wish of my heart." Ripley replied, "We will see."[3]

On July 8 Jones informed Beauregard, then at Petersburg, Virginia, of the increased activity and clashes on James and Johns Islands, and again pleaded for Colonel Harris to be sent to Charleston immediately. The heavy firing on Fort Sumter continued throughout July, which Mitchel considered as damaging as any of the bombardments that year. He asked Ripley to send men to help repair the recent damages and later acknowledged the "laborers thankfully received." On July 8, from daylight until dusk, Sumter received nearly 350 shots and only 20 missed the fort. From then until the twentieth, Mitchel sent reports to Ripley every day, often sending three or four messages a day.

Ripley promised to send more troops or laborers to Sumter as soon as possible but would send an additional medical officer and a private engineer, J. Fraser Mathewes, to assist in repairing the fort's damaged boom. He also informed Mitchel that he would open fire on the enemy when they are "annoying you" but that he was limited by a shortage of mortar powder. Ripley enclosed instructions with a cipher for the most important words for Mitchel to use in any telegraphed messages.

In August, Jones finally sent Cooper his report of the operations in the Charleston area during those hectic first ten days of July. He mentioned that Ripley's lines were not attacked but were constantly threatened. As his forces had been reduced to aid General Taliaferro, Ripley quickly met the situation with "increased vigilance."[4]

Pleased with the performance of the command at Fort Sumter, on July 16 Ripley petitioned General Cooper requesting that Captains John C. Mitchel of the 1st South Carolina Artillery and John Johnson of the engineers be promoted to major. He praised Mitchel's work as commander and the efforts of the previous commander, Lieutenant Colonel Elliott. Mitchel had been often on duty at Sumter since its capture and "commands the respect and commendation of every officer with whom he has been associated." Ripley praised his months of ceaseless vigilance, which "fairly earned his promotion."

Ripley commended Johnson, the fort's engineer officer since early April 1863, for his activity, energy, and skill, which enabled the garrison to withstand the unprecedented cannonade and bombardment they endured. Jones, who previously had recommended Johnson for promotion, endorsed Ripley's recommendations. Ripley also took time to notify Captain J. R. Tucker of the navy that the need for the steamer *Chicora* to be off Sullivan's Island was not now so urgent and thanked Tucker for his prompt assistance.[5]

On the day Ripley requested promotions for his two subordinate officers, Mitchel reported that Sumter received a much heavier than usual fire the previous night, and of the nearly 150 shells fired, only 32 missed the fort. The enemy's fire slackened on the morning of the sixteenth, and "our batteries fired remarkably well and with good effect." On July 19 Sumter received another devastating bombardment, the heaviest since the current series began. Mitchel recorded nearly 550 shells and mortars during the barrage but noted that, fortunately, many had missed the target and only three privates and one African American were slightly wounded.[6]

The next day, a sentinel on a parapet asked permission to move to a bomb-proof sentry box because of the extraordinarily heavy bombardment. When Mitchel went to the ramparts to assess the situation, a large fragment from a shell bursting directly overhead severely wounded him. After learning of Mitchel's mortal wounds, Ripley ordered one of his most trusted officers, Captain Huguenin, to the fort to replace Mitchel. Huguenin received the order from Ripley by signal; it stated, "Captain Mitchel is killed, you will take command of Sumter. I need not tell you to hold it."

Colonel Alfred Rhett advised Sumter's newly appointed commander not to risk the crossing in daylight, but Huguenin thought he should lose no time getting to the fort as "the general in command" might expect him to be there immediately. Under a very heavy fire, Huguenin and his crew reached Sumter at about sunset, and as he leaped ashore, the first thing Huguenin saw was the coffin containing "the body of my gallant predecessor; this was not an inspiriting sight."

Captain Mitchel's remains were taken to the city that night and reposed at St. Paul's Church under guard of the cadets. A solemn burial service was held the following afternoon attended by Generals Jones and Ripley in full dress uniform. At the conclusion of the service, the band of the 1st South Carolina Artillery led the procession of officers and cadets to Magnolia Cemetery, where Captain Mitchel was laid to rest.[7]

Huguenin continued the daily reports to Ripley on the fort's condition as the bombardment continued through July and August, finally ending on September 22. During the first sixty days of this third major bombardment, the fort received 14,666 shot and shell, which killed sixteen men and wounded sixty-five. Captain Johnson became a casualty in the early dawn of July 28; while inspecting some works on the eastern angle of the gorge at 3:45 A.M., he was severely wounded on the top of his head by a mortar shell fragment. Lieutenant E. J. White of the engineers replaced Johnson and served at Sumter until Charleston was evacuated. Johnson survived his serious injury to later write *The Defense of Charleston Harbor*.[8]

In early August, Jones contacted General Foster requesting a permit for a sixteen-year-old girl to pass through Federal lines at Hilton Head. Usually, all persons passing through Federal lines into the Confederacy were required to enter at Fort Monroe, but Foster made an exception as a courtesy to Generals Jones and Ripley. The girl was Marie Alice Sparks, Ripley's stepdaughter. It is not known exactly how long Marie had been in the North, but she crossed into South Carolina without incident.

On November 25, 1863, Charles K. Prioleau, the influential partner of Fraser, Trenholm & Company in England had written to an "H. U. Le Court (?) Esq." in New York City thanking him for the kind attention he had shown "these unfortunate ladies, Mrs. Bower and Miss Sparks." Prioleau had opened credit for the women, and if it was exhausted before they left New York, it was to be resumed indefinitely. Prioleau asked for separate receipts for Marie and Mrs. Bower so that "we may charge them appropriately." It appears that the two women may have been stranded in New York since November 1863, nearly eight months.[9]

During the summer of 1864, Ripley asked Henry Hotze, a Confederate agent in London and editor of the Confederate propaganda paper the *Index,* to negotiate a writing agreement for him with the *Herald and Standard*. On September 10 Hotze advised Ripley, "The desired arrangement is as complete as a third party can make it." The paper would be contacting Ripley directly, and Hotze hoped that Ripley would be "able to conclude a mutually advantageous engagement." Hotze stressed that the greatest difficulty would be preventing interruptions in transmitting articles and advised Ripley to take as many precautions as possible. There is no evidence that Ripley and the *Herald and Standard* ever signed an agreement or published any articles.[10]

In early September the situation in Charleston deteriorated further with the arrival of more Union prisoners. Ripley informed Jones's staff that the number imprisoned in the city was far greater than he could safely guard. Any increase in their numbers would compromise the defense of the city during an attack. Ripley advised the removal of prisoners from Charleston to the interior of the state, as he could guard only "from 500 to 1,000," noting that "such numbers as are now coming in jeopardize the safety of the city." Aware that yellow fever had struck the city, he realized that conditions would become worse if "the numbers crowded together in jails and prisons are not reduced at once." Meanwhile, Federal activity to the northeast of Sullivan's Island near Dewees and Long Islands concerned Ripley, and on September 12 he stressed once again that Battery Marshall should "be finished up without delay."[11]

On September 18 Jones's aide, Major John F. Lay, notified Ripley that telegrams from the recently exchanged Major Warley, then in command of the prison camp at Florence, indicated that the prisoners were "in a state of mutiny." Warley feared that he could be overpowered and that if the prisoners escaped, they would likely destroy the railroad line. Jones directed Ripley to send every available man he could spare and a detail of cavalry to Florence as soon as possible. Ripley's frustration must have mounted with the continued attempts to transfer units from his district while he faced another possible threat against Battery Marshall and Sullivan's Island.

Soon, more time and effort were expended on prisoner issues. Ripley notified Feilden that a boat, under flag of truce, had delivered fifteen boxes of clothing, letters, and greenbacks to Battery Marshall for naval prisoners being held in Charleston. Ripley had the clothing delivered to the quartermaster and kept the letters and money at his office. The delivery had no messages for the department, so Ripley proposed that unless he heard otherwise from headquarters, he would turn the whole shipment over to the provost marshal to examine and distribute.

Two days later Ripley received a terse response from Jones and Feilden. Jones instructed Ripley to send all the material to the chief quartermaster, where it was to be kept "subject to the orders from these headquarters." Jones directed Ripley to detain, in the future, all flags of truce until he telegraphed their presence to headquarters and was given permission to receive them. Never shy about expressing his opinion, Ripley replied that he wanted to expedite the process and, as he had not heard from headquarters, he had disposed of the material as he indicated he would and sent it to the provost marshal. In regard to receiving flags of truce, Ripley claimed that when Jones agreed to receive the shipment from Admiral Dahlgren, he gave Ripley permission to allow the commanding officer at Battery Marshall to receive the fifteen boxes. Ripley asked whether the commanding general wished "to rescind those instructions."[12]

By the end of September, Jones asked Cooper to order the commissary general of prisoners, John H. Winder, not to send any more prisoners to either Charleston or Savannah. There were more prisoners in Charleston than they could guard, and the yellow fever epidemic compelled Jones to move all prisoners away from Charleston. In addition, because of the epidemic, Jones notified his subordinate officers that if they wished, they could move as he had to Summerville, in the pinewoods north of Charleston. Joseph Barnwell recalled that Ripley, who could "be caustic when he chose to be, replied that the removal of higher officers to safe places would have a bad effect on the troops, and he would not take advantage of the kind permission given him."[13]

In late September, Jones tried a different approach to get the engineering expertise he believed he needed in South Carolina. He stopped asking Beauregard for Colonel Harris, and wrote to Cooper requesting that a "general officer that is well instructed in engineering and the use and management of heavy artillery, be assigned to the immediate command of all of the works and troops for the defense of this harbor." The duties were so varied, numerous, and important that the position called for an officer of "a high ability." However, Jones wanted any general appointed to the position to be under his command.

Although acknowledging that Ripley was in command of "the works in the city and harbor, Sullivan's Island and Christ Church Parish" and only those works on James Island were in General Taliaferro's command, Jones evidently did not believe that Ripley had the engineering training or expertise required for the position.[14]

On September 25, 1864, Ripley addressed a letter to General Cooper, igniting a firestorm that ultimately raged all the way to President Davis. Ripley initiated the problem when he asked Cooper for a decision regarding a point "which has caused some little difficulty" in the department. Evidently, Ripley was totally unaware that Cooper would not support him in any controversy. Cooper would obviously remember Ripley for "going over his head" when he involved Senator Shields, Secretary of War Conrad, and President Fillmore in his resignation process from the army in early 1853.

This difficulty started after Jones temporarily left Charleston on September 17 for the relative safety of Summerville. In his letter to Cooper, Ripley described his exchange with Major Lay when Jones's aide brought telegrams of a potential mutiny at the prison camp in Florence. Ripley ordered "certain troops" sent to Major Warley.

Soon afterward, Major Lay sent an order to Ripley, signed by Captain Feilden, stating that General Jones "directed certain dispositions," some of which Ripley believed "injudicious, and others impracticable." Ripley made dispositions with the means at his disposal to "best meet the case." Ripley told Captain Feilden not to send him any orders in the future that were unauthorized by the commanding general. Ripley soon received more telegrams and orders from Lay but was unable to communicate with Jones as to what actions he should take. Ripley rebuked Lay for sending him unauthorized directions and informed Cooper that he previously had reported Lay to Jones, once in writing and several times orally, for "taking unauthorized and irregular action as a staff officer."

The next morning, after Jones returned to Charleston, Ripley reported to him in person describing his actions and the conduct of Jones's staff officers. Ripley objected to "being ordered by staff officers upon an unforeseen and unprovided-for contingency in the absence of the commanding general." Ripley knew that standing orders could be written for certain events that might occur in the absence of the commanding general, but he did not believe it was correct for a staff officer to take original action on an unforeseen event.

Surprisingly, the day Ripley wrote to General Cooper, the news of the dispute had already reached Richmond. Beauregard notified Jones that President Davis had verbally ordered him to Charleston to await further orders. In the meantime he was "to inquire into the difficulty" between Jones and Ripley, as well as examine the condition of the defenses in and around Charleston. Ripley would now be investigated and judged by two of his most powerful detractors, Cooper and Beauregard. D. B. Harris, chief engineer, and Alfred Roman, chief inspector, would accompany Beauregard to Charleston, with Harris scheduled to remain on Jones's staff.[15]

It was well known that Ripley drank and thus gave his detractors an opportunity to attack him personally, regardless of whether or not his drinking affected his performance. After arriving in Charleston, Beauregard inquired into the "difficulty" between Jones and Ripley by looking for witnesses to the confrontation with Major Lay. Beauregard focused on Ripley's habits and behavior, rather than on the disputed orders questioned by Ripley.

Beauregard found two aides-de-camp, First Lieutenants P. C. Warwick and James L. Fraser, who were asked whether they had at any time since June 30, 1863, observed General Ripley "intoxicated or under the influence of liquor." Both officers claimed that on the morning of July 2, 1864, they were unable to locate Ripley at his home to inform him of the enemy's landing on the south end of James Island. Warwick met Ripley as he was arriving at his office and believed that the general "from his looks . . . had been up all night, and from his manner and general appearance . . . had been freely indulging in intoxicating liquors." Warwick concluded that the general's judgment was impaired and that he was "in no condition to properly discharge his duties." Ripley told Warwick to inform Jones that he was going over to Sullivan's Island and would remain there. Warwick incorrectly surmised that all orders responding to the enemy's landing on James Island were given from department headquarters and not by Ripley.

Fraser told a slightly different story. After finding Ripley was not at home on Rutledge Street, he soon located the general at his headquarters and gave him Jones's orders, instructing him to transfer a portion of his command to James Island and call out the local city troops. During this exchange, Fraser concluded that Ripley was under the influence of alcohol, but he had "no other evidence he was drunk." However, he believed "him to have been so from his boisterous manner, excited tone, and general appearance." Both aides relayed their assessment to Major Lay, who informed General Jones. In his final report of these operations, Jones gave no indication that he had experienced problems with Ripley. In fact, Jones commended Ripley and his officers, as the reduction of their forces "imposed greatly increased vigilance" on them, which they met "with alacrity."[16]

In his explanation of the situation to General Cooper, Jones claimed that before he left headquarters on the morning of September 17, he had conferred fully with Major Lay and given him directions, which he thought would cover any contingency likely to arise. Jones was to be sent for in case of any emergency while he was at Summerville, only about twenty-one miles from Charleston and on the South Carolina Railroad. Jones maintained that during his absence, when "perfectly proper orders, in accordance with my instructions and such as I would have given had I been present, were sent [to Ripley] he not only refused to receive and obey them but came in person to my headquarters, very much excited, and in a violent, rude, and insulting manner and language, accompanied with threats to Major Lay, refused to obey or receive orders from my headquarters."[17]

Ripley had previous problems with anger management, dating back to his youthful days at St. Lawrence Academy, his difficulties with Governor Pickens, his confrontations with Major Childs at the Charleston armory, his criticisms of Harris, and now his disastrous outburst against Major Lay. This time the results would be costly.

General Cooper endorsed Beauregard's report on the situation through the office of James A. Seddon. Cooper at least began by discussing the issue raised by Ripley, rather than his behavior. Cooper claimed that "according to long practice in the army," if Major Lay had quoted the authority of the commanding general, Ripley could not question whether the commanding general authorized the order before he obeyed it. Cooper argued that even though absent, Jones was within the geographic limits of his command, obviating Ripley from assuming command. Also, Cooper claimed that Ripley was not the highest-ranking officer in the department, evidently referring to Major General Lafayette McLaws, in command of the District of Georgia and the Third Military District of South Carolina. Cooper accused Ripley of insubordination and violently seeking to control the action of General Jones's staff officers, and he recommended relieving Ripley of his present assignment. Seddon agreed with Cooper's recommendation.[18]

Beauregard began his report to President Davis by suggesting that the enclosures from Fraser, Warwick, Jones, Cooper, and Seddon were evidence that Ripley could not be entrusted at this critical time with the important command of the First Military District of South Carolina. Beauregard thought that Charleston offered Ripley "such great temptations and facilities for indulging in his irregular habits."

However, Beauregard believed that Ripley's past "efficient service" might entitle him to "some consideration" by the president. He recommended that Ripley be ordered to active service in the field, "where time, reflection and stricter discipline might have a favorable effect on him." Specifically, Beauregard suggested that Ripley could be placed in temporary command of Elliott's brigade at Petersburg until either General W. S. Walker or Stephen Elliott Jr. returned to service.

Beauregard recommended his close friend, Colonel D. B. Harris, for promotion to brigadier or major general and to assume command of the First Military District in place of Ripley. As he closed his report, Beauregard mentioned that Warwick and Fraser reported to Jones in early July that they believed Ripley was "too much excited by liquor to be relied on" but that when Jones asked for the "particulars of General R's manner and conduct . . . he was satisfied that a charge to that effect could not have been sustained before a court, and thought it best not to prefer the charge." According to Beauregard, Jones came to this conclusion because of "his knowledge of the general, and his experience as judge-advocate of the difficulty of convicting officers of intoxication." Jones knew Ripley's temperament and personality and the young lieutenants did not; in addition, Jones had expressed satisfaction with Ripley's responses to his orders in early July despite the aides' critical comments.[19]

Neither Captain Feilden nor Major Lay, holdovers from Beauregard's staff, had an especially congenial relationship with Ripley. Feilden, of aristocratic English lineage, would have identified more closely with the refined P. G. T. Beauregard and the gentleman Virginia planter D. B. Harris than he would have with Ripley, who at times was described as blustery and rough, unceremonious in manner, and frequently obstinate.

Feilden believed that Beauregard was the best military man in the Confederacy and described Harris as "just the man I should like to serve under." However, Feilden would have agreed with Ripley regarding Major Lay. Beauregard's loyal English aide had a poor opinion of Lay, whom he described as "insufferable."

The Englishman, in a letter to his future wife, quoted Beauregard nearly word for word in criticizing Ripley's "irregular habits and indulging in Charleston." Feilden also referred to Ripley as an "old scoundrel . . . a worse old dog does not hold a position of importance in the Confederacy." After the war, reflecting on Ripley's military service, Feilden would annotate this letter in a much friendlier manner.[20]

On October 17 General Cooper added a new charge to the accusation that Ripley had evinced "arrogant insubordination to the authority of his commanding general." In addition, Cooper now referred to a subsequent, inexplicit report, found in the *Official Records*, which alleged that Ripley was in some way involved with Mrs. Mason and was guilty of "looseness of morals." Cooper concluded that "both instances are calculated to bring the military service into discredit." The "<u>beautiful</u> Mrs. Mason," who according to Susan Middleton had "scandalized" Columbia the previous year "by being a guest in the home of Dr. Gibbes," had apparently returned to Charleston. Susan described her as being General Jordan's friend and "relation," and apparently she had been the topic of gossip in Charleston before moving to Columbia. Somehow, Jordan avoided being linked with Mrs. Mason, but regardless of whether the allegation was true or not, Ripley was not so fortunate.[21]

On October 25 President Davis responded to the charges and allegations against Ripley. He concluded that the case did not seem quite clear. If General Ripley learned from the staff officer before the order was issued that it did not emanate from General Jones, he was not bound to obey it. If, however, the conclusion was that Ripley was guilty of insubordination, he should be arrested and brought before a court, not relieved for assignment to another command, as Beauregard intended.[22]

This tumultuous confrontation, which ultimately involved the president, resulted in drastic changes in the command of the Department of South Carolina, Georgia and Florida. President Davis ordered Lieutenant General W. J. Hardee from the Army of Tennessee to command the department, and Jones was reassigned to the new command of the District of South Carolina, which included all the state except for its Fifth Sub-District. By the middle of October, Ripley had been demoted to command the Second Sub-District of South Carolina.

After he returned to Charleston, Beauregard's choice to replace Ripley, Colonel Harris, became a yellow fever victim and soon died. Jones was in "wretched health" and unable to assume command. As a result, General Robert Ransom replaced Jones, and although Hardee agreed that Ripley should be relieved, compensating for the temporary loss of Jones was "more important than the immediate removal of Ripley."[23]

On October 25, from the headquarters of the Second Sub-District, Ripley wrote a curious, unaddressed memorandum. It likely was a response to a new superior officer in the area, Hardee or Ransom. As requested, Ripley addressed the possibility of recapturing and occupying Morris Island, an idea long abandoned as impractical by most officers in Charleston. Ripley wrote a long, comprehensive plan but began by warning that it could succeed only by surprise, as a regular attack would almost certainly fail. The memorandum is an example of Ripley's innovative thinking and attention to detail, but he welcomed modifications at every step. Ripley admitted that his complicated plan would result in the probable loss of three steamboats and three thousand men if it failed. As Ripley must have hopefully anticipated, the plan was not attempted.[24]

By November word of Ripley's besieged command reached elected officials and representatives in Charleston and the adjoining parishes. Deeply troubled that authorities planned to relieve Ripley, his loyal supporters rallied to his defense. They petitioned that their faith "in his present and future usefulness is justified by his past conduct and military views . . . and because he has the confidence of the troops under his command." His removal would be "a public calamity." They obviously discounted the accusations made against him and forwarded their petition to Governor Bonham, who endorsed it and had Senators Orr and Barnwell present the paper to President Davis. On November 23 the petition appeared on the front page of the *Mercury*.[25]

In late November conditions were deteriorating in Georgia as Sherman and his forces drove toward Macon and Augusta. One of Ripley's last communications, while in command of the Second Sub-District, was to notify General McLaws in Savannah that he was unable to fill General Fry's request to send five hundred small arms to Augusta. Ripley asked McLaws to send Fry all he could spare and inform Fry how many he could send. Sherman cut a wide swath from Milledgeville to Sandersville and Millen, but Savannah was his ultimate goal. On November 22 Major General Robert Ransom replaced Ripley and assumed command of the Second Sub-District of South Carolina.[26]

A few days later, Lieutenant E. B. Middleton entered in his journal, "General Ransom has relieved General Ripley of the command of the 2nd sub-district and it is rumored the latter is to be shelved. I am sorry for it, as he is most eminently qualified for this service. Our band, accompanied by several officers from our regiment on Sullivan's Island, serenaded him the other night." A notice of the event appeared in the *Mercury* and described the group as the Sullivan's Island Band, who with several officers "serenaded General Ripley last evening at his residence on Rutledge Street. As the general is relieved, it was intended to show the high appreciation in which he is held by the artillerists on Sullivan's Island and to express their desire for his return to the command of his sub-district."[27]

Evidently, Hardee granted Ripley a thirty-day leave of absence on November 22, and on December 13 Beauregard informed President Davis that Generals Hardee and Jones now agreed that Ripley was "unfit for command in Charleston Harbor owing to his unreliable habits." Beauregard planned to order Ripley to the field when his leave expired, despite Davis's opinion to the contrary expressed at the end of October.[28]

At the same time, Beauregard attempted to further discredit Ripley. He instructed Alfred Roman to begin a full investigation into allegations that while on a visit to Fort Sumter, late in October or early November, "Brigadier General Ripley was under the influence of intoxicating drink, and participated in acts subversive of good order and military discipline." Interestingly, whoever brought the allegations was quite vague and unsure as to when the incident occurred.

The inquisition involved five of Ripley's subordinates. Four were at Fort Sumter: Captain T. A. Huguenin, in command; Captain G. W. Lamar, commissary officer; Lieutenant Edwin I. White, engineer; and Lieutenant W. G. Ogier, adjutant. The fifth officer was Major Motte A. Pringle, quartermaster in Charleston.

Roman visited the four officers at Sumter on the evening of December 14 and questioned them as to whether, in late October or November, Ripley was at the fort and under the influence of intoxicating liquor and as a result had committed acts subversive of good order and military discipline. All four responded in writing later that day or the next, and Beauregard's inspector entered their letters as "exhibits A through E."

Captain Huguenin could only remember Ripley being at Fort Sumter on the night of October 8. Ripley visited the fort as requested by Huguenin to discuss "a mutiny, which had occurred among a portion of my garrison." While General Ripley was present, "we invited him to partake of refreshments," an invitation usually given to general officers, and while he "did take one or more drinks,"

Huguenin definitely did not think his faculties were in any way impaired by what he had to drink: "General Ripley did not participate in any act subversive of good order or military discipline."

Captain Lamar believed that on the night of October 8, "General Ripley was under the effect of intoxicating liquor. I can recall no other act which I considered subversive of military discipline." Roman concluded that Lamar must have believed that having anything to drink was in itself "subversive to military discipline."

Lieutenant White stated that on the night of October 8, while at Fort Sumter, Ripley was slightly under the influence of "spirituous liquors, but not to such an extent as to impair his usefulness or capacity to command. I did not witness any act which was subversive of good order or military discipline."

Lieutenant Ogier recalled that "to my knowledge he had been drinking, was not drunk, or in any way incapable of attending to his duties. I am unaware of anything in his conduct on that occasion prejudicial to good order and military discipline."

In his report to Beauregard's adjutant, J. M. Otey, Roman was "sorry to say those statements are not as explicit as they could have been. They speak of opinions, of impressions, and say nothing of facts." Roman believed that the officers disclosed as little as possible about the incident and was obviously disappointed they had defended Ripley. Roman believed the officers' defense of Ripley indicated that an officer "may drink as freely as he chooses," and, if he could move about his command with his faculties and capacity to command unimpaired, "he is not considered drunk."

Roman interviewed Major Motte A. Pringle at his quartermaster's post in Charleston, and although Pringle was not at the fort that night, for some reason Roman thought, or hoped, that the quartermaster would comment on the inquiry. Pringle discussed the situation with Roman but afterward "consulted a friend," who advised him not to respond to Roman's inquiry. Pringle's letter, enclosed as Roman's exhibit E, stated that he would gladly testify in court but did not feel bound to give a "voluntary statement about the Fort Sumter affair." Pringle did not want his refusal to convey "any unfavorable impression toward Ripley." He stressed that he reconsidered responding without consulting Ripley or his friends, none of whom knew Roman had even contacted him. Roman was infuriated, believing "his request had the weight of an order; therefore, Pringle was guilty of disobedience and should be made to account for it."[29]

Beauregard's attempt to discredit Ripley failed because of the strong support from Ripley's junior officers, who held him in high regard and respect. Roman refused to believe the testimony of these officers and their conclusion that Ripley was not impaired and definitely did not commit any acts "subversive of good order or military discipline that night."

General Jones, who supposedly had finally agreed with Beauregard to remove Ripley, would later describe the general as "an officer of distinguished ability, great energy, and fertile in resource; no more accomplished artillery officer could have been found in either army. He was especially charged with the defenses of the harbor, and the completeness of the preparations was in a great measure due to his skill and energy." He added that Ripley was the one "to whom, perhaps, more than any other officer, Charleston was indebted for the system of defensive works that enabled a comparatively small force to hold the enemy at bay and keep them away from the city."[30]

By the end of the year, Governor Magrath learned of Ripley's proposed transfer and reacted by sending Captain E. M. Seabrook to Richmond to meet with Senator R. W. Barnwell. Magrath admitted that he did not know the details of the problem between Beauregard and Ripley, but he did know that this was no time "for an indulgence in personal likes and dislikes. The great usefulness of Genl. Ripley is not only in the harbor, and other water defenses of the city, but also . . . for the selection and construction of the defenses around Branchville." The governor claimed that if he had known Beauregard planned to transfer Ripley, and if he had been in a position to intercede, he would have "asked the President to consider all circumstances before he decided." If the matter was definitely decided, he could only "express my regret that it has been done. I have never known an officer here more efficient and untiring, nor do I believe there is one more thoroughly devoted to the defense of this place to the last extremity."[31]

CHAPTER 27

Death of the Confederacy

Twenty years after the war, a *New York World* reporter interviewed Roswell Ripley regarding a letter he wrote to South Carolina's last wartime governor, Andrew G. Magrath. Dated December 25, 1864, Ripley's recently published letter may have been found in captured South Carolina archives. During the interview Ripley acknowledged that he offered to resign his Confederate commission and accept a position under the command of Governor Magrath. When asked whether his letter to the governor was insubordination, Ripley claimed it definitely was not. The precedent had been set when General Gustavus W. Smith resigned his commission and accepted a military position with the governor of Georgia. Ripley volunteered to lead South Carolina troops hastily being raised by the governor for the defense of the state and criticized the Confederate government for its failure to provide the forces necessary to defend South Carolina against Sherman's invading armies: "The government at Richmond was doing practically nothing to defend our borders, and we had to raise a force from the little material left to us." South Carolina "had been drained of all able-bodied men," and only youths under eighteen and men over fifty were left for the defense. "That force was to be under the control of the State Government, but it was to cooperate with the regular army," Ripley noted.

Ripley complained of "studied neglect and injustice done himself on the part of the Richmond authorities." Ripley, who was on leave during the month of December 1864, stated, "I had been ordered, just at that critical juncture, to leave the State for a command in Mississippi." Ripley believed that Beauregard's order was the "culminating act of a continued policy of injustice to me."

Beauregard contended that on December 23, 1864, he had ordered Ripley to join General John Bell Hood's Army of Tennessee and Ripley disobeyed the order. On November 30 Hood's army had been devastatingly defeated at the Battle of Franklin, Tennessee, and lost six general officers either killed or mortally wounded. Following that disaster, Hood's army was badly beaten at the Battle of Nashville on December 15–16. After Hood's ill-advised, catastrophic Tennessee Campaign, Beauregard claimed that he was "absolutely required at this moment [to be] at Montgomery with the Army of Tennessee." At Beauregard's request, Davis removed him from the Department of South Carolina, Georgia and Florida, and replaced him with Lieutenant General William J. Hardee.[1]

Ripley protested the order transferring him to the West in his letter to Governor Magrath, who "did not return a formal answer, but in a conversation advised me to go to Richmond. This I did and remained in Richmond until all was over." Either time had dimmed Ripley's memory, or possibly he chose not to discuss the details of his last months of the war, for in fact he did not remain in Richmond "until all was over." Motivated by a commitment to defend his adopted state and to avoid any contact with Beauregard, Ripley used the governor's advice as justification for ignoring Beauregard's orders. Ripley believed that in Richmond he could accurately explain the military crisis in South Carolina and plead for troops to be sent to the state. Evidently, soon after Magrath discussed the military situation with Ripley, the governor asked President Davis to detach Conner's brigade, originally Kershaw's brigade, from the Army of Northern Virginia and send it to South Carolina. On January 5, 1865, Davis agreed to transfer these South Carolinians, then under the command of Brigadier General John D. Kennedy, back to the Palmetto State.[2]

On January 6 Secretary James A. Seddon's Special Order No. 4, paragraph LI, granted Ripley a ninety-day extension to his leave. This leave, which Seddon thought had been granted in December, appears to have been based on a statement made by South Carolina senator James L. Orr to President Davis, claiming that Ripley "had been placed on furlough, etc." Davis forwarded this information to Seddon, who in December tried unsuccessfully to document the leave but nevertheless granted the extension. As Governor Magrath suggested, Ripley traveled to Richmond and conferred with General Robert E. Lee, most likely after first meeting with Davis. On January 8 Lee notified the president that he had met with Ripley and "listened with great pleasure to the account given by General Ripley of the affairs in S.C. and Charleston. It is painful to me to contemplate the evacuation of the city. . . . I think it safer & perhaps easier to prevent the enemy from reaching Charleston. I hope by concentration of all their forces that Sherman may yet be arrested in his course."[3]

The discussions with Ripley evidently impressed Davis and Lee with the situation in South Carolina. As a result, Davis began implementing Lee's plan to concentrate and consolidate forces to stop Sherman "in his course." On January 7 Davis notified Hardee that "Conner's brigade, from Lee's army, is en route to aid you," and he asked whether Hardee had heard "from Hood as to sending troops to Augusta?" Hardee had "no information whatever from Hood and have no reason to expect re-enforcements from that quarter." Also confirming that Ripley's pleas were influential, Hardee received word from Davis that more South Carolinians were on their way to defend the state. Davis "hoped" that Major General Matthew C. Butler's cavalry division would "soon be with you," as they had been "directed to proceed as rapidly as possible to South Carolina." Symptomatic of the Confederacy's disorganization and deteriorating communications, Davis "supposed" that General Wade Hampton was also on his way.[4]

In early January, after being replaced in South Carolina by General Hardee, Beauregard reached the headquarters of Hood's army in Montgomery, Alabama, where he ultimately was to "resume control of operations against Sherman." On January 9 Major General Daniel H. Hill, who also had been ordered to Hood's Army of Tennessee, reached Montgomery and Beauregard's headquarters. Two days later, as the Confederate command struggled, General Cooper ordered Hill to return to Charleston and serve with General Hardee rather than remain with Hood, who in fact had resigned as commander of the Army of Tennessee. Eight days after leaving Montgomery on his way to Charleston, Hill finally reached and was placed on duty at Augusta, Georgia. Word finally reached Cooper on January 14 that Ripley, who was on extended leave, had previously been ordered to report to General Hood.[5]

By January 20 Ripley had returned to South Carolina and wrote to General Cooper regarding his extended leave. Having learned of Roman's "inquisition" at Sumter, Ripley wrote, "I have respectfully to request that when the extension shall have expired, or it may be necessary to place me upon duty, it may not be under the command of General G. T. Beauregard." He cited Beauregard's "avowed personal motives of hostility" as the reason for this request. Ripley believed that his length of "responsible service" allowed him this concession. Obviously, he thought he was on a valid extended leave and seems to have been oblivious to how his request would be received by Cooper. Given Ripley's history with the adjutant general dating back to 1852–53 and his creative efforts to resign his U.S. Army commission, Cooper would not have been understanding or sympathetic. The next day, through the Adjutant General's Office, the secretary of war issued a directive revoking Ripley's ninety-day extension.

On January 25 Beauregard received word of the revocation of Ripley's extended leave and learned that Ripley would be ordered to report to the general whom he so desperately wanted to avoid. When Hill assumed command at Augusta, he notified General Hardee, "Our need of artillery officers, men, and harness is very urgent. We have twelve 6-pounders, four 3-inch rifles, two 20 and two 10-pounder Parrotts, but no men, horses or harness. If you could send me a chief of artillery, and some artillery officers, I would try to extemporize three or four batteries and man them from the hospitals." Beauregard telegraphed Hill on January 28 that he would be coming to Augusta and asked, "If General Ripley should be in Augusta, detain him and order him to report to General Cheatham for assignment to Gist's brigade." States Rights Gist was one of the six Confederate generals killed at the Battle of Franklin.

There is no record of whether Hill, Hardee, or Beauregard ever considered the possibility of appointing Ripley to be the chief of artillery Hill had requested. As Ripley had been an aide to the detested Gideon Pillow and authored *The*

War with Mexico, Hill intensely disliked the Ohio-born general. He would later strongly criticize Ripley's actions during the Peninsula Campaign and at South Mountain. An assignment with Hill would have been contentious, and Hill also did not know Ripley's whereabouts.[6]

Although Hill believed Sherman was moving toward Augusta, some of his staff admitted that "we are somewhat puzzled to know what Sherman is about." Hill complained, "We are working in the dark, and may lose the city." Hill reported that reinforcements from the remnants of the Army of Tennessee were beginning to arrive in Augusta but "destitute of everything—arms, clothing, etc. Nine hundred arrived out of 1600 started; the rest deserted. . . . More than half of the two advanced brigades have deserted."[7]

While the Confederates were ineffectually attempting to coordinate their defenses against Sherman, the Union army was on the move from Savannah into South Carolina. Sherman continued his strategy of advancing the army on two wings as he had during his march through Georgia. This inexorable force presented a front nearly forty miles wide and alternately appeared to threaten Charleston, Augusta, or Branchville, the last remaining rail center directly linking Virginia and Georgia.[8]

On February 2 Beauregard called Generals W. J. Hardee, D. H. Hill, and G. W. Smith, commander of the Georgia militia, to a council of war at Green's Cut Station near Augusta and estimated their total effective force available to oppose Sherman to be 33,450. However, Cheatham's and Stewart's corps from the Army of Tennessee had not yet reached Augusta. Therefore, Hardees and Hill's forces remained divided between Charleston and Augusta.

Amazingly, Beauregard asked Davis to send ten or twelve thousand troops from North Carolina and Virginia to Columbia, and with Davis's approval he would assume command of all forces there and "would defeat, and might destroy, Sherman's army." Davis responded by reemphasizing that "the necessity for the rapid concentration of your forces and . . . every available means must be employed to delay the advance of the enemy." Instead, Beauregard attempted to defend all four points—Augusta, Branchville, Charleston, and Columbia—and made no effort to consolidate his forces as recommended by Lee and the president. Lee unfortunately believed that Beauregard was concentrating his forces at Columbia as had been suggested.

On February 5 Beauregard dramatically informed Governor Magrath, "The crisis is again upon your state," and asked him to assemble all available state forces at Columbia. Beauregard did not know whether the enemy, after reaching Branchville, would move on Augusta, Charleston, or Columbia, or possibly both of the latter two cities. Because of Beauregard's inability to determine Sherman's objective, and with the Confederate forces so widely dispersed, a direct confrontation with the Union army in South Carolina was impossible. Sherman drove a wedge between the Confederates defending Augusta and Charleston and aimed directly for Columbia.[9]

After Ripley wrote to General Cooper from Charleston, there is no record of his activities for nearly two weeks. If he knew that his leave had been revoked on January 21 and that he had been ordered to report to General Beauregard in Montgomery, he disobeyed those orders. His desperation to avoid serving under Beauregard may have been overwhelming but did not justify his actions. If he kept on the move and no one knew where he was, he may not have received the orders. However, he should have informed his superiors where he was, and obviously he did not. During this time, he may have visited his family in Society Hill, where Alicia and her daughters probably sought refuge from the devastation of Charleston, and most likely stayed with Alicia's former in-laws, the Sparks family. As early as 1862, women of the Pringle family and other families began moving for safety to Society Hill and Darlington Court House. Some believed this was the only area where the inhabitants treated families properly and good inexpensive board could be obtained.[10]

With Confederate forces still in disarray, Ripley may have gone to Columbia and conferred again with Governor Magrath. It is not known whether the governor encouraged Ripley to make a second trip to Richmond, but once again Ripley entrained for the capital. Early in February, Colonel James H. Burton, superintendent of Confederate armories in Macon, Georgia, planned a meeting with Josiah Gorgas, the Confederate chief of ordnance. After an overnight stay in Columbia, on February 5 at 7:30 P.M. Burton boarded the train for Charlotte, then proceeded nonstop to Richmond. After boarding the train, Burton was surprised to meet and renew "acquaintances with General Ripley," whom he remembered from Ripley's business calls at the Royal Armory in Enfield before the war. Because of a heavy early morning storm, the train pulled into a snow-covered Richmond on February 7 at 1:30 P.M. Confederate clerk John B. Jones claimed, in his first diary entry for that date, that there were four inches of snow on the ground and that it was still snowing.[11]

In July 1860 Burton claimed he resigned his position at Enfield as a "consequence of ill health." Privately, Burton admitted that he had been corresponding for months with his father-in-law, George Mauzy of Harpers Ferry, as well as Governor Letcher and others in Virginia regarding an appointment as master armorer at the Virginia State Armory. The state had reactivated the armory in Richmond after John Brown's raid on Harpers Ferry in October 1859. Burton, a native of Jefferson County, Virginia, arrived in the United States on October 12, then traveled to New England in November and examined the machinery at the Sharps Rifle Manufacturing Company in Hartford. Burton ordered machinery for the Richmond Armory from the Ames Manufacturing Company and upon returning to Richmond began supervising its layout. In the spring of 1862, after

Burton's success refurbishing and restarting the armory, Gorgas placed him in charge of constructing a Confederate States armory on a forty-seven-acre site in Macon, Georgia. The armory later produced Spiller & Burr revolvers, and Burton, a partner of Spiller & Burr, used his influence with the Confederate government to secure a lucrative contract for his company; some may consider him to have been guilty of war profiteering.[12]

After Ripley arrived in Richmond, he visited President Davis and presented his views of the evolving military situation in South Carolina. Beauregard's recalcitrant general impressed the president enough for him to notify Lee that "General Ripley visits you" to present his views regarding matters in South Carolina and more particularly the city of Charleston. Davis hoped that Lee would grant Ripley "an audience on these subjects and . . . your suggestions to General Beauregard." Lee, now general-in-chief of the Armies of the Confederate States, must have been consumed with the difficulties presented by General Ulysses S. Grant's siege of Petersburg. If Ripley traveled to Petersburg and met with Lee as Davis requested, there is no record of Lee's response to the meeting. If Beauregard learned that Ripley visited Davis and Lee to present his opinions on the proper defense of South Carolina, he would not have been pleased.

Meanwhile, as Sherman drove deeper into the state, Beauregard took time to question the whereabouts of his missing general. On February 11, from his headquarters in Columbia, the embattled commander telegraphed Hardee in Charleston. "Should General Ripley still be in Charleston, inquire for [what] reason he has not joined his brigade in Augusta, and order him there forthwith, via Columbia. Should he disobey send him in arrest." The next day an incredulous Beauregard telegraphed General Cooper that "General Ripley is again in Richmond, notwithstanding repeated orders to join his brigade now fronting the enemy near Augusta. I request he be ordered to his post forthwith." The same day Hardee received a similar message: "Ripley's leave was canceled by the War Department," and he "ought to be with his command fronting the enemy near Augusta."[13]

Beauregard finally learned that Ripley had requested that any duty in the future "may not be under General G. T. Beauregard [as] that officer has on one occasion, at least, avowed personal motives of hostility as a reason for interfering with my official position." Ripley claimed he had good reason to believe Beauregard's actions against him in other instances were also from personal hostility. Beauregard's endorsement to Ripley's January plea to Cooper, although not added until February 13, 1865, has become the basis, without further research or substantiation, for many historiographers' assessment of Roswell Sabin Ripley's complete Confederate military career. Beauregard wrote, "Brigadier General Ripley is active, energetic, intelligent, ambitious, cunning and faultfinding. He complains of every commanding officer he has served under, and has quarreled (or had difficulties) with almost every one of his immediate subordinate commanders since his promotion to his present rank in 1861." Beauregard claimed that Ripley "obeys orders only so far as they suit his purposes, provided, by disobeying them, he does not incur the risk of a court-martial, which, however, he does not much fear, trusting to his intelligence and ability to get clear of the consequences thereof." Beauregard thought Ripley should be brought to trial, and if acquitted he would approve his application to be transferred out of his command, for "I will consider myself fortunate to be rid of such an element of discord."

Beauregard had previously recommended Ripley for promotion "on account of his zeal, activity, and intelligent discharge of his duties during the siege of Charleston," but since then his habits had become unreliable. Beauregard withdrew his recommendations "until there can be a guarantee that his habits have become more reliable."[14]

After meeting in early February with Davis and Lee, Ripley headed back to South Carolina while Sherman continued his nearly unchecked advance into the state. On February 14 Ripley again received orders from the Adjutant General's Office, and to his dismay learned he was to proceed to Columbia "and report to General G. T. Beauregard for assignment to duty with his proper command." That same day General Wade Hampton notified Beauregard that his scouts had reported Sherman's four army corps were on the move toward Columbia. Not having concentrated his forces as Lee had advised and expected, Beauregard's force in Columbia consisted of portions of Wheeler's cavalry, a small contingent of Stephen D. Lee's corps from the Army of Tennessee, and General Matthew Butler's newly arrived but undersized cavalry division.

Two days later, Beauregard informed Lee that his forces of about twenty thousand more or less demoralized infantry and artillery, occupied an arc of about 240 miles from Augusta to Charleston, admitting he had not concentrated his forces. He described Sherman's army as being double the size of his—organized, disciplined, flushed with success, and concentrated directly at Columbia. Beauregard intended to defend Columbia for as long as possible but doubted he could hold it for long. The shelling of Columbia began on February 16, and the beleaguered Confederates evacuated the city the next morning, retreating toward Chester and Charlotte. Beauregard, previously uncertain where Sherman would strike, now informed Lee that he was "positive the enemy intends moving on Charlotte."[15]

As the situation deteriorated, Lee increasingly doubted Beauregard's ability to confront Sherman. On February 19, after the fall of Columbia, Lee wrote to Seddon's replacement, Secretary of War John C. Breckenridge, and to Davis regarding Beauregard: "I do not know where his troops are, or on what lines they are moving. His dispatches only give movements of the enemy. I have also heard that his own health is indifferent, though he has never so stated. At the present rate of retreat, [Sherman] will soon be within striking distance of Roanoke. General Beauregard makes no mention of what he proposes, or what he can do. From his dispatches he does not appear able to do much."[16]

Three days after evacuating Columbia, Beauregard was still attempting to track down his elusive general. From White Oak, located between Columbia and Chester, Beauregard ordered Ripley to await orders in Charlotte. Unfortunately, Ripley had already passed through Charlotte, and on February 20 he again conferred with Governor Magrath, this time in Chester. The governor and his staff left Columbia for Chester and Union, and ultimately established offices in Spartanburg. On February 23 Magrath wrote, "The Government at Richmond seems at last to have been partially aroused. General Ripley, whom I met at Chester, [on February 20] has been ordered to the command of all Artillery of the Army." No confirmation of this "appointment" has been found. Ripley also told Magrath "there was no doubt that Johnson [sic] would be ordered to take the place of Beauregard."[17]

On February 21 Beauregard reached Chester and sent a telegram to Davis that the president described as "startling." The general wrote, "Should enemy advance into North Carolina toward Charlotte and Salisbury, as is now almost certain, I earnestly urge a concentration in time of at least 35,000 infantry and artillery at latter point, if possible, to give him battle there, and crush him, then to concentrate all forces against Grant, and then to march on Washington to dictate a peace."

Two days later Lee responded to Beauregard's "startling" telegram, which Davis had forwarded to him. Tactfully, Lee responded that it was a good idea and wished that "it was in our power to carry out his plan, but the means are lacking." Lee "heard from many sources that General Beauregard's health was very feeble and feared he might entirely give way." Various ailments, including chronic throat inflammations since childhood, sporadically plagued Beauregard throughout the war. In January 1862, before he left Richmond for Columbus, Kentucky, Beauregard required throat surgery, possibly an incision and drainage of a peritonsillar abscess. On January 28, 1865, Beauregard delayed his departure from Montgomery to Augusta as he claimed to be "confined to house by severe cold." Early in February, Hardee considered it "of great importance" for Beauregard to come to Charleston "if your health will permit it." One wonders whether Beauregard's "startling" delusional telegram and poor grasp of reality may have been a side effect of pain medication taken for an exacerbation of his chronic throat infections or possibly due to his being very ill and febrile.[18]

Early in February, Lee received a personal plea from General James Longstreet and his "friends at the South" to restore General Joseph E. Johnston to the command of the Army of Tennessee. Longstreet believed that only that act would "restore the army to organization, morale and efficiency." On February 4 Vice

President Alexander Stephens and others advised assigning Johnston to command the Army of Tennessee. Lee responded on February 13 that he was reluctant to do so as "an engagement with the enemy may be expected any day & a change now would be particularly hazardous." Nevertheless, Beauregard's telegram, rumors of his impaired health, and his inability to confront Sherman led Lee to appoint Johnston in command of the army operating against Sherman. Lee directed Beauregard to report to Johnston "for assignment to such duty as he deems most advisable."[19]

While Ripley was returning to South Carolina, Burton continued discussions with Gorgas in Richmond, "relative to armory management." On February 23 Burton proposed "a scheme" for establishing an "armory abroad." Gorgas asked the colonel to put the subject in writing and referred it to Secretary of War Breckenridge, who approved the project. Burton did not mention where the proposed "armory abroad" might be located. The armorer planned to return to Macon that night and at 7:30 P.M. boarded the train for Charlotte. He arrived there at 6:00 P.M. on March 1, registered at the Mansion House hotel, and "called at once on General Jos. E. Johnston and had [an] interview with him." The general informed Burton of the "total destruction of the ordnance stores, machinery, etc. at Columbia" and thought Burton should not visit Columbia expecting to find "anything in a serviceable condition." Secretary of War Breckenridge on February 16 had urged Beauregard to take prompt and efficient measures to save the machinery at the Columbia armory. When Beauregard was unable to respond quickly, the armory, consisting of warehouses, machine shops, a foundry, and offices, was totally destroyed. Union soldiers sledgehammered the machinery in the shops, as well as a large amount of machinery still uncrated. Gun-making tools, still in their original packing, were destroyed along with many gunstocks and barrels. Ten tons of Confederate machinery, including a stationary engine and lathe, were demolished. The Union army then burned all buildings in the complex.[20]

Burton's interest in Columbia concerned the machinery being stored there and destined for the Confederate armory in Macon. During the 1850s, while at the Royal Small Arms Factory in Enfield, Burton had established an important business relationship with Greenwood & Batley, Machinists, and their Albion Works at Leeds. He also developed a strong social relationship with the owners, Thomas Greenwood and John Batley, and their families. When Burton decided to leave Enfield in 1860, Greenwood & Batley offered him a position in Leeds the following year. He declined, and even had he considered it, the onset of the war prevented his return to England.[21]

In April 1863, a year after being appointed superintendent of the Macon armory, Burton proposed returning to England to purchase arms manufacturing machinery for the new armory. Secretary of War Seddon accepted Burton's proposal, and on June 8 Burton arrived in England with letters of introduction from

Seddon to commissioners John Slidell and James M. Mason. The government authorized the expenditure of nearly $300,000 for machinery capable of producing fifteen hundred rifles per week and allocated additional funds for four thousand barrels, fifty thousand bayonets, and an Anderson bullet-making machine featuring four complete machines on one frame.

Working with Major Caleb Huse, the Confederate purchasing agent in Europe, Burton mediated a contract between Charles K. Prioleau, president of Fraser, Trenholm & Company of Liverpool and Greenwood & Batley's Albion Works in Leeds. On July 28 Greenwood & Batley agreed to supply the requested machinery and other items, which Fraser, Trenholm & Company was to deliver at Bermuda, and then ship through the Union blockade. The contract was to be fulfilled by October 1, 1864, and payment would be made with cotton shipped to Fraser, Trenholm & Company. After three months of conferences and successful negotiations, Burton planned to leave Liverpool and return to the Confederacy. In an expression of their friendship, Greenwood & Batley presented Burton with an emerald-encrusted gold bracelet for his wife, Eugenia.[22]

As a result of the Union blockade of the eastern seaboard, all of Greenwood & Batley's shipments from Bermuda or the Bahamas were at risk of seizure. The first recorded shipment, dated October 2, 1863, sailed from Liverpool on the schooner *Honesta*, transporting two tons of steel privately purchased by Burton for Spiller and Burr revolvers. On January 11, 1864, the first known shipment from Greenwood & Batley, consisting of sixty-nine pieces of Confederate arms machinery, departed Liverpool on the *Princess Royal*. The *Queen of Britain* left Liverpool ten days later with "fifteen cases and sixty-six loose pieces of machinery." Both vessels sailed for St. George's, Bermuda, and by April 18 the Confederate agent in Bermuda, N. S. Walker, indicated that the *Queen of Britain* had "arrived & commenced to discharge. Nothing has been heard of the *Princess Royal* & some apprehensions are felt for her safety."

This may have been a second ship named the *Princess Royal*, for on January 29, 1863, the Union navy ran a ship aground with the same name near Charleston Harbor. That ship was then sold in a Northern prize court. The ultimate fate of this "second" *Princess Royal*, with its cargo of Confederate machinery, is not known.[23]

From Bermuda most shipments went to the closest Confederate port at Wilmington, North Carolina. On June 11, 1864, the *Captain Hawthorne* and the *Caroline Goodyear* shipped out of Liverpool with all the machinery that Fraser, Trenholm & Company had received from Greenwood & Batley up to that time. On August 3 Fraser, Trenholm expressed concerns regarding payment for the machinery and informed Burton they had not received "any cotton to be applied towards this contract." Regardless, shipments continued, and on September 2 the ordnance office in Wilmington notified Burton that they were sending him fifteen cases just unloaded from the *Helen*. On September 13 Wilmington notified Burton that the *Hope* had arrived with twenty-five cases of machinery, which they would transport as soon as possible to Columbia for storage.

The Confederate agent at Nassau, Louis C. Heyliger, on September 19 advised Burton of a shipment containing a "second lot of machinery" leaving for Charleston on the *Ella*. This shipment consisted of over 120 packages and pieces of machine parts plus three crates of machinery. The *Ella* was not large enough to transport either of the boilers included in the shipment from Liverpool, so the agent kept them in Nassau until a larger blockade-runner was available. Burton sent a copy of the *Ella*'s inventory to Major N. R. Chambliss at the Charleston Arsenal to check for any missing machinery. Although some pieces were slightly damaged, the cargo was intact and sent to Columbia for storage.[24]

On October 18 Heyliger advised Burton that he was sending the remaining machinery and one boiler on the *Hope* but that he still had three boilers on hand. In an attempt to disguise the boilers, the agent had them "painted a lead color" before loading them onto the blockade-runner. The attempted disguise did not save the *Hope* for on October 22 the huge side-wheeler, along with Burton's machinery and boiler, was captured by the U.S. Navy's *Eolus*, taken to Boston, and sold by a prize court.

One of the last reported sailings from Liverpool was on January 19, 1865, when the brig *Henry Holman* shipped out with another load of arms-manufacturing machinery. Since the ship was leaving England this late, it is unlikely the *Henry Holman*'s cargo was delivered to any open Confederate port. The Union army captured Fort Fisher on January 15, closing access to Wilmington, and the Confederates evacuated Charleston on February 17, effectively closing the last port available to the blockade-runners.[25]

From December 31, 1863, through October 18, 1865, Greenwood & Batley recorded nine loads of machinery being crated for shipment to Fraser, Trenholm & Company in Liverpool. Between January 11 and December 9, 1864, at least seven ships from Fraser, Trenholm, carrying the first four shipments from Greenwood & Batley, reached Confederate ports. Sixteen pages of inventory made up these first four shipments of over one thousand items, including everything from boilers, girders, and steel plating to large numbers of complex milling machines, as well as drilling, tapping, and threading machinery. One hundred fifty pieces of new machinery, ten steam engines, one hundred thousand pounds of copper, one thousand tons of cast iron, four hundred tons of bar iron, and immense quantities of chemicals apparently reached Macon, only to be destroyed by the Union army, as was any machinery stored in Columbia. In addition, the *Hope* was captured, and at the end of the war some machinery was stranded in Bermuda and/

or Nassau. At least one ship, the second *Princess Royal,* was probably lost at sea early in 1864. Burton, after returning to England in October 1865, completed six pages listing "machinery lost in the U.S."[26]

The paths of Burton and Ripley crossed once again in March 1865, this time in Charlotte at the Mansion House hotel. On March 2, the day after learning from General Johnston of the total destruction of the machinery and ordnance stored at Columbia, Burton wrote that he had also "met General Ripley at the hotel." Burton departed Charlotte by train on March 6 and finally reached Macon on the sixteenth. He would spend the final days of the war at Macon witnessing its occupation by Federal troops and the destruction of his armory and machinery.[27]

While he served in Charleston, Ripley would have been aware of the construction of an armory of great size and importance in Macon. Unanswered is what Burton actually told Ripley about the Greenwood & Batley machinery shipments, and more important, whether he revealed the extent of their destruction and losses. In any event, for his financial survival, Ripley became totally committed and doggedly pursued what would become the impossible dream of gaining control of this machinery. Ripley, his wife, and daughter, Alicia, would travel to England after the war, and the Greenwood & Batley machinery would become as complete an obsession with Roswell as Matildaville had been with his father. Ripley went to England for understandable political reasons, but it is difficult to comprehend why he pursued the Greenwood & Batley machinery so determinedly if he knew a great percentage of it had been shipped and destroyed, lost at sea, or stranded in Bermuda and the Bahamas. It would seem he did not.

CHAPTER 28

Chaos and Flight to England

In Charlotte, Generals Joseph E. Johnston and G. T. Beauregard finally caught up with Ripley and tentatively placed their delinquent general in command of Brown's Division, Cheatham's Corps. Ripley waited at the Manor House hotel for the division's arrival, but that road-weary unit from the Army of Tennessee did not reach Charlotte until March 11. General Johnston established his headquarters at Smithfield, North Carolina, on March 15, and hurriedly attempted to reorganize the disparate forces now under his command. The following day Beauregard ordered his assistant adjutant-general, Colonel George W. Brent, to Chester, South Carolina, "to expedite movement of troops and trains to Smithfield." Beauregard also ordered staff officers to the Georgia towns of Augusta, Milledgeville, and Winnsboro "to inspect and direct movement of troops and supplies." The next day Beauregard surprisingly ordered Brent to join him "wherever I may be."

Before the Confederates attempted to stop Sherman's forces at Bentonville, North Carolina, Johnston effectively removed Ripley from any significant field command. Although Ripley continued to be listed as commanding Brown's Division, on March 21 General Frank Cheatham actually led that recently arrived division on the last day of the Battle of Bentonville. Probably much to the relief of Ripley and Beauregard, Johnston relegated Ripley to a secondary role at Chester, thus preventing any interaction between the two adversaries. Ripley's mission, which originally had been assigned to Colonel Brent, was to facilitate the movement of troops through Chester and into North Carolina. This cannot be confirmed in the *Official Records* but is based in part on information attributed to Colonel E. M. Seabrook.[1]

From his vantage point at Chester, Ripley witnessed the flood of fleeing Confederate officials and their families evacuating Richmond. By the end of March, Davis and his cabinet members were the only remnants of the government remaining in the capital. On March 25 Davis ordered his wife and children to leave Richmond as soon as possible, and six days later the president's family departed by train for Charlotte, later traveling through Chester bound for Abbeville, South Carolina.

After the Confederate defeat at Five Forks, Davis attempted to transfer the seat of government to Danville, Virginia. Late in the night of April 2, the president and most of his cabinet officials, including Secretary of State Judah P. Benjamin, departed Richmond and arrived in Danville the next day. Six days later, on Palm Sunday, Robert E. Lee surrendered the Army of Northern Virginia at Appomattox Court House and the vestiges of the government were on the move again, this time for Greensboro, North Carolina.

At cabinet meetings in Greensboro on April 12 and 13, Generals Johnston and Beauregard, two of Davis's most implacable generals, strongly advised negotiating the surrender of their armies to General Sherman, thus ending all bloodshed and any organized Confederate resistance in the East. Every official agreed with Johnston except President Davis and his most loyal cabinet member, Judah Benjamin, both of whom advocated continuing the war in the West. The next day the cabinet convinced Davis to move what remained of the government from Greensboro to Charlotte, which they reached on April 18. Davis hoped to join his family In Charlotte; however, his wife, Varina, fearing a raid on the city, departed Charlotte five days prior to the president's arrival.[2]

South Carolinian Mary Boykin Chesnut, known for her reconstructed Civil War "diary," witnessed the bombardment of Fort Sumter and the beginning of the war in Charleston. In March 1865 Mary Chesnut joined her husband, James, who, after a varied career in the Confederacy, served as a brigadier general of reserves in Chester. After leaving Charlotte on April 13, Varina Davis and her entourage reached Chester in the early morning hours of April 15. Mary Chesnut met Varina at the rail station and invited "my dear Mrs. Davis, calm and smiling as ever, for a luncheon or breakfast." She "accompanied the president's wife back to the station and the group departed at 5:00 P.M. for Abbeville." Ripley probably knew the president's wife was in town and would have done what he could to assure her safety. It is not recorded whether Ripley met with Mrs. Davis, but it is unlikely that he would have missed the opportunity.[3]

Earlier that week Chesnut noted in her diary that Louis T. Wigfall and his wife, Charlotte, and their daughters, Francis (Fanny) and Louise (Louly), passed through Chester on their way to Texas. The Chesnuts apparently did not visit with the Wigfalls in Chester, but Louly evidently told General John Bell Hood that "they were bound for the Rio Grande and intended to shake hands with Maximilian, emperor of Mexico."

A South Carolina native and confirmed secessionist since 1844, the fiery and financially irresponsible Wigfall moved to Texas in the fall of 1846. The state elected him to the U.S. Senate during the Thirty-Sixth Congress, 1859–61. After Texas seceded, he remained in Washington fomenting trouble. Wigfall then served in the Confederate Congress, and in the early days of the Confederacy, he was a friend and nominal "aide" to President Davis. In time his relationship with Davis deteriorated, and the Texan became one of the president's harshest critics. After Congress adjourned for the final time on March 18, 1865, Wigfall journeyed to

North Carolina in support of General Johnston and attempted to stem the tide of Confederate desertions following the Battle of Bentonville. When Wigfall learned that Richmond had been abandoned, he and his family traveled from western North Carolina to Chester, then on to Abbeville, South Carolina. Despite their differences, Wigfall and Davis independently came to the same conclusion and planned to travel west through the Deep South to Texas, where they hoped to continue the fight. Wigfall's resolve to fight on was likely reinforced by his belief that if captured, he would be executed.

The Wigfalls pushed on from Abbeville, crossed the Savannah River, and headed for Washington, Georgia. In late May, when he learned that President Andrew Johnson's amnesty proclamation did not include him, Wigfall shaved off his beard and dressed as a paroled private in the 1st Texas Infantry Regiment. Escorted by a group of paroled Texas soldiers, the family reached the outskirts of Montgomery, where Wigfall decided it would be safer for the family to remain in Alabama with friends rather than continue with him to Texas. In Montgomery, Wigfall's son Halsey joined his mother and sisters.

Wigfall and his band of Texas veterans completed the journey on foot, but after reaching Texas, conditions were so bad that he did not send for his family; instead, they spent nearly a year with Charlotte's mother in Providence, Rhode Island. There is little record of Wigfall's activities in Texas, but he somehow accumulated enough money to escape to England, probably arriving in April 1866. Charlotte, Fanny, Louly, and Halsey joined him several months later, and they became socially involved with the Ripleys.[4]

Shortly after arriving in Charlotte, President Davis received a telegram notifying him of Lincoln's assassination. Davis believed "it could not be regarded otherwise than as a great misfortune to the South." Davis and his cabinet remained in Charlotte until they learned that the government in Washington had rejected a settlement negotiated by Generals Johnston and Sherman to end the war. On April 26, stunned to learn that Johnston had again met with Sherman and this time surrendered his army, Davis, Judah Benjamin, and a few remaining cabinet members left Charlotte. Accompanied by about two thousand men in five small brigades of reorganized cavalry, the group planned to travel through South Carolina and head west to the Mississippi. After passing north of Chester, Davis and Benjamin reached Abbeville early on May 2, only to learn that Varina and the children had left two days before they arrived.

After spending the morning and afternoon in Abbeville, the group headed for the Savannah River and crossed into Georgia. Davis's steadfast supporter, Judah Benjamin, decided it was time to leave his president and escape alone. He ostensibly planned to head south into Florida, try to reach Cuba or the Bahamas for "diplomatic business," and then possibly meet Davis in Texas. In fact, Benjamin never intended to return to the United States.[5]

Benjamin, probably the most prominent Jewish American political figure of the nineteenth century, was born on August 11, 1811, in St. Croix, then part of the British West Indies. He spent his early youth in Charleston, South Carolina, then moved to New Orleans. He married Natalie St. Martin, the daughter of a prominent French-Creole, Roman Catholic family. Benjamin gradually prospered in his law practice, his career flourished, and he purchased a sugarcane plantation, Bellechasse, becoming the owner of 140 slaves. Although he did well financially, his marriage deteriorated, and in 1844 Natalie, Judah's wife of eleven years, and their one-year-old daughter, Ninette, left New Orleans and sailed for Paris.

During his legal career Benjamin argued cases before the U.S. Supreme Court and "had a power of argument rarely, if ever, surpassed." He became active in Louisiana politics and in 1852 was elected to the U.S. Senate and reelected to a second term in 1858. In 1860, as the nation drifted toward disunion, some Southerners, including Benjamin, opposed secession except as a last resort. After South Carolina seceded, secession sentiment soared in Louisiana. Benjamin delivered an eloquent farewell speech to the Senate on New Year's Eve 1860: "We beseech you, let this parting be in peace . . . indulge in no vain delusion that duty or conscience, interest or honor, imposes upon you the necessity of invading our States or shedding the blood of our people. You have no possible justification for it." Shortly after Louisiana's secession on January 26, 1861, Benjamin and John Slidell, his fellow senator from the Bayou State, officially resigned their Senate seats.[6]

The same day the senators from Louisiana resigned, the Convention of Seceded States met in Montgomery, Alabama, to draft the Provisional Constitution of the Confederate States of America. On February 18, 1861, Jefferson Davis was inaugurated as the provisional Confederate president. Soon after, impressed "with the lucidity of his intellect, his systematic habits and capacity for labor," Davis appointed Judah P. Benjamin attorney general. Benjamin served in that position until September when disappointment with Secretary of War Leroy Walker led Davis to select Benjamin to replace him. As secretary of war, Benjamin, who lacked any military training, lasted only until March 1862. Davis then appointed Benjamin secretary of state, the post for which he perhaps was best suited. In Richmond, Benjamin and Davis visited every morning to update each other on the news and met in conference for several hours during the day. Benjamin held this post for the duration of the war, and the friendship matured between these two often-beleaguered officials.[7]

When Benjamin and Davis parted on May 3, 1865, the disguised secretary of state, clothed in rags, clattered off in an old wagon. The former Confederate statesman eventually reached Tampa, and at nearby Ellenton a Confederate commissary agent sheltered Benjamin at his home. Formerly the Gamble Plantation, this is now the site of the Judah P. Benjamin Confederate Memorial. With a price of $40,000 on his head, Benjamin enlisted an ex-Confederate officer to take him by boat from Sarasota to the Florida Keys. In early July Benjamin reached Knight's Key near the present city of Marathon.

Benjamin sailed by small boat from the Keys to the Bimini Islands, often nearly swamped by waterspouts and squalls. From Bimini, Benjamin made his way to Nassau and Havana, and then on to England. On August 30, 1865, the former secretary of state arrived at Southampton, nearly four months after he and Davis parted company. Nearly penniless, Benjamin successfully restarted his life and legal career in England, where he later assisted Roswell Ripley in his legal struggles.[8]

After his secretary of state departed, Davis continued on to Washington, Georgia, and somewhere between Abbeville and Sandersville, deep in southern Georgia, the president's party caught up with Varina and his family. They had only a short time together before being captured near Irwinsville by troopers of the 4th Michigan Cavalry and taken north to Macon. Jefferson Davis was detained only four hours in Macon before being transported north to imprisonment in Fortress Monroe, Virginia.[9]

Federal troops occupied Macon on April 20, a little over a month after James Burton returned from Richmond. From Macon, Burton resumed his correspondence and sought employment with Greenwood & Batley. Burton received a letter from the firm looking forward to his arrival "in the old country where you will be able to dwell in peace and quietude." Burton apparently enjoyed a fair amount of "peace and quietude" in Macon and was not fleeing for his life as were Davis, Benjamin, and Wigfall. On October 9, 1865, Burton, his family, and their hired nurse entrained for Louisville, Kentucky. From Louisville they traveled by steamboat up the Ohio River to Cincinnati and on October 14 arrived in New York City after a thirty-seven-hour train ride from Cincinnati.

With the Confederacy destroyed, its infrastructure in ruins, and the vast majority of its citizens impoverished, Burton was surprisingly well off financially. He could afford a full-time family nurse, traveled to New York City, and paid $850 in gold for his family's passage to England on a Cunard Lines steamship. Before departing New York, Burton dined on oysters at the Fulton Fish Market and bought "over garments" for his wife and daughters. Burton obviously profited from his business with Spiller & Burr and the Confederate government, and apparently had the foresight to convert his proceeds into gold. On October 18 Burton and his family sailed from New York for England on the S.S. *Persia,* arriving in Liverpool ten days later.[10]

After Johnston surrendered to Sherman on April 26, 1865, Ripley, who was still in Chester, received a curt reply from Johnston's adjutant in Greensboro, North Carolina. Told that it was "impossible to send infantry," Ripley was to keep a cavalry guard as long as possible, send the horses off to find forage, and then use any remaining men as guards. The Chesnuts left Chester on May 1 or

2 in a wagon train southbound for Winnsboro and their home near Camden. As they had to pass through a region devastated by Sherman, Ripley may have requested guards for the Chesnuts. In her diary in late April, Mary Chesnut confirmed Ripley's presence in Chester: "We began with Ripley—with Ripley we end. He is here in command."[11]

After destroying Columbia, the Union army's foragers, or "bummers," preceded the main body of the army headed north toward Chester. After burning and pillaging downtown stores and private homes in Winnsboro, the army pivoted to the northeast. The bummers spread across the countryside, plundering and burning farmsteads across the northeastern portion of the state. As the Federals continued their eastward march toward Fayetteville and Goldsboro, North Carolina, they found warehouses full of civil and military stores at Cheraw. In three days of occupation, nearly all of Cheraw's business establishments were sacked and burned.

Nearby Society Hill, where Ripley's wife and daughters sought refuge, did not escape unscathed as foragers roamed through and around the village. Mrs. Allston Pringle noted that even though her home was three miles from Society Hill, the Yankees found them "and paid us two visits of about a half hour each. However, they were not insolent to us. . . . Most everyone suffered some, but no violence [was] offered to the ladies." Rebecca Pringle wrote,

> Only one party entered the house—they robbed our trunks of what they pleased—searched our drawers, ate our breakfast and then put our silver spoons in their pockets. They took from Papa's plantation every four-footed animal and destroyed everything, but the un-ground corn. . . . They robbed the Negroes of everything, taking their shoes from their feet, and the handkerchief from the women's heads. . . . They have plundered everyone of everything most valuable. Every bottle of wine is gone; all of our beautiful china and glass is gone. The people in the village had an awful time . . . the wretches were walking in and out of their houses from sunrise to sunset.

It is not recorded whether the marauders visited Alicia Ripley and her daughters, but it is unlikely they escaped a visit from the foragers. Ripley probably left Chester in early May to join his family, and as he traveled from Chester to Society Hill, he would have seen the destruction wrought upon South Carolina. The depredations inflicted on the residents of that region would have intensified Ripley's hatred of the U.S. government.[12]

About one hundred miles south of Society Hill, Charleston had been virtually destroyed. Ripley's friend and the *London Times* special correspondent, Francis Lawley, on March 6 and 7, 1865, described the destroyed and evacuated city of Charleston:

Fully two thirds of this once beautiful and thriving city have been reduced to ashes, the other third, fronting the sea having been so riddled by shot and shell during the last eight months as to be virtually uninhabitable. Charleston is silent and deserted for the most part. Some houses appear unscathed, but a shell passing through the roof [tore] walls, lath and plaster, and ceilings into splinters. Street pavement and sidewalks have deep round holes from 200-pound Parrott shells. British Consulate walls have two holes and the nearby Spanish Consulate has three. Destruction is accentuated by the broad belt of ruins from the great fire of 1861, which swept from river to river.[13]

As the last of the Confederate army evacuated Charleston during the night of February 17–18, explosions and about twenty fires ripped through the city. On Sunday, February 18, the 21st U.S. Colored Troops, now in the possession of the city, began breaking into homes and stealing anything they could. The plundering continued despite General Orders No. 8 issued on February 28 by the occupying Union general, John P. Hatch. These orders "invited" all loyal citizens of the United States residing in Charleston or its vicinity to register, take an oath of allegiance to the government, and receive a certificate verifying their allegiance. Without a certificate, no passes or "other favors" would be granted. No guards would be posted to protect private property, but the orders advised all property owners to display a United States flag to discourage depredations.[14]

As the overwhelming power of the Union armies prevailed, the South's dream of independence was crushed and the Confederacy disintegrated. The South would be forced back into the Union and severely subjugated following the assassination of President Lincoln. With the South's infrastructure destroyed, Ripley and many others faced the overwhelming challenge of supporting themselves and their families. Ripley refused to live under "Radical Republican" rule and what he considered a tyrannical government. He concluded that he must leave South Carolina as soon as possible, and England was the logical destination.

The publication of Ripley's history of the Mexican War suggested that he possibly could support himself through writing. However, Ripley's previous business experience involving the sales of Sharps rifles, Adams revolvers, and arms-manufacturing machinery promised a more profitable course. His experience in England in the 1850s and his successful sale of arms to the British Government must have led Ripley to believe his best chance of prospering would involve a return to the arms industry. Through his contact with James Burton, Ripley probably learned that the master armorer would return to England with Greenwood & Batley. He and Burton most likely discussed the undelivered Confederate arms machinery intended for Macon but still in the hands of Greenwood & Batley. It is unclear whether Burton disclosed how much of the machinery had been lost or destroyed. Ripley was determined to gain control of the undelivered machinery and capitalize on the probability of war between France and Prussia.[15]

Ripley now faced the problem of how to get to England. His first known attempt occurred on August 17, 1865, when he made arrangements to sail from Charleston for New York and then on to Europe. Augustine Smythe had returned to Charleston and wrote to his wife telling her of his safe arrival and meeting with Ripley. As Ripley waited in Charleston, Smythe wrote, "a written order reached him saying he would be arrested if he tried it, and that he must remain quiet. So he is here and slightly tight tonight too."[16]

Later Ripley may have visited his mother in Ogdensburg, crossed the St. Lawrence River into Canada, and then sailed for England. Sometime in early October 1865, Ripley wrote to General William Preston in Quebec regarding the ultimate destination of former Confederate secretary of war John C. Breckinridge, who at the time was in Toronto. Ripley's letter has not been found, but Preston referred to it in his letter of October 21 to Colin McRae in London.[17]

In late 1865 and early 1866, Judah Benjamin, James Burton, Louis Wigfall, and Roswell Ripley all sought refuge in England, where their paths would be interwoven.

CHAPTER 29

England, 1866–1869

The exact date of Ripley's arrival in England is not known. However, indications are that he, accompanied by his wife and daughter, probably reached London in the spring of 1866. His stepdaughter, Marie Sparks, remained in South Carolina and on August 14, 1866, married Colonel Alfred Moore Rhett. The family registered at the Alexandra Hotel, 16–20 St. George's Place, Hyde Park Corner. Little has been preserved regarding the Alexandra, although it was considered "the first of any importance" in that part of the city. Built in 1858, it was enlarged in 1864 and renamed the Alexandra in honor of the wedding of the Prince of Wales (later King Edward VII) to Princess Alexandra of Denmark.[1]

Shortly after arriving, Ripley began negotiations with, Charles K. Prioleau, president of Fraser, Trenholm & Company of Liverpool. This prestigious firm had handled the machinery order for James H. Burton and the Confederate government. Ripley wanted to purchase any machinery remaining with Greenwood & Batley, and Prioleau had authorized the firm to dispose of any on hand. On July 5 Burton acknowledged receiving Ripley's letter the previous day, which he read with "much interest." Ripley had asked whether Greenwood & Batley could supply him with machinery "pertaining to the fitting up of armories." Burton claimed the company was in a good position to supply the machinery, provided "you acquire the business." Burton invited Ripley to Leeds to meet with him, Greenwood, and Batley at their office to discuss the matter. Burton claimed that if Ripley could secure the business, Greenwood & Batley "will be glad to assist you to the fullest extent of our power." Ripley was to come to the Albion Works in Leeds and let Burton know when he arrived. Unfortunately, nothing is known of this proposed meeting.

Burton, master machinist and armorer, arrived in England with his family in late October 1865, secured a residence in the spa city of Harrogate, then commuted daily by train to Greenwood & Batley's Albion Works in Leeds. The company owners accepted Burton and his family socially as they frequently wined and dined together. Burton worked for two months at the Albion Works compiling cost estimates for a small arms factory to be built at Lucca, Italy. In addition, Greenwood & Batley was involved in armories proposed by the Turkish and Egyptian governments. Burton also conducted studies evaluating Spencer and Whitworth rifles, and claimed he devised a simpler breech mechanism, which he incorporated into a Spencer rifle.[2]

In June 1866 Thomas Dudley, the U.S. consul in Liverpool, visited Ambassador Charles F. Adams in London and claimed he would try to get the Confederate machinery, which he believed was in the hands of Caleb Huse or Ripley. Although Ripley was just beginning his quest for the Greenwood & Batley machinery, evidently some government officials thought he already had it in his possession.

In August, Ripley began his negotiations with Greenwood & Batley and at the same time was in contact with the French government for the sale of the machinery, for which he expected to make a considerable profit. Meanwhile, Ripley endeavored to maintain a positive relationship and ingratiate himself with Burton, informing him of possible business for the Spencer rifle featuring Burton's modified breech. On September 21 Ripley wrote to Burton, enclosing "a copy of an extract from influential people in the War Department at Florence to Messrs. Castille and Ortega concerning breech loading guns." Ripley asked whether Burton wanted to show his gun to the Italian Government through these people: "If so drop me a note at the *Alexandra Hotel* and make an appointment at the *Castle & Falcon* for Monday at three o'clock P.M. to let them see it." Ripley was not certain but thought there might be business for Burton with the Italians.[3]

In 1866, following Prussia's defeat of Austria and the formation of the North German Confederation, both France and Prussia believed war was probable. In April 1866 the British Ordnance Select Committee received word that the French government had decided to evaluate a new breech-loading rifle invented by M. Chassepôt and in June ordered five hundred of these rifles for trials. After successful tests at Chalons in August, Emperor Napoleon III decided the government should adopt the Chassepôt breech-loader as the standard rifle for the army. Although approved, certain modifications were required, delaying production for six to eight weeks. The French planned to have four factories, located at St. Etienne, Châtellerault, Tulle, and Mutzig, capable of manufacturing up to 165,000 rifles by the end of 1867. Ripley's letter to Burton in July as to the availability of arms manufacturing machinery confirmed his attempt to gain a foothold in the French armament program.[4]

Any discussions Ripley had with Burton concerning the Greenwood & Batley machinery manufactured for the Confederate armory in Macon have not been preserved. Ripley must have known about the machinery and the intended armory. However, Burton apparently did not inform Ripley that much machinery had been destroyed in Macon and Columbia and that some had been lost at sea or stranded in Bermuda and the Bahamas. If Burton cautioned Ripley, his caveat was ignored. Ripley relentlessly attempted to gain control of whatever machinery Greenwood & Batley still had in their possession.

Rashly, Ripley borrowed a total of £20,000 from Francis Lawley, his brother Reverend Stephan Lawley, and others to purchase rights to the machinery. The fact that Greenwood & Batley also required Ripley to pay them a commission for

Francis C. Lawley, correspondent for the Times *of London, covered the Confederacy during the war. He befriended Ripley and invested in Ripley's failed effort to obtain the Greenwood & Batley arms-making machinery. He also assisted Ripley in his literary efforts with* Blackwood's *Magazine. From W. S. Hoole,* Lawley Covers the Confederacy, *1964, frontispiece.*

the machinery arouses suspicion that Burton, possibly for personal gain, encouraged Ripley to enter into this arrangement. As mentioned, Burton had a strong personal relationship with Greenwood & Batley, and the master machinist had a strong penchant for making money.[5]

Louis T. Wigfall is thought to have arrived in England in April 1866 and settled temporarily at the Langham Hotel. In an undated and unidentified newspaper clipping, the "Radical London" correspondent claimed, "Poor Wigfall is here too. . . . his friends at *Langham* say he looks very dejected, seedy, and disappointed." Although "poor Wigfall" appeared "seedy" to his friends, the magnificent Langham certainly was not. Opened in June 1865 with a reception for two thousand guests, including the Prince of Wales, it was reputed to be Europe's first "Grand Hotel." It featured three hundred bedrooms as well as "the first hydraulically powered lifts in the world, its own steam-pumped artesian well, hot and cold running water, and WCs in every bedroom . . . previously unheard of in hotels" [Langham]. Because of his limited finances, Wigfall's stay at the Langham was brief while he sought housing for his family.[6]

Wigfall eventually found a residence at 57 Gloucester Place, Portman Square, for his family, with Charlotte, Halsey, Louly, and Fanny joining him in July. Benjamin Branson owned 57 Gloucester Place, which was one of several lodging houses on the street. During his early days in England, Wigfall remained optimistic about his financial situation even though a Confederate bond scheme, as well as various

Louis T. Wigfall, Southern "fire-eater" and Confederate official self-exiled to England. He, his family, and the Ripleys were part of the Confederate social network in London. From the Library of Congress.

cotton and railroad ventures, failed. The *Dallas Herald* urged Wigfall to write an account of the war, and he evidently asked Ripley to write a description of the April 7, 1863, Federal ironclad attack on Fort Sumter. In an undated, unsigned, five-page reply in Ripley's handwriting, Wigfall received a detailed account of the assault. Ripley included a two-page abstract, "The Organization of Artillery." Ripley mentioned that his wife intended to "call on Mrs. Wigfall today." There is no evidence Wigfall finished his account of the war.

Ultimately, Wigfall could not earn enough money through his odd jobs as a legal assistant to provide for his family. To survive, the Wigfalls depended on aid from Halsey and from Charlotte's mother in the United States. Judah Benjamin noted that when Wigfall came to London, he "called on everybody but me when he arrived, and it was very agreeable to me not to meet him. I do not know how he continues to exist, but I suppose he must receive remittance from the other side." The family's financial condition forced Charlotte and her daughters to return to the United States in 1870. Louis joined them in 1872.[7]

Lacking a sustainable means of support, the Wigfalls and the Ripleys experienced increasingly difficult times, although Ripley's situation gradually became more and more problematic. These two self-exiled Confederates were in contact socially, and references to the Ripleys can be found in Wigfall's correspondence. On October 31, 1866, Charlotte wrote to her son Halsey, "Mrs. Jack Hamilton has paid a very long visit and she says Gen'l Ripley has heard nothing from France, meanwhile they are still at the *Alexandra Hotel*." Lieutenant Jack R. Hamilton, CSN, served on the floating ironclad battery with Ripley in Charleston at the onset of the war. His father, a former governor of South Carolina, was Louis Wigfall's cousin. Benjamin Moran, secretary to Ambassador Charles Adams, described Hamilton as "the little fellow who used to be in our Navy and was here in 1858 with the *Niagara* to lay the first Atlantic cable. He was a dangerous rebel, and although civil now, don't [sic] exhibit any very loyal feeling to the government."[8]

Although Prioleau allegedly instructed Greenwood & Batley to sell the machinery to Ripley, the negotiations failed. Ripley believed the machinists "endeavored to obstruct the sale." By the end of the year Ripley's "treaty" with the French government "went off."

Regardless of his precarious financial status, Ripley still tried to provide for his young daughter, Alicia. On December 28, 1866, Louly Wigfall wrote to her brother, "We had a visit from Gen. Ripley & his little daughter [then thirteen years old] this evening to ask Fannie to go with them tomorrow evening to see the Grand Pantomime at Drury Lane." According to Louly, "The pantomimes are a peculiarly English Christmas institution & are performed with the most gorgeous scenery & are particularly interesting to children, with the giants, fairies, etc." During the 1866 season the Ripleys and Wigfalls would have viewed Drury Lane's new pantomime entitled *Number Nip: or, Harlequin and the Gnome King of the Giant Mountain*.[9]

On February 3, 1867, Charlotte Wigfall mentioned in a letter to Halsey, "Whilst we were out Mrs. Hamilton, Mrs. Ripley & little Alicia called & I was sorry to miss them. The condition of Mrs. R. is very deplorable . . . and his suit has not been tried. I don't know how he himself manages. The *Alexandra Hotel* man has some interest in the suit and Gen'l Ripley stays there I think." Ripley attempted to move his family to rooms on Clifford Street but was unable to make the payments. Charlotte wrote that Ripley's "wife and daughter have been staying all winter at the Hs [Hamiltons]. I went there three or four weeks ago & was glad to hear that Mrs. R. had heard from her Charleston agents & that her brother Motte, who owes her several thousand dollars, would send almost immediately quite a large sum to her. Fate somehow seems to be decidedly against her, for the next news I heard was that Motte Middleton's house and crops had all been burnt by the negroes in their last outrages near Savannah. What they will do I don't know, but I feel deep sympathy for them."[10]

In 1867 Ripley continued to negotiate with the French government in his attempt to establish an armory near Paris. The British Ordnance Committee reported on April 8, 1867, that "the [French] Government are in a treaty with a person calling himself General Ripley, who proposes to establish a factory at Poissy, near Paris, and who would engage to deliver 150,000 arms of the approved pattern within two years; but it is a fortnight since they have seen him or any of his agents." In May arrangements with Greenwood & Batley again fell through when the machinists and Major Caleb Huse "tried to dispose of the machinery in various foreign countries." Huse had actually received a £290 advance for traveling expenses.

In June the French belatedly realized that the manufacture of Chassepôt rifles was not moving as quickly as they had hoped and decided to convert 400,000 muzzle-loading rifles into breech-loaders. Unfortunately, Ripley was running out of time in which to take advantage of this opportunity. Although Ripley still had not gained control of the machinery, Greenwood & Batley and Charles K. Prioleau continued to hold his money.[11]

In 1867 the Hamiltons also were having financial problems. They "left town for the economy and are pleasantly fixed in a little village, Brentwood near the Kew Gardens." Although the Hamiltons were twenty minutes by rail from the Wigfalls, the two families continued to socialize during the winter and spring. Later in the year Hamilton got a job with the Ordnance Works at Southwark. The nature of his job is not known, but he became one of the few Confederates in this circle of friends to be gainfully employed. To be nearer his work, Hamilton moved his family back to town, where they stayed "at Gen'l Ripley's old quarters on Clifford St."

On November 15 Hamilton wrote to Burton from the ordnance works: "General Ripley mentioned today that you had the report of Col. Raines' experiments made at the Augusta Arsenal with the 'gas chamber' in ordnance of different calibers." He asked Burton to share the report, as the ordnance was working on a "very heavy gun" and Hamilton wanted all the information he could get on the subject. It is not known whether Burton complied with this request or whether Ripley ever sought, or was considered for, employment with the Southwark Ordnance Department.[12]

In an inscrutable diary entry on February 4, 1868, Burton wrote, "Went to consult my solicitor in regard to my agreement with Ripley." Unfortunately, Burton does not reveal anything about this "agreement." Surprisingly, Ripley claimed that he employed James Burton to verify the condition of the machinery and then "subsequently engaged him as consulting and directing engineer with regard to completion and adaptation of the machinery for the purpose for which it was intended"—conceivably, Chassepôt rifles.

Two days later Burton noted that he wrote to Ripley but again does not mention anything specific about the letter. The men were obviously in contact, and it may be that Greenwood & Batley were not pleased to have their employee also working for Ripley. With little fanfare, on March 20 Burton and his family boarded the SS *Helvetia* and returned to Virginia.[13]

With his borrowed £20,000, Ripley paid Charles Prioleau £5,000, as well as an unknown amount in commissions to the Leeds machinists, and had not gained control of the machinery. Therefore, Ripley began "an action of Trover at Common Law" against the machinists, claiming that they wrongfully converted the machinery to their own use. Greenwood & Batley hired the firm of Brook,

Freeman and Batley to represent them in this suit. Concurrently, the United States government, through its consul, Thomas H. Dudley, in Liverpool and Secretary of State William Seward, brought legal action against both Fraser, Trenholm & Company and Greenwood & Batley. They claimed the government had rightful ownership of the machinery; therefore, Ripley now faced impossible odds in his efforts to acquire it. It is astounding that despite his intelligence, Ripley refused to admit his plan was now nearly unachievable.[14]

In early 1868 Ripley hired Abbott, Jenkins & Company of 8 New Inn, Wych Street, Strand, to be his solicitors in legal proceedings against Greenwood & Batley. On May 21 Ripley and Abbott interviewed John Batley regarding the machinery still in the firm's possession. Five days later Ripley and a "Mr. Adams" of the Abbott law firm met with John Batley and "produced *Letters of Authority* from Fraser, Trenholm, & Co." They demanded "inspection of the machinery comprising the Burton contract and also discussed the claims of the United States Government." On June 9 U.S. commissioners formally served Greenwood & Batley with a notice claiming ownership of the machinery. The *Times* reported that "on June 25 the Leeds machinists filed a Chancery Suit restraining Ripley's lawsuit in which he sought to recover £100,000." Ripley's suit was for "non-delivery of certain plant and machinery for the manufacture of Enfield rifles, originally ordered [from] the plaintiffs for the Confederate Government. The defendant, General Ripley, formerly was an officer in the Confederate army." The plaintiffs claimed that "they were willing to deliver the machinery to whoever was entitled to it."[15]

By this time Ripley's scheme of equipping an arms factory in Poissy had essentially collapsed, and he based his suit against Greenwood & Batley on his alleged sale of the machinery to Peter Pritchard, a Congreve rocket manufacturer. Pritchard supposedly agreed to pay £40,000 for the machinery, which incredibly was to be delivered in fourteen days in completed condition. Ripley produced two written documents, which he contended formed his contract with Pritchard. Ripley alleged that he sustained damages resulting from the failure of Greenwood & Batley to deliver the machinery. In July, in addition to the legal team of Abbott, Jenkins, & Company, Judah Benjamin appeared for Ripley's defense. The *Times* reported:

> Mr. Benjamin's argument was one of the ablest Vice-Chancellor Sir R. Malins had ever heard, but the vice-chancellor must express his conviction that, on the evidence and correspondence, this action was a most unrighteous one, although whether this Court could restrain it was another question. The plaintiffs, most eminent manufacturers of machinery; General Ripley, a gallant soldier, so well known in connection with Charleston, and all parties up to a

Judah P. Benjamin, the Confederate official who was especially effective as secretary of state, fled to England after the war, was admitted to the bar, and served as legal counsel for Ripley in his dispute with Greenwood & Batley, Machinists. From the National Archives.

certain point appeared to have acted with perfect fairness; but, unfortunately a change of views then occurred, and the contract with Mr. Pritchard was so improbable that His Honour [the vice-chancellor] could not believe it was entered into with any *bona fide* intention.

The vice-chancellor hoped that some arrangement might be reached, as the suit "had not been pleaded."[16]

Judah Benjamin had arrived at Southampton in August 1865 and by September 1866 had become a renowned barrister. He was well accepted in England and considered a natural-born British citizen based on his birth to British parents in St. Croix, British West Indies. The fifty-five-year-old former Confederate secretary of state humbly enrolled at Lincoln Inn in January 1866 to study for admission to the bar. However, through the power of influential friends, after just six months of study Benjamin was called to the bar. He elected to serve the English Northern Circuit, which included Liverpool and its core of Confederate sympathizers. These shipping firms and mercantile houses had supported the South and knew Benjamin as the South's most acclaimed international lawyer. Benjamin's reputation grew as his eloquent, persuasive oratory made deep impressions on judges and juries, and among his colleagues he was almost universally admired. Remarkably, Benjamin did his best to support Ripley's legal efforts and save him from economic ruin; however, Ripley's situation continued to deteriorate.[17]

On July 4 Batley's solicitors pressed Ripley to produce "the letters alleged to have passed between him and Mr. Peter Pritchard forming the contract on which his claim of damages was founded." In August the company's solicitors, Brook, Freeman & Batley, investigated the alleged suit against Ripley by Peter Pritchard and found no record of such a suit. As the litigation moved into July, Greenwood & Batley was stunned by rumors against its credit, which caused the firm's bankers to ask for an explanation of the suit. The machinists brought James Burton into the litigation by preparing draft affidavits and instructions, which were to be sent to him in Virginia. On August 22 Batley's solicitors examined Judah Benjamin's arguments, requesting better information on certain legal points in the case. On August 31, as the case dragged on, Ripley's solicitors requested a change of venue to London. From Virginia, Burton wrote to his London solicitors, Cattarns & Jehn, and enclosed letters from Ripley, the content of which is unknown.[18]

In another desperate effort to survive financially, Ripley attempted to purchase Enfield rifles on behalf of the French. Ripley corresponded with former Union general William B. Franklin, director of the Colt Fire Arms Manufacturing Company. Franklin graduated first in Ripley's class of 1843 at West Point and served during the Peninsula Campaign and at the Battles of South Mountain and Antietam during Ripley's service with the Army of Northern Virginia. On September 7 Ripley wrote to Franklin, claiming he could sell 100,000 good-quality, used muskets of the Enfield pattern for $3.50 in gold per musket without delay. He asked Franklin to "state price, time and place of delivery." Ripley believed that no one else had bid on his market for these arms, and if they acted quickly it could be a profitable deal. It is unlikely this came to fruition as Ripley's financial situation continued to deteriorate.[19]

By November 1868 the Wigfalls had moved from 57 Gloucester Place, Portman Square, to a new address on the same street, No. 79. This block of Gloucester Place appears to have been more elegant. Number 79, owned by George Isaac Leon in 1867, had previously been the home of General Sir William Robert Clayton, Baronet. The street also was the home to the Consul-General of Venezuela, an admiral, several physicians, surgeons, and dentists. The homes on the street have been renumbered and Wigfall's No. 79 is now No. 89, but its grand Georgian façade has been preserved.

Louise informed Halsey, "The Hamiltons are just the same. The poor Ripleys have been having a rather hard time, and Mrs. R. and little Alicia are now on a visit to Mrs. Hamilton, temporarily of course, but it is not pleasant to be under even temporary obligation to people." Louise asked Halsey not to say anything about this, as Mrs. Ripley was very sensitive about it being known in America. "If Motte Middleton [Mrs. Ripley's brother] had paid her what he owed, there would have been no trouble. Gen. R. has sent to sue him . . . as they have received no replies to their letters, that is their only course," she wrote.

Former residence of Louis T. Wigfall and family at 79 (now 89) Gloucester Place. The Ripleys and Wigfalls often met here socially. Photograph courtesy of Charles Priestley, London, American Civil War Roundtable, U.K.

In December, John Batley met with Thomas Dudley at the U.S. Consulate in Liverpool regarding the litigation. Batley reported to his solicitors that "it appeared unlikely the United States would assent to the proposed arrangements, or do anything to recognize Fraser, Trenholm & Co., or Ripley's right to the machinery"[20]

On January 2, 1869, Louise wrote to Halsey disclosing that after luncheon she was planning to visit Mrs. Hamilton, then living on Victoria Street, adding, "Mrs. Ripley and little Alicia are still there and are in a most painful state. Mrs. R. has been there about three months and they are getting very tired of her. It strikes me as almost inhuman. General R. has utterly failed, though his case about the machinery has not yet been tried." Ripley's lack of funds prevented him from doing anything, and he was "living on sufferance, as it were, at the *Alexandra,* having given the proprietor some interest in his affairs. . . . His poor wife & child are dependent on the charity, but coldly given I am afraid by the Hamiltons." They were treated politely and kindly by Mrs. Hamilton, "but you know there are two ways of being kind; one is from duty & necessity, & the other from the overflowing of a generous & loving heart. One is chilling as the winter blast, the other as warm and comforting as the glorious Sun of Heaven." Mrs. Hamilton told the Wigfalls that they were so "pressed and hampered that Jack had gone to General Ripley and told him he could not keep his wife and child any longer, and the poor man with tears in his eyes replied '. . . if he did not they would be turned in the street, that he had no roof to shelter them.' I thought it not only the bitterest cruelty I had ever heard of, but also the greatest indecency from one gentleman to another. And fancy her telling it!" Mrs. Hamilton was "perfectly unfitted to bear poverty in its mildest form. She is a nice little woman, kind at heart too, but not anyone to suffer inconvenience for others." The Wigfalls were going to the pantomime at Drury Lane and, Louise noted, "Fannie has asked Alicia Ripley to go with us. She wrote a refusal, which we fancied was only an excuse & we hope today to induce her mother to let her go. . . . be careful not to let a word of all I have written escape you."[21]

On February 3 Batley's solicitors received a telegram from Burton agreeing with the evidence in the depositions sent him. Batley's solicitors informed Consul Dudley they were sending a commission to the United States to examine Mr. Burton as a witness. The next day the Leeds machinists notified Dudley, "We understand Gen. Ripley is going to appeal against V. C. Manlius' [Malins's?] decision," rendered by the vice chancellor the previous July. "We have used every effort to bring about a friendly arrangement, but without effect, so now we are preparing for the struggle." Later in the month, the two sides met in London for a conference, then convened in the judge's chambers, where Benjamin represented Ripley. As a result, the parties agreed to a stay of two months. Burton's solicitors received copies of Ripley's letters to Burton, but wanted the <u>originals</u> "verified by someone acquainted with Ripley's handwriting."[22]

Ripley's world disintegrated on March 5, 1869, when Abbott informed Batley's solicitors that "the plaintiff [Ripley] had been arrested for debt and was lying in prison & they wished nothing further to be done." Burton's solicitors, who also planned to sue Ripley, were also informed that Ripley had been "adjudicated a bankrupt." On March 27 Charlotte Wigfall wrote to her son, "Jack Hamilton, who has a regular salary in the Iron Works of £400, is the only Confederate I know who is making his bread. I enclose Ripley's experience." The undated, unattributed newspaper clipping regarding his bankruptcy reads:

> General Ripley of the Confederate Army, and who long held the command at Charleston has been arrested for debt this week in London. His debts are £37,834. He stated that he had a claim on certain machinery, which was made for the Confederate Government, and is now in the hands of Greenwood and Baxley [sic] of Leeds and which he estimates at £50,000. The application was opposed on the ground that the bankrupt was about to leave the country. It was incidentally stated that the bankrupt was the man who fired the first gun

at Fort Sumter on the outbreak of the late war. His Honour, Mr. Commissioner Bacon, did not think the objection sustained and granted the release.[23]

The *Times* of London on March 12 printed a similar account of Ripley's bankruptcy, brief arrest, and subsequent release. He was described as being "late of the *Alexandra* and *Grosvenor Hotels*. The Court, on the ground that there was no sufficient evidence that the bankrupt was about to quit the country, granted the order of release."

Another notice appeared in the same day. The *London Gazette* reported that "Roswell Sabine Ripley, late of the *Alexandra Hotel,* Hyde-park, and now of the *Grosvenor Hotel,* Pimlico," who formerly was a general in the Confederate Army, but now has no occupation, is a "Prisoner for Debt in the Debtors' Prison for London and Middlesex." After having been adjudged bankrupt on March 8, Ripley was required to surrender to a "Registrar of the Court" at the first meeting of creditors to be held April 9 at 1:00 P.M.

Benjamin Moran noted, "Several ex-rebels are here in destitution. With the exception of J. P. Benjamin and Gen. Wigfall, every rebel of consequence in London has been in Whitecross Prison for debt." The days of Whitecross as a debtors' prison ended in October 1870. Originally intended to house up to five hundred debtors, by 1870 the number was reduced to thirty, and very few were imprisoned when the prison closed.

Adjudged bankrupt, Ripley somehow managed to secure lodging at the Grosvenor Hotel adjacent to Victoria Station. Construction on this stone and white brick edifice began in 1860. This six-story hotel featured two hundred bedrooms and had 120 bathrooms. The ten staircases had an adjacent "lifting room." Although the interior has been remodeled numerous times, the structure still is a hotel. How Ripley could afford his room is unknown.[24]

The bankruptcy notices in London newspapers are the first known examples of Ripley's given middle name, Sabin, with an added terminal *e*. Possibly the newspapers inadvertently related Ripley to a famous British general, Sir Edward Sabine. General Sabine, an artillerist, served in the colonies during the War of 1812. His fame in England centered on his postmilitary career in science, especially terrestrial magnetism and a magnetic survey of the planet. Ripley would have been flattered if the newspapers mistakenly connected him with the well-known General Sabine. Thereafter, Sabine appears to be the prevalent spelling of Ripley's middle name.

Charlotte Wigfall disclosed Ripley's final ignominy in a letter to her son dated April 14, 1869: "Mrs. Ripley and Alicia sailed on Saturday [April 12] for Baltimore. They have gone thru such humiliations, as you would be sorry to hear. A subscription was taken to send them home where I hope they will reach safely." Wigfall thought Ripley's suit would be tried and, if decided in his favor, would give him something, but "too late to save his family the mortification they have had to endure."[25]

On April 8 Ripley's "debts were partially proved in court to nearly £4,000." A Mr. Theodore Schweitzer, whom Ripley owed over £508, "was appointed assignee." The breadth of Ripley's indebtedness is evidenced by the inclusion of George La Cont and Charles Ollier, theatrical agents, for a sum of £56. 4s. Evidently, Ripley had been charging the tickets for his young daughter's entertainment at Drury Lane Theater. On April 30 the *London Gazette* reported that Ripley was to have a "Public sitting to pass his last examination, and make application for his Discharge before James Bacon Esq., a commissioner of the said Court." On May 24, "an order of discharge was granted to Roswell Sabine Ripley. He appeared before the Court on his own petition and attributed his present difficulties to the non-delivery of certain machinery by the vendors. The accounts returned debts to the amount of £36,923 and a surplus of £13, 223."[26]

During this time John Batley corresponded regularly with U.S. Consul Dudley in Liverpool regarding the case. Batley notified Dudley that their solicitors would serve Schweitzer with a summons to determine whether he intended to continue Ripley's suit. Batley also informed Dudley that he believed Prioleau perjured himself in the suit against them and that they would seek every means to punish him. Batley did not believe that "Ripley's case against us has a leg to stand upon, but the law is gloriously uncertain." By July 2, 1869, Batley informed Dudley that Schweitzer had "retired from the field" but that "Mr. Prioleau has taken up the game and I am told he is to sue us for having wrongfully converted his machinery." Ripley appeared still to be in London, Batley noted, supposedly funded by Prioleau. Someone who saw Ripley the other day told us "he is certain the fund voted by Congress to carry on this litigation will soon be exhausted, and he is sure Congress will grant no more funds, the whole affair will come to an end, and they will make us pay. I suppose we may rely upon your support in court?"

Ripley's continued optimism was unjustified. He remained in debt, mortgaged to the Lawley brothers and others. For Roswell, his inability to gain control of the Greenwood & Batley machinery and his failed dream of establishing an armory at Poissy, France, became an even greater financial disaster than his father's failure to develop Matildaville. Adding insult to injury, on July 5 Consul Dudley notified Greenwood & Batley that they were "at liberty to sell the plant and machinery in your possession forming the subject matter of the suit."[27]

Charlotte Wigfall recognized the humiliation that Alicia Ripley and her daughter endured as a result of Roswell's financial ruin. Although Ripley would have been humiliated when a collection was needed to fund his wife and daughter's return to South Carolina, it is questionable whether he was mortified by the bankruptcy itself. Ripley believed that he had purchased the rights to the remainder of the machinery ordered by James Burton from Greenwood & Batley. The

Leeds machinists and Charles K. Prioleau kept his money, and Consul Dudley and the U.S. government helped thwart Ripley's attempt to gain control of the machinery. As a result, his plans for equipping an armory in France failed. His forceful, self-assured personality, which had prevailed so often in the past, prevented him from realizing the weakness of his position and the overwhelming strength of his legal opposition. The courts ultimately decided that Ripley, in his desperation, had concocted an implausible, quasi-contract with Peter Pritchard, the Congreve rocket manufacturer. His final flawed attempt to gain control of the machinery or exact damages from Greenwood & Batley failed. For political reasons, Ripley resolutely refused to return to the United States. His unsuccessful legal battle over the machinery could only have intensified his loathing of the Republicans in control of the United States government.

CHAPTER 30

Financial Struggles, 1869–1873

Incredibly, Ripley continued to believe he would triumph in the British courts and be awarded £100,000 in damages from Greenwood & Batley. He may have believed the presence of Judah Benjamin on his legal team would assure his success. As John Batley had mentioned in his letter to Consul Dudley, Ripley may also have thought the U.S. government would eventually quit the case and he would be awarded the specified damages or rights to the machinery. In any event, Ripley astonishingly pledged £100,000 in the articles of agreement he signed with Charles D. Poston, who represented the Arizona Mining Company.

In February 1851 Charles Poston, a native of Kentucky and strong Unionist, immigrated to San Francisco, California. In February 1854 Poston set out for the newly acquired Gadsden Purchase on the southern border of what would become the Arizona Territory. In 1856 he founded the Sonora Exploring and Mining Company and located its headquarters in the deserted Spanish presidio of Tubac. Poston's mining company purchased the twenty-thousand-acre, Mexican-land-grant-based Arivaca Ranch. Poston reopened old Spanish mines and located new ones including the "celebrated Cerro Colorado or Heintzelman Mine." Unfortunately for Poston, all his mines were closed and abandoned at the onset of the Civil War. In 1863 President Lincoln signed the Senate bill granting territorial status to Arizona, and Poston, a friend of Lincoln's Kentucky family, was appointed superintendent of Indian affairs in the territory. The next year Poston became the Arizona Territory's delegate to Congress.

Following the appointment of Poston's longtime friend J. Ross Browne minister to China, the U.S. Department of Agriculture commissioned Poston to study agriculture conditions and practices in the Far East. In August 1868 Browne and Poston embarked from San Francisco for Asia. After Browne reached his post, Poston continued around the world, sightseeing in the East Indies, India, and Egypt before spending the summer of 1869 in Europe. During his stay in London, Poston attempted to "salvage" the Arizona mines he had worked so diligently to establish, but his efforts ultimately failed. Many years later, Poston's ownership of the Arivaca Ranch was challenged, and the courts rejected the Mexican land grant on which his ownership was based.[1]

In London on August 25, 1869, Ripley, bankrupt and penniless, met with Poston and signed an agreement to purchase, for £100,000, the "Arivaca Ranche with all the mineral rights; the Colorado or Heintzelman Mine in the Cerro Colorado Mountains, with all appurtenances, personal property, the reduction works, tenements and other property of said premises." Ripley signed the document "Roswell *Sabine* Ripley," using his "new" middle name. Ripley agreed "to occupy the property on, or before, January 1, 1870, or earliest practicable date." He was to begin "stocking and cultivating the pasture and arable lands, renewing the buildings, reopening the Heintzelman Mine, and opening other mines in connection with the property." The title documents were to be delivered at the offices of the Arizona Mining Company in New York City. With his unwarranted but characteristic optimism, Ripley entered into a real estate transaction with virtually no chance of success—a scenario reminiscent of his father's real estate misadventure with Matildaville. It would be interesting to know Poston's thoughts as he hoped to close this deal and rid himself of these properties.[2]

In September, Louly Wigfall wrote to her brother Halsey, "Mrs. Hamilton was here yesterday looking as pretty & young as usual & full of little items of news." She had heard from Mrs. Ripley in Charleston, described as penniless but with a kind landlady, who allowed her to remain "until Motte Middleton's crops come in, when she will be paid. The old general is still here and has, by his account, a brilliant prospect. Something about a mine with some chance of success, though he is getting somewhat impatient to have the deal concluded." Ripley is reported to have said, "If they don't make haste he would melt the ore they have given him as specimens. Little Mrs. Hamilton shrewdly observed, 'who knows, he might already have done so.'" Ripley obviously could never fulfill this contract, and another of his dreams of fortune went awry.[3]

Although Ripley no longer was a principal in the Greenwood & Batley lawsuit, the case continued in litigation. In November the solicitors discussed with Prioleau and potential buyers the proposed terms and means for selling the machinery, the best way to obtain Ripley and his assignee's consent, and "the payment of their costs." The solicitors advised, "a payment should be made to Ripley's assignees to obtain their and Mr. Lawley's consent."[4]

In desperation, in early January 1870 Ripley was finally forced to sell the Charleston property on East Bay Street he had placed in trust for his daughter. Ripley gave Wilmot G. DeSaussure power of attorney to work with the remaining trustee, Theodore Wagner, as John Middleton had died the previous year. As Alicia had not reached the age of twenty-one and was unmarried, Ripley was legally able to sell the property; he embarrassingly stated that he was planning to reinvest the proceeds from the sale but did not claim it would be for Alicia. As mentioned, Alicia and her mother returned to Charleston in April 1869, but it is unclear how much DeSaussure and Wagner knew about Ripley's financial condition. In early February, Trustee Wagner completed the sale of the property to Charles O. Witte. Ripley's $25,000 investment in 1863 returned only $5,000 in February 1870. It is not known how much the attorney's and trustee's fees reduced Ripley's share, but a $200 revenue stamp was on the paperwork.[5]

The hounding of Ripley continued in July when on two occasions Greenwood & Batley's solicitors wrote to James Burton's legal team in Virginia "as to whether Mr. Burton had proved his debt against Ripley's estate." Throughout the latter months of 1870, Greenwood & Batley's solicitors were involved in negotiations regarding the sale of the remaining Confederate machinery to the London Armoury Company.[6]

On the continent, during the late 1860s and 1870, the relationship between Prussia and France continued to deteriorate. By 1860 France had defeated two of its three chief European adversaries. The French army had been victorious, with help from the British, against the Russians in the Crimea in 1854–55, and in 1859 France defeated Austria. France won these wars despite serious inadequacies in training, military administration, and the disastrous mismanagement of their supply lines. Fortunately for France, its adversaries were in a significantly worse state of military preparedness. In 1860 France's third major opponent, Prussia, presented little to fear militarily, but during the early 1860s the Crown clashed with the Prussian Assembly over military appropriations and taxes. In 1863 Otto von Bismarck disbanded the assembly and within six months involved Prussia in a war with Denmark. A confrontation with Austria in 1866 served to unite Prussia with various other German states and resulted in the formation of the North German Confederation, which could field an army of over one million men.

After 1866 France was perceived to be a first-class power in decline and considered war inevitable after the German Confederation upset the balance of power in Europe. Chancellor Bismarck provoked France into declaring war on July 15, 1870, well before the French had fully mobilized. In early August, French armies advanced on Saarbrucken, where after a successful but limited attack, the French initiative stalled. Prussian counterattacks drove the French back, and on August 6 the full-scale invasion of France began, with the Prussians advancing irrepressibly against French resistance.[7]

As the war intensified, the new Chassepôt rifle could not be manufactured in sufficient quantities, and French agents searched markets in England and the United States for rifles. On August 25, 1870, French agent Charles H. DeBruin wrote to General W. B. Franklin of the Colt Firearms Manufacturing Company in Hartford, Connecticut. He claimed that Roswell Ripley suggested he might be able to buy a large quantity of Enfield rifles from Colt and "would pay cash on delivery at New York." DeBruin asked Franklin to contact him "in care of W. Hope, Esq., 8 Finch Lane, London."

Two days later, from the same address, Ripley posted a letter to his old classmate, General Franklin, regarding arms for the French. He wrote of DeBruin's efforts and mentioned, "I am certain he has the money here in London and under any circumstances will have it for some months. They are buying here, but will soon exhaust this market, and would like to get enough to move the Prussians out of France if they can." Ripley did not expect a speedy end to the war despite the Prussian advances and suggested that Franklin should write to DeBruin.[8]

These two letters, written on stationary imprinted "8 Finch Lane" and containing the mention of "W. Hope, Esq.," at the address, are the first indication of Ripley's friendship and business partnership with William Hope. Their association spanned most of Ripley's years in England and helped him survive his self-imposed exile.

Hope, born on April 12, 1834, in Edinburgh, was educated at Hatfield and Trinity College before volunteering for the British Army. In the Crimea, Lieutenant William Hope of the 7th Regiment, Royal Fusiliers, received the Victoria Cross for heroism under fire on June 18, 1855. Hope's bravery occurred during the British attempt to capture the strongly defended earthworks, referred to as the Redan, at Sevastopol. Sergeant Major William Bacon, who was wounded in the attack, informed Hope that a badly wounded Lieutenant Hobson had been left in the field. Hope returned to the battlefield and found Hobson, then returned to his lines and recruited four men to go with him to rescue the lieutenant. Finding they needed a stretcher, Hope went back to his lines for one. All of this was done under heavy enemy fire, and for his heroic action Hope personally received the Victoria Cross from Queen Victoria in Hyde Park on June 26, 1857. Thereafter, Hope was permitted the honor of placing "V.C." after his name. Hope served briefly as the military attaché to Lord Francis Napier, the British ambassador at Washington, and then as an attaché at The Hague. Following his years as an attaché, Hope became a colonel in the 1st City of London Artillery Volunteers.

Between 1860 and 1875 Hope was the most ambitious advocate of the use of sewage irrigation to reclaim barren land and transform it into farmland. Hope and the Honorable William Napier collaborated on plans to divert north London sewage into a model "sewage farm." These visionary schemes ultimately failed as costs outweighed the income generated. Ripley's business association with Hope likely involved his participation in these projects. In the late 1870s and 1880s, Hope and Ripley would collaborate on British patents for metallurgical processes and ordnance. London Directories listed "Wm. Hope, V.C." as a civil engineer at 8 Finch Lane and 38 Nicholas Lane between 1870 and 1875.[9]

Ripley, in his letter to General Franklin, overestimated the ability of the French to withstand the Prussian military onslaught and significantly misjudged the length of the Franco-Prussian War. Ripley also must have lamented his failure to establish his weapons factory at Poissy, as he was relegated to searching for arms for the French. While Ripley endeavored to find serviceable rifles, the French military situation steadily deteriorated. On September 2 the French resistance totally disintegrated at Sedan, where Emperor Napoleon III surrendered along with the bulk of his army. The disaster at Sedan stunned Paris and a new "Government of National Defense" was hurriedly created to replace the Second Empire of Napoleon III. Immediately, the new government began measures to improve fortifications around Paris. On September 7, shortly after the capitulation at Sedan, the Prussians began their assault on Paris.[10]

On Monday, September 12, 1870, Benjamin Moran entered the following in his diary: "At 9:30 yesterday morning the rebel Gen'l R.S. Ripley came to my house while I was in bed and wanted me to go with him to the Legation and give him a passport; but I did not see it. I met him there at 1 P.M. however and gave him the document. He is a native of Ohio and as great a rebel as ever."

Ripley's business relationship with the French agent Charles DeBruin would have kept him apprised of the situation on the continent. The former Confederate general Samuel G. French believed that Ripley "was at one time engaged in planning the defenses of Paris pending the Franco-German War." Circumstantial evidence indicates Ripley's involvement, but no direct record has been found of his role in the city's defense. The rapid Prussian advance on Paris must have prompted Ripley's urgent visit to Benjamin Moran's home early on that Sunday morning. Apparently, Ripley needed a passport to travel to Paris before the Prussians isolated the city. In France, Ripley would have been comfortable with the language. He attended a French-Canadian boarding school near Montréal as a young boy, studied French at St. Lawrence Academy, and continued his study at West Point, where he ranked high in French. He would have been conversant, if not fluent, in the language.

The Prussians advanced with two armies in a pincers movement, cutting Paris off from the rest of the world on September 20. This gave Ripley only a week to reach the beleaguered capital. In Paris redoubts were constructed, and all roads and railway entrances to the city were obstructed. Workshops in the city were converted to produce ammunition or transform muzzle-loading rifles into breech-loaders. Over fifteen hundred heavy guns were positioned, woods were felled, and buildings demolished to provide fields of fire. Ripley's expertise in artillery defenses would have proved invaluable.

The Prussian bombardment of Paris began on January 5, 1871, and continued until January 28, when the adversaries signed an armistice. It is not known whether Ripley, either by choice or necessity, remained in Paris and endured the entire siege. The end of hostilities would have enabled him to return to England if he had not already done so.[11]

In early 1871 Ripley must have finally realized that his business ventures and his hopes and aspirations, as well as his marriage, had all come to a disastrous end. Ripley had borrowed a significant amount of money from Frank and Stephen Lawley in his attempt to gain control of the remaining Confederate arms machinery in the hands of Greenwood & Batley. He bought, or so he thought, the rights to the machinery from Charles K. Prioleau of Fraser, Trenholm & Company. In addition, he paid a commission to James H. Burton and Greenwood & Batley for the machinery in their possession; they readily accepted and kept his money. The U.S. government's claim to the machinery as Confederate property and the government's legal intimidation of Greenwood & Batley, precluded delivery of the machinery, although it is doubtful that was ever the machinists' intent. Unable to gain control of the machinery, Ripley's plan for establishing an arms factory in France failed. With so much of the machinery having been sent to the Confederacy and destroyed or missing, one wonders whether the remaining machinery would have been sufficient to equip a productive arms factory. His lawsuit against the Leeds machinists for nondelivery did not succeed, and he went bankrupt. With Ripley unable to support his wife and daughter, they were forced to return to South Carolina. Without the judgment against Greenwood & Batley, his dream of buying the Arivaca ranch in the Arizona Territory and developing its silver mines collapsed. Ripley then attempted to buy arms for the French in their impending war with the Prussians. If profitable at all, the commissions generated from any arms purchased would have been only a temporary solution to his financial problems, as the Franco-Prussian War ended much too quickly to provide any lasting support. Once again Ripley found himself not only on the losing side of a devastating war but also bankrupt and heavily in debt.

Frank Lawley, in a letter dated May 27, 1871, described Ripley's condition as "wretched," a confirmation of his depression and financial distress. Despite this, Ripley managed to find accommodations at the Great Western Hotel in London. Adjacent to Paddington Station, it was the first of the great railway hotels in London and finished in a baroque style. From this hotel on July 5, 1871, Ripley responded, surprisingly on his own personally monogrammed stationary, to a letter from Colonel Charles Colcock Jones Jr. The colonel was preparing a Confederate "roster" and requested information concerning Ripley's military career. In his response Ripley described "being second to Beauregard who commanded the Department," but he refrained from mentioning the intense hostility that developed over the years between the two men. He acknowledged being sent in May 1862 to Virginia, where he "commanded a Brigade in D. H. Hill's Division." He added, "After the battle of Sharpsburg I returned to South Carolina." He did not disclose his participation in the Battles of Mechanicsville, Malvern Hill, and South Mountain, nor did he mention the serious throat wound he suffered at Sharpsburg.[12]

Even more difficult years for Ripley in London were now beginning. In early 1872 his bankruptcy case was reopened following the death of Theodore E. Schweitzer, the assignee of Ripley's bankrupt estate. Ripley apparently had moved from the Great Western Hotel back to the Grosvenor Hotel, where he received a notice to appear in the Court of Bankruptcy on February 16. The court was to appoint a new assignee or assignees to replace the deceased Schweitzer. Any creditors who had not already proved their debts were to come forward with proof of the same. Ripley was described as a general in the Confederate army but "now of no occupation."

In March 1872 Ripley corresponded twice with the former Confederate general Bradley T. Johnson, then living in Richmond, Virginia. Generals Johnson and Ripley had been in contact in March 1865, when Johnson commanded the prisoner of war camp in Salisbury, North Carolina. The content of these two 1872 letters is baffling as so little is known, or has been preserved, as to why Ripley and Johnson were communicating. The letters refer to a legal problem between Colonel Middleton Biddulph of England and a Mr. Broome who apparently lived in the United States, probably near Richmond. Ripley enigmatically wrote, "this mornings paper announces the death of Col. Middleton Biddulph, the presenter in the case, who will have to settle his business about chicken cocks and green houses somewhere else." Ripley appears to have been a middleman between Bradley Johnson and a third party, J. R. Lee-Bellasyse. This letter, dated March 23, was on stationary imprinted with William Hope's business address, indicating that he and Ripley continued to work together. Ripley wrote his second letter on March 25 using his own monogrammed stationary, but indicated that he had moved back to the Great Western Hotel. It appears that Bellasyse represented Biddulph, and Johnson may have been Broome's attorney in this unexplained legal dispute. Why Bellasyse needed Ripley to be a conduit to Johnson is a mystery. These letters are of significance only insofar as they document Ripley's dealings with Bellasyse, who would in a few years vent his wrath on Ripley. During this time something divisive must have occurred between Ripley and Bellasyse, which generated the Englishman's bitter enmity.[13]

In October 1872, the Newport Oregon Coal Company planned to issue sixteen thousand shares of preferred stock at the price of £10 per share, which would pay 10 percent interest per year. Advertisements announcing this offer appeared at least nine times between October 12 and 19 in London-area periodicals such as the *Pall Mall Gazette* and the *Spectator* magazine.

The Newport Company was formed to purchase the "extensive and valuable" coal property at Coos Bay, Oregon, which had been mined for sixteen years. The existing plant, facilities, and wharves were capable of shipping, by steamer, eighty thousand tons of coal per year, primarily to San Francisco. The company's prospectus and regulations could be viewed at the offices of their solicitors, Abbott, Jenkins and Abbott, 8 New Inn, Strand. The present owners selected Ripley to represent them in the sales process, most likely at the recommendation of Abbott and Jenkins, who may have applied some of the proceeds from Ripley's sales efforts toward his legal fees. This was another attempt by the beleaguered Confederate to find a source of income to support himself and pay off his debts.[14]

On January 23, 1873, the *Cheshire Observer* of Chester, England, noted that "General Ripley, Mr. John R. Lee Ballentyne, and a mineral agent for the Marquis of Westminster, Mr. Isaac Shone, sailed aboard the *Oceanic* to inspect the extensive property of the coal company." Inexplicably, the three Newport agents changed to the *Java* in Queenstown, Ireland, and arrived in New York on February 13. The *Java* manifest lists Ripley and Isaac Shone, but interestingly Ballentyne is now none other than J. R. Lee-Bellasyse. What could have transpired between Ripley and Bellasyse during this trip for the coal company may never be known. There is no record of how long Ripley was absent in this regard or when he returned. The first record of his return to England shows up in May 1874.[15]

CHAPTER 31

Literary Career, 1874–1875

In May 1874 Ripley received a letter from one of his former regimental commanders, Colonel William Lord de Rosset, informing him of his planned visit to London. De Rosset, a member of one of the oldest and most prominent families of Wilmington, served with the 3rd North Carolina Infantry. Assigned to Ripley's Brigade, the 3rd served during the Peninsula Campaign and at the Battles of South Mountain and Sharpsburg. De Rosset assumed command of the regiment after Colonel Gaston Meares was killed at the Battle of Malvern Hill. At Sharpsburg severe wounds of his hip and thigh disabled de Rosset.[1]

On May 13 Ripley replied that he was "very glad" to have received de Rosset's letter and would "be still more pleased to see you. A letter will always reach me addressed c/o W. Hope, Esq., V.C. at this office [38 Nicholas Lane] and I will meet you as soon as I know you are in London." De Rosset arrived and secured lodging at the Langham Hotel. At 10:00 P.M. on May 20, Ripley went to the Langham and left a note for de Rosset on hotel stationary: "I called as soon as I got your card, which came to me by mail as I did not go to the city today. I shall be at 38 Nicholas Lane tomorrow at 12:30 & will call here [the Langham] or anywhere else that I may have the pleasure of seeing you, and at such hour as you may approve."[2]

William Hope, who previously had been located at 8 Finch Lane, now maintained his civil engineer's office at 38 Nicholas Lane, a small building in which five other businesses were located. In 1874 the Anglo-German Tunneling Company, of which Charles H. DeBruin was secretary, occupied one of these offices. In 1870, when French agent DeBruin wrote to General Franklin for arms, he used Hope's address at 8 Finch Lane as his contact. Interestingly, in 1874 DeBruin, now working for an Anglo-German company, maintained contact with Hope and Ripley at Nicholas Lane. Both Finch and Nicholas Lanes were located in what is now referred to as the "City," or the original Roman City of London. Except for a few old churches, nearly all of the original buildings have been destroyed, either by the Luftwaffe during World War II or, more recently, by developers.[3]

Ripley advised de Rosset, "My private address is '8 Stanhope Terrace, Gloster [*sic*] Road, South Kensington.' I am there every morning until 10:30 and every evening, God knows when. Best tell me where to spot you by note or person tomorrow at Nicholas Lane. I shall be awfully glad to see you." The next day Ripley notified de Rosset that he would "come by the *Langham* at 6 o'clock this evening." A few days later Ripley wrote, "I had hoped to have called yesterday or today, but I was called off on matters of importance which will take me until late this evening. I shall look in tomorrow afternoon at the *Langham* & if I have the good luck to find you, I shall hope for another pleasant chat. If you are engaged, leave word at the office."

De Rosset remained in London for another month, but no other correspondence from Ripley has been preserved, except for a letter written on June 24 as de Rosset departed England: "I duly received your letter and should have answered it had I not mislaid your Liverpool address. I have given a letter of introduction to my friend Mr. Behr who goes out in the *Scotia,* and whom you will find a very agreeable companion." Fritz Bernard Behr was secretary of the Government & Guaranteed Securities Permanent Trust with offices also at 38 Nicholas Lane. Ripley closed his note, "Please remember me kindly to all my old friends, especially those of the old 3rd North Carolina Regiment . . . with my heartfelt sympathies with you in your bereavement." Evidently a death in de Rosset's family necessitated his return to North Carolina, and on June 25 he departed from Liverpool on the steamer *Scotia*.[4]

Knowing now that eleven years later de Rosset would write, in his letter of June 1885 to General D. H. Hill, a scathing denunciation of Ripley, one wonders why he chose to seek out and visit Ripley in London. In 1886 de Rosset responded to an article authored by Hill and published in the *Century*. In "The Battle of South Mountain or Boonsboro," Hill derisively wrote, "I received a note from Ripley saying that he was progressing finely; so he was, to the rear of the mountain on the west side. Before he returned the fighting was over, and he did not fire a shot that day."

De Rosset believed that statement also impugned his reputation, as well as that of the men of the 3rd North Carolina. In a letter to the *Century* dated September 24 and published in the December issue, de Rosset explained why the brigade "did not fire a shot that day." In this letter de Rosset stated that Ripley remained near him and directed him "to advance slowly up the mountain with a strong line of skirmishers in front. Upon reaching the summit, after toiling through the dense undergrowth of laurel, Captain Thruston, in command of the skirmish line, reported troops were in his front, a few minutes later confirming his first impression that they were G. B. Anderson's brigade, presenting their left flank and advancing toward his left."

However, in his letter to Hill the year before, de Rosset stated that he told Ripley the enemy was in front, after which Ripley ordered the brigade to fall back, a much more damning accusation. De Rosset claimed that it was much later when he learned that the troops in his front were those of Anderson's brigade. Thruston had refuted the charge that the enemy was in his front in his letter to Governor Vance describing his personal reconnaissance at the time.

Ripley's letters to de Rosset describe a cordial reunion. If de Rosset had berated Ripley at Sharpsburg, as he claimed to Hill, Ripley did not let it negatively influence their relationship. His parting note to de Rosset was most felicitous. As Samuel French would say in his eulogy of Ripley, "he harbored no resentments."[5]

During the early 1870s two Englishmen contributed significantly to Ripley's survival. Ripley developed a friendship and business relationship with William Hope that lasted throughout his many years in England. Surprisingly, despite his financial loss in the Greenwood & Batley legal fiasco, journalist Francis "Frank" Lawley maintained his friendship with Ripley and continued to be of assistance to the troubled ex-Confederate. Lawley returned to London in May 1865 after serving as a special correspondent for the *Times* of London in Charleston, Richmond, and throughout the Confederacy. His pro-Confederate dispatches were admired in England for both their style and substance. Lawley also corresponded with John Blackwood of *Blackwood's Edinburgh Magazine* and submitted articles for publication. Lawley, familiar with Ripley's *The War With Mexico*, encouraged Ripley to begin writing again.[6]

Fortuitously for Ripley, in July 1874 the first chapters of a proposed seven-volume publication appeared in the French magazine *Revue des Deux Mondes*. Entitled "L'Histoire de la Guerre Civile en Amerique," the volumes were the work of his Royal Highness the Comte de Paris, who served briefly as an aide-de-camp to General George McClellan. Ripley condemned the Comte's interpretation of events and believed the Frenchman had an "absolute ignorance of the real causes of the war." Ripley was especially angered as the Comte condemned states' rights, the Southern cause, and its leaders. Rebutting the Comte's prejudiced work provided Ripley with an opportunity to reenter the literary field.[7]

On July 13, 1874, Francis Lawley wrote to John Blackwood, stating, "a Confederate general of eminence and ability, General Ripley, the gallant defender of Charleston during the American War, has just called upon me, bringing with him a 'brochure' from his pen. It is a spirited and striking answer to the attack upon the South that the Comte de Paris has just published. General Ripley feels, and so do I, that his paper will make a sensation upon both sides of the Atlantic. I have begged Gen. Ripley to let me write to you asking if you will allow him to send his paper to you for inspection." Both Lawley and Ripley believed the immediate publication of his rebuttal was essential to discredit the Frenchman's anti-Southern chapters. Lawley urged Blackwood to notify him by telegram tomorrow, for "I should be sorry to let this go into other hands."

Blackwood responded quickly to Lawley's letter, and the next day Ripley wrote, "At the request of my friend, the Hon. Francis Lawley, I send you the manuscript of my remarks on the Comte de Paris' opening chapters of his 'History of the Civil War in America.' Should the number be worthy of publication they will command a circulation in France if translated & published speedily."

Ripley asked whether Blackwood wanted his agents, in the event that his article was published, to "attend to its publication in France, or for me to do so?"[8]

On July 17 Lawley wrote to *Blackwood's,* concerned that Ripley may not have forwarded his article. He explained, "I sent your telegram on Wednesday evening to Gen. Ripley with a request that he would immediately send you his 'brochure,' and I sincerely hope he has done so, & that you will find it worth printing, The only misgiving I have is his style should be too rough and unkempt, but I feel satisfied that it will not lack vigor." John Blackwood must have agreed with Lawley's "misgivings." On July 21 Ripley received a note with proofs from Blackwood and responded, "have seen Mr. Lawley, and we proceed at once to comply with your suggestions & shall mail the corrected matter tomorrow evening. I regret my late inexperience in writing for the press should have caused the delay, but now that the matter is in print I can recognize the force of your suggestions, and hope with the assistance of an 'old hand' like Lawley to make it satisfactory."

The next day Ripley tactfully informed *Blackwood's* that he and Lawley had carefully gone through the proofs and amended them. He hoped that "we have corrected a sufficient quantity of faults to make the document passable. You will notice that I have put it in the form of a letter to the editor. Of course you can put in such a heading as you deem most suitable." Ripley discussed his personal remarks criticizing the Comte with Lawley, who wrote to the publisher notifying him, "I have gone carefully over Gen. Ripley's 'brochure' and have done my best to amend it, but as regards the advisability of toning down the suit against the C. de Paris' military qualities, I don't think one word is said which he does not justly deserve. He and his kinsmen entered into the American strife, solely for political gain in France" but did not have "the pluck to wait until the side with which they took part prevailed." Having read the Comte's two volumes, Lawley offered the view that " they deserve a severer stroke of the lash than Gen. Ripley has applied. I think there is nothing in the General's paper that you will regret printing."[9]

Ripley's twenty-page article, "The Civil War in America, by the Comte de Paris," was printed as a letter to the editor as he proposed and appeared in the August 1874 issue of *Blackwood's Edinburgh Magazine.* As usual for that era, the magazine did not list Ripley as the author but attributed it to "A General Officer of the Late Confederate Army." Despite Lawley's and Blackwood's editing, the article is verbose and has awkward sentence structure. Some of Ripley's opinions and beliefs, though not uncommon for that era, would be considered "politically incorrect" today.

Ripley ridiculed the Comte's role in the war, as he served only a few months "as an aide-de-camp to General M'Clellan [sic] in his operations before Richmond, which resulted in the expulsion of the Federal Armies from Virginia. With them went the Comte de Paris." The count returned to Europe and described "the battle of the seven days as a successful and victorious change of base." Actually, these battles lost General McClellan his command, as he was driven, with great losses in men, artillery, munitions, and matériel, from every position "for thirty or forty miles to the protection of his fleet."

Nearly ten years after the end of the war, Ripley resolutely defended the South. He vigorously attacked the Comte's premise that "the foundation of despotism in America was prevented by the victory of Federal arms," which indicated to Ripley the Comte's "absolute ignorance of the real causes of the war." Ripley claimed inaccuracies and errors were on every page and correctly refuted the Comte's assertion that Lincoln had received a majority of the votes in the election of 1860. In fact, Ripley charged, he had received "barely two-fifths" of the popular vote and "a fraction of American society proceeded to seize and administer the government, [and] found the despotism which has ever since reigned at Washington."

Ripley claimed the citizens of South Carolina, believing there to be "no protection from the impending despotism of the Radical party . . . passed the *Ordnance of Secession,* which was respectfully communicated to the Federal authorities. Propositions were immediately made for the speedy and amicable adjustment of all questions relating to finance, public property, fortifications, and administration." The U.S. government met the action of the state "first by shuffling delays, and then by threats of coercion."

Ripley mistakenly believed that Virginia, "the largest and most influential of the Southern States," seceded after the Federal government "dispatched a fleet and troops" to coerce South Carolina. In fact, Virginia did not secede until after the bombardment of Fort Sumter and President Lincoln's call for those states that had not seceded to raise seventy-five thousand militiamen to suppress the rebellion.

Ripley briefly discussed the constitutionality of secession, remarking that the issue had been "considered and expounded to exhaustion, and opinions still remain divided; but the victorious Federals have never been so confident of the legality of their acts as to bring to trial any one of the so-called rebels for treason."

Much to Ripley's disgust, the Comte described states' rights as a "fatal doctrine." Ripley argued that a return to states' rights was "the only hope for the restoration of a tolerable state of affairs in the South" and would also put an end to the Radical Republicans' "schemes of plunder and oppression." Ripley believed that the Comte's inability to understand states' rights caused him to condemn those officers who religiously believed that it was their duty to fight for their respective states against an oppressive government in Washington.

Ripley objected vehemently to the Comte's justification and praise of John Brown's actions at Harpers Ferry. According to Ripley, "During and since the war this felon has been honored as a martyr; and his case stands as a notorious example of the perversion of the first principles of civilized society."

Ripley argued that the Comte based "all statements, arguments, descriptions, and conclusions on Northern sources," thus displaying his "ignorance of his subject." Ripley had "no intention of discussing the abstract right or wrong of the institution of slavery." He admitted that there were instances of slaves being "mistreated by unworthy persons with cruel severity" but maintained that time and progress had remedied this situation. He also contended, "the slaves, connected by a common interest, lived on the best of terms with their masters, and when the struggle came, were quite ready to assist the cause of the South in any way. No attempts at insurrection occurred throughout the length and breadth of the Confederacy during the four long years of agonizing strife. Hardly an instance of outrage on the part of the Negroes is recorded."

Ripley acknowledged that the African American "has received personal license. Political liberty he has not, for he is the abject slave and tool of the Northern Radical faction. While the [Southern] whites have been degraded, the slaves have not risen." Ripley argued that Northern men regarded blacks with aversion and only tolerated them "as an instrument of defeating and oppressing political opponents." Failure of the Radical Congress to pass the civil rights bill, "aimed at enforcing the social equality of the Negroes in Northern as well as Southern society," proved the insincerity of the Radical Republicans toward African Americans.

Ripley agreed with the Comte's claim that "the existence of slavery in the South prevented the settlement of Southern lands by immigrants from Europe and therefore gained immunity from an element which has pervaded the Northern States; the continued introduction into American society of multitudes of the lower order of emigrants from various countries in Europe." This foreign vote "was a marketable commodity amongst professional politicians, who plundered it not only for themselves, but for a host of their followers. The South was happy in the absence of this avalanche of corruption and infamy." Partly as a result, wrote Ripley, "the South remained for a long period Conservative and only demanded that they should be let alone in their local affairs."

Ripley contended that the causes of the war had been a problem for many years before the conflict. As early as 1835, politicians in the North began to look for strength "from the Abolitionists, and a combination of political factions coalesced with ultra-Abolitionists under the name of Republicans." When the Republicans "nominated Mr. Lincoln for the Presidency in 1860 they adopted the principles of the Abolitionists to secure their support. As a result, a fraction of American society pledged to violate the sacred stipulations of the Constitution under which America had progressed and prospered for eighty years."

Ripley claimed that Southerners were "denounced as wrong-doers and criminals, and threatened with subversion of their institutions." As a result they tried to "free themselves from the section of the Union that threatened and maligned them." Ripley defended the South and believed that the seceding states were justified in leaving the Union: "They sought and demanded no advantage; they took no steps against the interests or powers of those who chose to remain under the Federal compact. Believing it was better to separate in peace than to dwell together in anger, the Secession was declared and attempted."

Ripley anticipated that the "Royal author" in succeeding chapters "will undoubtedly assert, in common with the Northern editors of the period, that the Southern people commenced hostilities when they reduced Fort Sumter." Ripley countered, "This fort lay within the limits of South Carolina and its Federal commander," Major Robert Anderson, while negotiations were pending "committed an act of war by destroying public property at [Fort Moultrie] and assumed an attitude of defiance against State authorities." Even then nothing was attempted against Anderson, and he was undisturbed until it was officially announced that "a fleet of men-of-war and transports was off the coast to commence the work of coercion." In response to these threats, "Southern leaders could no longer delay. With inefficient and improvised means, they proceeded to reduce the fort defiantly occupied by its Federal commander. It was not hard to do." Major Anderson "succumbed after thirty hours' cannonade and bombardment." Ripley claimed the Federals made "a noisy, but harmless resistance" but did not mention his role in restoring Fort Moultrie, in the bombardment of Fort Sumter, or in Sumter's reconstruction following the Union withdrawal.

As interpreted by Ripley, "the shambling and miserable defense of Fort Sumter was lauded as an act of heroism. Unhappily, appeals to passion succeeded where those to reason had failed; and the whole strength of twenty-four million people was brought out to crush one-third their number. The war ended in 1865, the Southern armies unable to withstand the overwhelming masses brought against them. It was a triumph of the despotism of a fraction of American society which rules with unmitigated severity and injustice to this day."

Ripley concluded that "the work will remain a partisan history, written by a Royal Prince who was an intruder in a stranger's quarrel with which he had no concern." Ripley doubted any good would come to the American people by the publication of the Comte's work. He believed "the course of time would overthrow the despotic rule of the Radical Party. Even now the best men of all parties are striving to soften the asperities and enmities left by the war and would forget, if they could, the fatal mistakes which led to it." As for President Grant, Ripley stated that all "are weary of the atrocious and disgraceful corruption which has existed under . . . his administration."[10]

On October 27, 1874, buoyed by the publication of his "letter to the editor," Ripley submitted another manuscript for *Blackwood's* consideration. He enclosed a note to John Blackwood explaining that the story concerned the adventures of a friend that occurred at the close of the "American War." The tale took place on board a steamer with "conversations" inserted in a few places. Ripley suggested that if the story was too long it could be easily divided into two parts and proudly informed Blackwood that he had heard from his friends in America regarding his rebuttal of the Comte de Paris's history: "My friends like it amazingly. However they are of course all good old Rebels."

In early November, Ripley wrote to Blackwood requesting three or four copies of the August issue featuring his article "for friends in America who wish to get & keep the article." Ten days later Ripley received the issues and, probably to his surprise, was billed for the requested copies. When forwarding his payment on November 23, he complained that he had not received an answer regarding his recently submitted manuscript. In December, still not having received a response, Ripley wrote, "As it [the manuscript] appears to be of no use to you, will you kindly return it. It will save me the labor of rewriting from the notes." With a trace of sarcasm, he added, "I enclose eighteen pence in postage stamps. Please accept my apologies for having troubled you." A note added in Blackwood's offices to this letter indicates that his "book" was returned on December 19.[11]

Undeterred by this rejection, Ripley submitted his twenty-nine-page article to the *Southern Magazine,* and it was accepted. As Ripley had suggested to John Blackwood, his article appeared in two installments, July and August 1875. The tale, entitled the "The Last Confederate Flag on the Atlantic," describes the activities of a Confederate naval party that leaves Richmond in February 1865. They are under orders to leave the Confederacy "to gain the high seas." In this allegedly true story, the final objective of this party of sixteen is not mentioned, and the lieutenant in command is not identified. Ripley presented the story in the style of an adventure novel, occasionally featuring conversations, some rather humorous, between characters in the appropriate vernacular.

In the story, the party travels overland from Richmond northeast to the Chesapeake Bay. By a stealthily executed and bloodless ruse, the Confederates capture a schooner and its cargo bound from Baltimore for Norfolk and Charleston. Off Fort Monroe, the lieutenant bluffs his way through an inspection of the schooner by a Union boarding party and gains clearance from Chesapeake Bay into the Atlantic. Although hampered by heavy seas and a lack of nautical instruments and ocean charts, the Confederates continue on, headed for the West Indies. Along the way they seize another Yankee ship's cargo but parole the crew. On April 18 they anchor at Salt Key, the quarantine station for Nassau. While in port the lieutenant arranges for the sale of his prize cargo to a former blockade-runner. Ripley's fourteen-page first installment ends when the senior British naval officer allow the Confederates four days in port to complete necessary repairs.[12]

Ripley's second installment begins on April 23, 1865, with the Confederates transferring the captured prize cargo to the former blockade-runner's ship. Unaware that Lee has surrendered at Appomattox, they on-load ammunition and a deck cannon for future seizures. They then capture, plunder, and burn a Yankee whaler, the *Hope*. Following this they seize the *Daniel Webster*, whose captain argues unsuccessfully that the war is over and his ship should be spared. After looting the ship, they run it "full sail" onto a reef. The *Hope* and *Daniel Webster*'s crews are uninjured and safely paroled. However, the Rebels suspend further activity until the captain's claim that the war is over can be verified.

The story describes in great detail the crew's adventures in the Caribbean while they await news of the war and the delivery of their prize money. The Confederates soon receive catastrophic news. Robert E. Lee has indeed surrendered, the Confederacy has collapsed, and the former blockade-runner has taken all their prize money. Sailing on, the lieutenant and his crew reach Haiti, only to discover the nation in the throes of a violent revolution, "plundering and burning as the Federals exhibited in their conquering march through Georgia and the Carolinas." The lieutenant observes that Haiti "was in decay, filth and squalor were predominant." More Caribbean adventures follow with stops in Jamaica and Grand Cayman before most of the crew board ships for England.

As Ripley neared the conclusion of his adventure tale, he discussed blockade running in the Bahamas, and presented his evaluation of Confederate, British, and French war policies. He first derided the early Confederate policy of withholding cotton from the European market as "stupid." Pursued in the belief that it would force England and France to recognize the Confederacy, the policy "utterly failed." Ripley realized that after Great Britain had satisfied "the popular cry for abolition," its government would be reluctant to come to the aid of a country "whose avowed policy was the perpetuation of slavery." Ripley also believed the British had "no way of knowing what interference might lead to and British ministries have for a good many years preferred cheap and brief hostilities with weak powers rather than undertake anything like a great war for expediency or principle. France would do nothing without Great Britain, and the rest of the world had little interest in the matter." Springing from his perpetual readiness to speak his mind regardless of the consequences, Ripley's candid criticism of British policy may have influenced *Blackwood's* not to publish the piece.[13]

CHAPTER 32

An Eventful 1875

Return of the 54th Massachusetts Volunteer Infantry Flag

Ripley's nearly ten grievous years of self-imposed exile, tragic personal crises, and economic ruin intensified his loathing of the Radical Republican administration. Ripley did not renounce his U.S. citizenship but waited expectantly for the demise of the Republican Party. Ripley began to believe the tide was turning against the Republicans when in November 1874 the state of Massachusetts elected a Democrat, William Gaston, to the office of governor. When Ripley learned of Gaston's election, he responded quickly to what he thought was a repudiation of Radical Republican policies. Ripley probably did not know that Gaston's election resulted from his support for the repeal of the state's prohibition law, leaving the matter to be determined at the local level. After the law was repealed, Gaston lost his reelection bid in November 1875.[1]

On January 12, 1875, Ripley wrote to the governor of Massachusetts and forwarded the Regimental Colors of the 54th Massachusetts Volunteers. Ripley claimed that the garrison of Battery Wagner, being under his command in Charleston, seized the colors during the assault on the night of July 18, 1863. He added, "Since the close of the Civil War in America I have generally been absent from the country, and have seen with regret the failure of expedients attempted to restore peace and content to the Southern States." Ripley believed a "less embittered state" now existed and thought it was his duty to promote the "oblivion of the animosities which led to the war."

Ripley asserted that the flag exemplified the "gallant conduct of men like Shaw, Putnam, and the other sons of Massachusetts [who] sealed their devotion to their cause with their lives." Ripley believed the custodians of the flag "should be the authorities of the State served by these gallant men, and I therefore transmit the flag to your Excellency." Ripley shipped the flag and his letter to "an old friend," Lewis Carr, in New York City. By February 23 Carr had received Ripley's package and sent it to C. F. Adams Jr., son of the U.S. ambassador to Britain. Carr asked Adams to contact the governor and present the flag and letter to him.[2]

An interesting story circulated in Massachusetts after the war when the flagstaff, minus the 54th Regiment's flag, was returned to the state and its Republican governor, John A. Andrew. Boston newspapers, the *Herald* and the *Daily Globe*, reported that after the assault on Battery Wagner, members of the 54th Regiment carried off the remaining fragments of their flag as personal trophies. The state issued a replacement flag, which was attached to the original staff and placed in Doric Hall at the State House. The Herald reported that, in reality, during the bloody assault on Wagner, Sergeant William H. Carney reached the parapet and planted the regiment's flag. However, "a daring rebel seized it and in the darkness and struggle the flag was torn from the staff." The staff remained in possession of the regiment, and Ripley reported that the flag was later found in a "ditch in front of the battery."

The *Herald* article indicated that "Capt. Fielder, a staff officer in the southern army, carried off the captured ensign." The captain took the flag to Charleston, where it remained until the city was evacuated in February 1865. "Capt. Fielder" was in fact Captain Henry Wemyss Feilden of Beauregard's staff. In England, sometime after the war, Feilden presented the flag to Ripley. The *Daily Globe* disclosed, "Endeavors were made by friends of the regiment to secure its return, but its custodian refused to give it up. General Ripley made a solemn resolve never to restore the flag until a Democrat should be elected Governor of Massachusetts. He waited ten years, and upon Gov. Gaston's election," returned the flag.

Feilden and Ripley were not close during the war, but in England they evidently became more socially connected. In 1920 Feilden annotated some of his letters written during the war. In a letter dated September 25, 1864, Feilden referred to Ripley as an "old scoundrel, . . . and a worse old dog does not hold a position of importance in the Confederacy." His annotation indicated that his opinion of Ripley had changed remarkably. Feilden acknowledged getting to know "old Rip well when he was afterwards in quasi-exile, and many a dinner we had together in London. He was a most amusing old Reprobate, and really a splendid officer, but drank like a proverbial fish."[3]

On March 5 Governor Gaston sent the flag and Ripley's letter to the legislature for their disposition and recommended placing the flag in Doric Hall along with the staff from which the regimental flag was torn. Gaston asked the legislature to express their "appreciation of the generous courtesy of Gen. Ripley in returning the flag." By March 24 a resolution to that effect passed both houses of the legislature. A week later the governor wrote to Ripley, "Please accept my thanks for your courtesy in returning the flag, [and] for the just tribute which you have rendered to the brave men who served their country with so much credit to themselves and so much honor to the State."[4]

Chief of Chinese Defense

Even though his income from civil engineer William Hope's projects was now supplemented by payments received for his magazine articles, Ripley continued to search for a more stable position and regular salary. In 1875 two individuals met with Ripley on separate occasions and later reported their extraordinary conversations. Ripley made assertions that must have some basis in fact.

In the 1870s former commander Hunter Davidson of the Confederate States Provisional Navy obtained a position with the Argentine government. Davidson tried to recruit other ex-Confederates, then living in England, for employment in Argentina. On January 18, 1875, Davidson wrote to General G. T. Beauregard stating that he had just spent much of the day with Ripley and that they had dined together. Ripley told Davidson that he had just been appointed to the command of the "Northern defenses of China" and would be leaving shortly with his staff for that destination. Davidson did not mention whether he had offered Ripley a position in Argentina.[5]

The second instance occurred on June 3, 1875, when F. A. K. W. von Oppen, the liege and London agent for Colt Firearms, wrote to the home office in Hartford. He claimed that Edgar T. Welles of the Gatling Gun Company told him that Ripley "had been nominated Chief of the Chinese Defense." Von Oppen arranged a meeting with Ripley, who admitted that "his appointment was not yet certain" but that he thought a decision would be made in two or three months. If appointed, Ripley planned to proceed to China via the United States. In America, Ripley intended to call on Colt Firearms and the Gatling Gun Company. Ripley took copies of Welles's various Gatling gun pamphlets and spoke very highly of Colt's new army pistol. Von Oppen claimed that Ripley "spoke very friendly of General Franklin as having been his school fellow at West Point."

The Colt Firearms Company had dealt with the Chinese since 1869 when, through their London houses, they filled orders for pistols and proposed selling fifty thousand rifles to the Chinese government. Colt's business interest picked up in June 1875 when director Franklin responded to von Oppen's report on Chinese trade. Franklin hoped to be able to do "something in the way of pistol trade with the Chinese, but the poor style of arms they require renders it nearly impossible to deal with them." A month later Colt's agent reported that Firth & Company was sending samples of breech-loading rifles to China with "tenders for their supply." On July 6 von Oppen and Welles visited Firth & Company and the "China merchants."

The astounding offer Ripley apparently received to become the chief of Chinese defense may have resulted from his long-standing acquaintance with General Franklin, Colt's Firearms Company, and their dealings with the Chinese. Clearly, the position in China never materialized and would be added to Ripley's list of failed opportunities. It could only have been worse if Ripley had been offered but declined a position with Davidson in Argentina.[6]

The Stonewall Jackson Monument

On October 26, 1875, the *Richmond Daily Dispatch* heralded the dedication of "England's Gift to the Old Dominion." The event would feature the unveiling of a bronze statue of General Thomas J. "Stonewall" Jackson by the renowned

General Thomas J. "Stonewall" Jackson Monument, Richmond, Virginia. British sculptor John H. Foley consulted Ripley regarding Jackson's appearance. Author's photograph.

British sculptor John H. Foley. A procession of survivors of the Stonewall Brigade, other veterans, civic societies, and citizens would "welcome the first sight of the statue." Governor Kemper was to preside at the unveiling and the distinguished Reverend Dr. M. D. Hoge, a personal friend of Jackson's, would be "orator of the day." Businesses were closed, and "an illumination and fireworks" were to be held that night.[7]

Early in the war a significant number of British papers, pamphlets, and books favoring the Confederacy appeared in circulation. One of the strong pro-Confederates was Alexander James Beresford-Hope, a man of considerable wealth and culture, who served as a member of Parliament from 1841 to 1852, and from 1859 to 1861. Beresford-Hope presented three lectures, which were printed separately in 1861 and then combined and published together a year later as *The American Disruption*. Beresford-Hope believed that Confederate independence was in Britain's best interest and continued to support the South despite his opposition to the "abominable institution of slavery."

The British followed the progress of the war closely, and no Confederate general received more attention and tributes than Thomas J. "Stonewall" Jackson. His death on May 10, 1863, prompted outpourings of pity and sympathy. The *Times* of London compared Jackson's death to that of Lord Nelson at Trafalgar and called him "one of the most consummate generals that this century has produced."

Following Jackson's death, the Confederate propaganda newspaper in London, the *Index,* announced a proposal to "raise a subscription in England for the erection in the Confederate States of A BRITISH MONUMENT to this gallant man." Sixteen prominent Confederate sympathizers formed a committee to manage the "British Jackson Monumental Fund" with Beresford-Hope serving as treasurer. The group commissioned Foley, the eminent Irish-born sculptor, to create the statue based on a recent photograph. By the end of August 1863, more than £600 had been contributed and work began soon after. In October 1865 Benjamin Moran at his post in the U.S. Legation angrily noted, "These rogues are up to all kinds of tricks. They have the name of 'Mr. B. Moran' as a subscriber to the Stonewall Jackson Statue Fund. The amount being one pound." Some members of the legation pretended to believe that "it was me and so do the rebels."[8]

There were many delays in the casting "caused by the sculptor's desire for perfection, other commissions competing for his time, and his increasingly ill health." Foley was "a very conscientious and fastidious workman consulting his friends as to his designs, and altering them continually in course of execution." On March 5, 1874, Ripley wrote to General Bradley T. Johnson, stating that Charles K. Prioleau had informed him Johnson wanted the statue "transported home to Virginia."

At the request of Beresford-Hope, Ripley went to see Foley and gave him a photo of a Jackson painting Johnson had recently sent him. Ripley claimed, "Foley's first attempt, being modeled after the old humbugging photos, was a failure." Ripley believed this second photo was a better likeness of Jackson than the images with which Foley had been working. Ripley offered to help the sculptor and informed Johnson that "the other day he sent for me to take a look." Ripley arranged for Frank Lawley to go with him and they noted, "there is a very great improvement, though not now as good a likeness as we could wish, it is a likeness and a good statue."

Foley informed Ripley that the statue was to be in bronze and placed outdoors. Ripley believed "the work would look far better in marble" and cautioned Johnson to be careful it is not "<u>dwarfed</u>" by putting it on the capitol grounds. Ripley wanted, if possible, to "countermand the bronze, which will not be done for five or six months." Actually, Foley completed the statue soon after Ripley's visit in early March. The famed sculptor, who also designed the Seal of Confederate States of America, died on August 27, 1874.[9]

The *Alabama* Claims

Early in the war the Confederacy began the groundwork for a program in which Ripley would become entangled, at least by implication. The Confederate government appointed Lieutenant James D. Bulloch, formerly of the U.S. Navy, to be the purchasing agent charged with buying and arming ships in Europe for the proposed Confederate States Navy. Bulloch arrived at Liverpool, England on June 4, 1861, and began to engage the British shipbuilding industry. In June 1861 British shipbuilders embarked on the clandestine production of the commerce-raiders built to terrorize U.S. shipping. The first of these raiders was the *Oreto,* which was launched from Liverpool on March 22, 1862, and, as a Confederate raider, renamed the *Florida.*

Construction on *No. 290* began in August 1861, and on July 29, 1862, this most notorious raider was launched. Rechristened the *Alabama* and under the command of Captain Raphael Semmes, the *Alabama* wrought havoc among Northern merchant vessels. The last of the more famous raiders, the *Shenandoah,* was purchased from the British on September 20, 1864, and entered the war quite late. Nevertheless, in the north Pacific the *Shenandoah* destroyed thirty-eight whaling vessels and dispersed much of the American fleet.[10]

As early as February 1862, rumors reached Benjamin Moran at the U.S. Legation that a steamer, the *Oreto,* was being built in Liverpool for the Confederacy. Operating as the *Florida,* it would capture or destroy nearly seventy vessels. On April 7 Moran wrote that construction of a second Confederate raider, *No. 290,* was underway. Throughout 1862 Secretary of State William H. Seward and the U.S. minister to England, Charles F. Adams, protested the Confederate shipbuilding in Liverpool. On November 20, 1862, Adams demanded compensation from the British Foreign Office for "vessels destroyed by the British pirate *No. 290.*"

In March 1863 Moran wrote, "Lord Russell has written several dispatches to Mr. Adams, all of which are couched in a tone of studied insolence." He refused to "pay for the property of American citizens destroyed by the British pirate *No. 290.*" Undeterred, on November 22 Adams sent a long, argumentative dispatch to Russell, again claiming compensation for the property "destroyed by the English pirates, *No. 290* and *Oreto.*" In these protests, to closely associate the Confederate ships with the British, Adams and Moran always referred to them by their British "construction names."[11]

Following the war, the Republican-controlled administration increased pressure on the British to compensate the United States for its maritime losses suffered at the hands of the *Florida, Shenandoah,* and *Alabama.* Advocates and the press on both sides of the Atlantic argued over the merit and extent of these damages termed the "*Alabama* Claims." In April 1867 Moran discussed a dispatch from Washington that he described as being "by no means friendly.... This is ugly and may lead to war." A month later Moran described a dispatch from Secretary of State Seward as being "very ugly and shows an evident disposition to quarrel with England. In talking of it, Mr. Adams condemned the policy, as his mission was peace, and if Congress should war on the Alabama Claims as Mr. Seward seemed to think, he would resign and go home."[12]

Charles F. Adams did return to the United States in June 1868, and Reverdy Johnson replaced him as ambassador to England. In an attempt to solve the claims dilemma, Johnson worked diligently with the British foreign secretary, Lord Clarendon, to write the Johnson-Clarendon treaty, which the Senate in April 1869 overwhelmingly defeated. As vitriolic accusations raged against England, Senator Charles Sumner, Republican of Massachusetts, demanded even harsher monetary penalties against the British for additional "indirect claims," which increased Great Britain's "penalty" to over $2 billion. With these demands, Sumner attempted to force Great Britain to cede all or part of Canada to the United States and drive the British out of North America. Adams believed this demand "of reparation was an insult and a humiliation" to England. To solve the crisis, the two countries formed a commission to study the issue, and on May 7, 1871, they signed the Treaty of Washington. The new British representatives expressed "the regret felt by her Majesty's government for the escape of the *Alabama* and other vessels from British ports, and for depredations committed by those vessels." However, the American indirect claims remained in the treaty and were to be arbitrated at Geneva.

A board of five arbitrators—one each from Great Britain, the United States, Italy, Switzerland, and Brazil—were to determine the amount of the settlement. The British press seized on the indirect claims issue, labeling the Americans "imbeciles and fools." The general public seethed at the possibility of war over the unfair American demands, which would lead to "national degradation and financial ruin."

Meeting at Geneva in May 1872, Charles Adams represented the United States on the five-member arbitration tribunal. Adams, who never believed in the merit of the indirect claims, peremptorily removed them all to save the negotiations. The arbitration tribunal dissolved on September 14 after awarding the United States $15.5 million in damages but nothing for the indirect claims.[13]

There are no letters or papers documenting Ripley's position on the *Alabama* Claims. However, given his loathing of the Radical Republicans, he doubtless saw it as an example of their outrageous excesses and most likely he would have sided with the British.

Two years after the claims were completely settled, Benjamin Moran entered in his diary on August 11, 1874, "Mr. W. Frank, the American detective, . . . called to see if I could get from His Majesty's War Office a memoir of our forts which the Rebel General Roswell Ripley furnished His Majesty's Government." Submission of the "memoir" allegedly occurred when Ripley thought that war was likely over the claims. "I doubted the release of the paper," Moran wrote, "[and] said we could not apply officially for it, but I would try it privately." He continued, "Ripley is a treacherous fellow to act in this way." The legation's secretary offered no further comments or information regarding the document Ripley supposedly gave the British.[14]

Two years later, on May 11, 1876, accusations of Ripley's involvement with the British War Office resurfaced. J. R. Lee-Bellasyse of Brighton, with whom Ripley had communicated in regard to the mysterious Colonel Middleton Biddulph legal dispute, reappeared. Bellasyse claimed that when Ripley returned the Massachusetts battle flag, a British newspaper published a copy of Ripley's letter to the governor. Bellasyse had just recently found the old newspaper article and disparaged Ripley's sincerity and intentions in returning the flag. Bellasyse wrote to the governor of Massachusetts and sent copies of his letter to "leading journals" in the United States. Bellasyse asserted that in March 1872, at the height of the *Alabama* Claims dispute, "General Ripley wrote a long letter to our War Office, giving them all the information he possessed as regards the defenses of America, pointing out the best places to land troops, what support might be expected from the South, and sketching out a plan of our entire campaign."

Bellasyse stated that this information was published anonymously in a pamphlet for circulation among Ripley's friends. He claimed Ripley gave him a copy of the pamphlet but cautioned him "not to let any Yanks get hold of it." Bellasyse maintained that the War Office acknowledged Ripley's communication and thanked him for it. He concluded that Ripley was a traitor because he betrayed "his country to a foreign power." Ripley would have argued that with the Radical Republicans still in power, the United States was not his country, and he was still at war against it.

In closing his letter to the governor, Bellasyse described his relationship with Ripley and included a newspaper paragraph from the January 1875 issue of the *London Cosmopolitan:* "General Ripley, who skillfully defended Charleston during the American War, has been appointed to a command in the Chinese army with a salary of £5,000 a year." Bellasyse sarcastically added that Ripley did not get the position and happily referred to his bankruptcy.

The Massachusetts Archives preserved Ripley's letter accompanying the return of the flag, but no record of correspondence between Bellasyse and Governor Gaston exists. The archives index contains no references to Mr. J. R. Lee-Bellasyse. As a result, the details of the Ripley-Bellasyse relationship, as related to the governor, are forever lost. Somehow their relationship deteriorated, resulting in Bellasyse's profound enmity and vindictiveness. The government of Massachusetts valued the return of their flag and must not have been influenced by, nor did they keep, Bellasyse's bitter letter.[15]

There is circumstantial evidence but no proof that in 1872, at the height of the *Alabama* Claims crisis, Ripley may have provided the British War Office with information on U.S. defenses. Considering how deeply Ripley despised the

Republican administration in Washington, he may have viewed the *Alabama* Claims dispute as a chance to retaliate for the depredations committed against the South during the war and its postwar subjugation.

Three years had passed since the *Alabama* Claims crisis and Ripley saw the election in Massachusetts as a turning point. Thinking that political change was on the horizon, Ripley mellowed enough to return the regimental flag of the 54th Massachusetts.

CHAPTER 33

Ripley's "The Situation in America"

There is a dearth of information regarding Ripley's activities in 1876. On January 21 Ripley applied to the Court of Bankruptcy "to pass his examination." His balance sheet showed a debt of £9,056 and no assets. When adjudged bankrupt on March 5, 1869, Ripley's debt was £37,834. How this figure had been reduced is not known. The *Times* reported, "it appeared from the examination of the bankrupt that he was not engaged in any business. He had been trained as a soldier and had acted as a general in the Confederate Army. He was not possessed of any means and lived on money advanced by friends." The *Times* disclosed that Ripley, late of Gloucester Road, South Kensington was staying at the Royal Hotel on New Bridge Street.

With this move Ripley returned to living in hotels after his nearly three-year stay at 8 Stanhope Terrace, Gloucester Road. After 1875 all Stanhope Terrace addresses were renumbered and listed as part of Gloucester Road. Surprisingly, there were two No. 8 Stanhope Terrace addresses, one north of and the other south of No. 11, the Stanhope Arms Pub. Ripley never indicated at which of the two addresses he lived. The north No. 8 building no longer exists, but the south No. 8 is still standing and is now 103 Gloucester Road. In 1875 a saddler, George Martin, occupied this No. 8, and Ripley may have lived in a flat above Martin's establishment. Most likely, Ripley would have visited the pub just three doors from his No. 8. After all these years the Stanhope Arms is still a flourishing pub in the same building but now numbered 97 Gloucester Road.[1]

There is no record of Ripley's activities between February and December 1876. On November 30, 1876, Julia Ripley died in Ogdensburg at the home of her son-in-law, Judge Amaziah B. James. Sometime in December the self-exiled Confederate must have received news of his mother's death, but there is no record of how he received the news or his immediate response.[2]

Political events in the United States over the previous eight years certainly must have aroused Ripley's disgust. In 1876 Ripley's West Point classmate, President Ulysses S. Grant, completed his second term in office, his administration riddled with corruption. The first scandal, Black Friday of September 24, 1869, involved speculators attempting to corner the gold market, resulting in the financial ruin of many investors. During Grant's second presidential campaign of 1872, the next major scandal became public. Officers of Credit Mobilier skimmed huge profits from the federally subsidized Union Pacific Railroad, and the involvement

Stanhope Arms Pub, Gloucester Road. In continuous operation as a pub since around 1860, it was three doors from Ripley's flat, 1874–75. Photograph courtesy of Charles Priestley, London, American Civil War Roundtable, U.K.

of prominent Republicans further damaged Grant's administration. In 1874 Grant's secretary of the treasury resigned over a delinquent tax scandal in which he allowed his personally appointed tax agent to keep 50 percent of all taxes collected. In 1875 the newly appointed secretary of the treasury uncovered a scandal involving liquor distillers who diverted millions of dollars in liquor taxes to themselves. Finally, in 1876 it became known that the secretary of war had been receiving annual kickbacks from traders at Indian posts, but he resigned before he could be impeached.[3]

In June 1876 the Republican Party convened in Cincinnati and nominated Rutherford B. Hayes for president. The Democratic Party nominated the governor of New York, Samuel J. Tilden, and their platform pledged to replace the corrupt Grant administration with "honest, efficient government, and end the rapacity of carpetbag tyrannies" in the South. The backlash against the Grant administration's scandals and corruption gave Tilden the lead going into the final days of the election, and Hayes actually believed he had lost. Tilden did win the popular vote and was ahead in electoral votes, but the electoral votes of three states—South Carolina, Louisiana and Florida—were in dispute. Several months would pass before a congressional commission, appointed to study the situation, would announce the winner.[4]

In England, Ripley followed the election intently and began writing an article on the situation. In early December 1876 Ripley told Frank Lawley that he was "very anxious" to have his paper published in the February 1877 issue of *Blackwood's Magazine*. Lawley appealed to John Blackwood, claiming that Ripley would write a good article "with much more knowledge of detail than is usually possessed by English writers on American topics." Blackwood approved and agreed to publish Ripley's article in February.

On January 16 Ripley mailed his corrected proofs to Blackwood and asked to receive about "twenty copies to send to particular individuals in America." Three days later Ripley advised Blackwood he had received new information, which if approved would probably add a page to the article. Ripley mailed the corrected final proofs with his additions to the publisher on January 20.

Ripley believed that Tilden would be declared the winner but mentioned to Blackwood that he was concerned with the Democratic candidate's health. Ripley "ardently hoped that Tilden would keep his health and strength, and devote himself to his work. He is not young, but like all old politicians of any prominence, exceedingly tough. Besides, when so many people are anxious for a man to die, it is astonishing how long they hold on." Ripley believed his article would be important if it "helps keep the Americans up to their work and destroys the vicious system of rotation in office." As Ripley developed his essay, he explained the meaning of "rotation in office," which eventually would come to be known as "political patronage."[5]

In his article, entitled "The Situation in America," Ripley acknowledged that the British were not usually interested in American politics. Nevertheless, he claimed that how the situation was resolved could have serious consequences for the Western world but that there was enough time to resolve the dispute before it endangered peace. Ripley endeavored to explain the crisis and its cause, discussing political figures and events in early American history, as well as contemporary public figures, some of whom he knew personally. Interestingly, he doubted whether the men drafting the Constitution truly believed, as stated in the Declaration of Independence, that "all men are created equal." The framers of the Constitution must have distrusted the judgment of the masses of "equal whites" to elect the president, as they mandated that electors would choose the president and vice president. Over time the electors became "mere nominees in the hands of the party leaders." Ripley also faulted the system that could elect "a President unacceptable to the majority of the people," and the election of Lincoln verified his concern.[6]

Party officials who sought rewards from public funds, "for service rendered to the party, negatively influenced the destiny of the country." It soon became apparent that "buying votes with promises of places had certain inconveniences." There were only a limited number of positions available, but the number of applicants was infinite. In recounting the brief term of William Henry Harrison, Ripley, with his unusual sense of humor, wrote, "The rush for offices was so great, and the pertinacity of the applicants so annoying, that the estimable old soldier escaped his troubles by dying within two months of his inauguration." Harrison, during what little time he had in office, spent it "fending off an army of office seekers [and] the first floor of the White House was thick with job hunters." After General Zachary Taylor's election, "The rush for office was even greater than in Harrison's time, much to the disgust and annoyance of the fine old warrior." Ripley thought that Taylor, who also died in office, was a victim of the furor caused by these office seekers.[7]

Under the administrations of Democrats Franklin Pierce and James Buchanan, Ripley believed that the country enjoyed prosperity and sound currency and that "nothing could be desired, except that the people should be left alone." The Democrats' "most covetous and greedy place-hunters," Van Buren and his followers, left to form the Free Soil Party. The Free Soilers became more "venomous" when the Democrats returned to power without them. Many of the Whigs, now lacking a formal political party, joined these angry Free Soil former Democrats. Realizing they still were in a minority, the party courted the small group "of fanatical, odious, abolitionists and fanned the elements of disturbance in the Southern States."[8]

Ripley believed that all was well during the Pierce administration, but he minimized the effects of the Kansas–Nebraska Act of 1854. Viewing it as a compromise, Pierce firmly supported the bill allowing these two states, under the concept of popular sovereignty, to decide whether or not to permit slavery. In February 1854 opponents of the bill met in Wisconsin and formally organized the Republican Party. In Kansas the issue was bitterly contested, and following the violent encounters between Northern abolitionists and proslavery Missouri "Border ruffians," the state became known as "Bleeding Kansas." Ripley mentioned the "disturbances" in Kansas but attributed them to "a few thousand settlers from New England who were forming a territorial government from which . . . Southerners and their slaves were to be excluded."[9]

In his essay Ripley failed to mention that in 1856 the Democratic Party did not renominate Franklin Pierce but selected James Buchanan instead. Buchanan, who served as Pierce's ambassador to Great Britain, defeated the first Republican Party candidate, John C. Fremont. Ripley claimed that the Republican doctrine was "unacceptable to the Northern people, odious to the South and inaugurated a contest on sectional grounds." The Republicans "were defeated, but had fully adopted the abolitionists, and spared no means of exasperating the South."

Ripley wrote nothing about events during the Buchanan administration but commented on the developing divisions within the Democratic Party. Because of the previous successes of his party, Senator Stephen A. Douglas of Illinois "was clamorous for himself and his partisans; and as he could not be satisfied, he trafficked with the Republicans, broke up the Democratic Party and threw the election to Mr. Lincoln." Lincoln "and his faction were thoroughly detested in a large portion of the Union, disliked and disavowed by a strong minority in the remainder, and fell short of a popular majority by nearly one million votes." The three regional opposing candidates, Douglas, Breckinridge, and Bell, received 60 per cent of the votes in a losing effort.[10]

Immediately, South Carolina, "implicitly believing it to be her right, seceded," and the Gulf States of the Deep South soon followed. When Lincoln assumed office, "the Union had been dissolved, and the Border States were as good as gone." The Republican Party was unable to "reward its hungry partisans." Therefore, the Federal government went to war to "open a flood of public expenditure, to richly endow their friends and . . . buy up a portion of the needy or greedy opposition." The government "brought about hostilities in a manner to throw the onus on the seceders, who only asked to be let alone." The Republicans "shouted aloud for the preservation of the Union. The Constitution was thrown aside, a military despotism established, and the war begun." Ripley claimed that the "allurement of high military office brought numbers of professional politicians to their ranks." Benjamin Butler of Massachusetts was a prime example of a political general who "distinguished himself by being disgracefully beaten on every field . . . and by officially insulting his country-women." At the end of four years of war, "the Southern Confederacy succumbed from exhaustion," and the states that tried to "retain their Constitutional rights lay powerless at the feet of the Republican Party."[11]

Ripley admitted that if Lincoln had lived, he might have attempted to "restore the Constitution, and possibly could have controlled his Party." However, after Lincoln's assassination, his vice president, Andrew Johnson, a pro-Union Democrat, "odious to the South, commenced Reconstruction in as hostile a manner as the most venomous . . . Republican could desire." Evidently, Ripley did not know or ignored the fact that Johnson was in disfavor with the Radical Republicans for his "lenient" Reconstruction policy. Ultimately, the Republican-controlled Congress impeached and nearly convicted Johnson.

The former slaves, who had been emancipated "to punish the Southern whites," were used during Reconstruction to "secure and continue the power of the Republican Party." To facilitate this, Southern whites were "disenfranchised to permit the easy manipulation of votes." Northern "carpet-baggers" preyed on these powerless whites and with the aid of Federal troops, soon "appropriated all places of power." After several years, whites gradually regained power in some of the states in which blacks were in the minority. Nevertheless, in Louisiana, South Carolina, and Florida, Republicans still used the black majority to maintain control.[12]

General Ulysses Grant, "the successful Federal general of the civil war," succeeded President Andrew Johnson. Ripley, as one might expect, evaluated his former classmate's performance harshly. Grant graduated from the United States Military Academy "with a mediocre standing in his class, and entered the army as a subaltern of infantry." Grant served creditably in the war with Mexico and was brevetted captain, but his service after the war was "not so creditable," as "certain habits incompatible with military efficiency compelled him to leave the army." Ripley mistakenly believed that with the onset of the Civil War, Grant immediately reentered the army with the rank of brigadier general because of his "friendship of some of the political associates of the President." Ripley claimed that Grant "was often beaten during his military career, but achieved one of the most important Federal successes of the war with the capture of Vicksburg in 1863." Ripley tempered his praise of Grant's grand victory at Vicksburg by asserting that he completely outnumbered the Confederates and "was opposed by probably the weakest and most unfortunate of all the Confederate commanders." Ripley chose not to mention the name of the commander at Vicksburg—his old nemesis in Charleston, John C. Pemberton.

Following the victory at Vicksburg and later triumphs at Lookout Mountain and Missionary Ridge in Tennessee, Grant was promoted to lieutenant general and given command of all Union forces facing Robert E. Lee in Virginia. According to Ripley, "This happened at a time when the Federal Government had exhausted the list of generals at their disposal. . . . seven had been thrust aside in less than three years. The hope of winning through the skill of generals or good fighting of troops had been abandoned." The Union would now rely on "the lavish expenditure of overwhelming forces of men and material. General Grant had bravery . . . great tenacity of purpose, and wrote and spoke but little." Ripley thought this last characteristic might have been from the lack of ideas, but it saved him from the risk of "offending an exceedingly domineering and captious secretary of war," Edwin M. Stanton.

Ripley maintained that few, even among Grant's admirers, considered him "to be a scientific commander." Only one maxim of war, Ripley claimed, had been attributed to General Grant: "Keep pegging away." This "is not a bad maxim, nor is it entirely new. . . . it has often led to success, provided the supply of pegs is ample. Nevertheless, it does not particularly commend itself to the pegs of humanity who are to be expended." As Grant advanced against Lee, he "was beaten again and again, expended two fifths of his army in three weeks, nevertheless he kept pegging away." Some Federal officers complained bitterly of Grant's "frightful waste of his troops, or in the language of the camp, a longer butcher's bill." Finally, the "exhausted and outnumbered" forces under the command of Grant's "illustrious adversary," Robert E. Lee, were forced to surrender at Appomattox.[13]

As for Grant's presidency, Ripley acknowledged that the president was not a "bad sort of man" but sarcastically noted that he shared his good fortune with family and old army friends. These individuals got "the first news concerning opportunities for lucrative operations, appointments and control of contracts." Grant's generosity included a few old Confederates, who had been personal friends before the war, and "were willing to rat and embrace the faith of the Republican Party, got comfortable positions, with enough salary to keep the wolf from their doors."

By 1872, when the corruption in Washington became so glaring, some Republicans attempted to deny Grant a second term in office. These Republicans, who advocated reform in Washington and amnesty for the South, nominated Horace Greely to represent them. To combat this challenge, incumbent Republicans revived war issues and "the necessity of a great military President to keep the white Southrons in check." Grant could have been defeated, but the nomination of Horace Greely was unacceptable to a majority of voters "for though Mr. Greely was known to be an honest, well-intentioned man, he was *bizarre* to a degree . . . and had been mixed up in the advocacy of women's rights, socialism, and other absurdities."

Finally, Ripley focused on the disputed presidential election. His opinions are interesting but obviously reflect his fervent anti–Republican Party views. He placed much of the blame for the crisis on increasingly greedy politicians of both parties and their supporters seeking public appointments as a reward for party service. Ripley discussed the midterm elections of 1874 that resulted in the Democratic Party gaining a majority in the House of Representatives. He condemned the Federal response to Democratic Party victories in Louisiana state elections and the unseating of "certain members of the Legislature by Federal troops." When the newly elected Congress met in 1875 they investigated the conduct of public affairs and "discovered outrageous and disgraceful corruption." These findings ended any possibility of Grant seeking a third term. However, Grant's "friends were powerful enough to prevent the nomination of more prominent aspirants" and the convention nominated Rutherford B. Hayes, governor of Ohio. Republican Party managers blatantly revived Civil War issues and again electioneered by "waving the bloody shirt."

The Democratic Party platform stressed reform in government and "complete amnesty for the Southrons." Democratic candidate Samuel J. Tilden, "a gentleman of high character, with administrative ability and energy, had vigorously suppressed abuses and corruption in New York." All southern states were expected to vote for Tilden with the possible exceptions of Louisiana, South Carolina, and Florida.

These three contested states accounted for 19 electoral votes: Louisiana, with 8; South Carolina, with 7; and Florida, with 4. With them Tilden would have received 203 electoral votes to 166 for Hayes. As it was, Tilden had 184 untouchable electoral votes and any one of the three states would give Tilden the electoral victory. If these states' votes could be diverted from Tilden to Hayes, he would then have had 185 votes to 184 for Tilden. Ripley devoted the next eight pages to a thorough discussion of the Republican machinations employed to discredit and divert the electoral votes of the three closely contested Southern states.[14]

The issue still had not been decided when Ripley submitted his article. He did not know that the congressional commission consisted of fifteen members, five each from the House, Senate, and Supreme Court. He would have been dismayed to learn that it included five Republicans and five Democrats, plus two Republican and two Democratic-appointed justices and a supposedly "independent" fifth justice who had been appointed by Grant. Ripley offered different scenarios describing how the commission would reach its conclusion but had little doubt Tilden would be declared the winner, predicting, "If the present Administration enforces the inauguration of Mr. Hayes, it would bring speedy trouble." Happily, it seemed so utterly repugnant that it was unlikely to happen. Ripley presumed Tilden's presidency and eagerly anticipated his solemn pledge to reform the abuses of the U.S. government. Southerners "will have immediate relief from the great evils under which they have labored for the past ten years." They should be content with that and "exercise forbearance in the day of political triumph."[15]

Remarkably, at the end of his paper, Ripley concluded that the nation's troubles were due "almost entirely to the frequency of presidential elections and the methods resorted to for securing party success, rotation in office. A class of professional and venal politicians made . . . National policy and interests secondary to party aspirations and appropriated public offices as rewards for party service. Needy idlers plunged into party politics and . . . nearly seventy thousand Federal offices became coveted goods for at least one million of the most objectionable class of society. Agitation on one subject or another, increasing at each successive Presidential election, brought about civil war, and has kept large portions of the South under the most odious tyranny."

Ripley believed that to correct "rotation in office," government administrative office holders should be prohibited from contributing funds to a political party or participating in party activities. He also concluded that presidential elections should be held less often. Presidential elections held every four years caused "disgraceful frauds of immense magnitude, embittered Party animosities, arrayed one section of the country against the other, incited the most stupendous civil war known to history, and inflicted years of misery on the fairest portion of the land."

Illogically, Ripley feared that the current situation in America could bring about a renewal of the deadly struggle "in a greater intensity than before. If the Republican Party remains in power the danger is especially threatening. Their continued incumbency, in the face of a large popular majority against them . . . offers only the continued oppression of the Southern whites." However, he believed Tilden would probably be inaugurated. The Democrats and "their candidate are now pledged to Reform, and it undoubtedly will be required of them." Ripley concluded that to be settled peacefully, the succession to the presidency must definitely be decided within a month.

Soon after Blackwood's published Ripley's article, the congressional commission settled the crisis but undoubtedly not to Ripley's liking. Voting strictly on party lines the commission, eight to seven, awarded all contested electoral votes and the election to Hayes. The final electoral vote tally was Hayes 185, Tilden 184; however, Tilden carried the popular vote, 4,284,757 to 4,033,950 for Hayes.[16]

On March 5, 1877, now fully aware of the election's outcome, Ripley addressed a letter to John Blackwood. He was pleased to report that his article "has made quite a stir in America." As was the custom at the time, the magazine did not list Ripley as the author of "The Situation in America." Ripley claimed that in America the essay often had been "attributed to Lawley, which perhaps is well." Commenting on the election, Ripley wrote, "Mr. Hayes has got in, but he holds his place by virtue of an acknowledged fraud. As I thought when I wrote the article in February, there is trouble ahead. How it will work out is the question. Mr. Hayes must . . . abandon his party and deliver to punishment the very people who perpetrated the fraud." Ripley thought the House of Representatives, having declared Tilden the winner, made matters more "precarious." He believed the Democratic members would probably denounce the fraud "and suggest some kind of action. They are not going to rest quiet whatever reports may say. It is not a nice look out." He advised Blackwood "not to hold American securities without a continual watch of the times."

Ripley's dire predictions did not materialize. Tilden restrained his followers, and Hayes implemented the Compromise of 1877, which ended the military occupation of the South. Hayes promised to support genuine reconstruction of the South and add a Southern Democrat to his cabinet. In June 1877 Ripley would have approved of President Hayes's executive order banning U.S. government employees from participating in political activities, but Congress failed to act on Hayes's attempts to reform civil service.[17]

Buoyed by the successful publication of his treatise on the political situation in America, Ripley met with Frank Lawley to plan future literary efforts. On February 25, 1877, Lawley wrote to John Blackwood praising Ripley's recently published essay and mentioned that he had suggested to Ripley that he write an article about John Paul Jones. Lawley claimed Ripley "is better acquainted with the life and exploits of Jones than any man I know. He will do it well I think." Lawley said he had planned to write about Jones, "who is an interesting hero in Leith and Edinburgh" but that his work prevented it. Lawley asked Blackwood whether the magazine had any interest in Ripley's proposed article.

On March 5 Ripley informed Blackwood that he had, at Frank Lawley's suggestion, written a seventeen-page article on the American naval hero. Ripley mailed his paper to Edinburgh two days later and claimed he had included "all that anybody would care to know about him." Ripley apparently began his article with an anecdote in Scottish dialect and asked Blackwood to check its authenticity and had included a "scrap or two of old sea doggerel, which if you don't like, please strike out." Ripley claimed that he "treated the subject rather lightly, for although Paul was a very remarkable man, he was not by any means of the very highest class of heroes."[18]

On April 14 Ripley expressed concern that he had not heard from the magazine in over a month. He notified the publication that he was sailing for America on the eighteenth or nineteenth and that if *Blackwood's* planned to publish his article, it should send Francis Lawley the proof sheets for corrections. If the article was unacceptable, "kindly send the M.S. to Mr. Lawley at your earliest convenience." On July 4 Lawley wrote to the editor "on behalf of General Ripley, who is now in New York." Lawley asked whether he had received Ripley's "John Paul Jones" paper and whether was it suitable for publication. If the editor planned to reject the paper, Lawley asked him to return the manuscript, "As the General is in a position to find even a few guineas valuable." If returned, Lawley would submit the paper to some other magazine. About a week later, when Lawley learned the paper had been rejected and replied, he was "not surprised at your decision, for to say the truth, when he read it aloud to me in a hurried way, I did not at all think it well done." Regardless, Lawley planned to try elsewhere but was skeptical that another magazine would accept it. There is no evidence the article was ever published.[19]

On April 18 or 19, Ripley had indeed boarded the SS *Egypt* in Liverpool, bound for New York by way of Queenstown, Ireland. Ripley was listed among a number of salon passengers and arrived in New York City on April 30, 1877. It is not known why the ex-Confederate returned to New York at this time, and the trip is replete with conjecture and supposition. The total time he spent in the United States is unknown. It can be inferred that Ripley returned because of his mother's death in November 1876. During the freezing winter weather of upstate New York, burials were postponed until the spring thaw. Ripley certainly would have wanted to attend his mother's burial if at all possible. In his destitute condition, he also would have wanted to return if he was to receive any inheritance. Christopher Ripley's will has been preserved, and when he died in September 1851, Roswell and his sisters, Lucia and Laura, appeared in court to probate the will. Julia's will has not been found to determine whether Roswell appeared in court at that time, or confirm his presence in Ogdensburg in May 1877. However, he may have returned home for his mother's burial.[20]

Ripley probably stayed at the New York Hotel while he was in the city, having lodged there in the late 1850s while he marketed Adams's revolvers and dealt with the Robbins and Lawrence Company. An examination of the *New York Herald* in May and June 1877 found several of Ripley's friends listed as guests at the New York. On Saturday, May 19, General Gideon Pillow of Tennessee registered at the hotel. On June 18 General John S. Preston of South Carolina checked in, and on June 28 General James Conner of South Carolina arrived at the New York. On the same day, the former South Carolina governor Judge A. G. Magrath registered at the Westminster Hotel. Ripley had been in England for twelve years, and it is difficult to believe that these fellow Confederates would be in New York at the same time without contacting him. On June 11 Ripley's brother-in-law, Amaziah B. James, checked into the Fifth Avenue Hotel, possibly for a follow-up meeting regarding legal matters pertaining to Julia's death. No record has been found to confirm any of these possible meetings.

Knowing how strongly Ripley opposed the election of Hayes, he would have discussed the election if he met with the arriving Confederates. He previously mentioned that he thought Democrats would denounce the fraud and "suggest some kind of action." Unwisely, some Southern Democrats did threaten open rebellion rather than submit to "rank usurpation" of the presidency. Ripley would have participated in any action decided upon, but as previously mentioned, Tilden advocated restraint and the Democratic Party acted accordingly.[21]

Although *Blackwood's Magazine* rejected Ripley's "John Paul Jones" article, he continued to write for publication. He based his next literary effort on his role in defense of Charleston in 1863. This paper recounted the acrimonious controversy with General Beauregard and the engineer department over the fortification of Morris Island. His forty-three-page treatise, published in 1878, was based on his many months of correspondence with Beauregard's staff and entitled *Correspondence Relating to Fortification of Morris Island and Operations of Engineers*.[22]

An act of Congress on June 23, 1874, appropriated funds for the publication of *The War of the Rebellion: A Compilation of the Official Records of the Union and Confederate Armies*. This compilation would include all reports, letters, telegrams, and general orders from the war. Ripley may have traveled to Washington and gained access to the correspondence between Beauregard's staff and himself as government scribes were copying the material. These fourteen letters, endorsements, and interrogatories would later appear in the *Official Records,* series 1, volume 14, and volume 28, part 2. However, these documents were not printed as part of the *Official Records* until 1885 and 1890, respectively. In Ripley's article, the correspondence spans the months of May 1863 to January 1864. Obviously the documents did not bear the notations assigned in the *Official Records,* but the dates and content are the same. It seems unlikely Ripley saved copies of this material and transported it twice across the Atlantic Ocean to write it in New York.[23]

It is unclear why Ripley chose this time to disclose his frustration with the engineer department's "dilatory" efforts in fortifying Morris Island during the summer of 1863. Ripley's recent return of the 54th Massachusetts Infantry's flag may have focused attention on the regiment's ill-fated attack on Battery Wagner and created interest in the island's defense.

Ripley digressed from his main topic, Morris Island, and criticized the lack of progress on Battery Marshall at the eastern end of Sullivan's Island. He restated his criticisms of the chief engineer, Lieutenant Colonel David B. Harris, and his "inferior and oftentimes incompetent officers." He advocated a change in what he believed to be a failed system. On January 6, 1864, Beauregard ended this dispute and returned Ripley's paper "because the subject matter cannot legitimately enter into a communication from him to these Headquarters."[24]

Ripley's "Fortification of Morris Island Correspondence" was published in New York City in 1878. He may have remained in the United States to guide it to print and could have been in America for nearly one year. There is no evidence that he returned to Charleston during this time.

CHAPTER 34

Inventor

Ripley must have finally realized he could not support himself by his writing efforts. His success had been quite limited, and he had not achieved the acclaim accorded his *War with Mexico*. The full extent of his writings is not known, but in addition to his published and known rejected papers, he may have had other manuscripts rejected. There is no record of any payments Ripley received for his articles, but it is clear he did not earn enough money to keep him from being financially dependent on his English friends. He obviously would have concluded that he needed to capitalize on his other strengths and expertise. His education at West Point prepared him well for a military career, and he excelled as an artilleryman. As an artillery officer, Ripley would have been well aware of the inability of cannon to withstand the increasingly powerful charges used in attempts to improve their range. Ordnance and artillery officers began the process of banding barrels, hoping to prevent barrel bursts caused by these increased charges. Ripley would have known that improved metallurgical technology could increase the strength of cannon barrels. At West Point he graduated seventh in his class and ranked high in engineering, mathematics, geology/mineralogy, and chemistry. In addition, he gained a significant amount of knowledge and experience while in the arms-manufacturing industry before the war. These factors would play a significant role in Ripley's future endeavors.

It is not known when Ripley returned to England from his trip to America, but the first record of his return came in April 1878. While in New York, Ripley must have contacted William Harkness, who listed his occupation simply as "gas patents" in the 1880 New York City census. In early 1878, Harkness transmitted letters patent to Ripley for "Improvements In The Process And Apparatus For The Manufacture Of Gas For Heating And Other Purposes." On April 29, 1878, Ripley signed and sealed the specifications at the Office of the Commissioners of Patents. Ripley listed his address as 8 New Inn, Wych Street, Strand, which was that of his attorneys, Jenkins and Abbott, during his legal disputes with Greenwood & Batley. On May 23 the commissioners granted Patent No. 2069 to Roswell Sabine Ripley for this submission. Throughout the documentation for this and all future patents, Ripley used his adopted middle name, Sabine. Interpreting the inventors' technical language and condensing it into readable text has proved to be challenging.

Ripley's submission included three detailed pages of specifications and one page with three cross-sectional figures of the proposed machinery. The intended purpose of the machinery was to produce heating or other gasses by passing steam mixed with air through burning or incandescent coal, coke, or charcoal. The heating gas would be generated not only from the decomposition of the steam but also from the gases produced by the combustion of the coal or any other fuel. Ripley, after a detailed explanation of the process, concluded the specifications with six claims as to what Harkness's invention would accomplish.[1]

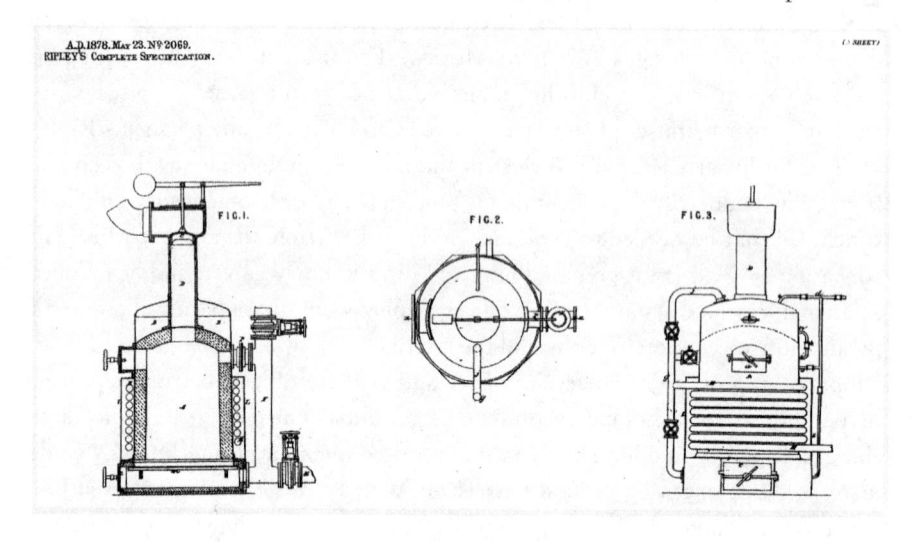

On December 13, 1878, Ripley visited the British Patent Office again, this time with two additional ideas forwarded to him by Harkness from New York. Ripley signed and submitted specifications for the two new patents, and on December 30 the office granted him Patent Nos. 5314 and 5315. The first, 5314, was for "Improvements In Puddling And In Furnaces, More Especially Such As Are Employed in Puddling." The process of "puddling" is the conversion of pig iron into wrought iron or steel by subjecting it to heat and frequent stirring in a furnace in the presence of oxidizing substances. Ripley submitted six pages of detailed specifications for this new and improved puddling furnace, plus three sheets of cross-sectional diagrams of the required machinery. Ripley intended to adapt the puddling furnace to gaseous fuel and would thereby improve the process he described in his previous gas retort Patent No. 2069.

The second of Ripley's year-end patents, 5315, contained the specifications for "Improvements In Gas Retorts, And In The Manufacture of Gas." This two-page document, with a single page of mechanical drawings, described the conversion of the retort in Patent 2069 into a compound type. The compound retort featured three circular compartments arranged in a triangular form and covered by two arched flues. Vaporizers in the retort converted the hydrocarbons into a vapor and prevented them from contacting the retort in a liquid form. These three patents originally were the work of Harkness and were complete when filed. Ripley's future patents were provisional and required the submission of a final version with specific claims to be evaluated by the patent office.[2]

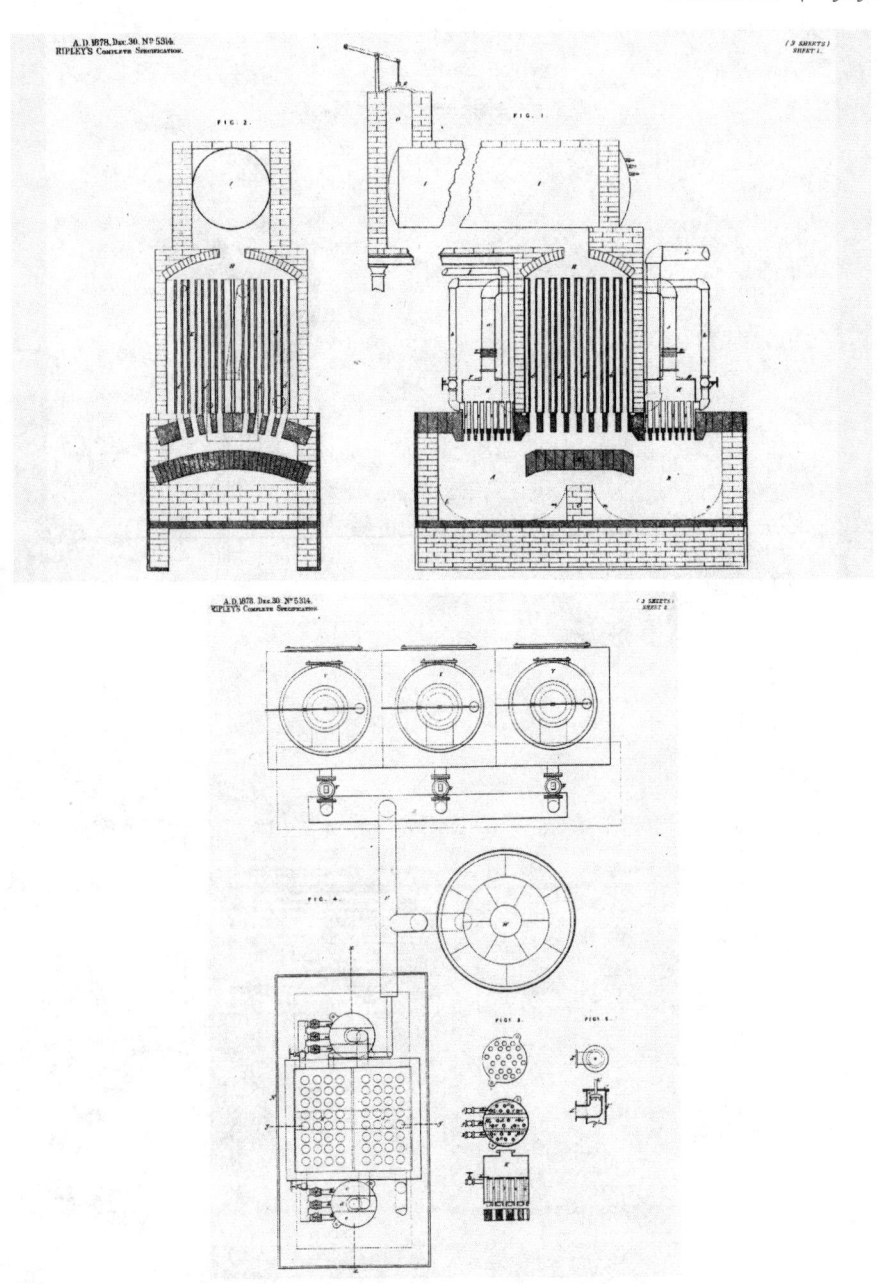

A.D. 1878. Dec. 30. Nº 5314.
RIPLEY'S Complete Specification.

(3 SHEETS)
SHEET 3.

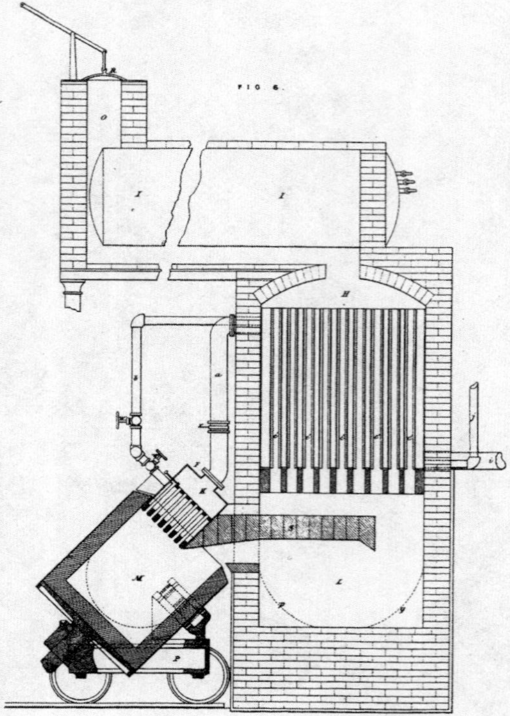

A.D. 1878. Dec. 30. Nº 5315.
RIPLEY'S Complete Specification.

(1 SHEET)

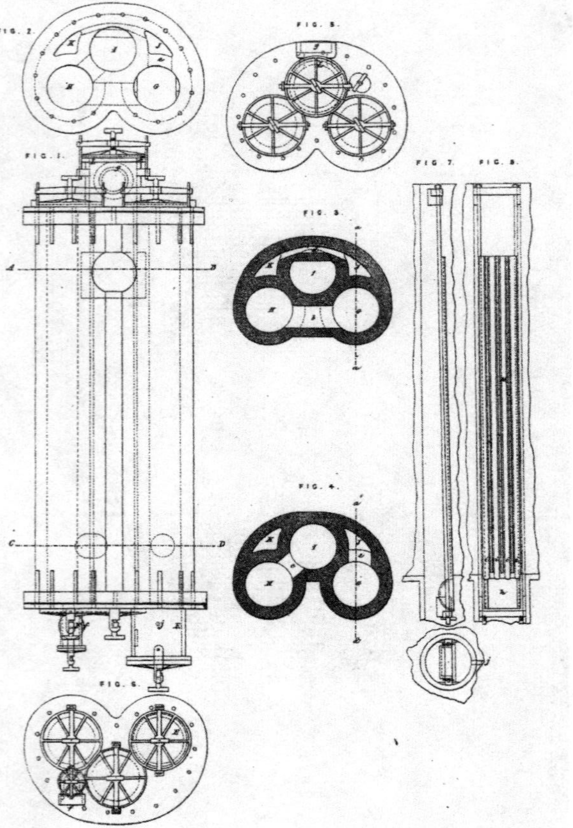

In April 1879 these three patents served as the basis for Ripley's ultimate goal, improvements in the manufacture of ordnance. In this endeavor Ripley collaborated with his long-time friend Lieutenant Colonel William Hope, V.C. After the Crimean War, while Hope served as military attaché to Lord Napier at The Hague, he was assigned to report on Dutch rifled guns. He became interested in metallurgy, especially in the strong and durable bronze the Dutch used in casting their cannon. Hope believed, although he had not learned the Dutch metallurgical secret, that he had discovered an analogous one. Hope would later serve with the 1st City of London Artillery, where his interest in ordnance continued to evolve.

Not only did Hope and Ripley have a close business relationship, but they also enjoyed a congenial social life. Beginning in 1867, William Hope leased the manor house at "Parsloes," an estate at Dagenham just east of London, where he raised a herd of shorthorn cattle. Hope's granddaughter, Margaret Hope, spent a good part of her childhood at the estate. During a March 1955 interview of descendants of Victoria Cross winners, Miss Hope recalled, "Many soldiers visited my Grandfather as he was very interested in designing guns . . . grandfather entertained Lord Napier and many distinguished visitors on the estate, one being an American general who had fought in the Civil War. The story was that he had a bullet embedded in his throat, as he spoke in such a deep and growling voice." Although Miss Hope did not remembered his name, the "distinguished visitor" was clearly Roswell Ripley. This interview is the only known account of Ripley's impaired speech, the result of his wound at Sharpsburg. The "bullet" possibly damaged Ripley's larynx as well as his recurrent laryngeal nerve. The embedded ball and fabric from his cravat, which some thought saved his life, probably caused scarring and chronic inflammation in his neck. Most likely, his life was spared because the ball was well spent when it struck him.

Unfortunately, a Hope family financial crisis in 1878 "due to grandfather's optimistic, but unfortunate speculations" caused the family to leave the estate. It is unclear whether the "family financial crisis" of 1878 was a factor in Hope joining forces with Ripley in their quest for improvements in ordnance.[3]

In the spring of 1879, Henry Clay Bull joined Ripley and Hope in their patent efforts. The introduction to this patent indicated that Ripley and Bull were staying at the Westminster Palace Hotel, while Hope listed his address as the Army and Navy Club, Pall Mall. On April 9, 1879, the three inventors filed provisional specifications at the Patent Office for "Improved Processes And Apparatus For Reducing, Melting, Purifying, And Otherwise Working Ores, Metals, Metalloids, And Similar Substances." The trio stated that their improved processes were designed for the manufacture of ordnance but could be used for other purposes. The provisional specifications filled approximately two and one-half pages and for some reason required a revision. William Hope returned to the Patent Office on October 7, 1879, with three pages of revised specifications.

William Hope, V.C., was a civil engineer who befriended and employed Ripley. In collaboration, they received patents for improved ordnance. Photograph courtesy of Ben Fellows, National Army Museum, U.K. Acc. No. Ref. 1974.07. 83.

Their improvements attempted to produce a "perfect quality of iron or steel for the manufacture of a cannon of power never before attained." Instead of using a coal-fired furnace, their "improved process" would use a furnace heated by gas, as described in Ripley's three earlier patents.

In a rather disjointed and confusing paragraph, the inventors described the process in two parts. The first part of the "new process" involved blasting heated gases through ore in a furnace at a high temperature to "produce a pure metal." The trio designed the furnace with two or more receptacles for molten metal between the fire and the chimney, and included detailed paragraphs describing the structure and workings of the furnace.

The second part of their "improved process" consisted of rotating "molten metals in a heated mould at a high velocity, the higher the better, which compresses the metals by centrifugal force." The metal after purification would not be cast in the "usual manner" but would be "worked up to a very high density and strength by being rotated while liquid, until it solidifies and sinks to a dull red heat." After the rotation the whole mass was to be cooled down as rapidly as possible to a solid state.

The inventors believed their process was especially applicable to the manufacture of ordnance from the molten metal stage. In the case of ordnance, rotating a gun while in one liquid mass of chemically pure iron or steel under a steady, continuous, circular pressure would result in a stronger barrel. There would be no joints or welds, and as a result, "the maximum possible strength both longitudinal and transverse will be attained." They determined this would be an advantage over ordnance that had been forged or rolled in the solid stage. They envisioned their process could also be used for the manufacture of armor plate or railway wheels.

In conclusion, they claimed current furnaces could be modified to use their "improved process." But if a new furnace was to be built, Ripley and his associates advocated the type of furnace then employed in the manufacture of "Rodman" guns but emphasized that it was most important to add "our improvements." The inventors did not submit mechanical drawings with these specifications. The patent commissioners granted the trio Patent No. 1421 dated April 9, 1879, the date of the original submission.

In October, just two weeks after Hope submitted the revised specifications for Patent No. 1421, the inventors realized that there were additional design problems with the furnace. Ripley and Hope returned to the patent office on October 27, 1879, with three pages of new, provisional specifications for two modifications of their original furnace design. For unknown reasons Henry Clay Bull was no longer with the group and never reappeared as part of the design team. Possibly he was a factor in the problem with the prototype.

Ripley and Hope found that in constructing the furnace as previously described, "the flame was not well placed [and] too much heat escaped up the chimney." In their new plans the flame was moved to just outside the "melting pot" and thereby maintained heat on the melting metal for an unlimited time. The inventors described in detail how the gas flames should be repositioned relative to the purifying/melting pot. The two revised provisional submissions differed in construction details, but the inventors claimed both furnaces worked on the same principle.[4]

Ripley and Hope did not return to the patent office with the final specifications for the revisions of Patent No. 1421 until April 21, 1880. The final revision of this patent would be designated Patent No. 4363 and was sealed in April 1880 but dated October 27, 1879, the day Hope and Ripley submitted the final revised plans. The final drafts covered four pages of detailed furnace mechanics for two "improved furnaces," accompanied by a page of mechanical drawings featuring three cross-sectional figures. Figures one and two were cross-sections of the first improved furnace; figure three was a cross-section of the second improved furnace.[5]

On May 1, 1879, concurrent with Hope and Ripley's patents relating to metallurgical furnaces, Ripley submitted provisional specifications for "Improvements In The Treatment Of Illuminating Gas, And An Apparatus Therefore."

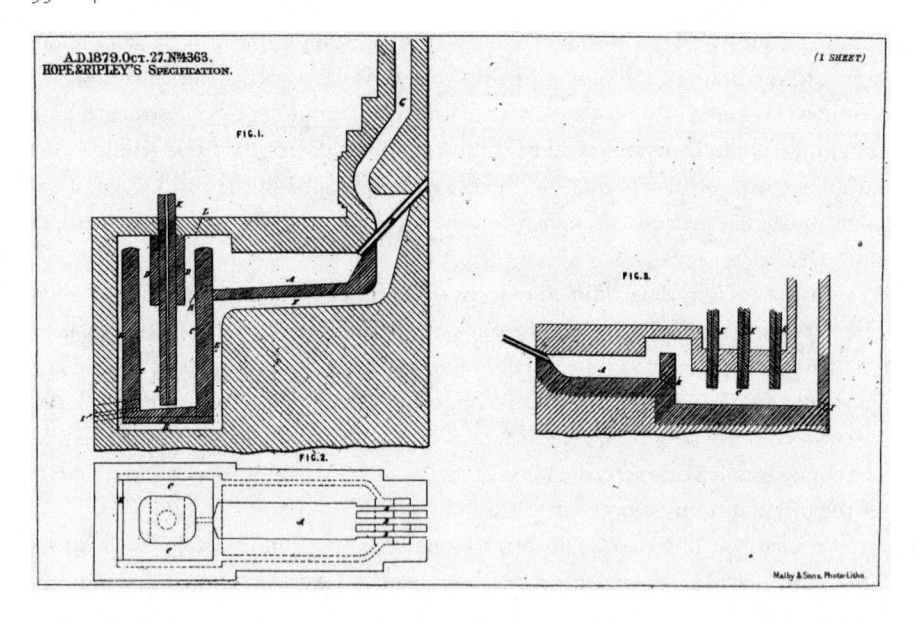

Ripley filed this one-page document after William Henry St. John, an engineer from Bay Shore, Long Island, forwarded his original work to England. As with the specifications forwarded to Ripley by Harkness, this document was also sent to Ripley's attorneys at 8 New Inn, Wych Street. Ripley claimed that "his correspondent," St. John, received Patent No. 2527 for this process on July 24, 1873. The title of this submission is somewhat misleading and does not at first appear to have any relationship to the preceding Ripley patents. However, a closer reading indicates that St. John's process of passing illuminating gas, or in this case, heating gas through a series of three separate chambers resulted in the removal of tar, naphthalene, a large quantity of sulfur compounds, and other impurities from the gas. This apparatus supposedly increased the volume of gas produced from a given amount of coal and contributed significantly to the efficiency of the metallurgical furnace.

On October 28, 1879, Ripley returned to the patent office with a final version of this submission. To the original document he added a "Description of the Drawings, in order that the invention may be most fully understood." Therefore, these two cross-sectional mechanical drawings were definitely the work of Ripley. The commissioners granted Patent No. 1733 for "Treating Illuminating Gas" to Ripley on May 1, 1879.[6]

On July 15, 1880, Hope and Ripley appeared once again at the patent office and presented provisional specifications for the most definitive of the patents relative to their ultimate goal: the production of ordnance. Hope was still residing at the Army and Navy Club; however, the introduction to this patent described

INVENTOR | 331

Roswell Sabine Ripley, residing at the Westminster Hotel, as a "late Major General in the Service of the Confederate States, and formerly Major in the United States Artillery." His fancied promotion, one that he, and even Beauregard at one time, believed he deserved, may have been an effort to give the specifications more credibility. Hope and Ripley entitled their submission "Improvements Relating To Ordnance And Firearms And Ammunition For The Same," for which they would be granted Patent No. 2923. The provisional specifications totaled eight and one-half pages and included two pages of cross-sectional drawings.

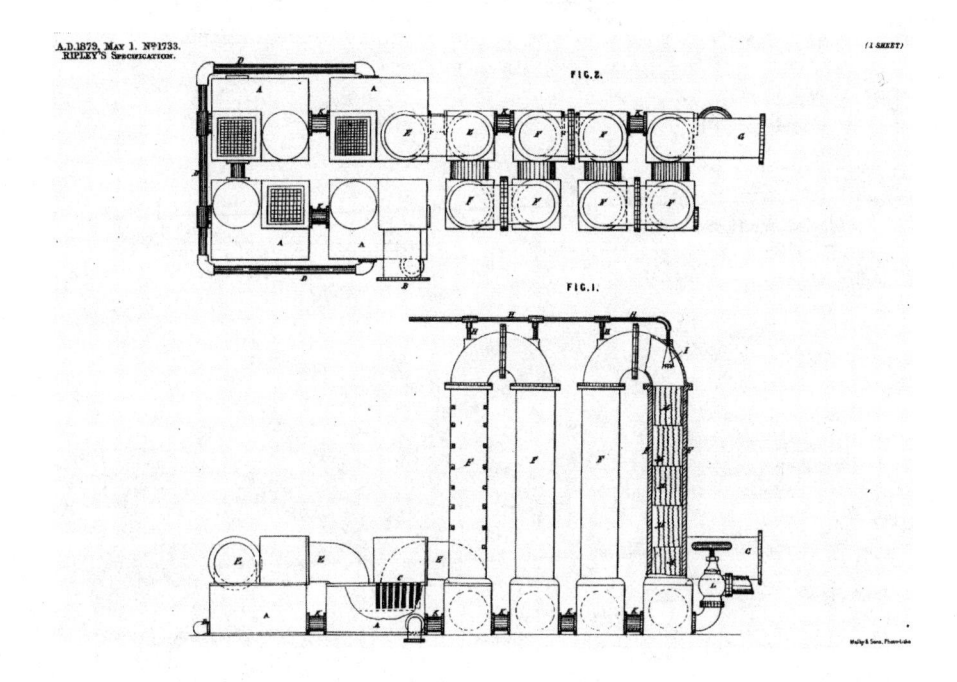

The inventors named their proposed cannon the "Hope" gun. Ripley and Hope intended their improved breech-loading cannon to resist the strains caused by "fired gunpowder and prevent dangerous waves of pressure in the cannon" and at the same time "convert the entire charge of gas within the gun." They also described "mechanisms of breech loading cannon, as well as rifling and boring cannon and small arms." Also included were methods of lubricating and self-cleaning the cannon and ejecting empty cartridge-cases. The inventors covered improved processes for "manufacturing cannon, jackets and steel tubes for cannon, and projectiles." As for ammunition, the patent included "cartridges, wads, and the ignition and combustion of gunpowder pellets." The goal was to "produce a perfect ballistic weapon of war."

Ripley and Hope's specifications began by referring to the first page of cross-sectional drawings in which they compared their approximately 6-ton cannon with that of a 38-ton Woolwich gun. Ripley and Hope directed attention to how significantly their cannon differed in form and proportion with the massive Woolwich cannon. They intended to increase the velocity of the fired projectiles, thereby increasing "the range, penetration, accuracy and flatness of trajectory of the guns." The "effective power of the gun for armor piercing and battering purposes depends directly upon the amount of powder converted into gas before the shot leaves the bore." Ripley believed it was most important to greatly increase "the feeble charges of powder presently used in all existing guns in every country of the world."

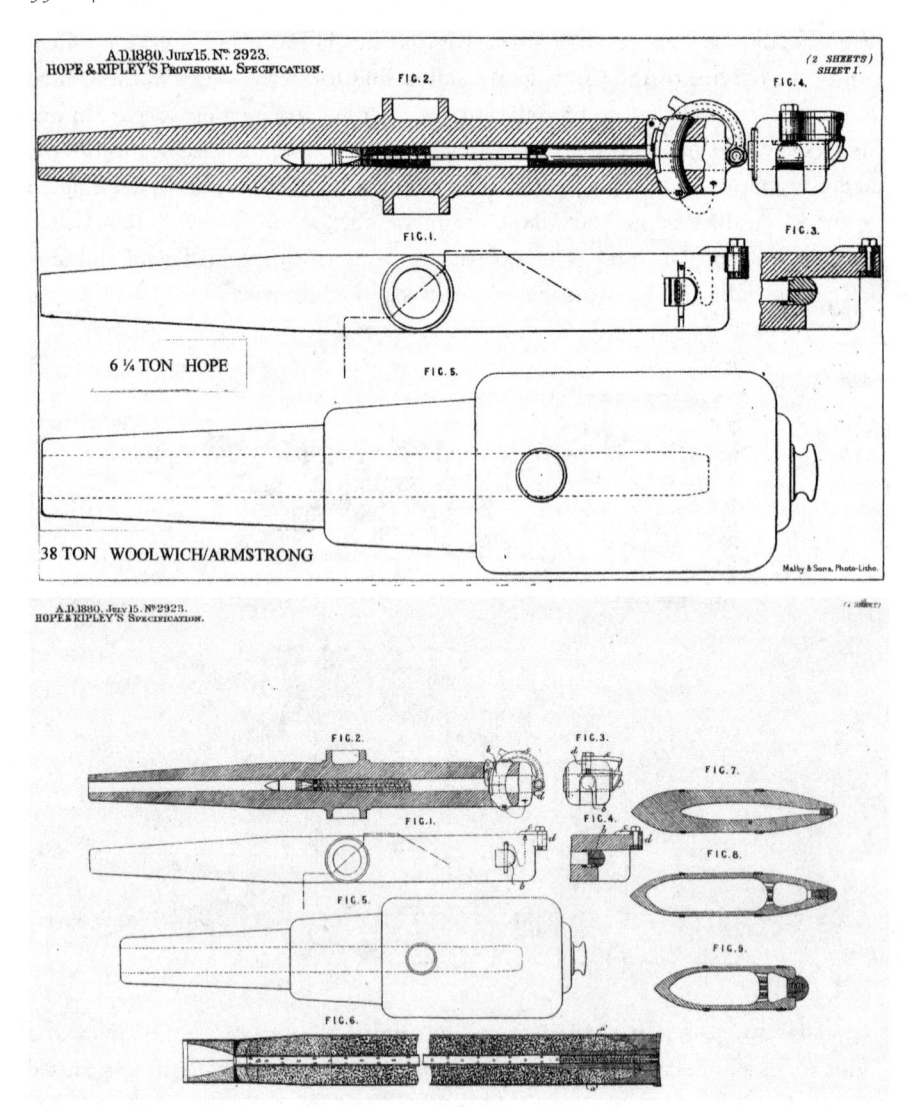

Ripley and Hope increased the length of the gun in the rear of the projectile, enabling the chamber to hold much more powder and thereby increasing the explosive power of the charge compared to existing guns. They did not propose increasing the length of the gun forward of the projectile but almost doubled the length of the projectile to achieve armor-piercing capability. They recommended using "quick burning gun powder" in the "unprecedentedly large powder chamber" to prevent the pressure inside the chamber from falling below a critical level.

In a unique modification, the charge would be ignited along its entire length. They believed increasing the charge in the current single-point ignition system resulted in a wave of pressure and caused either violent recoil or the barrel to burst. Ripley and Hope's solution involved placing the gunpowder in a "peculiar cartridge," made preferably of bronze or brass, through which a perforated tube ran the entire length. An "igniter" charge would send an intense flame as rapidly as possible along the perforated tube, insuring simultaneous ignition and combustion and thus preventing waves of pressure.

They described another innovation as the "Hope Breech Loading System," which featured an improved empty-cartridge ejector, actuated when the breechblock was opened. The inventors' specifications included a detailed description of how to modify the breech system for twin guns mounted in ships' turrets. The charge could be ignited by either an ordinary friction tube or by electricity through a vent cut into the breechblock, but only when "the breechblock is home."

Ripley and Hope devoted several paragraphs to the techniques involved in rifling cannon. They also recommended distributing the recoil over a larger surface by making the trunnions nearly the full size of the gun but with enough room to assure free elevation and depression of the barrel. The larger trunnion size, they maintained, would decrease the strain on the gun carriage. In addition, the trunnions were to be "bored out" rather than made solid to decrease the total weight of the gun.

Several pages described various shells for armor piercing and siege battering. For use against infantry they recommended a canister shell Hope had invented in 1856. Critical to the success of the cannon was their "patented metallurgical process to make guns and gun jackets." They believed this new process of casting cannon in one piece would give them a great advantage over older methods and prevent barrel bursts.

Ripley and Hope criticized the practice of casting cannon in successive layers of metal, termed coils or rings, and were especially critical of Woolwich and Armstrong guns. They claimed such guns "are the worst and are built on the same faulty principle," explaining that "in the deliberate defiance of the laws of nature and the teaching of science," these guns used a weaker coil of wrought iron over an inner core of steel. Sarcastically, Ripley wrote, "The authors of this system boast . . . they 'equalize the tension' throughout the wall of the gun. They do in fact accomplish this to a great extent, and consequently they succeed in bursting guns of maximum thickness with minimum charges of powder." Hope and Ripley did not return to the Patent Office with their final specifications for Patent No. 2923 until October 13, 1881, over a year after the first submission. Very few changes were noted and the inventors summarized their five major claims for the proposed cannon.[7]

Not totally satisfied with the patent No. 4363 for metallurgical furnaces and processes, dated October 27, 1879, Ripley appeared alone at the Patent Office on April 17, 1882. His provisional specifications of that date were followed on October 17 by the final submission. For this patent, "A Novel Method Of And Apparatus For Reducing And Purifying Metals Directly From Their Ores By Gaseous Fuel," Ripley was granted Patent No. 1831. Ripley enclosed two cross-sectional drawings of his "apparatus," or furnace, with his final two-page document. Ripley proposed a "novel method of treating metallic ores, by causing them, in suitable admixture and in a pulverized state, to be propelled along a tube into which inclined blowpipes project their flames, with the molten metal collected in reservoirs." From the reservoirs, molten metal "can be treated according to the product required, and iron may be treated directly for the manufacture of steel." Only a metallurgical engineer, well versed in the history of this technology, could evaluate Ripley's specifications and drawings."[8]

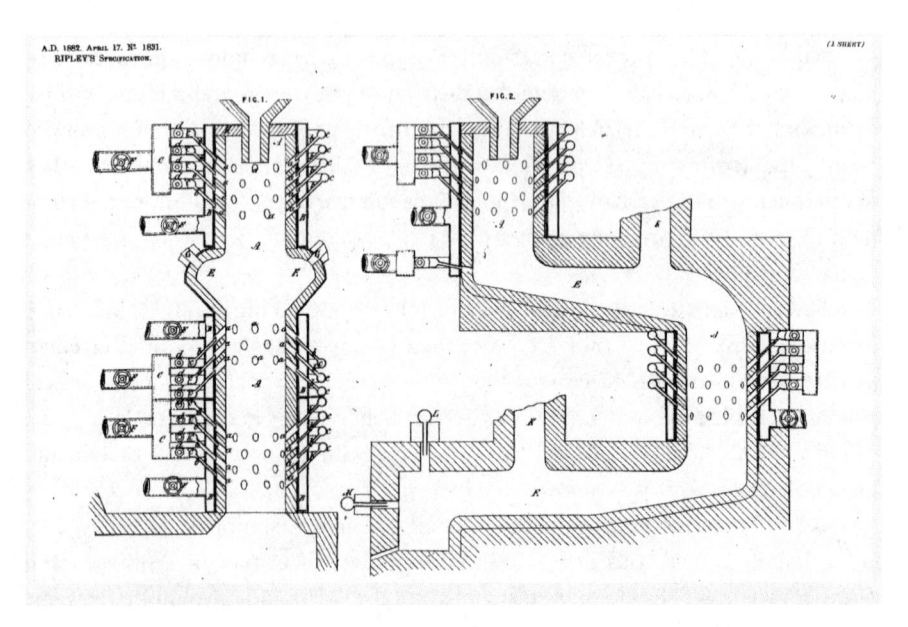

Ripley and Hope spent years attempting to improve metallurgical technology for the manufacture of ordnance. Hope claimed he acquired the metallurgical expertise necessary for these improvements as a military attaché in the Netherlands. He and Ripley submitted specifications and were granted patents to develop a gas-fired furnace to purify ores to be used for the manufacture of ordnance. Ultimately, the Patent Office awarded them a patent for ordnance, firearms, and ammunition. It is not known how Ripley and Hope financed their engineering and manufacturing processes. Ripley may have inherited money from his mother, or possibly during his trip to America he interested some of his friends in investing in his plans. William Hope also may have been able to recruit investors for their project. There are indications that prototype "Hope" cannons were cast at the immense steelworks of Jessop & Company at Sheffield.

The inventors also submitted their specifications for "Ordnance and Firearms and Ammunition for Same" to the French government, and on July 24, 1880, they were granted Patent No. 137,920 in France. Soon after, Hope and Ripley assigned their French patent to the Société des Fonderies et Forges de Terre-Noire. To what extent the inventors profited from their patent is not known.[9]

The Terre-Noire Foundries and Forges were a group of three foundries located in the cities of St. Etienne, Besseges, and La Voulte sur Rhone in southern France. The company no longer exists, and French military historian Pierre Lorain believes that the pertinent archives have long since been "destroyed by war or rats." Sometime after October 1882, Ripley left England for France, and several documents confirm Ripley's residence in St. Etienne and Paris in 1883 and 1884. Ripley would be returning to France, where nearly fifteen years before he tried to help thwart the Prussian advance on Paris. Once again his proficiency in French would be invaluable. It is likely Ripley worked with the foundry in St. Etienne and assisted in the French production of a "Hope" cannon.[10]

While at the St. Etienne foundry, Ripley sent provisional specifications for a breech-loading cannon and ammunition to Sydney Pitt in the London suburb of Sutton. It is not known why Ripley sent these specifications to Pitt; perhaps he was working with Hope. Pitt submitted the information to the British Patent Office for "Improvements in Breech Loading Cannon and Ammunition Therefore" on June 19, 1883. The introduction to this patent indicated that "Roswell Sabine Ripley, formerly an Officer of Artillery, of Charleston, South Carolina, U.S.A., temporarily residing at St. Etienne, France," sent the specifications to Pitt. The mention of Ripley being a resident of Charleston is interesting as it had been so long since he lived in the city, but it reaffirms Ripley's allegiance to the city and the South. The provisional specifications Ripley sent to Pitt were revisions of Patent No. 2923. On December 15, 1883, Pitt submitted the final specifications, which focused on an improved method of closing the cannon's breech, as well as different methods for igniting the unique elongated cartridge. These improved modifications received Patent No. 3042 and must have been solely the work of Ripley.[11]

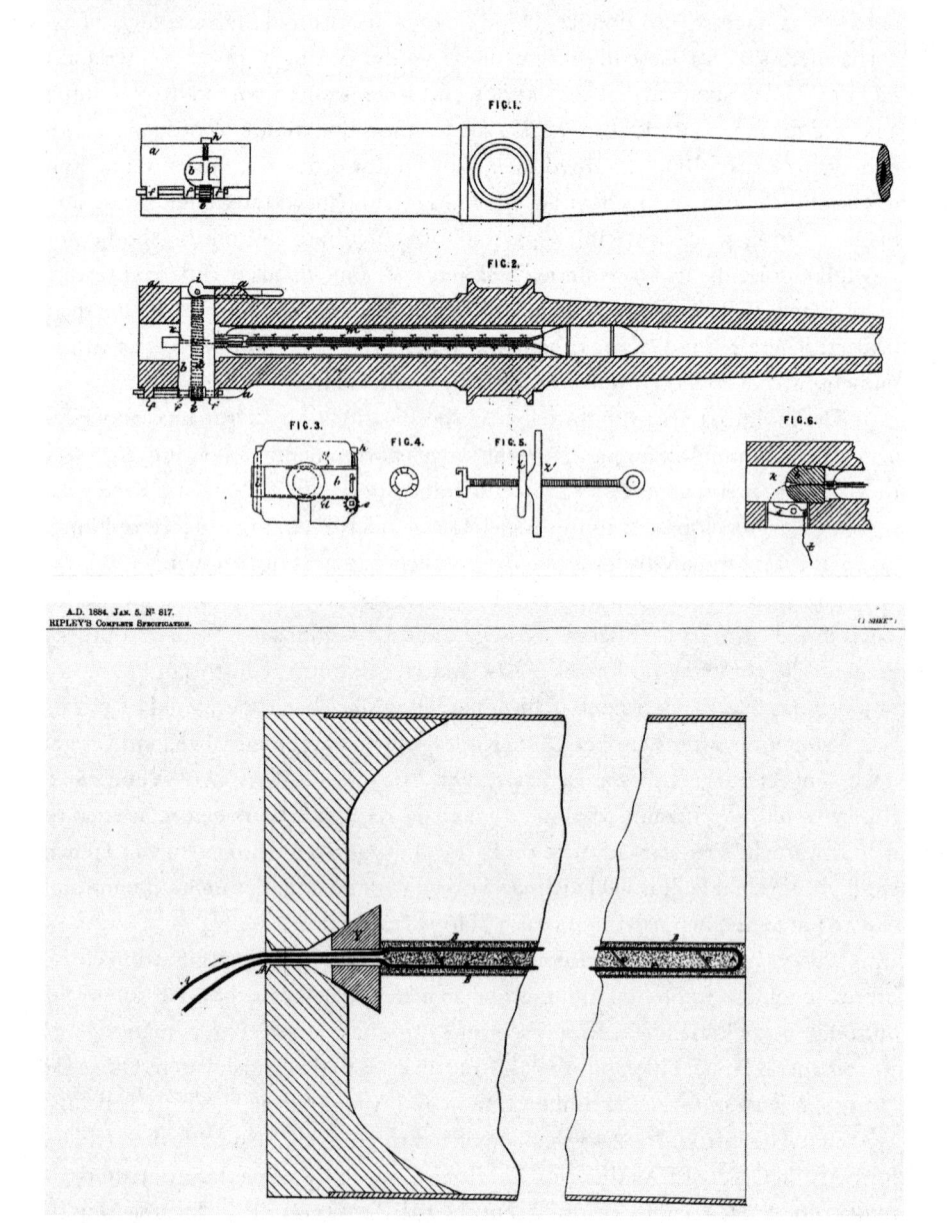

While Ripley was at St Etienne, the British director of artillery notified their Ordnance Committee of "a specification and other papers describing a new

(No Model.)

W. HOPE & R. S. RIPLEY.
CARTRIDGE FOR ORDNANCE.

No. 314,127. Patented Mar. 17, 1885.

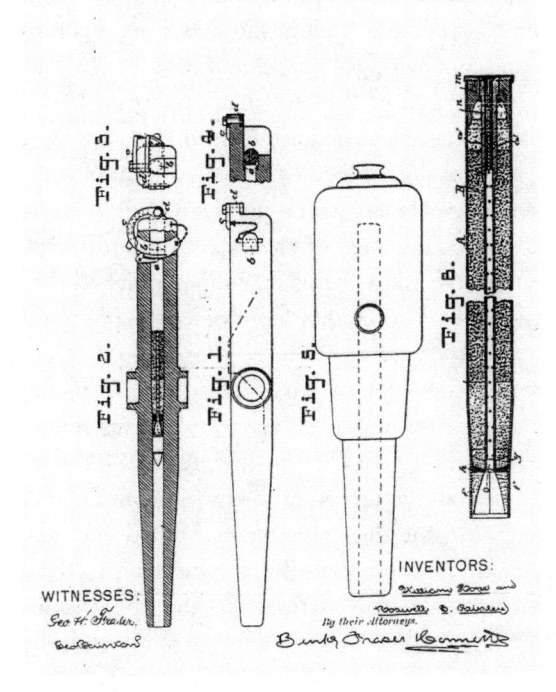

system of ordnance patented *No. 2923* by Lieut. Col. Hope and Major-General Ripley." On September 3, 1883, the British Ordnance Committee notified Hope that he would be given the opportunity of appearing before the committee, and on October 26 they examined Hope "on the subject of his proposed system of Ordnance." Although Hope agreed to receive nothing for the gun unless the government adopted it, the committee refused to test his gun after hearing negative testimony about it. Intent on expanding the protection for Patent No. 2923, after the inventors were awarded their French patent, they received Belgian Patent No. 64,672 on December 27, 1883; and on January 5, 1884, they filed a patent application, register Volume XXXII, No. 262, in Italy.[12]

While living in France, Ripley continued to work on improving ammunition for breech-loading cannon. On January 5, 1884, from St Etienne, he submitted his last known British patent while living in Europe. Through patent agents Carpmael & Company he entered provisional specifications for "Improvements In Ammunition For Breech Loading Cannon" and would be granted Patent No.

817. Once again Ripley listed his home as Charleston, "temporarily residing at St. Etienne, France." William Hope again was not involved and did not participate in the submission. Ripley claimed the two improvements were in the method of firing ammunition by electricity and preventing the explosive gas from escaping through an opening at the ignition point, thus dampening the explosive charge.

On April 22, 1884, Hope, in England, and Ripley, who now listed his residence as Paris, jointly filed a two-and-one-half-page application with the U.S. Patent Office covering the ammunition portion of British Patent No. 2923. Under the heading "Cartridge for Ordnance," one sheet detailed their unique cartridge, "comprised of a tubular brass case, which was provided with a perforated igniting tube, with the object of igniting the main charge throughout its length." The inventors claimed this decreased the lateral force of the explosion and recoil, minimized the possibility of a barrel burst, and achieved maximum initial velocity of the projectile. Although entered in April 1884, the patent office did not grant Patent No. 314,127 until March 17, 1885.[13]

In early May 1884, after nearly twenty years of self-imposed exile in Europe, Ripley traveled from Paris to the port city of Le Havre, where his stay in France ended. Now sixty-one years of age, he had spent the previous six years diligently attempting to develop a new and improved process for the production of ordnance—a remarkable effort after the disappointments he had endured. Although on occasion Ripley evidently drank heavily, his commitment to these years of rigorous, inventive effort counters any accusations that this impaired his responsibility or creativity.

During his last few years in Europe, Ripley must have done well financially, the result of his agreement with Terre-Noire Foundries and Forges. No longer destitute, he could afford to purchase a first-class ticket on the SS *Normandie*. He packed his possessions into three valises and sailed for New York. Surprisingly, on the ship's passenger manifest, Ripley listed his occupation as "U.S. Army." The SS *Normandie* arrived in New York City on May 14, 1884, and Ripley would spend his remaining days in the United States.[14]

CHAPTER 35

Return to America

When Ripley arrived at the Port of New York in May 1884, the nation was preparing for the coming presidential election, which may have played a part in his return. In 1875 Ripley returned the battle flag of the 54th Massachusetts Infantry because that state had elected a Democratic governor, and he saw this as a rebuke of the Radical Republicans. In 1884 Ripley would have been aware of the political issues in America. He must have believed that the demise of the Republicans in Washington and a national revitalization of the Democratic Party was close to fulfillment.

In 1880 President Rutherford B. Hayes kept his pledge not to seek a second term. The Republican convention, deadlocked after thirty-three ballots, finally nominated a compromise candidate, James A. Garfield of Ohio. That fall Garfield defeated Democrat Winfield Scott Hancock by less than ten thousand votes out of nearly nine million cast but won the electoral vote handily. Only four months after Garfield's inauguration, a disappointed Republican office seeker who was denied a diplomatic post mortally wounded the president, and Vice President Chester A. Arthur completed the remainder of Garfield's term. For years reformers had been calling for an end to the "spoils system," or patronage, as had Ripley in his article "The Situation in America." After Garfield's assassination, national sentiment spurred Congress into action. Passage of the Pendleton Act in 1883 started the modern civil service system. Because President Arthur supported the act and advocated governmental reform, the Republican Party refused to nominate him in 1884.

Ripley would have known about the divisions within the Republican Party and the narrow margins of victory in recent presidential elections. The Democratic Party was making progress, and the "bloody shirt" Radical Republicans were in disarray. More important, the Democrats now had a strong presidential candidate, Grover Cleveland. The former "honest and efficient" mayor of Buffalo, New York, had been overwhelmingly elected governor of the state in 1883. As governor, Cleveland turned down requests for patronage, insisted on appointments based on merit, and promoted and signed into law the state civil service bill. At the Democratic Party's convention in July, Cleveland easily won the nomination. Ripley would have strongly supported the Democrat, and with the overwhelming help of the Deep South, Cleveland defeated Republican candidate James G. Blaine in a close election.[1]

Finally back in New York City, Ripley gravitated to his favorite hotel, the New York. The *New York World* reported that he joined a group of former Union and Confederate officers "who distinguished themselves in that struggle" and made the hotel their headquarters. His fellow officers enjoyed Ripley's company as he was "a noted raconteur and had a stock of clever anecdotes about celebrated people ever at his command." The officers who either resided at the New York, or met there to dine and socialize, included Ripley's friend General John Newton, who was the New York commissioner of public works. A Virginian, Newton graduated second in his class at West Point in 1842, served with the U.S. Army Engineer Corps during the war, and retired as the army's chief engineer in 1886. Ripley and Newton saw action during the Seven Days and the Maryland Campaign. The New York Hotel group included General Thomas L. Clingman, a native of North Carolina. Clingman, a lawyer and former North Carolina senator, served as a colonel with the 25th North Carolina Infantry Regiment and later in 1863 as a brigadier general with Ripley in South Carolina. Another member of the group, General Gustavus W. Smith, was also in the West Point class of 1842 and served with the engineers during the Mexican War. Following his resignation from the army in 1854, Smith followed civil pursuits and from 1858 to 1861 served as the street commissioner of New York City. A native of Kentucky, Smith opposed the candidacy of Abraham Lincoln and supported an attempted Democratic "fusion" ticket in 1860. With the election of Lincoln and the start of the war, Smith resigned as street commissioner and in September 1861 was appointed a major general in the Confederate Army. Following the war, Smith returned to New York City.[2]

The New York Hotel, built at a cost of nearly $500,000, opened in 1844. At that time its location, far uptown at 721 Broadway (actually 715–722) between Washington Square and Waverly Place, was considered to be a "wild and perilous place." The six-story, two-hundred-room hotel was the first in New York to have hall bathrooms, and a salon with billiard tables provided entertainment for its guests. Always popular with Southerners, the New York was thought to have been the headquarters of Confederate spies during the war. Secret service agents were known to follow many of the hotel's Southern guests when they left the hotel.[3]

After arriving in New York, Ripley continued to work on his most recent British patent, No. 817, "Improvements in Ammunition for Breech Loading Cannon." Ripley had submitted the original work from France on January 5, 1884, and on October 4, 1884, still working through his agents Carpmael & Company in London, he filed the lengthier and more detailed complete specifications. Ripley submitted drawings of the truncated cone he designed to prevent the escape of the ignition gas and included a more detailed description of the electrical system. This system involved supplying a current through an insulated wire connected to a series of "fine platinum wires." The platinum wires were arranged along the

The New York Hotel, 715–722 Broadway, prior to 1880. Ripley's base of operations during the late 1850s, when he was a sales representative for Sharps Rifles, it became his postwar home with Union and Confederate officers after he returned from England. He died here following a stroke on March 29, 1887. Photographer unidentified. Courtesy of the New-York Historical Society, negative # 41061.

"axis of the cartridge," which was filled with fine-grained powder. The final patent was dated January 5, 1884, the original submission date.[4]

The 1884 *City of Charleston Yearbook* featured an article by Major Robert C. Gilchrist on the defense of Morris Island and Charleston Harbor, which later was published as a pamphlet. The author served with the Gist Guard Light Artillery along the southeast coast and in the defense of Charleston. Gilchrist believed the city was indebted for its defense to General Ripley "more than to any other man." Gilchrist praised Ripley's command of Fort Moultrie's artillery, especially his use of red-hot shot to set the barracks of Fort Sumter on fire, which compelled the fort to surrender. "What he accomplished with the limited material of war and the small force at his disposal was superhuman," wrote Gilchrist. "The success that crowned his efforts was his only reward."

As to who was at fault for the failure to fortify the southern end of Morris Island, Gilchrist recounted, "There were mutual recriminations and much 'bad-blood' between those who were thought to be responsible for the Federal success on 10 July." Gilchrest claimed that "the truth is General Beauregard did not believe an attack would be made by this route, and was firmly persuaded the enemy would again advance over James Island," as they did in 1862. Gilchrist defended Ripley's efforts to fortify the southern tip of the island against Union forces on Little Foley Island. Gilchrist placed the blame on Beauregard for undermining and impeding Ripley's efforts, which led to the attack across Light House Inlet, the siege of Battery Wagner, and ultimately its evacuation. At the conclusion of his fifty-five-page treatise, the author lauded Ripley "for erecting batteries along the shores of the inner harbor and within the city itself . . . by which the gallant defense was prolonged."[5]

Alfred Roman, Beauregard's friend and fellow Creole, served as a lieutenant colonel in the 18th Louisiana Volunteers until his horse was shot from under him at the Battle of Shiloh. Later that year he became Beauregard's aide and inspector-general during the general's second tour of duty in South Carolina. After the war Beauregard had attempted to write an account of his war experiences and accumulated numerous notes and material, but had written very little. Beauregard engaged Roman to organize this information and ghostwrite a two-volume history, *The Military Operations of General Beauregard,* published in 1884. Roman saw the deterioration of Beauregard and Ripley's relationship and barely mentioned Ripley in the book. He did not describe Ripley's role in restoring Fort Moultrie or his role in the bombardment of Fort Sumter. Roman briefly noted that Ripley was in command of Fort Sumter after Major Robert Anderson surrendered but gave no credit for Ripley's role in repairing and rearming the fort. Roman recounted the return of Beauregard to Charleston after his tours of duty in Virginia and the Western Theater. He contended that Beauregard, "at the suggestion of the leading men of the city, called for and obtained the services of Brigadier General R. S. Ripley." Roman described Ripley as a West Pointer, an officer of merit, quick, and intelligent. However, he was "erratic at times, and inclined to an exaggerated estimate of his own importance." Roman failed to mention that Beauregard and Ripley previously had worked well together and upon his return to Charleston Beauregard notified Adjutant General Cooper that he would be "pleased to have Ripley assigned to his command for the defense of Charleston."[6]

In late February 1885 Ripley received a letter from a Captain Ramsay. Most likely this was Captain William M. Ramsay, who served with Ripley as an engineer at Fort Pemberton. Ramsay inquired as to what Ripley remembered about the chief commissary of South Carolina, Major H. C. Guerin. On March 3 Ripley responded, "Guerin was a faithful and hard working fellow and did very well on the whole. . . . my recollections are very indistinct, as we certainly were never very bad off for subsistence in Charleston during the war." Ramsay asked Ripley whether he had seen Beauregard's recently published books and papers, to which Ripley answered that he had, saying, "They are very absurd, but I have something else to do and am too poor to spend time dressing up old corpses. Beauregard may blow as much as he likes against me."[7]

On March 17, 1885, the U.S. Patent Office granted Hope and Ripley Patent No. 314,127 describing improvements in Cartridge for Ordnance, which they originally submitted on April 22, 1884. The basis for this patent was the pair's British patent No. 2923, dated July 15, 1880, granted to them "or to our assignees, *La Cie Des Fonderies Et Forges De Terre-Noire, France.*" This final patent, with one exception, included all the additional patented improvements granted to British patent No. 2923 since July 1880. The only improvement not included was Ripley's British patent No. 817, which described an electrical system for firing the ignition cartridge. That patent could not be included because it was not finalized until October 1884, a date later than the original submission of Hope and Ripley's U.S. patent.[8]

The same day Hope and Ripley received their U.S. patent, the *New York World* published a conversation between one of their reporters and Ripley. The impetus for the interview, cited in a previous chapter, was the publication of a letter from Ripley to Governor Magrath of South Carolina. Dated December 25, 1864, the letter concerned Ripley's response to Sherman's invasion of South Carolina and the lack of adequate forces to defend the state. The interview focused on a postwar controversy between Jefferson Davis and General William T. Sherman. It seems that Sherman had alleged that South Carolina wanted to secede from the Confederacy and Davis planned to establish a dictatorship. All of this Ripley denied, stating that South Carolina never considered seceding: "That would have been ruin, indeed. Nor was there any fear that Mr. Davis would attempt a dictatorship. He is not the kind of man dictators are made of. . . . Mr. Davis would never have been given such power, nor could he have seized it. Gen. Sherman has found a mare's nest." Asked whether there were internecine troubles in the Confederate army, Ripley responded, "Well, Mr. Davis had a great ability in placing round pegs in square holes."

The interviewer questioned Ripley about the use of slaves for the defense of South Carolina. "I had long suggested that the Negroes be used as troops," he replied. "In the attack on Sumter they had shown themselves to be brave and cool under fire. I had several thousand of them in the earthworks and they actually sang while shot and shell hissed above them." The interviewer claimed the Confederates would have needed a regiment of white soldiers to guard every regiment of blacks, but Ripley strongly denied this assertion: "The Negro is not a coward. . . . it would have been easy to arouse an *esprit de corps.* Their new position and comparative responsibility would have flattered their vanity, and their habits of obedience would have made discipline easy. They fought well in the

Federal ranks." Ripley claimed that early in the war he "advocated the abolition of slavery. Get the credit with the world of abolishing slavery. If you don't abolish it, it will be done in spite of you." Ripley, when pressed why slaves were not used as soldiers, offered two reasons. The first was "sentimental. It seemed hardly the square thing that slaves with none of the rights as citizens, should be compelled to fight for those rights." Second, "the Negro was property, and property whose value would be less with a bullet through it." Even when Sherman invaded the state, we "could not have taken so radical a step as to put arms in the hands of the Negroes without the consent of the other states and the authority of Congress."[9]

In 1885, at the request of the mayor of Charleston, W. A. Courtenay, Ripley wrote his last published article, "Charleston and Its Defenses." Appearing as an appendix to the *City of Charleston, 1885 Yearbook,* this compact, twelve-page article primarily covered the period from December 1860 until the evacuation of Battery Wagner on September 9, 1863. Ripley feared his "memoranda on the fortifications of Charleston" was incomplete as it was "written entirely from memory." Although most of the credit for restoring Fort Moultrie had previously gone to Ripley, he did not mention himself in this regard. His description of the efforts to repair Fort Sumter after its evacuation was similarly bereft of self-acclaim, although he clearly was in command of the restoration. Ripley unselfishly credited General Beauregard with devising a system for fortifying the Carolina coast from Winyah Bay to Hilton Head, including Cole's Island, the Battery Islands, North and South Edisto, and the entrance to Port Royal Harbor. In early November 1861, Port Royal fell to an overwhelmingly strong Federal fleet, and Union forces established a foothold at Hilton Head. According to Ripley, in the little time available, Beauregard did all that could be done to defend Port Royal, and it would have been impossible to repel the Federal forces.

Regarding Robert E. Lee's replacement of Beauregard in the Department of South Carolina, Georgia and Florida, Ripley argued that General Lee realized the need to consolidate the coastal defenses, ordered the evacuation of smaller harbors, and advocated that only the defenses of "Georgetown, Charleston, and Savannah" should be maintained. In the *Official Records* Lee mentioned defending "the water approaches to Savannah and Charleston" but not Georgetown. According to Ripley, Lee considered the evacuation of Cole's Island but "after considerable discussion and consideration" ultimately decided to maintain it as "an outwork of Charleston." Ripley claimed Lee realized that the fortification of Cole's Island prevented access to the Stono River and "that it be continually and carefully strengthened." The *Official Records* confirm that Lee advised Ripley: "If it is necessary to maintain these batteries [on Cole's Island] they should be made as strong as possible." This indicates that Lee probably was transferred to Virginia before a definitive decision on Cole's Island was reached. Lee may have privately conveyed his decision regarding Cole's Island to Ripley, but it cannot be confirmed in the *Official Records*. Ripley, knowing that Lee became the heart and soul of the Confederacy after he left South Carolina, probably did not want to involve Lee in the unpopular abandonment of Georgetown and Cole's Island ordered by Pemberton.[10]

Ripley described at length the difficulties encountered in fortifying the Charleston area: "The Confederates were deficient in everything. There were no engineer officers, no laborers, no money and everything had to be improvised." The first engineers were the young cadets of the Citadel, and Ripley surprisingly claimed, "In a short time stalwart field hands, accompanied by their owners and overseers, were available in large numbers."

In March 1862 Pemberton, "who had peculiar ideas and was obdurate . . . speedily and peremptorily ordered the evacuation of Cole's Island, and opened the Stono River to the enemy." Ripley recounted the Union incursion up the Stono River and their overland assault across James Island. Fortunately, the Confederates repulsed the Union forces at the Battle of Secessionville on June 16, 1862, while Ripley was in Virginia. Although Pemberton also ordered the abandonment of Georgetown, Ripley refrained from charging Pemberton with that decision. However, Ripley correctly claimed that Pemberton advocated "abandoning all of the advanced works for the defense of Charleston, including Forts Sumter and Moultrie, and mounting the guns on the city wharves. Then, as if to prepare for the bombardment he proposed to invite . . . he converted some cellars, uncovered by the fire of December 1861, into bomb cellars." Pemberton advocated much of this in a dispatch dated May 21, 1862, but made no mention of "basement bomb cellars." Ripley believed there was little consolation in Pemberton's claim that "however great might be the damage to the city itself from bombardment, [the enemy's] feet could be kept from polluting its streets." Ripley maintained that Lee and the government in Richmond disapproved Pemberton's plan and it obviously was not implemented. Beauregard, on his second tour of duty in South Carolina, relieved Pemberton in September 1862, and strengthening the area's fortifications became a priority. In April 1863 Federal ironclads, under the command of Admiral Du Pont, attacked Fort Sumter and other installations in Charleston Harbor, but were repulsed after two and one-half hours of vigorous shelling. Union forces on Cole's Island remained in control of access to the Stono River, and their presence on Folly Island threatened Morris Island. Ripley once again related the deficiencies of Colonel Harris and his engineers in fortifying the southern end of Morris Island. He claimed he tried to construct batteries against Folly Island but was countermanded by Beauregard. On July 10, 1863, the Federals opened an overwhelming artillery barrage from Folly Island and gained a foothold on Morris Island. Ripley briefly described the siege of Battery Wagner and lauded the engineering abilities of Captain John Johnson, who made Fort Sumter "almost impregnable to assault" despite being shelled almost continually. Ripley concluded his last article by enumerating the "two notably egregious errors" that caused Charleston's material hardships and the majority of the destruction. The first was the abandonment of Cole's Island, "by which the enemy was practically invited to make his base within a few miles of the city." The second was the neglect, which allowed the enemy to attack and capture of Morris Island.[11]

"Charleston's Acknowledgements to General Ripley," a two-page addendum dated April 1886, followed Ripley's article and recognized that Ripley "stood by the people of Charleston during their trials and suffering, and never hesitated day or night to give support and confidence to the citizens. His mind was unsurpassed for devising means for attack and for defense and he imparted his persistent courage to all. He possessed not only military skills, but also the practical ability to apply those skills" to protect the city from its dangers. "Even in times of greatest stress and turmoil . . . he never lost the sympathies of the man." On one occasion, when the enemy threatened an attack on an adjacent island, "all available forces in the city were hastily summoned for resistance. Among them, the young Cadets of the Citadel were marched to the wharf to be embarked for the defense of the threatened position. The thought of devoting these young lives to what might be a useless sacrifice, deeply affected the General; looking with evident emotion on the corps . . . he said he would not make such a sacrifice," and ordered the cadets back to the Citadel. Those present "will remember the incident as exhibiting a tenderness of feeling" not expected in the "bluff and rough soldier." It was well for the city to "cherish one who served us so truly and manfully in our great trial. No one is, or deserves to be, more gratefully remembered than General Ripley."[12]

In comparison, after the war Beauregard waged intense literary battles against Jefferson Davis, Joseph E. Johnston, and Albert Sidney Johnston's son over their appraisals of his [Beauregard's] military skill and achievements. Beauregard detested Davis and was unable to stop Thomas Jordan, the general's former chief of staff, from writing a vicious denunciation of Davis while the former president was imprisoned.

More significantly, Beauregard strongly resented the postwar adoration of Robert E. Lee, who he claimed had "little military foresight . . . or great powers of deduction, but he had great nerve, coolness & determination—the greater the danger the greater was his presence of mind, although not very fertile in resources. He was perhaps a little too cautious in civil as well as military matters." Jordan notified Beauregard that he wanted to write more articles and thereby "demonstrate that Beauregard was the real genius of the South." Jordan and Beauregard aspired to discredit Lee, the man they thought was wrongly considered to be the Confederacy's greatest general.[13]

During these postwar years Beauregard also learned that the citizens of Charleston were enthusiastically praising Ripley for his efforts to defend the city.

Beauregard was angered; he not only had to deal with Davis, the Johnstons, and the adoration of Lee, but also with the citizens of Charleston, who basically ignored him in favor of the despised Ripley. Beauregard attacked Ripley in an article published in the May 1886 issue of the *North American Review*. That diatribe, spawned by Beauregard's damaged ego, was actually written by Alfred Roman from the general's notes and later condensed as "The Defense of Charleston" when it appeared in *Battles and Leaders of the Civil War*.

Beauregard began his denigration of Ripley by claiming that on February 8, 1863 he sent Ripley "minute instructions, because though he was an able artillery officer, he possessed scant knowledge and no experience of military engineering." In Beauregard's view, his best assistant for planning the construction of batteries and selecting their sites was Major D. B. Harris, the chief of the engineer department. Harris, said Beauregard, "always thoroughly understood and entered into my views"; in short, Harris was a perfect sycophant. Beauregard continued:

> It is an error to state, as I am informed one or two writers have done, even in South Carolina, that the erection of the batteries along the shores of the inner harbor, and in the city of Charleston itself, was due to what has been termed the untiring zeal, forethought, and engineering ability of General Ripley. My letters of instruction and my official orders to General Ripley, from his arrival in my department up to the time of my leaving it in April 1864, conclusively show that those batteries were all planned and located by me, and I passed upon all questions relative not only to their armament, but even to the caliber of the guns that were to be placed in them.

Beauregard made no mention of Ripley's "irregular habits."

In addition, Beauregard added his voice to those condemning Pemberton for abandoning Cole's Island. After the Confederates shelled and captured the gunboat *Isaac Smith* on the Stono River, Beauregard was convinced Union ironclads were not as formidable against land batteries as previously thought. He reasoned that "Cole's Island, if fortified properly, could have stopped an ironclad attack and prevented Union access to the Stono River."[14]

Ripley's friends in Charleston thought that he supported himself primarily by writing after he returned to America. However, there is no record of him having anything published after his article appeared in the 1885 *Charleston Yearbook*. Major Thomas A. Huguenin served the entire war in various capacities under Ripley, and after his death Huguenin suggested another source of income for Ripley. He claimed that Ripley worked in New York as a sales representative for a London paving company. The firm attempted to introduce wooden blocks as a replacement for paving stones in the streets of New York City. There is some credence to this as Huguenin and two of Ripley's close friends in New York, Smith and Newton, were, or had been, involved in public street works.

At the time there were several companies in London involved in the wood block paving business—the Asphaltic Wood Paving Company, Green's Wood Paving Company, and Improved Wood Paving Company. All intended their work to be an improvement over the wooden plank roads of that era. No record could be found linking Ripley with any wood block paving firm in London.[15]

CHAPTER 36

Death in New York and Honors in Charleston

It is unclear how long Ripley may have had respiratory problems, but after he returned to New York, he consulted John W. S. "Stump" Norris, M.D. Dr. Norris, who maintained an office in the New York Hotel, made the diagnosis of asthma. Ripley's friends believed he was in "perfect health, except for occasional attacks of asthma during which he suffered considerably and would walk the corridors of the hotel at all hours of the night." Ripley, who had always been overweight, was described by his friends in New York as being "large and stout," which definitely increased the likelihood he would have respiratory problems. His damaged larynx and trachea, with the projectile still embedded in his throat, would have contributed to the respiratory issues that made sleeping difficult. Evidently, on some nights he could breathe better being upright, so at times he roamed the hallways from his room on the third floor.[1]

During these last years in New York, Ripley managed to keep in touch with some old friends in Charleston, but there is no evidence he ever visited the city again. Mayor Courtenay had prevailed upon the old Confederate to write an account of the defense of Charleston for the 1885 *Charleston Yearbook*. When a Charleston lawyer, William H. Brawley, traveled to New York City, he often visited with Ripley and probably stayed at the Southerners' favorite hotel, the New York. Brawley, a native of Chester, South Carolina, had not known Ripley in Charleston during the war but saw "a great deal of him in New York . . . his interest in Charleston seemed to be very great during the whole of his life. He was perfectly loyal to this City, and always spoke of it with much feeling and sentiment."[2]

By 1887 it had been eighteen years since Ripley's marriage ended in separation. In April 1869 his wife, humiliated by her descent into poverty, returned to Charleston with their fifteen-year-old daughter, Alicia, their return voyage funded by money raised by Ripley's friends. Ripley's wife continued to live in Charleston and probably never wanted to see her estranged husband again. The sentiment may very well have been mutual, as many unpleasant memories must have haunted the couple. Ripley's daughter, Alicia Middleton Ripley, married Savage Deas Trenholm on August 7, 1873. Any desire Ripley may have had to see his daughter was complicated by the fact that for a time his wife lived with Alicia and her husband at 2 South Battery in Charleston. The family often spent summers in, and later moved to Flat Rock, North Carolina, located in the mountains not far from Asheville. Alicia's mother and husband, S.D. Trenholm, died in Flat Rock between 1895 and 1898. Ripley's daughter, Alicia Trenholm, died in Hendersonville, North Carolina on January 22, 1926.[3]

On March 29, 1887, two weeks after Ripley's sixty-fourth birthday, General John Newton "called at the [New York] hotel to see him on business and the two went to breakfast together. While they were talking, General Ripley's power of speech suddenly became paralyzed. He arose from the table and attempted to walk, but staggered and would have fallen had not General Newton grasped him by the arm and assisted him to his room." Ripley became insensible and the hotel staff summoned Dr. Norris. The doctor declared that Ripley had suffered "an attack of apoplexy [stroke] and his recovery was very doubtful." Probably the projectile and any extraneous material embedded in his neck caused inflammation and scarring. This chronic process may have affected his carotid artery and contributed to the stroke. All attempts "to restore him to conscious were unsuccessful." The general appeared to be suffering great pain from difficulty breathing". Attended by Dr. Norris and his nurse, Ripley's condition continued to deteriorate, and his physician pronounced him dead at 8:00 P.M.

General Newton took charge of the situation, contacting an undertaker, J. Chas Burton, and making arrangements for a funeral service for his good friend. The next day the manager of the hotel, H. Cranston, telegraphed Mayor William A. Courtenay of Charleston that he had been requested to notify the mayor of Ripley's death and of Ripley's wish to be buried in Magnolia Cemetery. When the mayor received the news, he asked Cranston to send Ripley's remains as soon as possible to Charleston by express.[4]

At 3:30 P.M. on April 1, Ripley's funeral service was held in the corridor of the New York Hotel. About thirty old comrades in arms and personal friends attended the service read by the Reverend Dr. Charles F. Deems. In attendance were Generals John Newton, T. L. Clingman, G. W. Smith, and Martin T. McMahon. Also attending were Colonel A. G. Dickenson of Virginia and a Captain H. R. Garden (probably Captain Hugh R. Garden of the Palmetto Battery, who served at Sharpsburg). The *New York Times* report of the funeral erroneously gave Ripley the promotion he had long desired, describing him as "a Major General in the Confederate Service." The undertaker prevailed upon Dr. J. T. Nagle of the New York City Health Department to allow transportation of the remains while he retrieved information required for the obligatory transit permit. That night the deceased was transported by rail to Charleston for a public service and burial in Magnolia Cemetery.[5]

Ripley's obituary in the *Ogdensburg Journal* claimed his name "will be familiar to the older residents of this city." As might be expected, the paper trivialized the basis for Ripley's Confederate service: "he married a southern lady, adopted southern views and took the confederate [sic] side during the great rebellion. He leaves a widow and one daughter, Mrs. Trenholm residing in Charleston. His sisters, Mrs. A. B. James and Mrs. Charles Shepard, both residents here, survive him." Roswell's sister, Lucia R. James, provided the undertaker with the information required for the transit permit.[6]

The front page of the *Charleston News and Courier* reported Ripley's death under the headline "The Sad and Sudden End of Charleston's Gallant Defender." According to the article, Ripley's "whole heart was in the service of South Carolina and the Confederacy, and many of the most essential things done for the protection of this city were originated by him and executed under his orders." This was a statement General Beauregard most certainly would have disputed. Mayor Courtenay telegraphed Ripley's family in Asheville, North Carolina, asking "if they had any special wishes in the matter." The mayor requested that surviving Confederate veterans and friends of Ripley meet at noon on March 31 in the city council chamber to make arrangements for his funeral and burial. Those present in the chamber included Brigadier General T. A. Huguenin, 4th Brigade, S.C.V.T.; General George D. Johnston, superintendent of the Citadel; Colonel E. M. Seabrook, who had been Ripley's aide-de-camp; Colonel P. C. Gaillard, Colonel Joseph A. Yates, Major W. H. Brawley, Major R. C. Gilchrist, Reverend C. E. Chichester, Reverend Dr. W. T. Thompson, Reverend John Johnson (formerly a major of engineers), and "many others." Reverend Johnson consented to officiate the ceremonies at St. Luke's Church.

Major Gilchrist addressed the group in the city council chamber, hoping nothing would be left undone to pay proper respect to Ripley's memory. Gilchrist maintained that if Charleston had been taken during the war, it would have been razed to the ground, but that did not happen because of Ripley's "gallant and heroic defense." He claimed that because of Ripley's "untiring energy, sleepless zeal, devotion and concentration, Charleston withstood the attacking fleets, and the most determined efforts of the enemy to reach the City."

The mayor believed that "General Ripley's remains should be shown every possible respect and honor upon their arrival," and those best able to fulfill this duty were "his old fellow officers and friends." General Huguenin proposed, and the group passed, a resolution forming a committee of five to assist the mayor in making all arrangements. The Committee of Arrangements included Huguenin, Seabrook, Gaillard, Brawley, and the former captain and now Reverend Chichester, whose wife would later write of Ripley's surprise visit to Castle Pinckney and their oyster dinner.

Immediately after the meeting adjourned, the Committee of Arrangements met in Mayor Courtenay's private office and selected eighteen former Confederate officers as pallbearers They were to assemble at the church at the designated hour and without further invitation. The army pallbearers, with their Confederate

Captain THOMAS A. HUGUENIN First Regiment S. C. Infantry, Commanding Fort Sumter 1864-65.
From a Photograph.

(left) Captain Thomas A. Huguenin, the last commander of Fort Sumter, from July 1864 until Charleston's evacuation in February 1865. He organized the prestigious memorial service, funeral, and burial of Ripley. From John Johnson, The Defense of Charleston Harbor, 1863–1865 (1889), facing p. 230. *(right)* Major John Johnson, commanding engineer at Fort Sumter, 1863–64. He was seriously wounded in July 1864. After the war, Reverend Johnson officiated Ripley's memorial service at St. Luke's. From John Johnson, The Defense of Charleston Harbor, 1863–1865 (1889), facing p. 276.

rank, included Ripley's son-in-law Colonel Alfred M. Rhett, Captain E. M. Seabrook, Colonel B. H. Rutledge, Colonel P. C. Gaillard, Major R. C. Gilchrist, Major T. A. Huguenin, Major F. L. Childs, and seven others. It is enlightening that Major Childs, who had a serious confrontation with Ripley over the rifling and banding of artillery in 1862, readily served as one of the pallbearers. Commander D. N. Ingraham and three others represented the Confederate navy. Former governor A. G. Magrath was also one of the pallbearers.[7]

On April 2 General Huguenin issued General Orders, No. 3, detailing his brigade's duties for the funeral. The brigade and regimental field officers, with their staffs, were to assemble at the Northeastern Railroad Depot at 9:00 A.M. on Sunday, April 3. In uniform and with side arms, they were to escort Ripley's remains to St. Luke's Church and attend the ceremonies and service at 10:00 A.M.

Huguenin continued his praise of Ripley, saying that "those of us now living, will give cheerful testimony to his worth as a soldier, and his kind and generous qualities as a man. His eminent services, particularly in defense of this city, will ever be remembered by a grateful people, and duly chronicled in the annals of history." Ripley was "inseparably connected" with Forts Sumter and Moultrie and Battery Wagner and "their glorious record is his also." Huguenin would be dismayed to learn that this is not the case. Ripley is not mentioned in the National Park handbook at Fort Moultrie. The Fort Sumter handbook pictures Ripley's subordinates Colonel Alfred Rhett, Major John Johnson, Major Stephen Elliott, Captain John Mitchel, and Captain Thomas A. Huguenin. Ripley is ignored and omitted.[8]

Ripley's body arrived at the Charleston depot at 5:00 A.M. Sunday, much earlier than expected. According to the *Charleston Yearbook*, the brigade was summoned and transported the "handsome casket" to the vestibule of St. Luke's Church. Ripley's "features were well preserved, his hair, beard, and moustache were nearly silver white. The coffin was literally covered with flowers and evergreens and draped with silver moss." Early in the morning thousands began passing through the vestibule to view the "gallant general" and pay their last respects. "Many of the old companions-in-arms paused sadly and reflectively over the coffin." Several wreaths of white French immortelles, one in the shape of a large anchor, were variously inscribed in purple flowers, *Charleston, Sumter, Moultrie,* and *Wagner.* "Around these most conspicuous memorials were various other loving contributions, bunches of simple flowers . . . coronals and wreaths of the richest and rarest roses, some offered by the relatives, and others by the more intimate friends of the deceased. It should also be stated . . . some affectionate friend or friends of General Ripley had placed upon his breast in New York a bouquet of gold roses, which were as fresh and un-faded as on the day they were placed."

The *Yearbook* continued, "The day was one full of sunshine—bright, balmy and beautiful. . . . No more fitting day could have been selected . . . a quiet reposeful Sunday . . . a day of rest so typical of the event being commemorated." Municipal flags, private flags throughout the city, and even the flags of the ships in port "were at half-staff in respect for the memory of General Ripley. The wardens and vestry of St. Michael's Church tolled the bells from 8 to 10 o'clock A.M. on Sunday." Prior to the funeral service the streets around the church were lined "for a long distance on every side with citizens attracted through respect for the departed soldier. The entrance to the church was blocked with people eager to enter. . . . the church was filled, there being a very large representation of ladies." General Johnson Hagood of Barnwell attended as a guest of the city. The cadets of the Citadel and their officers, in full dress uniform, were seated under the north gallery. The officers of the Huguenin Brigade were present in their Confederate grey uniforms with side arms.[9]

Reverend John Johnson, the pastor of St. Phillip's, read the funeral service assisted by Reverend Robert Wilson of St. Luke's. Reporters described the scene as solemn, instructive, and impressive: "Those who had survived the fight were assembled to pay tribute . . . to one of the foremost champions of the Lost Cause, and there were few of those present as pallbearers who had not seen service under the 'Old Commander.'" Following the funeral service, "the remains were placed in a hearse drawn by four handsome black horses," and a long line of carriages followed the hearse to Magnolia Cemetery. "Many people had already assembled at the cemetery" and somberly greeted the funeral procession when it arrived at about 11:15 A.M. The interment took place at a site previously selected by the city with the approval of the deceased's family. Ripley's daughter, Alicia, was present, along with "other near relatives" and all of the officers previously mentioned. Following the interment, the grave was covered with moss and adorned with the wreaths from the church service. "Immediately thereafter two ladies, one of whom was the daughter of General Ripley also approached the grave, deposited graceful memorials, paused awhile, and then retired." Most likely the unidentified lady was Ripley's stepdaughter, Marie Alice Sparks, who had married Colonel Alfred Rhett, one of the pallbearers. A few minutes after the memorials the attendees returned to the city. "The people whom he served so well and defended so bravely will ever cherish his memory."[10]

The *Charleston News and Courier* reported, "The City of Charleston honored itself in the manner in which it repaid its debt of gratitude and exhibited its appreciation of its heroic defender. . . . it has been many years since an event of so much significance has taken place in this old city." Beauregard would not have been pleased with the adoration showered on Ripley. The egocentric, self-serving Beauregard may have been the architect of Charleston's defenses, but Ripley was actively on site and personally involved in the work of the city's defense.[11]

After Ripley's burial the Survivors Association of Charleston District and the friends of General Ripley proposed to erect "an enduring monument, suitably inscribed, which will preserve to posterity his name and services." Voluntary contributions began, and in November 1892, at a meeting of the Washington Light Infantry, a committee was formed to complete the project. T. A. Huguenin chaired the fourteen-member executive committee that included E. M. Seabrook, John Johnson, Johnson Hagood, and former mayor William A. Courtenay. Treasurer Courtenay announced that only $1,000 was needed to complete the monument. By 1893 the additional sum had been raised, bringing the total collected to $2,000—an impressive sum for the postwar South. The monument marking Ripley's grave was unveiled and dedicated during a ceremony held on April 3, 1894, exactly seven years after his interment. Colonel Seabrook delivered the address, a short biography of Ripley with a comprehensive accounting of Ripley's Confederate military career and his service in the defense of Charleston. Defensively and defiantly facing north, the front of the polished Carolina granite monument is inscribed:

IN MEMORY OF
BRIG. GEN. R. S. RIPLEY, CSA
BORN AT WORTHINGTON, OHIO 14TH MARCH, 1823

GRADUATED AT WEST POINT 1843

The South face of the monument bears the inscription:

IN RECOGNITION OF HIS MILITARY SKILLS
AND HIS

DEVOTED SERVICES IN THE DEFENSE OF CHARLESTON HARBOR
1861–1865

THE SURVIVORS ASSOCIATION AND OTHER CITIZENS UNITE IN
ERECTING THIS ENDURING MEMORIAL
1893

The north and the south face of the monument each have one stanza from Henry Timrod's poem, "Ripley," written in the general's honor during the defense of Charleston. The east and west sides of the monument are etched respectively with the battles from the Mexican War and Civil War in which Ripley was

Brigadier General R. S. Ripley, C.S.A., grave monument, Magnolia Cemetery, Charleston. Author's photograph.

engaged. Regrettably, the west face incorrectly lists his presence at Seven Pines and Second Manassas and omits both Mechanicsville and South Mountain. A low rectangular wall encompasses the monument with a cannonball placed on each of its four corners.[12]

Although South Carolina's heroic cavalry commander, General Wade Hampton, could sympathize with Confederates who left the South after the war, he advised his former comrades to remain and rebuild. Hampton asserted that they "should take the oath of allegiance to the United States government so that they may participate in the restoration of civil government to our State . . . [and] devote their energies to the restoration of law and order, the re-establishment of agriculture and commerce, the promotion of education, and the rebuilding of our cities and dwellings which have been laid in ashes."[13]

The citizens of Charleston had not seen Ripley in over twenty years and could have become embittered by his absence during their reconstruction struggles. Obviously this did not happen and their respect for Ripley remained resolute. No one would have known General Roswell Ripley better than his staff officers, and to them, as evidenced by their honors and solemn tributes to him at his death, he would always be "Charleston's Gallant Defender."

Epilogue

Following Ripley's return to New York in 1884, Colonel William Hope continued to promote his cannon in Great Britain. That year, Hope attempted to have his gun tested by the British Ordnance Committee, but the committee refused to sanction a trial. However, in November 1886 rumors reached the Ordnance Committee that the Admiralty planned to give the "Hope Gun" a field trial. Belatedly, the committee decided that the gun should be presented again, and brought Hope before the committee for an interview. They intended to assess his qualifications as a gun maker and determine whether there was enough evidence to justify field-testing his cannon.[1]

When Hope appeared before the Ordnance Committee in late November 1886, he responded positively when asked whether he considered himself to be a "practical gun-maker." Hope claimed his experience came from studying and observing the works and results of others. Although he owned no gun works, he continued to work with Jessup & Company in Sheffield and asserted that he had "an order for six guns from one Foreign Government." The committee asked Hope whether his cannon had been given any practical trials. He admitted the gun had not been tried in England but it had been tested in France. Hope apparently was referring to the gun made in France in 1884 by the Fonderies et Forges des Terre-Noire under Ripley's supervision. Hope told the committee the metallurgical process for producing the gun was a secret, but he did have a gun in London and offered to present it to them. Hope claimed that years ago, when he served as an attaché in The Hague, he discovered an innovative steel-making process similar to a secret Dutch metallurgical method for casting cannon.[2]

On December 1, 1886, the committee heard testimony refuting Hope's claims for his gun and declaring that his "practically indestructible" secret metal "has never been made." The witness claimed that Hope's proposed trial in 1884 actually was suspended because the French company Terre-Noire filed a protest with the British War Office. According to the witness, the French company claimed they had purchased the rights "to all of Hope's patents, past, present and I think future . . . in payment probably for the gun made by them." At that time Ripley was in France working with Terre-Noire and using their steel to produce a French version of the "Hope Gun." The French company forwarded documents to the War Office supporting their claims and asked the British government to cease all dealings with Colonel Hope. The War Office asked Hope to refute these charges, and as he was unable to do so, the contract fell through. During this testimony it was claimed that the "Hope Gun" tests in France were "unsatisfactory and a dead failure." Ripley must have concluded that there was no future in pursuing this venture any further and did not return to England to join Hope in his continued efforts. Ripley left France in May 1884, apparently paying for his Atlantic crossing with his share of the proceeds from Terre-Noire.[3]

The Ordnance Committee continued in session into late January 1887. The committee learned that since the French gun's failed trials, Terre-Noire had been "waiting to see if there is any result at all [here] before they step in again." Consequently, the committee granted Hope a private trial of his cannon. It is unclear exactly when the Ordnance Department conducted the trial, but abstracts of the results were received on October 13, 1887, and were reported in the November 28 Proceedings of the Ordnance Committee. The tests probably took place sometime after Ripley's death in New York.

Jessop & Sons Company of Sheffield forged a solid-steel gun, supposedly to Colonel Hope's specifications and designed to withstand rigorous tests. They shipped the gun to Maudsley & Field's for boring and rifling, then bolted a breechblock designed by Hope onto the barrel. The trial took place near Hounslow, conducted by Hope and witnessed by his son and representatives of Jessop's and Maudsley & Field's, as well as a few of Hope's friends.

Colonel Hope loaded the 2.5-inch gun, "built in one piece, somewhat revolutionary for those days," with a low charge and fired it successfully. He then loaded the cannon with a larger charge "and was entreated by the bystanders to proceed cautiously and by degrees, or at least fire the charge by electricity." He declined to do either, and after placing the spectators under cover of some earthworks, he pulled the lanyard. There was a "hang-fire," and "when the discharge took place, the breechblock was blown entirely off; a piece of steel flew a half-mile into the air, narrowly missing Hope when it slammed to earth. The entire gun was lifted about fifteen feet and turned a somersault, lighting with the muzzle pointing toward the colonel. The case was split longitudinally for the great part of its length and is now at Maudsley's."

Colonel Hope claimed the cannon burst was "due to the steel for which he paid 98*l* per ton. The facts show clearly that this was not so." Maudsley's engineers said that Hope used too much powder; Jessop's & Sons countered that it was "due to the quality of the steel that Colonel Hope owes his life."[4]

Evidently, Hope continued to keep his "secret" metallurgical method or process a secret, as he blamed the quality of the steel for the burst. The "specifications" he sent to Jessop's & Sons must have been for the caliber, weight, and proportions of the gun. Evidently it was not "back to the drawing board," as there is no evidence Hope continued his efforts in cannon technology. Ripley must have expected his "Cartridge for Ordnance" to be the defining factor in preventing barrel bursts, but his earlier test in France fared no better.

NOTES

To avoid too many intrusions into the text, sources for the most part are cited every few paragraphs rather than on every occurrence or every paragraph, and are given in the order in which materials are cited or referenced.

Abbreviations

AGO	Adjutant General's Office
BPO	British Patent Office
Duke	Duke University, David M. Rubenstein Rare Book and Manuscript Library
HL	Dudley Collection. Huntington Library, American Historical Manuscripts Division
LOC	Library of Congress
M	Microfilm (used with NARA citations). Each reference followed by an identification number—e.g., M727
NARA	National Archives and Records Administration
NLS	Blackwood Papers. National Library of Scotland
OR	*The War of the Rebellion: A Compilation of the Official Records of the Union and Confederate Armies.* All references are to series 1 unless otherwise noted
ORN	*Official Records of the Union and Confederate Navies in the War of the Rebellion.* All references are to series 1
RG	Record Group (used with NARA citations). Each reference followed by an identification number—e.g., RG94
SCAH	South Carolina Department of Archives and History
SCHM	*South Carolina Historical Magazine*
SCHS	South Carolina Historical Society
SCL	University of South Carolina, Columbia, South Caroliniana Library
SHC	University of North Carolina, Chapel Hill, Southern Historical Collection
SLU	Ripley/Shepard Papers. St. Lawrence University, Owen D. Young Library
SO	Special Order(s)
TNA	The National Archives, U.K.
USMA	U.S. Military Academy Library. With the exception of the Ripley Papers, these records are listed under RG404, National Archives and Records Administration, in the bibliography.
Yale-1	R. S. Ripley Papers. Yale University Library, Beinecke Rare Book and Manuscript Library
Yale-2	James H. Burton Papers. Yale University Library, Manuscripts and Archives

Preface

1. Justification for the historical marker and the inscribed text written by the author. Presented for approval to the Ohio Historical Society by the Brigadier General R. S. Ripley Camp 1535, Sons of Confederate Veterans.

2. Cummings, *Seven Ohio Confederate Generals*, 749–51, 700; Cummings, "Fruit of a Restless Spirit," 146, 51, 53–54.

3. Sifakis, "Ripley, Roswell Sabine," *Who Was Who*, 545–46; Warner, *Generals in Gray*, 257; Dowdey, *Seven Days*, 186.

4. Seabrook, *Unveiling of the Ripley Monument*, 12; French, "Roswell S. Ripley," 63–64; Eggleston, *Rebel's Recollections*, 164–65.

5. R. S. Ripley to Francis Pickens, Oct. 20, 24, 1861, Law Papers, SHC; OR, vol. 6, 366; Freeman, *R. E. Lee*, 1:617; OR, vol. 47, pt. 2, 1031; Warner, *Generals in Gray*, 257, Dowdey, *Seven Days*, 187; National Park Service, *Fort Sumter*, 1–63.

6. "Death of Gen. R. S. Ripley," *New York World*, Mar. 30, 1887; "The Late Gen. Ripley," *Charleston News and Courier*, Mar. 30, 31, 1887, 1; "Our Warrior's Grave," *Charleston News and Courier*, Apr. 4, 1887, 1; Monument Committee, 2, R. S. Ripley Papers, SCHS.

Chapter 1: Family and Early Years

1. Cummings, *Seven Ohio Confederate Generals*, 1:382; Ripley, *Genealogy of a Part of the Ripley Family*, 17; Family Record, SLU.

2. Cummings, *Seven Ohio Confederate Generals*, 1:373–75; Caulkins, "Migration to Ohio," 433–53.

3. Ripley, *Genealogy of a Part of the Ripley Family*, 5, 11–17; Cummings, *Seven Ohio Confederate Generals*, 1:378n10, citing "Ralph Ripley's Military Record," *DAR Lineage Book* 142:151; Manley, "Ripley Papers and Matildaville," 4; Sifakis, "Ripley, James Wolfe," *Who Was Who*, 545.

4. Manley, "Ripley Papers and Matildaville," 4, 5; C. Ripley Papers, Feb. 21, Mar. 20, 1810, Connecticut Historical Society.

5. C. Ripley Papers, Mar. 20, 23, Apr. 21, 1813; C. Ripley Ledger, Apr. 30, May 25, June 18, July 25, 1813, Apr. 15, 1815. All items archived at Connecticut Historical Society.

6. Manley, "Ripley Papers and Matildaville," 5; Martin, *History of Franklin County*, 42; Family Record, SLU; Cummings, *Seven Ohio Confederate Generals*, 1:379–84; McCormick, *Probing Worthington's Heritage*, 30, 47; Family Record, SLU.

7. Julia Ripley to Christopher Ripley, Apr. 1, May 3, 1827, SLU; McCormick, *Probing Worthington's Heritage*, 54.

8. Julia Ripley to R. S. Ripley, Aug. 2, 1833, SLU.

9. Manley, "Ripley Papers and Matildaville," 5, 7, 8.

10. Durant, *History of St. Lawrence County*, 249–50; R. S. Ripley to Julia Ripley, Oct. 3, 1836, SLU.

11. D. S. Sheldon to Christopher Ripley, Dec. 5, 1836, R. S. Ripley to Christopher Ripley, Feb. 9, 1837, D. S. Sheldon to Christopher Ripley, Mar. 1, 1837, SLU.

12. Appelbaum, *William Wordsworth*, 34; Cook, *Life of Florence Nightingale*, 1:13.

Chapter 2: West Point

1. Clyde, *Life of James H. Coffin*, 154–55; James H. Coffin to Christopher Ripley, Sept. 21, 1837, SLU.

2. Cummings, *Seven Ohio Confederate Generals*, 391–93; U.S. Congress, *Biographical Directory*, 946, 1637, 1835, 824; Cadet Applications, Feb. 26, 1838, Feb. 9, 10, 16, 26, Mar. 1, 1839, RG94, NARA.

3. Asbury Dickins to Christopher Ripley, Mar. 6, 1839, SLU; Christopher Ripley to Joel Poinsett, Apr. 6, 1839, Cadet Applications, RG94, NARA.

4. Christopher Ripley to R. S. Ripley, n.d.; Notice, Preparatory School at West Point, Apr. 22, 1839. Both items at SLU.

5. Cadet Candidates, 1839, Order Book, 1837–1839, S.O. 38, USMA; Pappas, *To the Point,* 220, 120; Cummings, *Seven Ohio Confederate Generals,* 394; Register of Officers and Graduates, 1840, Conduct, 20, 23, USMA; Delinquencies, 1838–1844, 76, USMA; Order Book, Feb. 1838–June 1842, S.O. 89, 148, USMA; Register of Officers and Cadets, 1840–1843, Conduct, 23, 20, 19, 18, USMA.

6. Pappas, *To the Point,* 102; Order Book, 1838–1842, S.O. 64, 154, S.O. 96, 157, USMA; Julia Ripley to R. S. Ripley, May 10, 1840, Scope and Content, SLU; Shepard, "Lincoln's Assassination," 917–18; Creekman, *106th New York Volunteers,* 2.

7. Register of Officers and Graduates, 1840, Merit, Fourth Class, 16, USMA; Order Book, 1838–1842, S.O. 32, 81, USMA; Sifakis, "Hancock, Winfield Scott," *Who Was Who,* 279–80; Register of Officers and Graduates, 1841, Conduct, 20, USMA; Delinquencies, 1838–1844, 76, USMA; Order Book, 1838–1842, S.O. 82, 130, USMA; Julia Ripley to R. S. Ripley, Feb. 7, 1841, SLU; Register of Officers and Graduates, 1841, Merit, Third Class, 13, 14, USMA.

8. Julia Ripley to R. S. Ripley, May 9, 1841, SLU; Order Book, 1838–1842, S.O. 42, 216, USMA; Christopher Ripley to R. S. Ripley, Nov. 22, 1841, R. S. Ripley to Julia Ripley, May 17, 1842, SLU; personal visit, Magnolia Cemetery, Charleston, S.C.

9. Register of Officers and Graduates, 1842, Merit, Second Class, 9, 10, and Conduct, 19, USMA; Christopher Ripley and Julia Ripley to R. S. Ripley, July 29, 1842, SLU; Order Book, No. 2, 1842–1846, S.O. 25, 63, USMA; Register of Officers and Graduates, 1843, First Class, Merit, 8, and Conduct 18, USMA; Order Book, No. 2, 1842–1846, S.O. 50, 92, USMA; Register of Officers and Graduates, 1843, First Class, Merit, 7, and Conduct 1840–1843, 23, 20, 21, 18, USMA.

10. French, "Roswell S. Ripley," 63–68.

Chapter 3: Prelude to War

1. Order Book, S.O. 61, 63, USMA; Cummings, *Seven Ohio Confederate Generals,* 404; R. S. Ripley to AGO and Delafield to AGO, Aug. 13, 1843, Letters Rec'd, AGO, RG94, NARA.

2. Returns from Artillery, 3rd Regiment, Nov., Dec. 1843, and Mar., Apr., 1844, M727, NARA; Sheads, *Fort McHenry,* 1, 5–7.

3. R. S. Ripley to AGO, July 16, 25, 29, 1844, Letters Rec'd, AGO, RG94, NARA; Eisenhower, *So Far from God,* 80, 379–80; Winders, *Mr. Polk's Army,* 24; Samuel Ringgold to AGO, Aug. 29, 1844, Letters Rec'd, AGO, RG94, NARA; Returns from Artillery, 3rd Regiment, July 1844, M727, NARA.

4. R. S. Ripley to AGO, Sept. 26, 1844, Letters Rec'd, AGO, RG94, NARA; Returns from Artillery, 3rd Regiment, Oct. 1844 and Jan. 1845, M727, NARA; Kneitel, *Directory of U.S. Army Forts,* 77; Returns from Artillery, 3rd Regiment, Oct.–Dec. 1844, Jan. 1845, M727, NARA.

5. Henry, *Story of the Mexican War,* 17, 1, 20–21; Johannsen, *To the Halls,* 7.

6. Returns from Artillery, 3rd Regiment, Sept. 1845, M727, NARA; Scott, *Forgotten Valor,* 312.

7. W.S. to AGO, Jan. 24, 1846, Letters Rec'd, AGO, RG94, NARA; Returns from Artillery, 3rd Regiment, Feb.–June 1846; "Harbor of Annapolis," Maryland State Archives; J. N. Vinton to AGO, Feb. 20, 1846, Letters Rec'd, AGO, RG94, NARA.

8. R. S. Ripley to Julia Ripley, Mar. 9, Apr. 7, 1846, Yale-1; Henry, *Story of the*

Mexican War, 31; Returns from Artillery, 2nd Regiment, July 1846, M727, NARA; R. S. Ripley to Julia Ripley, June 1, 1846, Yale-1.

9. R. S. Ripley to Christopher Ripley, June 8, 1846, Yale-1; Winders, *Mr. Polk's Army*, 140, 239n2.

10. R. S. Ripley to Christopher Ripley, June 8, 1846, Yale-1; R. S. Ripley to Christopher Ripley, undated enclosure, SLU; R. S. Ripley to Julia Ripley, June 11, 1846, Yale-1.

Chapter 4: Mexico, 1846

1. R. S. Ripley to Julia Ripley, July 21, 26, 1846, Yale-1; Henry, *Story of the Mexican War*, 40; Winders, *Mr. Polk's Army*, 161; Johannsen, *To the Halls*, 124; Eisenhower, *So Far from God*, 80.

2. R. S. Ripley to Julia Ripley, July 26, Aug. 27, 1846, Yale-1; Eisenhower, *So Far from God*, 109–10.

3. Eisenhower, *So Far from God*, 118, 122–23; R. S. Ripley to Julia Ripley, Sept. 11, 1846, Yale-1.

4. Eisenhower, *So Far from God*, 128, 130; R. S. Ripley to Julia Ripley, Sept. 27, 1846, Yale-1; Eisenhower, *So Far from God*, 131–41, 147.

5. R. S. Ripley to Adeline Ripley, Oct. 6, 1846, Yale-1; Ripley, *Genealogy of a Part of the Ripley Family*, 18; R. S. Ripley to Julia Ripley, Oct. 26, 1846, Yale-1.

6. Eisenhower, *War with Mexico*, 167–68; R. S. Ripley to Julia Ripley, Nov. 19, 1846, R. S. Ripley to Lucia (Ripley) James, Dec. 6, 1846, Yale-1.

Chapter 5: Mexico, 1847

1. R. S. Ripley to Julia Ripley, Jan. 1, 1847, R. S. Ripley to Lucia (Ripley) James, Feb. 12, 1847, Yale-1.

2. Henry, *Story of the Mexican War*, 200–201; Johannsen, *To the Halls*, 91; R. S. Ripley to Julia Ripley, Mar. 16, 1847, Yale-1; Eisenhower, *So Far from God*, 255; R. S. Ripley to Julia Ripley, Mar. 27, 1847, Yale-1; Winders, *Mr. Polk's Army*, 161; R. S. Ripley to Julia Ripley, Apr. 3, 1847, Yale-1.

3. Eisenhower, *So Far from God*, 267; R. S. Ripley to Laura (Ripley) Shepard, May 2, 1847, Yale-1; Eisenhower, *So Far from God*, 110–11, 269, 272, 279–82.

4. R. S. Ripley to Julia Ripley, Apr. 23, 1847, Yale-1; McSherry, *El Puchero*, 220, 223; R. S. Ripley to Laura (Ripley) Shepard, May 2, 1847, Yale-1; Henry, *Mexican War*, 286; Cullum, "R. S. Ripley," *Biographical Register of the Officers*, 157.

5. R. S. Ripley to Laura (Ripley) Shepard, May 2, 1847, R. S. Ripley to Julia Ripley, May 21, June 3, 1847, Yale-1; Henry, *Story of the Mexican War*, 299–303, 318–19.

6. R. S. Ripley to Julia Ripley, Aug. 27, 1847, Yale-1; Henry, *Story of the Mexican War*, 405; Eisenhower, *So Far from God*, 382–83; Hughes and Stonesifer, *Gideon J. Pillow*, 93–96; Henry, *Story of the Mexican War*, 69; Eisenhower, *So Far from God*, 334–36.

7. Hughes and Stonesifer, *Gideon J. Pillow*, 98–101, 104, 107–11; R. S. Ripley to Julia Ripley, Oct. 25, 1847, Yale-1; McSherry, *El Puchero*, 170; *Aztec Club of 1847*, 3–23.

8. Hughes and Stonesifer, *Gideon J. Pillow*, 76–77, 79–80, 111–12; R. S. Ripley to Julia Ripley, Nov. 27, 1847, Yale-1; Winders, *Mr. Polk's Army*, 133; R. S. Ripley to Julia Ripley, Dec. 8, and 27, 1847, Yale-1.

Chapter 6: Postwar, 1848–1849

1. Hughes and Stonesifer, *Gideon J. Pillow*, 114–21; R. S. Ripley to AGO, Dec. 26, 1848, Feb. 8, 1849, Letters Rec'd, AGO, RG94, NARA; Hughes and Stonesifer, *Gideon J.*

Pillow, 122–23; William Marcy and James K. Polk to AGO, Feb. 22, 1849, Letters Rec'd, AGO, RG94, NARA.

2. R. S. Ripley to Gideon Pillow, Mar. 8, 1849, Pillow Letters, UCLA; Hughes and Stonesifer, *Gideon J. Pillow,* 123–24; Scaife, *Diary of James K. Polk,* 4:418, 421.

3. Johannsen, *To the Halls,* 241–44, 250–55; Ripley, *War with Mexico,* 1:xv–xvii.

4. Eisenhower, *So Far from God,* 407, 412; Ripley, *War with Mexico,* 2:72, 73; "H," "Battle of Cerro Gordo," 145; Johannsen, *To the Halls,* 214; Ripley, *War with Mexico* 1:53, 73, appendix, vol. 1: nos. 1 and 2.

5. Ripley, *War with Mexico,* xv; Contract, Ripley, R. S.–Harper & Bros., Harper & Brothers Records, Columbia University; Ripley, *War with Mexico* 645–46, 641–42.

Chapter 7: Florida, 1849–1850

1. Returns from Artillery, 2nd Regiment, June 1848–Aug. 1849, M727, NARA; Kneitel, *Directory of U.S. Army Forts,* 94.

2. Tidball, *John C. Tidball,* 104; Grunwald, *The Swamp,* 31–38, 40–41, 52–53.

3. Tidball, *John C. Tidball,* 110–12, 109.

4. Returns from Artillery, 2nd Regiment, Sept.–Nov. 1849, M727, NARA; Grunwald, *The Swamp,* 12, 42–44; Returns from Artillery, 2nd Regiment, Dec. 1849, M727, NARA.

5. Returns from Artillery, 2nd Regiment, Jan.–Apr. 1850, M727, NARA; Kneitel, *Directory of U.S. Army Forts,* 51; R. S. Ripley to Dear Sister, Feb.12, 1850, SLU; Grunwald, *The Swamp,* 53.

6. Thompson, "Notices of New Works," 63; Johannsen, *To the Halls,* 24; Hammond, "Battle of Buena Vista," 149–61; Kneitel, *Directory of U.S. Army Forts,* 36; Johannsen, *To the Halls,* 254; Returns from Artillery, 2nd Regiment, May–Dec. 1850, M727, NARA.

Chapter 8: Twilight of a Career

1. Returns from Artillery, 2nd Regiment, Oct. 1850–June 1851, M727, NARA; Weinert and Arthur, *Defender of the Chesapeake,* 1, 18, 31, 40, 45, 48, 60, 76, 66–68, 82.

2. Returns from Artillery, 2nd Regiment, July–Aug. 1851, M727, NARA; Manley, "Ripley Papers and Matildaville," 5, 7–9; Joel Buttles Diaries, Ohio History Connection.

3. C. Ripley resigns rights, Feb. 25, no year given, SLU; U.S. Census, 1850, St. Lawrence County, N.Y., C. Ripley, 103B; personal correspondence, Ms. Persis Boyesen, Ogdensburg (N.Y.) Public Library; *St. Lawrence Republican,* Sept. 23, 1851; Returns from Artillery, 2nd Regiment, Sept.–Dec. 1851, M727, NARA.

4. Returns from Artillery, 2nd Regiment, Jan.–Mar. 1852, M727, NARA; Sandburg, *Abraham Lincoln,* 4:318, 334; Shepard, "Lincoln's Assassination," 917–18; R. S. Ripley to AGO, AGO to R. S. Ripley, Jan. 23, 1852, R. S. Ripley and James Bankhead to AGO, Jan. 25, 1852, AGO to R. S. Ripley, Feb. 6, 1852, James Bankhead to AGO, Feb. 12, 1852, AGO to James Bankhead, Feb. 18, 1852, AGO to Charles Conrad, Feb. 21, 1852, Charles Conrad to AGO, Mar. 2, 1852, Bankhead to AGO, Mar. 22, 1852, Letters Rec'd, AGO, RG94, NARA.

5. James Shields to AGO, Mar. 31, 1852, Letters Rec'd, AGO, RG94, NARA; Callan, *Courage and Country,* 107–8, 111–16; Winders, *Mr. Polk's Army,* 46.

6. Callan, *Courage and Country,* 126–27, 130–33, 139; U.S. Senate, *Journal of the Senate,* Mar. 17, 1852, 282, Mar. 23, 1852, 299; U.S. Senate, *Bills and Resolutions,* 1852, S. 304; Returns from Artillery, 2nd Regiment, Apr. 1852, M727, NARA.

Chapter 9: A New Life in South Carolina

1. Stokeley, *Fort Moultrie*, 31, 36; Cullum, "James W. Ripley," *Biographical Register of the Officers*, 120.

2. Returns from Artillery, 2nd Regiment, Apr.–Dec. 1852; R. S. Ripley to AGO, Dec. 6, 1852, James Bankhead to AGO, Dec. 17, 1852, Letters Rec'd, AGO, RG94, NARA.

3. Cheves, "Middleton of South Carolina," 230, 237–38; Miles, *East Cooper Gazetteer*, 80–81; Russell E. Bidlack, "The Sparks Family of the Welch Neck Section of South Carolina: 9.1.1.3.4, Dr. William Alexander Sparks," *The Sparks Family Online*, http://www.sparksfamilyassn.org./pages/040-B.html (accessed Aug. 23, 2011).

4. Miles, *East Cooper Gazetteer*, 81–82; Miles, *Writings of the Islands*, 95–96.

5. "The War with Mexico," *Charleston Mercury*, July 30, 1852; Ripley, *Genealogy of a Part of the Ripley Family*, 23; R. S. Ripley to AGO, Dec. 31, 1852, Letters Rec'd, AGO, AGO, RG94, NARA; R. S. Ripley to Laura (Ripley) Shepard, May 2, 1847, Yale-1.

6. James Bankhead to AGO, Jan. 6, 1853, R. S. Ripley to AGO, Jan.10, 1853, AGO to Paymaster General, Jan. 13, 1853, 1853, James Shields to Charles Conrad, Jan. 16, 1853, R. S. Ripley to AGO, Jan. 21, 1853, James Conrad to AGO, Jan. 24, 1853, R. S. Ripley to AGO, Mar. 2, 1853, AGO to R. S. Ripley, Mar. 19, 1853, Letters Rec'd, AGO, RG94, NARA; Degregorio, "Millard Fillmore," *Book of U.S. Presidents*, 193.

7. Scharf, *History of Baltimore*, 629. North Carolina Death Certificate #143 Alicia Ripley Trenholm.

8. Ripley, *Genealogy of a Part of the Ripley Family*, 23; Chamberlain and Taylerson, *Adams' Revolvers*, 32, 34–35, 38; Bowes-Click and Kelleher, *Royal Regiment Fusiliers*, 23–25.

9. Chamberlain and Taylerson, *Adams' Revolvers*, 36, 22; R. S. Ripley to Ordnance Select Committee, Jan. 20, Feb. 28, Mar. 8, 14, 24, 26, 28, Apr. 19, May 8, 1855, TNA; Chamberlain and Taylerson, *Adams' Revolvers*, 41; Ordnance Select Committee to R.S. Ripley, May 16, June 7, July 26, 1855, TNA.

10. Captain William Dixon to Woolwich Royal Arsenal; May 28 correspondence between Captain William Dixon and Viscount Henry Hardinge; Captain Dixon to Henry, Viscount Hardinge, June 5, Aug. 28, 1855; Viscount Hardinge to Captain Dixon, Nov. 6, 1855; Captain Dixon to Viscount Hardinge, Nov. 13, 1855. Letters. Ordnance Select Committee, TNA.

11. Edwards, "One-Man Armory," 30; Chamberlain and Taylerson, *Adams' Revolvers*, 36; Burton Diaries, Apr. 2, 19, May 31, June 15, Aug. 15, 26, 29, 31, 1855, Yale-2.

12. Chamberlain and Taylerson, *Adams' Revolvers*, 38–40, 45, 47, 73–74, 45, 69, 70.

13. Letter Book, Sept. 18, 19, 22, and Oct 6, 1856, Robbins and Lawrence Co., Connecticut Historical Society; R. S. Ripley to D. N. Ingraham, Sept. 9, 1856, Letters Rec'd, Bureau Ordnance and Hydrography, RG74, NARA; Burton Diaries, Nov. 20, Dec. 10, 1856, and Jan. 19, 1857, Yale-2; Chamberlain and Taylerson, *Adams' Revolvers*, 75.

14. R. H. K. Whitely to H. K. Craig, Feb. 10, 1837, and Craig to Whitely, Feb. 13, 1857, Letters Rec'd and Sent, Chief of Ordnance, RG156, NARA; R. S. Ripley to D. N. Ingraham, Mar. 1, 1857, Letters Rec'd, Bureau Ordnance and Hydrograph, RG74, NARA; Chamberlain and Taylerson, *Adams' Revolvers*, 91, 74.

15. "Certificate of Incorporation," May 2, 1857, New York Department of State; R. S. Ripley to D. N. Ingraham, May 25, 27, July 31, 1857, Letters Rec'd, Bureau of Ordnance and Hydrography, RG74, NARA.

16. Chamberlain and Taylerson, *Adams' Revolvers*, 74; Burton Diaries, Aug. 18, Feb. 19, June 30, July 1, Sept. 7, Oct. 20, 24, 1857, Yale-2.

17. Chamberlain and Taylerson, *Adams' Revolvers*, 74–75; "Lieutenant-Colonel Ripley Interview," *Charleston Mercury*, July 20, 1861.

Chapter 10: Secession

1. Degregorio, "Abraham Lincoln," *Book of U.S. Presidents*, 231–32; Sifakis, "Brown, John," *Who Was Who*, 79.
2. Cisco, *States Rights Gist*, 40; R. S. Ripley to W. H. Gist, Mar. 3, 1860, Service Record, R. S. Ripley, SCAH.
3. A. B. Moore to R. S. Ripley, Mar. 22, 1860, J. E. Brown to R. S. Ripley, Apr. 3, 1860, Service Record, R. S. Ripley, SCAH.
4. Degregorio, "Abraham Lincoln," *Book of U.S. Presidents*, 232–34.
5. R. S. Ripley to W. H. Gist, May 16, 1860, Service Record, R. S. Ripley, SCAH; Cisco, *States Rights Gist*, 52; R. S. Ripley to S.R. Gist, Nov. 7, 1860, Service Record, R. S. Ripley, SCAH; Chamberlain and Taylerson, *Adams' Revolvers*, 75; Ripley to Gist, Nov. 7, 1860, Service Record R. S. Ripley, SCAH.
6. Cisco, *States Rights Gist*, 46–47; Long, *Civil War Day by Day*, 13.
7. Swanberg, *First Blood*, 94, 109–11.
8. OR, vol. 1: 2, 3, 252, 124–25; Swanberg, *First Blood*, 123.
9. Seabrook, *Unveiling of the Ripley Monument*, 4–6; OR, vol. 1: 9–10, Swanberg, *First Blood*, 144–48, 153.
10. S.C. Senate to Francis Pickens, Jan. 28, 1861, Law Papers, SHC; R. S. Ripley to R. G. M. Dunovant, Jan. 31 and Feb. 1, 1861, Dunovant Papers, Duke; Cisco, *States Rights Gist*, 55.
11. R. S. Ripley to Walter Gwynne, Feb. 1, 1861, R. S. Ripley to R. G. M. Dunovant, Feb. 2, 1861, Dunovant Papers, Duke.
12. Long, *Civil War Day by Day*, 21–25, 27, 29–31, 33–34, 38–39.
13. *Charleston Mercury*, Feb. 11, 1861, 2.
14. Rhett, "Flag, 1st S.C. Artillery," 126; "Flag, 1st S.C. Artillery," 6–7, Charleston City Council Proceedings.
15. R. S. Ripley to Captain George James, Feb. 8, 9, 1861, Misc. Ripley Papers, SCL.
16. OR, vol. 1: 260; R. S. Ripley to L. P. Walker, n.d., W. Porcher Miles, J. H. Trapier, and G. T. Beauregard to Jefferson Davis, Mar 8–15, 1861, Service Record, R. S. Ripley, SCAH; OR, vol. 1: 262–65, 267.
17. Swanberg, *First Blood*, 221, 220, 226–31.
18. OR, vol. 1: 277, 279, 283.
19. *Charleston Mercury*, Apr. 1, 1861, 1; OR, vol. 1: 228–29.
20. Swanberg, *First Blood*, 254–55; OR, vol. 1: 226–27, 229, 284, 286–89; Swanberg, *First Blood*, 271.
21. OR, vol. 1: 285; Swanberg, *First Blood*, 269.

Chapter 11: The Bombardment

1. Swanberg, *First Blood*, 270, 280–81.
2. Ibid, 270; OR, vol. 1: 297, 301, 298–300.
3. Swanberg, *First Blood*, 291–92; "Talk with Gen. Ripley," *New York World*, Mar. 17, 1885.
4. OR, vol. 1: 39–40.
5. Dudley, *Going South*, 5.
6. OR, vol. 1: 13–14; Swanberg, *First Blood*, 295–96; OR, vol. 1: 40; "Talk with Gen. Ripley," *New York World*, Mar. 17, 1885.
7. *Charleston Mercury*, Apr. 13, 1861; OR, vol. 1: 40; de Fontaine, "Second Day of the War," 205.
8. Chester, "Inside Sumter in '61," 67–68.

9. Doubleday, *Reminiscences of Forts Sumter and Moultrie*, 161–62.
10. *OR*, vol. 1: 41.
11. Doubleday, *Reminiscences of Forts Sumter and Moultrie*, 153–57; *OR*, vol. 1: 311.
12. King, *Louis T. Wigfall*, 118–19; Swanberg, *First Blood*, 317–20; Ringold, "William Gourdin Young," 31–32.
13. *OR*, vol. 1: 63–66; Swanberg, *First Blood*, 320, 326–29.
14. *OR*, vol. 1: 42, 43; Swanberg, *First Blood*, 330.
15. Johnson, *Defense of Charleston Harbor*, 18–20; Marszalek, *Emma Holmes*, 60–61.
16. Seabrook, *Unveiling of the Ripley Monument*, 6; R. S. Ripley to Pickens, May 13, 1861, Pickens Papers, Duke; *Charleston Mercury*, May 21, 1861, 1; *OR*, ser. 4, vol. 1, 317–18.
17. Sifakis, *Who Was Who*; Russell, William Howard, 563; Williams, *P. G. T. Beauregard*, 64–67; *Charleston Mercury*, June 6, 1861, 1; July 20, 1861, 1.
18. de la Cova, *Cuban Confederate Colonel*, 150, 125, 141–42, 147.
19. Chichester, *Inside the Forts*, 1, 2, 3, 7.
20. Seabrook, *Unveiling of the Ripley Monument*, 7; *Charleston Mercury*, Aug. 16, 1861, 1; *OR*, vol. 6: 267.
21. *Charleston Mercury*, Sept. 9, 1861, 2; *ORN*, vol. 12: 379, 428, 445, 446.
22. *OR*, vol. 6: 269–71, 273–74.
23. Nepveux, *Trenholm*, 21; *OR*, ser. 4, vol. 1: 616, 623.
24. F. L. Childs to wife, Sept. 3, 4, 8, 1861, Childs Papers, SCL.
25. General R.S. Ripley to Captain F. L. Childs, Oct. 24, 1861; Captain F.L. Childs to General R.S. Ripley, Oct. 25, 1861; Captain F. L. Childs to Lt. Colonel J. Gorgas, Oct. 26, 1861; Lt. Colonel J. Gorgas to Secretary of War J. P. Benjamin, Nov. 2, 1867. Letters, War Department, M437, NARA.

Chapter 12: Robert E. Lee in Command

1. *OR*, vol. 6: 168–71; Burton, *Siege of Charleston*, 68; Leland, "Middleton Correspondence," *SCHM* (Jan. 1862): 35.
2. Edmunds, *Francis W. Pickens*, 164, 10; F. W. Pickens to R. S. Ripley, Oct. 3, Ripley to Pickens, Oct. 5, 20, 24, 1861, Law Papers, SHC; Edmunds, *Francis W. Pickens*, 164.
3. Burton, *Siege of Charleston*, 69–71; *OR*, vol. 6: 306, 309.
4. *OR*, vol. 6: 309; *Charleston Mercury*, Nov. 8, 1861, 2; *OR*, vol. 6: 9, 13–14; Marszalek, *Emma Holmes*, 104, *OR*, vol. 6: 312–13.
5. de la Cova, *Cuban Confederate Colonel*, 147, 151–56, 158–59, 171.
6. Sifakis, "Rhett, Robert Barnwell," *Who Was Who*, 541; *Charleston Mercury*, Nov. 11, 1861, 1; *OR*, vol. 6: 323–24.
7. *OR*, vol. 6: 327, 329; F. W. Pickens to Jefferson Davis, Nov. 24, 1861, Pickens Papers, SCAH; *OR*, vol. 6: 334.
8. *OR*, vol. 53: 193; *OR*, vol. 6: 336–37, 339; *OR*, vol. 53: 196–98; *OR*, vol. 6, 344–45.
9. *Charleston Mercury*, Dec. 12, 1861, 2; Chichester, *Inside the Forts*, 3, 4; *Charleston Mercury*, Dec. 13, 16, 25, 1861.
10. *OR*, vol. 6: 346–47, 42–44; *ORN*, vol. 12: 423; *OR*, vol. 6: 352–54, 358–59, 361.
11. *OR*, vol. 6: 363–64, 366, 361–62, 384.
12. Ibid., 367, 369–71, 382.
13. Leland, "Middleton Correspondence," *SCHM* (Jan. 1962): 40.
14. *OR*, vol. 6: 385–86, 389; *Charleston Mercury*, Feb. 19, 1862, 2.
15. *OR*, vol. 6: 387–88, 390–91.

16. Ibid., 391–93; Long, *Civil War Day by Day*, 171–72; *OR*, vol. 6: 394.

17. Freeman, *R. E. Lee*, 1:617; Freeman, *Lee's Lieutenants*, 1:273; *OR*, vol. 6: 400.

Chapter 13: General John C. Pemberton

1. *OR*, vol. 6: 400–402; Ballard, *Pemberton*, 24, 25, 64, 84–89.

2. Long, *Civil War Day by Day*, 172; *OR*, vol. 6: 398, 400, 420; *OR*, vol. 14: 481.

3. Crute, *Confederate States Army*, 247–48; Caldwell and Wallace, *Brigade of South Carolinians*, 32–33; *OR*, vol. 6: 267, 285; Boutelle, *Map of Charleston Harbor*.

4. J. F. Marshall to R. S. Ripley, Feb. 16, 1862, Marshall Letter Book, SCL; Boutelle, *Map of Charleston Harbor*.

5. W. H. Trescott to W. P. Miles, Mar. 10, 1862, Miles Papers, SHC; *OR*, vol. 6: 405, 414; Ballard, *Pemberton*, 90; *OR*, vol. 6: 415.

6. *Charleston Mercury*, Mar. 26, 1862, 2; Burton, *Siege of Charleston*, 211–12.

7. Bennett Diary, 11–14, 20, 23, Duke; *OR*, ser. 2, vol. 3: 323–25.

8. J. F. Marshall to R. S. Ripley, Mar. 28, 1862, Marshall Letter Book, SCL.

9. *OR*, vol. 6: 417; Hagood, *Memoirs of the War*, 57–60.

10. *OR*, vol. 6: 417–18, 423–26.

11. W. H. Trescott to W. P. Miles, Apr. 3, 1862, Miles Papers, SHC; Brennan, *Secessionville*, 23–24; *OR*, vol. 14: 495.

12. J. F. Marshall to R. S. Ripley, Apr. 6, 10, 12, 1862, Marshall to Jefferson Davis, Apr. 8, 1862, Marshall to George W. Randolph, Apr. 10, 1862, Marshall to James L. Orr, Apr. 12, 1862, Marshall to Ripley and Ripley to Marshall, Apr. 19, 1862, Marshall Letter Book, SCL; Caldwell and Wallace, *Brigade of South Carolinians*, 35, 66.

13. W. H. Trescott to W. P. Miles, Apr. 22, 1862, Miles Papers, SHC.

14. Brennan, *Secessionville*, 24–25; Botkin, *Civil War Treasury*, 151–53; *OR*, vol. 14: 14–15, 502–3.

15. Brennan, *Secessionville*, 25–27.

16. "George C. Eggleston Obituary," *New York Times*, Apr. 23, 1911; Eggleston, *Rebel's Recollections*, 142, 164–68.

17. *OR*, vol. 14: 503–4.

18. Brennan, *Secessionville*, 36, 38; *OR*, vol. 14: 16, 17, 507.

19. *OR*, vol. 14: 505–6, 503.

20. Ibid., 501–2, 509–10, 523–24.

21. Horres, "Affair of Honor," 9–11; *OR*, vol. 14: 504, 515–18.

22. Ibid., 519–21.

23. *ORN*, vol. 13: 139–40.

24. *Charleston Mercury*, May 31, 1862, 1.

25. Brennan, *Secessionville*, 69–73, 169–94, 303; Beauregard, "Defense of Charleston," 7; Cisco, *States Rights Gist*, 77, 85; Hagood, *Memoirs of the War*, 61; Johnson, *Defense of Charleston Harbor*, 25.

Chapter 14: Peninsula Campaign

1. Dowdey, *Seven Days*, 19, 21–22; Freeman, *R. E. Lee*, 1:556–602, 605–8; Dowdey, *Seven Days*, 21–23.

2. Sears, *To the Gates of Richmond*, 3–5, 12–14, 17–19; *OR*, vol. 5: 1099.

3. Sears, *To the Gates of Richmond*, 24, 34–39, 46–48, 61–62.

4. Ibid., 117–21, 138; Smith, *Battle of Seven Pines*, 129–30, 179.

5. *OR*, vol. 11, pt. 3: 563; Smith, *Battle of Seven Pines*, 130; Sears, *To the Gates of Richmond*, 25; Smith, *Battle of Seven Pines*, 130.

6. Sears, *To the Gates of Richmond*, 143; Smith, *Battle of Seven Pines*, 131, 136; Sears, *To the Gates of Richmond*, 144–45.

7. OR, vol. 14: 519; Crute, *Confederate Army*, 110–11; OR, vol. 11, pt. 2: 484–85; Bridges, *Lee's Maverick General*, 59–61.

8. Gallagher, introduction, *Lee's Maverick General*, xvii–xviii.

9. Bridges, *Lee's Maverick General*, 18, 23–26, 35.

10. Hughes and Stonesifer, *Gideon J. Pillow*, 41, 80, 96, 115.

11. OR, vol. 11, pt. 3: 573; OR, vol. 11, pt. 2: 651; Crute, *Confederate States Army*, 110–11, 109, 212, 214.

12. Reese, "Letters from J. B. Reese," Apr. 29, June 17, July 26, 1862; Thomas, *Doles-Cook Brigade*, 489–90.

13. OR, vol. 11, pt. 3: 595, 601; OR, vol. 11, pt. 1: 1051–52, 1047–50; OR, vol. 11, pt. 3: 609.

14. OR, vol. 11, pt. 1: 48; Sears, *To the Gates of Richmond*, 161–62, 174–77; Pollard, *Second Year of the War*, 311. Pollard claimed Ripley attended this meeting but listed the date as June 25.

15. Bridges, *Lee's Maverick General*, 62; Sears, *To the Gates of Richmond*, 181–88; OR, vol. 11, pt. 2, 498–99.

16. Bridges, *Lee's Maverick General*, 65; OR, vol. 11, pt. 2: 647, 756.

17. Bridges, *Lee's Maverick General*, 63; Sears, *To the Gates of Richmond*, 194–95, 201–3.

18. Sears, *To the Gates of Richmond*, 203–6; OR, vol. 11, pt. 2: 647, 756.

19. OR, vol. 11, pt. 2: 623, 835–36, 647–48, 657–58, 648–49.

20. Herring, "Hard Service in Camp," 19; OR, vol. 11, pt. 2: 976.

21. Reese, "Letters from J. B. Reese," July 12, 26, 1862.

22. Dowdey, *Seven Days*, 185–88, 191; Freeman, *Lee's Lieutenants*, 1:515; OR, vol. 11, pt. 2: 836.

23. Boykin, "Battle Pictures" July 24, 1862; Reese, "Letters from J. B. Reese," Aug. 16, 1862; Thomas, *Doles-Cook Brigade*, 494; Fleming Jourdan to wife, June 16, 1862, University of Georgia Libraries.

24. OR, vol. 11, pt. 2: 649, 624, 631, 649, 626.

25. Jones, "Campbell Brown's Memoirs," 54.

26. OR, vol. 11, pt. 2: 649, 494; Sears, *To the Gates of Richmond*, 310, 338; OR, vol. 11, pt. 2: 950–51.

27. Sears, *To the Gates of Richmond*, 329; OR, vol. 11, pt. 2: 629, 975–77, 623.

28. Law, "Fight for Richmond," 654.

Chapter 15: Maryland Campaign

1. Ferguson, *Ashes of Glory*, 150; OR, vol. 11, pt. 2: 629.

2. Sears, *To the Gates of Richmond*, 343–44, 156; Bridges, *Lee's Maverick General*, 87; Leach Diary, Jul. 20, 1862, SHC; OR, vol. 11, pt. 3, 658.

3. Sears, *To the Gates of Richmond*, 350–53.

4. Ibid., 354; OR, vol. 11, pt. 2: 956–64.

5. OR, vol. 11, pt. 3: 668–69.

6. OR, vol. 11, pt. 3: 671; OR, vol. 51, pt. 2: 1075; OR, vol. 12, pt. 3: 938, 965.

7. OR, vol. 19, pt. 1: 808, 1019; OR, vol. 12, pt. 3: 942; Thomas, *Doles-Cook Brigade*, 68, 468–69; Sifakis, "Hotchkiss, Jedediah," *Who Was Who*, 319; *Supplement to the Official Records*, pt. 1, *Reports*, vol. 2, serial no. 2: 598, Freeman, *R. E. Lee*, 2:340.

8. *OR*, vol. 19, pt. 1: 1019; Bridges, *Lee's Maverick General*, 89–90; *OR*, vol. 19, pt. 1: 1019; Thomas, *Doles-Cook Brigade*, 469.
9. *OR*, vol. 19, pt. 2: 603–4; Bridges, *Lee's Maverick General*, 91–94.
10. *OR*, vol. 19, pt. 1: 1019; Sears, *Landscape Turned Red*, 96.
11. *OR*, vol. 19, pt. 1: 1019, 816; Bridges, *Lee's Maverick General*, 94–96.
12. *OR*, vol. 19, pt. 1: 816–17, 1019, 817, 1031.
13. Sears, *Landscape Turned Red*, 125–29; *OR*, vol. 19, pt. 1: 817, 1019–20.
14. Sears, *Landscape Turned Red*, 129–30; Bridges, *Lee's Maverick General*, 108–9; *OR*, vol. 19, pt. 1: 1020, 1031–32.
15. *OR*, vol. 19, pt. 1: 1020, 804–5, 1031, 908, 1032, 1021.
16. Ibid., 908–9, 922, 1032.
17. Hill, "Battle of South Mountain," 143.
18. W. L. De Rosset to D. H. Hill, June 18, 1885, Hill Papers, Library of Virginia; Sears, *Antietam*, 134.
19. *Supplement to the Official Records*, pt.1, *Reports*, vol. 3, serial no. 3, 584–86.
20. Hill, "Battle of South Mountain," 143; Bridges, *Lee's Maverick General*, 111, 292n22.
21. Leach Diary, Sept. 14, 1862, SHC.
22. *OR*, vol. 19, pt. 1: 1032; Grattan, "The Battle of Boonsboro Gap," 40.
23. Bridges, *Lee's Maverick General*, 113–14; Murfin, *Gleam of Bayonets*, 191–92; Thomas, *Doles-Cook Brigade*, 68–69.
24. Thomas, *Doles-Cook Brigade*, 469; *OR*, vol. 19, pt. 1: 1032–33; Priest, *Antietam*, 23–24, 44, 46.
25. Thomas, *Doles-Cook Brigade*, 469–70; *OR*, vol. 19, pt. 1: 1033.
26. *OR*, vol. 19, pt. 1: 1027, 1033.
27. W. L. De Rosset to D. H. Hill, June 18, 1885, Hill Papers, Library of Virginia; Bridges, *Lee's Maverick General*, 108; Freeman, *Lee's Lieutenants*, 2:277.
28. Long, *Civil War Day by Day*, 267–68.

Chapter 16: Return to Charleston

1. *OR*, vol. 19, pt. 1: 1031; *Charleston Mercury*, Sept. 23, 1862, Sept. 24, 1862.
2. Ballard, *Pemberton*, 107; *OR*, vol. 53: 247; *OR*, vol. 14: 560–61, 567, 581–82, 585.
3. F. W. Pickens to Jefferson Davis, July. 29, 1862, Pickens Papers, SCAH; *OR*, vol. 14: 597–98; Pickens to Davis, Aug. 20, 1862, Pickens Papers, SCAH.
4. *OR*, vol. 14: 601, 603–4, 608–9; *OR*, vol. 15: 820.
5. Horres, "Affair of Honor," 9, 18–20; Rosen, *Confederate Charleston*, 104.
6. Marszalek, *Diary of Miss Emma Holmes*, 196; Horres, "Affair of Honor," 20–21.
7. R. S. Ripley to G. T. Beauregard, Dec. 29, 1863, Ripley to Beauregard, Sept. 29, 1862, Service Record, R. S. Ripley, SCAH.
8. S.C. Congressmen to Jefferson Davis, Sept. 30, 1862, Letters Rec'd, War Department, M474, NARA.
9. *OR*, vol. 14: 616, 581; Sifakis, "Smith, William Duncan," *Who Was Who*, 608; *OR*, vol. 14: 632, 635.
10. *Charleston Mercury*, Oct. 15, 1862, 2; *OR*, vol. 14: 581, 641.
11. *OR*, vol. 14: 656, 649–52.
12. Ibid., 652–56.
13. R. S. Ripley to Thomas Jordan, Oct. 30, 1862, Letters Rec'd, Adjutant and Inspector General (hereinafter A&IGO), M474, NARA.

14. Horres, "Affair of Honor," 21–22; *OR*, vol. 14: 515; Horres, "Affair of Honor," 22.
15. Leland, "Middleton Correspondence," *SCHM* (Oct. 1962): 209; Horres, "Affair of Honor," 22.
16. *Charleston Mercury*, Nov. 1, 1862, 2.
17. F. W. Pickens to R. S. Ripley, Nov. 29, 1862, Pickens Papers, SCAH.
18. de la Cova, *Cuban Confederate Colonel*, 182.
19. *OR*, vol. 14: 689–92.
20. F. L. Childs to wife, Dec. 11, 1862, Childs Papers, SCL; *OR*, vol. 14: 745–46, 761; Manarin, *North Carolina Troops*, 3:342.
21. Leland, "Middleton Correspondence," *SCHM* (Oct. 1962): 210.
22. Cisco, *Henry Timrod*, 24, 38–40, 42, 78–79, 81, 83.
23. *Charleston Mercury*, Jan. 1, 1863, 2; Vouchers and Accounts, Dec. 1861–July 1863, Service Record, R. S. Ripley, SCAH.
24. Hayne, *Poems of Henry Timrod*, 99–100.

Chapter 17: The Impending Storm

1. *OR*, vol. 14: 732–35.
2. Miscellaneous Ripley Papers, SCL.
3. *OR*, vol. 14: 743–45.
4. *Charleston Mercury*, Jan. 20, 1863, 2; Hoole, *Vizetelly Covers the Confederacy*, 63.
5. Augustine Smythe to wife, Jan. 25, 1863, Smythe Papers, SCHS; *Supplement to the Official Records*, pt. 2, *Record of Events*, vol. 64, serial no. 76: 394.
6. *ORN*, vol. 13: 505, 509, 521, 526–28; *OR*, vol. 14: 200–1.
7. *OR*, vol. 14: 756; *ORN*, vol. 13: 566; Burton, *Siege of Charleston*, 123.
8. G. T. Beauregard to Samuel Cooper, Feb. 7, 1863, Service Record, R. S. Ripley, SCAH.
9. *OR*, vol. 14: 204; *ORN*, vol. 13: 660–61; *OR*, vol. 14: 204–6; Burton, *Siege of Charleston*, 130.
10. *Charleston Mercury*, Feb. 13, 1863, 1.
11. Leland, "Middleton Correspondence," *SCHM* (Jan. 1863): 35.
12. *OR*, vol. 14: 790–91.
13. *OR*, vol. 14: 776, 802–7.
14. Ibid., 812–13.
15. Leland, "Middleton Correspondence," *SCHM* (Jan. 1863): 36; Edgar, *South Carolina*, 292, photograph following 406; personal visit to Roper House; Leland, "Middleton Correspondence," 36.
16. *OR*, vol. 14: 829–34.
17. Ibid., 749–50, 818, 825–26, 847.
18. Hoole, *Vizetelly Covers the Confederacy*, 68–69.

Chapter 18: Attack of the Ironclads

1. *ORN*, vol. 13: 493–94, 503–4, 531, 543–44, 547, 549.
2. Ibid., 692, 736–37.
3. Ibid., 756, 745–46, 766, 787; *OR*, vol. 14: 846; *ORN*, vol. 13: 802.
4. *Charleston Mercury*, Mar. 31, 1863, 2.
5. Johnson, *Defense of Charleston Harbor*, 43–47.
6. Ibid., 48–49.
7. Ibid., 49–50, 32; *OR*, vol. 14: 948–52.
8. *ORN*, vol. 14: 11–13; Johnson, *Defense of Charleston Harbor*, 50–51.

9. Ibid., 51; *ORN*, vol. 14: 9–13.
10. Ibid., 13–16.
11. Johnson, *Defense of Charleston Harbor,* 49; *ORN*, vol. 14: 16–20.
12. *ORN*, vol. 14: 21–23; *ORN*, vol. 13: 631; *ORN*, vol. 14: 10, 12.
13. Johnson, *Defense of Charleston Harbor,* 43; *ORN*, vol. 14: 23–25.
14. *OR*, vol. 14: 257.
15. *Charleston Mercury,* Apr. 9, 1863, 2.
16. *Charleston Mercury,* Apr. 10, 1863, 2.
17. *OR*, vol. 14: 257–61.
18. Ibid., 893; Leland, "Middleton Correspondence," *SCHM* (April 1963): 96.
19. *ORN*, vol. 14: 44, 45, 141; Johnson, *Defense of Charleston Harbor,* 63; *ORN*, vol. 14, 110; *OR*, vol. 14, 261.
20. Johnson, *Defense of Charleston Harbor,* 64, 65; *OR*, vol. 14: 243.
21. Johnson, *Defense of Charleston Harbor,* 65–71; *ORN*, vol. 14: 212–13; *OR*, vol. 14: 243.
22. *OR*, vol. 14: 286–87, 921–23.
23. Ibid., 923, 925–26.
24. Ibid., 933, 936–37.
25. Ibid., 938–42.

Chapter 19: The Defense of Morris Island

1. *OR*, vol. 14: 1024, 880–81.
2. Ibid., 776, 1024.
3. Wise, *Gate of Hell,* 58.
4. *OR*, vol. 14: 938, 956, 1021–23.
5. Cullum, "David B. Harris," *Biographical Register of the Officers,* 542; Wise, *Gate of Hell,* 19; Beauregard, "Defense of Charleston," 8.
6. *OR*, vol. 14: 956–57.
7. Ibid., 956–59.
8. Rhett, "Mitchel at Fort Sumter," 6–7; *OR*, vol. 28, pt. 2: 140–41.
9. Ibid., 147–50.
10. Ibid., 151.
11. Fremantle, *Three Months in the Southern States,* v, 179.
12. Ibid., 180–82.
13. Ibid., 182; Emerson and Stokes, *Confederate Englishman,* x–xiii, 1.
14. Fremantle, *Three Months in the Southern States,* 182–83, 179, 185–87.
15. Ibid., 188–90, 185, 190.
16. Ibid., 191–92, 193, 195–96, 198–99.
17. Ibid., 200, 202–5.
18. *OR*, vol. 28, pt. 2: 164–65.
19. Ibid., 166.
20. Ibid., 166–67.
21. Ibid., 167.
22. Ibid., 167–68.
23. Ibid., 168–69, 174–75, 148.
24. *OR*, vol. 35, pt. 2: 634.
25. *OR*, vol. 28, pt. 2: 171–72.
26. Ibid., 177–80.
27. Ibid., 180–83.

28. Ibid., 183–84; Pressley, "Diary of Lieutenant-Colonel John G. Pressley," 54–55.
29. Wise, *Gate of Hell*, 59–61, 77, 226.

Chapter 20: Attacks on Battery Wagner

1. Wise, *Gate of Hell*, 25, 36; OR, vol. 28, pt. 1: 1; Wise, *Gate of Hell*, 42–43, 66–67.
2. OR, vol. 28, pt. 2: 186–87; Wise, *Gate of Hell*, 74.
3. Ibid., 68; OR, vol. 28, pt. 2: 186.
4. Wise, *Gate of Hell*, 69, 70; OR, vol. 28, pt. 2: 188.
5. OR, vol. 28, pt. 1: 370; Wise, *Gate of Hell*, 73, 71; OR, vol. 28, pt. 1: 368–69, 371, 523; Wise, *Gate of Hell*, 82.
6. Wise, *Gate of Hell*, 76, 78, 229; OR, vol. 28, pt. 1: 371.
7. *Charleston Mercury*, July 11, 1863, 1.
8. OR, vol. 28, pt. 1: 60–62, 371.
9. Olmstead, "Reminiscences of Service in Charleston Harbor," 124.
10. Wise, *Gate of Hell*, 81; Susan Middleton to Harriott Middleton, July 9, 1863, Correspondence, Cheves-Middleton Papers, SCHS.
11. OR, vol. 28, pt. 1: 371; Wise, *Gate of Hell*, 84; OR, vol. 28, pt. 1: 372, 549; Pressley, "Diary of Lieutenant-Colonel John G. Pressley," 58; OR, vol. 28, pt. 1: 372; Wise, *Gate of Hell*, 48–51.
12. Wise, *Gate of Hell*, 93, 95–96, 21, 100; OR, vol. 28, pt. 1: 372–73.
13. Ibid., 373; Wise, *Gate of Hell*, 97–98.
14. Wise, *Gate of Hell*, 232, 48–49, 98–101.
15. Ibid., 99, 232–33, 101–6.
16. Ibid., 107–8.
17. Ibid., 109–12; OR, vol. 28, pt. 1: 373.
18. Wise, *Gate of Hell*, 112; OR, vol. 28, pt. 1: 373; Wise, *Gate of Hell*, 114.
19. Wise, *Gate of Hell*, 121–22; OR, vol. 28, pt. 2: 211–14, 216–19, 223, 231; OR, vol. 28: pt.1, 377.
20. Stiles, "Roll of Honor," 136–38; Stiles, "Victoria Cross of the Confederacy," 304.
21. OR, vol. 28, pt. 1: 374; Gilchrist, *Defense of Morris Island*. 36; Stiles, "Roll of Honor," 137; Johnson, *Defense of Charleston Harbor*, 144.
22. OR, vol. 28, pt. 2: 176, 226–27; OR, vol. 28, pt. 1: 374, 391.
23. OR, vol. 28, pt. 2: 221–22.
24. Ibid., 223–24.
25. Ibid., 224, 251.
26. Register of Mesne Conveyances, Aug. 1863, U 14, 45–46, Charleston County Records.
27. Augustine Smythe to aunt, Apr. 23, 1863, Smythe Papers, SCHS; C. K. Prioleau to Theodore Wagner, May 1, 1863, Fraser Trenholm Collection, Maritime Archives; Wise, *Lifeline of Confederacy*. 252, 256, 238, 247, 280, 324.

Chapter 21: Siege and Bombardment

1. Wise, *Gate of Hell*, 119–20.
2. OR, vol. 28, pt. 1: 421; Gilchrist, *Defense of Morris Island*, 26–27.
3. OR, vol. 28, pt. 2: 225–26; Ripley, *Siege Train*, map, xxi.
4. OR, vol. 28, pt. 2: 228, 233–34.
5. Ibid., 237–39.
6. OR, vol. 28, pt. 1: 381–82.
7. OR, vol. 28, pt. 2: 253–54.

8. Ibid., 255–57; Williams, *P. G. T. Beauregard*, 33.
9. *OR*, vol. 28, pt. 2: 257.
10. *OR*, vol. 28, pt. 1: 382; *OR*, vol. 28, pt. 2: 258.
11. *OR*, vol. 28, pt. 1: 385
12. Wise, *Gate of Hell*, 154–56.
13. *OR*, vol. 28, pt. 1: 386–87.
14. Ibid., 387–88.
15. *OR*, vol. 28, pt. 2: 287; *OR*, vol. 28, pt. 1: 388–89; Johnson, *Defense of Charleston Harbor*, 119–21.
16. *OR*, vol. 28, pt. 1: 389–90; Wise, *Gate of Hell*, 132–33.
17. Johnson, *Defense of Charleston Harbor*, 124; *Charleston Mercury*, Aug. 20, 1863, 2.
18. Johnson, *Defense of Charleston Harbor*, 125–27.
19. Sturgill and Price, "McCabe's Impression," 266–69.
20. Johnson, *Defense of Charleston Harbor*, 128; *OR*, vol. 28, pt. 1: 393–94.
21. Johnson, *Defense of Charleston Harbor*, 131–32, 137–39.
22. *OR*, vol. 28, pt. 2, 311, 309.
23. Ibid., 322.
24. *OR*, vol. 28: 57–62; Wise, *Gate of Hell*, 168–72; *Charleston Mercury*, Aug. 31, 1863, 1.
25. Wise, *Gate of Hell*, 173–77.
26. *OR*, vol. 28, pt. 1: 57–59, 94–100.
27. *OR*, vol. 28, pt. 2: 328–32; *OR*, vol. 28, pt. 1, 398–99.
28. *OR*, vol. 28, pt. 2: 334–36; *OR*, vol. 28, pt. 1: 399–400, 621.
29. Augustine Smythe to aunt, Sept. 5, 1863, Smythe Papers, SCHS.
30. *OR*, 400–401; Wise, *Gate of Hell*, 201–2.
31. Rhett, "Morris Island," 336–42.
32. Huguenin, Journal and Record, 23, 32–33, Citadel Archives and Museum.

Chapter 22: The *H. L. Hunley* Arrives

1. Johnson, *Defense of Charleston Harbor*, 154–56; *OR*, vol. 28, pt. 2: 344.
2. Johnson, *Defense of Charleston Harbor*, 159–63.
3. *OR*, vol. 28, pt. 2: 350–51.
4. Ibid., 358–59, 365.
5. Ibid., 364, 366–67, 374.
6. Ibid., 380–81.
7. Ibid., 365, 388–89.
8. G. T. Beauregard to Samuel Cooper, Oct. 2, 1863, Service Record, R. S. Ripley, SCAH.
9. *OR*, vol. 28, pt. 2: 400.
10. Ibid., 398.
11. *OR*, vol. 14: 1015–17; *Charleston Mercury*, April 9, 1863, 2.
12. *Charleston Mercury*, Oct. 10, 1863, 2.
13. R. S. Ripley to G. T. Beauregard, Oct. 10, 1863, Beauregard to Samuel Cooper, Oct. 26, 1863, J. T. Trezevant to Josiah Gorgas, Nov. 1, 1863, Letters Rec'd, A&IGO, M474, NARA.
14. Vouchers and Accounts, March 1864, Service Record, R. S. Ripley, SCAH.
15. Ragan, *The Hunley*, 41–45, 62–69.
16. Ibid., 73; *OR*, vol. 28, pt. 2: 351; Ragan, *The Hunley*, 78.
17. Ragan, *The Hunley*, 81–100.

18. Vouchers and Accounts, July–Oct. 1863, Service Record, R. S. Ripley, SCAH.
19. Harriott Middleton to Susan Middleton, Oct. 22, 1863, Correspondence, Cheves-Middleton Papers, SCHS.
20. Johnson, *Defense of Charleston Harbor*, 170; OR, vol. 28, pt. 2: 463.
21. Ibid., 466.
22. Williams, *P. G. T. Beauregard*, 198–99.
23. *Charleston Mercury*, Nov. 4, 1863, 2; Rosen, *Confederate Charleston*, 127; *Charleston Mercury*, Nov. 6, 1863, 2.
24. OR, vol. 28, pt. 2: 484; OR, vol. 28, pt. 1: 155; OR, vol. 28, pt. 2: 488–90, 503.
25. Ibid., 495–98.

Chapter 23: Ripley Rebuked

1. OR, vol. 28, pt. 2: 502.
2. Ibid., 502–3, 171.
3. Ibid., 515–16.
4. Ibid., 516–18.
5. Ibid., 518–19.
6. Ibid., 519–20.
7. Ibid., 523, 527.
8. Ibid., 528–29; OR, vol. 14: 825–26.
9. OR, vol. 28, pt. 2: 539–41; OR, vol. 14, 1024, 881; OR, vol. 28, pt. 2: 541.
10. OR, vol. 28, pt. 2: 548–49.
11. Ibid., 556–59.
12. Ibid., 565, 593.
13. Ragan, *Hunley*, 108–15, 118–19; OR, vol. 28, pt. 2: 553.
14. Susan Middleton to Harriott Middleton, Dec. 23, 1863, Correspondence, Cheves-Middleton Papers, SCHS.
15. R. S. Ripley to Jordan, Dec. 29, 1863, Service Record, R. S. Ripley, SCAH.
16. OR, vol. 35, pt. 1: 502, 506.
17. OR, vol. 28, pt. 2: 520.
18. Ibid., 559.
19. Johnson, *Defense of Charleston Harbor*, 180–82; Rosen, *Confederate Charleston*, 121.

Chapter 24: The *H. L. Hunley* Lost at Sea

1. OR, vol. 35, pt. 1: 513–16.
2. OR, vol. 28, pt. 2: 560.
3. OR, vol. 35, pt. 1: 518, 557, 518–19.
4. Ragan, *The Hunley*, 115, 124, 118–19, 114, 152, 143, 147, 145, 156.
5. OR, vol. 35, pt.1: 534.
6. Sears, *To the Gates of Richmond*, 41, 43, 53–54; OR, vol. 35, pt.1: 543, 547–48.
7. OR, vol. 35, pt.1: 578, 582, 598–99, 602, 606–7.
8. Ragan, *The Hunley*, 145, 147, 150–53, 156–57.
9. Susan Middleton to Harriott Middleton, Jan. 31, 1864, Correspondence, Cheves-Middleton Papers, SCHS; OR, vol. 35, pt. 1: 466–68.
10. Ragan, *The Hunley*, 164, 170, 166, 171.
11. OR, vol. 35, pt. 1: 262.
12. Ragan, *Hunley*, 184–85; OR, vol. 35, pt. 1: 620.

13. *OR*, vol. 35, pt. 1: 621, 633; R. S. Ripley to Thomas Jordan, February 22. 1864, Service Record, R. S. Ripley, SCAH.

14. *OR*, vol. 35, pt. 1: 112–13.

15. *Statutes at Large of South Carolina*, 227; Register of Mesne Conveyances, Dec. 1864, 296–99, Charleston County Records.

16. Cuthbert and Hoffius, *Northern Money, Southern Land*, 4, 68.

Chapter 25: Ripley Returns and Reacts

1. *OR*, vol. 35, pt. 2: 404.
2. Ibid., 409, 414, 415–22.
3. Ibid., 415–16.
4. Ibid., 417.
5. Ibid., 417–18.
6. Ibid., 418–19.
7. Ibid., 419–20.
8. Ibid., 420–21.
9. Ibid., 421–22.
10. Ibid., 425–26.
11. Ibid., 26, 428–29, 434–36.
12. Ibid., 427, 443; Emerson and Stokes, *Confederate Englishman*, 13–14; *OR*, vol. 14: 306–7.
13. *OR*, vol. 35, pt. 2: 451, 473.
14. Ibid., 474, 478, 480.
15. Ibid., 482–84.
16. Ibid., 484–85.
17. Ibid., 489–90, 493–94, 496.
18. *OR*, vol. 35, pt. 1: 137–39, 264, 271.
19. *OR*, vol. 35, pt. 2: 132, 134–5,
20. Ibid., 143, 147–48.
21. *OR*, ser. 2, vol. 7: 415–16; *OR*, vol. 35, pt. 2: 163, 198; *OR*, ser. 2, vol. 7: 571–72.

Chapter 26: Ripley in Crisis

1. *OR*, vol. 35, pt. 1: 207–15.
2. *OR*, vol. 35, pt. 2: 537, 545–48, 555.
3. Huguenin, Journal and Record, 34, 35, Citadel Archives and Museum.
4. *OR*, vol. 35, pt. 2: 570; *OR*, vol. 35, pt. 1: 221–26; *OR*, vol. 35, pt. 2: 575–76; *OR*, vol. 35, pt.1: 123–26.
5. *OR*, vol. 35, pt. 2: 589–90.
6. *OR*, vol. 35, pt. 1: 225–26.
7. Rhett, "Mitchel at Fort Sumter," 6, 7; Huguenin, Journal and Record, 35, 36, Citadel Archives and Museum; Rhett, "Mitchel at Fort Sumter," 7.
8. *OR*, vol. 35, pt. 1: 227, 230–43; Johnson, *Defense of Charleston Harbor*, 235–36, 231.
9. *OR*, vol. 35, pt. 2: 213–14; C. K. Prioleau to H. U. Le Court, Nov. 25, 1863, Prioleau Papers, SCHS.
10. Henry Hotze to R. S. Ripley, Sept. 10, 1864, Hotze Letter Book, LOC.
11. *OR*, ser. 2, vol. 7: 805; *OR*, vol. 35, pt. 2: 622; *OR*, ser. 2, vol. 7: 841.
12. *OR*, ser. 2, vol. 7: 878, 886, 890–91.

13. *OR,* vol. 35, pt. 2: 627; "Life and Recollections Joseph W. Barnwell," 136, Charleston Library Society.
14. *OR,* vol. 35, pt. 2: 623–24.
15. Ibid., 628–29, 630.
16. Ibid., 631–32; *OR,* vol. 35, pt. 1: 126.
17. *OR,* vol. 35, pt. 2: 629.
18. Ibid., 630.
19. Ibid., 632–33.
20. Emerson and Stokes, *Confederate Englishman,* x, 78–80.
21. *OR,* vol. 35, pt. 2, 633–34; Susan Middleton to Harriott Middleton, Dec. 23, 1863, Correspondence, Cheves-Middleton Papers, SCHS.
22. *OR,* vol. 35, pt. 2: 630.
23. Ibid., 635, 637, 639, 643–44, 646, 649–50.
24. Ibid., 640–43.
25. Ibid., 646–47; *Charleston Mercury,* Nov. 23, 1864, 1.
26. *OR,* vol. 44: 872, 873, 877–85.
27. Edw. B. Middleton Diary, Nov. 27, 1864, Cheves-Middleton Papers, SCHS; *Charleston Mercury,* Nov. 25, 1864, 2.
28. G. T. Beauregard to Jefferson Davis, Dec. 13, 1864, Beauregard to Samuel Cooper, Dec. 16, 1864, P.G.T. Beauregard Papers. LOC.
29. J. M. Otey to Alfred Roman, Dec. 13, Roman to Otey, Dec. 16, 1864, Exhibits A-E, Civil War Misc. Collection, U.S. Army Military History Institute.; T. A. Huguenin to Roman, Dec. 14, 1864, Beauregard Papers. SCL.
30. Jones, *Siege of Charleston Harbor,* 5–7, 167, 196.
31. Andrew Magrath to R. W. Barnwell, Jan. 1, 1865, Civil War Misc. Collection, U.S. Army Military History Institute.

Chapter 27: Death of the Confederacy

1. "Talk with Gen. Ripley," *New York World,* Mar. 17, 1885; *OR,* vol. 47, pt. 2: 1031, 1001; Long, *Civil War Day by Day,* 603, 610–11; *OR,* vol. 44: 1009–10.
2. "Talk with Gen. Ripley," *New York World,* Mar. 17, 1885; *OR,* vol. 47, pt. 2: 991; Wyckoff, *3rd S.C. Infantry,* 33, 215–16.
3. Sifakis, "Seddon, James Alexander," *Who Was Who,* 578; *OR,* vol. 47, pt. 2: 992; *OR,* vol. 35, pt. 2: 647–48; Freeman and McWhiney, *Lee's Dispatches,* 312–14.
4. *OR,* vol. 47, pt. 2: 997, 1000, 1014, 1018.
5. Ibid., 991, 1001–2; Bradley, *Last Stand,* 28; *OR,* vol. 47, pt. 2: 1023, 1001.
6. *OR,* vol. 47, pt. 2: 1030–32, 1043, 1038, 1051; Cisco, *States Rights Gist,* 142; Hughes and Stonesifer, *Gideon J. Pillow,* 58, 80, 86, 96, 115.
7. *OR,* vol. 47, pt. 2: 1058, 1061.
8. Bradley, *Last Stand in the Carolinas,* 4, 5, 21–22
9. *OR,* vol. 47, pt. 2: 1083–84, 1090, 1098, 1104, 1107.
10. Seabrook, *Unveiling of the Ripley Monument,* 12; Côté, *Mary's World,* 197; Middleton, *Life in Carolina,* 161–62.
11. Burton Diaries, Feb. 1–7, 1865, Yale-2; Jones, *War Clerk's Diary,* vol. 2, 411.
12. J. H. Burton to John Anderson, July 18, 1860, Yale-2; Burton Diaries, Feb. 24, Apr. 26, June 5, 1860, Yale-2; Norman, *Burton's Revolver,* 2, 6–9; Burton Diaries, Sept. 29, Oct. 12, Nov. 5–Dec. 15, 1860, Yale-2; Edwards, "One-Man Armory," 30; Norman, *Burton's Spiller and Burr Revolver,* 63–66, 14–16, 101–5.

13. *OR*, vol. 47, pt. 2: 1120, 1158, 1165–66.

14. Ibid., 1030–31.

15. Ibid., 1181, 1185; Bradley, *Last Stand in the Carolinas*, 23; *OR*, vol. 47, pt. 2: 1202, 1208–9, 1193.

16. *OR*, vol. 47, pt. 1: 1044; Dowdey and Manarin, *Wartime Papers of Robert E. Lee*, 904–6.

17. *OR*, vol. 47, pt. 2: 1232; Andrew Magrath to W. H. Trescott, Feb. 23, 1865, Magrath Papers, SCAH.

18. *OR*, vol. 47, pt. 2: 1238; Dowdey and Manarin, *Wartime Papers of Robert E. Lee*, 909; Welsh, *Medical Histories of Confederate Generals*, 18–19; *OR*, vol. 47, pt. 2: 1050, 1113.

19. *OR*, vol. 47, pt. 2: 1078–79, Dowdey and Manarin, *Wartime Papers of Robert E. Lee*, 894, 909; *OR*, vol. 47, pt. 2: 1248.

20. Burton Diaries, Feb. 23–Mar. 1, 1865, Yale-2; *OR*, vol. 47, pt. 2: 1201, 503.

21. J. M. Payne to J. H. Burton, Sept 13, 1864, Yale-2; Burton Diaries, Aug. 13, 14, Sept. 3, 4, Oct. 12, 24, 1857, July 12, 31, Aug. 1, 1858, Feb. 10 and 25, 1859, Feb. 23, May 3, 5, June 5, 23, July 23, 24, Sept. 18, 19, 1860, Yale-2; Greenwood & Batley to Burton, Sept. 25, 1860, Yale-2.

22. Josiah Gorgas to J. H. Burton, Apr. 2, 1863, James Seddon to J. M. Mason and John Slidell, Apr. 25, 1863, Burton to Gorgas, Apr. 13, July 11, 30, 1863, Yale-2; Wise, *Lifeline*, 46; Burton Diaries, Sept. 5, 1863, Yale-2.

23. J. H. Burton to Fraser, Trenholm, Oct. 2, 1863, *Princes Royal* invoice, Jan. 11, 1864, *Queen of Britain* invoice, Jan. 21, 1864, N. S. Walker to Burton, Apr. 18, 1864, Yale-2; Wise, *Lifeline*, 118–19, 317; Fraser, Trenholm to Burton, May 6, 1864, Yale-2.

24. Wise, *Lifeline*, 133; Fraser, Trenholm to J. H. Burton, June 11, Aug. 3, 1864, Payne to Burton, Sept. 2 and 13, 1864, Heyliger to Burton, Sept. 19, 1864, Yale-2; Wise, *Lifeline*, 165; Burton to Chambliss, Oct. 7, 1864, Payne to Burton, Oct. 14, 1864, Yale-2.

25. Louis C. Heyliger to J. H. Burton, Oct. 18, 1864, with Burton's added memo, Yale-2; Wise, *Lifeline of the Confederacy*, 305; Fraser, Trenholm to Burton, Jan. 19, 1864, Yale-2; *OR*, vol. 47, pt. 2: 74, 483.

26. Inventories, Greenwood & Batley to Fraser, Trenholm, Dec. 31, 1863, Apr. 20, July 12, Sept. 28, Dec. 1, 1864, Feb. 14, Apr. 26, Aug. 1, Oct. 18, 1865, Yale-2; Deliveries to C.S.A., June 5, 6, Sept. 16, Dec. 9, 1864, Yale-2; Norman, *Burton's Spiller and Burr Revolver*, 90–91; Memo, Machinery lost in U.S., compiled Oct.–Nov. 1865, Yale-2.

27. Burton Diaries, Mar. 2–16, Apr. 20, 1865, Yale-2; Norman, *Burton's Spiller and Burr Revolver*, 91.

Chapter 28: Chaos and Flight to England

1. *OR*, vol. 47, pt. 1: 1082–83; Bradley, *Last Stand in the Carolinas*, 137; *OR*, vol. 47, pt. 2: 1399, 1412; Bradley, *Last Stand in the Carolinas*, 441, 375, 386; Seabrook, *Unveiling of the Ripley Monument*, 12.

2. Davis, *Jefferson Davis*, 601–3, 420, 611–19, 623.

3. Woodward, *Mary Chesnut's Civil War*, xxx, 596, 755, 783–85; Sifakis, "Chesnut, Mary Boykin," *Who Was Who*, 118–19.

4. Woodward, *Mary Chesnut's Civil War*, 783; King, *Louis T. Wigfall*, 8, 31–34, 41, 47, 79, 111–13, 127–31, 184–89, 213, 217–23.

5. Davis, *Rise and Fall of the Confederate Government*, 2:579–80, 584, 587–88, 585; Davis, *Jefferson Davis*, 626–28, 631–32.

6. Evans, *Judah P. Benjamin*, xx, 4–5, 23, 26–29, 31–33, 102–3, 108–10, 403.
7. Long, *Civil War Day by Day*, 31, 38, 39; Evans, *Judah P. Benjamin*, 116, 120–22, 154–55, 172–73.
8. Evans, *Judah P. Benjamin*, 312–14; personal visit, Gamble Plantation; McKay, "Judah Philip Benjamin"; Evans, *Judah P. Benjamin*, 318–21.
9. Davis, *Jefferson Davis*, 633–38, 640–44.
10. Burton Diaries, Apr. 20, May 9, July 11–Sept. 3, 1865; Greenwood & Batley to Burton, Sept. 18, 1865; Burton Diaries, Oct. 9–28, 1865. All sources Yale-2.
11. *OR*, vol. 47, pt. 3: 843–44, 871; Woodward, *Mary Chesnut's Civil War*, 800–801, 793.
12. Barrett, *Sherman's March Through the Carolinas*, 95–98, 108–11; Côté, *Mary's World*, 235–37.
13. Lawley, "The Civil War in America," *Times* (London), Mar. 6, 1865, 6, and "The Confederate States," *Times* (London), Mar. 7, 1865, 5.
14. Burton, *Siege of Charleston*, 318–22; *OR*, vol. 47, pt. 2: 616.
15. Howard, *Franco-Prussian War*, 40–41.
16. Augustine Smythe to wife, Aug. 17, 1865, Smythe Papers, SCHS.
17. William Preston to Colin McRae, Oct. 21, 1865, McRae Collection, South Carolina Confederate Relic Room.

Chapter 29: England, 1866–1869

1. Greenwood vs. Ripley, 1–2, TNA; Heyward, "Descendants of Col. William Rhett," 63; Clunn, *Face of London*, 173; Bayne and Priestley, "Ripley in London," 7.
2. Greenwood vs. Ripley, 2, TNA; J. H. Burton to R. S. Ripley, July 5, 1866, Yale-2; Burton Diaries, Oct. 31–Dec. 23, 1866 Yale-2.
3. Moran Diaries, June 30, 1866, LOC; Greenwood vs. Ripley, 2, TNA; R. S. Ripley to Burton, Sept. 21, 1866, Yale-2.
4. Howard, *Franco-Prussian War*, 40–41; Abstracts of Proceedings, Ordnance Committee, 1866: Apr. 30, June 11, Aug. 31, Sept. 17, 21, Dec. 31, TNA.
5. Thomas Dudley to W. H. Seward, Dec. 24, 1868, HL.
6. King, *Louis T. Wigfall*, 223; Wallace, "Confederate Exiles in London," 75–77; The Langham: a (hi)story of Glory and Grace: Innovation in Hospitality; Bennett, *London Confederates*, 12.
7. Bayne and Priestley, "Ripley in London," 9; King, *Louis T. Wigfall*, 223–27; R. S. Ripley to L. T. Wigfall, undated seven pages, Wigfall Papers, LOC; Evans, *Judah P. Benjamin*, 348; King, *Louis. T. Wigfall*, 227, 230–31.
8. Charlotte Wigfall to Halsey Wigfall, Oct. 31, 1866, Wigfall Papers, LOC; *OR*, vol. 1: 316–17; King, *Louis T. Wigfall*, 6; Moran Diaries, Oct. 28, 1868, LOC.
9. Greenwood vs. Ripley, 3–4, TNA; Louise Wigfall to Halsey Wigfall, Dec. 28, 1866, Wigfall Papers, LOC; *Times* (London), "Drury Lane Theater," Dec. 19, 1866, 6.
10. Charlotte Wigfall to Halsey Wigfall, Feb. 3, 1867, Wigfall Papers, LOC.
11. Abstracts of Proceedings, Ordnance Committee, Apr. 8, 1867; Greenwood vs. Ripley, 24, 25; Abstracts of Proceedings, Proceedings Ordnance Committee, June 19, 1867. All sources at TNA.
12. Louise Wigfall to Halsey Wigfall, June 29, 1867, Charlotte Wigfall to Halsey Wigfall, Nov. 5, 1867, Wigfall Papers, LOC; J. R. Hamilton to Burton, Nov. 15, 1867, Yale-2.
13. Burton Diaries, Feb. 4, 6, Mar. 20, and Apr. 29, 1868, Yale-2.
14. Thomas Dudley to W. H. Seward, Dec. 24. 1868, Official Dispatches, HL.

15. Ripley's Claims vs. Greenwood & Batley, Sept. 10, May 26, June 9, 11, 1868, HL; *Times* (London) June 29, 1868, 10.

16. *Times* (London) July 21, 1868, 11, July 28, 1868, 9.

17. Evans, *Judah P. Benjamin*, 326, 4–5, 330, 333, 327, 372–73, 377.

18. Brook, Freeman & Batley, Bill of Costs, July 4, 1868, HL; Proceedings at Law, Aug. 5, July 31, Aug. 15, 17, 20, 31, 1868, HL; Burton Diaries, Sept. 14, 1868, Yale-2.

19. Sifakis, "Franklin, William Buel," *Who Was Who*, 227–28; R. S. Ripley to William Franklin, Sept. 7, 1868, author's collection, original letter.

20. Bayne and Priestley, "Ripley in London," 9; Louise Wigfall to Halsey Wigfall, Nov. 7, 1868, Wigfall Papers, LOC; Bill of Costs, Dec. 17, 1868, HL.

21. Louise Wigfall to Halsey Wigfall, Jan. 2, 1869, Wigfall Papers, LOC.

22. Proceedings, Feb. 3, 1869, HL; Official Dispatches, Joseph Batley to Thomas Dudley, Feb. 10, 1869, Greenwood & Batley to Dudley, Feb. 11, 1869, HL; Proceedings at Law, Feb. 22, 25, 1869, HL.

23. Proceedings at Law, Mar. 5, 11, 1869, HL; Charlotte Wigfall to Halsey Wigfall, Mar. 27, 1869, Wigfall Papers, LOC.

24. *Times* (London), Mar. 12, 1869, 11; *London Gazette*, Mar. 12, 1869, 1674; Moran Diaries, Dec. 28, 1869, LOC; *Times* (London), Oct. 11, 1870, 8; image, *Illustrated London News*, July 7, 1860, 13; Bayne and Priestley, "Ripley in London," 7.

25. "Obituary, Sir Edward Sabine," *Times* (London), June 27, 1883, 12; Charlotte Wigfall to Halsey Wigfall, April 14, 1869, Wigfall Papers, LOC.

26. Proceedings at Law, April 8, 1869, HL; "General Ripley B2/30"; *London Gazette*, Apr. 30, 1869, 2605–6; *Times* (London) May 25, 1869, 11.

27. Official Dispatches, John Batley to Thomas Dudley, Apr. 19, May 6, July 21, 1869, HL; Bill of Costs, June 30, July 5, 1869, HL.

Chapter 30: Financial Struggles, 1869–1873

1. Sacks, "Charles Debrille Poston," 3–11.

2. C. D. Poston and R. S. Ripley, "Articles of Agreement," Poston Papers, Arizona Historical Foundation.

3. Louise Wigfall to Halsey Wigfall, Sept. 18, 1869, Wigfall Papers, LOC.

4. Bill of Costs, Nov. 3, 4, 5, 1869, HL.

5. Charleston County Records, Mesne Conveyances, 1870, Book O, no. 15, 28–29, 98–101.

6. Bill of Costs, July 9, 13, through Nov. 22, 1870, HL.

7. Howard, *Franco-Prussian War*, 17–23, 40–41, 56–57, 81–85, 120–82.

8. Ibid., 246–47; Charles H. DeBruin to W. B. Franklin, Aug. 25, 1870, R. S. Ripley to Franklin, Aug 27, 1870, Colt Papers, Connecticut State Library.

9. Bowes-Click and Kelleher, *Regiment of Fusiliers*, 24–25; *Dagenham Post and Chadwell Heath News*, May 9, 1956, 14; "Wm. Hope Obituary," *Times* (London), Dec. 19, 1909; Goddard, "19th Century Recycling," 32–36; *Kelly's Directory*, 1870–75.

10. Howard, *Franco-Prussian War*, 217–26, 319, 229.

11. Moran Diaries, Sept. 12, 1870, LOC; French, "Roswell S. Ripley," 68; Howard, *Franco-Prussian War*, 229–30, 361, 441.

12. Francis Lawley to wife Jenny Lawley, May 27, 1871, Lawley Documents, Hull History Center; Betjeman, *London's Historic Railway Stations*, 109; R. S. Ripley to Charles C. Jones Jr., July 5, 1871, Jones Papers, Duke.

13. *London Gazette*, Feb. 2, 1872, 399; R. S. Ripley to Gen. Bradley Johnson, telegram, Mar. 9, 1865, and letters, Mar. 23, 25, 1872, Johnson Letters and Papers, Duke.

14. Ads, "Newport [Oregon] Coal Co. Ltd.," *Pall Mall Gazette,* Oct. 12–19. 1872.

15. *Cheshire Observer,* Jan. 25, 1873, 5; Passenger Lists, Arriving in New York, 1873, R. Ripley, Roll 371, Line 15, M237, NARA.

Chapter 31: Literary Career, 1874–1875

1. W. L. de Rosset to R. S. Ripley, de Rosset Letters, Duke; Koonce, *Doctor to the Front,* 206; *OR,* vol. 11, pt. 2: 657–59, 976–77; *OR,* vol. 19, pt. 1: 1031–33.

2. R. S. Ripley to W. L. de Rosset, May 13, 1874, de Rosset Letters, Duke.

3. *Kelly's Directory,* 1870–1875, 473; Bayne and Priestley, "Ripley in London," 8.

4. R. S. Ripley to de Rosset, May 21 [20], June 24, 25, 1874, de Rosset Letters, Duke; *Kelly's Directory,* 1870–1875, 473.

5. Hill, "Battle of South Mountain or Boonsboro," 143; W. L. de Rosset to D. H. Hill, June 18, 1885, Hill Papers, Library of Virginia; de Rosset, Letter to the *Century*; French, "Roswell S. Ripley," 63.

6. Stephens and Lee, "Lawley, Francis Charles," *Dictionary of National Biography,* 426–27.

7. Ripley, "Civil War in America," 211.

8. Francis Lawley to John Blackwood, July 13, 1874, R. S. Ripley to Editor, July 14, 1874, NLS.

9. Francis Lawley to John Blackwood, July 17, 1874, R. S. Ripley to Blackwood and to Editor, July 21, 1874, Ripley to Blackwood, July 22, 1874, Lawley to Blackwood, July 22, 1874, NLS.

10. Ripley, "Civil War in America," 211, 229, 212–14, 216–17, 220–21, 224–28, 230.

11. R. S. Ripley to Editor and John Blackwood, Oct. 27, 1874, Ripley to Editor, Nov. 4, 23, Dec. 5, 1874, NLS.

12. Ripley, "Last Confederate Flag," July 1875, 56–69.

13. Ripley, "Last Confederate Flag," Aug. 1875, 129–43.

Chapter 32: An Eventful 1875

1. "William Gaston, Governor," Massachusetts State Archives.

2. R. S. Ripley to William Gaston, Jan. 12, 1875, Lewis Carr to C. F. Adams Jr., Feb. 23, 1875, Gaston Files, Massachusetts State Archives.

3. "54th Regiment (colored)," *Boston Herald* and *Boston Daily Globe,* Dec. 22, 1885; Emerson and Stokes, *Confederate Englishman,* 79–80.

4. William Gaston to Legislature, Mar. 5, 1875, Resolution, Mar. 20 and 24, 1875, Gaston to R. S. Ripley, Mar. 31, 1875, Gaston Files, Massachusetts State Archives.

5. Hunter Davidson to G. T. Beauregard, Jan. 18, 1875, Beauregard Papers, Tulane University, Louisiana Research Collection.

6. F. A. K. W. von Oppen to W. B. Franklin, June 3, 1875, June 19, 1869, Franklin to von Oppen, June 20, 1875, von Oppen to Franklin, July 3, 8, 1875, Colt Papers, Connecticut State Library.

7. *Richmond Daily Dispatch,* Oct. 26, 1875, 1.

8. Bennett, *London Confederates,* 39, 40, 114–15; Moran Diaries, Oct. 23, 1865, LOC.

9. Stephens and Lee, "Foley, John Henry," *Dictionary of National Biography,* 353–54; R. S. Ripley to Bradley T. Johnson, Mar. 5, 1874, Johnson Letters and Papers, Duke; *Dictionary of National Biography,* "Foley, John Henry," 353–54.

10. Stern, Introduction to *Secret Service of the Confederate States in Europe,* 1:ix, xxii, xviii, xix; Bulloch, *Secret Service of the Confederate States in Europe,* 1:177–78, 235, 275–77, 2:152–54.

11. Wallace and Gillespie, *Journal of Benjamin Moran*, 2:953n5, 975, 1023–24, 1044–45, 1092, 1135, 1227–28.
12. Morison, *Oxford History of the American People*, 726–29; Moran Diaries, Apr. 11, May 22, 1867, LOC.
13. Adams and Morse, *Charles Francis Adams*, 377, 380–82, 384–86, 392, 395–97.
14. Moran Diaries, Aug. 11, 1874, LOC.
15. "Ex-Rebel Gen. Ripley," clipping, unknown newspaper, enclosed with J. R. Lee-Bellasyse to Governor of Massachusetts, May 11, 1876, Cullum File, Ripley Papers, USMA; J. Michael Comeau, archivist, Massachusetts State Archives, Columbia Point, personal communication, Sept. 17, 1992.

Chapter 33: Ripley's "The Situation in America"

1. "Court of Bankruptcy," *Times* (London), Jan. 21, 1876; Bayne and Priestley, "Ripley in London," 7; Charles Priestley, American Civil War Round Table, U.K., personal communication.
2. "Death of Mrs. Julia C. Ripley," *Ogdensburg (N.Y.) St. Lawrence Republican*, Dec. 6, 1876.
3. Degregorio, "Ulysses S. Grant," *Book of U.S. Presidents*, 271.
4. Degregorio, "Rutherford B. Hayes," *Book of U.S. Presidents*, 284–86.
5. Francis Lawley to John Blackwood, Dec. 18, 1876, R. S. Ripley to Blackwood, Jan. 16, 19, 20, Feb. 1, 1877, NLS.
6. Ripley, "Situation in America," 196–98.
7. Ripley, "Situation in America," 198–99; in Degregorio, *Book of U.S. Presidents*, see "William Henry Harrison," 145, and "Zachary Taylor," 181; Ripley, "Situation in America," 199.
8. Ripley, "Situation in America," 199–200.
9. Degregorio, "Franklin Pierce," *Book of U.S. Presidents*, 204–5; Ripley, "Situation in America," 200.
10. Degregorio, "James Buchanan," *Book of U.S. Presidents*, 215–16; Ripley, "Situation in America," 200; Degregorio, "Abraham Lincoln," *Book of U.S. Presidents*, 234.
11. Ripley, "Situation in America," 200–201.
12. Ripley, "Situation in America," 201; Degregorio, "Andrew Johnson," *Book of U.S. Presidents*, 253–54; Ripley, "Situation in America," 202–3.
13. Degregorio, "Ulysses S. Grant," *Book of U.S. Presidents*, 264; Ripley, "Situation in America," 203–4.
14. Ripley, "Situation in America," 205–12.
15. Degregorio, "Rutherford B. Hayes," *Book of U.S. Presidents*, 285–86; Ripley, "Situation in America," 214–17.
16. Ripley, "Situation in America," 217–20; Degregorio, "Rutherford B. Hayes," *Book of U.S. Presidents*, 286.
17. R. S. Ripley to John Blackwood, Mar. 5, 1877, NLS; Degregorio, "Rutherford B. Hayes," *Book of U.S. Presidents*, 286–88.
18. Francis Lawley to John Blackwood, Feb. 25, 1877, R. S. Ripley to John Blackwood, Mar. 5, 7, 1877, NLS.
19. R. S. Ripley to Editor, April 14, 1877, Francis Lawley to Editor, July 4, Francis Lawley to John Blackwood, July 9, 1877, NLS.
20. Passenger Lists, Arriving in New York, 1877, R. S. Ripley, Roll 408, Line 36, M237, NARA; Last Will and Testament, Christopher Ripley, Sept. 30, 1851, New York State Historical Association.

21. "New York Hotel Arrivals," *New York Herald,* May 19, June 18, 28, 11, 1877; Degregorio, "Rutherford B. Hayes," *Book of U.S. Presidents,* 286.

22. Ripley, *Correspondence Relating to Fortification of Morris Island,* 1–43.

23. OR, vol. 14: iii, 1021–25; OR, vol. 28, pt. 2: 140–41, 147–50, 164–68, 174, 515–19, 523, 527, 539–41, 548–49, 556–59, 520; title pages to OR, vols. 14 and 28, pt. 2.

24. Ripley, *Correspondence Relating to Fortification of Morris Island,* 23, 25, 29, 43.

Chapter 34: Inventor

1. U.S. Census, 1880, New York, N.Y., William Harkness, 299D; Patent no. 2069, BPO.
2. Patents no. 5314 and 5315, BPO.
3. Ordnance Inquiry Commission, "Hope Testimony," *Minutes of Evidence,* Nov. 30, 1886, 93, no. 2467; Hope, "A Crimean V.C. Who Lived in Dagenham."
4. Patent no. 1421, BPO.
5. Patent, no. 4363, BPO.
6. Patent, no. 1733, BPO.
7. Patent, no. 2923, BPO.
8. Patent, no. 1831, BPO.
9. Ordnance Inquiry Commission, "Hope Testimony," *Minutes of Evidence,* Nov. 30, 1886, 93, nos. 2470, 2471; Patent no. 314,127, U.S. Patent Office.
10. Personal communication with Pierre Lorain, French military historian, Paris.
11. Patent no. 3042, BPO.
12. Abstracts of Proceedings, Ordnance Committee, "Hope, V.C. and General Ripley," Sept. 3, Oct. 19, 26, 1883, 3288/10, 540, 694, TNA; Ordnance Inquiry Commission, "Hope Testimony," *Minutes of Evidence,* Dec. 7, 1886, 137, nos. 3523, 3527; Patent no. 314,127, listing French, Belgian, and Italian patents, U.S. Patent Office.
13. Patent no. 817, BPO; Patent no. 314,127, U.S. Patent Office.
14. Passenger Lists, Arriving in New York, 1884, Roswell Sabine Ripley, Roll 476, Line 19, no. 64, M237, NARA.

Chapter 35: Return to America

1. In Degregorio, *Book of U.S. Presidents,* see "James A. Garfield," 299, 300–302, "Chester A. Arthur," 311, 313–14, and "Grover Cleveland," 324–26.
2. "Death of Gen. R. S. Ripley," *New York World,* Mar. 30, 1887; "Gen. Ripley's Funeral," *New York Times,* Apr. 2, 1887; in Sifakis, *Who Was Who,* see "Newton, John," 470, "Clingman, Thomas Lanier," 128–29, and "Smith, Gustavus Woodson," 602–3; Smith, *Confederate War Papers,* 360–64.
3. Evans, "Knickerbocker Hotels, 1800–1850," 380, 382–84, 392–93.
4. Patent no. 817, BPO.
5. Gilchrist, *Defense of Morris Island,* 5–7, 48.
6. OR, vol. 10, pt. 1: 521; OR, vol. 14: 726, 804; Williams, *P. G. T. Beauregard,* 309–10, 314; Roman, *Military Operations of General Beauregard,* 1:42, 48, 2:26; OR, vol. 14: 616.
7. OR, vol. 14: 522; R. S. Ripley to William Ramsay, Mar. 3, 1885, Ripley Papers, USMA.
8. Patent no. 314,127, U.S. Patent Office.
9. "Talk with Gen. Ripley," *New York World,* Mar. 17, 1885.
10. Johnson, Appendix, *Defense of Charleston Harbor,* clxv; Ripley, Appendix, "Charleston and its Defenses," 347–50; OR, vol. 6: 307–12, 327, 394.
11. Ripley, "Charleston and its Defenses," 350–58; OR, vol. 14: 509–10.

12. Ripley, "Charleston and its Defenses," 358–60.
13. Williams, *P. G. T. Beauregard*, 304–5, 307–8, 316–18.
14. Ibid., 317; Beauregard, "Defense of Charleston," 1, 2, 7–9.
15. *OR*, vol. 1: 51; *OR*, vol. 35: 644; Ripley Papers, USMA; *Kelly's Directory* 1885–1887.

Chapter 36: Death in New York and Honors in Charleston

1. Trow, "Norris, John W. S., Physician," *Trow's New York City Directory*, 1309; "Death of Gen. R. S. Ripley," *New York World*, Mar. 30, 1887; Certificate of Death, Gen. R. S. Ripley, New York City Health Department.
2. "Mortuary—Roswell S. Ripley," 267; U.S. Census, 1870, Chester, Chester County, S.C., William H. Brawley, 58A.
3. "S. D. Trenholm," *Charleston City Directory*, 1882; Holmes, "Trenholm Family," 161; Cheves, "Middleton of South Carolina," 238. North Carolina Death Certificate #143, Alicia Ripley Trenholm.
4. "General Ripley Dead." *Democrat and Chronicle*, Rochester, New York, Wed. March 30, 1887. 2. "Death of Gen. R. S. Ripley," *New York World*, Mar. 30, 1887; "Death of Gen. R. S. Ripley: The Sad and Sudden End of Charleston's Gallant Defender," *Charleston News and Courier*, Mar. 30, 1887, 1.
5. "Gen. Ripley's Funeral," *New York Times*, Apr. 2, 1887; *OR*, vol. 37, pt. 1: 61; *OR*, vol. 19, pt. 1: 805, 926; Certificate of Death, Gen. R. S. Ripley, New York City Health Department.
6. "Death of Gen. Ripley," *Ogdensburg (N.Y.) Journal*, Mar. 31, 1887.
7. "The Late Gen. Ripley," *Charleston News and Courier*, Mar. 30, 31, 1887, 1; "Mortuary—Roswell S. Ripley," 265–68.
8. "Mortuary—Roswell S. Ripley," 269, 265; Stokeley, *Fort Moultrie*; National Park Service, *Fort Sumter*.
9. "Mortuary—Roswell S. Ripley," 270–74.
10. Ibid., 274–76, 265.
11. "Our Warriors Grave," *Charleston News and Courier*, Apr. 4, 1887, 1.
12. Ripley Monument Committee, 2, Ripley Papers, SCHS; Breese, "Confederate Monuments in South Carolina," 60; Seabrook, *Unveiling of the Ripley Monument*, 3–14; Hayne, *Poems of Henry Timrod*, 99–100; personal visit, Magnolia Cemetery, Charleston, S.C.
13. Wellman, *Giant in Gray*, 198.

Epilogue

1. Ordnance Inquiry Commission, "Hope Testimony" *Minutes of Evidence*, 137, 65.
2. Ibid., 92–93.
3. Ibid., 137–38.
4. Ibid., 138; Abstracts of Proceedings, Ordnance Committee, "Trial of Gun," Nov. 28, 1887, 935–36, 3288/10, TNA; Hogg, *Jane's Military Review*, 165.

BIBLIOGRAPHY

Archival Sources

Arizona Historical Foundation, State of Arizona Library and Archives, Tempe.
Poston, Charles D. Papers, 1847–1962. FM MSS #44, Box 1, Folder 10.

British Patent Office, Newport, Gwent, U.K.
Patent no. 2069. May 23, 1878. R. S. Ripley. "Manufacture of Gas for Heating, &c." From William Harkness.
Patent no. 5314. December 30, 1878. R. S. Ripley. "Puddling Furnaces." From William Harkness.
Patent no. 5315. December 30, 1878. R. S. Ripley. "Gas Retorts and the Manufacture of Gas." From William Harkness.
Patent no. 1421. April 9, 1879. Henry Clay Bull, William Hope, and R. S. Ripley. "Reducing and Purifying Ores or Metals for the Manufacture of Ordnance, &c."
Patent no. 1733. May 1, 1879. R. S. Ripley. "Treating Illuminating Gas."
Patent no. 4363. October 27, 1879. William Hope and R. S. Ripley. "Metallurgical Furnaces and Processes."
Patent no. 2923. July 15, 1880. William Hope and R. S. Ripley. "Ordnance and Firearms and Ammunition for Same."
Patent no. 1831. April 17, 1882. R. S. Ripley. "Reducing and Purifying Metals."
Patent no. 3042. June 19, 1883. Sidney Pitt. "Improvements in Breech Loading Cannon and Ammunition Therefor." From R. S. Ripley.
Patent no. 817. January 5, 1884. R. S. Ripley. "Improvements in Ammunition for Breech Loading Cannon."

Charleston City Council, Charleston, S.C.
"The Flag of the 1st S.C. Regular Artillery." Council Proceedings, November 14, 1893.

Charleston County Records, Charleston, S.C.
Register of Mesne Conveyances. August 1863, Book U 14, 45–46; December 1864, Book U 14, 296–99; January 1870, Book O 15, 27–28; and February 1870, Book O 15, 98–101.

Charleston Library Society, Charleston, S.C.
"Life and Recollections of Joseph W. Barnwell." Hinson Collection, Manuscript no. 372, 1929.

The Citadel Archives and Museum, Charleston, S.C.
Huguenin, Thomas A. Journal and Record, Part First, C.W. A1985.7.

Columbia University, Rare Book and Manuscript Library, New York, N.Y.
Harper & Brothers Records, 1817–1929.

Connecticut Historical Society, Hartford.
Ripley, Christopher. Letter Book and Ledger, 1813–1815.
Ripley, Christopher. Papers.
Robbins and Lawrence Co. Corporate Records and Letter Book, 1856.

Connecticut State Library, Hartford
Colt Patent Firearms Manufacturing Co. Papers. Record Group 103, Box 11, Incoming Correspondence.

Duke University, David M. Rubenstein Rare Book and Manuscript Library, Durham, N.C.
Bennett, Frank T. Papers and Diary.
de Rosset, William L. Letters.
Dunovant, R. G. M. Papers.
Johnson, Bradley Tyler. Letters and Papers.
Jones, Charles Colcock, Jr. Papers.
Pickens, Francis W. Papers.

Hull History Centre, University of Hull, U.K.
Lawley, Francis C. Documents. U DDFA/39/54, Forbes Adam Family Papers.

Huntington Library, American Historical Manuscripts Division, San Marino, Calif.
Dudley, Thomas Haines. Collection. Letter Press Book of Official Dispatches, Bill of Costs, and Proceedings at Law, DU 361–367, "Greenwood & Batley vs. R. S. Riley" Lawsuit.

Library of Congress, Manuscripts Division, Washington, D.C.
Beauregard, P. G. T. Papers.
Hotze, Henry. Papers and Letter Book, May 1864 to June 1865.
Moran, Benjamin. Diaries.
Wigfall, General Louis T. Family Papers.

The Library of Virginia, Richmond.
Hill, D. H. Papers, 1860–1888. Accession 32032, Box 3.

Maritime Archives and Library National Museums, Liverpool.
Prioleau, Charles K. Letter Book. Fraser, Trenholm Collection, B/FT/Box8/1.

Maryland State Archives, Annapolis, Md.
"The Harbor of Annapolis, U.S. Coast Survey, Washington, 1846." Huntington Corporation Map Collection.

Massachusetts State Archives, Boston.
Gaston, Governor William. Files, January, February, March 1875.
"William Gaston, Governor of the Commonwealth, 1875–1876." Massachusetts Governors.

The National Archives, Kew, Richmond, UK. Formerly the British Public Records Office.
Abstracts of Proceedings and Reports of the Ordnance Select Committee, 1855.
   Ordnance Board Minutes: WO 45/273, correspondence, R. S. Ripley to Ordnance Board and to Dixon; Ordnance Board Entries: WO 44/701, Dixon correspondence, 53S 5222/1, 53S 5222/2, L10055, and S 10295, Hardinge to Dixon, C 8047.

Abstracts of Proceedings, Ordnance Committee, 1866: 2020/2, 370, 607, 608, 863.
Abstracts of Proceedings, Ordnance Committee, 1867: 2020/2, 369, 370.
Greenwood vs. Ripley. C 16/494/G99 (1868), Chancery.

National Archives and Records Administration, Washington, D.C.
M237. Passenger Lists of Vessels Arriving in New York, N.Y., 1820–1897: 1873, 1877, 1884.
M437. Letters Received by the Confederate War Department.
M474. Letters Received by the Confederate Adjutant and Inspector General.
M727. Returns from Regular Army Artillery Regiments, June 1821–January 1901.
  Second Regiment of Artillery, July 1846.
  Third Regiment of Artillery, November, December 1843, and March, April 1844.
RG74. Bureau of Ordnance and Hydrography, U.S. Navy.
RG94. Adjutant General's Office, Records Relating to the U.S. Military Academy, "Cadet Application Papers, 1838–1839."
RG94. Letters Received by the Office of the Adjutant General, AGO, (Main Series) 1822–1860.
RG156. Letters Received and Sent, the Office of the Chief of Ordnance.
RG404. U.S. Military Academy Records, National Archives–Affiliated Archives. Records on deposit at United States Military Academy Library (USMA), West Point, N.Y.
  Register of Cadet Delinquencies, 1838–1844. Administrative Records, Records of the Department of Tactics.
    Annual Descriptive Lists of Cadet Candidates, 1839. Personnel Records, Records Relating to Cadet Candidates, Records of the Deputy Chief of Staff.
    Orders Pertaining to the U.S. Military Academy, 1837–1842 (Order Book). Orders and Other Issuances, Records of the Deputy Chief of Staff, Personnel and Administration.
    Register of Officers and Graduates of the U.S. Military Academy, 1840–1843. Records of the Deputy Chief of Staff, Personnel and Administration.

National Library of Scotland, Edinburgh.
Blackwood Papers. MSS 4320, 4324, 4365.

New York City Health Department.
Gen. R. S. Ripley Death Certificate.

New York Department of State, Albany.
Adams' Revolving Arms Co., New York. Certificate of Incorporation.

New York State Historical Association, Cooperstown.
Proof of the Last Will and Testament of Christopher Ripley, St. Lawrence County, N.Y.

Ohio History Connection, Columbus.
Buttles, Joel. Diaries, vol. 1205: July 20, 1842; vol. 1206: September 29, 1843, May 17, 1845.

St. Lawrence University Libraries, Canton, N.Y.
Ripley, Christopher, and Charles Shepard. Papers, 1801–1870. MSS. Coll. No. 012. This collection includes a typescript by Atwood Manley entitled "The Ripley Papers."

South Carolina Confederate Relic Room and Military Museum, Columbia.
McRae, Colin J. Collection.

South Carolina Department of Archives and History, Columbia.
Magrath, Governor Andrew G. Papers, 1865.
Pickens, Governor F. W. Papers, 1860–1862.
Ripley, R. S. 1st South Carolina Artillery, Compiled Service Records of Confederate General and Staff Officers. MC 331, Roll 212, Correspondence, Voucher and Accounts.

South Carolina Historical Society, Charleston.
Middleton, Harriott. Correspondence. Cheves-Middleton Papers,.
Middleton, Lt. Edw. B. Diary and Journal, 1864–1865. Cheves-Middleton Papers.
Ripley, R. S. Papers.
Prioleau, Charles K. Papers.
Smythe, Augustine T. Papers. Smythe-Stoney-Adger Collection.

Tulane University, Louisiana Research Collection, New Orleans.
Beauregard, G. T. Papers.

University of California, Los Angeles, Charles E. Young Research Library.
Pillow, Gideon J. Letters. Misc. Manuscripts collection (Collection 100, Box 31).

University of Georgia Libraries, Special Collections,
Hargrett Rare Book and Manuscript Library, Athens, Ga.
Jourdan, Captain Fleming. Letters, MS #826.

University of North Carolina at Chapel Hill, Southern Historical Collection,
Wilson Library.
Law, Evander M. Papers, 1860–1864, Acc. 1393. Loaned for microfilming by Mrs. Miles F. Storm, Winter Haven, Fla., March 1948.
Leach, Calvin. Diary and Letters, 1861–1867. Coll. #1875-z.
Miles, William P. Papers. M-508 letters, Jan–Mar, 1862.

University of South Carolina, Columbia. South Caroliniana Library.
Beauregard, P. G. T. Papers. 2MSS.
Childs, Frederick L. Papers. Manuscript Collection #410.
Marshall, Colonel J. Foster. Official Letter Book. Manuscripts Collection #1367.
Miscellaneous Ripley Papers, February–March 1861.

U.S. Army Military History Institute, Carlisle Barracks, Pa.
Civil War Miscellaneous Collection.

U.S. Military Academy Library, West Point, N.Y.
Ripley, Roswell S. Papers. Special Collections and Archives Division, Cullum File no. 1173. See also National Archives and Records Administration, RG404.

U.S. Patent Office, Alexandria, Va.
Patent no. 314,127, March 17, 1885. W. Hope and R. S. Ripley. "Cartridge for Ordnance."

Yale University Library, Beinecke Rare Book and Manuscript Library, New Haven, Conn.
Ripley, R. S. Papers. Western Americana Collection, WA MSS S-1691. The papers in the collection are dated 1846 and 1847. Although a note included in the collection states "R. S. Ripley Papers 1846–1848," there are no 1848 papers.

Yale University Library, Manuscripts and Archives, New Haven, Conn.
Burton, James H. Papers. MS 117. Also in the Charles W. Ramsdell Collection, microfilm, Dolph Briscoe Center for American History, The University of Texas at Austin.

Printed Sources

Adams, Charles F., Jr., and John T. Morse, ed. *Charles Francis Adams.* New York: Houghton, Mifflin, 1900.

Appelbaum, Stanley, ed. *William Wordsworth: Favorite Poems.* Mineola, N.Y.: Dover, 1992.

Aztec Club of 1847. Washington, D.C.: Judd & Detwiler, 1893.

"A Crimean V.C. Who Lived in Dagenheim." Margaret Hope interview. *Dagenheim Digest,* no. 27, March 1955.

Ballard, Michael B. *Pemberton: A Biography.* Jackson, Miss.: University Press of Mississippi, 1991.

Barrett, John C. *Sherman's March Through the Carolinas.* Chapel Hill: University of North Carolina Press, 1956.

Bayne, Greg, and Charles Priestley. "Roswell Ripley in London." *Crossfire Magazine* (London) 95 (Spring 2011): 6–9.

Beauregard, G. T. "The Defense of Charleston." In *Battles and Leaders of the Civil War,* ed. Robert U. Johnson and Clarence C. Buhl, 4:1–23. 4 vols. 1887. Reprint, Secaucus, N.J.: Castle, n.d.

Bennett, John D. *The London Confederates: The Officials, Clergy, Businessmen, and Journalists Who Backed the American South During the Civil War.* Jefferson, N.C.: McFarland, 2008.

Betjeman, John. *London's Historic Railway Stations.* London: John Murray, 1972.

Botkin, B. A. *A Civil War Treasury of Tales, Legends, and Folklore.* New York: Random House, 1960. In House Report No. 3505, 49th Congress, 2nd Session.

Boutelle, C. O. *General Map of Charleston Harbor.* U.S. Coast Survey, Government Printing Office, Washington, D.C. 1865.

Bowes-Click, Colin, and Jim Kelleher, *The Royal Regiment of Fusiliers.* Derby, U.K.: English Life Publishers, 1999.

Boykin, S. "Battle Pictures." *Macon (Ga.) Daily Telegraph,* July 24, 1862.

Bradley, Mark L. *Last Stand in the Carolinas: The Battle of Bentonville.* Campbell, Calif.: Savas Woodbury, 1996.

Breese, Wm. E. "Confederate Monuments in South Carolina." *Confederate Veteran* 1 (January 1893): 60.

Brennan, Patrick. *Secessionville: Assault on Charleston.* Campbell, Calif.: Savas, 1996.

Bridges, Hal. *Lee's Maverick General: Daniel Harvey Hill.* 1961. Reprint, Lincoln, Neb.: University of Nebraska Press, 1991.

Bulloch, James D. *Secret Service of the Confederate States in Europe, or How the Confederate Cruisers Were Equipped.* 2 vols. New York: Thomas Yoseloff, Sagamore Press, 1959.

Burton, E. Milby. *The Siege of Charleston 1861–1865.* Columbia: University of South Carolina Press, 1970.

Caldwell, J. F. J., and Lee A. Wallace Jr., ed. *A History of a Brigade of South Carolinians, Known First as Gregg's, and Subsequently as McGowan's Brigade.* Dayton, Ohio: Morningside, 1984.

Callan, J. P. Sean. *Courage and Country: James Shields, More Than Irish Luck.* Lake Forest, Ill.: Irish Quill, 2004.

Caulkins, Julia. "Narrative of the Family Migration to Ohio." In *History of Delaware Co. Ohio*, 433–53. Chicago: O. L. Baskin, 1880.
Chamberlain, W. H. J., and A. W. F. Taylerson. *Adams' Revolvers*. London: Barrie & Jenkins, 1976.
Chester, Captain James. "Inside Sumter in '61." In *Battles and Leaders of the Civil War*, ed. Robert U. Johnson and Clarence C. Buel, 1:59–73. 4 vols. 1887. Reprint, Secaucus, N.J.: Castle, n.d.
Cheves, Langdon, Esq. "Middleton of South Carolina." *South Carolina Historical and Genealogical Magazine* 1 (July 1900): 228–62.
Chichester, Mrs. C. E. *A Lady's Experience Inside the Forts in Charleston Harbor During the War*. Charleston: n.p., 1895.
Cisco, Walter Brian. *States Rights Gist: A South Carolina General of the Civil War*. Shippensburg, Pa.: White Mane, 1991.
———. *Henry Timrod: A Biography*. Teaneck, N.J.: Farleigh Dickinson Univ. Press, 2004.
Clunn, Harold P. *The Face of London*. London: Simpkin Marshall, 1932.
Clyde, Rev. John C. *Life of James H. Coffin, LL.D.* Easton, Pa.: New Library Press, 1881.
Cook, Sir Edmund. *The Life of Florence Nightingale*. Vol. 1. London: Macmillan, 1914.
Côté, Richard N. *Mary's World*. Mount Pleasant, S.C.: Corinthian Books, 2004.
Creekman, Charles Todd, Jr. *The 106th New York Volunteers: A Civil War Heritage*. New York, 1985.
Crute, Joseph H., Jr. *Units of the Confederate States Army*. Midlothian, Va.: Derwent Books, 1987.
Cullum, George W. *Biographical Register of the Officers and Graduates of the U.S. Military Academy at West Point, N.Y.* Vols. 1 and 2. 3rd ed. Boston: Houghton Mifflin, 1891.
Cummings, Charles M. *Seven Ohio Confederate Generals: Case Histories of Defection*. Vols. 1 and 2. Ann Arbor, Mich.: UMI Dissertation Services, 1963.
———. "Fruit of a Restless Spirit." *Ohio History* 73 (Summer 1964): 144–56.
Cuthbert, Robert B., and Stephen G. Hoffius, eds. *Northern Money, Southern Land: The Lowcountry Plantation Sketches*. Columbia: University of South Carolina Press, 2009.
Davis, William C. *Jefferson Davis: The Man and His Hour*. New York: HarperCollins, 1991.
Davis, Jefferson. *Rise and Fall of the Confederate Government*. Richmond, Va.: Garrett & Massie, 1938.
de Fontaine, F. G. "The Second Day of the War." *Southern Bivouac* 2 (September 1886): 201–7.
de la Cova, Antonio Rafael. *Cuban Confederate Colonel: The Life of Ambrosio José Gonzales*. Columbia: University of South Carolina Press, 2003.
de Rosset, William R. Letter to the *Century* 33 (December 1886): 308–09.
Degregorio, William A. *The Complete Book of U.S. Presidents: From George Washington to Bill Clinton*. New York: Wing Books, 1993.
Doubleday, Brevet Major-General Abner. *Reminiscences of Forts Sumter and Moultrie*. New York: Harper & Brothers, 1876.
Dowdey, Clifford. *The Seven Days: The Emergence of Robert E. Lee*. 1964. Reprint, Wilmington, N.C.: Broadfoot, 1988.
Dowdey, Clifford, and Manarin, Louis H. eds. *The Wartime Papers of Robert E. Lee*. 1961. Reprint, New York: Da Capo, 1987.
Dudley, William S. *Going South: U.S. Naval Officer Resignations and Dismissals on the Eve of the Civil War*. Washington, D.C.: Naval Historical Foundation, 1981.
Durant, Samuel. *History of St. Lawrence County, New York*. Philadelphia: Everts, 1878.

Edgar, Walter. *South Carolina: A History*. Columbia: University of South Carolina Press, 1998.

Edmunds, John B. *Francis W. Pickens and the Politics of Destruction*. Chapel Hill: University of North Carolina Press, 1986.

Edwards, William B. "One-Man Armory: Colonel J. H. Burton." *Virginia Cavalcade* 12 (Autumn 1962): 28–33.

Eggleston, George C. *A Rebel's Recollections*. New York: Herd & Houghton, 1875.

Eisenhower, John S. D. *So Far from God: The U.S. War with Mexico 1846–1848*. New York: Random House, 1989.

Emerson, W. Eric, and Karen Stokes, eds. *A Confederate Englishman: The Civil War Letters of Henry Wemyss Feilden*. Columbia: University of South Carolina Press, 2013.

Evans, Eli N. *Judah P. Benjamin: The Jewish Confederate*. New York: Free Press, 1988.

Evans, Meryle R. "Knickerbocker Hotels and Restaurants, 1800–1850," *New York Historical Society Quarterly* 36, no. 4 (1952): 377–409.

Ferguson, Ernest B. *Ashes of Glory: Richmond at War*. New York: Vintage Books, 1997.

Freeman, Douglas Southall, *R. E. Lee: A Biography*. 4 vols. New York: Charles Scribner's Sons, 1934.

———. *Lee's Lieutenants: A Study in Command*. 3 vols. New York: Charles Scribner's Sons, 1942.

Freeman, Douglas Southall, and Grady McWhiney, eds. *Lee's Dispatches: Unpublished Letters of General Robert E. Lee, C.S.A., to Jefferson Davis and the War Department of the Confederate States of America 1862–1865*. New York: G. P. Putnam's Sons, 1957.

Fremantle, Arthur J. L. *Three Months in the Southern States, April–June 1863*. 1863. Reprint, New York: Time-Life, 1984.

French, Samuel G. "Roswell S. Ripley." In *Eighteenth Annual Reunion of the Association of the Graduates of the USMA, at West Point, New York*, 63–68. East Saginaw, Mich.: Evening News Printing, 1887.

Gallagher, Gary W. Introduction to *Lee's Maverick General: Daniel H. Hill*, by Hal Bridges, xii–xxi. Lincoln: University of Nebraska Press, 1991.

"General Ripley, B2/30." *Gaoler's Book for the Debtors Prison for London and Middlesex at Whitecross St.* City of London.

Gilchrist, Major Robert C. *The Confederate Defense of Morris Island, Charleston Harbor*. Charleston: News and Courier Book Presses, 1884.

Goddard, Nicholas. "19th Century Recycling: Victorians and the Agricultural Use of Sewage." *History Today* 3 (June 1981): 32–36.

Grattan, Judge George D. "The Battle of Boonsboro Gap or South Mountain." *Southern Historical Society Papers* 39 (April 1914): 31–44.

Grunwald, Michael. *The Swamp: The Everglades, Florida, and the Politics of Paradise*. New York: Simon & Schuster, 2006.

"H." "Battle of Cerro Gordo." *Southern Quarterly Review* 5 (January 1852): 121–53.

Hagood, Brig. Gen. Johnson. *Memoirs of the War of Secession*. Columbia, S.C.: State Co. 1910.

Hammond, M. C. M. "Battle of Buena Vista," *Southern Quarterly Review* 3 (January 1851): 146–89.

Hayne, Paul H., ed. *The Poems of Henry Timrod*. New York: Arno Press, 1972.

Heitman, Francis B. *Historical Register and Dictionary of the U.S. Army*. Washington, D.C.: Government Printing Office, 1903.

Henry, Robert Self. *The Story of the Mexican War*. 1950. Reprint, New York: De Capo Press, 1989.

Herring, Marcus D. "Hard Service in Camp and Battle." *Confederate Veteran* 22 (January 1914): 18–19.

Heyward, Barnwell Rhett. "The Descendants of Col. William Rhett, of South Carolina." *South Carolina Historical and Genealogical Magazine* 4 (January 1903): 36–74.

Hill, D. H. "The Battle of South Mountain, or Boonsboro." *Century Magazine* 32 (May 1886): 137–53.

Hogg, Ian V., ed. *Jane's Military Review*. London: Jane's Information Group, May 1987.

Holmes, Henry Schulz, comp. "The Trenholm Family." *South Carolina Historical and Genealogical Magazine* 16 (October 1915): 151–63.

Hoole, W. Stanley. *Vizetelly Covers the Confederacy*. 1957. Reprint, Wilmington, N.C.: Broadfoot, 2000.

Hope, Miss Margaret. "A Crimean V.C. Who Lived in Dagenham" (interview). *Dagenham Digest*, no. 27 (March 1955).

Horres, C. Russell, Jr. "An Affair of Honor at Fort Sumter." *South Carolina Historical Magazine* 102 (January 2001): 6–26.

Howard, Michael. *The Franco-Prussian War: The German Invasion of France, 1870–1871*. 1961. Reprint, New York: Dorset Press, 1990.

Hughes, Nathaniel Cheairs, Jr., and Roy P. Stonesifer Jr. *The Life and Wars of Gideon J. Pillow*. Chapel Hill: University of North Carolina Press, 1993.

Johannsen, Robert W. *To the Halls of the Montezumas*. New York: Oxford University Press, 1985.

Johnson, John. *The Defense of Charleston Harbor, Including Fort Sumter and the Adjacent Islands, 1863–1865*. 1889. Reprint, Freeport, N.Y.: Books for Libraries Press, 1970.

Jones, J. B. *A Rebel War Clerk's Diary: At the Confederate States Capital*. 1866. Reprint, New York: Time-Life, 1982.

Jones, Samuel. *The Siege of Charleston Harbor and the Operations on the South Atlantic Coast in the War Among the States*. New York: Neale, 1911.

Jones, Terry L., ed. "Campbell Brown's Memoirs of the Seven Days Battles." In *The Peninsula Campaign of 1862: Yorktown to Seven Days*, ed. William J. Miller, 2:40–71. Campbell, Calif.: Savas Woodbury, 1995.

Kelly's Directories. London: Kelly & Co., 1866–75, 1885–87.

King, Alvy L. *Louis T. Wigfall: Southern Fire-eater*. Baton Rouge: Louisiana State University Press, 1970.

Kneitel, Tom. *Directory of U.S. Army Forts, Camps, and Airfields (1790–1945)*. Commack, N.Y.: CRB Books, 1992.

Koonce, Donald B., ed. *Doctor to the Front: Recollections of Confederate Surgeon Thomas Fanning Wood*. Knoxville: University of Tennessee Press, 2000.

Law, E. M. "The Fight for Richmond, 1862." *Southern Bivouac* 2 (April 1887): 649–60.

Lawley, Francis, special correspondent. "The Civil War in America." *Times* (London), March 6, 1865.

———. "The Confederate States." *Times* (London), March 7, 1865.

Leland, Isabella Middleton, ed. "Middleton Correspondence 1861–1865." *South Carolina Historical Magazine* 63 (January 1962): 33–41.

———. "Middleton Correspondence 1861–1865." *South Carolina Historical Magazine* 63 (October 1962): 204–10.

———. "Middleton Correspondence 1861–1865." *South Carolina Historical Magazine* 64 (January 1963): 28–38.

———. "Middleton Correspondence 1861–1865." *South Carolina Historical Magazine* 64 (April 1963): 95–104.

Long, E. B., with Barbara Long. *The Civil War Day by Day: An Almanac 1861–1865*. Garden City, N.Y.: Doubleday, 1971.

Manarin, Louis H. *North Carolina Troops 1861–1865: A Roster*. Vol. 3, *Infantry*. Raleigh: North Carolina Office of Archives and History, 2004.

Manley, Atwood. "The Ripley Papers and Matildaville." *Quarterly* 5 (April 1960): 3–12. Published by the St. Lawrence County Historical Association, Canton, New York.

Marszalek, John F., ed. *The Diary of Miss Emma Holmes 1861–1866*. Baton Rouge: Louisiana State University Press, 1979.

Martin, William T. *History of Franklin County*. Columbus, Ohio: Follett, Foster, 1858.

McCormick, Robert and Jennie. *Probing Worthington's Heritage*. Worthington, Ohio: Cottonwood, 1990.

McKay, D. B. "Judah Philip Benjamin." *Tampa Sunday Tribune*, February 14, 1954.

McSherry, Richard. *El Puchero*. Philadelphia: Lippincott, Grambo, 1850.

Medical and Surgical History of the War of the Rebellion (1861–1865). Washington: Government Printing Office, 1870.

Middleton, Alicia Hopton. *Life in Carolina and New England During the 19th Century*. Bristol, R.I.: Privately printed, 1929.

Miles, Suzannah Smith. *East Cooper Gazetteer: History of Mount Pleasant, Sullivan's Island and the Isle of Palms*. Charleston, S.C.: History Press, 2004.

———. *Writings of the Islands: Sullivan's Island and the Isle of Palms*. Charleston, S.C.: History Press, 2004.

Morison, Samuel Eliot. *Oxford History of the American People*. New York: Oxford University Press, 1965.

"Mortuary—Roswell S. Ripley." In *City of Charleston Yearbook, 1887*. Charleston, S.C.: Lucas, Richardson, Steam Book Printers, 1887.

Murfin, James V. *The Gleam of Bayonets: The Battle of Antietam and the Maryland Campaign of 1862*. New York: Bonanza Books, 1965.

Naylor, Ron. "They Won the Highest Award for Gallantry." *Dagenham Post and Chadwell Heath News*, May 9, 1956, 14.

National Park Service. *Fort Sumter: Anvil of War*. Washington, D.C.: Division of Publications, U.S. Dept. of Interior, 1984.

Nepveux, Ethel S. *George Alfred Trenholm and the Company That Went to War, 1861–1865*. Charleston, S.C.: Comprint, 1973.

Norman, Matthew W. *Colonel Burton's Spiller and Burr Revolver: An Untimely Venture in Confederate Small Arms Manufacturing*. Macon, Ga.: Mercer University Press, 1996.

Official Records of the Union and Confederate Navies in the War of the Rebellion. 31 vols. Washington, D.C.: Government Printing Office, 1894–1927.

Olmstead, Colonel Charles C. "Reminiscences of Service in Charleston Harbor in 1863." *Southern Historical Society Papers* 11 (February–March 1883): 118–25.

Ordnance Inquiry Commission. *Minutes of Evidence, Royal Commission, Warlike Stores, Index, 1886–1887*. London: Eyre & Spottiswoode, 1887.

Pappas, George C. *To The Point: The United States Military Academy, 1802–1902*. Westport, Conn.: Praeger, 1993.

Pollard, Edward A. *The Second Year of the War*. Richmond, Va.: West & Johnson, 1863.

Priest, John M. *Antietam: The Soldier's Battle*. Shippensburg, Pa.: White Mane, 1989.

Pressley, John G. "Extracts from the Diary of Lieutenant-Colonel John G. Pressley, Twenty-Fifth South Carolina Volunteers." *Southern Historical Society Papers* 14 (1886): 35–62.

Ragan, Mark K. *The Hunley: Submarines, Sacrifice, and Success in the Civil War*. Revised ed. Charleston, S.C.: Narwhal Press, 1999.

Ravenel, Mrs. St. Julien. *Charleston: The Place and the People.* New York: Macmillan, 1916.

Reese, Joseph B. "Letters from J. B. Reese." *Countryman* (Turnwold, Ga.), April 29–August 16, 1862.

Rhett, Claudine. "Morris Island." *Southern Historical Society Papers* 12 (1884): 336–42.

——. "Flag of the First Regiment South Carolina Regular Artillery." *Confederate Veteran* 2 (April 1894): 126.

——. "Captain John Mitchel at Fort Sumter," *Confederate Veteran* 4 (January 1896): 6–7.

Ringold, May Spencer. "William Gourdin Young and the Wigfall Mission—Fort Sumter April 13, 1861." *South Carolina Historical Magazine* 73 (January 1972): 27–35.

Ripley, Hezekiah W. *Genealogy of a Part of the Ripley Family.* Newark, N.J.: A. Stephen Holbrook, 1867.

Ripley, R. S. *The War with Mexico.* 2 vols. 1849. Reprint, New York: Burt Franklin, 1970.

——. "The Civil War in America." *Blackwood's Edinburgh Magazine* 116 (August 1874): 211–30.

——. "The Last Confederate Flag on the Atlantic." *Southern Magazine* 10 (July 1875): 56–69.

——. "The Last Confederate Flag on the Atlantic." *Southern Magazine* 10 (August 1875): 129–43.

——. "The Situation in America," *Blackwood's Edinburgh Magazine* 121 (February 1877): 196–220.

——. *Correspondence Relating to the Fortification of Morris Island and Operations of the Engineers in Charleston, S.C.* New York: John J. Caulon, 1878.

——. "Charleston and Its Defenses in the Late War Between the States." *City of Charleston Yearbook, 1885.* Charleston: News and Courier Presses. 1885.

Ripley, Warren. *Artillery and Ammunition of the Civil War.* Charleston, S.C.: Battery Press, 1984.

——, ed. *Siege Train: The Journal of a Confederate Artilleryman in the Defense of Charleston.* Columbia: University of South Carolina Press, 1986.

Robertson, James I., Jr. *Stonewall Jackson: The Man, The Soldier, The Legend.* New York: Macmillan, 1997.

Roman, Alfred. *The Military Operations of General Beauregard in the War Between the States, 1861–1865,* New York: Harper & Brothers, 1884.

Rosen, Robert. *Confederate Charleston: An Illustrated History of the City and the People During the Civil War.* Columbia: University of South Carolina Press, 1994.

Sacks, Dr. B. "Charles Debrille Poston: Prince of Arizona Pioneers." *Smoke Signal* (Tucson, Ariz.), Spring 1963, 3–11.

Sandburg, Carl. *Abraham Lincoln: The War Years.* New York: Harcourt Brace, 1939.

Scaife, Milo Milton, ed. *The Diary of James K. Polk During His Presidency, 1845 to 1849.* Vol. 4. Chicago: A. C. McClurg, 1910.

Scharf, John Thomas. *History of Baltimore City and County.* Philadelphia: Louis H. Evarts, 1881.

Scott, Robert Garth, ed. *Forgotten Valor: The Memoirs, Journals and Civil War Letters of Orlando B. Wilcox.* Kent, Ohio: Kent State University Press, 1999.

Seabrook, Col. E. M. *Address Delivered at the Unveiling of the Ripley Monument, April 3, 1894.* Charleston, S.C.: Daggett, 1894.

Sears, Stephen W. *Landscape Turned Red: The Battle of Antietam.* New Haven, Conn.: Ticknor & Fields, 1983.

---. *To the Gates of Richmond: The Peninsula Campaign.* New York: Ticknor & Fields, 1992.

Sheads, Scott. *Fort McHenry: A History.* Baltimore: Nautical and Aviation Publishing Company of America, 1952.

Shepard, Julia Adelaide. "Lincoln's Assassination." *Century Magazine* 77 (April 1909): 917–18.

Sholes' Directory of the City of Charleston. N.p.: A. E. Sholes, 1882.

Sifakis, Stewart. *Who Was Who in the Civil War.* New York: Facts on File, 1988.

Smith, Gustavus Woodson. *Confederate War Papers.* New York: Atlantic Publishing, 1884.

---. *The Battle of Seven Pines.* 1891. Reprint, Dayton: Morningside, 1974.

Statutes at Large of South Carolina. Vol. 13, Dec. 1861–Dec. 1866. Columbia, S.C.: Republican Printing, 1875.

Stephens, Sir Leslie, and Sir Sidney Lee, eds. *Dictionary of National Biography.* Supplement, January 1901–December 1911. London: Oxford University Press, 1973.

Stern, Philip Van. Introduction to *Secret Service of the Confederate States in Europe, or How the Confederate Cruisers Were Equipped,* by James D. Bulloch, v–xix. 2 vols. New York: Thomas Yoseloff, Sagamore Press, 1959.

Stiles, John C. "Victoria Cross of the Confederacy." *Confederate Veteran* 23 (July 1915): 304.

---. "Roll of Honor." *Confederate Veteran* 30 (April 1922): 136–38.

Stokeley, Jim. *Fort Moultrie: Constant Defender.* Washington D.C.: National Park Handbook, Department of the Interior, 1985.

Sturgill, Claude C., and Charles L. Price, eds. "McCabe's Impression of the Bombardment of Charleston, 1863." *South Carolina Historical Magazine* 70 (October 1970): 266–69.

Supplement to the Official Records of the Union and Confederate Armies. Wilmington, N.C.: Broadfoot, 1994.

Swanberg, W. A. *First Blood: The Story of Fort Sumter.* New York: Charles Scribner's Sons, 1957.

Thomas, Henry W. *History of the Doles-Cook Brigade, Army of Northern Virginia, C.S.A.* 1908. Reprint, Dayton, Ohio: Morningside, 1988.

Thompson, John Reuben. "Notices of New Works." *Southern Literary Messenger* 16 (January 1850): 61–64.

Tidball, Eugene C. *The Life of John C. Tidball: No Disgrace to My Country.* Kent, Ohio: Kent State University Press, 2002.

Trow, John F. *Trow's New York City Directory.* Vol. 98. New York: Trow City Directory Co., 1887.

U.S. Congress. *Biographical Directory of the U.S. Congress.* Washington, D.C.: Government Printing Office, 1961.

U.S. Senate. *Bills and Resolutions.* S 304, 1st Session, 32nd Congress.

U.S. Senate. *Journal of the Senate of the United States of America, 1789–1873,* vol. 43 (1852).

Wallace, Sarah Agnes, and Frances Elma Gillespie, eds. *The Journal of Benjamin Moran, 1857–1865.* Chicago: University of Chicago Press, 1949.

---. "Confederate Exiles in London, 1865–1870: The Wigfalls." *South Carolina Historical and Genealogical Magazine* 52 (July 1951): 74–87.

---. "Confederate Exiles in London, 1865–1870: The Wigfalls." *South Carolina Historical and Genealogical Magazine* 52 (October 1951): 198–206.

The War of the Rebellion: A Compilation of the Official Records of the Union and Confederate Armies. 128 vols. Washington, D.C.: Government Printing Office, 1880–1901.

Warner, Ezra T. *Generals in Gray: Lives of Confederate Commanders.* Baton Rouge: Louisiana State University Press, 1983.
Weinert, Richard P., and Colonel Robert Arthur. *Defender of the Chesapeake: The Story of Fort Monroe.* 3rd ed. 1989. Reprint, Shippensburg, Pa.: White Mane, 1989.
Wellman, Manly Wade. *Giant in Gray: A Biography of Wade Hampton of South Carolina.* Dayton, Ohio: Press of Morningside Bookshop, 1998.
Welsh, Jack D., M.D. *Medical Histories of Confederate Generals.* Kent, Ohio: Kent State University Press, 1995.
Williams, T. Harry. *P. G. T. Beauregard: Napoleon in Gray.* Baton Rouge: Louisiana State University Press, 1955.
Winders, Richard Bruce. *Mr. Polk's Army: The American Experience in the Mexican War.* College Station: Texas A&M University Press, 1997.
Wise, Stephen R. *Lifeline of the Confederacy; Blockade Running During the Civil War.* Columbia: University of South Carolina Press, 1988.
———. *Gate of Hell: Campaign for Charleston Harbor, 1863.* Columbia: University of South Carolina Press, 1994.
Woodward, C. Vann, ed. *Mary Chesnut's Civil War.* New Haven, Conn.: Yale University Press, 1981.
Wyckoff, Mac. *A History of the 3rd South Carolina Infantry: 1861–65.* Fredericksburg, Va.: Sergeant Kirkland's Museum and Historical Society, 1995.

INDEX

Page references appearing in *italics* indicate illustrations or material contained in their captions. Names of military units are alphabetized as spelled rather than by numerical order. For example, the 29th South Carolina Regiment will appear before the 23rd South Carolina Regiment.

Abbeville (S.C.), 263, 264, 265
Abbott, Jenkins & Company (British law firm), 277
Abbott, Jenkins and Abbott (British law firm), 291
abolition movement, 41, 63, 183, 184, 298
A Company (2nd Artillery Regiment; U.S.A.), 46–47
A Company (3rd Artillery Regiment; U.S.A.), 17
A Company (South Carolina Artillery; C.S.A.), 182, 183
Adams, Charles F., 272, 274–75, 307, 308
Adams, Charles F., Jr., 302
Adams, James, 65
Adams, Robert, 58–60
Adams, Warren, 231
Adams' Revolvers (Taylerson and Chamberlain), 61
Adams' Revolving Arms Company, 60, 61
African Americans: as Morris Island fortification labor, 171, 177; as POWs, 224; Radical Republicans and, 298; Ripley on, 298, 343–44; S.C. labor shortages of, 168, 214, 238; as Union soldiers, 183, 184–85, 269
Alabama, 67
Alabama, CSS, 307, 308
Alabama Claims crisis, 307–10
Alabama General Assembly, 63
Albion Works (Leeds, England), 259, 271
Alexander, William, 208, 218–19, 222
Alexandra Hotel (London, England), 271, 274, 275, 280, 282
Alexandria (Va.), 80
Alice (steamer), 186
Almonte, Juan N., 41
American Disruption, The (Beresford-Hope), 305
American Line Steamship Company, 12
American Review, 40
Ames Manufacturing Company, 255
Amissville (Va.), 124

Ampudia, Pedro de, 23, 25, 26
Anderson, E. C., 186
Anderson, George B.: in Hill's Division, 110, 124; Maryland Campaign (1862), 127, 128, 130–31, 132, 294; Peninsula Campaign (1862), 110, 120
Anderson, George T., 127–29, 130
Anderson, J. R., 86
Anderson, Richard H., 11, 118, 119, 125, 127
Anderson, Robert, 79; command transferred from Fort Moultrie to Fort Sumter, 65, 299; correspondence of, 73; C.S.A. ultimatum to, 75–76; Doubleday and, 77; Fort Sumter occupied by (1861), 65, 66; safe conduct offered to, 70; surrender of (1861), 78, 342
Andrew, John A., 302
Anglo-German Tunneling Company, 293
Antietam, Battle of (1862), 132–36, *133* map, *134*, 140, 279, 290, 293, 327
Antietam Creek, 132
Appomattox Court House (Va.), Lee's surrender at (1865), 264, 300–301
Arabia (steamer), 59
Argentina, 304
Arivaca Ranch, Ripley purchase of, 285–86, 290
Arizona Mining Company, 285
Arizona Territory, 285
Army and Navy Club (London, England), 327, 330
Army Artillery Battalion, 22, 23, 24
Army of Northern Virginia (C.S.A.): Lee as commander of, 110; Lee's dissatisfaction with leadership in, 122; Maryland Campaign (1862), 125, 126, 136; reinforcements sent to S.C. from, 252; Ripley's brigade in, 142, 279; Smith (G. W.) as commander of, 110; surrender of (1865), 264
Army of Tennessee (C.S.A.), 247, 251, 253, 254, 257, 258–59
Army of the Potomac (U.S.A.), 108, 122–23
Army of the Valley (C.S.A.), 113

Army of Virginia (U.S.A.), 122–23
Arthur, Chester A., 339
Articles of War, 142–43
Ashepoo River, 88, 89
Asphaltic Wood Paving Company (London, England), 348
Augusta (Ga.), 253, 256, 263
Augusta, USS, 82
Augusta Arsenal (Ga.), 16–17, 18–19, 276
Augusta Arsenal (Maine), 13
Austro-Prussian War (1866), 272
Aztec Club, 34

Bacon, William, 288
Bahamas, 261–62, 272, 301
Baker, H. S., 123
balloons, 223
Baltimore (Md.), 55–56, 64
Baltimore and Ohio Railroad, 125
Bankhead, James, 47, 49–50, 53, 55
Barnum's Hotel (Baltimore, Md.), 19, 20
Barnwell, Joseph, 242
Barnwell, Robert, 65, 83, 247
BASF (German company), 226
Basinger, William S., 231, 235
Batley, John, 259, 277, 280, 281, 285. *See also* Greenwood & Batley (Leeds, England)
Battery Beauregard (Sullivan's Island, S.C.), 98, 148, 208–9, 219, 229–30
Battery Bee (Sullivan's Island, S.C.), 148, 163, 165, 193, 218
Battery Cheves (James Island, S.C.), 190, 192
Battery Gary (Mount Pleasant, S.C.), 211
Battery Glover (James Island, S.C.), 149, 153, 192
Battery Gregg (Morris Island, S.C.): Battery Wagner (July 18, 1863), 183; Beauregard inspection of, 192; C.S.A. loss of, 201, 202, 205, 213, 220; engineering work and, 213; Fort Sumter weaponry moved to, 191, 194; materiel shortages at, 192; Signal Corps at, 186; Union guns directed at, 193
Battery Haskell (James Island, S.C.), 191, 192, 194, 233
Battery Island (S.C.), 137, 177, 344
Battery Marion (Sullivan's Island, S.C.), 231, 234
Battery Marshall (Sullivan's Island, S.C.), 98, 208–9, 212–15, 219, 222, 228–29, 238
Battery Ramsay (White Point Garden, S.C.), 165, 204
Battery Rutledge (Sullivan's Island, S.C.), 210, 229
Battery Ryan (James Island, S.C.), 209

Battery Simkins (James Island, S.C.), 191, 193
Battery Tatom (Charleston, S.C.), 209
Battery Wagner (Morris Island, S.C.): Beauregard visit to, 192; black POWs captured at, 224; committee recommendations for, 155; C.S.A. loss of, 202, 205, 213, 220, 344; C.S.A. objectives concerning, 178; First Battle of (July 10–11, 1863), 179–81; fortification work on, 170; Ripley's report on defenses at, 141; Second Battle of (July 18, 1863), 183–86, 302–3; torpedoes connected to, 159; Union siege/bombardment of, 190, 193–94, 195, 206
"Battle of South Mountain, or Boonsboro, The" (D. H. Hill), 129, 131, 294
"Battle Pictures" (Boykin), 118
Battles and Leaders of the Civil War, 347
Baylor, Charles G., 56
B Company (3rd Artillery Regiment; U.S.A.), 17
Beasley, William, 58
Beaufort (S.C.), 85
Beaumont, F. B. E., 58–60
Beauregard, P. G. T.: ammunition economization directive and, 202–3; as Aztec Club member, 34; Carolinas Campaign, 254–55; Charleston fire relief supported by, 90; Charleston Harbor (April, 1863), 163, 164; Clingman brigade ordered to N.C. by, 216; Cole's Island abandonment and, 107; correspondence of, 144, 145, 256, 304; Davis Charleston visit and, 209; Davis vs., 346; Feilden as staff member of, 173, 246; during Fort Sumter bombardment, 196; Gillmore ultimatum to, 197, 236; Gonzales as artillery chief under, 144; Grant as viewed by, 173; Hardee as replacement for, 251; Harris and, 169, 207–8, 218, 220, 221–22, 233, 347; health problems of, 258, 259; *Hunley* and, 206–8, 219, 224–25; Johnston replaces, 259; Jones (Samuel) as replacement for, 232; Jordan as chief of staff of, 168, 228; *Keokuk* salvage and, 164–66; Lee and, 257–58; Lincoln ultimatum and, 73; Mexican War service of, 32, 33; micromanaging style of, 208; Morris Island fortifications and, *171;* Ordnance Dept. vs., 203–4; Pemberton and, 345; postbellum writings of, 342–43, 347; as Provisional C.S.A. Forces commander, 68; reassigned to Virginia, 232, 239; Rhett-Calhoun duel and, 138, 143; Ripley postbellum writings on, 344; Sherman's Carolina Campaign and, 257–58; as South Carolina, Georgia, and Florida Dept. commander, 69, 344; as South Carolina and Georgia Dept. commander, 138, 139, 344; Union

INDEX | 401

amphibious landing precautions of, 209–11; weaknesses of, 192; as West Department commander, 251; as West Point cadet, 169

Beauregard, P. G. T.—Ripley's relationship with: ammunition economization and, 202–3; in Beauregard's postbellum writings, 342–43; during Charleston defense preparations, 68–69, 69, 139, 140, 190; deterioration of, 69, 169, 191–92; disobedience of orders, 252, 255, 257; "fire-ship" idea and, 187–88; intoxication allegations, 248–49; Jones (Samuel)-Ripley conflict and, 243–44, 245–46; Morris Island interrogatories, 213, 215–18, 221–22; official rebuke, 219–20, 221; promotion recommendations, 151–52, 204, 257, 331; reinforcement orders and, 223; Ripley's engineer complaints and, 69, 169, 212, 218, 219; Ripley's leave of absence request denied, 219–20; Ripley's postbellum reputation in Charleston, 346–47

Beauregard, R. T., 91–92, 93

Beaver Dam Creek, Battle of (1862). *See* Mechanicsville, Battle of (1862)

Bee, Barnard E., 34, 81
Bee, J. S., 180
Bee, W. C., 226
Behr, Fritz Bernard, 294
Belgian Patent No. 64,672, 337
Bell, John, 64, 315
Benbow, H. L., 222
Benham, Henry, 106, 107
Benjamin, Judah P., 270, 274, 277–78, 278, 282, 285; background of, 266; Charleston defense preparations and, 91; as Confederate Secretary of War, 83; flight of, after Lee's surrender, 264, 265–67; Port Royal (1861), 85; Ripley's arms deals and, 83
Benjamin, Natalie St. Martin, 266
Benjamin, Ninette, 266
Bennett, Frank T., 98–99
Bentonville, Battle of (1865), 263, 265
Beresford-Hope, Alexander James, 305, 306
Berkshire (Ohio), 1
Bermuda, 260, 261–62, 272
Besseges (France), 335
Biddulph, Middleton, 291, 309
Big Cypress Swamp (Fla.), 44
Bimini Islands, 267
Bismarck, Otto von, 287
Blackwood, John, 295–96, 299–300, 313, 319
Blackwood's Edinburgh Magazine, 208, 273, 295, 296–99, 301, 313
Blaine, James G., 339
Blake, Walter, 173

blockade running, 82, 91, 101, 166, 172, 188–89, 206, 223, 226, 260–62, 300–301
Bohicket Creek, 93
Bonham, Milledge L., 139, 167, 177, 181, 247
Boonsboro (Md.), 126, 132
Booth, John Wilkes, 49
Boston Daily Globe, 302, 303
Boston Herald, 302–3
Bower, A., 61
Boykin, S., 118
Boylston, S. C., 164–65
Bradford, Hannah, 1
Bragg, Braxton, 204, 209
Brainard, Asa, 6, 11
Branchville (S.C.), 233, 250, 254
Branson, Benjamin, 273
Brawley, William H., 349, 351
Brazos Santiago (Mexico), 21
Breach Inlet, 222, 224–25, 229
Breach Inlet Battery (Sullivan's Island, S.C.), 141
Breckinridge, John C., 64, 257, 259, 270, 315
Brennan, Patrick, 106
Brent, George W., 263
Bridges, Hal, 131
British Arms Commission, 58
British Coldstream Guards, 172
British Court of Bankruptcy, 290–91
British Foreign Office, 307
British Jackson Monumental Fund, 306
British Ordnance Select Committee, 57, 272, 275, 336–37
British Patent Office: Patent No. 817 ("Improvements in Ammunition for Breech Loading Cannon"), 337–38, 340–41, 343; Patent No. 1421 ("Improved Processes and Apparatus for Reducing, Melting, Purifying, and Otherwise Working Ores, Metals, Metalloids, and Similar Substances"), 327–29; Patent No. 1733 ("Treating Illuminating Gas"), 330, *331*; Patent No. 1831 ("A Novel Method of and Apparatus for Reducing and Purifying Metals Directly from Their Ores by Gaseous Fuel," *334, 334*; Patent No. 2069 ("Improvements in the Process and Apparatus for the Manufacture of Gas for Heating and Other Purposes"), 323–24, *324*, 325–27; Patent No. 2527 ("Improvements in the Treatment of Illuminating Gas, and an Apparatus Therefore"), 329–30; Patent No. 2923 ("Improvements Relating to Ordnance and Firearms and Ammunition for the Same"), 330–34, *332*, 335, 336–37, 343; Patent No. 3042 ("Improvements in Breech Loading Cannon and Ammunition Therefore"), 335–36;

British Patent Office (*continued*)
  Patent No. 4363 ("Improved Processes and Apparatus for Reducing, Melting, Purifying, and Otherwise Working Ores, Metals, Metalloids, and Similar Substances"), 329; Patent No. 5314 ("Improvements in Puddling and in Furnaces, More Especially such as Are Employed in Puddling"), 324, 325–26, 325–27; Patent No. 5315 ("Improvements in Gas Retorts, and in the Manufacture of Gas"), 324–27, *326;* British War Department, 57, 308, 309
Broadfoot, David, 207, 208
Brook, Freeman and Batley (British law firm), 276–77, 279
Brown, Campbell, 119
Brown, H. A., 118, 120
Brown, John, 63, 255, 297
Brown, Joseph E., 64
Browne, J. Ross, 285
Brunswick (Ga.), 88
Buchanan, James, 34, 65, 98, 314–15
Buena Vista, Battle of (1847), 29
Bull, Henry Clay, 327–29
Bull Island (S.C.), 150
Bulloch, James D., 306–7
Bunch, Robert, 105–6
Burnet, B. S., 231
Burns, Archibald W., 37
Burroughs, Mary, 53
Burton, Eugenia, 260, 267
Burton, James H.: as acting Harpers Ferry Arsenal master armorer, 58; arms machinery order of, 255–56, 259–62, 271, 283; correspondence of, 272, 276; C.S.A. armory plans and, 256; as Enfield chief engineer, 58, 59; as Greenwood & Batley employee, 269, 290; relocation to England, 270; relocation to Virginia, 276; Ripley and, 59, 61, 255, 269, 272, 290; Ripley's Greenwood & Batley lawsuit and, 279, 281, 287
Butler, Benjamin, 315
Butler, Matthew C., 252, 257
Butler, William O., 27, 205
Buttles, Joel, 3, 4, 5, 47, 48

Calhoun, Ransom, 138–39, 142–43, *143*
Camargo (Mexico), 22, 27
Cameron, Simon, 71, 73
Campbell, John A., 69–70
Camp Palo Alto (Mexico), 27
Camp Ripley (Richmond, Va.), 117
Cañete (Mexican actress), 35
Capers Island (S.C.), 223

Captain Hawthorne (ship), 260
Carney, William C., 184, 185, 303
Carolina (steamer), 70–71
Caroline Goodyear (ship), 260
carpetbaggers, 315–16
Carpmael & Company, 337, 340
Carr, Lewis, 302
"Cartridge for Ordnance" (Patent No. 314, 127), *337,* 338, 343
Castle Pinckney (Charleston, S.C.), 65, 81, 90, 99, 149, 186, 208
Catholic Church, 36
Catoctin Mountain, 126
Catskill, USS, 159, 161, 162, 179
Cattarns & Jehn (British law firm), 279
Caulkins, Chloe (aunt), 1
Caulkins, Eunice (grandmother), 1
Caulkins, Julia. *See* Ripley, Julia Caulkins (mother)
Caulkins, Lovewell (uncle), 1
Caulkins, Roswell (grandfather), 1
C Company (3rd Artillery Regiment; U.S.A.), 16–17, 21
Centreville (Va.), 124
Century Magazine, 12, 129
Cerralvo (Mexico), 22–23, 24
Cerro Gordo, Battle of (1847), 29–30, 36, 40–41, 50
Chamberlain, W. H. J., 61, 64
Chamberlain & Company, 226
Chambliss, N. R., 261
Chantilly (Va.), 125
Chantilly, Battle of (1862), 124
Chapultepec, Battle of (1847), 32–33
Charleston (S.C.), 346; C.S.A. control of military operations in, 68; Davis visit to (1863), 209; Democratic National Convention in (1860), 64; destruction of, 268–69; evacuation of, 182, 220, 252, 255, 261, 268; fortification of, 52, 70, 74 map; Fort Moultrie evacuation in, 65–66; Great Fire of (1861), 89–90, 145, 172; Marshall defense plans for, 99; ordnance placement in, 208–9; Pemberton defense plans for, 104–5; Pemberton reassigned from, 137–38; Rhett-Calhoun duel in (1862), 138–39, 142–43, *143;* Ripley defense preparations, 87–89, 90–95, 140–42, 148–50, 159, 209–11, 250, 341–42, 344–46; Ripley family return to, from England, 283, 286, 290, 349–50; Ripley funeral in, 351–54, *352;* Ripley gravesite in, 14, 350, 354–56, *355;* Ripley return to (1862), 139–40, 144; Ripley's allegiance to, 335, 338; Ripley's daughter's trust property in, 188, 286–87; Ripley's postbellum reputation

INDEX | 403

in, 346–47; Union blockade of, 91, 102, 150–51, 152, 158, 206; Union bombardment of (1863), 197–98, 220, 224, 235–36; Union POWs as human shields in, 235–37, 241; as Union target, 84, 139, 228; wartime cost of living in, 224; weaponry available in, before Civil War, 64. *See also* Fort Moultrie (S.C.); Fort Sumter (S.C.); Fort Sumter, Battle of (1861); *specific battery; island*
Charleston, CSS, 206
"Charleston and Its Defenses" (Ripley), 344–46, 347
Charleston Arsenal, 83, 144, 209, 245, 261
Charleston Battalion (C.S.A.), 180, 183
Charleston City Hall, 209
Charleston Club (Charleston, S.C.), 138
Charleston Harbor, First Battle of (April, 1863), 159–64, 160 map, 204–5, 345
Charleston Harbor, Second Battle of (July–September, 1863): Battery Wagner (July 10–11, 1863), 179–81; Battery Wagner (July 18, 1863), 183–86; Battery Wagner siege/bombardment (late summer, 1863), 190, 193–94; British sympathizer visits preceding, 172–74; casualties during, 194, 195; C.S.A. James Island fortifications, 171–72; C.S.A. Morris Island fortifications, 168, 169, 170–71; Fort Sumter siege/bombardment, 194–97; ordnance placement during, 190–93; press coverage of, 205; Ripley-engineer conflict affecting, 168–72, 174–77, 190; Ripley "fire-ship" idea during, 187–88; Ripley HQs during, 208; Ripley investments during, 188–89, 206; Secessionville (July 16, 1863), 182–83; Union movements/fortifications preceding, 168, 173–74, 176, 177–78
Charleston Hotel (Charleston, S.C.), 55, 90, 145–46, 150, 172
Charleston Light Dragoons (C.S.A.), 209
Charleston Mercury, 54, 62, 67, 70, 76, 80–81, 82, 86, 94, 98, 106, 136, 139–40, 146–47, 159, 163, 165, 176, 181, 195, 205, 247, 248
Charleston News and Courier, 351, 354
Charleston Oaks Club (Charleston, S.C.), 138
"Charleston's Acknowledgements to General Ripley," 346
Charleston-Savannah railroad, 86, 88, 93, 94
Charleston Zouave Cadets (C.S.A.), 81
Charlotte (N.C.), 257, 259, 262, 263, 264
Chase, Philander, 3–4
Chassepôt, M., 272
Châtellerault (France), 272
Chatfield, John L., 180
Cheatham, Frank, 253, 254, 263

Cherokee (blockade-runner), 189
Cheshire Observer, 292
Chesnut, James, 264, 267–68
Chesnut, Mary Boykin, 105, 264, 267–68
Chester (S.C.), 257, 258, 263, 267–68
Cheves, Langdon, 169, 170–71, 174–75, 176, 180
Chew, Robert, 73
Chichester, Charles E., 81, 178, 186, 190, 351
Chickahominy River, 109, 113, 114
Chickamauga, Battle of (1863), 209
Chicopee Falls (Mass.), 59
Chicopee Journal Weekly, 61
Chicora (C.S.A. warship), 98, 152, 164, 193, 239
Childs, F. L.: Beauregard vs., 144–45, 218; as Charleston Arsenal chief ordnance officer, 82, 83, 144, 175; credit lines of, 82; as Ripley pallbearer, 351–52; Ripley's arrest of, 145, 171; Ripley vs., 83, 84, 144–45, 146, 171, 175, 245, 352; Trezevant as replacement for, 205
China, 304
Churubusco, Battle of (1847), 31
Cincinnati (Ohio), 267
Circular Church (Charleston, S.C.), 90
Cisco, W. B., 65
Citadel (Charleston, S.C.), 346, 353
City of Charleston Yearbook, 341–42, 344–46, 347, 349, 353
civil service system, 339
Civil War (1861–1865), 94, 159–61, 256, 316; beginning of, 76–78, 264, 340; end of, 299; mortality rate during, 20; Southern negotiation attempts preceding, 65, 69–70, 71–72, 73
Civil War (1861–1865)—battles: Bentonville (1865), 263, 265; Chantilly (1862), 124; Charleston Harbor (April, 1863), 159–64, 160 map, 345; Chickamauga (1863), 209; Cold Harbor (1864), 12; Five Forks (1865), 263–64; Fort Donelson (1862), 94, 97; Fort Henry (1862), 97; Fort Pulaski (1862), 183; Franklin (1864), 251, 253; Gettysburg (1863), 22; Manassas (1861), 80, 81, 108, 169; Manassas (1862), 101, 124; Nashville (1864), 251; Olustee (1864), 225; Petersburg (1864–1865), 256; Port Royal (1861), 84, 85–87; Secessionville (1863), 106, 182–83, 345; Seven Pines (1862), 109–10; Shiloh (1862), 342; Vicksburg (1863), 316; Yorktown (1862), 108–9. *See also* Fort Sumter, Battle of (1861); Maryland Campaign (1862); Peninsula Campaign (1862)
Civil War (1861–1865)—Ripley's military service during: Beauregard's assessment of, 256–57; Carolinas Campaign, 263; Charleston defense preparations, 87–89, 90–95,

404 | INDEX

Civil War (1861–1865) (*continued*)
140–42, 148–50, 159, 209–11, 250, 341–42, 344–46; Charleston fire (1861), 90; Charleston Harbor (April, 1863), 159–64; demoted to Second Sub-District commander, 247–48; as First Military District commander, 139–40, 149, 152, 157, 158; Foster courtesy extended to, 240–41; Gonzales as aide-de-camp to, 87; Gonzales criticism of, 144; Hill (D. H.) vs., 110–11, 129; historiographical assessment of, 256; *Hunley* and, 225; Jones (Samuel) assessment of, 250; *Keokuk* salvage, 165–66; Lee and, 92–93, 103; Northern impression of, 98–99; Pemberton and, 97, 101, 104–5, 106, 140, 316; Pickens vs., 91–92; *Planter* loss, 102–3, 104; Port Royal (1861), 85–87; POW issue and, 236, 237, 241–42; profiteering by, 152–53, 188–89, 206; promotions, 151–52, 204; Ripley postbellum writings on, 344–46; Seven Pines (1862), 109–10; social life, 93; staff members of, 106. *See also* Beauregard, P. G. T.—Ripley's relationship with; Charleston Harbor, Second Battle of (July–September, 1863); Maryland Campaign (1862); Peninsula Campaign (1862)
"Civil War in America, by the Comte de Paris, The" (Ripley), 296–99
Clarendon, Lord, 308
Clark (8th Infantry adjutant), 25
Clayton, William Robert, 279
Cleveland, Palmer, 5
Clingman, Thomas L., 179, 181–82, 210, 213, 214, 216, 340, 350
Cobb, Howell, 124–25
Coffin, James H., 9
Colcock, Charles J., 226
Colcock, Thomas H., 226, 227
Cold Harbor, Battle of (1864), 12
Cole's Island (S.C.): Beauregard defenses on, 344; Hagood as commander of, 99–100; Lee's fortification of, 91, 93, 94–95; Pemberton's abandonment of, 99–101, 102, 104, 106–7, 153, 167, 344–45, 347; reoccupation proposals/suggestions, 137, 153, 155, 171; Ripley postbellum writings on, 344–45, 346; Secessionville (1863) and, 140; significance of, in Charleston defense, 93, 94–95; Union forces on, 176
Colquitt, Alfred H., 203; as Battery Wagner commander, 186; casualties suffered by, 120; Charleston defense preparations, 167, 179, 182; Maryland Campaign (1862), 124, 126, 127; Peninsula Campaign (1862), 110, 115, 120; in Savannah, 223; staff members of, 132

Colt, Samuel, 58
Colt Fire Arms Manufacturing Company, 279, 287, 304
Columbia (S.C.), 182, 254–55, 257–58, 261, 262, 268, 272
Columbia (Tenn.), 39
Columbus (Ky.), 258
Combahee River, 88–89
commerce raiders, 306–7
Committee on Military Affairs, 51
Committee on the District of Columbia, 51
Comte de Paris, 295
Confederate Adjutant and Inspector General's Office, 186
Confederate Army, 351–52; Lee as general-in-chief of, 256; Pemberton promotions within, 96–97; Provisional Forces of, 68; Ripley application for commission in, 68. *See also specific army*
Confederate bond scheme, 273–74
Confederate Congress, 82, 186, 264
Confederate Engineer Corps, 122, 174
Confederate Navy, 142, 152, 187, 193, 234, 239, 274, 352
Confederate Ordnance Department, 110–11, 171, 175, 203, 205–6, 218, 221
Confederate Senate, 97
Confederate States of America (C.S.A.): armories in, 255–56; Charleston military operations controlled by, 68; collapse of, 315; communications in, 252; economy of, 227, 301; Europe-based shipbuilding program of, 306–7; final days of, 263–69; foreign recognition of, 152, 301; Lincoln's attitude toward, 72; negotiation efforts of, 69–70, 71–72, 73; official seal of, 306; press coverage of, 273; provisional government formed (1861), 67, 266; Timrod as "poet laureate" of, 146
Confederate States Provisional Navy, 304
Confederate Treasury Department, 206
Confederate War Department, 71, 87, 145, 204
Conner, James, 252
Conrad, Charles, 50, 51, 55, 56, 152, 243
Constitutional Union Party, 64
Continental Hotel (Philadelphia, Pa.), 64
Contreras, Battle of (1847), 31
Convention of Seceded States (Montgomery, Ala.; 1861), 266
Cook, Edward, 8
Cooper, Samuel, 52, 55, 85, 93, 139, 144, 145, 151–52, 177, 179, 187–88, 202, 203, 233, 239, 342; correspondence of, 243, 255; Jones (Samuel)-Ripley conflict and, 244, 245; Ripley denied promotions by, 204; Ripley

vs., 243, 253; troop movements ordered by, 233–34
Cooper River, 207
Coosawatchie (S.C.), 89, 140
Coos Bay (Oreg.), 291
Countryman, 112, 115–18
Courtenay, William A., 349, 350, 351, 354
Craig, H. K., 60
Crampton's Gap, 127
Credit Mobilier, 311–12
Crimean War (1853–1856), 56, 58, 62, 287, 288
C. Ripley & Company, 4
Crowfield Estate (S.C.), 53
Culpepper Court House (Va.), 124
Cumberland Sound, 88
Cummings Point Battery, 180, 191, 192
Cunard Steamship Lines, 267
Cushing, Caleb, 37

Dahlgren, John A., 179, 183, 202, 242
Daily American Times, 56
Dallas Herald, 274
Dantzler, O. M., 224–25
Danville (Va.), 263–64
Darlington Court House (S.C.), 255
Davidson, Hunter, 304
Davis, Jefferson, 101; Beauregard vs., 346; capture/imprisonment of, 267, 346; Charleston defense and, 139; Charleston visit of (1863), 209; Confederate capital moved to Danville (Va.) by, 263–64; correspondence of, 79–80, 92, 124, 137; as C.S.A. provisional president, 67; flight of, after Lee's surrender, 265, 266–67; Gonzales and, 87; heroism medals awarded by, 186; Jones (Samuel)-Ripley conflict and, 245, 246–47; Pemberton and, 137–38; Pickens-Ripley conflict and, 92; Richmond defense ordered by, 108, 109; Ripley postbellum writings on, 346; Ripley resignation threat and, 79–80; Ripley visits to, 256; Sherman vs., 343
Davis, Varina, 263, 264, 265
DeBruin, Charles H., 287–88, 289, 293
Deems, Charles F., 350
Defense of Charleston Harbor, The (Johnson), 165, 171, 240, 352
Delafield, Robert A., 16
Delaware County (Ohio), 1
Deleon (doctor), 25
De Lisle (engineer), 159–61
Democratic National Convention (1844), 29
Democratic National Convention (1860), 64
Democratic Party, 32, 41, 50–51, 302, 303, 312, 314–15, 319, 339

Democratic Review, 40
Denmark, 287
De Pass, William, 182
De Rosset, William L., 115, 129–30, 132, 134, 135, 293–95
DeSaussure, Wilmot G., 286
Dewees Inlet, 238
D. H. Hill Division (C.S.A.), 122, 124
Dickenson, A. G., 350
Dickins, Asbury, 9, 10
Dixon, George E., 207, 208, 218–19, 222, 223–24
Dixon, William M., 57, 58
Doles, George P., 127, 132, 134, 135, 139, 142
Donnolly (Georgia private), 182
Doty, James D., 10
Doubleday, Abner, 11, 77
Douglas, Stephen A., 63, 315
Dowdey, Clifford, 117
Drayton (*Passaic* captain), 161
Drayton, Thomas F., 85, 86–87, 127–29, 130, 131
Drury Lane Theatre (London, England), 275, 283
Dubuquois, Captain (French captain), 152
Dudley, Thomas H., 272, 277, 280, 281, 283, 284, 285
Duncan, James, 35, 37
Duncan's Artillery Battery (U.S.A.), 22, 25
Dunovant, R. G. M., 66, 88
Du Pont, Samuel F., 84, 85, 102, 158, 159, 164, 179, 345

Early, Jubal, 96
Eason & Company, 144–45
Echols, William H., 163, 169, 176, 233
E Company (First Charleston Battalion; C.S.A.), 150
E Company (2nd Artillery Regiment; U.S.A.), 53
Edisto Island (S.C.), 89, 93, 344
Edisto River, 88, 89
Eggleston, George Cary, 102–3
Egypt, 271
18th Battalion (C.S.A.), 180
18th Georgia Battalion (C.S.A.), 231, 233, 234
18th Louisiana Volunteers (C.S.A.), 342
18th South Carolina Regiment (C.S.A.), 92, 225
8th Georgia Battalion (C.S.A.), 167
8th Infantry Regiment (U.S.A.), 22, 25
Eisenhower, John D. S., 23–24, 31, 40
Elements of Algebra (D. H. Hill), 110
11th South Carolina Regiment (C.S.A.), 232
Ella (ship), 261
Ellenton (Fla.), 266

Ellerson's Mill (1862). *See* Mechanicsville, Battle of (1862)
Elliott, Stephen, 196, 202, 203, 208, 238, 239, 245
Elliott, Stephen, Jr., 245
emancipation, 315
Enfield (England), 58, 59–60, 61, 255, 259
England: Benjamin legal career in, 267, 278; Confederate shipbuilding program in, 306–7; Confederate social network in, 265, 274, 275, 280; Confederate sympathizers in, 305, 306; C.S.A. unrecognized by, 301; Stonewall Jackson Monument sent from, 304–6; Wigfall self-exile in, 273–74. *See also* London (England)
England—Ripley postbellum self-exile in, 270, 271; arrival date, 269; business ventures, 303–4; financial difficulties, 267, 274, 275, 279, 281–83; residences, 323, 331; transportation, 270; trips to US, 323
Eolus, USS, 261
Etiwan (transport ship), 165
Eutaw House (Baltimore, Md.), 55–56
Evans, Nathan G., 88, 91, 92, 93, 98, 167, 216, 228, 232
Everglades (Fla.), 43, 44
Ewell, Richard S., 119

Fayetteville (N.C.), 268
Fayetteville (N.C.) Arsenal and Armory, 145
Feilden, Henry Wemyss, 172–73, 232, 233, 234, 242, 243, 246, 303
Fenwick's Island (S.C.), 88
Ferguson (civilian), 207
Ferguson, J. B., 91–92
Ferguson, John, 189
Ferguson's Light Battery (C.S.A.), 167
5th Brigade (D. H. Hill's Division; C.S.A.), 110
5th Infantry Regiment (U.S.A.), 23
Fifth Military District (C.S.A.), 98
5th North Carolina Regiment (C.S.A.), 127
55th Pennsylvania Regiment (U.S.A.), 98–99
51st North Carolina Regiment (C.S.A.), 182, 183
54th Massachusetts Regiment (U.S.A.), 183, 184–85, 302–3, 310, 339
Fillmore, Millard, 47, 50, 56, 152, 243
1st Brigade (Army Artillery Battalion; U.S.A.), 22, 24–25, 27
First Charleston Battalion (C.S.A.), 150
1st City of London Artillery (GB), 327
First Division (U.S.A.), 23
1st Georgia Volunteers (C.S.A.), 180, 182

First Military District (C.S.A.): Beauregard involvement in, 192–93, 208; defense preparations, 158; Evans's brigade ordered to, 216; Harris replaces Ripley as commander of, 245–46; manpower problems in, 232–34; Pemberton's defense plans for, 220; Ripley as commander of, 139–40, 149, 152, 157, 158; Ripley ordered to send troops from, 241–42; Smith (W. D.) as commander of, 139; subdivisions within, 157
1st North Carolina Regiment (C.S.A.), 110, 111, 112, 115, 120, 122
1st Regiment (South Carolina Artillery; C.S.A.), 143
1st Regiment Rifles (C.S.A.), 70
1st South Carolina Artillery (C.S.A.), 67, 151, 153, 159, 170, 178, 183, 197, 239, 240
1st South Carolina Regiment (C.S.A.), 101, 222, 229, 230
1st Texas Infantry Regiment (C.S.A.), 265
Five Forks, Battle of (1865), 263–64
Flambeau (Union steamer), 153
Flat Rock (N.C.), 152, 225, 349–50
Florence (S.C.), 241–42, 243
Florida: Indian Scare of 1849, 43–44; manpower problems in, 233; presidential election (1876), 312–13, 318; Ripley avoidance of service in, 52–53, 54; Ripley service in, 43–45, 46; secession of (1861), 67; Seminole Wars (1818; 1835–1842), 43; Union troop movements in, 223, 225
Florida, CSS, 307
Florida Keys, 267
Floyd, John B., 65
Flynn, William, 224
F. M. Jones shipyard (Charleston, S.C.), 82
Foley, John H., 305, 305, 306
Folly Island (S.C.), 167, 168, 176, 177–78, 179, 215, 216, 236, 345
Foot Point Plantation (S.C.), 226–27
Fort Beauregard (S.C.), 86
Fort Columbus (N.Y.), 19
Fort Concepcion (Mexico), 29
Fort Donelson, Battle of (1862), 94, 97
Fort Drum (Fla.), 44
Fort Fisher (N.C.), 261
Fort Griswold (Groton, Conn.), 3
Fort Henry, Battle of (1862), 97
Fort Johnson (Charleston, S.C.), 149, 153, 190, 196, 210, 218, 233
Fort Johnston (N.C.), 16, 17
Fort Macon (N.C.), 16
Fort Marion (Fla.), 43, 44
Fort McAllister (Ga.), 158

Fort McHenry (Md.): Ripley (James) as commander of, 16; Ripley stationed at, 16–17, 18, 46–47
Fort Monroe (Va.), 16, 47, 49–50, 51, 53, 108, 267
Fort Monroe Artillery School of Practice, 47
Fort Moultrie (S.C.), 16, 51, 52; Charleston Harbor (April, 1863), 159, 162; Fort Sumter weaponry moved to, 193; NPS brochure on, 353; ordnance placement at, 204, 208, 238; Pemberton's planned abandonment of, 104–5; pre-Confederate flags at, 67; remodeling of, 230; Rhett-Calhoun conflict at, 105; Ripley as artillery commander at, 341; Ripley defense preparations, 98, 148, 230–31, 344; Ripley reports/memos on defenses on, 141, 230–31; S.C. seizure of, 65, 221, 299; Union evacuation of, 65–66; Union siege/bombardment of, 216
Fort Pemberton (S.C.), 151, 186, 204
Fort Pickens (Fla.), 71
Fort Pierce (Fla.), 43–44
Fort Pulaski, Battle of (1862), 183
Fort Ripley (Charleston, S.C.), 94, 99, 149, 186, 208
Fort Sumter (S.C.): Beauregard decision to hold at all costs, 202; Beauregard visit to, 192; as C.S.A. symbol, 202; during Fort Wagner (July 18, 1863), 183; guns moved to, 238; guns removed from, 190–91, 194–95; Huguenin as commander of, 352; ironclad attack on (1863), 143, 159–64, 204–5; *Keokuk* gun mounted at, 165, 173, 196; materiel shortages at, 239; NPS brochure on, 353; Pemberton's planned abandonment of, 104–5; Rhett as commander of, 143; Ripley complaints about engineers' work on, 213–14; Ripley defense preparations, 148–49, 150, 345–46; as Ripley HQs, 149, 163; Ripley intoxication allegations while at, 248–49, 253; Ripley report on defenses at, 142; Ripley visits to, 195–96; Union amphibious attacks against, 202; Union amphibious landing threats at, 210; Union demand to evacuate, 202; Union siege/bombardment of, 194–97, 208, 212, 220, 224, 234–35, 238, 239, 240; Union technological innovations against, 212
Fort Sumter, Battle of (1861): background of, 65–72; bombardment, 76–78, 264; Confederate fortifications, 73–75, 74 map; Confederate ultimatum delivered, 75; Lincoln ultimatum and, 73; Northern press coverage of, 299; Ripley popularity following, 80–81,

82, 151–52; Ripley's official report on, 78–79; Ripley's resignation threat following, 81–82; secessions following, 297; Southern negotiation attempts preceding, 65, 69–70, 71–72, 73; Union defenses, 76–77; Union reinforcement efforts, 66, 75–76; Union surrender, 67, 78, 221, 341, 342
Fort Wagner (Morris Island, S.C.). *See* Battery Wagner (Morris Island, S.C.)
Fort Walker (Hilton Head, S.C.), 85, 86–87
48th Georgia Regiment (C.S.A.), 110, 111, 112, 114–15, 119–20, 124
48th New York Regiment (U.S.A.), 180, 184, 185
44th Georgia Regiment (C.S.A.), 110, 111–12, 115–17, 119–20, 124, 129, 135
46th Georgia Regiment (C.S.A.), 167
Foster, J. G., 71
Foster, John G., 235–36, 240–41
14th South Carolina Regiment (C.S.A.), 101
4th Artillery Regiment (U.S.A.), 21–22
4th Georgia Infantry Regiment (C.S.A.), 124, 127, 132
4th Michigan Cavalry (U.S.A.), 267
Fourth Military District (C.S.A.), 166
4th North Carolina Regiment (C.S.A.), 128
Fox's Gap, 127, 128, 130, 135
France: armament program in, 272; C.S.A. unrecognized by, 152, 301; military preparedness of, 287; Ripley armory plan in, 272, 275–76, 283, 290; Ripley as inventor in, 335, 336–38; Sedan defeat and, 288–89
Franco-Prussian War (1870–1871), 270, 287–89, 335
Frank, W., 308
Franklin (Tenn.), Battle of (1864), 251, 253
Franklin, William B., 279, 287–88, 293
Franklinton (Ohio), 3
Fraser, James L., 244, 245
Fraser, Trenholm & Company, 241, 260, 277, 280, 290
Frederick (Md.), 37–38, 125
Freeman, Douglas Southall, 117, 135
Free Soil Party, 314
Fremantle, Arthur J. L., 172, 173–74, 176, 208
Fremont, John C., 314
French, Samuel G., 15, 289, 295
Frost, Edward, 178
Fry, Birkett D., 248–48

Gadsden Purchase, 285
Gaillard, P. C., 351–52
Gaines' Mill, Battle of (1862), 118–19, 120
Garden, Hugh R., 350
Garfield, James A., 339

Garland, Samuel, 110, 120, 124, 126, 135
Garrison, William Lloyd, 41
Gaston, William, 302, 303
Gatling Gun Company, 304
G Company (2nd Artillery Regiment; U.S.A.), 21–22
General Clinch (steamer), 70–71
General Order No. 42, 16
General Orders No. 3 (U.S.A.), 352
General Orders No. 75, 113
General Orders No. 95 (C.S.A.), 170, 176, 213
General Ripley (schooner), 82
George Parish and Company, 5, 13
Georgetown (S.C.), 99, 233, 345
Georgia, 67; manpower problems in, 233; Sherman's campaign in, 247–48, 254–55
Georgia, District of, 245
Gettysburg, Battle of (1863), 22
Gibbes (doctor), 219, 246
Gibson, William, 105, 110, 111
Gilchrist, Robert C., 341–42, 351–52
Gillet, Ransom H., 9, 10
Gillmore, Quincy A., 179, 183, 184, 190, 193, 197, 202, 236
Gist, States Rights, 63, 64–65, 107, 140, 150, 153–54, 166–67, 253
Gist, William Henry, 63, 64
Gist Guard Light Artillery (C.S.A.), 341
Goldsboro (N.C.), 111–12, 268
Gonzales, Ambrosio J., 81, 87, 89, 144, 146, 191, 204
Gordon, John B., 120
Gordonsville (Va.), 122
Gorgas, Josiah: Beauregard as viewed by, 145; Beauregard vs., 203, 204, 218, 221; as bureaucrat, 171; Burton and, 255, 256, 259; Charleston Arsenal under control of, 83; correspondence of, 83, 221; Hill (D. H.) vs., 110–11; Northern background of, 110; as Richmond chief of ordnance, 83; Ripley vs., 83, 84, 145, 171, 175, 204, 205; Trezevant and, 205, 206
Governors Island (N.Y.), 43
Graham, R. F., 168, 170, 174, 178, 180
Grant, Ulysses S.: as Aztec Club member, 34; Beauregard on, 173; during Civil War, 173, 233, 256, 316–17; as president, 299, 311–12, 317; Ripley on, 299, 316–17; Supreme Court appointees of, 318; as West Point cadet, 10, 15, 316
Grattan, George D., 132
Great Britain, 53; *Alabama* Claims against, 307–10; Crimean War (1853–1856), 56–57, 62; C.S.A. unrecognized by, 152, 301; Oregon boundary dispute, 19; Ripley as arms merchant in, 57–62, 269; Southern sympathizers from, 172–73
Greeley, Horace, 317
Green Pond (S.C.), 223
Greensboro (N.C.), 264, 267
Green's Wood Paving Company (London, England), 348
Greenwood, Thomas, 259
Greenwood & Batley (Leeds, England): arms machinery from destroyed/lost at sea, 260, 261, 262, 272; Burton employed by, 259, 260, 267, 269; Ripley arms machinery purchase from, 271, 272–73, 273, 275–76, 289–90; Ripley lawsuit against, 276–79, 278, 280, 281, 282–84, 285, 287, 290, 295, 323; undelivered Confederate arms machinery from, 269–70
Gregg, Maxcy, 34
Gregg, William, 226
Gregg's/McGowan's Brigade (C.S.A.), 101
Grosvenor Hotel (London, England), 282, 290
Guerin, H. C., 149, 342
Gwynne, Walter, 66–67, 80

Hagerstown (Md.), 125, 126–27
Hagood, Johnson, 203, 223; Battery Wagner (July 18, 1863), 185; as Battery Wagner commander, 186; Charleston defense preparations, 94; as Cole's Island commander, 99–100, 107; as James Island commander, 181, 182, 183; at Ripley funeral, 353; Ripley monument and, 354; as Second Military District commander, 167; Stevens as replacement for, 101; Taliaferro relieved by, 185–86
Halleck, Henry W., 122–23, 236
Hamburg Pass, 127, 132
Hamilton, Archibald, 59–60
Hamilton, D. H., 210, 212–13, 214
Hamilton, John R. ("Jack"), 75, 78, 274–75, 276, 279, 280
Hamilton, Mrs. John R., 274, 275, 276, 279, 280–81
Hammond, M. C. M., 45–46
Hampton, Wade, 252, 257, 356
Hampton Roads (Va.), 85
Hancock, Winfield Scott, 12, 339
Hardee, William J., 247, 251, 252, 253, 254, 256
Hardinge, Henry, 1st Viscount Hardinge, 57–58
Harkness, William, 323, 324, 325, 330
Harper & Brothers, 40, 45
Harpers Ferry (Va./W.Va.): Battle of (1862), 125–26; Brown's raid on (1859), 63, 255, 297
Harpers Ferry Arsenal (Va./W.Va.), 58
Harriet Lane (Union steamer), 71

Harris, David B.: background of, 169, 246; Battery Marshall fortification work of, 213; Battery Wagner (July 18, 1863), 185; Beauregard and, 69, 169, 204, 207–8, 218, 220, 221–22, 233, 347; Charleston defense preparations, 163; Davis Charleston visit and, 209; death of, 247; as First Military District commander, 245–46; during Fort Sumter bombardment, 196; *Hunley* and, 207–8; Jones (Samuel) demand for, 239, 242; *Keokuk* salvage and, 164–65; Morris Island fortifications and, 174; Ripley vs., 69, 168–70, 169, 176–77, 213, 218, 245
Harrison, George P., 185
Harrison, William Henry, 314
Harrison's Landing (Va.), 119, 122
Harrogate (England), 271
Hartington, Marquis of, 150
Haskell, Charles T., 180
Hatch, John P., 269
Hayes, Rutherford B., 312–13, 317, 318, 339
Heckman, C. A., 236
Heintzelman Mine, 285, 286
Helen (ship), 261
Helvetia, SS, 276
Henry, Robert Self, 31
Henry Holman (brig), 261
Henry Pratt (ship), 19, 21
Herald and Standard, 241
Herring, Marcus D., 115
Heyliger, Louis C., 261
Hill, A. P. (Ambrose Powell), 113–14, 117, 125
Hill, D. H. (Daniel Harvey), 126; academic background of, 110; in Augusta, 253–54; casualties suffered by, 120; character of, 124–25; correspondence of, 294; division led by, 122, 124; Holmes replaced by, 122; Lee vs., 110, 124; Malvern Hill (1862), 119–20, 123; Maryland Campaign (1862), 124–26; military background of, 11, 110; Pillow vs., 111; Ripley vs., 110–11, 121, 129, 253–54; writings of, 129, 131, 294
Hilton, Henry, 45
Hilton Head (S.C.), 85–87, 236, 240–41
Hingham (England), 1
Hingham (Mass.), 1
Histoire de la Guerre Civile en Amerique, L' (Comte de Paris), 295
History of Delaware County, 1
H. L. Hunley (submarine), 206–8, 218–19, 222, 223–25, 226
Hoffman, William, 236–37
Hoge, M. D., 305
Holcombe Legion (C.S.A.), 225, 232

Holmes, Emma, 79, 139
Holmes, Theophilus, 109, 122
Honesta (schooner), 260
Hood, John Bell, 129, 251, 253, 264
Hooker, Joseph, 34, 38
Hoole, W. S., 273
Hope (ship), 261–62
Hope, Margaret, 327
Hope, William, 287, 288, 293, 295, 303, 327–34, 335, 338, 343
"Hope Breech Loading System," 333–34
"Hope" gun, 330–34, 335
Horres, C. Russell, Jr., 138
Horse Artillery (C.S.A.), 127
Hotchkiss, Jedediah, 124
Hotze, Henry, 241
Housatonic, USS, 224, 226
Howard, John, 169
Howland, C., 2–3
Huger, Benjamin, 110, 120, 122
Hughes, Joseph, 3
Huguenin, Thomas A., 229, 235, 238–39, 240, 248–49, 347, 351–53, 352
Hunley, Horace L., 206, 207
Hunter, David, 102, 179
Huse, Caleb, 260, 272, 275

I Company (2nd Artillery Regiment; U.S.A.), 52–53, 54
Illinois Senate, 63
Illustrated London Times, 150
"Improved Processes and Apparatus for Reducing, Melting, Purifying, and Otherwise Working Ores, Metals, Metalloids, and Similar Substances" (Patent No. 1421), 327–29
"Improved Processes and Apparatus for Reducing, Melting, Purifying, and Otherwise Working Ores, Metals, Metalloids, and Similar Substances" (Patent No. 4363), 329, 330
Improved Wood Paving Company (London, England), 348
"Improvements in Ammunition for Breech Loading Cannon" (Patent No. 817), 337–38, 340–41, 343
"Improvements in Breech Loading Cannon and Ammunition Therefore" (Patent No. 3042), 335–36
"Improvements in Gas Retorts, and in the Manufacture of Gas" (Patent No. 5315), 324–27, 326
"Improvements in Puddling and in Furnaces, More Especially such as Are Employed in Puddling" (Patent No. 5314), 324–27, 325–26

"Improvements in the Process and Apparatus for the Manufacture of Gas for Heating and Other Purposes" (Patent No. 2069), 323–24, 324, 325–27
"Improvements in the Treatment of Illuminating Gas, and an Apparatus Therefore" (Patent No. 2527), 329–30
"Improvements Relating to Ordnance and Firearms and Ammunition for the Same" (Patent No. 2923), 330–34, 332, 335, 336–37, 343
Index (Confederate propaganda paper), 241, 306
Indian Chief, CSS, 207, 219, 222
Indian Scare of 1849, 43–44
Ingraham, Duncan N., 59, 61, 93, 187, 191, 351–52
Institute Hall (Charleston, S.C.), 90
ironclads, 99, 140, 141, 142, 148–49, 159–64, 179, 194, 345
Isaac Smith (US gunboat), 151, 173, 347
Island Belle (blockade runner), 82
Italy, 337

Jackson (Miss.), 167
Jackson, Andrew, 43, 47, 52
Jackson, Thomas J. ("Stonewall"), 112–13, 114, 124, 125, 304–6, 305
Jalapa (Mexico), 30
James, Amaziah B., 6, 48, 49, 311
James Island (S.C.): Cole's Island abandonment and, 100, 106–7, 167; commissary situation on, 149–50; C.S.A. fortifications on, 98, 106, 171–72, 190; C.S.A. offensive on, 182–83; Davis inspection of, 209; Gist as commander of, 140; manpower problems at, 232, 234; ordnance placement at, 204, 209; Pemberton inspection of, 98; Ripley complaints about engineers' work on, 214, 233; Ripley review of forces on, 205; Taliaferro as commander of, 243; transportation problems at, 169; Union attack threats at, 167, 209; Union landings at, 182, 238–39; Union siege/bombardment of, 106, 107, 233; Union targets triangulated from, 212
Jamison, D. F., 84
Jessop & Company (Sheffield, England), 335
Jewish Americans, 266
Johannsen, Robert, 40, 46
John Fraser & Company, 226
"John Paul Jones" (unpublished; Ripley), 319–20
Johns Island (S.C.), 93, 223, 238, 239
Johnson, Andrew, 265, 315
Johnson, Bradley T., 291, 306

Johnson, John, 107, 165, *171*, 186, 196, 239, 240, 345, 351, *352*, 353–54
Johnson, Reverdy, 308
Johnson-Clarendon Treaty, 308
Johnston, Albert Sidney, 346
Johnston, George D., 351
Johnston, Joseph E., 262; as Army of Tennessee commander, 258–59, 263; as Aztec Club member, 34; Burton and, 259; Carolinas Campaign, 263, 264, 265; Charleston defense preparations, 238; Fair Oaks (1861), 108; McClellan's plan against, 108; negotiations with Sherman, 265; Pemberton and, 96; Ripley and, 140, 263; Ripley postbellum writings on, 346; surrender of (1865), 265, 267; in Virginia, 108, 109
Jones, Charles Colcock, Jr., 290
Jones, D. R., 123
Jones, John B., 255
Jones, John Paul, 319–20
Jones, Roger, 32, 38, 39, 49–50
Jones, Samuel: engineering officer request of, 242–43; Foster courtesy extended to, 240–41; health problems of, 247; Ripley and, 232–33, 243–45, 246–47; as South Carolina, Georgia, and Florida Dept. commander, 232; as South Carolina District commander, 247; Union POWs placed in Charleston by, 235–36
Jordan, Thomas, 171, 173, 176, 180; Beauregard and, 163; as Beauregard's chief of staff, 168, 228; Charleston Harbor (April, 1863), 163; correspondence of, 174, 216; Davis vs., 346; Fort Sumter defenses and, 196–97; *Hunley* and, 225; Mason scandal and, 219; postbellum writings of, 346; Ripley complaints about engineers' work to, 168–69, 175; Ripley "fire-ship" idea and, 187; Ripley insubordination charges and, 246; Ripley leave-of-absence applications submitted to, 219; Ripley memoranda submitted to, 218, 223, 228–32; Roman interrogatories and, 215–16; troop movements ordered by, 232
Jourdan, Fleming, 118
Judah P. Benjamin Confederate Memorial (Ellenton, Fla.), 266

Kansas-Nebraska Act (1854), 314
K Company (2nd Artillery Regiment; U.S.A.), 43–44, 46, 51, 52
Keitt, Ellison S., 233–34
Keitt, Lawrence M., 146, 150, 186, 188, 209–10, 214
Kemper, James L., 305
Kennedy, John D., 252

Keokuk, USS, 158–59, 161, 162–65, 173, 196, 204–5
Kerr, James, 58–60
Kershaw, Joseph B., 252
Kiawah River, 104
Kilbourne, James, 3
Kimberley and Brace (brokerage firm), 2
Kinard, John P., 146
Kirkland, William, 106
Knowlton, Miner, 16

La Cont, George, 283
La Coste, Adolphus W., 165, 166
Lamar, G. W., 248, 249
Lamar Battery (S.C.), 182
Langham Hotel (London, England), 273, 293–94
Langnel, Col. (Fayetteville Arsenal commander), 145
"Last Confederate Flag on the Atlantic, The" (Ripley), 299–301
La Voulte sur Rhone (France), 335
Law, Evander McIvor, 120–21
Lawley, Francis C.: correspondence of, 290; as *London Times* correspondent, 268–69, 273, 295; Ripley in debt to, 272, 273, 283, 289; Ripley literary efforts assisted by, 273, 295–96, 313, 319–20; Ripley's Greenwood & Batley lawsuit and, 286; Stonewall Jackson Monument and, 306
Lawley, Stephen, 272, 283, 289
Lawley Covers the Confederacy (Hoole), 273
Lawton, Alexander R., 86
Lay, John F., 232, 241, 243, 244–45, 246
Leach, Calvin, 122, 131
Lee, Robert E.: as Army of Northern Virginia commander, 110; as Aztec Club member, 34; Beauregard and, 257–58, 344; Charleston fire relief supported by, 90; Cole's Island abandonment and, 344–45; as Confederate Armies general-in-chief, 256; correspondence of, 124; Grant vs., 316–17; Hill (D. H.) vs., 110, 124; injury suffered by, 124; Maryland Campaign (1862), 86, 123–24, 125, 126, 132, 136; Mexican War service of, 32; military districts as defined by, 98; Pemberton and, 88, 89, 97, 100, 104, 105; Peninsula Campaign (1862), 86, 109–10, 119, 122; Pickens and, 92; postbellum adoration of, 346, 347; recalled to Virginia, 96, 108, 344–45; Rhett-Calhoun duel and, 105; Ripley assigned Charleston defenses by, 87–89, 90–95, 139–40; Ripley's relationship with, 92–93; Savannah HQs of, 94; Sherman's Carolina Campaign and, 257–58; as South Carolina, Georgia, and Florida Dept. commander, 86, 86; surrender of (1865), 264, 300–301; West Virginia campaign, 108
Lee, Stephen D., 78, 82, 257
Lee-Bellasyse, J. R., 291, 292, 309
Leeds (England), 259
Le Havre (France), 338
Leicester (Mass.), 4
Leon, George Isaac, 279
"Leonidas" article, 33, 37
Leslie, Charles, 150
Letcher, John, 255
Libby Prison (Richmond, Va.), 197–98
Lifeline of the Confederacy (Wise), 188–89
Light Division (C.S.A.), 113
Lighthouse Inlet, 168, 342
Lincoln, Abraham, 84; Arizona Territory bill signed by, 285; assassination of (1865), 12, 49, 265, 269, 315; debates with Douglas (1858), 63; elected president (1860), 297, 313, 315, 340; Fort Sumter reinforcement ordered by, 71, 73; Halleck appointed general-in-chief by, 122; inauguration of (1861), 69; McClellan and, 108; POW issue and, 236; as Republican presidential nominee (1860), 64–65
Lippincott & Company, 110
Literary World, 40
Little Folly Island (S.C.), 168, 170, 173, 176, 183, 342
Liverpool (England), 82–83, 260, 261, 267, 278, 280, 294, 307
London (England): Confederate propaganda papers in, 306; Confederate social network in, 274, 275, 280; De Rosset visit to Ripley in, 293–95; Ripley imprisoned for debt in, 281–82; Ripley residences in, 311, 312, 331; Ripley self-exile in, 271; Wigfall self-exile in, 273–74, 279, 280
London Armoury Company, Ltd. (London, England), 58, 59, 61, 287
London Cosmopolitan, 309
London Gazette, 282, 283
Long, E. B., 65
Long Island (S.C.), 97, 229
Longstreet, James: Army of Tennessee command and, 258–59; Maryland Campaign (1862), 123, 125, 126, 127, 129, 132; Peninsula Campaign (1862), 109, 110, 111, 112, 113; as West Point cadet, 11
Louisiana, 67, 266, 312–13, 318
Louisville (Ky.), 267
Lowell, James Russell, 41
Lowndes, Rollins, 106

Macbeth, Charles, 167, 182
Macbeth, J. Ravenel, 178
Macon (Ga.), 247, 255, 261, 267, 272
Macon Telegraph, 117–18
Madison, James, 3
Magnolia Cemetery (Charleston, S.C.), 240, 350, 354–56, *355*
Magrath, Andrew G., 84, 103, 176, 177, 250, 251–52, 254, 255, 258, 351–52
Magruder, John B., 34, 122
Malins, R., 277
Malins, V. C., 281
Malvern Hill, Battle of (1862), 119–20, 290, 293
Malvern Hill, McClellan's attempt to reoccupy, 123
Manassas, Battle of (1861), 80, 81, 108, 169
Manassas, Battle of (1862), 101, 124
Maney, Thomas, 39
Manigault, A. M., 100
Manley, Atwood, 48
Manor House (Charlotte, N.C.), 263
Mansion House (Charlotte, N.C.), 259, 262
Marcy, William L., 34, 37, 38–39
Markoe, F., Jr., 186
Marshall, Jehu Foster, 97–98, 99, 101
Martin, George, 311
Martinsburg (Va.), 125
Maryland Campaign (1862), 86; Antietam, 132–36, *133* map, 134, 137, 140, 279, 290, 293, 327; casualties during, 136; C.S.A. positioning preceding, 122–25; De Rosset service in, 293; Harpers Ferry, 125–26; Hill (D. H.) criticism of, 110; Lee's plan for, 125, 126; McClellan learns Lee's plan for, 126; Newton service in, 340; Pickens-Pemberton conflict during, 137; Ripley-Hill conflict during, 254; Ripley wounded during, *134*, 134–35, 146, 327; South Mountain, 126–32, 135, 137, 254, 279, 290, 293, 294
Maryland Heights, 125
Mason, "beautiful Mrs.," 219, 246
Mason, James M., 260
Massachusetts, 302, 303, 310, 339
Massachusetts Archives, 309
Massachusetts Arms Company (Chicopee Falls, Mass.), 59, 60, 61
Massachusetts State House (Boston, Mass.), 303
Matamoros (Mexico), 22
Mathewes, J. Fraser, 169–70, 178, 207, 239
Matildaville tract (Ogdensburg, N.Y.), 5, 13, 47–48, 61, 227, 262, 283, 286
Mauzy, George, 255
McCabe, W. Gordon, 195–96

McClellan, George B., 34; as Army of the Potomac commander, 108; cautious strategy of, 108; Comte de Paris as aide-de-camp to, 295, 296; Maryland Campaign (1862), 122–23, 126; Peninsula Campaign (1862), 108–9, 119, 122, 296–97; as Union general-in-chief, 108, 125, 297
McConochie, Alexander, 60
McConochie, James, 60
McCormick, Jennie, 3
McCormick, Robert, 3
McCulloch, Benjamin, 23
McDowell, Irwin, 108
McGowan, Samuel, 34
McLaws, Lafayette, 11, 120, 123, 124, 125, 245, 247–48
McMahon, Martin T., 350
McRae, Colin, 270
McRae, Duncan K., 127, 132
Meade, George Gordon, 22
Means Battery (Charleston, S.C.), 153
Meares, Gaston, 111, 114, 118, 120, 293
Mechanicsville, Battle of (1862), 113–18, *116* map, 120–21, 129, 135, 290
Mercedita (C.S.A. warship), 152
Mercer, H. W., 105, 179, 204
Mexican-American War (1846–1848): armistice during (1847), 31, 32; beginning of, 17–18; end of hostilities (1847), 33; Grant military service during, 316; Hill (D. H.) as veteran of, 110; mortality rate during, 20, 22; opposition to, 41; peace agreement in, 34–35; personal advancement opportunities during, 50; Pillow-Scott conflict during, 32, 33, 34–35; Ripley's history of (see *War with Mexico, The* (Ripley)); Smith (G. W.) service in, 340
Mexican-American War (1846–1848)—battles: Buena Vista (1847), 29; Cerro Gordo (1847), 29–30, 36, 40–41, 50; Chapultepec (1847), 32–33; Churubusco (1847), 31; Contreras (1847), 31; Monterrey (1846), 22–24, 26; Palo Alto (1846), 19, 21; Resaca de la Palma (1846), 19, 21; Veracruz (1847), 27–29, 50
Mexican-American War (1846–1848)—Ripley's military service in: as battalion quartermaster staff, 22, 23; at Cerro Gordo (1847), 29–30, 40–41; Mexico City social life, 34–36; at Monterrey (1846), 22–24; promotions, 24–25, 29–30, 33; transportation to, 19–20, 21; at Veracruz (1847), 27–29
Mexico City campaign (1847), 29–34
Middleton, Alicia. See Ripley, Alicia Middleton Sparks (wife)
Middleton, E. B., 248

Middleton, Edward, 53
Middleton, Frances Motte, 53
Middleton, Harriott, 84, 143, 146, 152–53, 161, 219, 224
Middleton, J. Motte, 186, 276, 279, 286
Middleton, John (ancestral in-law), 53
Middleton, John (father-in-law), 53, 286
Middleton, Mary Burroughs, 53
Middleton, Susan, 84, 146, 152–53, 161, 164, 219, 224, 246
Milan (French ship), 145–46, 150, 152
Miles, William Porcher, 68, 78, 98, 100, 103, 139, 167, 181, 216
Military Operations of General Beauregard, The (Roman), 342
Milledgeville (Ga.), 263
Mills House (Charleston, S.C.), 90, 145–46, 180
Mississippi, 67
Mississippi and East Louisiana, Dept. of (C.S.A.), 166–67
Mitchel, John C., 170, 171, 173, 175, 177, 178, 238, 239, 240
Mitchell, Julian, 106
Mobile (Ala.), 206, 207, 208, 218, 219, 223–24
Molino del Rey (Mexico), 32, 33
Molson Davies and Company, 4–5
Monitor, USS, 99
Montauk, USS, 158, 159, 161, 179
Monterrey, Battle of (1846), 22–24, 26
Montgomery (Ala.), 67, 253, 265, 266
Montréal (Québec, Canada), 4–5
Moore, A. B., 63, 105
Morales, Juan, 29
Moran, Benjamin, 274–75, 282, 289, 306, 307, 308–9
Morrill, J. T., 99
Morris Island (S.C.): Beauregard interrogatories about defense/loss of, 213, 221–22; Beauregard visit to, 192; Cole's Island abandonment and, 167; C.S.A. loss of, 180, 205, 213, 220, 345–46; fortification failures on, 341–42; Ripley complaints about engineers' work on, 175, 212, 214, 345; Ripley postbellum writings on, 345–46; Ripley's report on defenses on, 141; Roman interrogatories about Union movements on, 215, 216–17; Sullivan's Island artillery aimed at, 230–31; transportation problems at, 169; Union artillery placements on, 190, 191, 193, 195, 216–17; Union attack threats at, 177–78; Union bombardment of Fort Sumter from, 194–97, 234–35; Union command on, 236; Union landings at, 179, 180; Union reinforcement ship attacked from, 66; Union siege/bombardment of, 179; Yates as artillery commander on, 180. *See also* Battery Gregg (Morris Island, S.C.); Battery Wagner (Morris Island, S.C.)
Motte, Frances, 53
Motte, Jacob Rhett, 44, 53
Moultrie Creek, Treaty of (1823), 43
Moultrie House (Charleston, S.C.), 53–54, 203
Moultrieville (S.C.), 53
Mount Pleasant (S.C.): *Hunley* repairs in, 222; Keitt inspection of, 150; manpower problems at, 232, 238; name of, 53; Ripley HQs in, 208, 221, 222, 224; Ripley reports on defenses at, 141–42, 210–11
Mount Pleasant Plantation (S.C.), 53
Murrells Inlet (S.C.), 166
Mutzig (France), 272
"My Heart Leaps Up When I Behold" (Wordsworth), 8

Nagle, J. T., 350
Nahant, USS, 158, 159, 162, 179
Najera, Juan de, 23
Nance, William F., 178, 180, 224–25
Nantucket, USS, 159, 161–62
Napier, Francis, 288, 327
Napier, William, 288
Napoleonic Wars (1793–1815), 16
Napoleon III (Emperor of France), 272, 288–89
Nashville (Tenn.), 39
Nashville, Battle of (1864), 251
Nassau (Bahamas), 261–62
National Hotel (Washington, D.C.), 49
National Park Service, 353
New Ironsides, USS, 158, 159, 161, 183, 187, 188, 194, 202
New Orleans (La.), 266
New Orleans Daily Picayune, 33, 37
Newport Oregon Coal Company, 291–92
Newton, John, 11, 340, 347, 350
New York (N.Y.), 60; Burton flight to, after Lee's surrender, 267; Ripley (Christopher) relocation to, 5; Ripley as author in, 42, 344–46, 347; Ripley death/funeral in, 350; Ripley income sources in, 347–48; Ripley invention work in, 323, 340–41, 343; Ripley patent application in, 59; Ripley return to (1884), 339, 340, 341
New York City Health Department, 350
New York Herald, 105–6
New York Hotel (New York, N.Y.), 59–60, 340, 341, 350
New York Times, 350
New York World, 251, 340, 343–44
19th South Carolina Regiment (C.S.A.), 92

9th Maine Regiment (U.S.A.), 180, 181
Normandie, SS, 338
Norris, John W. S. ("Stump"), 349, 350
Norris, William, 209
North American Mining Company, 5, 47
North American Review, 347
North Carolina, District of (C.S.A.), 122, 124, 232
North Carolina Cavalry (C.S.A.), 123
North Edisto Island (S.C.), 344
North German Confederation, 272, 287
No. 290, CSS, 307
"Novel Method of and Apparatus for Reducing and Purifying Metals Directly from Their Ores by Gaseous Fuel, A" (Patent No. 1831), 334, 334
Nullification Crisis (1832), 52

Oak Grove, Battle of (1862), 113
observation balloons, 223
Ogdensburg (N.Y.), 6; Ripley (Christopher) death in, 48; Ripley (Christopher) family in, 5; Ripley (Christopher) relocation to, 4; Ripley (Julia) death in, 311; Ripley-Caulkin family ties and, 23; Ripley visits to, 13, 16, 42, 46, 47, 48, 270, 321; Ripley West Point application in, 10; Staniford in, 25. *See also* Matildaville tract (Ogdensburg, N.Y.)
Ogdensburg Academy (Ogdensburg, N.Y.), 9
Ogdensburg Cemetery (Ogdensburg, N.Y.), 48
Ogdensburg Journal, 350–51
Ogier, W. G., 248, 249
Ollier, Charles, 283
Olmstead, C. H., 180, 182
Olustee (Fla.), Battle of (1864), 225
100th New York Regiment (U.S.A.), 184
Onward, USS, 102
Oppen, F. A. K. W. von, 304
"Ordnance and Firearms and Ammunition for Same" (Patent No. 137,920), 335
Ordnance of Secession, 90
Oregon boundary dispute, 19
Oreto (commerce raider), 307
Orr, James L., 65, 97, 101, 139, 247, 252
Orr's Rifles (C.S.A.), 97, 101
Osceola (Seminole chief), 43
Osceola (steamer), 99
Otey, J. M., 249
Otter Island (S.C.), 88
Oyster Point (Morris Island, S.C.), 178

Palmetto Artillery Battalion (C.S.A.), 151, 182
Palmetto Band, 70
Palmetto Battery (C.S.A.), 350

Palmetto State (C.S.A. warship), 98, 152
Palo Alto, Battle of (1846), 19, 21
Panic of 1837, 61
Paris (France), 289, 335, 338
Parish, George, 13, 14, 47, 48
Passaic, USS, 158, 159, 161
Patapsco, USS, 158, 159, 161
patronage system, 313, 339
Pawnee (Union steamer), 71
Paw Paw River, 89
Payne, John, 206–7
Peabody, George, 59
Pemberton, John C., 153–54; assigned to Lee, 88, 89; as Aztec Club member, 34; Beauregard and, 345; Cole's Island abandoned by, 99–101, 102, 104, 106–7, 153, 167, 344–45, 347; First Military District defense plans of, 220; as Mississippi and East Louisiana commander, 138, 166–67; Pickens vs., 100, 137–38; promotions of, 96–97; reassigned from Charleston, 97, 137–38, 139, 345; Ripley and, 97, 101, 104–5, 106, 140, 316; Ripley postbellum writings on, 344–45; S.C. reinforcements sent to, 166–67; as South Carolina and Georgia Dept. commander, 96, 103; Vicksburg (1863), 316
Pemberton, Martha Thompson, 96
Pender, William Dorsey, 114, 120–21
Pendleton Act (1883), 339
Peninsula Campaign (1862), 86; balloon use during, 223; C.S.A. casualties during, 115, 120, 135; De Rosset service in, 293; Franklin service in, 279; Gaines' Mill, 118–19, 120; Lee's dissatisfaction with leadership in, 122; Lee's plan for, 112–13; Malvern Hill, 119–20, 290, 293; McClellan's attempt to restart, 123; Mechanicsville, 113–18, 116 map, 120–21, 129, 135, 290; Newton service in, 340; Oak Grove, 113; Pickens-Pemberton conflict during, 137; Ripley-Hill conflict during, 129, 254; Savage Station, 119; success of, 122; White Oak Swamp, 119; Yorktown, 108–9
Persia, SS, 267
Peterkin (company commander), 223
Petersburg (Va.), 239, 245
Petersburg, Siege of (1864–1865), 256
Petrel, HMS, 150, 152
Philadelphia (Pa.), 64
Phoenix Iron Works (Charleston, S.C.), 90
Pickens, Francis W., 69; Cole's Island abandonment and, 100; correspondence of, 79–80, 137; criticism directed at, 84–85, 85; Fort Moultrie evacuation as viewed by, 65; Gonzales as aide-de-camp to, 81, 87; Lee as

viewed by, 92; Lincoln ultimatum to (1861), 73; military meddling by, 84–85, 85, 91–92, 137; Pemberton vs., 100, 137–38; Rhett-Calhoun duel and, 105, 142; Ripley appointed S.C. Militia major of ordnance by, 66; Ripley commended by, 79; Ripley resignation threat and, 79–80; Ripley vs., 245; as S.C. governor, 65
Pierce, Franklin, 34, 314
Pillow, Gideon: Aztec Club and, 34; at Fort Donelson (1862), 94; Hill (D. H.) vs., 111, 121; influence on Ripley, 51; during Mexican War, 29, 30, 32–33; Polk and, 39, 111; Ripley as aide-de-camp to, 32, 36, 38, 43, 111, 121, 253–54; Ripley's Mexican War history and, 38–40, 46; Scott vs., 32, 33, 34–35, 37–38
Pitt, Sydney, 335
Planter (steamer), 102, 103
Pocahontas (Union steamer), 71
Pocotaligo (S.C.), 140
Poinsett, Joel R.: Ripley (James) and, 52; Ripley's West Point appointment and, 9–10; as secretary of war, 52
Point Isabel (Mexico), 21
Poissy (France), 275–76, 283, 290
Polk, James K.: as Democratic presidential nominee (1844), 29; departure from office, 39; military preparedness under, 18; Pillow and, 29, 32, 34, 36, 38, 39, 111; Ripley and, 19, 38–39, 41, 49, 55; Santa Anna bribery attempt and, 34–35, 37; Scott vs., 32, 50; Shields senate run and, 50–51; Sparks appointed consul by, 53
Pope, John, 11, 122–23, 124, 125
Porter, Fitz John, 113
Porter, W. D., 103
Portland (Ohio), 4
Port Royal (S.C.), 150, 158, 159, 183, 344
Port Royal, Battle of (1861), 84, 85–87
Poston, Charles D., 285–86
Potsdam (N.Y.), 5–8, 6
Powhatan (Union steamer), 71
Pressley, John G., 177, 182–83
Preston, William, 270
Princess Royal (ship), 260, 262
Princeton (ship), 28
Pringle, Motte A., 248, 249
Pringle, Rebecca, 268
Pringle family, 255
Prioleau, Charles K.: Burton as contract mediator for, 260; correspondence of, 188, 189, 241; as Fraser, Trenholm & Co. partner, 241, 260, 271; as Fraser & Co. office manager, 82–83; Ripley commission held by, 276, 284,
290; Ripley negotiations with, 271, 275; Ripley's Greenwood & Batley lawsuit and, 283, 286; Stonewall Jackson Monument and, 306; *Thistle* and, 188, 189
prisoners of war, 81, 98–99, 153, 186, 197–98, 224, 235–37, 241–42, 243, 291
Pritchard, Peter, 277–78, 284
Prussia, 287, 289. See also Franco-Prussian War (1870–1871)
Prussian Assembly, 287
Pryor, Roger, 78
Puebla (Mexico), 30–31, 34, 37
Pulaski House (Savannah, Ga.), 63, 225
Putnam, H. S., 184, 185
Putnam Volunteers (C.S.A.), 111–12

Quebec (Canada), 269
Queen of Britain (ship), 260

Rachel (brig), 2–3
Radical Republicans, 108, 184, 269, 284, 297, 308, 315, 339
Rains, G. W., 33, 276
Raleigh (N.C.), 90
Ramble (British brig), 2
Ramsay, William M., 342–43
Ramsey, Captain (engineer), 172
Randolph, George W., 139
Ransom, Robert, 247, 248
Rapidan Station (Va.), 124
Ravenel, Frank, 106
Ravenel, William, 226
Raymond, Sewell, 5
Rebel's Recollections, A (Eggleston), 102–3
Reconstruction Era, 315–16
Redoubt No. 1 (James Island, S.C.), 192, 204
Reese, Joseph B., 111–12, 115–18, 129
Relyea, C. J., 102
Reno, Jesse Lee, 127, 132
Republican National Convention (1860), 64
Republican Party, 302, 309–10, 312, 314, 315, 319, 339. See also Radical Republicans
Resaca de la Palma, Battle of (1846), 19, 21
Reynolds, J. J., 16
Rhett, A. Burnet, 115
Rhett, Alfred Moore: as Charleston inner batteries commander, 200, 232; duel with Calhoun, 105, 138–39, 142–43, 143, 146, 153; Elliott as replacement for, 200; as Fort Sumter commander, 143, 153, 159, 162, 163, 173, 196, 197, 203, 205; Huguenin and, 240; *Keokuk* salvage and, 164; marriage to Ripley's step-daughter, 143, 271, 354; as Ripley pallbearer, 351–52

416 | INDEX

Rhett, R. B., Jr., 226
Rhett, Robert Barnwell, 87, 176
Rhind, Alexander C., 158–59, 162
Richmond (Va.): armories in, 255–56; Army of the Valley march to, 113; Beauregard in, 80; Confederate abandonment of, 263, 265; C.S.A. defense plans, 109, 122; Feilden in, 172; Fremantle in, 174; Gorgas as ordnance chief in, 83, 259; Lee in, 96, 108, 122; Magrath in, 251–52; ordnance supplies from, 155, 195; Pemberton in, 96, 138; POWs sent to Charleston from, 197–98; reinforcements sent to, 234; Ripley in, 105, 106, 252, 255, 256; Ripley recuperation in, 139; Ripley's Brigade forwarded to, 104, 110, 111; Seabrook (E. M.) in, 250; Signal Corps in, 209; Stonewall Jackson Monument sent from England to, 304–6, 305; Union attack plans against, 108, 112
Richmond Armory, 255–56
Richmond Examiner, 197–98
Richmond Weekly, 208
Riley, Bennet, 111
Ringgold, Samuel A., 16, 17, 47
Rio Del Plan, 29
"Ripley" (poem; Timrod), 146–47, 355
Ripley, Adeline (cousin), 24
Ripley, Alicia Middleton (daughter), 56, 62, 188, 255, 275, 276, 279, 283, 290, 349–50, 354
Ripley, Alicia Middleton Sparks (wife), 188; children of, 53, 56, 62, 240–41; in England, 276, 279; evacuation from Charleston, 182, 225, 255, 268; family background of, 53, 84; financial difficulties of, 53; Ripley's courtship of/marriage to, 53–54; separation from Ripley, 283, 286, 290, 349–50; social life of, 93, 173
Ripley, Christopher (father): birth of, 2; children of, 1; correspondence of, 6, 13, 14, 19–20; employment history of, 2–3, 4–5; final illness/death of, 47–49, 55; influence on son, 51; legal problems of, 5–6, 13, 47–48, 61, 227, 262, 283, 286; marriage of, 3; real estate owned by, 48; religious orientation of, 3–4; Ripley's West Point appointment supported by, 9–10, 55; War of 1812 military service of, 3, 48
Ripley, Hannah Bradford (ancestor), 1
Ripley, James Wolfe (uncle): artillery training of, 47; birth of, 2; Civil War military service of, 2; employment history of, 4; as Fort McHenry post commander, 16; at Fort Moultrie (S.C.), 52; as US Army Ordnance Corps officer, 2, 10

Ripley, Joshua (ancestor), 1–2
Ripley, Julia Caulkins (mother): children of, 1; correspondence of, 4, 5, 6, 11–13, 14, 18–19, 20, 27, 35; death of, 311; as husband's business agent, 4; marriage of, 3; real estate owned by, 48; Ripley visits to, 270
Ripley, Laura (sister), 1, 3–4, 12, 30–31, 351
Ripley, Lucia (sister), 1, 3–4, 6, 26, 27–28, 351
Ripley, Roswell Sabin, 188; *Alabama* Claims crisis and, 308–10; anger management problems of, 245; appearance of, 9, 19, 34, 57, 102, 196; as arms merchant, 56–62, 269, *341*; artistic talent of, 12–13, 14, 22; as author, 241, 273, 295–301, 303, 313–20 (*see also War with Mexico, The* (Ripley)); biases/prejudices of, 36, 317; birth of, 1, 2, 14; bureaucracy as viewed by, 83, 84, 103, 149, 192; character of, 169, 284; children of, 56, 62, 240–41; competence of, 211; correspondence of, 6, 13–14, 18–20, 24, 25–26, 27–29, 30–31, 35, 39, 44–45, 54–55, 64–65, 68, 83, 168–69, 243, 255, 270, 272, 287–88, 291, 294, 295, 299–300, 306, 319; courtship/marriage of, 53–54; death of, 341, 350; detail orientation of, 211, 229, 247; Doubleday and, 77; drinking habit of, 144, 176, 244, 245–46, 248–50, 303; education of, 5–7, 6, 9; family background of, 1–4; financial difficulties of, 20, 53, 186, 227, 274, 275, 279, 281–83; Florida tour of duty, 43–45, 46; French language proficiency of, 5, 11, 289; funeral of, 351–54, *352*; gravesite of, 14, 354–56, *355*; health problems of, 349; horses owned by, 146; as journalist, 56; land-development investment of, 226–27; leaves of absence taken by, 16, 38–42, 47, 48–50, 51, 54–55, 111, 140, 152, 225, 228, 248, 253; marital separation of, 283, 286, 290, 349–50; middle name of, 1, 4, 282, 286, 323; at Mitchel funeral, 240; obituaries, 351–52; Pickens's military meddling and, 84, *85*; political affiliation of, 41, 269, 284, 309–10, 317; political connections of, 51, 55, 152, 243; press coverage of, 251, 343–44; rebellious character of, 6–8, 11; religious orientation of, 4; relocation to England, 269, 270; residence purchased by, 188; resignation from US military, 54–56, 243, 253; as Rhett-Calhoun inquiry witness, 142, 143, 146; as S.C. Militia major of ordnance, 66; sense of humor of, 314; Shields and, 51, 55; social skills of, 35–36, 56, 93, 152–53, 173; Southern armory proposal of, 63–64, 65; West Point appointment of, 9–10; as West Point assistant/instructor, 16, 18; as West

INDEX | 417

Point cadet, 10–15, 77, 323. *See also* Beauregard, P. G. T.—Ripley's relationship with; Civil War (1861–1865)—Ripley's military service during; England—Ripley postbellum self-exile in; *specific person; place*
Ripley, Roswell Sabin—as author: "Charleston and Its Defenses," 344–46; "The Civil War in America, by the Comte de Paris," 296–99; "John Paul Jones," 319–20; "The Last Confederate Flag on the Atlantic," 299–301; "The Situation in America," 313–19. See also *War with Mexico, The* (Ripley)
Ripley, Roswell Sabin—as inventor: educational background for, 323; in France, 335, 336–38; Hope collaborations with, 327–34, *328;* Patent No. 817 ("Improvements in Ammunition for Breech Loading Cannon"), 337–38, 340–41, 343; Patent No. 1421 ("Improved Processes and Apparatus for Reducing, Melting, Purifying, and Otherwise Working Ores, Metals, Metalloids, and Similar Substances"), 327–29; Patent No. 1733 ("Treating Illuminating Gas"), 330, *331;* Patent No. 1831 ("A Novel Method of and Apparatus for Reducing and Purifying Metals Directly from Their Ores by Gaseous Fuel," 334, *334;* Patent No. 2069 ("Improvements in the Process and Apparatus for the Manufacture of Gas for Heating and Other Purposes"), 323–24, *324,* 325–27; Patent No. 2527 ("Improvements in the Treatment of Illuminating Gas, and an Apparatus Therefore"), 329–30; Patent No. 2923 ("Improvements Relating to Ordnance and Firearms and Ammunition for the Same"), 330–34, *332,* 335, 336–37, 343; Patent No. 3042 ("Improvements in Breech Loading Cannon and Ammunition Therefore"), 335–36; Patent No. 4363 ("Improved Processes and Apparatus for Reducing, Melting, Purifying, and Otherwise Working Ores, Metals, Metalloids, and Similar Substances"), *330;* Patent No. 5314 ("Improvements in Puddling and in Furnaces, More Especially such as Are Employed in Puddling"), 324, 325–26, 325–27; Patent No. 5315 ("Improvements in Gas Retorts, and in the Manufacture of Gas"), 324–27, *326;* Patent No. 314,127 ("Cartridge for Ordnance"), 337, 338, 343
Ripley, William (ancestor), 1
Ripley's Brigade (C.S.A.), 293
Ripley/Shepard Papers (St. Lawrence University), 12, 13–14
Rivers, C. H., 229

Robbins and Lawrence (Windsor, Vt.), 56, 59
Robertson, Alexander, 188
Rodes, Robert E., 110, 120, 124, 127
Rodgers (*Weehawken* captain), 161
Roll of Honor, 186
Roman, Alfred: as Beauregard staff member, 170, 244; Fort Sumter inspected by, 153; military career of, 342; postbellum writings of, 342, 347; Ripley alcoholism investigation held by, 248–49, 253; Ripley engineering complaints and, 170–71, 174, 175, 176; Ripley sent interrogatories about Union movements by, 214–18
Rosalie (schooner), 101
Rosecrans, William, 11
Rosen, Robert, 138
Rosser, Thomas L., 127, 128
Royal Hotel (London, England), 311
Royal Small Arms Factory (Enfield, England), 58, 61, 255, 259
Ruffin, Thomas, Jr., 135
Russell, William, 80
Russia, 56, 287
Rutledge, B. H., 351–52
Rutledge, John, 187
Ryan, Captain (commissary officer), 149–50

Sabin, Chloe Caulkins (aunt), 1
Sabin, Josiah (uncle), 1
Sabine, Edward, 282
St. Andre (French consul), 152
St. Andrew's Hall (Charleston, S.C.), 90
St. Croix (British West Indies), 278
St. Etienne (France), 272, 335, 336–37, 338
St. George's (Bermuda), 260
St. John's Episcopal Church (Worthington, Ohio), 3–4
St. John, William Henry, 330
St. Lawrence Academy (Potsdam, N.Y.), 5–6, *6,* 9, 11, 245, 289
St. Lawrence Republican, 48
St. Lawrence University, 12
St. Luke's Church (Charleston, S.C.), 352, 353–54
St. Martin, Natalie, 266
Salisbury (N.C.), 291
Saltillo (Mexico), 25–26
San Jacinto, Battle of (1836), 17
San Luis Potosi (Mexico), 26, 27
Santa Anna, Antonio López de, 17, 26, 27, 29, 31, 34, 37
Savage Station, Battle of (1862), 119
Savannah (Ga.): Beauregard inspection of fortifications at, 140; Davis visit to (1863), 209;

418 | INDEX

Savannah (Ga.) (*continued*)
  reinforcements sent to, 191, 223, 225, 247–48; Ripley defense preparations, 88, 89, 94; Ripley in, 52, 63–64, 225; as Sherman's goal, 248; Union attack threats at, 94, 153–54, 158; Union POWs as human shields in, 242. *See also* Charleston-Savannah railroad
Scammon, E. P., 236
Schimmelfennig, Alexander, 236
Schweitzer, Theodore, 283, 290–91
Scotia (steamer), 294
Scott, Thomas A., 84
Scott, Winfield: arrival in Mexico, 27; Fort Sumter evacuation proposed by, 71; McClellan replaces as general-in-chief, 108; Mexico City campaign (1847), 29, 31, 32–33; Pillow vs., 29, 32, 33, 34, 37–38; Polk vs., 32, 50; recalled from Mexico, 111; in Ripley's Mexican War history, 40, 46, 49, 111, 121; Santa Anna bribery attempt by, 34–35; during Seminole Wars, 43; Veracruz (1847), 28; Worth vs., 34–35
Seabrook, E. M., 226, 250, 263, 351–52, 354
Seabrook, Henry, 226, 227
Seabrook, John A., 226
secession movement, 266; Fort Sumter as symbol of, 202; Harpers Ferry raid and (1859), 63; Nullification Crisis and (1832), 52; Ripley's view of, 63
Secessionville (S.C.), 140, 182, 209, 233
Secessionville, Battle of (1863), 106, 182–83, 345
2nd Artillery Regiment (U.S.A.), 21–22, 43–44, 46–47, 51, 52–53, 54, 55
Second Military District (C.S.A.), 167
Sedan, Battle of (1870), 288–89
Seddon, James A., 166, 167, 245, 252, 257, 259–60
Seminole Wars (1818; 1835–1842), 43
Semmes, Raphael, 307
17th South Carolina Regiment, 92
7th Connecticut Regiment (U.S.A.), 179–80, 181, 184
7th Infantry Regiment (U.S.A.), 23
7th New Hampshire Regiment (U.S.A.), 184, 185
7th South Carolina Battalion (C.S.A.), 180
76th Pennsylvania Regiment (U.S.A.), 180, 181
Seward, William H., 64, 69–70, 71, 72, 204, 307
Seymour, Truman, 183, 184, 236–37
Shaler, Alexander, 236
Sharps, Christian, 56
Sharpsburg (Md.), 132, 134. *See also* Antietam, Battle of (1862)

Sharps Rifle Manufacturing Company (Hartford, Conn.), 56, 255, *341*
Sharps Rifle Manufacturing Company (Philadelphia, Pa.), 64
Shaw, Robert G., 184–85
Sheldon, David, 6
Shenandoah, CSS, 307
Shepard, Charles (brother-in-law), 12, 48
Shepard, Charles William (nephew), 12
Shepard, Julia Adelaide (niece), 12, 49
Sherman, Thomas W., 84
Sherman, William T.: Beauregard operations against, 253, 257–58, 259; Carolinas Campaign, 86, 251, 254–55, 256, 257, 263, 268, 343, 344; C.S.A. negotiations with, 264; Davis vs., 343; Johnston operations against, 259; Johnston's surrender to, 265, 267; Lee's strategy against, 252; March to the Sea, 247–48; Savannah as goal of, 248
Shields, James, 50–51, 55, 56, 243
Shiloh, Battle of (1862), 342
Shone, Isaac, 292
Sickles, Daniel, 112
Signal Corps (C.S.A.), 150, 186, 209
Simonton, Charles H., 149, 176, 177
"Situation in America, The" (Ripley), 313–19
16th South Carolina Regiment, 92
6th Connecticut Regiment (U.S.A.), 179–80, 184, 185
Sixth Military District, 98
62nd Ohio Regiment (U.S.A.), 184
67th Ohio Regiment (U.S.A.), 184, 185
63rd Georgia Regiment (C.S.A.), 183
slavery, 172, 298, 301, 305, 315, 343–44
Slidell, John, 152, 260, 266
Small Arms Manufactories (Enfield, England), 57
Smalls, Robert, 102, 103, 104
Smith, Angus, 207, 208
Smith, Gustavus W., 174; as Aztec Club member, 34; background of, 340; Carolinas Campaign, 254; Maryland Campaign (1862), 124; Mexican War service of, 340; as Pemberton replacement, 137; Peninsula Campaign (1862), 109; postbellum employment of, 347; at Ripley funeral, 350; as West Point cadet, 11, 340
Smith, Robert A., 111, 115–17, 118
Smith, W. D., 139, 140
Smith, W. P., 122
Smithfield (N.C.), 263
Smythe, Augustine T., 150, 188, 189, 236, 269
socialism, 317

Société des Fonderies et Forges de Terre-Noire, 335
Society Hill (S.C.), 225, 255, 268
Sonora Exploring and Mining Company, 285
South, Department of the (U.S.A.), 179
Southampton (England), 278
South Atlantic Blockading Squadron (U.S.A.), 102, 150–51, 158, 179
South Carolina: black labor shortage in, 168, 238; delegation from sent to D.C. to discuss secession, 65; manpower problems in, 166, 232–34; military crisis in, 252; presidential election (1876), 312–13, 318; secession movement in, 52; secession of (1860), 65, 90, 266, 297, 315; Sherman's campaign in, 86, 251, 254–55, 343, 344
South Carolina, Department of (C.S.A.), 82, 83
South Carolina, Georgia, and Florida, Department of (C.S.A.), 69, 86, 86, 232–33, 247, 251, 344
South Carolina and Georgia, Department of (C.S.A.), 96, 103, 138, 139
South Carolina Artillery (C.S.A.), 115, 143, 151, 182
South Carolina Convention, 70–71, 84
South Carolina General Assembly, 65
South Carolina Militia, 64
South Carolina Palmetto Guard (C.S.A.), 79
South Carolina Senate, 66
South Carolina War Department, 66
South Edisto Island (S.C.), 344
Southern armory, Ripley's proposal for, 63–64
Southern Literary Messenger, 45
Southern Magazine, 300–301
Southern Quarterly Review, 39–40
South Mountain, 125
South Mountain, Battle of (1862), 126–32, 135, 254, 279, 290, 293, 294
South Tenement of Vanderhorst North Row (Charleston, S.C.), 188
Spain, 152
Sparks, Alexander, 53
Sparks, Alicia Middleton. *See* Ripley, Alicia Middleton Sparks (wife)
Sparks, Marie Alice (stepdaughter), 53, 240–41, 255, 271, 354
Spartanburg (S.C.), 258
Special Order No. 2, 38
Special Order No. 6, 18
Special Order No. 8, 18
Special Order No. 69, 38
Special Order No. 77, 16
Special Orders No. 56 (C.S.A.), 176
Special Orders No. 105 (C.S.A.), 167

Special Orders No. 191 (C.S.A.), 126
Special Orders No. 195 (C.S.A.), 140
Special Orders No. 202 (C.S.A.), 138
Special Orders No. 229 (C.S.A.), 144–45
Spencer, James B., 9
Spiller & Burr, 256
Stanhope Arms Pub (London, England), 311, 312
Staniford, Thomas, 25
Stanton, Edwin M., 99, 316
Star of the West (steamer), 66, 71
states' rights, 96, 297
State Troops (C.S.A.), 203
Stephens, Alexander, 258–59
Stevens, Clement, 101, 167
Stevenson, Thomas G., 184
Stewart, A. P., 11, 254
Stokes, M. S., 111, 115, 120
Stono (blockade runner), 151
Stono Inlet, 167, 168
Stono River, 89, 91, 93, 94–95, 99, 100, 102, 104, 150–51, 173, 177, 183, 344, 347
Strong, George C., 179, 180, 183–84
Stuart, J. E. B., 112, 126
submarines, 206–8
Sullivan's Island (Charleston, S.C.), 52, 53, 186; Beauregard interrogatories about, 217; C.S.A. artillery fire from, 218; Davis inspection of, 209; fortification of, 97–98, 228–32; Fort Sumter weaponry moved to, 193, 195; *Hunley* practice runs from, 223–24; mutinous conduct on, 222; ordnance placement on, 208–9; Ripley as commander of, 97, 221, 243; Ripley complaints about engineers' work on, 214, 229; Ripley ordered to send troops from, 223, 232; Ripley reports/memos on defenses on, 141–42, 228–32; Union amphibious landing threats at, 209–11, 213, 241–42; Union siege/bombardment of, 224, 235; Union targets triangulated from, 212
Sullivan's Island Band, 244
Summerville (S.C.), 97, 243, 244
Sumner, Charles, 308
Sumter (light-draft), 151
"Swamp Angel" (Parrot gun), 197
Swanberg, W. A., 71
Sykes, George, 11

Taliaferro, William B., 203, 210, 223; Battery Wagner (July 18, 1863), 184, 185; as Battery Wagner commander, 183, 186, 190; Charleston defense preparations, 179; Chichester as artillery chief of, 190; engineers criticized by, 233; Hagood relieves, 185, 186; as James

420 | INDEX

Taliaferro, William B. (*continued*)
  Island commander, 233, 243; as Morris Island commander, 181–82; promotion recommendations, 204; Ripley and, 239; Savannah orders of, 191
Taylerson, A. W. F., 61, 64
Taylor, Richard, 96
Taylor, Zachary, 18, 22, 25, 41, 42, 314
Tennessee Campaign, 251
Terre Noire Foundries and Forges, 335, 338, 343
Texas: annexation of (1845), 17–18, 41; Confederate officials' flight to, 264; secession of (1861), 67
Texas Mounted Volunteers, 23
Texas Revolution (1836), 17
3rd Artillery Regiment (U.S.A.), 16–17
Third Military District (C.S.A.), 245
3rd New Hampshire Regiment (U.S.A.), 180
3rd North Carolina Regiment (C.S.A.), 110, 111, 112, 114–15, 119–20, 134, 293, 294
13th North Carolina Regiment (C.S.A.), 135
13th South Carolina Regiment (C.S.A.), 101
38th North Carolina Regiment (C.S.A.), 114
31st North Carolina Regiment (C.S.A.), 183
32nd Georgia Regiment (C.S.A.), 234
37th Infantry Regiment (U.S.A.), 3
Thistle (blockade-runner), 188–89
Thompson, Martha ("Pattie"), 96
Thompson, W. T., 351
Thruston, Stephen Decatur, 129–31, 294
Tilden, Samuel J., 312–13, 317–18
Times (London), 80, 268–69, 273, 277, 282, 295, 305, 311
Timrod, Henry, 146–47, 355
Toronto (ON, Canada), 269
torpedoes, 99, 179, 180
Totten, Joseph G., 71
Tower, Zealous B., 32
Trapier, J. H., 68, 80, 82
"Treating Illuminating Gas" (Patent No. 1733), 330, 331
Treaty of Moultrie Creek (1823), 43
Trenholm, Savage Deas, 349, 350
Trescott, William H., 65, 84, 98, 100, 101
Trezevant, J. T., 205, 206, 218
Trist, Nicholas P., 34, 37
Tucker, J. R., 187, 188, 191, 206, 234, 239
Tulle (France), 272
Turkish Empire, 56, 271
Turkish Irregular Cavalry, 57
Turner's Gap, 126–27
12th Battalion (C.S.A.), 180
12th Georgia Battalion (C.S.A.), 233
12th South Carolina Regiment (C.S.A.), 101

20th South Carolina Regiment (C.S.A.), 92, 146, 151, 209–10, 224, 232, 233–34
20th South Carolina Volunteers (C.S.A.), 141
25th North Carolina Regiment (C.S.A.), 340
25th South Carolina Infantry (C.S.A.), 177, 182–83, 193
21st Colored Troops (U.S.A.), 269
21st South Carolina Infantry Regiment (C.S.A.), 168, 178
24th South Carolina Regiment (C.S.A.), 101, 167
29th South Carolina Regiment (C.S.A.), 232
22nd Georgia Battalion (C.S.A.), 183
22nd South Carolina Regiment (C.S.A.), 222
27th South Carolina Regiment (C.S.A.), 230
26th South Carolina Regiment (C.S.A.), 232
23rd North Carolina Regiment (C.S.A.), 127
23rd South Carolina Regiment (C.S.A.), 232
Twiggs, David E., 23, 67

Union Pacific Railroad, 311–12
United States: Oregon boundary dispute, 19; Ripley return to (1884), 338; Ripley trips to, from England, 323
United States Agriculture Department, 285
United States Army Corps of Engineers, 52, 340
United States Census (1850), 48
United States Coast Survey, 18, 19
United States Consulate (Liverpool, England), 280
United States House of Representatives, 317, 318
United States Military Academy (West Point, N.Y.): Beauregard as cadet at, 169; Class of 1842, 11, 340; Class of 1843, 279; Class of 1844, 12; clergy at, 13; demerit system at, 11; Doubleday as cadet at, 77; Grant as cadet at, 10, 15, 316; Harris as faculty member at, 169; Polk administration and, 20; Ripley (James) as cadet at, 2; Ripley appointed to, 9–10, 55; Ripley as assistant/instructor at, 16, 18; Ripley as cadet at, 10–15, 77, 323
United States Navy, 84, 85, 91, 189, 190, 261
United States Navy Ordnance and Hydrography Bureau, 59, 61
United States Ordnance Department, 58, 60
United States Patent Office, 338, 343
United States Secret Service, 340
United States Senate, 50–51, 264, 266, 308, 318
United States Senate Journal, 51
United States Supreme Court, 266, 318
United States War Department, 57

Van Buren, Martin, 52, 314
Vance, Zebulon, 130, 294

Vanderhorst, Arnoldus, 138
Vanning (company commander), 223
Veracruz, Battle of (1847), 27–29, 50
Vicksburg, Siege of (1863), 316
Victoria (Queen of England), 288
Vincent's Creek, 178, 193
Vinton, John R., 17, 18, 22, 24, 28, 47
Violet (British brig), 2
Virginia: reinforcements sent to, 101, 233–34; secession of (1861), 96, 169, 297; West Virginia secession from, 108. *See also* Peninsula Campaign (1862)
Virginia, CSS, 99
Virginia Provisional Army (C.S.A.), 96
Virginia State Armory (Richmond, Va.), 255–56
Vizetelly, Frank, 150

Wagner, Theodore D., 188, 189, 286
Walker, John, 125
Walker, Knox, 38
Walker, Leo D., 106
Walker, Leroy P., 68, 70, 73, 83, 266
Walker, N. S., 124, 260
Walker, W. H. T., 167
Walker, W. S., 140, 245
Wall, John, 184
Warley, Alexander F., 187
Warley, F. F., 236, 241, 243
Warlow (British captain), 58
War of 1812, 2–3, 47, 282
Warwick, P. C., 244, 245
War with Mexico, The (Ripley): acclaim accorded to, 54, 323; critical reviews of, 45–46, 54; Hill (D. H.) and, 111, 121, 253–54; Lawley's familiarity with, 295; profitability of, 269; publication contract for, 41–42; Scott as portrayed in, 49, 111, 121; Whig Party and, 49; writing of, 38–41, 43, 111
Washington (D.C.), 47, 49, 65
Washington (Ga.), 265
Washington, Treaty of (1871), 308
Washington Arsenal, 17
Washington Light Infantry, 354
Watson, Baxter, 206
Watter (battalion commander), 167
Weehawken, USS, 158, 159, 161, 179
Weldon (N.C.), 216
Welles, Edgar T., 304
Wessels, H. W., 236, 237
Westminster Palace Hotel (London, England), 327, 331
West Virginia, 108
Wheeler, Joseph, 257
Whig Party, 32, 38, 40, 41, 42, 45, 314

White, Edwin I., 248, 249
White, E. J., 240
Whitecross Prison (London, England), 282
Whitely, R. H. K., 60
White Oak Swamp, 123–24
White Oak Swamp, Battle of (1862), 119
White Point Battery (S.C.), 89, 149
White Point Garden (S.C.), 150, 165
Whiting, E. M., 139
Whiting, W. H. C., 73, 110, 177, 179
Whitney, B. A. ("Gus"), 206
Whittier, John Greenleaf, 41
Wigfall, Charlotte, 264, 265, 273, 274, 275, 281
Wigfall, Francis ("Fanny"), 264, 265, 273, 275
Wigfall, Halsey, 265, 273, 274, 276, 279, 281, 286
Wigfall, Louise ("Louly"), 264, 265, 273, 275, 279, 286
Wigfall, Louis T.: background of, 264; as Beauregard staff member, 78; Davis vs., 264–65; flight of, after Lee's surrender, 264–65, 267; Fort Sumter (1861), 78; Lincoln inauguration and, 69; resignation from US Senate, 69, 78; Ripley and, 282–83; self-exile of, in England, 270, 273–74, 274, 279, 280
Wigg, George, 188, 189
Wilcox, Orlando, 18
Willard Hotel (Washington, D.C.), 49
Williams, Seth, 11
Wilmington (N.C.), 228, 232, 260, 293
Wilson, Robert, 353
Wilton's Bluff (S.C.), 89
Winder, John H., 242
Windham (Conn.), 2
Winnsboro (Ga.), 263, 268
Wise, Henry A., 223
Wise, Stephen R., 188–89
Witte, Charles O., 286
Wolcott, Alexander, 3
women's rights, 317
Wool, John E., 27, 32, 49
Wordsworth, William, 8
Worth, William J., 22, 32, 34–35, 37
Worthington (Ohio): downtown described (early 1800s), 3; Ripley born in, 1, 2; Ripley family relocation from, 4; Ripley family relocation to, 3; Ripley nostalgia for, 14, 23
Worthington Manufacturing Company, 3, 4
Wyse, F. O., 17, 18

Yates, Joseph A., 151, 166, 170, 177, 180, 351
yellow fever, 242, 247
Yorktown, Siege of (1862), 108–9
Young, William C., 78